Digital Strategy and Governance in Transformative Technologies

Digital Strategy and Governance in Transformative Technologies offers a comprehensive exploration of how emerging technologies are reshaping business operations, governance structures, and societal interactions. This timely volume examines the complex interplay between digital strategies and governance frameworks across AI, blockchain, cryptocurrencies, and the metaverse. It provides crucial insights for navigating the digital frontier.

The book's strength lies in its multifaceted approach, moving from foundational concepts to specialized applications. It begins by examining technological convergence challenges and strategic foundations, then delves deep into pressing issues such as AI ethics in healthcare and law enforcement, blockchain's role in fostering trust and accountability, cryptocurrency regulation, and the legal implications of the metaverse. The authors address critical questions about the ethical deployment of digital technology, blockchain transparency, cryptocurrency governance, and virtual space regulation through detailed case studies and empirical research. What sets this book apart is its balanced treatment of both theoretical frameworks and practical applications. The authors do not just explore technological capabilities; they examine how these innovations intersect with ethical considerations, regulatory compliance, and sustainable practices. From analyzing Meta's political ad policies to examining e-waste management in the digital era, the book offers actionable insights for policymakers, business leaders, and practitioners.

This essential resource serves as a guide for organizations and institutions grappling with digital transformation challenges. Whether you are a technology strategist, policymaker, academic researcher, or business leader, this book provides the framework and insights needed to develop effective digital strategies while ensuring responsible governance in an increasingly complex technological landscape.

Digital Strategy and Governance in Transformative Technologies

Edited by Arif Perdana, S Vijayakumar Bharathi, Ridoan Karim, Saru Arifin, and Aashish Srivastava

CRC Press
Taylor & Francis Group
Boca Raton London New York

CRC Press is an imprint of the
Taylor & Francis Group, an **informa** business

Designed cover image: Shutterstock

First edition published 2026
by CRC Press
2385 NW Executive Center Drive, Suite 320, Boca Raton FL 33431

and by CRC Press
4 Park Square, Milton Park, Abingdon, Oxon, OX14 4RN

CRC Press is an imprint of Taylor & Francis Group, LLC

© 2026 selection and editorial matter, Arif Perdana, S Vijayakumar Bharathi, Ridoan Karim, Saru Arifin, and Aashish Srivastava; individual chapters, the contributors

Reasonable efforts have been made to publish reliable data and information, but the author and publisher cannot assume responsibility for the validity of all materials or the consequences of their use. The authors and publishers have attempted to trace the copyright holders of all material reproduced in this publication and apologize to copyright holders if permission to publish in this form has not been obtained. If any copyright material has not been acknowledged please write and let us know so we may rectify in any future reprint.

Except as permitted under U.S. Copyright Law, no part of this book may be reprinted, reproduced, transmitted, or utilized in any form by any electronic, mechanical, or other means, now known or hereafter invented, including photocopying, microfilming, and recording, or in any information storage or retrieval system, without written permission from the publishers.

For permission to photocopy or use material electronically from this work, access www.copyright.com or contact the Copyright Clearance Center, Inc. (CCC), 222 Rosewood Drive, Danvers, MA 01923, 978–750–8400. For works that are not available on CCC please contact mpkbookspermissions@tandf.co.uk

Trademark notice: Product or corporate names may be trademarks or registered trademarks and are used only for identification and explanation without intent to infringe.

ISBN: 978-1-032-76271-5 (hbk)
ISBN: 978-1-032-76268-5 (pbk)
ISBN: 978-1-003-47780-8 (ebk)

DOI: 10.1201/9781003477808

Typeset in Palatino
by Apex CoVantage, LLC

Contents

Editors ix
Contributors xi
Preface xvii

Part 1 Introduction to the Digital Frontier and Strategic Foundations

1 The Intersection of Digital Strategy and Technology Landscapes: Overcoming Convergence Challenges 3
Neelesh Kumbhojkar, Arun Menon, and S. Vijayakumar Bharathi

2 Strategic Foundations of the Digital Frontier 26
Neelesh Kumbhojkar, Arun Menon, and S. Vijayakumar Bharathi

3 Tracing the Evolution of Digital Strategy with AI, Blockchain, Cloud, and Cryptocurrencies 45
Manjari Sharma and Sharad Gupta

Part 2 AI in Strategy: From Law to Ethical Alignment

4 Strategizing AI: Integrating Ethics and Environmental Sustainability in Digital Healthcare and Legal Systems 73
Widyastuti Andriyani, Dian Tri Wiyanti, and Daniel C.A. Nugroho

5 Assessing the Efficacy of Artificial Intelligence (AI) Applications in Predictive Policing: A Systematic Review Method 94
Sofia Khatun and Sivananda Kumar K.

6 Neurobiological Foundations of AI: Tracing the Evolution of Neural Networks 119
Vishwas Gupta

7 The Urgency of Artificial Intelligence (AI) for the
   Enhancement of Maritime Cultural Heritage Management
   in Indonesia 145
   Hutomo Putra

8 Artificial Intelligence and the Future of Software Development:
   Transforming the Software Development Lifecycle in the
   Digital Era 168
   Siddharth Gaikwad, Suneel K. Prasad, and S. Vijayakumar Bharathi

Part 3 Blockchain and Governance: Enhancing Trust and Accountability

9 Immutable Transparency: Leveraging Blockchain Transparency
   Features to Foster Trust in Decentralized Systems 197
   Manisha Singh and Sonali Srivastava

10 The Ethical Ledger: A Review of Literature on the Alignment
   of Accounting Ethics and Blockchain Technology 216
   Priyanka Koundal, Minie Bhalla, and Manpreet Kailay

11 Using Blockchain Technology for Audit Trail.......................................239
   Bilal Alagha and İlker Özçelik

12 A Blockchain-Enabled Digital Strategy for Agriculture Trade 260
   Sneha Kumari, V. G. Venkatesh, and S. Vijayakumar Bharathi

13 Blockchain Accountability Strategy of ESG-Focused
   Cryptocurrency Projects 283
   K. Pallavi and Sonali Srivastava

Part 4 Cryptocurrencies: Strategizing in a Decentralized Financial Landscape

14 Cryptocurrency Integration in the Web 3.0 Ecosystem:
   Opportunities, Challenges, and Future Directions.............................. 305
   Adarsh Chandra Nigam and Ruby S. Chanda

15 Cryptocurrency Regulations in India: Opportunities and
   Challenges..331
   Maneesh Yadav and Gurudev Sahil

16 A Case Study on Cryptocurrency Strategy and Regulation in the Asia Pacific 344
Sandy Arief and Wikan Karis Basutama

Part 5 Navigating the Legal and Ethical Landscapes of the Metaverse

17 Navigating the Legal Landscape of the Metaverse 365
Aji Baskoro and Annisa Hafizhah

18 Virtual Rape: Parallels between Physical and Virtual Violation in the Metaverse 387
Stephin Sinu Oommen and Anushka Datta

Part 6 Policy and Governance in the Digital Era

19 An Analysis of Meta's Political Ad Policy Enforcement: Perspectives from Bangladesh 411
Mohammad Pizuar Hossain, Miraj Ahmed Chowdhury, and Partho Protim Das

20 Regulating E-Waste Management in the Digital Era: A Legal and Policy Analysis 434
Ridoan Karim, Md. Shah Newaz, and Andrea Appolloni

Index 455

Editors

Arif Perdana is an Associate Professor and the Director of Action Lab Indonesia at Monash University. He has held academic positions at the University of Queensland, the Singapore Institute of Technology, and Aarhus University. His expertise spans digital strategy and data science, with research focusing on responsible AI, blockchain, and machine learning. He has secured funding from institutions such as the Singapore Government, Bank Indonesia, and the Monash Data Futures Institute. Dr. Perdana has also led professional training workshops, presented at global conferences, and published in leading journals in information systems–related disciplines.

S Vijayakumar Bharathi is a Professor at the Symbiosis Centre for Information Technology, Symbiosis International (Deemed University). He holds postgraduate degrees in commerce and management and a PhD in computer science from Symbiosis International University, specializing in enterprise resource planning (ERP) risk assessment for Small and Medium Enterprises. A member of the SAP Academic Alliance Board (Asia Pacific and Japan), he is a global SAP trainer and researcher in intelligent ERP, blockchain, and technology adoption. He collaborates with SAP headquarters and leads global curriculum pilot projects.

Ridoan Karim is a Lecturer in Business Law and the Deputy Director of the Centre for Commercial Law and Regulatory Studies (CLARS), Malaysia Hub, Monash University Malaysia. His research spans contract and cyber law, energy transition, and sustainable finance. He has served as a consultant on government-funded projects and has been collaborating with the Monash Data Futures Institute. Recognized for his research excellence, he received the Monash School of Business Excellence Award in 2022. He earned a PhD at the University of Malaya.

Saru Arifin is an Associate Professor at the Faculty of Law, Universitas Negeri Semarang, Indonesia. He earned a PhD in human rights law at the University of Pécs, Hungary. His research focuses on public international law, human rights law, and legislation studies, with publications by Routledge, Brill, and Sage. Dr. Arifin is actively involved in academic organizations such as GAJE and ISILL. He also serves as the Director of Programs at the Institute for Migrant Rights and is a member of APJHI's Ethical Committee (2024–2029).

Aashish Srivastava researches law and technology. He earned a BS, LLB and Diploma in cyber law in India, and he earned a PhD in electronic signatures at Monash University. His dissertation was published by Springer, and he has published several articles in the area of IT law in journals such as *Information Technology and People, Journal of Business Law, Common Law World Review, Rutgers Computer and Technology Law Review, Computers Law and Security Review,* and *International Journal of Law and Information Technology*. Dr. Srivastava has more than ten years of experience in teaching commercial law, marketing law, and IT law to business students at Monash Business School. His research and supervision interests include e-commerce, cybersecurity, e-crimes, and legal issues in cyberbullying and hazing (ragging).

Contributors

Bilal Alagha is a cybersecurity engineer pursuing a master's in computer engineering at Eskisehir Osmangazi University, Turkey. He earned a bachelor's in communications and computer engineering at Al-Azhar University, Palestine. His research focuses on computer networks, information security, and blockchain technology.

Widyastuti Andriyani is a lecturer at Universitas Teknologi Digital Indonesia. His research focuses on intelligent systems, with works in medicine, law, forestry, and IoT in agriculture.

Andrea Appolloni is an associate professor in the Department of Management and Law, University of Rome Tor Vergata. Her research interests include supply chain management, sustainability, and innovation.

Sandy Arief is an assistant professor of accounting at Universitas Negeri Semarang. He earned a PhD in accounting and corporate governance at Macquarie University. Dr. Arief is a certified sustainable business coach at Arc Australia Consulting.

Aji Baskoro earned a Master of Law at the Faculty of Law, Universitas Gadjah Mada, Indonesia.

Wikan Karis Basutama is a Financial Surveillance Analyst at the Central Bank of Indonesia. He earned a master's degree at Macquarie University. He is certified in fraud prevention, detection, and AML CFT.

Minie Bhalla is an associate professor at Lovely Professional University, Punjab, India.

S. Vijayakumar Bharathi is a professor at the Symbiosis Centre for Information Technology, Symbiosis International (Deemed University). He earned a PhD in computer science with a focus on ERP risk assessment. His research interests include design thinking, technology adoption, immersive technologies, and blockchain.

Ruby S. Chanda is a professor at the Symbiosis Institute of Management Studies, Symbiosis International (Deemed University), Pune, Maharashtra, India. She earned a PhD in customer relationship management. Her research areas include CRM, services marketing, and brand management. She has published 35+ research papers in national and international journals.

Miraj Ahmed Chowdhury is the founder of Digitally Right in Bangladesh. He is a 2020 GNI-Internews Digital Rights Fellow and a board member of MRDI, Sustainable Journalism Partnership and What To Fix.

Partho Protim Das is a deputy manager of an Outreach Team at Digitally Right, Bangladesh. He has a decade-long experience in online and mass media development, focusing on digital innovation.

Anushka Datta is a final-year law student at Christ University, Delhi, specializing in intellectual property law and international law. She won the 2024 Bennett Client Counselling Competition and reached the quarterfinals in the Henry Dunant International Moot Court Competition. She has interned with legal journals and serves as a student editor for her university's publications. Her recent achievements include a paper presentation at GNLU and a publication in RGNUL.

Siddharth Gaikwad is an MBA-ITBM graduate of the Symbiosis Centre for Information Technology, Pune, India. He is a consultant specializing in managing cyber risks and conducting assessments to strengthen client organizations' security postures. With expertise in the information security domain, he focuses on providing strategic consulting and solutions to address security challenges and identify opportunities for improvement.

Sharad Gupta is an educator and corporate trainer with over 21 years of experience in industry and academia, specializing in HRM and organizational behavior. His research focuses on AI's role in education and blockchain applications in HR. He conducts workshops on stress management, conflict resolution, and leadership skills. His work explores how AI can enhance learning experiences and how blockchain can revolutionize HR processes.

Vishwas Gupta is an assistant professor at the Symbiosis Centre for Management Studies, NOIDA Camps of the Symbiosis International (Deemed University) specializing in QT, statistics, and operations. With an MBA from Rohailkhand, University and an MPhil from Madurai Kamraj University, he has industry experience with ICICI Prudential and Sarabhai Pharmaceuticals. His research focuses on consumer psychometric analysis and network techniques, with publications in national and international journals.

Annisa Hafizhah is a lecturer at the Faculty of Law, Universitas Sumatera Utara, Indonesia.

Mohammad Pizuar Hossain is a PhD scholar at Monash University, Melbourne, and a senior lecturer at East-West University, Bangladesh. He was the 2021–2022 Chevening Scholar at the University of Edinburgh and the 2022 Tech Policy Fellow at Digitally Right.

Manpreet Kailay is an assistant professor at Lovely Professional University, Punjab, India.

Ridoan Karim is a lecturer in business law at Monash University, Malaysia. His research focuses on science, technology and law, privacy and data protection law, energy justice, and Asian comparative law.

Sofia Khatun is a doctoral student at Christ University, Bangalore, with a history of exceptional academic performance and research skills.

Priyanka Koundal is a research scholar at Lovely Professional University, Punjab, India.

Sivananda Kumar K. is an associate professor at the School of Law, Christ University, Bangalore. He earned a PhD in corporate crime and violence regulation at Acharya Nagarjuna University.

Sneha Kumari is an assistant professor at Symbiosis School of Economics, Symbiosis International (Deemed University). He is an associate researcher at Circular Economy and Territories for the European Commission, and his publications have encompassed big data, the agriculture value chain, and sustainability.

Neelesh Kumbhojkar is Director of Symbiosis Centre for Alumni Engagement, Symbiosis International (Deemed University). He has 25+ years of research and industry experience with an earned PhD in nanotechnology/computational physics. His research focuses on strategic consultancy and disruptive technologies, including cloud, AI, ML, blockchain, and digital transformation.

Arun Menon is a global executive with 32+ years of IT services industry experience. He is part of the executive leadership team at Jade Global. He is a former Tech Mahindra executive leading transformation programs across North America, Asia Pacific, and Europe.

Md. Shah Newaz is a senior lecturer at North South University. His research interests include sustainable consumer behavior, SDG 12, intertemporal choice, technology diffusion, and waste management.

Adarsh Chandra Nigam is a partner for the Singapore and India office of Stanton Chase LLP. He is a PhD scholar at the Faculty of Management, Symbiosis International University, Pune, Maharashtra, India.

Daniel C.A. Nugroho is a lecturer at the Faculty of Medicine, Universitas Kristen Duta Wacana. His research focuses on health informatics, clinical informatics, and public health informatics.

Stephin Sinu Oommen is a student at Christ University, Delhi, with expertise in moot court competitions and research on digital exploitation. A quarterfinalist in the Henry Dunant Memorial Moot, he has interned with legal professionals and focuses on cyber and technology law, particularly the metaverse. He actively contributes to academic and cultural initiatives at his university.

İlker Özçelik is an assistant professor of software engineering and the director of Intelligent Systems Security Research Group at Eskisehir Osmangazi University. He earned a PhD in intelligent and interactive systems at Clemson University.

K. Pallavi is a research scholar at VIT Bhopal University studying green microfinance in sustainable development. He earned an MBA at MANIT, Bhopal.

Suneel K. Prasad is a retired professor from the Symbiosis Centre for Information Technology. His experience spans defense, corporate, and academics. His research interests include business process management, project management, and process mining, focusing on process reengineering, discovery and optimization, robotic process automation, and digital twinning. He specializes in enhancing operational efficiency and automation.

Hutomo Putra is a researcher at the Research Center of Society and Culture, National Research and Innovation Agency, Indonesia.

Gurudev Sahil is an assistant professor at Symbiosis Law School, Hyderabad, Symbiosis International (Deemed University), specialising in legal education and research. He supervises PhD students and leads initiatives in moot court, placement, and maritime law. His work focuses on innovative pedagogy and legal research, with significant contributions through publications and leadership at legal seminars.

Manjari Sharma is an associate professor at Christ University with 15 years of expertise in financial management and investment analysis. As an international affairs coordinator, she has launched global immersion programs. Her research covers stock market volatility and investment strategies. She has coauthored the books *WealthWise* and *Innovative Pedagogy* and previously served at Maldives Business School.

Contributors

Manisha Singh is an assistant professor at VIT Bhopal University's Business School. She earned a PhD in management at MANIT, Bhopal. She has 18 years of combined industry and academia experience.

Sonali Srivastava is an assistant professor at Jaypee Business School, JIIT, Noida. With a PhD in finance from Dayalbagh Educational Institute, she has published in Scopus and WOS journals and has authored books on auditing and accounting.

V. G. Venkatesh is a professor of supply chain management at EM Normandie Business School, France. He earned a PhD at Waikato University, New Zealand, and has published 60+ journal articles.

Dian Tri Wiyanti is a lecturer in statistics and data science at Universitas Negeri Semarang. She is currently studying at Taipei Medical University and researching machine learning and explainable AI in critical care.

Maneesh Yadav is a professor of law at TMU University, Moradabad, with over 16 years of experience as an academician, consultant, researcher, and trainer. His expertise spans business laws, CSR, international capital markets, and investor issues. He has previously worked at the Indian Institute of Management, Lucknow.

Preface

The landscape of digital technologies has undergone an unprecedented transformation. It reshapes business operations, governance structures, and societal interactions. Over the past decade, integrating artificial intelligence (AI), blockchain, cloud computing, and cryptocurrencies has transcended theoretical discussions, establishing itself as a cornerstone of digital transformation. This book, *Digital Strategy and Governance in Transformative Technologies*, examines the interplay between digital strategies and governance frameworks. It emphasizes the challenges and opportunities posed by emerging technologies.

This book is motivated by the recognition that digital transformation extends beyond mere technological adoption. Organizations and institutions worldwide grapple with the complexities of integrating emerging technologies while ensuring ethical considerations, regulatory compliance, and sustainable practices. This book addresses these challenges through a multifaceted lens. It explores the theoretical frameworks and practical applications across different sectors and geographical contexts.

The structure of this book reflects the interconnected nature of digital technologies and their governance implications. Beginning with foundational concepts in digital strategy, the narrative progresses through specialized domains of AI, blockchain applications, cryptocurrency regulations, and metaverse governance. Each chapter contributes to a broader understanding of how these technologies shape strategic decisions and policy frameworks in the digital age.

The Scope of Digital Strategies

The first section sets the stage by examining the foundational elements of digital strategies in the context of technological convergence. It highlights how organizations must navigate the complexities of overlapping technologies to achieve tangible outcomes. Through a discussion on strategic collaboration, data-driven decision-making, and technological synergies, this chapter provides a comprehensive overview of the digital frontier. The chapter "The Intersection of Digital Strategy and Technology Landscapes: Overcoming Convergence Challenges" emphasizes overcoming challenges posed by technological overlap, while the chapter "Tracing the Evolution of Digital Strategy with AI, Blockchain, Cloud, and Cryptocurrencies" explores the historical progression of key transformative technologies and their interplay, illustrating strategic opportunities.

The inclusion of real-world case studies further enriches the narrative, offering insights into how digital strategies can drive innovation while maintaining accountability and efficiency. The chapter "Tracing the Evolution of Digital Strategy with AI, Blockchain, Cloud, and Cryptocurrencies" underscores the pivotal role of AI, blockchain, cloud computing, and cryptocurrencies. By identifying the intersections of these technologies, the authors illustrate how strategic integration can redefine industries, enhance customer experiences, and create new marketplaces. The chapter establishes a foundational understanding that informs subsequent discussions on specific technologies and their governance implications.

AI: Balancing Innovation and Ethics

AI represents one of the most significant technological advancements of the 21st century. Its adoption is, however, fraught with ethical dilemmas and societal challenges. The second section explores the multifaceted role of AI in shaping digital strategies, with a particular focus on law enforcement, healthcare, and cultural heritage management. It describes how AI-driven solutions can enhance efficiency and decision-making while addressing the ethical considerations arising from algorithmic bias, data privacy concerns, and environmental sustainability.

The chapter "Strategizing AI: Integrating Ethics and Environmental Sustainability in Digital Healthcare and Legal Systems" demonstrates AI's transformative potential in healthcare diagnostics and legal systems while advocating for Green AI to reduce its environmental impact. The chapter "Assessing the Efficacy of Artificial Intelligence (AI) Applications in Predictive Policing" examines the use of AI in forecasting criminal behavior, emphasizing accuracy and ethical concerns.

One key theme of this chapter is the integration of ethical principles into AI systems. By aligning AI applications with societal values, organizations can ensure that technological advancements contribute to equitable and sustainable outcomes. The chapter "Neurobiological Foundations of AI: Tracing the Evolution of Neural Networks" explores the biological inspiration behind AI, highlighting advanced architectures like spiking neural networks, while the chapter "The Urgency of AI for the Enhancement of Maritime Cultural Heritage Management in Indonesia" showcases how AI enhances underwater heritage conservation. The subsequent chapter "Artificial Intelligence and the Future of Software Development" discusses AI's impact across all phases of software development.

The chapter also examines AI's transformative potential in predictive policing and software development, emphasizing the importance of transparency, accountability, and cross-disciplinary collaboration. By presenting a nuanced analysis of AI's capabilities and limitations, this chapter gives readers a deeper understanding of the balance required between innovation and ethics.

Blockchain: A Framework for Trust and Accountability

Blockchain technology has garnered significant attention for its potential to enhance transparency and trust in decentralized systems. This section explores the governance implications of blockchain, with a focus on its applications in accounting, agriculture, and environmental sustainability. By leveraging blockchain's inherent features, such as immutability, distributed ledger systems, and real-time data verification, organizations can address longstanding challenges in fraud prevention, resource management, and stakeholder accountability.

The chapter "Immutable Transparency: Leveraging Blockchain Transparency Features to Foster Trust in Decentralized Systems" examines blockchain's transparency in reducing dishonest behavior. The next chapter "The Ethical Ledger: A Review of Literature on the Alignment of Accounting Ethics and Blockchain Technology" explores how blockchain enhances professional integrity and fraud prevention in accounting practices. The chapter "Using Blockchain Technology for Audit Trail" investigates blockchain's role in creating tamper-proof audit systems.

This chapter also examines the alignment between blockchain technology and accounting ethics, highlighting its role in reinforcing principles such as integrity, confidentiality, and professional competence. The chapter "A Blockchain-Enabled Digital Strategy for Agriculture Trade" illustrates blockchain's capacity to streamline agricultural trade operations. At the same time, the chapter "Blockchain Accountability Strategy of ESG-Focused Cryptocurrency Projects" evaluates its application in managing ESG investments and promoting sustainability.

Through thematic literature reviews and case studies, the authors demonstrate how blockchain can enhance audit quality, improve data reliability, and foster stakeholder trust. Furthermore, the discussion extends to using blockchain in ESG-focused cryptocurrency projects, illustrating its capacity to support socially responsible investments and sustainable development goals.

Cryptocurrencies: Governance in a Decentralized Financial Landscape

The rise of cryptocurrencies represents a paradigm shift in global financial systems. Part 4 critically analyzes the opportunities and challenges associated with cryptocurrencies, particularly in the context of Web 3.0 ecosystems. It examines how decentralized finance (DeFi) platforms redefine traditional financial structures, offering increased accessibility, security, and efficiency. However, these benefits are accompanied by regulatory uncertainties, scalability issues, and concerns about market volatility.

The chapter "Cryptocurrency Integration in the Web 3.0 Ecosystem" explores real-world projects demonstrating how decentralized applications enable financial inclusion and innovation. The next chapter "Cryptocurrency Regulations in India: Opportunities and Challenges" provides insights into India's evolving stance on cryptocurrency regulation, while the chapter "A Case Study on Cryptocurrency Strategy and Regulation in the Asia Pacific" compares regulatory frameworks in Indonesia, China, and Japan.

Through comparative analyses of cryptocurrency regulations in India, Indonesia, China, and Japan, this chapter highlights the diverse approaches adopted by different jurisdictions. The discussion emphasizes the need for a balanced regulatory framework that fosters innovation while safeguarding consumer interests and financial stability. By addressing the convergence of traditional finance and DeFi, this chapter provides actionable insights into the governance strategies required to navigate this rapidly evolving landscape.

The Metaverse: Legal and Ethical Dimensions

The emergence of the metaverse has introduced new dimensions to digital interaction, blending virtual environments with real-world applications. Part 5 examines the legal and ethical challenges posed by the metaverse, focusing on issues such as intellectual property rights, data privacy, and jurisdictional complexities. As virtual spaces become increasingly integrated into daily life, the need for comprehensive legal frameworks becomes more urgent. The chapter "Navigating the Legal Landscape of the Metaverse" analyzes jurisdictional and intellectual property complexities in virtual environments. The next chapter "Virtual Rape: Parallels Between Physical and Virtual Violation in the Metaverse" discusses the urgent need for robust regulatory frameworks to address misconduct and protect users.

This chapter also addresses the psychological and emotional impacts of misconduct in virtual environments, drawing parallels between physical and virtual violations. By presenting empirical surveys and legal analyses, the authors underscore the importance of user protection and accountability in the metaverse. The chapter concludes with recommendations for interdisciplinary approaches to developing robust legal standards that align with the unique characteristics of virtual spaces.

Policy and Governance in the Digital Era

The final section explores the broader implications of policy and governance in addressing the societal impacts of digital technologies. By analyzing case studies on Meta's political ad policy enforcement and e-waste management, this chapter highlights the complexities of regulating technology-driven ecosystems. It emphasizes the need for adaptive governance strategies to keep pace with technological advancements while addressing ethical, environmental, and social considerations.

The chapter "An Analysis of Meta's Political Ad Policy Enforcement" highlights gaps in Meta's ad archiving system, revealing issues with over-enforcement and under-enforcement of political ads. The final chapter "Regulating E-Waste Management in the Digital Era" advocates for circular economy principles in e-waste policies to address environmental degradation. Meta's political ad policy enforcement serves as a case study for examining the challenges of content moderation and algorithmic decision-making. The findings reveal gaps in detection systems, highlighting the risks of over-enforcement and under-enforcement in political advertising. Similarly, the discussion on e-waste management advocates for a circular economy approach, integrating repairability, recyclability, and durability principles into product design and end-of-life management.

Conclusion

Digital Strategy and Governance in Transformative Technologies aims to comprehensively explore the intersections between technology, strategy, and governance. By presenting a diverse range of perspectives and case studies, this book seeks to inform readers about the complexities of navigating the digital frontier. The discussions emphasize the importance of ethical considerations, interdisciplinary collaboration, and adaptive governance in harnessing the transformative potential of emerging technologies. This volume represents a collaborative effort to advance the understanding of digital strategy and governance in the context of transformative technologies. The contributors have brought their expertise and research rigor to examine critical issues at the intersection of technology, strategy, and governance. By fostering dialogue and understanding, this book aspires to contribute to the development of inclusive, equitable, and sustainable digital ecosystems.

The editors acknowledge that this book represents a snapshot of a rapidly evolving field. As the digital landscape continues to evolve, the insights offered in this book will remain relevant for policymakers, academics, and practitioners seeking to address the challenges and opportunities of transformative technologies. We encourage readers to consider the insights presented here as part of an ongoing dialogue about the future of digital transformation and its governance implications.

Part 1

Introduction to the Digital Frontier and Strategic Foundations

1
The Intersection of Digital Strategy and Technology Landscapes: Overcoming Convergence Challenges

Neelesh Kumbhojkar, Arun Menon, and S. Vijayakumar Bharathi

1.1 Introduction

In the dynamic landscape of modern business, the intersection of digital strategy and technology is a pivotal focal point, especially in the face of the complex challenges of digital convergence (Teece, 2018; Drechsler et al., 2020). A robust digital strategy is a blueprint for leveraging data assets and technology-driven initiatives to their fullest potential. This endeavor typically necessitates the collaboration of a diverse array of talents, spanning executive leadership, marketing, and information technology (IT) expertise. Key to its success is the dismantling of silos between IT leaders and customer-facing departments, fostering a seamless digital customer experience (Taherdoost, 2024). Complementing this strategic framework are technology landscapes, offering a comprehensive overview of emerging technologies and their integration with an organization's overarching innovation objectives (Hanelt et al., 2021). Technology road mapping is central to this alignment – a versatile planning approach synchronizing short-term actions with long-term aspirations.

However, amid this digital evolution, enterprises encounter numerous formidable challenges. These include safeguarding data integrity and privacy, ensuring interoperability across diverse platforms, nurturing a skilled workforce, and confronting heightened market competition as traditional boundaries blur (Sharad Mangrulkar & Vijay Chavan, 2024). To navigate these hurdles effectively, businesses must cultivate a culture of innovation and collaboration, investing in continuous staff development and prioritizing user-centric experiences. Furthermore, forging strategic partnerships with technology providers and industry peers emerges as a cornerstone strategy in adapting to the shifting tides of digital convergence. Thriving in this era demands adept navigation of technological landscapes and a steadfast commitment to fostering agility, innovation, and customer-centricity at every turn (Omol, 2023).

1.1.1 Overview of Digital Strategy and Technology Landscapes

As per Hanelt (Hanelt & Bohnsack, 2021), digital transformation is the creation of new business models by leveraging technologies. When every company becomes a technology business, the business of a technology company undergoes a paradigm shift. In its special report for Technology Providers 2025, Gartner talks about technology and service providers needing to take a long-term view to see opportunities and threats, which are not always visible, while serving current market demands (Gartner, 2022). Innovation using technology can create new opportunities. The adaptability of technology and a call to make it more mainstream should depend on the technology's maturity, applicability within the industry context, and the total cost of ownership. It can help create a new path internally (evolutionary) or externally (revolutionary) for the organization. Having a revolutionary approach is not an optional path for any enterprise. It can be an existential crisis in the ever-changing world should this path not be adopted. In every industry, there will always be new entrants bringing in disruptive business models to alter the course of the industry. With the pace of technological change, the time required to bring in these disruptive models has been reduced. It is now or never for organizations to adopt a revolutionary approach and bring in a new model to disrupt their own business or create a new one.

In the world of fast-paced technological changes, there is a strong interplay of technologies such as artificial intelligence (AI), data, cloud, blockchain, Internet of Things (IoT), spatial computing, and quantum computing. Delivery mechanisms using dev-ops and microservices allow incremental development and quick prototyping to test outcomes.

1.1.2 Defining Convergence in the Digital Strategic Landscapes

Convergence is not about blending technologies but creating new synergies where the combined effect exceeds the sum of individual parts. It is all about moving from an inward looking to an externally focused strategy on developing partner networks and growing the customer base with new products and services. Contrary to homogeneous technology development, technological convergence will cause radical and discontinuous innovation in a market or industry (Kwak & Kim, 2022). New technologies develop interdependently, and technology integration and substitution can introduce a new technological paradigm, i.e., radical innovation (Dosi et al., 2022). The convergence of technologies should result in the creation of new business processes that were not feasible earlier.

1.1.3 Need for Addressing Convergent Challenges in Digital Strategy

A successful digital strategy is the roadmap for achieving a revolutionary approach in the digital age. It involves the effective use of technologies to drive a range of critical business outcomes. These outcomes include enhanced customer and employee experiences, increased productivity across various functions, reduced operational costs, faster time to market for new products and services, the ability to expand and serve customers in new geographic locations, improved security measures to protect data and assets, and finally, operational elasticity, which allows businesses to rapidly scale operations up or down in response to market demands.

As technologies such as AI, big data, cloud, and IoT converge, they open exciting possibilities for creating new markets and products (Bhattacharjee & Badhan, 2024). However, this convergence also presents challenges such as developing regulatory frameworks, security concerns, data privacy regulations, systems integration challenges, increasing computing requirements, and the need to upskill the workforce. A comprehensive strategy is needed to tackle all these issues. It is anticipated that more than 8 billion devices are connected to the internet. This interconnection and collation of data in real-time will propel increased convergence and new business processes and outcomes.

The key is to use technologies to deliver business outcomes rather than implement them as the strategy (Vomberg et al., 2024). Adopting business leads to continuous digital transformation, which is paramount for an organization to stay current and help develop new products and markets.

1.2 The Interplay of Technologies

1.2.1 Overview of Key Digital Technologies

A robust arsenal of technologies fuels the digital revolution, each offering unique business opportunities:

- Social Media: Creates a direct line of communication with customers, enabling real-time service and valuable customer insights.
- Mobility: Empowers a "connected everywhere" world, fostering personalized interactions with customers and employees.
- The IoT generates vast amounts of data through sensors, allowing for remote monitoring, data-driven decision-making, and automated operations.
- Blockchain: Provides a secure and transparent distributed ledger system, revolutionizing trust and security in areas like supply chain management.

- Cloud Computing: Offers unparalleled flexibility and scalability, enabling businesses to adopt pay-as-you-go models like software-as-a-service (SaaS) and platform-as-a-service (PaaS).
- AI: Processes massive datasets, uncovering valuable insights and enabling intelligent decision-making across various functions.
- Generative AI: Utilizes large or small language models to democratize AI-powered content creation, opening doors for personalized marketing and interactive experiences.
- Quantum Computing: Harnesses the power of quantum mechanics to solve complex problems beyond the reach of traditional computers, potentially revolutionizing fields like materials science and drug discovery.
- Spatial Computing: This technology blends the physical and digital worlds, creating immersive experiences through virtual reality and augmented reality. It has applications in areas like training, product visualization, and design.
- Big Data: Transforms large volumes of structured and unstructured data into actionable insights, driving data-driven decision-making and innovation.

By leveraging this technological landscape strategically, organizations can create a foundation for a successful revolutionary approach.

1.2.2 Identifying Overlapping Areas among Technologies

While AI, Blockchain, social media, and IoT offer immense potential, they all rely on two critical pillars: data and computing.

1. **Data** is the fuel that drives these technologies. The ever-growing volume of data generated by sensors (IoT), user interactions (social media), and complex simulations demands robust data management and governance strategies.
2. **Compute Power** is essential for processing massive datasets and running sophisticated algorithms. AI systems require specialized computing power to function effectively.

Figure 1.1 illustrates the significant decline in storage prices in U.S. dollars per terabyte (TB), adjusted for inflation. The term "Memory" refers to random access memory, while "disk" denotes magnetic storage. "Flash" indicates specialized memory for fast data access and rewriting, and "solid-state" pertains to solid-state drives. This rapid reduction in storage costs has transformed data management, enabling organizations to store vast amounts of information more affordably. As prices drop, businesses can leverage

The Intersection of Digital Strategy and Technology Landscapes 7

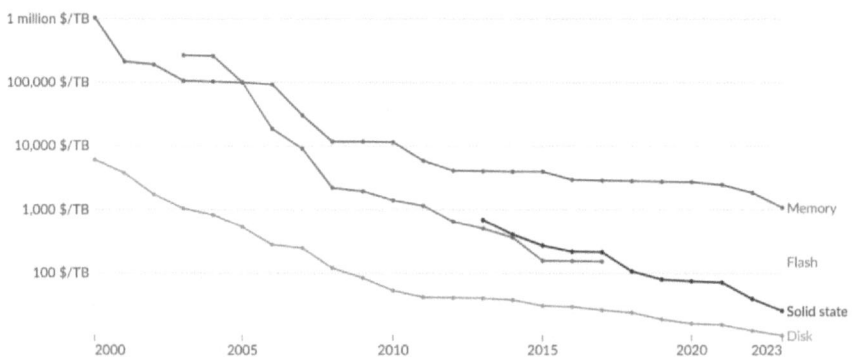

FIGURE 1.1
Rapid drop in storage prices

Source: https://ourworldindata.org/grapher/historical-cost-of-computer-memory-and-storage?time=2000.latest (Giattino et al., 2023).

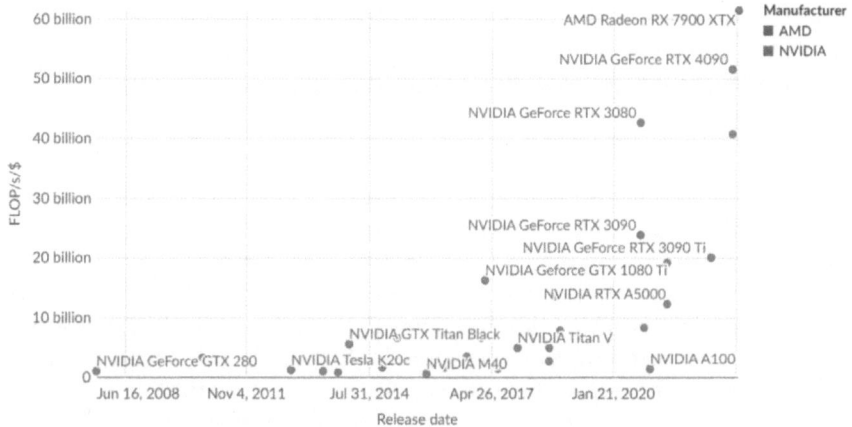

FIGURE 1.2
Performance of graphics processing units for AI systems in floating operations per second per U.S. dollar, adjusted for inflation

Source: https://ourworldindata.org/artificial-intelligence#all-charts.

advanced technologies and enhance their data capabilities, driving innovation and efficiency across various sectors.

Graphics processing units from AMD and Nvidia have become essential in AI systems, dominating the computing hardware landscape. Their performance is often measured in floating-point operations per second per U.S. dollar, adjusted for inflation, demonstrating a significant improvement in cost-effectiveness over time (Figure 1.2). Nvidia commands a substantial

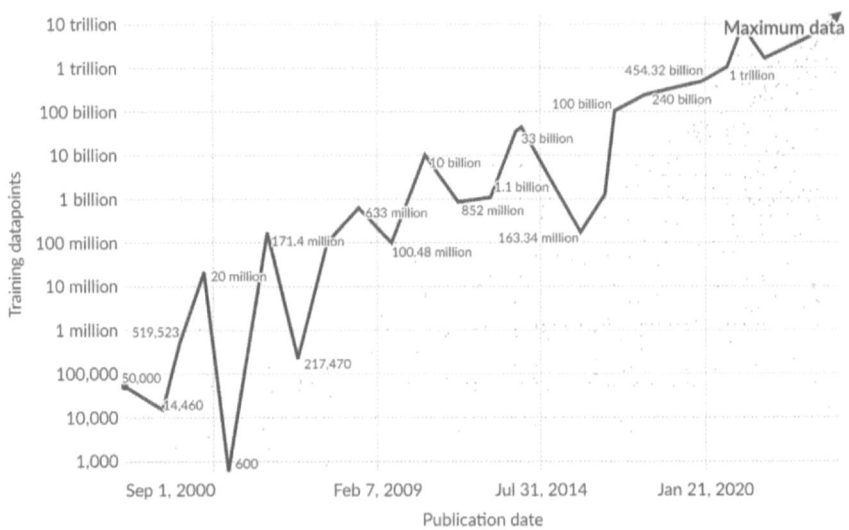

FIGURE 1.3
Datapoints used to train AI systems

Source: https://ourworldindata.org/artificial-intelligence#all-charts (Epoch, 2023).

market share due to its advanced architecture and robust software ecosystem. AMD is also making strides, offering competitive alternatives that emphasize value.

Figure 1.3 presents the proliferation of data points used to train AI systems over the last two decades. Training data size is critical in developing AI systems and machine learning models. It directly influences the model's learning depth; larger datasets enable a more profound and nuanced understanding of the subject matter. Moreover, an extensive training dataset enhances the model's recognition capabilities, allowing it to identify patterns and make accurate predictions more effectively. Consequently, the significance of robust training data cannot be overstated, as it plays a vital role in the overall performance and reliability of AI systems, driving advancements across various applications and industries.

1.2.2.1 Cloud as the Enabler

Cloud computing offers a compelling solution to these challenges. It provides flexibility and scalability, allowing cloud infrastructure to seamlessly scale to meet fluctuating data and compute demands, eliminating the need for upfront investments in on-premises hardware. In addition, cloud services handle infrastructure management and maintenance, freeing up internal IT resources to focus on strategic initiatives and reducing operational overhead.

This also helps leverage the newer compute strategies coming to the marketplace, lowering the overall cost structure and improving outcomes.

1.2.2.2 The Rise of Hybrid Cloud and Quantum Computing

The ever-increasing pressure on computing resources necessitates a strategic approach. A hybrid cloud model, which combines on-premises infrastructure with public cloud resources, balances cost optimization and control. This allows organizations to strategically allocate workloads based on specific needs.

In addition, quantum computing, though still in its initial stages, holds immense promise for tackling problems beyond the reach of traditional computers. By developing a cloud strategy incorporating future technologies like quantum computing, organizations can position themselves as early adopters and gain a significant competitive advantage.

1.2.3 Implications of Tech Intersections on Business Operations

Delivering a consistently positive customer experience hinges on robust applications and efficient business processes (Kaushal & Yadav, 2023). Often, organizations make the mistake of solely monitoring applications, overlooking the core business processes they support. This disconnect can lead to a disjointed customer experience and revenue loss. Advancements in technology offer solutions such as the business process observability tools. These tools go beyond application monitoring by providing insights into the actual performance of business processes, helping correlate business and application performance, identifying bottlenecks and issues, and fine-tuning processes.

While achieving a completely flawless operation may be ideal, striving for continuous improvement is a more realistic and achievable goal. Organizations can build predictable operations and proactive management by leveraging business process observability tools and fostering a culture of constant improvement.

1.2.4 Navigating Complexity in Digital Strategy

Technology is central to an organization's transformation. Getting the strategy right to use the right technology at the right time to ensure an outcome conformance with the vision requires a very well-thought-out approach (Saha et al., 2024). A key enabler of this approach is the recognition of the convergence of technologies, which brings forth new use cases and innovative approaches to doing things. Each technology has its hype, adoption, and maturity cycles. As Gartner explains in its hype cycle (Gartner et al.), every technology goes through the life cycle of "Innovation Trigger, Peak of inflated expectations, Trough of disillusionment, Slope of enlightenment,

Plateau of productivity." With the cycle being different, it is the timing of bringing the confluence of these technologies and creating use cases that can help create the sauce for success. In 2024, quantum computing is still a few years away from becoming mainstream, while AI, which was on the periphery for two decades, is mainstream and is rapidly getting adopted, while spatial computing is on the cusp of a big adoption wave and is waiting for the following innovative product to hit the marketplace. A roadmap to use these technologies as they move through their maturity path is critical to ensuring currency and optimal technology usage.

1.2.5 Complexity Theory and Its Application in Digital Strategy

In applications, the ever-increasing volume of data coupled with more significant problem sets creates a combinatorial explosion in complexity, often posing a major challenge to dissect this complexity and create an effective strategy to deal with it. Coevolution among disparate technologies under technology disequilibrium is a characteristic of technology convergence (San Kim & Sohn, 2020). A modular architecture incorporates flexible functionality where the internal structure is designed independently but, when combined, functions as an integrated whole. The industry has experienced previously unimaginable levels of innovation and growth because it embraced the concept of modularity, building complex products from smaller subsystems that can be designed independently yet function together as a whole (Baldwin & Clark, 2000; Hofmann & Jaeger-Erben, 2020). Modularity, in this sense, also suggests organizing complements (products that work with one another) to interoperate through public, nondiscriminatory, well-understood interfaces (Farell & Weiser, 2003; Teece, 2018; Holgersson et al., 2022).

1.2.6 Challenges Arising from Tech Overlaps

As systems span across technologies, data following through the various infrastructure layers within the organization or externally in the cloud becomes complex. Understanding the interplay of technologies in creating practical business lead use cases and ensuring that organizational goals are met is essential. One key to watch out for is security.

Security must permeate into everything in the organization. It takes only one security attack for an organization to lose credibility with investors, buyers, and employees. Security attacks are known to break companies and diametrically change their fortunes. A lockdown and hard ring-fencing might help from a security posture but will impact operations, development, and overall progress. Taking a practical approach to security strategy and intermixing it with AI, data, and cloud strategy is critical to ensuring progress while balancing security requirements. Implementing a "zero-trust" tools approach and having employees realize the value of following basic

The Intersection of Digital Strategy and Technology Landscapes

principles followed by a robust education program can help cover the multiple security angles (Buck et al., 2021).

1.2.7 Strategies for Managing Complexity in Digital Initiatives

Technologies can dramatically reduce the concept of actualization time. The more technologies in the basket, the greater the interplay and complexities. The strategy to use technologies must be business-driven, i.e., the unique selling propositions (USPs), financial goals, and vision of the organization must drive the adoption of technology and help create a clear differentiation from competitors (Yadav et al., 2023; Su et al., 2023).

An encompassing AI strategy is needed in the organization to develop true differentiation. AI needs to permeate every fabric of the organization. It requires a complete re-think of the business processes, data strategy, security, risk management, and AI governance strategy. This intersection of technology, strategy, governance, and business processes will drive the success of the organization in the long term. Figure 1.4 depicts AI performance in comparison to human performance, which is baselined at zero. With AI systems surpassing human performance, it is time for them to be interspersed into business processes, making them more effective.

SaaS products are here to stay in an IT stack. The era of on-premises software is over unless there is a compelling reason to retain it on-premise. Today's SaaS tools offer a basket of applications under one roof. With most

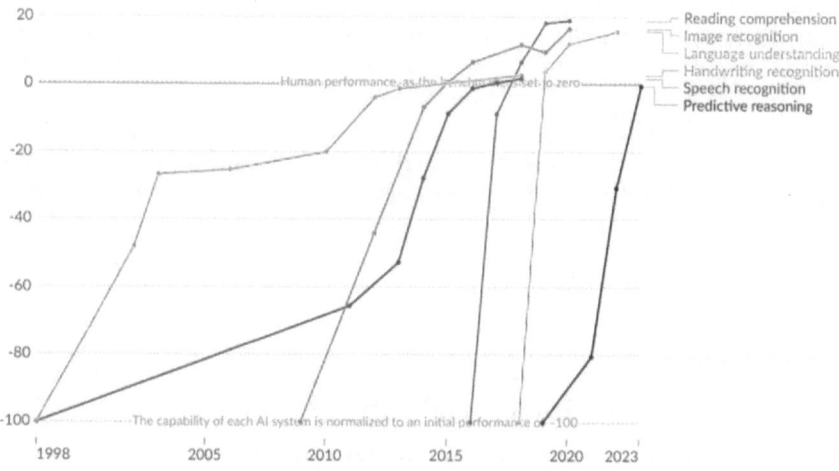

FIGURE 1.4
AI systems on various capabilities relative to human performance

Source: https://contextual.ai/blog/plotting-progress (Kiela, 2023).

of the backend management of the infrastructure database taken care of by the SaaS provider, the operational elements of the IT stack get a lot simplified (Frank et al., 2023).

Having off-the-shelf tools helps enable functions to help the organization focus on its true mission. There are a few considerations to consider when evaluating any product or platform to align with:

1. The vendor's size and financial stability. As most smaller vendors are acquired by the larger, more prominent players, service levels and roadmaps will change post-acquisition.
2. The vendor/provider's industry orientation. The vendor's focus is on investing in and providing industry-specific solutions.
3. The vendor's strategy is to become a PaaS vendor.
4. Rapidity of patches, upgrades offered, and flexibility to accept these upgrades/patches.
5. Financial flexibility with the commercial models offered and historical trends of price increases.
6. Integration ability to custom or legacy applications

Most SaaS providers have adopted a GenAI inclusion strategy. Today, GenAI systems provide an excellent natural language interface and accelerate content development (Feng et al., 2024). The use of co-pilots is now mainstream. With automated software code generation, the organization must develop new skills to ensure currency and leverage these technologies.

Today, most products and platforms claim to be AI-enabled. There is a clear differentiation between the marketing buzz of AI and having a true ground-up built product/platform around AI. The fitment of the vendor AI approach and strategy must be examined from the organizational view of AI and data (Mikalef & Gupta, 2021). It is recommended that the organization have an independent strategy and use the tools to help accelerate it rather than simply adopting them and making them the organization's strategy.

1.3 Integration and Interoperability

1.3.1 Importance of Integration in Digital Ecosystems

With the exponential number of systems that collect, process, and share data, systems must communicate without human intervention to deliver a common business objective.

The heart of any digital ecosystem is the integration layer, which integrates disparate systems and keeps data consistent, ensuring that all systems have a shared view of the data and a standard semantic view (Chen, 2022).

Integration using iPaaS solutions takes data from multiple cloud-based applications and routes it between systems (Frantz et al., 2021). Having a physical view of the journey that data takes to perform a business process will be key to understanding and appreciating security challenges, if any, latency involved, and the total time taken to execute the process and, in turn, impacting/enhancing the customer serviceability and the overall experience as well as time to market.

1.3.2 Addressing Interoperability Challenges

For systems to interoperate with a common state, they must have a set of common standards, protocols, and semantic understanding. Definitions of system owners of data enable consistency across data and propagation across from a sole source of truth. Syntactic interoperability establishes a standard data format and data structure protocols, while semantic interoperability establishes metadata to link data elements to a common vocabulary (Dang et al., 2023).

Breaking all processes into microservices, which enables a quick building of Lego blocks to assemble and re-assemble based on business dynamics and changing market conditions, will help organizations to be agile and nimble (Abouahmed & Ahmed, 2023). Having a balance and an enterprise architecture team closely reviewing the approach on what needs to be broken up and what needs to be built up as a combination of microservices is as much an art as a science.

1.3.3 Leveraging Application Programming Interfaces (APIs) and Standards for Seamless Integration

Application programming interfaces (API)-based integration can help implement multiple business processes. It provides organizations with access to rich data sources, synchronizes information across systems, improves productivity, and creates new business processes (Suzic, 2016). While providing access to data, API-based integrations help reduce operational friction and provide the flexibility to innovate continuously and create new processes.

It is vital to have an API integration strategy, which includes identifying requirements, goals, and data that needs to be transferred across systems and having a catalog of APIs. Security is integral to any integration strategy to ensure that only authorized users and systems can access the data. Every API-based integration implementation must handle error handling, scalability, and maintainability requirements. API strategy needs to tie closely with the data strategy so that data flow via APIs is captured correctly and a harmonious relationship exists between data, API, and business process transformation strategy.

1.4 Data Management across Overlapping Technologies

1.4.1 Role of Data in Digital Strategy

Data is the new oil that greases any organization and enables it to move forward rapidly. Technology convergence has increased the quantum of data generated. Gathering wisdom from the data generated and using it within data governance, privacy, and legitimate use requires a detailed data strategy for any organization, industry, or country (Yeung, 2018). In the last decade, data has moved from being an afterthought to having a seat at the head of the table to help drive business strategy decision-making and open new avenues of growth and improvement in the overall ecosystem, creating avenues for both evolutionary and revolutionary paths. Building a data fabric layer helps organizations run a federated data management model and helps build tools and processes to leverage data near its source.

1.4.2 Big Data and Its Implications

With the multitude of access points feeding in data, structured and unstructured, there has been an explosion in volume, variety, and velocity. Compared to traditional data warehouses, data updates are made at predefined intervals; in many big data implementations, data sets are updated near real-time (Mehmood & Anees, 2022).

The data's veracity, variability, and value present an opportunity to monetize. The collation and processing of this semi-structured, unstructured, and structured data requires storage and computing resources. Cleaning, parsing, and analyzing this data is complex and time-consuming. However, if done rightly, it can produce a wealth of knowledge and often provide the necessary USP for an organization to revolutionize itself.

1.4.3 Data Governance in a Convergent Environment

Data strategy involves empowering ownership, enhancing transparency and security, and facilitating business enhancement (Kouroubali & Katehakis, 2019). While data and insights derived from it can be a great power, if necessary, controls must be put in place to ensure veracity. Otherwise, wrong decision-making can occur, which might make the organization noncompliant with regulatory requirements.

Converged systems collect personal data as machines directly interface with end users (Asch et al., 2018). Most countries have laws defining this data's collection, storage, and use. Digital privacy takes a prime seat, as converged systems find it easy to co-relate data to help identify, locate, or track an individual (Pearlson et al., 2024).

Data security practices should include proactive measures to prevent data theft and user notifications in case of a breach. Converged technologies, such as IoT devices, offer users access from anywhere, anytime, using any device (Farahani et al., 2021). While this is convenient, it opens multiple opportunities for potential exploitation by malicious actors.

With AI transcending into all systems and processes, it is essential to have a data governance strategy to feed into the AI systems and have a strategy to deal with the outcomes generated by the AI systems. AI governance involves having the proper rules, responsibilities, and processes to derive the maximum value while mitigating risk and ensuring security and regulatory compliance (Janssen et al., 2020). For AI to succeed, it needs high-quality data and consistent data. While deploying AI systems as one grapples with a model-centric or data-centric approach, it is not one over the other but a complementary approach that will push the organization forward. Having data around the model performance that is trusted and high-quality data as output can build more confidence among the user base in the AI models and remove the black box effect. The whole approach must be quickly assembled, tested, and refined.

1.5 Agile Approaches to Convergent Challenges

1.5.1 Agile Methodologies for Managing Tech Overlaps

Converged technology implementations open a variety of use cases and require a shift in mindset within the organization. Agile methodologies advocate breaking organizational boundaries and helping businesses, and technologists come together with a common purpose. This requires fluid organization, effective communication, and alignment within the entire organization. Development approaches like dev-ops, agile, and hybrid-agile are here to stay and will only accelerate the cycle time to get outcomes quicker into the hands of the customer (Ambler & Lines, 2020).

The use and deployment of AI systems require a rethink from the traditional models of driving IT systems implementation from a requirement to deploy and forget models to more continuously evolving models getting trained based on the data being fed into the system, giving an ability to constantly improve and keep changing and improving based on incoming data. The better the quality and quantum of data used for training, the better the outcome.

1.5.2 Cross-Functional Teams in Convergent Projects

Convergent projects bring in many technologies to help create new business processes that transcend the organization (Kodama, 2021). This will require an agile, collaborative, non-siloed organization. For any project to succeed, cross-functional teams must come together with a common purpose. This is best facilitated as part of agile methodologies. An agile team should have members from streams focused on user experience, technology, business, and operations. Adhering to the methodology's main principles will help an organization become flexible and more customer-centered.

1.5.3 Iterative Development and Continuous Improvement

Rather than going for a big-bang, all-in-one approach, agile methodologies inherently advocate an iterative approach, allowing the business to see the output being produced and the ability to experiment with it in the marketplace (Mordi, 2021). It will enable feedback to ensure a more aligned product outcome in upcoming cycles. This iterative approach to continuous improvement also allows for course corrections based on the feedback received. This reduces the gap between the backend teams and the field, resulting in a better outcome.

1.6 Strategic Decision-Making amid Tech Overlaps

1.6.1 Identifying Opportunities in Tech Convergence

Organizations must prepare an outline for designing digital strategies in the technology convergence era by considering critical components, as presented in Figure 1.5.

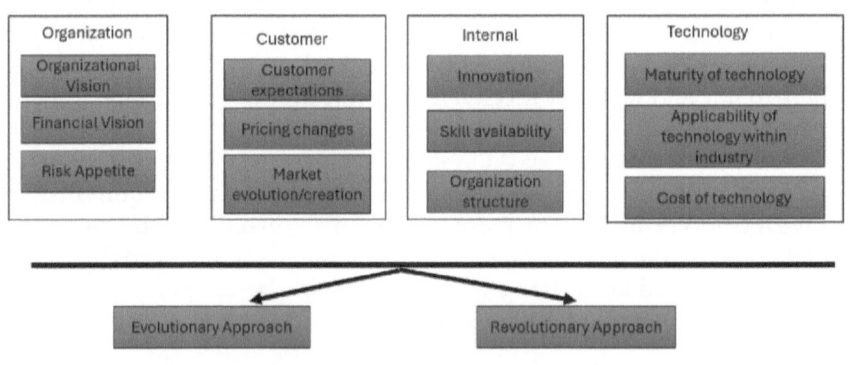

FIGURE 1.5
A blueprint for designing strategies in the era of technology convergence

In the era of technological confluence, the first step for the organization is to determine the radical quotient it would like to adopt to create a new market and product line for its services. This can forge a new industry and set the pace to move from evolutionary to revolutionary. Localized exploitation and internal integration of technology can help evolve the IT structure within an organization to help speed up the go-to-market and create new evolutionary products. Entire business processes and network redesign can help revolutionize the product set and market need. The strategy needs to be investigated in both contexts.

Inputs into the process from an organizational perspective are business risk-taking appetite, innovation quotient of the organization, financial vision, and organizational vision, which, when combined with internal skills readiness and organization structure, help define the path internally. Customer expectations are rapidly evolving. In the hyper-connected, personalized experience, demands for instant gratification are rising. Gartner says 80% of sales interactions between suppliers and buyers will occur in digital channels by 2025. The remorse cycle for customers is rapid. Crucial and pricing expectations form an essential market input for strategy definition. These customer expectations, market evolution, and pricing expectations form crucial market inputs for the strategy definition, and pricing expectations form key market inputs in the strategy definition.

1.6.2 Aligning Digital Strategy with Business Objectives

Any strategy must have clearly defined desired outcomes. In the era of rapid technology convergence, a strategy must focus on an outcome centered around personalized experiences, a significant reduction in transaction speed, the ability to scale up, better security, and overall reduced costs. To evolve and decide on the strategy, it is essential to go through an introspection exercise along the steps as shown in Figure 1.6.

1.6.2.1 Step 1: Vision Definition

Defining the desired visible end state for the evolutionary approach creates a goalpost that shapes the path to achieve it. Kelly Burke (Burke, 2011) defines a vision as brevity, clarity, abstraction, and challenge. It also states the organization's purpose, is future-focused, sets a desirable goal, and matches the organization's success criteria.

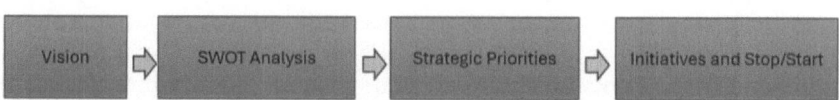

FIGURE 1.6
Taking vision to execution

The vision has two significant aspects to it – the organizational vision and the financial vision. An organization's vision determines what kind of organization is envisaged in the future. For example, General Electric CEO Jeff Immelt repositioned the firm as a digital industrial company looking to define the future of the Internet of Things (Immelt, 2017). This pivots the organization in a new direction and repositions it as it seems. Another example is Starbucks – when Howard Schultz returned as CEO, he repositioned the company to revert the focus to coffee rather than food items, setting the stage for the company to achieve greatness again.

Financial vision sets the goal from a financial view of what the organization should strive to achieve. It could be from a revenue perspective, margin perspective, source of revenue perspective, and markets from which revenue is achieved.

1.6.2.2 Step 2: Execution Path Definition

The first step of taking the vision to reality is to get a strengths–weaknesses–opportunities–threats (SWOT) analysis done. While strengths and weaknesses are inward-looking and mirror the organization's current state, the weaknesses look at the external world and the changing dynamics that will impact the organization. It helps generate the current position of the organization concerning its ecosystem. This reflection will prompt the action required to propel the organization forward. SWOT should lead to strategic priorities that an organization should take to mitigate the weaknesses and threats while capitalizing on the opportunities. These strategic priorities should lead to initiatives and activities with a timeline plan. Each initiative should have a clear charter, measurable goals, and a timeline of activities. It is also the time to review the current set of activities and see if there are activities that should be stopped, continued, or started. This approach to developing an execution blueprint takes it from the approach and desired end state to have an execution plan. A traceability matrix from the SWOT analysis to initiatives and activities also mirrors the impact of execution or nonexecution of these activities.

To determine which initiatives to pursue, one must understand the interplay of business, technology, operations, and customers. Evaluating the vision from each lens provides a view into what the organization needs to do to move forward.

1.6.3 Balancing Risks and Rewards

Technology convergence opens the doors to new markets and new products. It can bring many benefits, such as increased efficiency, innovation, competitiveness, and customer satisfaction. However, it also enters an arena where regulatory frameworks still play a catch-up game and challenges around data privacy, security, cultural resistance, and risk of security breaches. The way forward is to figure out the right balance.

1.7 Uber: A Case Study Illustrating Successful Navigation of Tech Overlaps

Uber is a technology company and not a taxi or a limousine company. It has a platform that connects service providers and consumers. It leverages technology to develop and improve the platform with a customer-centric approach. At the same time, it is quick to jump on external technology advancements around social media, smartphones, and AI. From its launch in 2009 and pivoting from an exclusive service to a mass-based mobility service, riding on the growing proliferation of smartphones and social media platforms, Uber has successfully navigated the regulatory hurdles while constantly evolving and tackling each market based on changing customer dynamics. The culture within the organization is to listen to customers and their needs, and the whole organization rallies around it. Its strategy to marry internal technology progress, external changing customer demand, and personas, and keep evolving its internal organization has helped it stand the tide of time and keep growing. Uber has grown from $10.4 billion in 2018 to $37.2 billion in 2023, a compound annual growth rate growth of 30%. This pace of growth is phenomenal, considering that there have been different organizations in the world that have tried to copy the same formula but have met with limited success.

From a regulatory perspective, Uber comes under transportation regulations when it uses the platform for mobility. When it uses the same platform for delivery, it can fall under the jurisdiction of health regulators. On top of it, when one adds the country, state, or city-specific regulations, the complexity expands multifold. With Uber being a platform, debates continue in various jurisdictions worldwide about treating the gig workers who work as drivers as part of Uber mobility. Every city, state, and country in the world is producing its interpretations, making it a daunting task to ensure compliance and, at the same time, keep the sanctity of the original model and purpose. Uber has not shied away from regulatory conflicts and, in turn, has used them to highlight its service and widen its user base.

Some key points to note about Uber:

1. Ability to eliminate wait times and have a ride on demand, compared to the earlier approach of booking limousines or taxis from smaller organizations and the inability to have a consistent experience.
2. Technology provides a view to the customer on the path the driver takes to reach the customer and during the ride, including the hassle-free payment process.
3. Use technology to implement dynamic pricing based on supply-demand, ensuring the organization can capitalize on demand surges, especially from customers ready to pay more.

4. Use of social media to propagate the brand.
5. Having an organizational structure and a culture within the organization of having the customer at the center of everything.
6. Ability to marry and continuously evolve business processes, technology, and strategy with changing dynamics.
7. During COVID-19, the ability to quickly flip the business to move from mobility to delivery/Uber eats.

What makes Uber stand out is its customer-centricity and the ability to put the customer before its technology-driven projects. The close association with the market enables the organization to listen to the changing demands and appropriately change its product mix and execution approach. Uber is known for its technological innovations, including dynamic pricing (surge pricing) that links fares to demand, a user-friendly mobile app with seamless payment options, and AI-based route planning. These innovations enhance the overall user experience and help develop a strong customer base in this growing sharing economy.

Uber's ability to continuously innovate and grow markets in different countries with a local strategy while leveraging its central technical capabilities, start-up culture, and great organizational culture makes it an organization that will endure technology change and market change.

1.8 Conclusion and Future Outlook: Navigating the Ever-Changing Digital Landscape

In his book *Great by Choice* (Jim Collins, 2011), Collins discusses innovation with discipline; this discipline will ensure that the organization continues on the 20-mile march principle and becomes a 10× organization.

Innovation and the ability to experiment small and have the element of try, learn, and proceed is the mantra for sustained growth. To create revolutionary pathways, it is essential to experiment and learn before taking more significant bets.

Defining a strategy requires recognizing interplay across technologies, whether AI, data, cloud, blockchain, or security in today's context or with the introduction of spatial computing or quantum computing. The technologies are not independent of each other and have a crucial bearing on the entire architectural landscape. It is also important to harness this interplay with business processes to deliver a new innovative customer experience or product or create a new marketplace. Regulatory and external geopolitical

The Intersection of Digital Strategy and Technology Landscapes 21

headwinds, controllable and noncontrollable, can be converted into opportunities. Rallying the organization and having a correct structure with appropriate financial backing are critical enablers of a successful executable strategy as shown in Figure 1.7.

Technological change is accelerating, demanding a nimble and adaptable organization and culture aligned with a clear vision. This strategic positioning allows organizations to leverage technological convergence at the opportune moment.

A key enabler for any successful strategy is aligning the organizational structure with desired outcomes. To capitalize on new products, markets, workstyles, and technologies, periodic restructuring is essential. It disrupts entrenched silos and lethargy associated with legacy systems, propelling the organization forward.

Many traditional businesses are transforming into technology companies. The "Chief Digital Officer" (CDO) is critical to this shift. The CDO marries innovative technologies with a strategic vision to drive this transformation. Similarly, the "Chief Customer Success Officer" reflects modern organizations' customer-centric focus, rallying all departments toward a singular goal: exceptional customer service. As AI continues to rise, organizations grapple with leveraging it to create a competitive edge. This is where the "Chief AI Officer" (CAIO) becomes crucial. The CAIO identifies and implements AI solutions that create clear differentiation from competitors.

These specialized C-suite roles underscore the growing importance of technology within organizations and their evolving business models. As

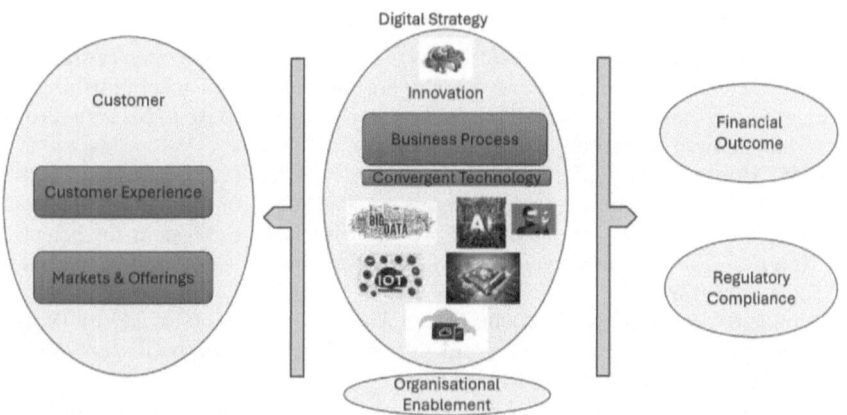

FIGURE 1.7
Synthesizing interrelationships as part of digital strategy

traditional factory-floor models fade, agile structures take center stage, aligning with the ever-changing marketplace, technology, and customer landscape.

In today's rapidly evolving technological landscape, adopting a revolutionary approach is no longer a choice – it is an existential imperative. Disruptive technologies empower new entrants to reshape markets and create groundbreaking products. Organizations must embrace this change or risk becoming obsolete.

The first step is crafting a clear vision for transformation. This necessitates a critical pivot, often identified through deep introspection into the organization's strengths, weaknesses, opportunities, and threats (SWOT analysis). This self-evaluation lays the foundation for strategic priorities and actionable initiatives.

Technology is a powerful tool, but it is only half the equation. To truly thrive, organizations must leverage the interplay of various technologies, crafting a unified strategy where each technology strengthens and complements the others. This synergistic approach creates a sum greater than its parts.

However, technology alone cannot drive success. A complete overhaul of business processes and organizational structure is necessary. Processes must be reimagined around the customer's journey, ensuring a seamless and engaging experience across all touchpoints. Similarly, organizational structures must adapt to become more agile and collaborative, fostering innovation and responsiveness to market shifts.

References

Abouahmed, M., & Ahmed, O. (2023). *Machine Learning in Microservices: Productionizing Microservices Architecture for Machine Learning Solutions*. Packt Publishing Ltd.

Ambler, S., & Lines, M. (2020, July). *Introduction to Disciplined Agile Delivery*. Project Management Institute.

Asch, M., Moore, T., Badia, R., Beck, M., Beckman, P., Bidot, T., . . . Zacharov, I. (2018). Big Data and Extreme-Scale Computing: Pathways to Convergence-Toward a Shaping Strategy for a Future Software and Data Ecosystem for Scientific Inquiry. *The International Journal of High Performance Computing Applications, 32*(4), 435–479.

Baldwin, C. Y., & Clark, K. B. (2000). *Design Rules: The Power of Modularity* (Vol. 1). The MIT Press. Retrieved from https://direct.mit.edu/books/book/1856/Design-RulesThe-Power-of-Modularity

Bhattacharjee, A., & Badhan, A. K. (2024). Convergence of Data Analytics, Big Data, and Machine Learning: Applications, Challenges, and Future Direction. In *Data Analytics and Machine Learning: Navigating the Big Data Landscape* (pp. 317–334). Singapore: Springer Nature. https://doi.org/10.1007/978-981-97-0448-4_15

Buck, C., Olenberger, C., Schweizer, A., Völter, F., & Eymann, T. (2021). Never Trust, Always Verify: A Multivocal Literature Review on Current Knowledge and Research Gaps of Zero-Trust. *Computers & Security, 110*, 102436.

Burke, K. (2011). *Characteristics of a Good Vision Statement: Integrated and Paraphrased from Various Sources, Including the Academic Leadership Journal*. University of Hawaii, HILO. Retrieved from https://hilo.hawaii.edu/strategicplan/documents/SPC_07_11_vision_characteristics.pdf

Giattino, C., Mathieu, E., Samborska, V., & Roser, M. (2023). *Artificial Intelligence*. Published online at OurWorldInData.org. Retrieved from https://ourworldindata.org/artificial-intelligence [Online Resource]

Chen, W. (2022). Digital Ecosystem. In *Encyclopedia of Big Data* (pp. 385–387). Cham: Springer International Publishing.

Dang, V. N., Aussenac-Gilles, N., Megdiche, I., & Ravat, F. (2023, May). Interoperability of Open Science Metadata: What About the Reality? In *International Conference on Research Challenges in Information Science* (pp. 467–482). Cham: Springer Nature Switzerland.

Dosi, G., Pereira, M. C., Roventini, A., & Virgillito, M. E. (2022). Technological Paradigms, Labour Creation and Destruction in a Multi-Sector Agent-Based Model. *Research Policy, 51*(10), 104565.

Drechsler, K., Gregory, R., Wagner, H. T., & Tumbas, S. (2020). At the Crossroads Between Digital Innovation and Digital Transformation. *Communications of the Association for Information Systems, 47*(1), 23.

Epoch. (2023). *With Minor Processing by Our World in Data: "Training Computation (petaFLOP)"* [dataset]. Epoch. "Large Language Model Performance and Compute" [original data].

Farahani, B., Firouzi, F., & Luecking, M. (2021). The Convergence of IoT and Distributed Ledger Technologies (DLT): Opportunities, Challenges, and Solutions. *Journal of Network and Computer Applications, 177*, 102936.

Farell, J., & Weiser, P. J. (2003). Modularity, Vertical Integration, and Open Access Policies: Towards a Convergence of Antitrust and Regulation in the Internet Age. *Harvard Journal of Law & Technology*, 86–134. Retrieved from https://scholar.law.colorado.edu/faculty-articles/539/

Feng, C. M., Botha, E., & Pitt, L. (2024). From HAL to GenAI: Optimize Chatbot Impacts with CARE. *Business Horizons, 67*(5).

Frank, R., Schumacher, G., & Tamm, A. (2023). Cloud: The Automated IT Value Chain. In *Cloud Transformation: The Public Cloud Is Changing Businesses* (pp. 75–113). Wiesbaden: Springer Fachmedien Wiesbaden.

Frantz, R. Z., Corchuelo, R., Basto-Fernandes, V., Rosa-Sequeira, F., Roos-Frantz, F., & Arjona, J. L. (2021). A Cloud-Based Integration Platform for Enterprise Application Integration: A Model-Driven Engineering Approach. *Software: Practice and Experience, 51*(4), 824–847.

Gartner. (2022). *Tech Providers 2025: Strategic Transformation Drives Growth*. Gartner. Retrieved from https://www.gartner.com/en/doc/tech-providers-2025-strategic-transformation-drives-growth

Gartner. (n.d.). *Gartner Hype Cycle*, 1–2. Retrieved from https://www.gartner.com/en/research/methodologies/gartner-hype-cycle?utm_source=google&utm_medium=cpc&utm_campaign=GTR_NA_2022_GTR_CPC_SEM1_BRANDCAMPAIGNMQ&utm_adgroup=141653137818&utm_term=hype%20cycles&ad=679713141030&matchtype=p&gad_source=1&gclid=EAIa

Hanelt, A., & Bohnsack, R. (2021, July). A Systematic Review of the Literature on Digital Transformation: Insights and Implications for Strategy and Organisational Change. *Journal of Management Studies, 58*(5), 1159–1197. Retrieved from https://doi.org/10.1111/joms.12639

Hanelt, A., Bohnsack, R., Marz, D., & Antunes Marante, C. (2021). A Systematic Review of the Literature on Digital Transformation: Insights and Implications for Strategy and Organisational Change. *Journal of Management Studies, 58*(5), 1159–1197.

Hofmann, F., & Jaeger-Erben, M. (2020). Organisational Transition Management of Circular Business Model Innovations. *Business Strategy and the Environment, 29*(6), 2770–2788.

Holgersson, M., Baldwin, C. Y., Chesbrough, H., & Bogers, M. L. (2022). The Forces of Ecosystem Evolution. *California Management Review, 64*(3), 5–23.

Immelt, J. (2017, September–October). Inside GE's Transformation. *Harvard Business Review*, 41–55. Retrieved from https://hbr.org/2017/09/inside-ges-transformation.Organisational#:~:text=During%20Jeff%20Immelt%27s%2016%20years,the%20profile%20of%20its%20workforce

Janssen, M., Brous, P., Estevez, E., Barbosa, L. S., & Janowski, T. (2020). Data Governance: Organizing Data for Trustworthy Artificial Intelligence. *Government Information Quarterly, 37*(3), 101493.

Jim Collins, M. T. (2011). *Great By Choice* (1st ed.). Denver: Random House Business. Retrieved from https://www.jimcollins.com/books/great-by-choice.html

Kaushal, V., & Yadav, R. (2023). Learning Successful Implementation of Chatbots in Businesses from B2B Customer Experience Perspective. *Concurrency and Computation: Practice and Experience, 35*(1), e7450.

Kodama, M. (2021). Knowledge Creation Through Collective Phronesis. *Knowledge and Process Management, 28*(3), 223–245.

Kouroubali, A., & Katehakis, D. G. (2019). The New European Interoperability Framework as a Facilitator of Digital Transformation for Citizen Empowerment. *Journal of Biomedical Informatics, 94*, 103166.

Kwak, K., & Kim, N. (2022). Industrial Leadership Changes Without Technological Discontinuity: Modularization, Institution-Led Market Discontinuity, and Market Development Strategy. *Technological Forecasting and Social Change, 180*, 121688.

Mehmood, E., & Anees, T. (2022). Distributed Real-Time ETL Architecture for Unstructured Big Data. *Knowledge and Information Systems, 64*(12), 3419–3445.

Mikalef, P., & Gupta, M. (2021). Artificial Intelligence Capability: Conceptualization, Measurement Calibration, and Empirical Study on Its Impact on Organisational Creativity and Firm Performance. *Information & Management, 58*(3), 103434.

Mordi, A. (2021). Agile Software Tools in the Field: The Need for a Tool Reflection Process. In *The Agile Imperative: Teams, Organisations and Society Under Reconstruction?* (pp. 55–89). Springer.

Omol, E. J. (2023). Organisational Digital Transformation: From Evolution to Future Trends. *Digital Transformation and Society, 3*(3).

Pearlson, K. E., Saunders, C. S., & Galletta, D. F. (2024). *Managing and Using Information Systems: A Strategic Approach*. John Wiley & Sons.

Saha, A., Agarwal, P., Ghosh, S., Gantayat, N., & Sindhgatta, R. (2024, January). Towards Business Process Observability. In *Proceedings of the 7th Joint International Conference on Data Science & Management of Data (11th ACM IKDD CODS and 29th COMAD)* (pp. 257–265). Association for Computing Machinery.

San Kim, T., & Sohn, S. Y. (2020). Machine-Learning-Based Deep Semantic Analysis Approach for Forecasting New Technology Convergence. *Technological Forecasting and Social Change, 157*, 120095.

Sharad Mangrulkar, R., & Vijay Chavan, P. (2024). Case Studies Using Blockchain. In *Blockchain Essentials: Core Concepts and Implementations* (pp. 203–227). Berkeley, CA: Apress.

Su, J., Zhang, Y., & Wu, X. (2023). How Market Pressures and Organisation Readiness Drive Digital Marketing Adoption Strategies' Evolution in Small and Medium Enterprises. *Technological Forecasting and Social Change, 193*, 122655.

Suzic, B. (2016, April). User-Centered Security Management of API-Based Data Integration Workflows. In *NOMS 2016–2016 IEEE/IFIP Network Operations and Management Symposium* (pp. 1233–1238). IEEE.

Taherdoost, H. (2024). *Digital Transformation Roadmap: From Vision to Execution.* CRC Press.

Teece, D. J. (2018). Profiting from Innovation in the Digital Economy: Enabling Technologies, Standards, and Licensing Models in the Wireless World. *Research Policy, 47*(8), 1367–1387.

Vomberg, A., de Haan, E., Fabian, N. E., & Broekhuizen, T. (2024). Digital Knowledge Engineering for Strategy Development. *Journal of Business Research*, 114632.

Yadav, S., Samadhiya, A., Kumar, A., Majumdar, A., Garza-Reyes, J. A., & Luthra, S. (2023). Achieving the Sustainable Development Goals Through Net Zero Emissions: Innovation-Driven Strategies for Transitioning from Incremental to Radical Lean, Green and Digital Technologies. *Resources, Conservation and Recycling, 197*, 107094.

Yeung, K. (2018). Algorithmic Regulation: A Critical Interrogation. *Regulation & Governance, 12*(4), 505–523.

2

Strategic Foundations of the Digital Frontier

Neelesh Kumbhojkar, Arun Menon, and S. Vijayakumar Bharathi

2.1 Introduction

Digital frontier is a multifaceted concept that encompasses technological, economic, social, cultural, regulatory, environmental, and educational dimensions (Komalasari, 2024). Understanding the scope is essential for an organization to navigate the digital era. Herbert (2017) talks about a company's ability to react and successfully utilize new technologies and procedures – now and in the future. It is the forward edge of technological impact with respect to an organization's usage of technology and their reliance upon it for day-to-day operations to achieve marketable productivity improvements (Doll et al., 2003). The digital frontier interrogates the World Wide Web and the digital ecosystem it has spawned to reveal how their conventions, protocols, standards, and algorithmic regulations represent a novel form of global power (Kumar, 2021).

Cutting-edge technologies around artificial intelligence (AI), spatial computing, quantum computing, cloud, Internet of Things (IoT), big data, and blockchain can spiral an organization upwards at an unprecedented speed or become an existential crisis for the organization (Nowotny, 2021). These technologies can create new business models, disrupt existing industries, and gain competitive advantage. A foundational change is required in this rapidly evolving digital world. It is an existential crisis for organizations. Ismail et al. (2017) discuss companies converging multiple new digital technologies, enhanced with ubiquitous connectivity, to reach superior performance and sustained competitive advantage. The need to transform permeates business models, customer experience models, operational models, internal people/resources management models (including skills, talent and culture), and networks (including the entire value system). Society at large is also transforming in the way it operates. Leodolter (2017) talks about it as a societal meta-development. It is in this context that there needs to be an awareness of this digital frontier and a conscious attempt to stay ahead of the curve.

2.1.1 Evolution of Digital Technologies

From the internet era of the late 1990s to all connected ecosystems of today, where each technology thrives on its ability to leverage each other, digital technologies have come a long way. The time to move from labs to commercial zones has shrunk rapidly. Earlier, when most technologies originated from defense establishments or universities, today, one sees commercial establishments equally investing in propelling the advancement of technology to gain a competitive advantage. Technologies such as IoT, AI, blockchain, cloud, and big data are catalysts to redefine business models, change efficiency models, and reshape customer experience paradigms (Sewpersadh, 2023).

2.1.2 Impact on Business, Society, and Economy

Rogers, in his book *The Digital Transformation Playbook* (Rogers, 2016), shows why traditional businesses need to rethink their underlying assumptions in five domains of strategy – customers, competition, data, innovation, and value. He reveals how to harness customer networks, platforms, big data, rapid experimentation, and disruptive business models and integrate these into existing businesses and organizations. Technological impact on society is evident in the example of Unified Payments Interface (UPI) payment adoption in India and its ubiquity across all strata of society. Interoperability and ability to connect with existing financial institutions, along with the dynamics of the COVID-19 pandemic, saw the usage move from 1,246 million transactions in March 2020 to 13,440 million transactions in March 2024 (UPI24). The continuously increasing interaction between digital technologies, business, and society has transformational effects and increases the change process's velocity, scope, and impact (Van Veldhoven & Vanthienen, 2019).

2.1.3 Historical Perspectives

In 1769, James Watt's steam engine opened the floodgates for an industrial revolution that was earlier constrained by human and animal power limits. "The Industrial Revolution thereby opened a new age of promise. It also transformed the balance of political power, within nations, between nations, and between civilizations; revolutionized the social order; and as much changed man's way of thinking as his way of doing" (Checkland, 1970). Today, AI, IoT, big data, blockchain, quantum computing, and spatial computing stand at this juncture with an ability to recreate the economy, society, geopolitical landscape, and the fundamental way we operate.

2.1.4 Milestones in Digital Innovation

Network speed and availability via mobile technology, computing power using graphics processing units, storage technologies that have made access to vast amounts of data accessible, and low-powered edge computing have proliferated sensors and data collection points. These enabling technologies allow technologies such as AI, IoT, and big data to interact with each other and help create a new digital frontier.

2.1.5 Challenges and Opportunities

Today, every business discusses digital transformation (Rogers, 2023). With the acceleration of new technologies, every organization must adapt to survive. However, according to their admission, 70% of businesses must transform. Across industries, established companies are held back by bureaucracy, inertia, and old working methods. How can businesses break through to drive real change? Rogers identifies the five most significant barriers to digital transformation: vision, priorities, experimentation, governance, and capabilities.

Some key challenges are the pace of innovation, the ability to adopt technology, digital culture, and the ability to reimagine (Arham et al., 2024). Any organization or society that can tackle these challenges stands at the forefront of a sea of opportunities. The investment must be in developing new technologies, mindsets, and business and operational models to improve work and competitiveness and deliver new and relevant value for customers and employees in an ever-evolving digital economy (Solis & Szymanski, 2016).

2.2 What Are the Strategic Foundations of the Digital Landscape?

Digital transformation requires a blend of the ability to adopt technology with a customer-centric approach (Khuntia et al., 2024). Reimagination of business models, execution models, and culture is critical to any digital transformation.

The digital strategy comprises four essential components (Figure 2.1): business processes and models adapted to a digital world, customer experience management, and customer value generation, the use of technology to enable the aforementioned components, and finally, an organization and culture that helps drive all the above.

These four components are interconnected and essential for a successful digital strategy. Together, they ensure that organizations can effectively leverage digital technologies to achieve their business objectives and remain competitive in the ever-evolving digital landscape.

All of these elements are interlinked (Keiningham et al., 2020). Customer experience and customer personalization drive business processes. New

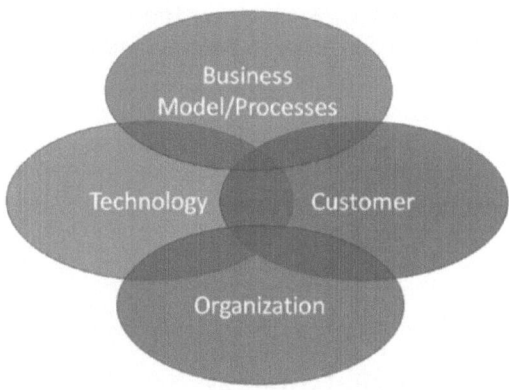

FIGURE 2.1
Digital strategy basic components

business models enabled by technological advances can help create new customer bases and open new business avenues. To take advantage of technology, organizations must become more innovative. Technology leaders should move from the back-office enablement functions to the driver's seat as part of the leadership.

2.2.1 Aligning Business Goals with Digital Initiatives

Digital initiatives can be short-term or long-term (Zhong & Ren, 2023). Using technology to ease the current business mechanisms will provide small incremental gains. A complete redefinition of business models and processes and the use of technology are required to enable it to leapfrog. The key elements to make the alignment are a clear vision, an understanding of the risk-taking capabilities, and financial strengths and weaknesses. Business processes fortified with AI can redefine business outcomes.

2.2.2 Importance of Data in Digital Strategy

For any AI-fortified business process to work, data is required. Data is a pillar that drives strategy. The advancement of technology has allowed for the collation of unstructured and structured data (Javaid et al., 2022). Moving from looking at historical data and predicting future conclusions is outdated. Today, data can provide near real-time intelligence, and AI-driven tools can help predict potential outcomes in the near future. The path forward is to move a federated data model that can go to the data source and tap it in near real time. It changes the entire decision-making process. Personalization is another crucial element that data can provide (Mejeh & Rehm, 2024). Having insight into the customer via all structured and unstructured communications with the customer can help bring a personalized experience, which was not feasible earlier.

To innovate and capitalize on new markets and buying patterns, data analytics can provide critical intelligence to help an organization correct or pivot itself to get a first-mover or competitive advantage (Sharma et al., 2024). The data's veracity, variability, and value present an opportunity to monetize.

2.3 Frameworks for Digital Strategy

2.3.1 Different Types of Analysis (SWOT Analysis in the Digital Context)

SWOT analysis, which stands for strengths, weaknesses, opportunities, and threats, considers internal and external factors to help businesses identify their strengths and weaknesses while spotting opportunities and threats. Examining these four quadrants in light of an organization's defined vision helps to determine the necessary steps for advancing in the digital context (Parra-López et al., 2021; Puyt et al., 2023).

Strengths involve identifying any market, technical, cultural, innovation, or organizational strengths that can be leveraged to accelerate the digital journey. Weaknesses focus on pinpointing gaps and areas that need improvement to ensure a smooth and rapid digital transformation. Opportunities aligned with the organization's vision involve identifying external factors that can be capitalized on to accelerate the digital journey and potentially outperform competitors. Finally, threats are external factors that could jeopardize an organization's digital strategy. Although they cannot be controlled, a well-prepared mitigation plan can help minimize their impact.

By conducting a thorough SWOT analysis and aligning it with the organizational vision, businesses can better understand their current position in the digital landscape and develop effective strategies to navigate challenges and capitalize on opportunities for successful digital transformation.

2.3.2 PESTLE Analysis for Digital Strategy

The transformative power of digital transformation and digital strategies in creating new markets, experiences, and processes necessitates a multifaceted approach to strategic planning and review (Parra-López et al., 2021). Considering the external factors that can influence a strategy's success or failure in today's dynamic landscape is essential. Utilizing the PESTLE (political, economic, social, technological, legal, environmental) analysis framework can provide valuable insights into these factors.

Politically, market disruptions caused by technology can impact job creation and redundancy. Tax policies, political tensions, employment laws, trade restrictions, and data privacy regulations can either facilitate or hinder strategy execution. In addition, geopolitical shifts and alignments can open or close market opportunities. Economically, the adoption (or lack thereof) of new technologies can create income disparities. Competitive pressures, readily available data and intelligence, and evolving market dynamics can significantly alter consumer behavior. Economic factors like tax and inflation rates, unemployment, exchange, and interest rates can also impact strategic outcomes.

Socially, work cultures are transforming. Shifting demographics, increasing cultural diversity, and evolving consumer lifestyles, coupled with pervasive technology use, have blurred the lines between work and personal life. Expectations for personalization in both spheres have also risen. Technologically, advancements in AI, big data, IoT, and supply chain automation have revolutionized various operations. However, these technologies and connected and personalized devices present growing security concerns.

Legally, intellectual property rights, data privacy and protection, and the ethical use of AI are areas subject to increasing legal scrutiny and regulation. Environmentally, e-waste management and pursuing net-zero carbon emissions are key priorities for organizations, societies, and governments worldwide.

By considering these PESTLE factors, organizations can develop a more comprehensive digital strategy that anticipates and adapts to potential challenges and opportunities in the dynamic digital landscape.

2.3.3 Porter's Five Forces in the Digital Age

Porter's five forces model remains as relevant in today's digital age as it was introduced in 1979 (Isabelle et al., 2020). The model focuses on identifying an organization's current position concerning competitive rivalry, supplier power, buyer power, substitution threat, and new entry.

The digital age is the age of market disruption. With every technological advancement, unknown entities have a high potential to become dominant players and change the market and consumer behavior patterns. Barriers to entry are small, and there is always the threat of a new way of doing business, which can completely usurp the market. Creating new substitutes is fast and is not limited by physical constraints or distribution channels.

Today, Alibaba and Google have a group of businesses. Alibaba has moved from an e-commerce company to a financial services and technology company. Companies like Google, Alibaba, and others are constantly evolving to disrupt markets with products or services based on the digital footprint and digital technologies that they continue to develop.

The most potent force today is buyer power and the ability of the buyer to discern the services/products from one organization over another (Hung et al., 2022). Customer experience is the crucial factor that can make or break an organization. There is a gap between what enterprises believe are "super experiences" they deliver and what customers want or have learnt to expect in the digital era (Allen, 2005).

2.3.4 Analyst and Practitioner Models of Digital Strategy

While technology undergoes constant evolution, businesses are ongoing entities with the daily imperative of maintaining operations and securing short-term and long-term profitability. The three-box solution can provide a valuable framework for established organizations that cannot simply pause operations to adapt (Govindarajan, 2016).

The first box focuses on managing the present, ensuring the current business model remains efficient and profitable, and meeting the needs of today's market. The second box involves selectively forgetting the past, recognizing that past successes may not guarantee future success. Companies must be willing to let go of outdated practices or no longer relevant strategies. Finally, the third box centers on creating the future. This entails exploring new opportunities, innovating, and developing new models to stay ahead of the curve and ensure long-term growth and relevance.

This three-box approach allows businesses to balance maintaining current operations, adapting to change, and proactively shaping their future. It recognizes the need for continuous improvement and innovation while acknowledging the realities and constraints of running an established organization.

We propose a Four-Lens Model, a practical framework that provides a comprehensive view of an enterprise, enabling organizations to navigate the complex and rapidly evolving business landscape. This model, shown in Figure 2.2, examines the enterprise through four critical lenses: external forces, business processes, customers, and technology. The external forces lens analyzes geopolitical dynamics, emerging markets, new competitors, and evolving regulatory requirements. By continuously monitoring these external factors, enterprises can proactively adapt their strategies and stay ahead of the curve. The business processes lens emphasizes the importance of a technology-fortified composable enterprise. This approach allows organizations to break down traditional silos and create flexible, modular processes that can adapt to changing conditions. The composable enterprise enables continuous process evolution in reaction to external forces and customer needs. The customer lens highlights the significance of personalization, experience management, and catering to new customer segments. By deeply understanding their customers' evolving needs and expectations, enterprises can deliver tailored solutions and exceptional experiences. The technology lens underscores the importance of segregated access, orchestration, and robust data core systems. Technology is crucial in building the

Strategic Foundations of the Digital Frontier

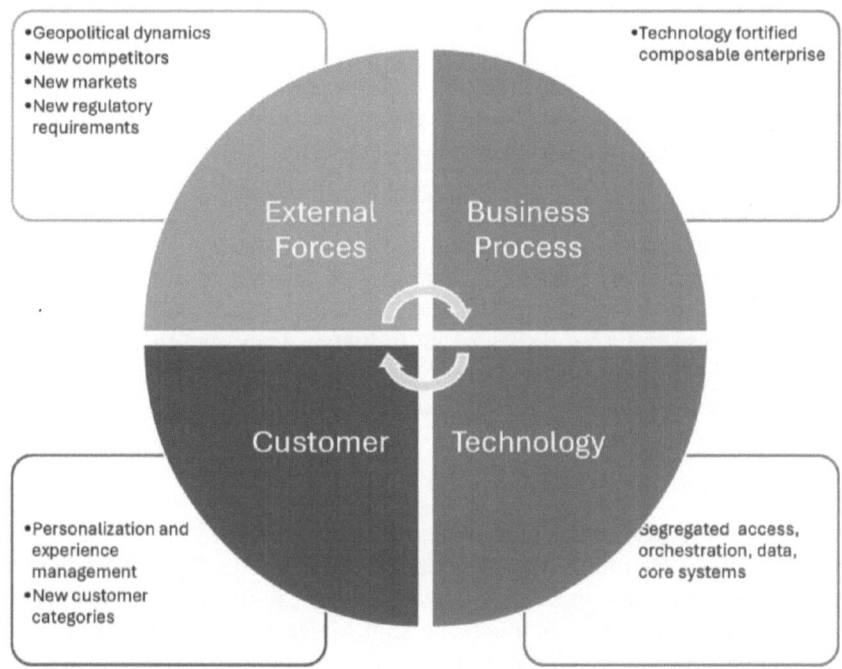

FIGURE 2.2
Four-lens model

core and developing a composable enterprise. Organizations can streamline processes, enhance decision-making, and drive innovation by leveraging the right technologies. The four-lens model encourages periodic assessments through each lens to ensure that the enterprise remains agile, responsive, and aligned with its strategic objectives. This holistic approach empowers organizations to navigate the complexities of the modern business world and thrive in an era of constant change.

2.4 Digital Ecosystems and Value Chains

With the changing technology landscape, organizations must come together to complement each other and deliver value in an ecosystem. The role of a digital ecosystem is to deliver value propositions to customers, taking into account the complementary capabilities of ecosystem participants – dynamic business models with evolving complex technical systems that best suit digital ecosystems. The COVID-19 pandemic has amplified the importance of digital interactions and has accelerated the adoption of digital-ecosystem business models.

For Moore (Moore, 1993, 1996), the success of innovative firms depends on their ability to mobilize resources owned by other organizations such as partners, suppliers, or customers. Moore suggests shifting the locus of strategic analysis from a firm's industry to its business ecosystem across various industries. Firms cooperate and compete within an ecosystem, while ecosystems compete against each other. He sees such ecosystems evolving from a dispersed group of organizations to a more structured community.

A firm's success depends on the success of its business ecosystem, which extends beyond the boundaries of its industry. They define ecosystems as many loosely interconnected participants who depend on each other for mutual effectiveness and survival (Barnett, 2006).

2.4.1 Mapping Digital Value Chains

A firm's competitive advantage depends on its ability to create more value than its rivals (Brandenburger & Stuart Jr, 1996; Porter, 2011). With technological advancements, the race is always to get the innovative product first to market and gain an advantage. In that quest, rather than developing a stand-alone product, it is better to put together an entire ecosystem, creating a better footprint to leverage the product and service. Success will depend on distributing the challenges and ecosystem value creation across components and complements (Kretschmer et al., 2022).

The first step is to identify the opportunity. Identify the ability to improve efficiency, reduce costs, or create new value propositions. The next step is to define the ecosystem in which the product or service will operate. Identify the complements and components. Define how the various components will interact with the entire value-creation process. Develop a shared understanding of the overall ecosystem.

Fostering an environment of co-creation and innovation is essential within digital ecosystems. This allows participants to collaborate, build upon each other's strengths, and create a value proposition that surpasses what any individual entity could achieve alone. Several value chain flows support this collaborative environment. Information flow, for instance, involves sharing crucial data such as customer insights, competitor activity, and market trends. This enables all complementors to leverage this knowledge for mutual benefit. Financial flow encompasses the transactions between complementors when serving a single customer based on pre-established agreements. Finally, material flow refers to the movement of physical or digital products between various players within the ecosystem to fulfill customer needs.

2.4.2 Identifying Stakeholders in the Digital Ecosystem

In digital ecosystems, it is essential to identify the role of the sponsor and their incentive to push some of the complements over others (Fu et al., 2024).

Interaction between complements is evolutionary based on the value each complement can bring to the table and the customer preferences on its interactions with the ecosystem.

It is important to recognize the key players. The sponsor, also known as the focal company, is the driving force behind the ecosystem, orchestrating collaboration and aligning other organizations to serve the customer. Complementors are organizations whose products or services enhance the ecosystem's value proposition. Enablers provide essential infrastructure or services, facilitating value creation for a fee. Finally, Customers are the consumers of the ecosystem's value, whose behaviors and preferences influence its evolution and future direction.

2.4.3 Leveraging Partnerships and Collaborations

The success of an innovating firm often depends on the efforts of other innovators in its environment (Adner & Kapoor, 2010). For an ecosystem to succeed, incentives must be aligned. The participants' motivations in the ecosystem must have a common objective of value generation for the customer. The sponsor of the ecosystem has to be seen as fair in promoting the complementors. Understanding the markets and kinds of customers, products which the ecosystem participants will cooperate, and the areas where they might compete.

Continued collaboration will hinge on all participants and their ability to contribute to the innovation and evolution of the ecosystem (Wei et al., 2020). It is expected that the sponsor will help some of the complementors innovate. Help can be financial or technological. Challenges arise when incentives across the ecosystem are not aligned (Casadesus-Masanell, 2007).

2.5 Customer-Centric Digital Strategy

In the fast-changing technology landscape, the customer is the central power determining the digital evolution roadmap. The ability of the customer to appreciate new services and markets generated by digital technology and their willingness to pay a price for the value ensures that the technology thrives. Personalization has moved from the personal arena to businesses. There is an expectation that every customer will continue to get personalized service that helps enhance their experience or generate additional value in their activities. Digital strategy must revolve around a reimagined set of business processes with the customer at the heart (Willcocks et al., 2024). Companies look to customer behavior to inform and lead change, which puts customer experience at the heart of accelerating digital transformation initiatives (Solis & Szymanski, 2016).

Customer experience improvement has to be the underlying theme of any digital transformation. Customer experience is the culmination of the experience at every touchpoint or interaction directly with the enterprise or through its products or services. Expectations of customer experience from the customer are constantly evolving, and expectations are ever-rising. Improvement of this perceived value factored with time makes customer experience improvement a journey and a continuous effort rather than a one-time initiative (Kumbhojkar & Menon, 2022).

2.5.1 Understanding Customer Journeys

Business processes must be aligned with customer journeys (Terho et al., 2022). Identifying all touch points in the customer journey, from the initial introduction to the final point of interaction, must be viewed from the lens of digital strategy. Customer journeys are not static and continuously evolve with technological advancement. Keeping pace with it and creating journeys for every segment of the customer base is a continuous activity for any organization.

2.5.2 Personalization and Customization in Digital Strategy

The expectations of personalization are on the rise for business to business and business to consumer customers. Segmenting the customers, listening to their asks, anticipating their needs, and giving them a service or a product that fulfils current and potential future needs will help an organization move up the customer-perceived value chain. It is essential to have a 360-degree view of the customer not only from the products and services it acquires from the organization but also from the entire ecosystem the customer operates to achieve personalization (Biswas et al., 2020). The ability to take advantage of the broader ecosystem data points and build on it to give a more wholesome experience will go a long way in making the customer a promoter of the organization's services and products. To achieve this customer experience, designers, business process analysts, technologists, and front-end sales/support teams must work in unison.

2.5.3 Building Relationships through Digital Channels

Customers thrive and operate in a digital ecosystem. They move between personal and business ecosystems. Personal and external factors influence people running businesses in their day-to-day dealings. For an organization to succeed in this complex ecosystem, it is vital to appreciate the various channels of conversations and connections and build on them to enhance customer lifetime value.

Strategic Foundations of the Digital Frontier 37

2.6 Risk Management and Change Management in Digital Strategy

Maintaining customer trust and loyalty in the digital age hinges on an organization's ability to proactively identify and mitigate evolving risks (Biswas et al., 2020). One such risk is security: the convergence of technology has expanded the number of touchpoints and entry points, increasing the potential for cyberattacks and exploitation by malicious actors. In addition, rapid technological change continually introduces new, more efficient, and cost-effective ways to deliver services, necessitating innovation, and out-of-the-box thinking for organizations to stay ahead. Regulatory risks and changes are also challenging, as regulatory frameworks often lag technological advancements. This means organizations need to adapt as regulations catch up, potentially requiring changes to their business models and ecosystem operations. Finally, organizational risks must be addressed: continuous reskilling is essential for organizations to thrive in a dynamic digital landscape, and organizational structures also need to evolve to prioritize technology adoption and integrate it into decision-making processes. As the shift toward remote and flexible work arrangements accelerates, attracting and retaining top talent becomes increasingly critical.

2.6.1 Assessing and Prioritizing Digital Risks

Risk identification is a continuous process, and so is the process of prioritizing risks. Resources – financially and physically are always a point of constraint, and it is in this environment that one needs to assess the risks that have the potential to make a significant impact on the vision of the organization, its current operations, and its ability to operate in the future (He et al., 2020). The organization does not have to deal with all risks on its own. It is helpful to have an ecosystem of complements or get like-minded organizations, sometimes competitors, together to tackle risks, especially risks like regulatory or security that have a broader impact.

2.6.2 Mitigation Strategies for Digital Risks

A successful digital strategy must incorporate operational safeguards. Key considerations include cybersecurity: implementing a comprehensive security policy with regular audits and strict enforcement creates a strong deterrent against cyber threats. It is also crucial to recognize the dependence on partners and suppliers, ensuring they adhere to the same security and data protection standards to mitigate any risks from their operations. In the digital world, risks can be controlled, but not eliminated, so developing a robust business continuity plan and disaster recovery plan and conducting regular mock drills is essential for preparedness. Finally, employing architectural strategies like microservices to break down the digital ecosystem into smaller, isolated components can limit the impact of any security breach.

2.6.3 Continual Monitoring and Adaptation

From the operational layer, it is essential to move to AIOps and have a predictable proactive operation (Dakkak et al., 2023). Observability tools today in the marketplace can link business processes, applications, and infrastructure and help correlate key performance indicators (Observability Tools & Platform Market, 2024). A robust security and operations setup with a well-defined incident management response plan is essential. Technology advances are rapid. There is a risk of becoming obsolete and failing to generate better value propositions using the latest technology. Technology, while it changes, brings newer players in the ecosystem, reduced robustness due to the newness of the technology, and, in turn, greater risk of compliance and security.

2.6.4 Responding to Change in the Digital Landscape

Response to changes in the digital landscape requires a holistic approach. Systems, processes, and organizations have to adapt to changing times. It requires an organizational change management office that drives changes systematically and works to reduce risk and leverage technology to generate value. Talent has to keep abreast of the happenings within the digital landscape and learn to be innovative in adopting it (Kiron et al., 2016).

Organizational structures have to be agile, and silos within organizations have to be broken to ensure that with technology change, the primary focus on the customer is not lost, and business processes keep changing with the customer at the center, leveraging the digital ecosystem.

Rapid digitalization, while offering numerous benefits, also carries several potential drawbacks, challenges, and ethical considerations. Job displacement and economic inequality can occur as automation and AI-driven technologies lead to job losses in specific sectors. This could increase economic inequality if not managed properly. The digital divide, resulting from unequal access to technology and digital skills, can further marginalize those without the necessary resources or knowledge. In addition, the increased collection and use of personal data raises significant concerns about privacy breaches, surveillance, and misuse of information. As digital systems become more interconnected, the risk of cyberattacks, data breaches, and ransomware attacks increases, potentially disrupting critical infrastructure and services. Algorithmic bias and discrimination can perpetuate or even amplify existing biases in society, leading to unfair outcomes in areas like employment, housing, and loan approvals. Overreliance on technology can also create vulnerabilities and disruptions in the event of system failures or outages.

Furthermore, digital device production, use, and disposal contribute to environmental challenges like electronic waste and increased energy consumption. The constant connectivity and digital overload associated with rapid digitalization can negatively impact mental health, leading to stress, anxiety, and social isolation. Excessive reliance on digital communication can also lead to a decline in face-to-face interactions and genuine human connection. Finally, the development and deployment of AI and other emerging technologies raise ethical concerns about their potential impact on society, including issues like job displacement, autonomous weapons, and the manipulation of human behavior.

Addressing these potential drawbacks and challenges requires careful planning, ethical considerations, and proactive measures to ensure that rapid digitalization benefits society as a whole while minimizing its negative impacts.

2.7 Case Studies and Examples

2.7.1 Real-World Examples of Successful Digital Strategies

The UPI has made digital payments in India a reality. Launched in 2016 by the National Payments Corporation of India, UPI has transcended the day-to-day life of over 1.4 billion population. The success of UPI is visible in the rise of monthly transactions from 5,405 million per month in March 2022 to 13,440 million transactions in March 2024 (Pushkarna, 2024). This astounding rise in transactions lies in its ability to use a simple virtual payment address linked to a bank account without sharing bank details. This interoperability across banks and wallets has made its adaptability easy. Leveraging the proliferation of smartphones and a mobile-first strategy has ensured digital inclusion across all strata of society.

The Recording Industry Association of America (RIAA) saw the release of a compression technology called MP3 that allowed music compression. The music industry did not picture this technology having an impact in conjunction with the rise of the internet. In 1999, Napster was formed to illegally store and distribute music on MP3 without paying any royalties. It brought the music industry to its knees as it ambushed its royalty fees. In 2003, Apple saw an opportunity and introduced the iPod and iTunes online music store. So, for a fee of $0.99, users could legally download and listen to music compared to $15 CDs from the record industry. RIAA rallied with Apple to make the best out of the bind it found itself. By 2011, Apple had sold 300 million iPods and 10 billion songs through iTunes (Wayte, 2023).

2.7.2 Lessons Learned from Digital Strategy Failures

The success of digital strategies lies in their ability to keep the customer at the center, leverage an ecosystem, build interoperability, and demonstrate value to the customer. For this to happen, there has to be a culture of innovation within the organization and the use of data and analytics to identify trends and predictive models.

Reimagining business models in a continuously evolving ecosystem is critical to not getting ambushed by new emerging competitors. RIAA used to cut CDs and enjoy hefty fees for every album CD sold. It all changed when a 19-year-old started a free service called Napster. RIAA was caught off-guard due to its inability to visualize a better distribution model in the internet world. Apple capitalized on the opportunity and introduced a new product with iTunes and iPod. It further evolved with Apple Music in 2015, creating an industry for streaming services with organizations like Spotify capitalizing on it.

2.7.3 Applying Concepts to Various Industries and Sectors

Organizations need to be open to taking their digital unique selling proposition across industries. Uber started as a platform that connects people who wanted a ride with available drivers. Uber took the delivery concept and moved into the food delivery business using the same platform. Reusing the same platform, it entered the freight business. Uber had a revenue of $10.4 billion in 2018 and grew its revenue to $37.2 billion in 2023. This rapid growth of Uber is an outcome of its strong customer-centricity and technological ability to take its products and services across industries and different customer needs.

2.8 Future Trends in Digital Strategy

2.8.1 Emerging Technologies and Their Impact

The proliferation of AI and machine learning leveraging big data and cloud infrastructure has brought the power of predictive modeling into the hands of many. It has taken customer personalization to new levels. Spatial computing and quantum computing can create an explosion of use cases and take customer centricity to new unheard-of heights. With big data, there is a 360-degree view of the customer. Human limitations and computing limitations are significantly reduced with AI and quantum computing; the use cases are limited only by the imagination of humans. These technologies will be adopted to create vertical solutions specific to industry and geography.

Customer bases will be attuned to getting services and products specific to their customized requirements rather than having to live with generic solutions.

To cater to this rapid change, there is a need to build a flexible architecture for systems that separate the experience layer, orchestration layer, data fabric layer and the core system layer. This segregation allows for a differential pace of change at each layer and an ability to adopt newer technological changes without disrupting the business's day-to-day running.

2.8.2 Anticipating Future Challenges and Opportunities

Newer technologies create an existential crisis for many organizations as older business methods become extinct, and the shifting customer base quickly adapts to new business models and newer ways of doing things. The success of an organization lies in understanding technology trends and, at appropriate times, investing in them to redefine their current business models and processes. Barriers and limitations like compute capacity, network speeds, data availability, and geographic boundaries stand to diminish in the days to come. With it come new opportunities to move from a deterministic system to a more probabilistic one, which can consume vast amounts of data and compute at incredible speeds to create a better predictable outcome.

2.8.3 Continuous Innovation in Digital Strategy

Innovation is critical to the survival of any organization in today's rapidly changing world. The fundamental approach should be to innovate quickly, test market results in a minor fashion, and expand based on success. Building an organization's culture of innovators is essential for it to herald forward in this new digital age. For it to happen, adopting design thinking, having an agile approach, and an organizational structure that is flexible and nimble-driven with a singular focus on the customer is critical.

The speed of disruption will require a composable enterprise architecture that allows for the recreation of business processes at a rapid pace in response to the four-lens model described in the earlier section.

2.9 Conclusion: Staying Ahead in the Digital Frontier

To stay ahead in this digital frontier, organizations have to take the approach of cannibalizing their current business models and coming up with new ones. This constant reinvention of the marketplace with customers at the center is critical. Evolutionary approaches can only give incremental advantages, and it will be soon that an unheard-of competition emerges and pivots the marketplace. Technology can help re-invent the marketplace or create new marketplaces, unseating long-established norms. Organizations must have a revolutionary approach, which has to be ingrained into the organization's DNA to stay ahead in this digital frontier.

References

Adner, R., & Kapoor, R. (2010). Value creation in innovation ecosystems: How the structure of technological interdependence affects firm performance in new technology generations. *Strategic Management Journal, 31*(3), 306–333.

Allen, J., Reichheld, F. F., Hamilton, B., & Markey, R. (2005). *Closing the delivery gap.* Bain & Co.

Arham, A. F., Norizan, N. S., Muhamad Hanapiyah, Z., Mazalan, M. I., & Yanto, H. (2024). Enhancing academic performance: Investigating the nexus between digital leadership and the role of digital culture. *The Bottom Line, 37*(3).

Barnett, M. L. (2006). The keystone advantage: What the new dynamics of business ecosystems mean for strategy, innovation, and sustainability by IansitiMarco and LevienRoy. Cambridge, MA: Harvard Business School Press, 2004. 272 pages, hard cover, $35.00. *The Academy of Management Perspectives, 20*(2), 88–90. https://doi.org/10.5465/amp.2006.20591015

Biswas, S., Carson, B., Chung, V., Singh, S., & Thomas, R. (2020). *AI-bank of the future: Can banks meet the AI challenge.* New York: McKinsey & Company.

Brandenburger, A. M., & Stuart Jr, H. W. (1996). Value-based business strategy. *Journal of Economics & Management Strategy, 5*(1), 5–24.

Casadesus-Masanell, R., & Yoffie, D. B. (2007). Wintel: Cooperation and conflict. *Management Science, 53*(4), 584–598.

Checkland, S. G. (1970). Landes, David S., "The unbound Prometheus: Technological change and industrial development in Western Europe from 1750 to the Present" (Book Review). *Business History Review, 44*(2), 238.

Dakkak, A., Bosch, J., & Holmstrom Olsson, H. (2023). Towards AIOps enabled services in continuously evolving software-intensive embedded systems. *Journal of Software: Evolution and Process,* e2592.

Doll, M. W., Rai, S., & Granado, J. (2003). *Defending the digital frontier: A security agenda.* John Wiley & Sons.

Fu, H., Xiao, X. H., & Zhu, H. M. (2024). Big gains in digital ecosystem niches: How facilitators emerge and develop into an organizational category. *Information & Management, 61*(4), 103957.

Govindarajan, V. (2016). *The three-box solution: A strategy for leading innovation.* Harvard Business Review Press.

He, Q., Meadows, M., Angwin, D., Gomes, E., & Child, J. (2020). Strategic alliance research in the era of digital transformation: Perspectives on future research. *British Journal of Management, 31*(3), 589–617.

Herbert, L. (2017). *Digital transformation: Build your organization's future for the innovation age.* Bloomsbury Publishing.

Hung, S. W., Cheng, M. J., & Lee, C. J. (2022). A new mechanism for purchasing through personal interactions: Fairness, trust and social influence in online group buying. *Information Technology & People, 35*(5), 1563–1589.

Isabelle, D., Horak, K., McKinnon, S., & Palumbo, C. (2020). Is Porter's five forces framework still relevant? A study of the capital/labour intensity continuum via mining and IT industries. *Technology Innovation Management Review, 10*(6).

Ismail, M. H., Khater, M., & Zaki, M. (2017). Digital business transformation and strategy: What do we know so far. *Cambridge Service Alliance, 10*(1), 1–35.

Javaid, M., Haleem, A., Singh, R. P., Suman, R., & Rab, S. (2022). Significance of machine learning in healthcare: Features, pillars and applications. *International Journal of Intelligent Networks, 3*, 58–73.

Keiningham, T., Aksoy, L., Bruce, H. L., Cadet, F., Clennell, N., Hodgkinson, I. R., & Kearney, T. (2020). Customer experience driven business model innovation. *Journal of Business Research, 116*, 431–440.

Khuntia, J., Saldanha, T., Kathuria, A., & Tanniru, M. R. (2024). Digital service flexibility: A conceptual framework and roadmap for digital business transformation. *European Journal of Information Systems, 33*(1), 61–79.

Kiron, D., Kane, G. C., Palmer, D., Phillips, A. N., & Buckley, N. (2016). Aligning the organization for its digital future. *MIT Sloan Management Review, 58*(1).

Komalasari, R. (2024). Navigating the digital frontier: A socio-technical review of Indonesia's NHS E-health strategy and healthcare transformation. *Inclusivity and Accessibility in Digital Health*, 174–194.

Kretschmer, T., Leiponen, A., Schilling, M., & Vasudeva, G. (2022). Platform ecosystems as meta-organizations: Implications for platform strategies. *Strategic Management Journal, 43*(3), 405–424.

Kumar, S. (2021). *The digital frontier: Infrastructures of control on the global web*. Indiana University Press.

Kumbhojkar, N. R., & Menon, A. B. (2022). Integrated predictive experience management framework (IPEMF) for improving customer experience: In the era of digital transformation. *International Journal of Cloud Applications and Computing (IJCAC), 12*(1), 1–13.

Leodolter, W. (2017). *Digital transformation shaping the subconscious minds of organizations: Innovative organizations and hybrid intelligences*. Springer.

Mejeh, M., & Rehm, M. (2024). Taking adaptive learning in educational settings to the next level: Leveraging natural language processing for improved personalization. *Educational Technology Research and Development*, 1–25.

Moore, J. F. (1993). Predators and prey: A new ecology of competition. *Harvard Business Review, 71*(3), 75–86.

Moore, J. F. (1996) *The death of competition: Leadership and strategy in the age of business ecosystems*. Chichester, England: John Wiley & Sons.

Nowotny, H. (2021). *In AI we trust: Power, illusion and control of predictive algorithms*. John Wiley & Sons.

Observability Tools & Platform Market (2024). https://www.marketsandmarkets.com/Market-Reports/observability-tools-and-platforms-market-69804486.html

Parra-López, C., Reina-Usuga, L., Carmona-Torres, C., Sayadi, S., & Klerkx, L. (2021). Digital transformation of the agrifood system: Quantifying the conditioning factors to inform policy planning in the olive sector. *Land Use Policy, 108*, 105537.

Porter, M. E. (2011) *Competitive advantage of nations: Creating and sustaining superior performance.* New York, NY: Free Press.

Pushkarna, A. (2024, April 1). UPI transactions jump 11% MoM in March, volume nears INR 20 lakh Cr mark. *Inc42 Media.* https://inc42.com/buzz/upi-transactions-jump-11-mom-in-march-volume-nears-inr-20-lakh-cr-mark/ (https://www.npci.org.in/what-we-do/upi/product-statistics)

Puyt, R. W., Lie, F. B., & Wilderom, C. P. (2023). The origins of SWOT analysis. *Long Range Planning, 56*(3), 102304.

Rogers, D. L. (2016). *The digital transformation playbook: Rethink your business for the digital age.* Columbia University Press.

Rogers, D. L. (2023). *The digital transformation roadmap: Rebuild your organization for continuous change.* Columbia University Press.

Sewpersadh, N. S. (2023). Disruptive business value models in the digital era. *Journal of Innovation and Entrepreneurship, 12*(1), 2.

Sharma, M., Singh, P., & Tsagarakis, K. (2024). Strategic pathways to achieve sustainable development goal 12 through Industry 4.0: Moderating role of institutional pressure. *Business Strategy and the Environment.* https://doi.org/10.1002/bse.3769

Solis, B., & Szymanski, J. (2016). *The six stages of digital transformation.* Altimeter Prophet.

Terho, H., Mero, J., Siutla, L., & Jaakkola, E. (2022). Digital content marketing in business markets: Activities, consequences, and contingencies along the customer journey. *Industrial Marketing Management, 105,* 294–310.

Van Veldhoven, Z., & Vanthienen, J. (2019). *Designing a comprehensive understanding of digital transformation and its impact.* Conference, Humanizing Technology for a Sustainable Society. KU Leuven, Faculty of Economics and Business, Leuven, Belgium.

Wayte, L. (2023). *Pay for play: How the music industry works, where the money goes, and why.* University of Oregon.

Wei, F., Feng, N., Yang, S., & Zhao, Q. (2020). A conceptual framework of two-stage partner selection in platform-based innovation ecosystems for servitization. *Journal of Cleaner Production, 262,* 121431.

Willcocks, L. P., Hindle, J., Stanton, M., & Smith, J. (2024). *Maximizing value with automation and digital transformation: A realist's guide.* Springer Nature.

Zhong, X., & Ren, G. (2023). Independent and joint effects of CSR and CSI on the effectiveness of digital transformation for transition economy firms. *Journal of Business Research, 156,* 113478.

3

Tracing the Evolution of Digital Strategy with AI, Blockchain, Cloud, and Cryptocurrencies

Manjari Sharma and Sharad Gupta

3.1 Introduction

The convergence of artificial intelligence (AI), blockchain, cloud computing, and cryptocurrencies represents a transformative shift in how digital strategies are formulated across industries. These technologies have evolved from theoretical constructs into integral components that drive innovation, efficiency, and governance in modern business and societal contexts. The article delves into the distinct historical evolution of each technology and emphasizes their individual and collective contributions to digital transformation.

AI has its roots in mid-20th-century academic pursuits, limited initially to problem-solving algorithms and symbolic reasoning. Over time, machine learning and deep learning advancements have enabled AI to transition from rule-based systems to autonomous models that drive decision-making across sectors, including healthcare, finance, and automotive industries. This evolution highlights the shift from early, narrow applications to today's comprehensive, data-driven AI systems that analyze massive datasets, enhance automation, and optimize operational processes.

Blockchain, introduced in 2008 as the foundational architecture of Bitcoin, has grown beyond its initial application in cryptocurrencies. Its decentralized ledger has found utility across industries like supply chain management and healthcare, providing secure, transparent, and immutable records that reduce reliance on intermediaries and enhance data security.

Cloud computing emerged in the late 1990s, facilitating the move from local servers to scalable, cost-effective remote data storage and processing. The cloud has since become essential in supporting AI and blockchain technologies, allowing companies to access powerful computational resources without investing in expensive infrastructure. Cryptocurrencies, built on blockchain technology, began as an alternative to fiat currencies but have expanded into decentralized finance (DeFi) platforms. These digital currencies challenge traditional financial institutions by offering secure, transparent, and decentralized methods of conducting cross-border transactions, enhancing financial inclusion on a global scale. This chapter critically examines the historical development and integration of AI, blockchain, cloud computing, and cryptocurrencies, exploring their roles in shaping digital strategies and highlighting their challenges and opportunities.

3.2 Historical Context and Evolution of AI

The development of AI, from its theoretical origins to its indispensable role in modern digital strategies, highlights a compelling narrative of human creativity and technological progress. Initially conceptualized in the mid-20th century, machines mimicking human intelligence were once a speculative idea confined to science fiction and academic theory. This period began a relentless pursuit to develop computational systems capable of performing tasks typically requiring human cognition.

The early stages of AI were marked by significant milestones, including creating simple algorithms to solve specific problems through basic logical processes. Early AI models, such as rule-based systems and symbolic reasoning, focused on replicating human decision-making in specific, narrow domains. However, these early systems were limited in scope and adaptability, leading researchers to push for more sophisticated models.

Over the decades, significant advancements in computer science have propelled AI from basic algorithms to advanced systems involving machine learning and deep learning. These technologies, which allow computers to learn from and make predictions based on data, represented a significant shift from hardcoded instructions to systems capable of adapting and improving over time. This progression was further enhanced by the advent of deep learning, employing complex neural networks that learn from vast amounts of unstructured data in ways that mimic human neural architectures.

Specific breakthroughs, such as the development of IBM's Watson, which revolutionized healthcare diagnostics by analyzing vast datasets to recommend treatment options, and Google's AlphaGo, which showcased AI's ability to surpass human capabilities in complex strategic games, represent pivotal moments in AI's evolution. These landmark innovations signaled AI's transition from academic research to practical, high-impact applications that reshape industries.

These advancements have been fueled by exponential increases in computational power, a phenomenon encapsulated in Moore's Law, and the explosion of available data – often called "Big Data." These vast datasets provide the essential raw material from which AI systems learn and refine their algorithms, enhancing their efficiency and capability. Today, as noted by Stuart Russell and Peter Norvig (2016), AI stands as a cornerstone of innovation across multiple industries, driving advancements that were unimaginable just a few decades ago. AI now underpins the strategic operations of sectors as diverse as healthcare, finance, automotive, and entertainment, transforming them with capabilities that range from predictive analytics to autonomous decision-making. The evolution of AI, driven by both technological advancements and human ingenuity, continues to be a dynamic force at the forefront of digital strategy and technological innovation.

3.3 Strategic Integration of AI in Business and Industry Contexts

The strategic incorporation of AI into business operations has profoundly transformed various industries, marking a pivotal shift in how organizations drive efficiency, foster innovation, and secure competitive advantages. As Brynjolfsson and McAfee (2017) articulate, AI technologies are no longer just tools but essential components that fundamentally reshape business performance frameworks and strategies. AI's ability to process vast amounts of data and make real-time decisions enables organizations to move beyond traditional operational methods toward more dynamic, predictive, and personalized approaches.

In the financial sector, AI has emerged as a transformative force by introducing predictive analytics that allows institutions to anticipate market trends, manage risks with precision, and offer personalized services at an unprecedented scale. AI models analyze complex datasets to identify emerging patterns, which enhances decision-making accuracy and boosts financial performance. Moreover, AI strengthens security and tailors customer experiences, raising industry customer interaction and service delivery standards. The integration of AI into finance not only reduces operational costs but also enhances client engagement by providing more customized, real-time solutions.

Similarly, AI is critical in transforming how businesses engage with customers in the retail sector. AI-powered algorithms analyze vast quantities of consumer data, enabling businesses to tailor marketing strategies that are both more efficient and customer-centric. This results in highly personalized shopping experiences where recommendations are based on individual preferences, past behaviors, and real-time interactions. Retailers leverage AI to optimize inventory management, predict consumer demand, and enhance customer loyalty through personalization, fundamentally reshaping customer relationships and driving revenue growth.

One of the most profound transformations AI brings is seen in healthcare. As highlighted by Jiang et al. (2017), AI-driven diagnostic tools and machine-learning models are revolutionizing how medical professionals diagnose and treat diseases. These tools analyze medical imaging, predict patient outcomes, and customize treatment plans individually, thus improving the accuracy and speed of diagnoses. In addition to improving patient outcomes, AI solutions address critical healthcare challenges by increasing access to quality care, reducing the time and costs associated with medical diagnostics, and ensuring that healthcare is practical and scalable. This shift toward AI-driven healthcare solutions enhances clinical efficacy and solves larger societal healthcare issues, such as the uneven distribution of care and resources.

Across these sectors – finance, retail, and healthcare – AI is a catalyst for business innovation and societal advancement. AI empowers organizations to overcome traditional operational limits and unlock new opportunities by automating complex processes, enhancing decision-making, and enabling personalized interactions. Its strategic integration within industries improves efficiency, innovation, and broader societal benefits, such as more inclusive healthcare, better financial services, and enhanced consumer experiences. This dual role as both a commercial driver and a societal innovator underscores the comprehensive impact of AI on modern industry and society.

Therefore, the strategic integration of AI into industries not only transforms business operations but also catalyzes a broader evolution in societal structures. AI's capacity to personalize, automate, and optimize processes enables industries to transcend traditional limitations, resulting in more innovative, inclusive, and efficient operations. AI plays a crucial dual role in enhancing business performance while driving societal progress.

3.4 Case Studies Illustrating the Pivotal Role of AI in Sectoral Transformation

A range of case studies highlights AI's profound and transformative impact across different sectors. These practical applications of AI demonstrate its versatility and ability to reshape industry practices and consumer experiences. The following cases from the automotive and financial sectors showcase how AI technologies are redefining industry landscapes and operational paradigms.

In the automotive sector, Tesla's AI-powered autonomous driving technology exemplifies innovation in transportation. Tesla's machine learning algorithms process real-time sensory data from multiple sources, allowing vehicles to make decisions that mimic human judgment. This technology significantly reduces accidents while enhancing the driving experience.

Tesla's use of AI advances automotive safety and efficiency and sets new benchmarks for the future of human-machine collaboration in transportation by reducing human error and optimizing traffic flow.

In the financial sector, Ant Financial's application of AI revolutionizes banking services by enhancing data security, analyzing customer behavior, and providing personalized financial products. AI facilitates credit assessments and fraud detection, resulting in faster and more accurate services. This strategic deployment of AI transforms financial service delivery, making banking more secure, efficient, and tailored to individual needs on a global scale while enhancing customer satisfaction.

These case studies illustrate how AI's strategic integration into industries drives innovation and enhances operational efficiency and consumer engagement. Tesla and Ant Financial exemplify AI's ability to set new performance, safety, and customer interaction benchmarks.

3.5 AI's Contribution to Technological Innovation and the Challenges Encountered

AI plays a pivotal role in technological innovation, fostering the creation of new products, services, and processes that redefine what is possible. AI's ability to analyze vast datasets, learn from trends, and make real-time decisions has revolutionized industries by introducing capabilities once deemed the realm of science fiction. AI's dynamic and adaptable nature has led to significant advancements in areas ranging from autonomous vehicles to personalized medicine, demonstrating its transformative potential across various sectors. AI has become a key driver of technological progress in healthcare, finance, logistics, and education by enabling businesses and institutions to automate complex tasks, derive insights from data, and develop intelligent systems.

However, alongside these remarkable contributions, AI's rapid evolution and widespread adoption present a series of profound challenges that must be addressed to harness its full potential responsibly. The key challenge, among others, is ethical considerations, prominently concerning privacy, bias, and the implications for the future of work. As noted by philosopher Nick Bostrom (2014), these ethical dilemmas arise from AI's capabilities to surpass human decision-making processes. This could lead to issues such as the invasion of personal privacy, the amplification of existing biases embedded within datasets, and the displacement of workers through widespread automation, potentially exacerbating inequality if not managed carefully.

One critical ethical concern is how AI systems can perpetuate or even worsen societal biases. Because AI systems learn from data, any biases present in the training data can be reflected or magnified in AI-driven decisions, particularly in sensitive areas like hiring, lending, and law enforcement. Moreover, the ability of AI to make decisions with limited transparency, often referred to as the "black box" problem, challenges the accountability of AI systems significantly when these decisions impact individuals' rights and opportunities.

Addressing these challenges necessitates a comprehensive and multidisciplinary approach. Regulatory frameworks must be developed to govern the use of AI, ensuring that its deployment in various sectors complies with ethical standards that protect individual rights and promote fairness. Moreover, stronger ethical guidelines must be established to ensure AI systems are transparent, explainable, and free from harmful biases. Efforts to ensure AI transparency – such as requiring developers to explain how decisions are made – are critical to building public trust and ensuring accountability when AI systems are used in high-stakes decisions.

Ongoing research is critical in this context, continually assessing AI's impact and evolving potential risks. Researchers must advance AI systems' technical capabilities and address AI's social implications, ensuring that innovation aligns with societal norms and ethical principles. This requires ongoing dialogue between technologists, ethicists, policymakers, and the public to balance AI-driven innovation and protecting fundamental ethical values. By fostering such dialogue, we can ensure that AI contributes positively to society, advancing technological innovation while safeguarding privacy, equity, and transparency.

3.6 Legal and Ethical Considerations in the Deployment of AI Technologies

Deploying AI technologies brings significant legal and ethical challenges, requiring a careful balance between fostering innovation and implementing necessary regulations. The integration of AI across various sectors must navigate a complex landscape of ethical dilemmas and legal constraints, emphasizing the need for an equilibrium that does not stifle technological advancement while ensuring adherence to ethical standards. The challenge lies in striking a balance where AI can drive progress and innovation without compromising fundamental human rights and freedoms, notably privacy, fairness, and accountability.

The European Union's General Data Protection Regulation (GDPR) is a prime example of regulatory efforts to address these challenges. Enacted to safeguard individual privacy in the burgeoning era of AI and digital technologies, the GDPR sets comprehensive rules for data protection and privacy. As highlighted by Goodman and Flaxman (2017), this regulation serves as a benchmark for global regulatory approaches, influencing how personal data should be handled worldwide in the context of AI applications. The GDPR underscores the importance of obtaining explicit consent from individuals for data usage, ensuring transparency in how AI systems process personal data, and giving individuals the right to access, rectify, or delete their data. These protections are essential as AI increasingly relies on vast datasets, which could lead to privacy and data security violations if misused.

Beyond legal frameworks, AI's ethical development and deployment necessitate a strong commitment to transparency, accountability, and fairness. According to Mittelstadt and colleagues (2016), these principles are essential to ensure that AI systems do not perpetuate existing societal biases or contribute to new forms of inequality. One of the key ethical challenges is ensuring that AI systems are designed to mitigate bias, as biased algorithms can exacerbate discrimination, particularly in areas like hiring, lending, and criminal justice. Addressing algorithmic fairness requires developers to ensure their datasets are representative and continuously audit AI systems for unintended outcomes that may harm marginalized groups.

In addition, accountability is a central ethical concern. As AI systems become more autonomous and decision-making becomes more opaque, AI's "black box" nature raises significant questions about responsibility when errors or harm occur. Legal frameworks must ensure a clear line of accountability for developers, operators, or organizations using AI systems. This would build trust in AI technologies and provide recourse for individuals affected by flawed or harmful AI-driven decisions.

AI stands at the forefront of the digital revolution, offering unparalleled opportunities for innovation, efficiency, and societal advancement. As AI continues to evolve, its integration into digital strategies will increasingly influence the trajectory of industries, economies, and governance. The future of AI requires a collaborative approach among technologists, policymakers, ethicists, and regulators. Only through such collaboration can we develop the legal and ethical frameworks that ensure AI serves as a tool for good, advancing human welfare without infringing on rights or exacerbating inequalities. By doing so, we can ensure that AI propels humanity toward a future where technology amplifies our capabilities, enriches our lives, and fosters sustainable and equitable progress (Table 3.1).

3.7 Blockchain: The Backbone of Cryptocurrencies and Beyond

The emergence of blockchain technology as the cornerstone of cryptocurrencies represents a significant development in the digital revolution. First introduced as the foundational architecture for Bitcoin in 2008 by an entity

TABLE 3.1

Overview of Technological Adoption

Technology	Year Introduced	Initial Use Cases	Current Trends	Key References
Blockchain	2008	Cryptocurrency (Bitcoin)	Supply chain transparency, healthcare data management	Nakamoto, S. (2008). Bitcoin: A Peer-to-Peer Electronic Cash System.
AI	1956	Problem-solving and symbolic methods in small domains	Machine learning, natural language processing, autonomous vehicles	McCarthy, J., Minsky, M. L., Rochester, N., & Shannon, C. E. (1956). A Proposal for the Dartmouth Summer Research Project on AI.
Cloud Computing	Late 1990s	Web-based email services and website hosting	Serverless computing, platform as a service (PaaS), infrastructure as a service (IaaS)	Vaquero, L. M., Rodero-Merino, L., Caceres, J., & Lindner, M. (2009). A break in the clouds: Towards a cloud definition. ACM SIGCOMM Computer Communication Review.
Cryptocurrency	2009	Digital Currency (Bitcoin)	Decentralized finance (DeFi), non-fungible tokens (NFTs), smart contracts	Nakamoto, S. (2008). Bitcoin: A Peer-to-Peer Electronic Cash System.

known under Satoshi Nakamoto, blockchain technology has since expanded beyond its initial role to become a transformative force across numerous sectors (Nakamoto, 2008). At its core, blockchain is a decentralized digital ledger that records transactions across a distributed network of computers, ensuring transparency, security, and immutability. This system operates without a central authority, making it resilient against tampering and fraud (Crosby et al., 2016). This pioneering innovation has redefined the concept of digital trust, establishing a new paradigm for secure and transparent digital transactions.

Blockchain technology is crucial in cryptocurrencies, extending beyond facilitating digital currencies like Bitcoin and Ethereum. Blockchain's decentralized framework enables secure, transparent transactions without intermediaries, which helps reduce fraud, lower transaction costs, and enhance privacy for users (Tapscott & Tapscott, 2016). Its resistance to tampering and ability to maintain an immutable record of transactions have made blockchain the benchmark infrastructure for digital currencies, presenting an innovative alternative to traditional financial systems and challenging long-standing norms of monetary exchange (Yli-Huumo et al., 2016).

Beyond cryptocurrencies, blockchain's potential extends to various sectors. In the supply chain industry, blockchain enables product traceability from origin to consumer, improving transparency and operational efficiency (Kshetri, 2018). In healthcare, blockchain is a secure platform for storing and exchanging patient data, enhancing system interoperability while safeguarding privacy (Mettler, 2016). Moreover, blockchain drives innovation in digital identity verification, smart contracts, and electoral systems, demonstrating its versatility and potential to transform business and governance models (Swan, 2015).

Practical examples highlight blockchain's transformative impact across industries. In the supply chain domain, collaborations between Maersk and IBM have led to the creation of TradeLens. This blockchain-based solution enhances the transparency and efficiency of global trade logistics (Jennings, 2018). In healthcare, projects like MedRec utilize blockchain to improve medical record management, giving patients secure, seamless access to their health information (Ekblaw et al., 2016). In the financial sector, blockchain technologies are streamlining processes like payments, remittances, and cross-border transactions, as exemplified by Ripple's growing network of financial institutions (Hackett, 2017).

As blockchain technology evolves, it faces regulatory challenges, mainly due to its decentralized nature and diverse applications across multiple jurisdictions. Governments and regulatory bodies are grappling with how to effectively regulate blockchain-based applications while fostering innovation and protecting consumers (De Filippi & Wright, 2018). To address these challenges, a nuanced approach to governance is needed to balance the necessary regulatory oversight with blockchain's potential for social and economic transformation (Tapscott & Tapscott, 2016).

Blockchain technology is a cornerstone of the digital age, and its legacy has reached far beyond the creation of cryptocurrencies to influence numerous aspects of business, governance, and society. As it matures, blockchain promises to usher in a new era characterized by greater transparency, enhanced security, and improved efficiency in digital transactions. Although the technology faces significant challenges – particularly in regulation and governance – these are surmountable with concerted efforts from stakeholders

TABLE 3.2

Blockchain Technology Applications across Sectors

Sector	Initial Use Cases	Current Applications	Benefits Realized	Future Directions
Finance	Cryptocurrency Transactions	Decentralized finance (DeFi), smart contracts	Reduced transaction costs, enhanced security	Integration with traditional banking, global payment networks
Supply Chain	Product Traceability	Real-time tracking, anti-counterfeiting	Transparency, reduced losses	Full lifecycle product management, integration with IoT
Healthcare	Patient Data Management	Secure data sharing, personal health records	Data security, improved patient care	Interoperable health records, AI-driven analytics
Government	Identity Verification	Voting systems, land registration	Fraud reduction, enhanced citizen engagement	Smart contracts for public services, blockchain in legislative processes
Education	Credential Verification	Secure record keeping, digital diplomas	Verification ease, reduced fraud	Lifelong learning portfolios, cross-institution recognition

across the spectrum. To realize blockchain's full potential while managing its complexities, a forward-thinking approach is required – one that prioritizes innovation, ethical considerations, and strategic governance. As we move further into the blockchain era, its evolving legacy will continue to reshape our digital landscape, offering new paradigms for transacting, interacting, and establishing trust in the digital realm (Table 3.2).

3.8 Cloud Computing: The Catalyst for AI and Blockchain Acceleration

In the current digital transformation era, cloud computing has emerged as a foundational technology that accelerates the adoption of AI and blockchain technologies. Offering scalable and flexible computing resources, cloud computing eliminates the need for extensive on-premises infrastructure, thereby democratizing access to cutting-edge technologies (Mell & Grance, 2011). Its pivotal role in the digital revolution provides the backbone for rapid innovation and the deployment of digital strategies across industries. By lowering the barriers to entry, cloud computing allows smaller enterprises and start-ups to access high-level computational resources previously available only to large organizations.

Cloud computing serves as a synergistic platform at the intersection of AI and blockchain, enhancing the capabilities and reach of both technologies. AI provides essential computational power and data storage solutions, facilitating the development and deployment of machine learning models and AI-driven applications at scale (Hashem et al., 2015). In the realm of blockchain, cloud services offer a decentralized and secure environment that enables networks to operate more efficiently and at lower costs (Zhang & Wen, 2017). This integration accelerates the adoption of these technologies and amplifies their impact across sectors. The flexibility of cloud computing ensures that AI and blockchain systems can scale as needed, supporting both intensive processing tasks and real-time data analysis.

The cloud meets the significant computational demands of AI, particularly deep learning algorithms, by providing scalable resources that allow for the processing of vast datasets and complex computations without hardware limitations (Li et al., 2020). Concurrently, blockchain applications benefit from the cloud's global infrastructure, which supports deploying decentralized applications (dApps) and smart contracts, ensuring high availability and reliability (Sultan et al., 2018). By hosting blockchain networks on the cloud, organizations can ensure uninterrupted access to services, reduce latency, and improve the overall security of decentralized operations.

Addressing Legal and Security Concerns in Cloud Computing: Despite its benefits, cloud computing introduces significant legal and security concerns, particularly concerning data protection, privacy, and compliance with regulations such as the GDPR (Hon et al., 2012). The shared responsibility model in cloud services necessitates a collaborative approach to security, wherein providers and users play critical roles in ensuring data integrity and protection (Pearson, 2013). The transnational nature of cloud computing also poses jurisdictional challenges that complicate regulatory compliance across different regions (Millard, 2013). To mitigate these challenges, organizations must develop comprehensive cloud security strategies that include encryption, data anonymization, and continuous monitoring to safeguard sensitive data.

The strategic adoption of cloud computing significantly impacts business efficiency and scalability. By leveraging cloud services, businesses can rapidly deploy and scale applications, respond flexibly to market demands, and reduce operational costs through efficient resource use (Marston et al., 2011). In particular, AI-powered services such as predictive analytics or personalized marketing solutions benefit from the ability to scale computing resources on demand, ensuring real-time responses to changing business conditions. This agility is especially crucial in AI and blockchain, where the speed of development and deployment can significantly influence competitive advantage and innovation (Iansiti & Lakhani, 2017).

Looking ahead, the convergence of cloud computing with emerging technologies such as edge computing and quantum computing is poised to redefine the landscape of digital strategies. Edge computing enhances cloud computing by processing data closer to the source, reducing latency and bandwidth use, which is particularly beneficial for real-time AI and blockchain applications (Shi et al., 2016). As more devices are connected to the Internet of Things (IoT), edge computing will enable faster data processing at the local level, improving efficiency and reducing the load on centralized cloud systems. In addition, quantum computing could exponentially increase computational capabilities, offering new possibilities for complex problem-solving in cryptography, AI model training, and beyond (Castelvecchi, 2017).

Cloud computing is indispensable in the current and future landscape of digital strategies, acting as a catalyst for the adoption and acceleration of AI and blockchain technologies. By providing scalable and flexible computing resources, cloud computing enables the deployment of advanced digital solutions, driving innovation and efficiency across industries. However, to realize its full potential, businesses must proactively address legal, security, and compliance challenges. As the technology continues to evolve, organizations need to integrate cloud computing strategically within their digital infrastructures to ensure they remain agile, secure, and competitive in a rapidly changing global landscape. The strategic integration of cloud computing into digital infrastructures will continue to play a critical role in shaping the future of technology, fostering a more connected, efficient, and innovative digital world (Table 3.3).

3.9 Cryptocurrencies: Navigating the Strategic and Regulatory Labyrinth

Cryptocurrencies, such as Bitcoin and Ethereum, have emerged as disruptive financial innovations since the inception of Bitcoin in 2009 (Nakamoto, 2008). Built on blockchain technology, these digital currencies offer decentralized and secure transaction mechanisms, challenging traditional banking systems (Catalini & Gans, 2016). Their key principles – decentralization, transparency, and immutability – redefine money and enable a new paradigm for global financial interactions (Swan, 2015). By eliminating intermediaries, cryptocurrencies create a peer-to-peer financial ecosystem that reduces dependence on central authorities and lowers transaction barriers.

TABLE 3.3
Blockchain Technology Applications across Sectors

Component	Description	Interactions	Benefits	Future Directions
Core Cloud Services (IaaS, PaaS, SaaS)	Infrastructure, platforms, and software provided over the internet, serving as the foundational layers for deploying and managing applications and services (Mell & Grance, 2011).	Serve as the backbone for AI and blockchain technologies, offering scalable resources and platforms for development and deployment (Zhang & Wen, 2017).	Enhanced efficiency, scalability, and accessibility (Marston et al., 2011).	Evolution toward more integrated and specialized cloud services to support emerging technologies like quantum computing and IoT (Castelvecchi, 2017; Shi et al., 2016).
AI	Technologies that simulate human intelligence processes by machines, especially computer systems (Russell & Norvig, 2016).	AI algorithms leverage cloud computing for data processing and storage, benefiting from the cloud's computational power for learning and analysis (Hashem et al., 2015; Li et al., 2020).	Accelerated innovation, improved decision-making, and automation (Jordan & Mitchell, 2015).	Advancements in AI-driven analytics and autonomous systems, further integration with IoT and edge computing
Blockchain Technology	A decentralized ledger that records transactions across a network of computers to ensure transparency and security (Nakamoto, 2008; Crosby et al., 2016).	Blockchain networks utilize cloud infrastructure for enhanced scalability and security, benefiting from cloud's global reach and robustness (Sultan et al., 2018).	Increased security, transparency in transactions, and trust (Tapscott & Tapscott, 2016; Yli-Huumo et al., 2016).	Expansion into various sectors beyond finance, such as healthcare and government, for secure and transparent data management

(Continued)

TABLE 3.3 (Continued)

Blockchain Technology Applications across Sectors

Component	Description	Interactions	Benefits	Future Directions
Benefits Realized	The integration of cloud computing with AI and blockchain yields numerous advantages	–	Reduced costs, enhanced security, increased innovation, and greater operational efficiency	–
Interactions	Describes how AI and blockchain technologies interact with cloud computing to create a synergistic ecosystem	Cloud services enable the deployment and scaling of AI models and blockchain networks, facilitating data sharing and processing (Zhang & Wen, 2017).	–	–
Future Directions	Predictions for how this ecosystem will evolve, emphasizing growth areas and emerging trends	–	–	More sophisticated AI and blockchain applications, edge and quantum computing integration, and stronger focus on privacy and regulatory compliance (Shi et al., 2016; Castelvecchi, 2017).

The strategic adoption of cryptocurrencies offers businesses several advantages, including lower transaction costs, faster settlements, and access to a global market without the limitations of traditional financial infrastructures (Tapscott & Tapscott, 2016). Moreover, blockchain's security features mitigate fraud risks, enhancing trust in digital transactions (Yli-Huumo et al., 2016). These benefits underscore cryptocurrencies' potential to revolutionize business operations, opening up opportunities for innovation and competitive advantage (Iansiti & Lakhani, 2017). Cryptocurrencies enable seamless cross-border transactions and enhance financial inclusivity, especially in under-banked regions.

However, the regulatory landscape for cryptocurrencies remains complex and varies widely across jurisdictions. Regulators worldwide struggle to categorize cryptocurrencies due to their hybrid nature, encompassing aspects of currencies, commodities, and securities (De Filippi & Wright, 2018). This has created both opportunities and risks, with countries adopting different cryptocurrency use and taxation policies, which affect market participation and innovation.

In some regions, stringent regulations and bans stifle innovation and limit market participation (Rauchs et al., 2018). In contrast, jurisdictions with clear guidelines and progressive policies have become hubs for cryptocurrency development and investment (Hileman & Rauchs, 2017). This disparity highlights the need for a harmonized global regulatory approach to ensure the stable integration of cryptocurrencies into the financial ecosystem (Böhme et al., 2015). Without such alignment, fragmented markets may hinder global scalability.

Case Studies on the Impact of Regulatory Decisions: The role of regulation in shaping cryptocurrency markets is evident in case studies from Japan and China. In 2017, Japan officially recognized Bitcoin as a legal payment method, catalyzing widespread acceptance and integration within its economy. This regulatory clarity boosted market growth, attracting significant investor interest and fostering innovation (Fujimura & Shin, 2018). Japan's supportive environment increased consumer and business engagement with digital currencies, enabling a thriving cryptocurrency ecosystem.

Conversely, China's regulatory crackdown in 2017 banned cryptocurrency exchanges and Initial Coin Offerings (ICOs), citing concerns over financial risks, fraud, and volatility. This action caused market instability and prompted blockchain enterprises to relocate to more favorable jurisdictions (Chen, 2018). The contrasting approaches in Japan and China underscore how regulatory decisions can either foster innovation or stifle market growth, driving enterprises to adapt or relocate.

These case studies show the critical role regulatory environments play in the evolution of cryptocurrencies. Japan's proactive engagement facilitated market growth and broader adoption, while China's restrictions demonstrate how stringent regulations can hinder innovation. The divergent strategies of these two countries illustrate how national regulatory philosophies

– from facilitative to prohibitive – shape national and global cryptocurrency markets.

Understanding the impact of these regulatory decisions is crucial for cryptocurrency stakeholders as they navigate the legal and market challenges. These case studies offer valuable lessons for other nations formulating or revising cryptocurrency regulations. Policymakers must strike a balance between fostering innovation and ensuring market stability to support cryptocurrencies' positive contributions to the global economy.

3.10 Shaping the Future of Cryptocurrencies through Regulation and Innovation

As the cryptocurrency sector matures, navigating its regulatory and innovation challenges becomes increasingly critical. The future of cryptocurrencies will largely depend on developing coherent regulatory frameworks that foster innovation while mitigating risks such as volatility, security vulnerabilities, and misuse of illicit activities (Gudgeon et al., 2020). Without effective regulation, cryptocurrency markets risk potential destabilization due to fraud, money laundering, and speculative behavior, which can erode user trust.

Regulatory bodies face the challenge of balancing consumer protection and market stability with an environment conducive to technological innovation. Effective regulation should integrate cryptocurrencies into the global financial system by leveraging their benefits – such as increased efficiency and reduced costs – while minimizing risks. Key measures like tax reporting and anti-money laundering compliance are essential to legitimizing cryptocurrencies and supporting broader adoption.

On the business side, entrepreneurs and companies play a pivotal role in shaping the future of cryptocurrencies. Companies must remain agile, adapting to new laws and policies to thrive in the evolving regulatory landscape. This involves complying with regulations and proactively engaging with developments to create innovative solutions that maximize the benefits of cryptocurrencies, such as faster transactions and global market access. Businesses that innovate within regulatory frameworks can capitalize on strategic advantages, including lower barriers to entry for financial services and increased transaction efficiency.

Innovation within these frameworks often leads to developing new products – such as more secure wallet technologies and enhanced fraud detection systems – that address security concerns while building user trust in digital currencies. In addition, innovations like stablecoins, which minimize volatility by pegging to traditional currencies, help address one of the major cryptocurrency concerns: price fluctuations.

The future of cryptocurrencies will be shaped by collaboration between regulators, industry participants, and the broader community. This cooperation fosters an ecosystem where technological innovation can flourish alongside sound regulatory practices. Ongoing stakeholder dialogue ensures that regulatory frameworks evolve alongside technological advances and market needs, creating a balanced environment that encourages innovation while managing systemic risks.

Engaging with the broader community, including users and tech enthusiasts, also provides regulators and businesses valuable insights into market demands and potential solutions. Such engagement ensures that cryptocurrency development aligns with broader economic goals, while user feedback helps improve the usability and security of cryptocurrency platforms, promoting wider adoption.

In summary, the dynamic interplay between regulation and innovation in the cryptocurrency sector calls for an informed approach considering digital currencies' global financial implications. By fostering a balanced regulatory environment where innovation thrives within a framework of trust and security, stakeholders can unlock cryptocurrencies' full potential to transform the financial sector and contribute to the global economy. The development of cryptocurrencies is not only a technological challenge but also a multifaceted effort that requires cohesive strategies, regulatory foresight, and collaborative innovation.

3.11 Integrated Digital Strategies: AI, Blockchain, Cloud, and Cryptocurrencies

In an era of rapid technological evolution, the convergence of AI, blockchain, cloud computing, and cryptocurrencies is shaping the future of modern digital strategies. While distinct in their capabilities, these technologies interconnect to create a powerful ecosystem that is driving transformative changes in how businesses, governments, and societies function, innovate, and interact. Together, they form a cohesive infrastructure for the digital age, enabling unprecedented efficiency, security, and scalability.

3.12 AI and Cloud Computing: Synergy and Scalability

Integrating AI with cloud computing is a critical driver of digital transformation. Cloud computing provides the scalable infrastructure necessary to deploy AI applications efficiently. AI algorithms, particularly those involving machine learning and deep learning, demand vast computational resources and data storage capacities. Cloud platforms like Amazon Web Services, Microsoft Azure, and Google Cloud offer virtually unlimited processing power and storage, allowing businesses to avoid the significant costs of on-premises infrastructure (Mell & Grance, 2011). This accessibility democratizes AI, enabling companies of all sizes to implement advanced AI solutions at scale without significant upfront investments in hardware.

The scalability of cloud computing empowers AI to process large datasets, enabling sophisticated analytics, real-time data processing, and the execution of complex algorithms at scale. These capabilities are essential for industries such as healthcare, finance, and retail, where AI-driven insights transform operations by providing predictive analytics, personalized services, and autonomous systems (Jordan & Mitchell, 2015). For example, AI in healthcare is utilized to analyze patient data, predict disease outcomes, recommend treatments, and assist in surgeries (Jiang et al., 2017). The ability of cloud platforms to provide flexible, on-demand resources accelerates innovation and improves responsiveness across sectors, ensuring that AI-driven solutions can be rapidly scaled as needs evolve.

3.13 Blockchain: Enhancing Security and Transparency

Blockchain technology, with its decentralized and secure ledger system, enhances the transparency and trustworthiness of digital systems, particularly when integrated with AI. Blockchain provides a tamper-resistant ledger for transactions and data exchanges, ensuring that AI-driven processes are verifiable and secure. This feature is especially valuable in industries such as finance and healthcare, where data integrity and security are paramount (Iansiti & Lakhani, 2017). By ensuring that data recorded through AI processes cannot be altered or tampered with, blockchain reinforces trust in AI-generated insights and decision-making.

In the financial sector, blockchain's decentralized nature eliminates the need for intermediaries, enabling secure, transparent, and efficient transactions. In addition, blockchain provides a framework for the secure exchange of data between AI systems, reducing the risk of fraud and data manipulation. Smart contracts – self-executing contracts with the terms of the agreement written directly into code – leverage AI to automate contract execution and blockchain to ensure the contract's integrity (Ojha & Niranjan, 2023). This combination fosters a secure, automated environment for business operations, reducing human error and increasing efficiency.

Integrating blockchain with cloud computing further enhances the reliability of cloud services by securing data against tampering and unauthorized access. Blockchain's immutable ledger addresses the inherent vulnerabilities of cloud computing, particularly about data security and privacy. For instance, using blockchain to record and secure cloud-stored data can ensure that it remains tamper-proof, even in decentralized or multi-cloud environments, mitigating concerns about data breaches or unauthorized alterations. A blockchain-based cloud can thus ensure that data remains secure and immutable, addressing the increasing concerns about data breaches and manipulation (Awadallah et al., 2021).

3.14 Cryptocurrencies: Decentralized Financial Systems

Cryptocurrencies, such as Bitcoin and Ethereum, represent a key application of blockchain technology, offering a decentralized alternative to traditional financial systems. These digital assets enable peer-to-peer transactions without reliance on central banks or financial intermediaries, reducing transaction costs and increasing financial inclusion (Tapscott & Tapscott, 2016). Blockchain's decentralized ledger ensures that cryptocurrency transactions are secure, transparent, and immutable, fostering trust in these digital currencies. By bypassing traditional financial gatekeepers, cryptocurrencies offer greater autonomy over financial transactions, expanding access to underbanked populations globally.

The role of AI in cryptocurrency markets is expanding, as AI algorithms analyze market trends, predict price movements, and execute trades automatically. AI-powered trading bots can process vast amounts of market data in real-time, making informed trading decisions based on predictive models and current market conditions (Shahbazi & Byun, 2022). Moreover, AI enhances the security of cryptocurrency ecosystems by detecting patterns and anomalies in blockchain transactions, helping identify and prevent fraudulent activities.

Cryptocurrencies are also being integrated into cloud computing and AI applications. For instance, blockchain platforms are increasingly supporting decentralized cloud computing services, where individuals and businesses can rent out unused computing resources in exchange for cryptocurrencies (Ojha & Niranjan, 2023). This model, known as blockchain-as-a-service, demonstrates how cryptocurrencies incentivize participation in decentralized networks, creating new business models and expanding the utility of cloud computing. Integration fosters decentralized cloud ecosystems, allowing for more efficient and secure sharing of computing power.

3.15 Synergistic Impact on Business and Society

The synergy between AI, blockchain, cloud computing, and cryptocurrencies creates an exponential impact. Together, these technologies enable the development of intelligent, secure, and decentralized digital ecosystems that are transforming industries from finance to healthcare.

Finance: AI-powered algorithms are enhancing risk assessment, fraud detection, and personalized banking services. Blockchain is transforming payment systems by providing a secure and transparent ledger, enabling low-fee cross-border transactions. Cryptocurrencies, built on blockchain, further decentralize the financial system, giving individuals and businesses greater control over their assets (Tapscott & Tapscott, 2016). This decentralization reduces reliance on traditional banks and increases access to financial services, particularly in emerging markets.

Healthcare: The convergence of AI, blockchain, and cloud computing is revolutionizing precision medicine. AI algorithms analyze patient data to tailor treatments to individual needs, while blockchain ensures that medical records are secure and accessible only to authorized personnel. Cloud computing provides the necessary infrastructure for storing and processing large volumes of medical data (Kumar et al., 2022). This synergy enhances patient care by improving accuracy and accessibility, while also reducing healthcare costs.

Supply Chain Management: Blockchain and AI are enhancing transparency and efficiency in supply chains. Blockchain provides an immutable record of transactions and the movement of goods, while AI analyzes supply chain data to optimize operations. For example, AI can predict demand fluctuations, while blockchain verifies the authenticity and provenance of goods, reducing fraud and ensuring quality (Ojha & Niranjan, 2023). This combination improves supply chain accountability, reducing costs and delays while ensuring product integrity.

3.16 Challenges and Opportunities

While the integration of AI, blockchain, cloud computing, and cryptocurrencies offers numerous benefits, it also presents several challenges:

(i) Technical Complexity: Implementing these technologies requires significant technical expertise and infrastructure. AI models must be trained on large datasets, and blockchain systems must be carefully designed to ensure scalability and efficiency (Akter et al., 2022). Achieving seamless integration between these technologies requires advanced skills and strategic planning to overcome compatibility and scalability issues.

(ii) Regulatory Uncertainty: Cryptocurrencies and blockchain technologies face regulatory challenges in many countries due to concerns about money laundering, fraud, and market volatility. Developing clear regulatory frameworks is essential for the widespread adoption of these technologies (De Filippi & Wright, 2018). The lack of standardized regulations across jurisdictions creates uncertainty, which can deter investment and hinder global adoption.

(iii) Ethical Considerations: The use of AI in decision-making processes raises ethical questions about bias, transparency, and accountability. Similarly, blockchain's decentralization can lead to governance issues and the concentration of power among miners or validators (Bostrom, 2014). Addressing these concerns is critical to ensuring that these technologies are used responsibly and that they promote equity and fairness.

Despite these challenges, the opportunities for innovation and societal advancement are vast. The convergence of AI, blockchain, cloud computing, and cryptocurrencies drives the next wave of digital transformation, offering new ways to create value, improve efficiency, and foster inclusion. As these technologies evolve, they will redefine industries and contribute to a more connected and equitable global economy.

3.17 Future Directions

The future of technological integration will continue evolving as quantum computing, the IoT, and edge computing converge with AI, blockchain, cloud computing, and cryptocurrencies. Quantum computing promises to transform blockchain and AI by enabling the execution of complex algorithms and transactions at unprecedented speeds. This will significantly accelerate cryptography, data security, and machine learning advancements, revolutionizing how businesses and governments handle large-scale data processing (Castelvecchi, 2017).

Edge computing, which processes data closer to its source (e.g., IoT devices), is another key growth area. Combining edge computing with AI and blockchain can reduce latency, improve real-time decision-making, and enhance applications such as autonomous vehicles and smart cities. For instance, edge computing allows AI-driven IoT devices to process data locally, while blockchain ensures data security and integrity. This integration improves efficiency by minimizing the need for centralized cloud storage and reducing vulnerabilities at single data points.

The ongoing integration of these technologies represents a leap in the digital revolution, providing new avenues for innovation, efficiency, and societal advancement. However, to fully realize the benefits of these technologies, key legal, ethical, and governance challenges must be addressed. Policymakers, strategists, and legal scholars will play a critical role in crafting the regulatory frameworks that allow these technologies to flourish while minimizing risks such as privacy breaches and market volatility.

Collaboration across industries, governments, and academia will be crucial to developing responsible and sustainable digital ecosystems. Quantum computing, IoT, and AI-driven solutions will redefine the digital landscape, pushing the boundaries of what is possible in business, governance, and society.

3.18 Conclusion

As we stand at the intersection of the Fourth Industrial Revolution, driven by advancements in AI, blockchain, cloud computing, and cryptocurrencies, it is evident that we are entering a transformative phase in digital strategy and governance. When integrated strategically, these technologies can reshape industries, redefine global interactions, and reform legal frameworks that govern them. AI and blockchain, particularly in combination with cloud infrastructure, drive operational efficiencies and challenge traditional systems, prompting reevaluating how businesses, societies, and governments operate in the digital age.

The future of digital strategies hinges on the responsible integration of AI, blockchain, and cloud computing with a forward-thinking approach to governance. These technologies can unlock unprecedented levels of efficiency and transparency across sectors. However, realizing this potential requires a balance between innovation and ethical considerations, particularly in ensuring inclusivity and fairness in their implementation.

The rapid pace of technological change demands that policymakers, strategists, and legal scholars work collaboratively to navigate these complexities. By fostering cross-disciplinary dialogue and embracing public-private partnerships, stakeholders can ensure that these innovations benefit all segments of society.

At the forefront of this transformation is the need for a governance model that prioritizes ethical considerations – such as equity and access – while mitigating risks like privacy breaches and market volatility. Only through careful governance can we ensure the sustainable growth of these technologies for the greater good.

In conclusion, the future of digital strategies lies in our collective ability to navigate the challenges and opportunities posed by these technologies.

Through collaboration and a shared vision, we can shape a digital landscape that drives innovation, fosters equity, and promotes responsible progress for all.

References

Akter, S., Michael, K., Uddin, M. R., McCarthy, G., & Rahman, M. (2022). Transforming business using digital innovations: The application of AI, blockchain, cloud, and data analytics. *Annals of Operations Research*, 308(1–2), 7–39. https://doi.org/10.1007/s10479-020-03620-w

Awadallah, R., & Samsudin, A. (2021). Using blockchain in cloud computing to enhance relational database security. *IEEE Access*, 9, 69513–69526. https://doi.org/10.1109/ACCESS.2021.3077633

Böhme, R., Christin, N., Edelman, B., & Moore, T. (2015). Bitcoin: Economics, technology, and governance. *Journal of Economic Perspectives*, 29.

Bostrom, N. (2014). *Superintelligence: Paths, Dangers, Strategies*. Oxford University Press.

Brynjolfsson, E., & McAfee, A. (2017). *The Second Machine Age: Work, Progress, and Prosperity in a Time of Brilliant Technologies*. W.W. Norton & Company.

Castelvecchi, D. (2017). Quantum computers ready to leap out of the lab in 2017. *Nature News*, 541(7635), 9–10.

Catalini, C., & Gans, J. S. (2016). *Some Simple Economics of the Blockchain*. MIT Sloan Research Paper.

Chen, Y. (2018). *The Blockchain Industry and Regulatory Environment in China: An Overview*. MDPI Information.

Crosby, M., Nachiappan, Pattanayak, P., Verma, S., & Kalyanaraman, V. (2016). Blockchain technology: Beyond bitcoin. *Applied Innovation Review*, 2.

De Filippi, P., & Wright, A. (2018). *Blockchain and the Law: The Rule of Code*. Harvard University Press.

Ekblaw, A., Azaria, A., Halamka, J. D., & Lippman, A. (2016). *A Case Study for Blockchain in Healthcare: "MedRec" Prototype for Electronic Health Records and Medical Research Data*. MIT Media Lab.

Fujimura, S., & Shin, L. (2018). Japan: The new heart of bitcoin. *Forbes*.

Goodman, B., & Flaxman, S. (2017). European Union regulations on algorithmic decision-making and a "right to explanation". *AI Magazine*, 38(3), 50–57.

Gudgeon, L., Werner, S., Perez, D., & Knottenbelt, W. J. (2020). *DeFi Protocols for Loanable Funds: Interest Rates, Liquidity and Market Efficiency*. arXiv preprint arXiv:2006.13922.

Hackett, R. (2017). Why big business is racing to build blockchains. *Fortune*.

Hashem, I. A. T., Yaqoob, I., Anuar, N. B., Mokhtar, S., Gani, A., & Ullah Khan, S. (2015). The rise of "big data" on cloud computing: Review and open research issues. *Information Systems*, 47, 98–115.

Hileman, G., & Rauchs, M. (2017). *Global Cryptocurrency Benchmarking Study*. Cambridge Centre for Alternative Finance.

Hon, W. K., Millard, C., & Walden, I. (2012). The problem of "personal data" in cloud computing: What information is regulated? The cloud of unknowing. *International Data Privacy Law*, 2(4), 211–228.

Iansiti, M., & Lakhani, K. R. (2017). The truth about blockchain. *Harvard Business Review*, 95(1), 118–127.

Jennings, R. (2018). How Maersk and IBM's blockchain could redefine global trade. *Forbes*.

Jiang, F., Jiang, Y., Zhi, H., Dong, Y., Li, H., Ma, S., Wang, Y., Dong, Q., Shen, H., & Wang, Y. (2017). Artificial intelligence in healthcare: past, present and future. *Stroke and Vascular Neurology*, 2(4).

Jordan, M. I., & Mitchell, T. M. (2015). Machine learning: Trends, perspectives, and prospects. *Science*, 349(6245), 255–260.

Kshetri, N. (2018). 1 blockchain's roles in meeting key supply chain management objectives. *International Journal of Information Management*, 39, 80–89.

Kumar, R., Arjunaditya, Singh, D., Srinivasan, K., & Hu, Y.-C. (2022). AI-powered blockchain technology for public health: A contemporary review, open challenges, and future research directions. *Healthcare*, 11(1), 81. https://doi.org/10.3390/healthcare11010081

Li, H., Ota, K., & Dong, M. (2020). Learning IoT in edge: Deep learning for the internet of things with edge computing. *IEEE Network*, 34(1), 9–14.

Marston, S., Li, Z., Bandyopadhyay, S., Zhang, J., & Ghalsasi, A. (2011). Cloud computing — The business perspective. *Decision Support Systems*, 51(1), 176–189. https://doi.org/10.1016/j.dss.2010.12.006

Mell, P., & Grance, T. (2011). *The NIST Definition of Cloud Computing*. National Institute of Standards and Technology.

Mettler, M. (2016). *Blockchain Technology in Healthcare: The Revolution Starts Here*. 18th International Conference on e-Health Networking, Applications and Services (Healthcom).

Millard, C. (2013). *Cloud Computing Law*. Oxford University Press.

Mittelstadt, B., Allo, P., Taddeo, M., Wachter, S., & Floridi, L. (2016). The ethics of algorithms: Mapping the debate. *Big Data & Society*, 3(2).

Nakamoto, S. (2008). *Bitcoin: A Peer-to-Peer Electronic Cash System*. https://bitcoin.org/bitcoin.pdf

Ojha, S., & Niranjan, R. (2023). *Potential Usage of AI in Blockchain Technology*. https://www.researchgate.net/publication/369939996_Potential_usage_of_AI_in_Blockchain_Technology

Pearson, S. (2013). Privacy, security and trust in cloud computing. *Privacy and Security for Cloud Computing*, 3–42.

Rauchs, M. et al. (2018). *2nd Global Cryptoasset Benchmarking Study*. Cambridge Centre for Alternative Finance.

Russell, S., & Norvig, P. (2016). *Artificial Intelligence: A Modern Approach*. Pearson.

Shahbazi, Z., & Byun, Y.-C. (2022). Machine learning-based analysis of cryptocurrency market financial risk management. *IEEE Access*, 10, 37848–37856. https://doi.org/10.1109/ACCESS.2022.3162858

Shi, W., Cao, J., Zhang, Q., Li, Y., & Xu, L. (2016). Edge computing:Vision and challenges. *IEEE Internet of Things Journal*, 3(5), 637–646. https://doi.org/10.1109/JIOT.2016.2579198

Sultan, N., Al-Jaroodi, J., & Mohamed, N. (2018). Integrating blockchain with edge computing for IoT applications: Opportunities, solutions, and challenges. *IEEE Access*, 7, 164184–164203.

Swan, M. (2015). *Blockchain: Blueprint for a New Economy*. O'Reilly Media.

Tapscott, D., & Tapscott, A. (2016). *Blockchain Revolution: How the Technology Behind Bitcoin Is Changing Money, Business, and the World*. Portfolio Penguin.

Yli-Huumo, J., Ko, D., Choi, S., Park, S., & Smolander, K. (2016). Where is current research on blockchain technology? A systematic review. *PLoS One*, 11(10).

Zhang, S., & Wen, J. (2017). The IoT electric business model: Using blockchain technology for the internet of things. *Peer-to-Peer Networking and Applications*, 10(4), 983–994.

Part 2

AI in Strategy
From Law to Ethical Alignment

4

Strategizing AI: Integrating Ethics and Environmental Sustainability in Digital Healthcare and Legal Systems

Widyastuti Andriyani, Dian Tri Wiyanti, and Daniel C.A. Nugroho

4.1 Introduction

The chapter explores the integration of artificial intelligence (AI) in medicine and law, highlighting its transformative potential across various sectors. In healthcare, AI's evolution marks a significant shift, offering new opportunities for innovation in diagnostics, treatment personalization, and overall healthcare management. By enhancing the accuracy of various medical processes, AI paves the way for a redefined patient care delivery system, raising the possibility of earlier interventions for more desirable outcomes. This chapter introduces the concept of a "unified digital space of trust," where AI-generated information can be authenticated and reliably used across different healthcare environments. This could bridge diverse variations in medical practice by ensuring that data are transparent and trustworthy (Chikhaoui et al., 2022; Dwivedi et al., 2021; Mennella et al., 2024).

Similarly, in the legal domain, AI is reshaping the roles of professionals by streamlining research, decision-making, and case review processes. This could alter how justice is delivered in an increasingly digital world. The legal implications of AI in healthcare are particularly critical, as we envision a future where legal frameworks must harmonize to govern AI's use, address developer and operator liability, and ensure equitable access. This approach requires national and international legal acts to affirm AI entities' legal status in healthcare (Shahid et al., 2023; Laptev et al., 2022)

AI is potentially revolutionizing medical imaging and diagnostics, driven by deep learning and neural network technologies (Fröhlich et al., 2018; Scherer, 2015). These advancements enable precise disease detection and treatment planning, showcasing AI's critical role in predictive analytics and personalized medicine (Elsayed et al., 2017; Marie-Sainte et al., 2019; Padhy et al., 2019; Saba et al., 2019). Yet, with such advancements come significant ethical and regulatory challenges. How do we protect patient privacy in an era of data-driven healthcare? How do we mitigate algorithmic biases that may inadvertently harm vulnerable populations? These dilemmas must be addressed as AI becomes more integral to healthcare delivery (Chikhaoui et al., 2022).

Furthermore, deploying AI in healthcare is not without its operational hurdles. Standardization, data quality assurance, and transparency in AI's "black box" processes are necessary to build trust in its outcomes. Collaborative efforts are essential to ensure AI's applicability across diverse clinical settings, focusing on patient-centered development, ethical guidelines, and the training of healthcare professionals (Feretzakis et al., 2024; Khalifa & Albadawy, 2024; Mennella et al., 2024). As AI reshapes medicine and law, this chapter explores how these sectors can balance technological innovation and ethical, legal, and environmental responsibilities. By focusing on equitable access, transparency, and sustainability, we set the stage for a future where AI can responsibly fulfill its transformative potential for society's benefit.

The research method employed in this chapter was a scoping review designed to explore the breadth of literature on integrating AI in medicine and law. A scoping review is a form of knowledge synthesis that employs a systematic and iterative process to explore and compile an established or developing body of literature on a specific subject (Mak & Thomas, 2022). A scoping review is ideal for mapping the key concepts and types of evidence and identifying research gaps, especially in rapidly evolving areas like AI. This approach allows for a comprehensive understanding of the current state of AI applications, challenges, and potential innovations in these domains.

This scoping review aimed to identify not only the technological advancements and innovations in AI but also the ethical dilemmas and regulatory challenges, focusing on how AI can be sustainably and ethically integrated into real-world medical and legal systems. The review explored key topics such as the application of AI in medicine and law, the ethical frameworks surrounding AI and its associated dilemmas, environmental sustainability in AI operations, strategic planning for ethical and sustainable AI, real-world integration and innovations, and a forward-looking perspective toward a sustainable and ethical AI future.

4.2 AI in Law and Legal Issues

AI's application aims to make justice more accessible, supporting the principle that law is the foundation of a fair society. The initial steps toward integrating technology in law involved creating legal research databases, which have evolved to incorporate AI and machine learning, revolutionizing legal research and analysis. The introduction of legal databases like LexisNexis and Westlaw in the 1970s marked the beginning of technology's role in the legal field, setting the stage for digitizing legal information. These platforms evolved to incorporate AI and machine learning, transforming legal research and analysis (*LexisNexis*, 2023; *Westlaw*, 2023). In the 1980s, expert systems emerged as early AI applications in law, simulating human expert decision-making to analyze legal issues and predict outcomes, significantly advancing legal technology. Recent developments in AI, such as deep neural networks and natural language processing (NLP), have further revolutionized legal tasks by enhancing the efficiency, accuracy, and processing of complex legal language. AI in legal practice increases work efficiency, democratizes legal services, and enables lawyers to broaden their expertise. As AI continues to evolve, it could redefine professional standards and ethical responsibilities in the legal sector, underscoring its growing importance in modern legal practices (Chalkidis & Kampas, 2019).

Integrating AI into the judicial system offers the potential to reduce human biases like fatigue and emotional influence, aiming to make judicial decisions more objective and consistent. However, AI can inadvertently carry biases from its development, including the legal frameworks it is based on and the data it is trained on, potentially affecting its fairness. A notable case is the Correctional Offender Management Profiling for Alternative Sanctions (COMPAS) tool, used in criminal justice to predict reoffending risks, which showed racial bias against African American defendants. This highlights the importance of thoroughly examining and refining AI systems in legal settings to ensure they're transparent and unbiased and effectively contribute to a more equitable and efficient judicial process (Buocz, 2018).

AI is transforming the legal industry by providing predictive analytics, giving legal professionals insights into case outcomes based on historical data analysis. This technology helps lawyers gauge their chances of success, making the legal research and decision-making process more efficient and strategic. Despite its benefits, challenges such as ensuring data accuracy and adapting machine learning models to fit the specific needs of legal contexts like the European Convention on Human Rights remain. The goal is not to replace judges but to enhance legal processes by making court decisions more transparent and predictable, thus supporting more informed and fair judicial outcomes. This innovative approach promises to improve legal research efficiency and contribute to a judicial system that is both more transparent and predictable (Aletras et al., 2016; Medvedeva et al., 2020).

The development of legal assistance chatbots stems from the urgent need to improve access to justice, addressing the gap caused by the lack of legal representation for many litigants. This gap is often due to high costs, geographical barriers, and the complexity of legal processes rather than a voluntary choice to forego legal aid. Chatbots like those from the LegalIA project and Éducaloi in Quebec are emerging as vital tools in making legal information more accessible and understandable, thus democratizing legal knowledge and aiding those unable to navigate the legal system independently. These AI-driven platforms provide tailored advice on various legal issues, bridging the knowledge gap. However, the effectiveness of these chatbots is limited by the complexity of legal language and the specificity of inquiries, posing challenges to AI's ability to grasp and respond to nuanced human concerns. Despite these hurdles, the evolution of legal chatbots represents a critical advancement toward making legal systems more accessible and transparent, marking a significant step forward in the intersection of law and technology (Queudot et al., 2020).

4.3 Ethical Frameworks for AI

4.3.1 Ethical Considerations in AI Applications in the Medical Field

The ethics of using AI in medicine is crucial for technological advancement. One of the main aspects that needs to be considered is patient privacy, as sensitive data must protect patient privacy and system control. Federated learning in healthcare and legal model prediction by AI are two innovative approaches to using AI that significantly impact the health and legal sectors (Gerke et al., 2020). The Federated Learning in Health Policy enables collecting medical data from various institutions without retaining patient information, thus safeguarding privacy and patient confidentiality. This technology improves diagnosis and clinical practice, even though patient data remains confidential and is only accessible to authorized personnel (Siala & Wang, 2022).

AI-based models for legal prediction help analyze complex data, such as crime risks or legal decisions. This model enhances efficiency and accuracy in the legal decision-making process. However, the main challenge is maintaining transparency and adequacy in AI's decisions and avoiding bias in algorithmic decision-making. This model helps prevent biased work and requires human oversight to ensure compliance with legal ethics (Lupo, 2022; Slimi & Carballido, 2023). AI integration in healthcare and law is crucial for efficient healthcare and improved legal predictive models, enabling transparent care processes and potentially transforming daily practices. The ethical considerations for AI use in healthcare involve balancing moral principles, preventing misuse of sensitive medical data, and promoting transparency and accessibility in AI clinical decision-making (Siala & Wang, 2022) (see Figure 4.1).

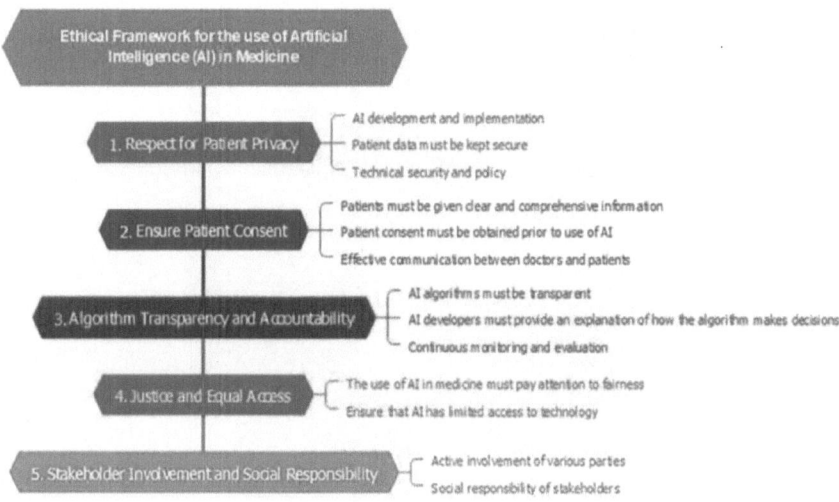

FIGURE 4.1
Ethical framework for the use of AI in medicine

4.3.2 The Ethical and Justice Dilemmas in Legal Decisions Regarding AI

4.3.2.1 Ethical Framework

AI in law enforcement requires ethical considerations like privacy, transparency, and accountability. Education on AI ethics can enhance technology use and improve ethical consequences. AI-based law enforcement can increase efficiency and accountability while upholding confidentiality, privacy, and transparency (Bird et al., 2020; El Mestari et al., 2024).

4.3.2.2 Ethical Dilemma

AI in legal decision-making is controversial due to its potential to disrupt individual privacy. Algorithms can analyze data from various sources to make predictions or recommendations related to legal decisions, such as criminal justice or deviations in criminal law. However, ethical issues arise when the potential to harm individual privacy becomes a significant concern. Data about a person's ethnicity or identity to predict health risks during data collection can lead to discrimination or inappropriate profiling (Naik et al., 2022; Saheb, 2024). Privacy concerns in AI-based legal decisions are crucial, as individuals need to be aware of their data and avoid unnecessary services. Ensuring privacy and preventing misuse of AI is essential, and regulations and policies prioritizing transparency, accessibility, and fair justice goals are necessary (Bird et al., 2020; Greenstein, 2022) (see Figure 4.2).

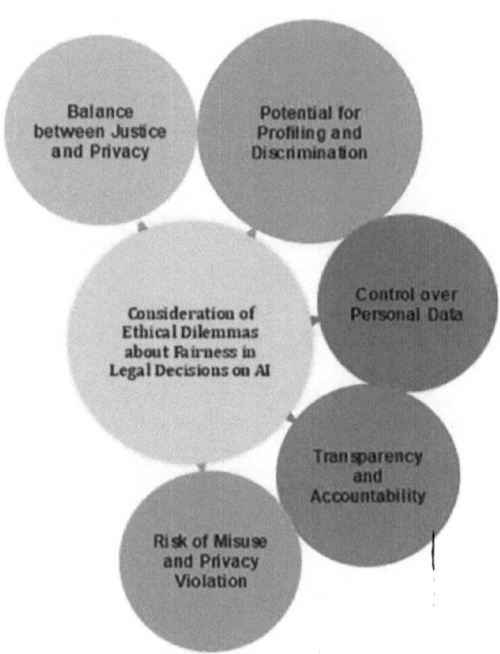

FIGURE 4.2
Ethical dilemma considerations on justice in legal decisions regarding AI

Privacy and data protection are crucial in law enforcement, especially when integrating AI into the legal realm. Sensitive personal information is vital for effective and reliable legal decisions. Transparency and accessibility in AI-driven legal processes are essential for public protection and upholding ethical standards of confidentiality, privacy, and nondiscrimination (Leslie, 2022; Akgun & Greenhow, 2021).

4.3.3 Integration of Ethical Guidelines into the Development and Application of AI in Medicine and Law

4.3.3.1 Development and Application of AI

Ethical principles are essential in developing and applying AI in education and law to ensure it respects moral and ethical values. AI can enhance diagnosis, patient care, and clinical decision-making while upholding privacy, individual rights, and fairness. Integrating ethical principles into AI development promotes accurate, fair, and accessible systems, protecting individual rights and promoting a harmonious society by embracing AI technology (Díaz-Rodríguez et al., 2023; Biondi et al., 2023) (see Figure 4.3).

The development of ethical guidelines for developing, practicing, and using AI is crucial in law and ethics. These guidelines must adhere to

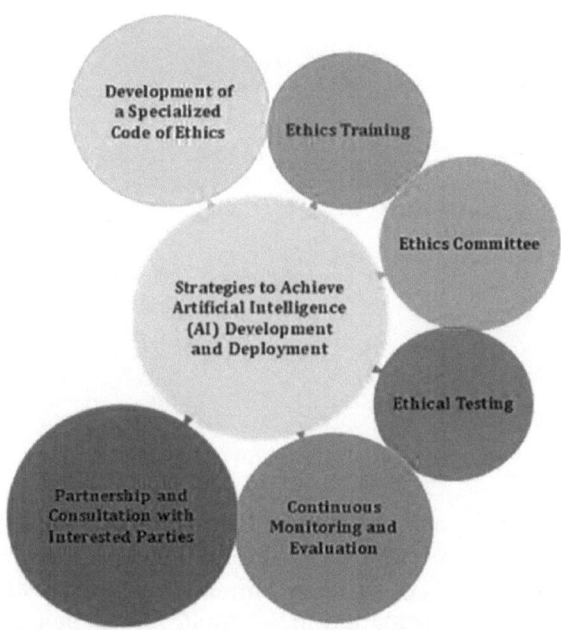

FIGURE 4.3
Strategies to achieve AI development and deployment

integrity, privacy, transparency, and accountability. Providing knowledge and resources to professionals to manage ethical complexities is essential for creating a safe and ethical AI environment and enhancing healthcare and legal services (El Mestari et al., 2024; Lupo, 2022; Slimi & Carballido, 2023).

4.3.3.2 Aspects of Integrating Ethics Guidelines

Integrating ethical guidelines ensures that AI-assisted legal decisions consider principles of justice, human rights, and privacy protection (El Mestari et al., 2024; Lupo, 2022; Slimi & Carballido, 2023). By prioritizing these ethical values in the development and application of AI, we can ensure that the technology provides significant clinical and legal benefits and upholds integrity, trust, and fairness in both fields (Joksimovic et al., 2023; Vargas-Murillo et al., 2024) (see Figure 4.4).

The development and application of AI in the legal sector aim to enhance the trust and competence of individuals by ensuring that AI-based legal decisions are fair and accurate for all individuals and groups. It is essential to minimize the risks of profiling and discrimination, as well as to integrate ethical principles into AI applications to ensure that society consistently upholds crucial ethical and moral standards (Arbelaez Ossa et al., 2024; Kinney et al., 2024; Ng et al., 2024; Rosemann & Zhang, 2022). Regulations and

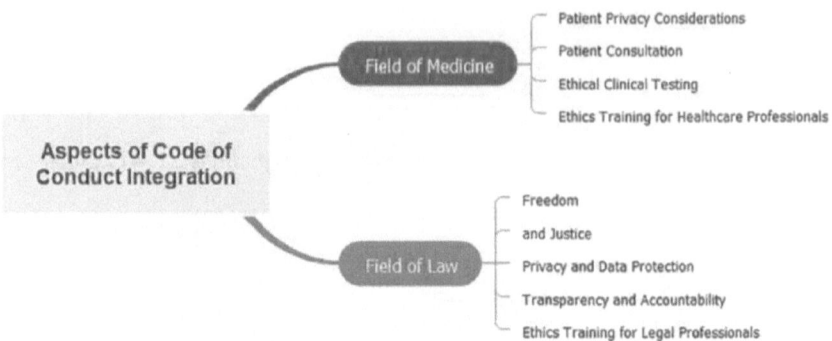

FIGURE 4.4
Aspects of code of ethics integration

ethical standards influence AI's potential to improve global health in the United States (US), Europe, and Asia. The Health Insurance Portability and Accountability Act (HIPAA), a federal law, ensures privacy and confidentiality of patient health information in AI applications (Siala & Wang, 2022; Mennella et al., 2024).

The General Data Protection Regulation (GDPR) regulates AI use in the European Union (EU), impacting companies and health institutions. It sets standards for personal data protection and mandates businesses to adhere to privacy principles, emphasizing data privacy (Meszaros et al., 2022). AI applications in Asia, especially China, are gaining traction for operational efficiency and diagnostic accuracy but raise ethical concerns about personal data privacy due to China's flexible regulations (M. Chen et al., 2024). The US and Europe prioritize data privacy and innovation. At the same time, AI's success in healthcare relies on its integration into regulatory systems and ethical practices despite a lack of regulation and ethics.

4.4 Environmental Sustainability in AI Operations

4.4.1 Environmental Impact of AI Technology

AI's use in medicine and law raises ethical and environmental concerns due to its extensive dataset, leading to increased computational and energy usage. However, AI development promotes ethical technology, demonstrating its positive impact on society without compromising the planet's health (Bekbolatova et al., 2024; Ramalingam et al., 2023).

4.4.2 Eco-Friendly AI

Due to advancements in technology, particularly in information and communication, AI is playing a crucial role in addressing environmental issues. It optimizes computer infrastructure, harnesses renewable energy, and develops solutions for environmental issues, reducing carbon footprints. AI's predictive power aids conservation efforts, balancing technological innovation with environmental protection (Mana et al., 2024) (see Figure 4.5).

Green AI intends to reduce environmental impact and contribute positively to environmental preservation. AI employs various technologies and practices to minimize its ecological footprint, such as optimizing energy-efficient algorithms and utilizing renewable energy sources. Green AI reduces carbon emissions associated with large-scale AI computation (Rodrigues, 2023). AI also utilizes transformative applications that AI can leverage to enhance efficiency, thereby increasing the environmental role in technological innovation (Ayoubi et al., 2023).

4.4.3 The Success of AI Integration in the Healthcare and Legal Sectors

One study highlights the potential of AI in improving medical diagnosis and treatment, particularly in the US, with a 25% increase in diagnostic accuracy and reduced analysis time in a project for early cancer diagnosis. Federated learning in multicenter studies has developed comprehensive model diagnoses without patient data, preserving patient privacy and improving model prediction quality (Mennella et al., 2024).

The study on using AI in legal decision-making reveals its potential to enhance the speed of decision-making processes. In Europe, a project utilizing AI to assist in the decision-making process for a criminal case

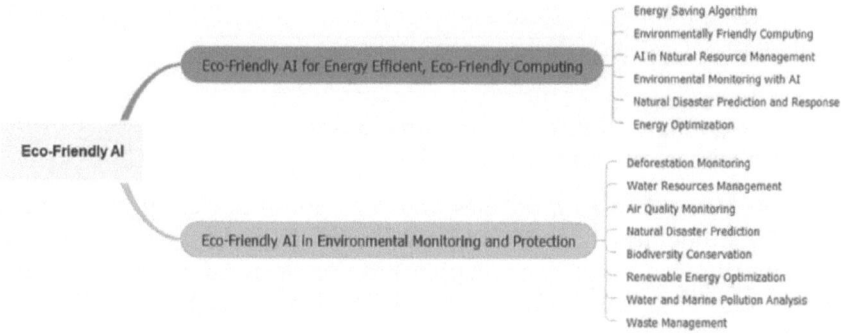

FIGURE 4.5
Environmentally friendly AI

demonstrated that integrating AI can cut decision-making time by 30%, with an accuracy rate of 85% for AI-generated recommendations. However, further research is necessary to prevent bias in AI algorithms (Slimi & Carballido, 2023). The application of AI in crime risk assessment systems shows that AI can provide more accurate risk assessments than manual methods. This model uses socioeconomic, criminal, and mental health data to help prevent crime, enhance rehabilitation efforts, and improve efficiency in the crime prevention system (Naik et al., 2022; Saheb, 2024). These studies illustrate how the integration of AI in the healthcare and legal sectors enhances accuracy and efficiency and significantly changes how decisions are made while continuously considering the critical ethical and privacy aspects of its implementation.

4.5 Strategic Planning for Ethical and Sustainable AI

Strategic planning for AI's ethical and sustainable use is the foundation for ensuring that AI technology benefits society and the environment (Telefonica, 2023).

4.5.1 Integration of Ethics and Environment

The special sector council, involving AI development companies, government agencies, environmental organizations, and local communities, is crucial in developing a risk evaluation framework for AI initiatives. This framework focuses on energy efficiency, language protection, and resource utilization, enabling continuous monitoring and evaluation of AI's impacts on ethics and the environment. Performance indicators, independent audits, and transparent reporting mechanisms are essential (Larsen et al., 2023; Podgórski, 2015; Vyhmeister & Castane, 2024).

4.5.2 Government, Industry Standards, Business Collaboration, and Public Policy

AI's role in implementing policies and regulations is crucial, with HIPAA providing guidelines for protecting patient privacy and personal health data, including the use, storage, and application of electronic health data in AI applications (Pesapane et al., 2021; Van De Sande et al., 2022). GDPR, despite being implemented in the US, has global implications for healthcare organizations and companies in the EU. Adhering to these regulations ensures AI use in healthcare complies with laws, promotes patient privacy, and protects data (Meszaros et al., 2022). Several rules and AI strategies in healthcare are relevant, particularly in the US. These regulations ensure that AI is used

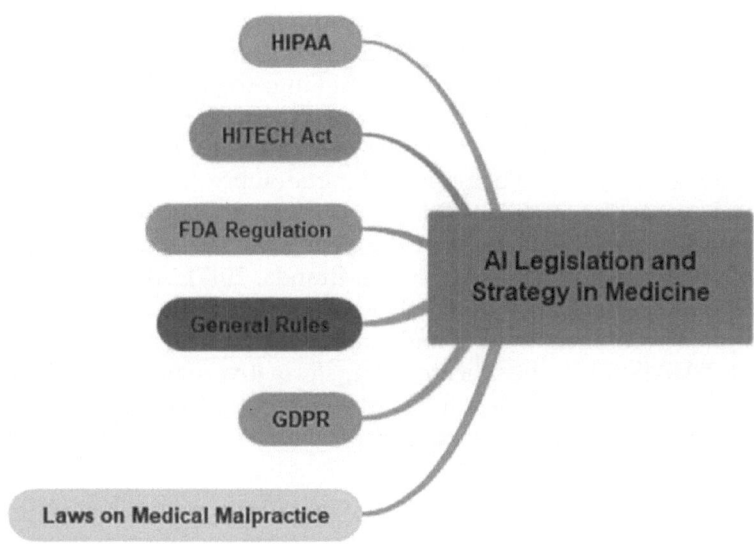

FIGURE 4.6
Legislation and AI strategies in medicine

responsibly and accountably, promoting a more sustainable and practical approach to AI-based decision-making (see Figure 4.6).

4.6 Real-World Integrations and Innovations

AI is revolutionizing the healthcare and legal sectors through extensive data analysis, task automation, and enhanced decision-making processes. AI facilitates early disease identification, customized therapies, and predictive analytics in healthcare. In legal practice, it enhances case analysis, automates document examination, and facilitates judgment prediction. This chapter analyzes AI's practical applications and advancements across several industries, highlighting ethical and environmental issues to ensure responsible and sustainable influence.

4.6.1 AI-Driven Healthcare Revolution

AI has significantly advanced healthcare, including early disease detection and personalized treatments (Rahmanti et al., 2022). It specializes in processing large datasets and delivering rapid analyses for complex medical issues. During the COVID-19 epidemic, AI techniques, like smartphone-based diagnostic imaging, alleviated the shortage of radiologists. Multitask learning models enhanced diagnostic accuracy and interpretability in resource-limited settings (Antony et al., 2023). AI decision support tools, like cardiotography in obstetrics, improve decision-making; trust and transparency are crucial for successful integration (Dlugatch et al., 2024).

AI also predicts epidemics, enabling quick responses. For example, an AI model using real-world data predicted dengue outbreaks, offering early warnings and prevention strategies (Mazhar et al., 2024). Beyond physical health, AI supports mental health by providing personalized, accessible counseling through generative models (Martínez-Miranda, 2017). AI also aids chronic disease management, such as a diabetes self-management platform offering customized recommendations and improving patient outcomes (Joachim et al., 2022). AI's role in healthcare is transformative, enhancing diagnostics, disease forecasting, and mental health support. Ethical and environmental concerns are essential to ensuring responsible and sustainable AI applications in healthcare.

4.6.2 AI Transformation in the Legal Sector

AI is transforming the legal sector by improving productivity, accessibility to justice, and creativity. Case analysis and document drafting are two tasks that can be streamlined by technologies such as NLP, machine learning, and AI-driven decision support systems. Ejjami (2024) claims these technologies improve legal labor's accuracy and efficiency. NLP helps lawyers to lower expenses and improve access to justice by facilitating the fast trend finding inside large volumes of data. Fairness depends on ethical issues, including openness, data privacy, and algorithmic bias being taken into account. Mainly targeting African-American offenders, the COMPAS algorithm – used for recidivism prediction – has drawn criticism for racial prejudice (Safdar et al., 2020). AI technologies such as ShotSpotter and PredPol also draw criticism for their disproportionate impacts on Black populations (Noiret et al., 2021).

Demands for enhanced transparency and equity in AI systems have resulted in calls for regular audits and the creation of fairness-oriented algorithms utilizing varied datasets (Noiret et al., 2021). In addition to these ethical concerns, AI is revolutionizing document handling within legal companies. NLP-driven solutions expedite document analysis, enabling solicitors to discern critical information more effectively (Rosca et al., 2020). AI forecasts judicial outcomes in certain nations, improving decision-making (Sushina & Sobenin, 2020). Notwithstanding these advantages, the environmental ramifications of AI present difficulties. The legal profession is urged to implement green computing techniques, including AI systems that employ renewable energy and carbon-neutral data centers (Díaz-Rodríguez et al., 2023). The EU's Ethical Charter on AI underscores the necessity of evaluating the enduring environmental consequences of AI (Brooks et al., 2020).

The incorporation of AI raises apprehensions about client confidentiality and the integrity of legal proceedings (Dronadul & Bhaskar, 2023). Addressing these challenges requires transparent algorithms, varied datasets, and ethical frameworks that ensure justice and accountability (Ejjami, 2024). Law schools must change curricula to prepare future lawyers for AI-driven systems (Dronadul & Bhaskar, 2023). AI is revolutionizing the legal system by enhancing efficiency and justice and presenting ethical and environmental challenges. The legal profession must establish transparent and sustainable protocols alongside regulatory frameworks to ensure AI's responsible and equitable use.

4.6.3 Comparative Analysis: Healthcare and Legal Sectors

Comparative analysis indicates that the healthcare and legal industries face similar ethical and regulatory concerns, including bias reduction, data privacy, and the necessity for transparent AI systems (Hjaltalin & Sigurdarson, 2024). AI enhances patient care by facilitating early diagnosis, personalizing medications, and monitoring health within the healthcare sector, improving accuracy and efficiency (Ali et al., 2023). In the legal domain, AI enhances administrative efficiency by streamlining document processing, legal research, and risk assessment (Hjaltalin & Sigurdarson, 2024). Both sectors emphasize reducing AI's environmental effect, with AI enabling energy-efficient practices and advancing digital transformation (Cruz Salazar et al., 2024). AI can reduce resource consumption and simplify legal service procedures, boosting sustainability (Hjaltalin & Sigurdarson, 2024).

The application of AI differs between rich and poor countries. Strong infrastructure and data security in wealthy nations like the US and Europe allow AI to be subtly included (Hjaltalin & Sigurdarson, 2024). Nevertheless, developing countries face financial and infrastructure challenges. In Colombia, small and medium-sized firms face difficulties implementing AI-driven Industry 4.0 technologies due to limited resources (Cruz Salazar et al., 2024). In Thailand, issues of trust and usability hinder the adoption of AI-driven digital wallets like Worldcoin (Kraiwanit et al., 2024). Although these sectors utilize AI for precision, efficiency, and sustainability, their deployment techniques vary according to rules, technological preparedness, and available resources. These disparities underscore the necessity for context-specific AI solutions to optimize advantages while mitigating ethical and environmental issues.

4.6.4 Lessons Learned and Best Practices

From the beginning, this strategy emphasizes the relevance of incorporating ethical and environmental considerations into AI plans. To maximize AI's benefits while adhering to ethical standards and fulfilling environmental duties, it is essential to involve stakeholders, carefully monitor and evaluate AI's consequences, and implement sustainable AI practices.

In the end, implementing AI in the healthcare and legal industries offers a glimpse into a future in which technology breakthroughs will enhance the delivery of services, the efficiency of operations, and the establishment of ethical and sustainable stakeholder confidence. When successfully integrating AI into various sectors, it is necessary to adopt a multidisciplinary strategy emphasizing continuous learning and adaptability. Using this strategy, we can successfully negotiate the complex problems associated with incorporating AI and guarantee that its revolutionary potential is utilized to foster justice, equity, and environmental responsibility.

4.7 Toward a Sustainable and Ethical AI Future

AI can markedly enhance healthcare outcomes when congruent with ethical principles. Explainable AI (XAI) guarantees openness, safety, and reliability in AI-generated judgments, which are crucial for healthcare decision-making and patient trust (Ahmad et al., 2024). XAI elucidates the rationale behind AI decisions, enhancing patient outcomes and bolstering trust among healthcare practitioners (Chaudhary, 2024). Ethical concerns such as accountability, equity, and prejudice are paramount in the legal domain. AI systems must guarantee impartial decision-making. XAI enhances the transparency of AI systems, especially in critical domains such as criminal justice, where routine audits are essential to mitigate prejudice (Chaudhary, 2024). The Green AI prioritizes energy-efficient algorithms that cut carbon emissions. AI can forecast climate-related illness outbreaks and assess environmental elements affecting public health, enabling proactive control and reduced environmental impact (Yigitcanlar et al., 2021). Decentralized AI and blockchain technologies improve healthcare and legal data privacy and security, minimizing data breaches and unethical behavior (Gupta, 2020). This technique enhances the sustainability and security of both sectors.

Investigation and global cooperation are essential to address AI's ethical and environmental challenges. Engineers, ethicists, and policymakers work to develop AI technologies that adhere to global environmental and ethical standards (Yigitcanlar et al., 2021). AI in healthcare enhances patient outcomes by promoting transparency and trust, while legal AI systems gain from algorithmic transparency and consistent ethical evaluations. Data-driven governance and energy-efficient AI foster holistic environmental sustainability throughout the sector.

4.8 Conclusion

The application of AI to legal institutions and healthcare marks a dramatic transformation that offers advantages, including improved decision-making, better diagnostics, and more efficiency. While in the legal sphere, AI improves research efficacy and strengthens justice through predictive analytics, in the healthcare field, it helps with early disease identification and tailored treatments. Still, these benefits are coupled by drawbacks. Resolution of ethical issues, including patient confidentiality, algorithmic bias, and openness, guarantees ethical and fair application.

Green AI approaches must be adopted considering AI's ecological consequences, particularly its significant processing needs. AI can improve sustainability while preserving technological advantages by utilizing algorithm development for energy efficiency and integrating renewable energy sources. Given that AI is being included in sectors handling sensitive, vast amounts of data, such as law and healthcare, this is especially important. In healthcare, AI holds the potential to improve patient outcomes and reduce the burden on healthcare professionals through automation and predictive analytics. Ensuring transparency in AI development is crucial. XAI can enhance trust by making decision-making processes clear. In addition, federated learning allows for collaborative AI model development while protecting patient privacy and promoting AI's growth while safeguarding data.

In legal systems, AI's ability to streamline case analysis and assist judicial decision-making could reshape the field. However, concerns about algorithmic biases, particularly in criminal justice, require continuous oversight. Legal professionals must work with technologists to ensure AI fosters fairness rather than perpetuating bias. Regular audits of AI tools are necessary to maintain ethical standards in legal decision-making. Strong regulatory structures are vital to oversee AI applications in law and healthcare. These models should ensure that AI application conforms to moral and societal norms. Governments and interested parties can create standards promoting openness, responsibility, and fairness. Legislation such as the GDPR and the HIPAA guarantees the protection of privacy and data security in healthcare.

Moreover, it should be examined how AI might help with sustainability. Green AI initiatives, including renewable energy consumption and energy-efficient algorithms, generally help lower AI's environmental impact. The correct application of AI can help solve environmental issues.

Even if AI offers revolutionary opportunities in law and medicine, a thorough, multidisciplinary approach is essential. Combining ethical, legal, and environmental considerations can help realize equitable and sustainable benefits from AI. Dealing with problems and ensuring suitable application of AI for the advantage of society depends on cooperation among technologists, policymakers, and professionals.

References

Ahmad, I., Zhu, M., Li, G., Javeed, D., Kumar, P., & Chen, S. (2024). A secure and interpretable AI for smart healthcare system: A case study on epilepsy diagnosis using EEG signals. *IEEE Journal of Biomedical and Health Informatics*, 1–12. https://doi.org/10.1109/JBHI.2024.3366341

Akgun, S., & Greenhow, C. (2021). Artificial intelligence in education: Addressing ethical challenges in K-12 settings. *AI and Ethics*, 2(3)(September 22), 431–440. https://doi.org/10.1007/s43681-021-00096-7

Aletras, N., Tsarapatsanis, D., Preoţiuc-Pietro, D., & Lampos, V. (2016). Predicting judicial decisions of the European court of human rights: A natural language processing perspective. *PeerJ Computer Science*, 2, e93. https://doi.org/10.7717/peerj-cs.93

Ali, O., Abdelbaki, W., Shrestha, A., Elbasi, E., Alryalat, M. A. A., & Dwivedi, Y. K. (2023). A systematic literature review of artificial intelligence in the healthcare sector: Benefits, challenges, methodologies, and functionalities. *Journal of Innovation & Knowledge*, 8(1), 100333. https://doi.org/10.1016/j.jik.2023.100333

Antony, M., Kakileti, S. T., Shah, R., Sahoo, S., Bhattacharyya, C., & Manjunath, G. (2023). Challenges of AI driven diagnosis of chest X-rays transmitted through smart phones: A case study in COVID-19. *Scientific Reports*, 13(1), 18102. https://doi.org/10.1038/s41598-023-44653-y

Arbelaez Ossa, L., Lorenzini, G., Milford, S. R., Shaw, D., Elger, B. S., & Rost, M. (2024). Integrating ethics in AI development: A qualitative study. *BMC Medical Ethics*, 25(1), 1–11. https://doi.org/10.1186/s12910-023-01000-0

Ayoubi, H., Tabaa, Y., & El Kharrim, M. (2023). Artificial intelligence in green management and the rise of digital lean for sustainable efficiency. *E3S Web of Conferences*, 412. https://doi.org/10.1051/e3sconf/202341201053

Bekbolatova, M., Mayer, J., Ong, C. W., & Toma, M. (2024). Transformative potential of AI in healthcare: Definitions, applications, and navigating the ethical landscape and public perspectives. *Healthcare (Switzerland)*, 12(2). https://doi.org/10.3390/healthcare12020125

Biondi, G., Cagnoni, S., Capobianco, R., Franzoni, V., Lisi, F. A., Milani, A., & Vallverdú, J. (2023). Editorial: Ethical design of artificial intelligence-based systems for decision making. *Frontiers in Artificial Intelligence*, 6. https://doi.org/10.3389/frai.2023.1250209

Bird, E., Fox-Skelly, J., Jenner, N., Larbey, R., Weitkamp, E., & Winfield, A. (2020). *The ethics of artificial intelligence: Issues and initiatives*. European Union (Issue March). http://www.europarl.europa.eu/thinktank

Brooks, C., Gherhes, C., & Vorley, T. (2020). Artificial intelligence in the legal sector: Pressures and challenges of transformation. *Cambridge Journal of Regions, Economy and Society*, 13(1), 135–152. https://doi.org/10.1093/cjres/rsz026

Buocz, T. J. (2018). *Artificial intelligence in court legitimacy problems of AI assistance in the judiciary* (Vol. 2, Issue 1). www.nytimes.com/2011/03/05/science/05legal.html

Chalkidis, I., & Kampas, D. (2019). Deep learning in law: Early adaptation and legal word embeddings trained on large corpora. *Artificial Intelligence and Law*, 27(2), 171–198. https://doi.org/10.1007/s10506-018-9238-9

Chaudhary, G. (2024). Explainable artificial intelligence (xAI): Reflections on judicial system. *Kutafin Law Review*, 10(4), 872–889. https://doi.org/10.17803/2713-0533.2023.4.26.872-889

Chen, M., Wang, S., & Wang, X. (2024). How does artificial intelligence impact green development? Evidence from China. *Sustainability (Switzerland)*, 16(3). https://doi.org/10.3390/su16031260

Chikhaoui, E., Alajmi, A., & Larabi-Marie-Sainte, S. (2022). Artificial intelligence applications in healthcare sector: Ethical and legal challenges. *Emerging Science Journal*, 6(4), 717–738. https://doi.org/10.28991/ESJ-2022-06-04-05

Cruz Salazar, L. A., Gil, S., Rueda Carvajal, G. D., Sánchez-Zuluaga, G. J., & Zapata-Madrigal, G. D. (2024). AI in assessing Industry 4.0 adoption in Colombia: A case study approach. *IFAC-PapersOnLine*, 58(8), 162–167. https://doi.org/10.1016/j.ifacol.2024.08.067

Díaz-Rodríguez, N., Del Ser, J., Coeckelbergh, M., López de Prado, M., Herrera-Viedma, E., & Herrera, F. (2023). Connecting the dots in trustworthy artificial intelligence: From AI principles, ethics, and key requirements to responsible AI systems and regulation. *Information Fusion*, 99(June), 101896. https://doi.org/10.1016/j.inffus.2023.101896

Dlugatch, R., Georgieva, A., & Kerasidou, A. (2024). AI-driven decision support systems and epistemic reliance: A qualitative study on obstetricians' and midwives' perspectives on integrating AI-driven CTG into clinical decision making. *BMC Medical Ethics*, 25(1), 6. https://doi.org/10.1186/s12910-023-00990-1

Dronadul, S. D., & Bhaskar, D. V. (2023). Impact of artificial intelligence (AI) on legal profession and justice system. *International Journal of Law Management & Humanities*, 6(2), 1084–1124. https://doij.org/10.10000/IJLMH.114491

Dwivedi, Y. K., Hughes, L., Ismagilova, E., Aarts, G., Coombs, C., Crick, T., Duan, Y., Dwivedi, R., Edwards, J., Eirug, A., Galanos, V., Ilavarasan, P. V., Janssen, M., Jones, P., Kar, A. K., Kizgin, H., Kronemann, B., Lal, B., Lucini, B., . . . Williams, M. D. (2021). Artificial intelligence (AI): Multidisciplinary perspectives on emerging challenges, opportunities, and agenda for research, practice and policy. *International Journal of Information Management*, 57, 101994. https://doi.org/10.1016/j.ijinfomgt.2019.08.002

Ejjami, R. (2024). AI-driven justice: Evaluating the impact of artificial intelligence on legal systems. *International Journal for Multidisciplinary Research*, 6(3). https://doi.org/10.36948/ijfmr.2024.v06i03.23969

El Mestari, S. Z., Lenzini, G., & Demirci, H. (2024). Preserving data privacy in machine learning systems. *Computers and Security*, 137(November 2023), 103605. https://doi.org/10.1016/j.cose.2023.103605

Elsayed, H. A. G., Galal, M. A., & Syed, L. (2017). HeartCare+: A smart heart care mobile application for Framingham-based early risk prediction of hard coronary heart diseases in middle East. *Mobile Information Systems*, 2017, 1–11. https://doi.org/10.1155/2017/9369532

Feretzakis, G., Juliebø-Jones, P., Tsaturyan, A., Sener, T. E., Verykios, V. S., Karapiperis, D., Bellos, T., Katsimperis, S., Angelopoulos, P., Varkarakis, I., Skolarikos, A., Somani, B., & Tzelves, L. (2024). Emerging trends in AI and radiomics for bladder, kidney, and prostate cancer: A critical review. *Cancers*, 16(4), 810. https://doi.org/10.3390/cancers16040810

Fröhlich, H., Balling, R., Beerenwinkel, N., Kohlbacher, O., Kumar, S., Lengauer, T., Maathuis, M. H., Moreau, Y., Murphy, S. A., Przytycka, T. M., Rebhan, M., Röst, H., Schuppert, A., Schwab, M., Spang, R., Stekhoven, D., Sun, J., Weber, A., Ziemek, D., & Zupan, B. (2018). From hype to reality: Data science enabling personalized medicine. *BMC Medicine*, 16(1), 150. https://doi.org/10.1186/s12916-018-1122-7

Gerke, S., Minssen, T., & Cohen, G. (2020). Ethical and legal challenges of artificial intelligence-driven healthcare. *Artificial Intelligence in Healthcare* (January). https://doi.org/10.1016/B978-0-12-818438-7.00012-5

Greenstein, S. (2022). Preserving the rule of law in the era of artificial intelligence (AI). In *Artificial intelligence and law* (Vol. 30, Issue 3). Springer Netherlands. https://doi.org/10.1007/s10506-021-09294-4

Gupta, I. (2020). *Decentralization of artificial intelligence: Analyzing developments in decentralized learning and distributed AI networks*. Issue arXiv preprint arXiv:1603.04467.

Hjaltalin, I. T., & Sigurdarson, H. T. (2024). The strategic use of AI in the public sector: A public values analysis of national AI strategies. *Government Information Quarterly*, 41(1), 101914. https://doi.org/10.1016/j.giq.2024.101914

Joachim, S., Forkan, A. R. M., Jayaraman, P. P., Morshed, A., & Wickramasinghe, N. (2022). A nudge-inspired AI-driven health platform for self-management of diabetes. *Sensors*, 22(12), 4620. https://doi.org/10.3390/s22124620

Joksimovic, S., Ifenthaler, D., Marrone, R., De Laat, M., & Siemens, G. (2023). Opportunities of artificial intelligence for supporting complex problem-solving: Findings from a scoping review. *Computers and Education: Artificial Intelligence*, 4(May), 100138. https://doi.org/10.1016/j.caeai.2023.100138

Khalifa, M., & Albadawy, M. (2024). AI in diagnostic imaging: Revolutionising accuracy and efficiency. *Computer Methods and Programs in Biomedicine Update*, 5, 100146. https://doi.org/10.1016/j.cmpbup.2024.100146

Kinney, M., Anastasiadou, M., Naranjo-Zolotov, M., & Santos, V. (2024). Expectation management in AI: A framework for understanding stakeholder trust and acceptance of artificial intelligence systems. *Heliyon*, 10(7), e28562. https://doi.org/10.1016/j.heliyon.2024.e28562

Kraiwanit, T., Limna, P., & Wattanasin, P. (2024). Digital wallet dynamics: Perspectives on potential worldcoin adoption factors in a developing country's *FinTech Sector. Journal of Open Innovation: Technology, Market, and Complexity*, 10(2), 100287. https://doi.org/10.1016/j.joitmc.2024.100287

Laptev, V. A., Ershova, I. V., & Feyzrakhmanova, D. R. (2022). Medical applications of artificial intelligence (legal aspects and future prospects). *Laws*, 11(1). https://doi.org/10.3390/laws11010003

Larsen, B., Desai, A., Jacob, J., K, S., Kumar, M., Saxena, R., & Tudu, H. (2023). *Adopting AI responsibly: Guidelines for procurement of AI solutions by the private sector*. World Economic Forum, June.

Leslie, D. (2022). Explaining decisions made with AI. *SSRN Electronic Journal*. https://doi.org/10.2139/ssrn.4033308

LexisNexis. (2023). https://www.lexisnexis.com

Lupo, G. (2022). The ethics of artificial intelligence: An analysis of ethical frameworks disciplining AI in justice and other contexts of application. In *Onati socio-legal series* (Vol. 12, Issue 3). https://doi.org/10.35295/OSLS.IISL/0000-0000-0000-1273

Mak, S., & Thomas, A. (2022). Steps for conducting a scoping review. *Journal of Graduate Medical Education*, 14(5), 565–567. https://doi.org/10.4300/JGME-D-22-00621.1

Mana, A. A., Allouhi, A., Hamrani, A., Rahman, S., el Jamaoui, I., & Jayachandran, K. (2024). Sustainable AI-based production agriculture: Exploring AI applications and implications in agricultural practices. *Smart Agricultural Technology*, 7(February), 100416. https://doi.org/10.1016/j.atech.2024.100416

Marie-Sainte, S. L., Saba, T., Alsaleh, D., & Alamir Alotaibi, M. Bin. (2019). An improved strategy for predicting diagnosis, survivability, and recurrence of breast cancer. *Journal of Computational and Theoretical Nanoscience*, 16(9), 3705–3711. https://doi.org/10.1166/jctn.2019.8238

Martínez-Miranda, J. (2017). Embodied conversational agents for the detection and prevention of suicidal behaviour: Current applications and open challenges. *Journal of Medical Systems*, 41(9), 135. https://doi.org/10.1007/s10916-017-0784-6

Mazhar, B., Ali, N. M., Manzoor, F., Khan, M. K., Nasir, M., & Ramzan, M. (2024). Development of Data-driven machine learning models and their potential role in predicting dengue outbreak. *Journal of Vector Borne Diseases*. https://doi.org/10.4103/0972-9062.393976

Medvedeva, M., Vols, M., & Wieling, M. (2020). Using machine learning to predict decisions of the European court of human rights. *Artificial Intelligence and Law*, 28(2), 237–266. https://doi.org/10.1007/s10506-019-09255-y

Mennella, C., Maniscalco, U., De Pietro, G., & Esposito, M. (2024). Ethical and regulatory challenges of AI technologies in healthcare: A narrative review. *Heliyon*, 10(4), e26297. https://doi.org/10.1016/j.heliyon.2024.e26297

Meszaros, J., Minari, J., & Huys, I. (2022). The future regulation of artificial intelligence systems in healthcare services and medical research in the European Union. *Frontiers in Genetics*, 13(October), 1–10. https://doi.org/10.3389/fgene.2022.927721

Naik, N., Hameed, B. M. Z., Shetty, D. K., Swain, D., Shah, M., Paul, R., Aggarwal, K., Brahim, S., Patil, V., Smriti, K., Shetty, S., Rai, B. P., Chlosta, P., & Somani, B. K. (2022). Legal and ethical consideration in artificial intelligence in healthcare: Who takes responsibility? *Frontiers in Surgery*, 9(March), 1–6. https://doi.org/10.3389/fsurg.2022.862322

Ng, J. Y., Cramer, H., Lee, M. S., & Moher, D. (2024). Traditional, complementary, and integrative medicine and artificial intelligence: Novel opportunities in healthcare. *Integrative Medicine Research*, 13(1). https://doi.org/10.1016/j.imr.2024.101024

Noiret, S., Lumetzberger, J., & Kampel, M. (2021). Bias and fairness in computer vision applications of the criminal justice system. *2021 IEEE Symposium Series on Computational Intelligence (SSCI)*, 1–8. https://doi.org/10.1109/SSCI50451.2021.9660177

Padhy, S., Takkar, B., Chawla, R., & Kumar, A. (2019). Artificial intelligence in diabetic retinopathy: A natural step to the future. *Indian Journal of Ophthalmology*, 67(7), 1004. https://doi.org/10.4103/ijo.IJO_1989_18

Pesapane, F., Bracchi, D. A., Mulligan, J. F., Linnikov, A., Maslennikov, O., Lanzavecchia, M. B., Tantrige, P., Stasolla, A., Biondetti, P., Giuggioli, P. F., Cassano, E., & Carrafiello, G. (2021). Legal and regulatory framework for AI solutions in healthcare in EU, US, China, and Russia: New scenarios after a pandemic. *Radiation*, 1(4), 261–276. https://doi.org/10.3390/radiation1040022

Podgórski, D. (2015). Measuring operational performance of OSH management system – a demonstration of AHP-based selection of leading key performance indicators. *Safety Science*, 73, 146–166. https://doi.org/10.1016/j.ssci.2014.11.018

Queudot, M., Charton, É., & Meurs, M.-J. (2020). Improving access to justice with legal chatbots. *Stats*, 3(3), 356–375. https://doi.org/10.3390/stats3030023

Rahmanti, A. R., Yang, H.-C., Bintoro, B. S., Nursetyo, A. A., Muhtar, M. S., Syed-Abdul, S., & Li, Y.-C. J. (2022). SlimMe, a chatbot with artificial empathy for personal weight management: System design and finding. *Frontiers in Nutrition*, 9. https://doi.org/10.3389/fnut.2022.870775

Ramalingam, D. A., Karunamurthy, D. A., Amalraj Victoire, D. T., & Pavithra, B. (2023). Impact of artificial intelligence on healthcare: A review of current applications and future possibilities. *Quing: International Journal of Innovative Research in Science and Engineering*, 2(2), 37–49. https://doi.org/10.54368/qijirse.2.2.0005

Rodrigues, M. P. (2023). Green computing and energy-efficient algorithms for sustainable computing. *International Journal of Computing and Digital Systems*, 14(1). https://journal.uob.edu.bh:443/handle/123456789/5045

Rosca, C., Covrig, B., Goanta, C., Van Dijck, G., & Spanakis, G. (2020). Return of the AI: An analysis of legal research on artificial intelligence using topic modeling. In N. Aletras, I. Androutsopoulos, L. Barrett, A. Meyers, & D. Preoţiuc-Pietro (Eds.), *Proceedings of the natural legal language processing workshop 2020*. CEUR-WS.org.

Rosemann, A., & Zhang, X. (2022). Exploring the social, ethical, legal, and responsibility dimensions of artificial intelligence for health – a new column in intelligent medicine. *Intelligent Medicine*, 2(2), 103–109. https://doi.org/10.1016/j.imed.2021.12.002

Saba, T., Khan, M. A., Rehman, A., & Marie-Sainte, S. L. (2019). Region extraction and classification of skin cancer: A heterogeneous framework of deep CNN features fusion and reduction. *Journal of Medical Systems*, 43(9), 289. https://doi.org/10.1007/s10916-019-1413-3

Safdar, N. M., Banja, J. D., & Meltzer, C. C. (2020). Ethical considerations in artificial intelligence. *European Journal of Radiology*, 122(November 2019), 108768. https://doi.org/10.1016/j.ejrad.2019.108768

Saheb, T. (2024). Mapping ethical artificial intelligence policy landscape: A mixed method analysis. *Science and Engineering Ethics*, 30(2), 1–26. https://doi.org/10.1007/s11948-024-00472-6

Scherer, M. U. (2015). Regulating artificial intelligence systems: Risks, challenges, competencies, and strategies. *SSRN Electronic Journal*. https://doi.org/10.2139/ssrn.2609777

Shahid, A., Qureshi, G. M., & Chaudhary, F. (2023). Transforming legal practice: The role of AI in modern law. *Journal of Strategic Policy and Global Affairs*, 4(1), 36–42. https://doi.org/10.58669/jspga.v04.i01.04

Siala, H., & Wang, Y. (2022). SHIFTing artificial intelligence to be responsible in healthcare: A systematic review. *Social Science and Medicine*, 296(February–June), 114782. https://doi.org/10.1016/j.socscimed.2022.114782

Slimi, Z., & Carballido, B. V. (2023). Navigating the ethical challenges of artificial intelligence in higher education: An analysis of seven global AI ethics policies. *TEM Journal*, 12(2), 590–602. https://doi.org/10.18421/TEM122-02

Sushina, T., & Sobenin, A. (2020). *Artificial intelligence in the criminal justice system: Leading trends and possibilities*. Proceedings of the 6th International Conference on Social, Economic, and Academic Leadership (ICSEAL-6-2019). https://doi.org/10.2991/assehr.k.200526.062

Telefonica. (2023). *Ethical use of artificial intelligence to build trust and economic value 2.* Telefonica.

Van De Sande, D., Van Genderen, M. E., Smit, J. M., Huiskens, J., Visser, J. J., Veen, R. E. R., Van Unen, E., Ba, O. H., Gommers, D., & Bommel, J. van. (2022). Developing, implementing and governing artificial intelligence in medicine: A step-by-step approach to prevent an artificial intelligence winter. *BMJ Health and Care Informatics*, 29(1), 1–8. https://doi.org/10.1136/bmjhci-2021-100495

Vargas-Murillo, A. R., Pari-Bedoya, I. N. M. de la A., Turriate-Guzman, A. M., Delgado-Chávez, C. A., & Sanchez-Paucar, F. (2024). Transforming justice: Implications of artificial intelligence in legal systems. *Academic Journal of Interdisciplinary Studies*, 13(2), 433. https://doi.org/10.36941/ajis-2024-0059

Vyhmeister, E., & Castane, G. G. (2024). TAI-PRM: Trustworthy AI – project risk management framework towards industry 5.0. *AI and Ethics*, 0123456789. https://doi.org/10.1007/s43681-023-00417-y

Westlaw. (2023). https://legal.thomsonreuters.com/en/westlaw

Yigitcanlar, T., Mehmood, R., & Corchado, J. M. (2021). Green artificial intelligence: Towards an efficient, sustainable and equitable technology for smart cities and futures. *Sustainability*, 13(16), 8952. https://doi.org/10.3390/su13168952

5

Assessing the Efficacy of Artificial Intelligence (AI) Applications in Predictive Policing: A Systematic Review Method

Sofia Khatun and Sivananda Kumar K.

5.1 Introduction

In the fight against criminal recidivism, data science has emerged as a leading field in recent years (Alice, 2021). Data scientists use quantitative and qualitative methodologies to answer pertinent questions and make predictions. Specifically, literature dating back to the 1920s outlines the potential of risk assessment tools and machine learning (ML) algorithms to anticipate the probability of criminal recidivism and minimize its spread (Burrington, 2018). The creation of several datasets and ML models that can support judicial judgments on probation, sentence duration, or the adoption of better rehabilitation measures has improved the reliability of the methodologies over time. Indeed, ML models have several potential uses in the criminal justice system. They help predict or track the impact of criminal justice policy on recidivism reduction at the group level. In the context of individual cases, they can be used to evaluate the likelihood of recidivism and so bolster court decisions (Alikhademi et al., 2022).

The main objective of this review is to delve further into these contentious subjects. Even though these methods have been around for a while and ML models have been evaluated well for their potential to aid criminal justice, they are still not used much in actual court proceedings (Sarzaeim et al., 2023). This results from the contentious viewpoints discussed in the legal and scientific literature. Based on what Rees said, "We would be entitled to feel uneasy, even if presented with compelling evidence that, on average, the machines make better decisions than the humans" (Ferguson, 2024). The main reason people are afraid to let algorithms determine all of their decisions. Ignoring the possibilities of applying ML models in the future is difficult to fathom, notwithstanding the perplexities (Bertovskiy et al., 2022). There has been a surge in interest in using ML systems to improve criminal justice and public policy in recent years due to their remarkable accuracy in predicting complicated outcomes (Friese, 2023). In order to enhance the accuracy of the ML model, researchers have been searching for firm indicators that predict distinct types of recidivism to improve prediction scales. While standardizing data collection and performing data preprocessing might improve ML model performances, paying attention to previously ignored elements and interactions is equally crucial (Trials, 2022). With the ever-changing ML techniques and the countless variables used to predict recidivism, there is a growing need for clarity in the extensive literature that has emerged in recent years. This literature aims to outline the state of the art in recidivism prediction techniques and critically analyze their potential and limitations (Hinman, 2022). It leverages the potential of a review written according to the Preferred Reporting Items for Systematic Reviews and Meta-Analyses (PRISMA) Statement.

5.2 Materials and Methods

5.2.1 Eligibility Criteria

The PRISMA Statement has organized the systematic review methodologies. There were no limits on language, publication date, or publication status. The studies' characteristics are as follows: The research aims to forecast recidivism, with a clear exposition of data gathering methods and detailed descriptions of the approaches, including the ML techniques. The authors excluded studies that aimed to reduce bias in ML models, predict psychiatric characteristics in offenders, or lack the necessary accuracy metrics to evaluate the models.

5.2.2 Information Sources and Search Strategy

Scopus and Pubmed were the two internet databases used to choose the studies. The following equation was used to search for bibliographic records using title, abstract, and keywords: ("crim*") OR ("offen*") OR ("violat*") AND ("recidiv*") OR ("relapse") AND ("machine learning") OR ("artificial intelligence") OR ("deep learning"), yielding 79 records. Literatures that fulfilled our inclusion and exclusion criteria were located by searching the references of the included papers. The period January 2022 was the most recent search. We started by eliminating titles that did not qualify based on our screening process. The papers were ultimately included or excluded based on the above criteria after abstracts were reviewed and complete texts were read.

5.2.3 Assessment of Risk of Bias

All incorporated systematic reviews had their potential for bias evaluated using the ROBIS tool. One way to evaluate the potential for bias in systematic reviews is using the ROBIS tool, which has three steps: (1) determining the review's relevance (which is optional), (2) pinpointing any issues with the review's methodology, and (3) determining the review's bias risk. Review eligibility criteria, study discovery and selection, data collecting and study appraisal, and synthesis and findings are the four domains that will be evaluated in phase two of the review. The second step identifies the concerns, and the third phase summarizes them.

5.3 Results

5.3.1 Study Selection

The original set of 79 preliminary results had 16 duplicates deleted. On top of that, 33 articles were omitted since their titles and abstracts alone needed to meet the requirements. After thoroughly evaluating the complete text, the remaining papers were either chosen or removed. Out of all the papers that were considered, 18 were not included because they did not meet the qualifying criteria:

- Thirteen articles failed to adequately detail their technique; one examined solely the psychological traits of recurrent offenders, and fourteen sought to lessen model bias.
- Twelve studies were ultimately chosen. Following the criteria given by Page and colleagues, Figure 5.1 shows a PRISMA flow diagram that summarizes the outcomes of the research selection.

5.3.2 Study Characteristics

We categorized the study results into three areas for presentation. The first one examines the dataset and ML techniques used in the research. Our initial focus was on the attributes of datasets. We then verified if the authors utilized ML techniques like data preprocessing or cross-validation (CV) in the studies. One strategy involves converting raw data into a comprehensible format for ML algorithms. The CV is a method used to assess ML models' ability to predict unseen data accurately. The initial section is crucial as various datasets and ML methodologies can significantly impact the ultimate performance of ML models. In the second section, we examined the type of recidivism targeted for prediction. We chose the ML model that

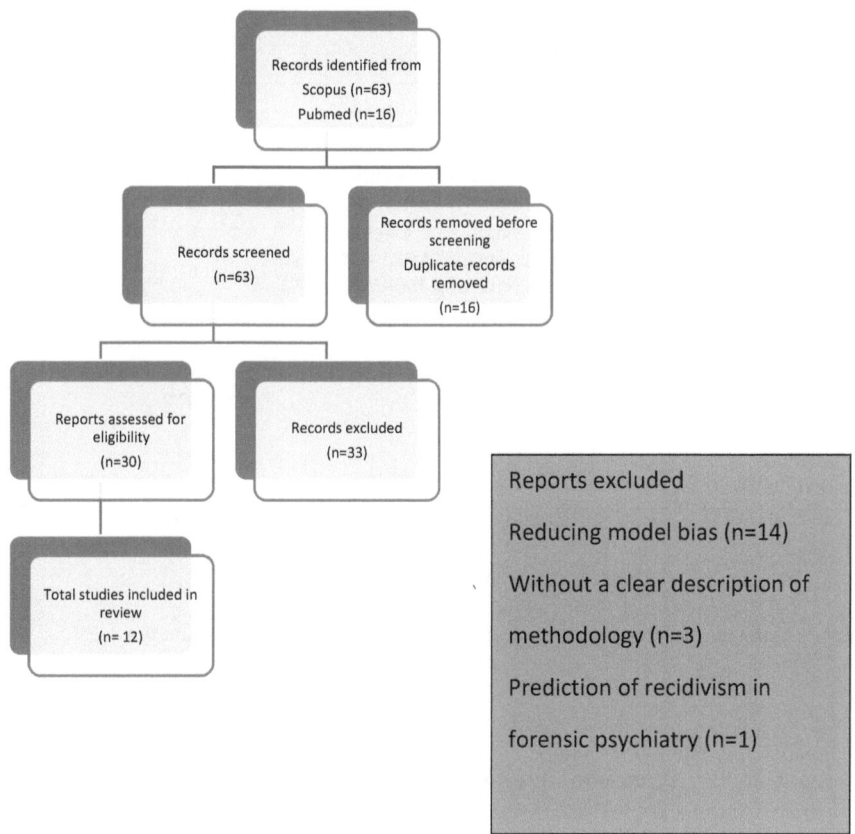

FIGURE 5.1
Flowchart showing the process of inclusion of publications.

demonstrated the highest performance for this study. In the third segment, we categorized the research into four groups depending on their objectives and then evaluated the effectiveness of each ML model using specific criteria.

5.3.3 Characteristics of Dataset and ML Techniques

The main features of the considered studies are listed in Table 5.1.

Every research uses a unique dataset, of which two relied only on information gathered from prisons or the legal system. The first one looked at sexual recidivism rates among juvenile offenders in Florida who were followed up with for more than two years following their first charge. Finding out if ML models could outperform traditional statistical methods was the primary goal of Ozkan and colleagues. Consequently, the writers utilized statistical models that used several predictor variables. These variables included a wealth of developmental factors and data from past risk assessments for

TABLE 5.1

Dataset Combined and ML Techniques Applied

Authors	Dataset Combined	ML Techniques
(Butsara et al., 2019)	Data by central correctional institution for drug addicts and central women correctional institution in Thailand	Data standardization + Feature selection and CV
(Duwe & Kim, 2017)	Minnesota Screening Tool Assessing Recidivism Risk (MnSTARR) + Minnesota Sex Offender Screening Tool-3 (MnSOST-3)	CV
(Ghasemi et al., 2021)	Level of Service/Case Management Inventory (LS/CMI)	CV
(Haarsma et al., 2020)	NeuroCognitive Risk Assessment (NCRA) + demographic feature set	Feature selection + CV
(Karimi-Haghighi & Castillo, 2021)	RisCanvi	CV
(Ozkan et al., 2019)	Florida Department of Juvenile Justice (FDJJ)	Feature selection
(Salo et al., 2019)	Finnish Risk and Needs Assessment Form (Riski-ja tarvearvio [RITA]) Finnish Prisoner Database + static predictors	CV
(Singh & Mohapatra, 2021)	Historical, Clinical, and Risk Management-20 (HCR-20) + clinical and nonclinical risk assessment factors	ANOVA + CV
(Ting et al., 2018)	Youth Level of Service/Case Management Inventory 2.0 (YLS/CMI)	
(Tolan et al., 2019)	Structured Assessment of Violence Risk in Youth (SAVRY) + static features	CV
(Tollenaar & van der Heijden, 2013)	StatRec with Dutch Offender's Index	
(Tollenaar & van der Heijden, 2019)	Dutch Offender's Index (DOI)	CV

Note: CV: cross-validation; ANOVA: analysis of variance.

all juveniles reported for delinquency by the Florida Department of Juvenile Justice (FDJJ). The second study, written by Butsara, drew on data collected from two Thai correctional institutions: one for female inmates and one for drug addicts. There are 298 female detainees and 300 male inmates in the sample. To determine the most important variables for predicting recidivism in drug distribution, the authors developed a method and studied the efficacy of ML in this area.

A total of five articles refer to national recidivism prediction risk assessment tools. Using RisCanvi, a risk assessment protocol for violence prevention implemented in the Catalan prison in 2009, Karimi-Haghighi and Castillo created a risk score based on several factors. Inmates' familial and social environments, clinical conditions, attitudes, and beliefs are potential danger zones. There are 2,634 examples in the dataset. Between 2003 and 2006, 27,772 inmates were released from Minnesota jails, according to Duwe and Kim's study. Using the Minnesota Sex Offender Screening Tool-3 (MnSOST-3), which analyzes the risk of sexual recidivism for sex offenders in Minnesota, the authors utilized a dataset from the Minnesota Screening Tool Assessing Recidivism Risk (MnSTARR). This dataset evaluates the likelihood of five distinct forms of recidivism. In two separate research, Tollenaar and colleagues utilized the StatRec scale in conjunction with static data from the Dutch Offender Index (DOI). General, criminal, and violent recidivism are the three types of recidivism that are predicted in both studies. The data set originates from a 2005 criminal case involving juvenile criminals found guilty. More recently, researchers looked into the results generalizability by adding public access data from a North Carolina prison to the dataset. All people freed between July 1977 and June 1978 and July 1979 and June 1980 are included in these data sets. Although ML models were applied to both cohorts, this evaluation solely considers the data from 1977–1978 (not including Tollenaar's 2019 study) because the 1980 cohort demonstrated a lower calibration probability. Salo and colleagues utilized the dynamic components of the Finnish Risk and Needs Assessment Form (RITA) to forecast both nonviolent and violent recidivism. A total of 746 males who were given further prison terms were included in the sample. The full RITA, which includes 52 topics, including aggressiveness, substance abuse, work issues, economic coping, and resistance to change, is required of all persons.

Tolan and colleagues combined statistical features and other risk assessment approaches in a separate investigation. After comparing various datasets and ML models concerning AUC, the authors demonstrated how the ML model performed better with Structured Assessment of Violence Risk in Youth (SAVRY) characteristics. The SAVRY considers 24 risk indicators and six predictive factors to assess potential aggression. There are three main types of risk factors: historical, personal, and social/contextual. The study's data set came from the juvenile justice system in Catalonia and comprised 853 SAVRY-analyzed juvenile offenders who completed their sentences in 2010 and were between the ages of 12 and 17.

One study attempted to predict FTO recidivism by combining the Historical, Clinical, and Risk Management-20 (HCR-20) with 16 additional clinical and nonclinical risk assessment variables. Data was gathered from different prisons all around the Indian state of Jharkhand. The majority of the 204 male convicts in the study lived in poverty, and their ages ranged from 18 to 30.

Last but not least, we must highlight the work of Haarsma and colleagues, who employed the NeuroCognitive Risk Assessment (NCRA), a program for risk assessment based on neurocognitive tests that can detect crucial criminogenic characteristics associated with recidivism. The NCRA was self-administered by 730 Harris County Department of Community Supervision and Corrections participants. A ML model was used to quantify the individual's recidivism risk score based on NCRA and demographic data.

Each study employed a unique combination of ML approaches to sift through the dataset, analyze it, and draw better conclusions. Four investigations improved the datasets by using preprocessing. Two of them preferred a feature selection strategy. Before using feature selection, one study utilized generic data standardization. Finally, one of them employed variance analysis to find essential characteristics for this dataset. Another critical point is the author's decision to measure ML models' capacity to generalize to data not yet observed using cross-validation (CV). Nine of the papers considered for the review used CVs.

5.3.4 Aim of the Studies and ML Model Applied

To facilitate a more accurate comparison of the studies, sorting can be done based on the type of recurrence they predict. The sorting results in four categories: general, sexual, violent, and other recidivism (Ajayi, 2022). The final category comprises research focused on a particular crime, exclusively involving males, or specifically targeted children.

The datasets from Table 5.1 were utilized to train ML models for predicting recidivism. You can choose from various models depending on the data and the specific target variable you aim to predict. The studies compared many models to determine the most effective in predicting recidivism. The models were compared based on accuracy (ACC) and area under the curve (AUC) metrics. The ACC measures the algorithm's rate of properly classifying data points by comparing the number of correctly classified observations to the total number of predictions. The AUC evaluates the ML models' capacity to differentiate between recidivism and nonrecidivism. Both measurements yield a result between 0 and 1. When the score approaches 0, it indicates that ML models have poor predictive performance. A score close to 0.5 suggests that the models randomly predict recidivism risk. A score near 1 indicates that ML models have excellent discrimination between recidivism and nonrecidivism.

In this review, we only included the ML models that demonstrated superior performance based on the author's assessment (Table 5.2). The most commonly utilized ML model is logistic regression, along with its variations LogitBoost and the generalized linear models with ridge and lasso regularization (Glmnet). The second most frequent model is the random forest, cited in references (Ghasemi et al., 2021; Ozkan et al., 2019; Salo et al., 2019; Liu et al., 2011). Other notable ML models include multilayer perceptron (MLP), linear discriminant analysis (LDA), and penalized LDA.

5.3.5 Results of Syntheses

Tables 5.3, 5.4, 5.5, and 5.6 present the results of the investigation of ACC and AUC for general, sexual, violent, and other types of recidivism, showing that

TABLE 5.2

Purpose of Datasets, ML Models, and Their Evaluation

Dataset	Type of Recurrence	Purpose	ML Model	Evaluation Metrics	Evaluation Value
Thailand (Mantri, 2023)	Other	Recidivism in drug distribution	Logistic Regression	ACC	0.90
MnSTARR+ (Hung & Yen, 2021)	General	General recidivism	LogitBoost	ACC AUC	0.82 0.78
LS/CMI (Verte, 2024)	General	General recidivism	Random Forest	ACC AUC	0.74 0.75
NCRA+ (Guariglia, 2022)	General	General recidivism	Glmnet	AUC	0.70
RisCanvi (Aitken, 2023)	Violent	Violent Recidivism	MLP	AUC	0.78
FDJJ (Singh, 2022)	Sexual	Sexual Recidivism in Youth	Random Forest	AUC	0.71
RITA+ (Heaven, 2020)	Other	General and violent recidivism in male	Random Forest	AUC	0.78
HCR-20+ (Hung & Yen, 2023)	General	General recidivism	Ensemble model with NBC, kNN, MLP, probabilistic neural networks, support vector machines	ACC	0.87
YLS/CMI (McDaniel, 2022)	Other	General Recidivism in Youth	Random Forest	ACC AUC	0.65 0.69
SAVRY+ (Ganguli, 2023)	Other	Violent recidivism in youth	Logistic Regression	AUC	0.71
StatRec (Lau, 2020)	General	General Recidivism	Logistic Regression	ACC AUC	0.73 0.78
	Sexual	Sexual recidivism	LDA	ACC AUC	0.96 0.73
	Violent	Violent recidivism	Logistic regression	ACC AUC	0.78 0.74

(Continued)

TABLE 5.2 (Continued)

Purpose of Datasets, ML Models, and Their Evaluation

Dataset	Type of Recurrence	Purpose	ML Model	Evaluation Metrics	Evaluation Value
DOI (Shapiro, 2019)	General	General recidivism	L1–Logistic Regression	ACC AUC	0.78 0.73
	Sexual	Sexual recidivism	L1–Logistic Regression	ACC AUC	0.96 0.77
	Violent	Violent recidivism	Penalized LDA	ACC AUC	0.78 0.74

Note: ACC: accuracy; AUC: area under the curve; Thailand: data by central correctional institution for drug addicts and central women correctional institution in Thailand; MnSTARR+: Minnesota Screening Tool Assessing Recidivism Risk + Minnesota Sex Offender Screening Tool-3; LS/CMI: Level of Service/Case Management Inventory; NCRA+: NeuroCognitive Risk.

TABLE 5.3

Evaluation of General Recidivism

	MnSTARR+	LS/CMI	NCRA+	HCR-20+	StatRec	DOI
ACC	0.82	0.74		**0.87**	0.74	00.78
AUC	**0.78**	0.75	0.70		**0.78**	00.73

Note: AUC: area under curve; ACC: accuracy; MnSTARR+: Minnesota Screening Tool Assessing Recidivism Risk + Minnesota Sex Offender Screening Tool-3; LS/CMI: Level of Service/Case Management Inventory; NCRA+: NeuroCognitive Risk Assessment + demographic feature set; HCR-20+: Historical, Clinical and Risk Management–20 + clinical and non-clinical risk assessment factors; StatRec: static recidivism risk (Static Recidiverisico); DOI: Dutch Offender's Index. The highest scores are highlighted in bold.

TABLE 5.4

Evaluation of Sexual Recidivism

	StatRec	DOI
ACC	0.96	0.96
AUC	0.73	**0.77**

Note: AUC: area under the curve; ACC: accuracy; StatRec: static recidivism risk (Static Recidiverisico); DOI: Dutch Offender's Index. The highest scores are highlighted in bold.

all ML models perform effectively. The ACC scores range from 0.65 to 0.96, whereas the AUC scores range from 0.69 to 0.78. The top scores are indicated in Tables 5.3, 5.4, 5.5, and 5.6. Table 5.3 displays the outcomes from various research forecasting general recidivism. The ensemble model trained using

TABLE 5.5

Evaluation of Violent Recidivism

	RisCanvi	StatRec	DOI
ACC		**0.78**	**0.78**
AUC	**0.78**	0.74	0.74

Note: AUC: area under curve; ACC: accuracy; RisCanvi: risk assessment protocol for violence prevention introduced in the Catalan prison; StatRec: static recidivism risk (Static Recidiverisico); DOI: Dutch Offender's Index. The highest scores are highlighted in bold.

TABLE 5.6

Evaluation of All the Other Recidivism

	Thailand	FDJJ	RITA+	YLS/CMI	SAVRY+
ACC	**0.90**			0.65	
AUC*		0.71	**0.78**	0.69	0.71

*AUC: area under curve; ACC: accuracy; Thailand: Thailand: data by central correctional institution for drug addicts and central women correctional institution in Thailand; FDJJ: Florida Department of Juvenile Justice; RITA+: Finnish Risk and Needs Assessment Form + static predictors; YLS/CMI: Youth Level of Service/Case Management Inventory 2.0; SAVRY+: Structured Assessment of Violence Risk in Youth + static features. The highest scores are highlighted in bold.

an HCR-20+ dataset demonstrates enhanced performance and appears to be the most efficient approach based on the ACC. The logistic regression model achieves the highest score based on the AUC metric when using the MnSTARR+ and StatRec datasets.

The comparison between the StatRec and DOI datasets in Tables 5.3, 5.4, and 5.5 indicates that they yield similar findings, except for overall recidivism, which differs by 0.05. Nevertheless, this outcome was expected as both investigations utilized information from the Dutch Offender's Index. The MLP trained with the RisCanvi dataset outperformed other approaches for violent recidivism, as shown in Table 5.5.

Table 5.6 displays the findings of studies that encompass all forms of recidivism. Comparing this research is challenging because of variations in sample types, such as juvenile offenders or males, and the particular focus on predicting distinct types of recidivism, including drug distribution recidivism. However, we noticed that the results indicate the overall efficacy of the prediction models. The Thailand dataset is particularly relevant due to its high accuracy of 0.90 achieved by logistic regression. The model achieved an AUC score of 0.78 when trained with the RITA+ dataset using a random forest.

5.3.6 Factors Involved in Predicting Recidivism

Some research in this review detailed the variables that had the most significant impact on the final assessment. Section 5.4 discusses many aspects of the results. We list the variables most involved in the outcomes of each model, as reported by the authors. Four key characteristics have been identified: royal pardons or suspension, age at first offense, familial encouragement, and frequency of substance abuse. The LS/CMI includes items such as A18 (previous charges, probation violations, parole suspensions during past community supervision), A14 (three or more current offenses), A423 (could utilize time more effectively), and A735 (current substance abuse issue). NCRA includes a selection of 13 tests, such as the balloon analog risk task (time taken), point-subtraction aggression paradigm (growth, punishment ratio), reading the mind through the eyes (accuracy, median time), emotional Stroop (test duration, time on black, time on icon color, time on positive and negative words), and Tower of London (aborted attempts, duplicate moves, illegal moves on the first move fraction). The most influential factors in this model predicting sexual recidivism are previous felony sex offense referrals, the quantity of prior misdemeanor sexual misconduct referrals, and the number of previous felony offenses.

The critical dynamic elements identified from RITA's items are effective management of one's finances for general reoffending and aggressiveness for violent reoffending. The most influential factors impacting the model's accuracy are the total YLS score, difficulties in managing behavior, age at first arrest, history of running away, and family conditions. The logistic regression model primarily incorporates static features such as sex, ethnicity, age at significant crime, and criminality in the next ten years, along with one SAVRY component, the expert's evaluation. Static features are deemed more significant than SAVRY features in the MLP model. The most influential variables for general recidivism in a logistic regression model are age, conviction density, specific offense types (property offense and public order offense), the number of previous offenses, and home country. The logistic regression model shows that the most significant factors influencing violent recidivism are the number of previous convictions, the most severe offense type (property crime with violence), the offense type in the current case (property crime without violence, public order, other offense), and the individual's country of origin. Finally, in terms of sexual reoffending (linear discriminant analysis), three primary coefficients have been identified: prior sexual offenses and country of origin have the most significant positive impact on the likelihood of sexual reoffending. In contrast, the number of previous public prosecutor's disposals has the most substantial negative impact.

5.3.7 Reporting Biases

This systematic review analyzed datasets and ML models concurrently. Considering the dataset used to train the ML model is essential while critically evaluating the results. The method of data collection varies in each study. Some articles source data from countries' organizations, whereas others obtain data from risk assessment tool checklists or neuropsychological testing. Thus, databases vary in aspects, including sample size, average age, kind of crime, and duration of recidivism follow-up. These variables can significantly alter the evaluation of the machine-learning model.

It is important to note that some articles need to disclose the use of data preprocessing or provide detailed details regarding the process employed. As previously stated, we utilized the ROBIS assessment to identify potential systemic bias. Table 5.7 and Figure 5.2 provide a summary of the bias risk. Table 5.7 provides a detailed breakdown of each study's relative risk of bias, categorizing it into low, high, or uncertain risk in four domains. Figure 5.2 illustrates the risk of bias (ranging from "high" to "low" and "unclear") for each domain evaluated in all the included research, along with the "overall risk." Nine studies were rated as low risk, one as high risk, and two had an uncertain risk assessment among those reviewed. The primary issues include the unevenness of the samples and the inadequate explanation of data preprocessing and analysis, which complicates the comparison of various ML algorithms.

5.4 Discussion

Data science indicates that ML algorithms can be highly effective (Owen, 2018). The results of the papers analyzed in this review demonstrate that each machine-learning model has strong performance. The median score for the ACC is 0.81. The mid-score for the AUC is 0.74. With ACC and AUC values ranging from 0 to 1, the mid-scores indicate the models' good predictability. Some studies employ a risk assessment to evaluate a particular type of recidivism, crime, or demographic, while others estimate the risk of overall recidivism. Nevertheless, no notable distinctions are seen when comparing the two types of investigations. This review only identified a 0.03 increase in ACC for a particular form of recidivism. There is no proof utilizing a more detailed risk assessment could notably enhance the capability to forecast criminal reoffending. This review assesses several ML techniques, algorithms, and datasets for predicting recidivism. Upon analyzing the available models, logistic regression emerges as the predominant technique for predicting recidivism in these studies, with more intricate algorithms being less prevalent (Moktali, 2023). Regarding performance, both a basic prediction model like logistic regression and more intricate ones like random forest exhibit comparable predictive accuracy and performance. The results suggest that focusing on model complexity is unnecessary to enhance criminal recidivism prediction.

TABLE 5.7
Tabular Presentation for ROBIS Results

Review (Name, Year)	Phase 2				Phase 3
	1. Study Eligibility Criteria	2. Identification and Selection of Studies	3. Data Collection and Study Appraisal	4. Synthesis and Findings	Risk of Bias in the Review
(O'Brien, 2024)	☺	☺	☹	☺	☹
(Jany, 2022)	☺	☺	☺	☺	☺
(Madia, 2022)	☺	☺	?	☺	☺
(Blount, 2021)	☺	☺	☺	☺	☺
(Al-Sibai, 2023)	☺	☺	☺	☺	☺
(Lee et al., 2024)	☺	☺	☹	☺	?
(Dubois, 2017)	☺	☺	?	☺	☺
(White, 2024)	☺	☺	☺	☺	☺
(Verma, 2022)	☺	☺	☺	☺	☺
(Chiancone, 2023)	☺	☺	☹	☺	?
(Dwivedi, 2023)	☺	☺	☺	☺	☺
(McCarthy, 2019)	☺	☺	☺	☺	☺

☺ = low risk; ☹ = high risk; and ? = unclear risk.

Assessing the Efficacy of AI Applications

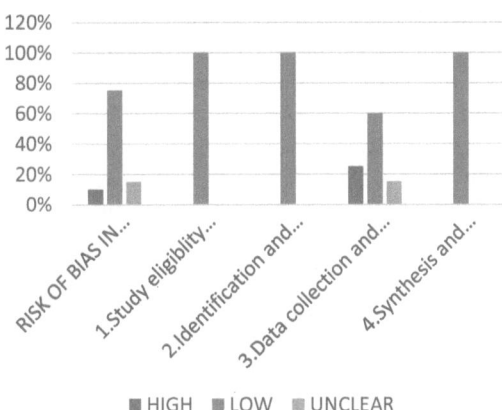

FIGURE 5.2
Graphical display for ROBIS results.

The literature examined in this systematic review identified certain limitations. The performance of each model is influenced by factors beyond only the ML model or dataset. Data collecting and data preprocessing methods are crucial. Both factors can have a substantial impact on model performance. It is rare in the literature to emphasize data preprocessing procedures, hindering the comparison of various investigations (McConvey, 2023). Furthermore, the ML models mentioned in the literature provide a binary outcome. Sometimes, it is challenging to discern the key variables that impacted the final evaluation based on the model's description. Recent research has emphasized the likelihood of racial bias in risk assessments, which have become more prevalent and successful. Biases linked to age estimation, which is essential in forensic science, should be considered (Lynn, 2021).

Section 3.6 details the variables with the most significant influence on evaluating each model's recidivism probability. It is advisable to take some factors into account in this matter. The authors state that the critical variables for the final assessment should focus solely on the ML model and the dataset it uses. Therefore, the findings may only apply to specialized subgroups or distinct subpopulations. Furthermore, during the final assessment, analyzing individual variables independently may not be feasible because ML algorithms examine how these variables are integrated. Explaining individual-level predictions becomes challenging due to the complexity of models incorporating interactions and nonlinear effects, with difficulty increasing as the model complexity develops.

The utilization of ML techniques for risk assessment in the criminal justice system to forecast recidivism has grown in recent years (Castets-Renard, 2021). Nevertheless, it remains a contentious subject because of the extensive study on algorithmic fairness. This paper aims to analyze the current strategies used to predict criminal recidivism. We did not intend to demonstrate the flawless accuracy of the ML method or suggest that it is feasible to depend entirely on the ML model for predicting recidivism. We will discuss the advantages and drawbacks of using data science in the humanities. It is crucial to emphasize the significance of focusing more on the dataset and data processing. By stepping back and concentrating on these characteristics, model performance could be enhanced and potential bias reduced. Furthermore, it is beneficial to compare models using identical evaluation metrics to enable comparison. We noted a solid overall performance of the models based on the metrics presented in the analyzed publications. This enables us to highlight the tangible assistance these tools can provide to human judgment, which is equally susceptible to bias. The binary outcome and algorithmic bias pose a constraint on this method. Modern ML models are often called "black boxes" due to their intricate design, making it challenging for users to comprehend how an AI system processes data to make judgments. The inaccessibility of the models and algorithms employed in judicial decisions may compromise openness, impartiality, and justice, resulting in prejudice against individuals or groups. Developing transparent algorithms or utilizing explainable AI might be beneficial (Schiff et al., 2023). Explainable AI refers to AI systems capable of justifying their reasoning to a human user and identifying their strengths and limitations. By utilizing these methodologies, we can determine the impact of each component on the outcome, providing valuable insights for criminal justice professionals to inform their decisions (Sarmah, 2019). Using a person-in-the-loop method that combines human and machine collaboration might enhance results by leveraging their respective capabilities and emphasizing the value of synergistic effort.

5.5 Thoughts Proposed

The swift advancement of AI technology in India has elicited apprehension regarding its possible application in criminal endeavors (Xue et al., 2019). An unusual type of criminal activity has arisen, employing AI algorithms for advanced cybercrimes and hacking incidents. The judicial system encounters difficulties in criminal identification and attribution, while AI evasion strategies and anonymizing technology hinder the tracking of perpetrators. AI-generated counterfeit content, such as deepfakes, presents novel issues for the Indian judicial system, with the potential to manipulate evidence, damage reputations, and disseminate misinformation. The criminal justice system is grappling with a significant issue: the lack of resources for investigating and resolving crimes (Halley, 2022). However, the potential of AI to expedite the investigative process is a ray of hope. AI can swiftly analyze extensive datasets, identifying patterns and correlations that would be arduous for humans to discern alone. This paves the way for more efficient and precise identification of suspects and evidence collection by law enforcement. AI's role in forensic analysis, a critical aspect of investigating various crimes, is particularly noteworthy (Purves, 2023). It can analyze fingerprints, DNA samples, and various forms of evidence to identify suspects or link crimes to prior incidents, thereby enhancing the efficiency of criminal investigations.

Our systematic literature analysis examined fairness in police and recidivism algorithms (Pearsall, 2010). The examination of the chosen publications uncovered several solutions designed to mitigate intrinsic biases in these algorithms, underscoring the multifaceted nature of fairness in the field (Data Centre, 2024). The productive use of AI in predictive policing that results in positive outcomes is contingent on AI compliance with human rights (Isafiade, 2022). Our analysis yields the following recommendations for future considerations: prejudice, transparency, and accountability.

- *Transparency*
    - Increased openness can be achieved if practitioners make their algorithms accessible and explainable. The starting point is the citizens' right to be informed that algorithms may be implemented in their vicinity (Behnam Shad, 2023). Data processing, data collecting, data processing purposes, algorithm developers, and algorithm users should all be transparently disclosed to the public. This respect for the public's right to know is crucial. Citizens should be able to inquire and get further details by publicizing contact information. Relying on in-house software developers instead of commercial organizations is crucial for developing predictive police software to enhance transparency (Berk, 2021). Although it may be expensive and time-consuming, hiring expert personnel allowed us to maintain control over the entire development process and the finished algorithm, allowing us to avoid the black box problem. Developers should be obligated to make data and code accessible for critical examination if needed by regulatory mechanisms if the hiring of commercial parties cannot be prevented (Perle, 2023).
- *Accountability*
    - The establishment of impartial oversight organizations is necessary to resolve the accountability issue. These organizations need sufficient resources and personnel. By bolstering and increasing faith in the police, the United Kingdom's oversight agencies have already established a promising practice (Huysman, 2019). In addition to reviewing algorithms, the body is responsible for overseeing the whole scope of police data utilization, including data collection methods, purposes, processing, storage, and use of results (including secondary use). Most member states have

existing oversight mechanisms; whenever required, their authority should be broadened to encompass all types of data gathering and processing within the context of predictive policing, and they should be equipped with the appropriate resources, knowledge, and know-how (Momsen, 2020).

- *Hypothetical AI results based on probability*
  - It is highly recommended that predictive policing not be fully automated to maximize accountability (Bhathal, 2022). Humans must ultimately make intervention decisions. The results of an algorithm should not be taken as absolute "facts" but rather as probabilities that have been built and can (and often must) be changed. Realize that chances are simply that – chance – and not the same as guarantees (Doerfler, 2021). Embracing and promoting critical reflection is crucial, especially in light of false positives, because AI is undoubtedly not a future-predicting oracle. AI can uncover relationships that may not be immediately obvious. These correlations can bolster police frameworks by providing probability (Waller & Fawcett, 2013). As a result, predictive policing should never take the role of long-term programs that deal with the causes of crime but rather serve as an adjunct to such programs.
- *Evaluate efficiency*
  - Investing in comprehensive comparative studies on the use and execution of predictive policing is another option to increase accountability (Diaz, 2021). Among the many facets of predictive policing that have received little research is its efficacy. Generalizing evaluation findings to other contexts is complex due to inconsistent standards (Newton et al., n.d.). Several factors can influence which variables are included or omitted from evaluation studies. These include the following:
  - The type of predictive policing (area-based, event-based, or person-based) (Hälterlein, 2021)
  - The data type (with or without facial recognition)
  - The application objective (risk assessments or risk reduction) (FSE Editors, 2023)
  - Contextual factors (such as trust in the police or the business interests of developers)
  - Programs can have excellent risk assessment capabilities but need to catch up when it comes to actually reducing risks. Consequently, it is difficult to draw definitive conclusions about causes and effects due to the abundance of possible confounding circumstances (McCray, 2024). Because of this, it is challenging to tell if predictive policing AI apps would make police more efficient and legitimate or if they

will lead to excessive surveillance. Thorough comparative studies and open reviews are required to provide a foundation of evidence about the costs and benefits of AI applications in policing prediction (Ziosi & Pruss, 2024).
- *Combating data bias issues*
  - The output quality is directly proportional to the data quality. A data-gathering and quality strategy can alleviate many issues (Stephens, 2024). Monitoring data quality and gathering is critical to prevent prejudice and biased applications. Countries like Austria and Estonia, which routinely evaluate the quality of their data, can serve as examples in this regard. Examples include Estonia, which established a dedicated analytic team to oversee data collecting and provide suggestions for software and quality enhancements (Pingen, 2023). There must be institutionalized training for police personnel and software operators who input, modify, or interpret the data. Training should focus on the algorithms' limits, such as the potential for automation bias and false positives, and on the roles of individuals and institutions in analyzing the data. One encouraging example is Austria, which educates its police officers on crime analysis and is thus aware of the dangers of predictive policing and the importance of proper conduct (Söderholm, 2023).

5.6 Conclusion

Using AI in criminal justice systems creates a multifaceted environment of prospects and obstacles. This research conducts a thorough literature review on the equity of predictive policing algorithms and the reduction of age-related bias in predictive policing. Our systematic literature review revealed the necessity to broaden the scope of protected qualities beyond the frequently examined domains of race to encompass gender, age, and socioeconomic position. These findings contest the widely held belief that fairness and accuracy are incompatible. The research enhances the conversation on the responsible application of AI in law enforcement, underscoring the necessity of constant evaluation and improvement of predictive policing tools to guarantee equitable public service. This paradigm underscores the necessity for ongoing human supervision, periodic evaluations of AI systems, and the creation of explicit accountability structures. We advocate for a balanced strategy that harnesses the advantages of AI while protecting individual rights and preserving the integrity of judicial processes.

Utilizing quantitative and qualitative methodologies to forecast criminal recidivism could be a valuable asset in criminal justice. Research in this field is growing, but its application in legal proceedings is restricted because of differing opinions. This systematic study presents the current status of using ML approaches to assess the risk of reoffending. It emphasizes essential insights that can be valuable for criminal justice professionals in utilizing these innovative technologies. The methods used all perform well, with an average ACC score of 0.81 and an average AUC score of 0.74. Nevertheless, the use of AI in this area remains contentious because of the substantial critical concerns. To address these crucial challenges, it is essential to confront a new challenge: ensuring algorithms are transparent and accessible to ensure that the use of these new technologies supports decisions grounded in transparency, impartiality, and justice. Integrating natural and social sciences methods with a systemic approach can help correlate e-tech data with human interpretation, ensuring the human operator remains central in the human-computer system in line with the integrated cognitive system. The application of AI in legal proceedings and the subsequent decision-making processes will be a topic of extensive contemplation among scientists, legal experts, and bioethicists. This systematic review comprehensively analyzes the most reliable findings and addresses ethical, deontological, and legal challenges.

References

Aitken, P. (2023, April 29). Police using AI could lead to "predictive" crime prevention "slippery slope," experts argue [Text.Article]. *Fox News.* https://www.foxnews.com/world/police-using-ai-lead-predictive-crime-prevention-slippery-slope-experts-argue

Ajayi, O. (2022, October 25). *Artificial intelligence is used for predictive policing in the US and UK – South Africa should embrace it, too.* https://www.uwc.ac.za/news-and-announcements/news/artificial-intelligence-is-used-for-predictive-policing-in-the-us-and-uk-south-africa-should-embrace-it-too

Alice, N. (2021, July 12). 4 benefits and 4 drawbacks of predictive policing. *Liberties.Eu.* https://www.liberties.eu/en/stories/predictive-policing/43679

Alikhademi, K., Drobina, E., Prioleau, D., Richardson, B., Purves, D., & Gilbert, J. E. (2022). A review of predictive policing from the perspective of fairness. *Artificial Intelligence and Law, 30*(1), 1–17. https://doi.org/10.1007/s10506-021-09286-4

Al-Shamsi, H. R. S., & Safei, S. (2023). Artificial intelligence adoption in predictive policing to predict crime mitigation performance. *International Journal of Sustainable Construction Engineering and Technology, 14*(3), Article 3.

Al-Sibai, N. (2023, October 7). Study finds that police "crime predicting" AI Fails miserably at predicting crimes. *Futurism.* https://futurism.com/the-byte/predictive-policing-ai-fails

Asaro, P. M. (2019). AI ethics in predictive policing: From models of threat to an ethics of care. *IEEE Technology and Society Magazine, 38*(2), 40–53. https://doi.org/10.1109/MTS.2019.2915154

Behnam Shad, K. (2023). Artificial intelligence-related anomies and predictive policing: Normative (dis)orders in liberal democracies. *AI & Society*. https://doi.org/10.1007/s00146-023-01751-9

Berk, R. A. (2021). Artificial intelligence, predictive policing, and risk assessment for law enforcement. *Annual Review of Criminology*, *4*, 209–237. https://doi.org/10.1146/annurev-criminol-051520-012342

Bertovskiy, L. V., Novogonskaya, M. S., & Fedorov, A. R. (2022). Predictive policing: High-tech modeling as a method to identify serial killers. *Kutafin Law Review*, *9*(2), Article 2. https://doi.org/10.17803/2713-0525.2022.2.20.329-342

Bhathal, H. (2022, June 13). Canada's predictive policing tech is poorly regulated under AI policy. *Truthout*. https://truthout.org/articles/canadas-predictive-policing-tech-is-poorly-regulated-under-ai-policy/

Blount, K. (2021). Seeking compatibility in preventing crime with artificial intelligence and ensuring a fair trial. *Masaryk University Journal of Law and Technology*, *15*(1), Article 1. https://doi.org/10.5817/MUJLT2021-1-2

Burrington, I. (2018, April 26). A pioneer in predictive policing is starting a troubling new project. *The Verge*. https://www.theverge.com/2018/4/26/17285058/predictive-policing-predpol-pentagon-ai-racial-bias

Butsara, N., Athonthitichot, P., & Jodpimai, P. (2019). Predicting recidivism to drug distribution using machine learning techniques. *2019 17th International Conference on ICT and Knowledge Engineering (ICT&KE)*, 1–5. https://doi.org/10.1109/ICTKE47035.2019.8966834

Castets-Renard, C. (2021). Human rights and algorithmic impact assessment for predictive policing. In A. Reichman, A. Simoncini, G. De Gregorio, G. Sartor, H.-W. Micklitz, & O. Pollicino (Eds.), *Constitutional challenges in the algorithmic society* (pp. 93–110). Cambridge University Press. https://doi.org/10.1017/9781108914857.007

Chiancone, C. (2023, October 3). *The role of artificial intelligence in law enforcement*. https://www.linkedin.com/pulse/role-artificial-intelligence-law-enforcement-chris-chiancone

Christie, L. (2021). *AI in policing and security*. https://post.parliament.uk/ai-in-policing-and-security/

Crevier, D. (1995). *AI: The tumultuous history of the search for artificial intelligence* (2nd print). Basic Books.

Dakalbab, F., Abu Talib, M., Abu Waraga, O., Bou Nassif, A., Abbas, S., & Nasir, Q. (2022). Artificial intelligence & crime prediction: A systematic literature review. *Social Sciences & Humanities Open*, *6*(1), 100342. https://doi.org/10.1016/j.ssaho.2022.100342

Data Centre. (2024, April 27). *Predictive policing: The use of AI in law enforcement – data center info*. https://datacenterinfo.com/predictive-policing-the-use-of-ai-in-law-enforcement/

Diaz, A. (2021, September 13). *Data-driven policing's threat to our constitutional rights*. Brookings. https://www.brookings.edu/articles/data-driven-policings-threat-to-our-constitutional-rights/

Doerfler, A. (2021, November 17). Countering bias in predictive policing. *News*. https://news.clas.ufl.edu/countering-bias-in-predictive-policing/

Dubois, C. (2017, February 28). *The future of AI and predictive policing – news*. https://www.allaboutcircuits.com/news/the-future-of-ai-and-predictive-policing/

Duwe, G., & Kim, K. (2017). Out with the old and in with the new? An empirical comparison of supervised learning algorithms to predict recidivism. *Criminal Justice Policy Review, 28*(6), 570–600. https://doi.org/10.1177/0887403415604899

Dwivedi, M. (2023). The tomorrow of criminal law: Investigating the application of predictive analytics and AI in the field of criminal justice. *International Journal of Creative Research Thoughts, 11*(9), a499–a509. DOI: http://doi.one/10.1729/Journal.36085

Evans, N. (2022, September 1). Artificial intelligence and policing: It's a matter of trust. *Policing Insight*. https://policinginsight.com/feature/opinion/artificial-intelligence-and-policing-its-a-matter-of-trust/

Ferguson, A. G. (2024, February 7). Predictive policing news, research and analysis. *The Conversation*. https://theconversation.com/global/topics/predictive-policing-22313

Friese, G. (2023, October 17). Advancing policing through AI: Insights from the global law enforcement community. *Police1*. https://www.police1.com/iacp/articles/advancing-policing-through-ai-insights-from-the-global-law-enforcement-community-3SzYuRViccy8vwQ3/

FSE Editors. (2023, September 12). *Ethical implications of AI in predictive policing*. https://falconediting.com/en/blog/ethical-implications-of-ai-in-predictive-policing/

Ganguli, P. (2023, August 21). Predictive policing and crime prevention: The role of AI. *INDIAai*. https://indiaai.gov.in/article/predictive-policing-and-crime-prevention-the-role-of-ai

Ghasemi, M., Anvari, D., Atapour, M., Stephen wormith, J., Stockdale, K. C., & Spiteri, R. J. (2021). The application of machine learning to a general risk–need assessment instrument in the prediction of criminal recidivism. *Criminal Justice and Behavior, 48*(4), 518–538. https://doi.org/10.1177/0093854820969753

Guariglia, M. (2022, January 1). *Police use of artificial intelligence: 2021 in review*. Electronic Frontier Foundation. https://www.eff.org/deeplinks/2021/12/police-use-artificial-intelligence-2021-review

Haarsma, G., Davenport, S., & White, D. C. (2020, January 24). *Frontiers | assessing risk among correctional community probation populations: Predicting reoffense with mobile neurocognitive assessment software*. https://www.frontiersin.org/journals/psychology/articles/10.3389/fpsyg.2019.02926/full

Halley, C. (2022, February 23). What happens when police use ai to predict and prevent crime? *JSTOR Daily*. https://daily.jstor.org/what-happens-when-police-use-ai-to-predict-and-prevent-crime/

Hälterlein, J. (2021). Epistemologies of predictive policing: Mathematical social science, social physics and machine learning. *Big Data & Society, 8*(1). https://doi.org/10.1177/20539517211003118

Heaven, W. D. (2020). Predictive policing algorithms are racist: They need to be dismantled. *MIT Technology Review*. https://www.technologyreview.com/2020/07/17/1005396/predictive-policing-algorithms-racist-dismantled-machine-learning-bias-criminal-justice/

Hinman, N. (2022). *AI and the law* [Online post]. https://stories.surrey.ac.uk/ai-and-the-law/index.html

Hung, T.-W., & Yen, C.-P. (2021). On the person-based predictive policing of AI. *Ethics and Information Technology, 23*. https://doi.org/10.1007/s10676-020-09539-x

Hung, T.-W., & Yen, C.-P. (2023). Predictive policing and algorithmic fairness. *Synthese, 201*(6), 206. https://doi.org/10.1007/s11229-023-04189-0

Huysman, M. (2019, November 4). *Beyond the hype of AI: Predictive policing in practice* [Online post]. Vrije Universiteit Amsterdam. https://vu.nl/en/news/2019/beyond-the-hype-of-ai-predictive-policing-in-practice

Indika. (2024, July 8). *AI in predictive policing: Enhancing law enforcement*. https://www.indikaai.com/blog/the-future-of-predictive-policing-with-ai-enhancing-law-enforcement-through-crime-pattern-prediction

Isafiade, O. (2022, October 24). Artificial intelligence is used for predictive policing in the US and UK – South Africa should embrace it, too. *The Conversation*. http://theconversation.com/artificial-intelligence-is-used-for-predictive-policing-in-the-us-and-uk-south-africa-should-embrace-it-too-191266

Jany, L. (2022, July 4). Researchers use AI to predict crime, biased policing in major U.S. cities like L.A. *Los Angeles Times*. https://www.latimes.com/california/story/2022-07-04/researchers-use-ai-to-predict-crime-biased-policing

Jenkins, R., & Purves, D. (2020). *Artificial intelligence and predictive policing: A roadmap for research*. https://www.academia.edu/44336908/Artificial_Intelligence_and_Predictive_Policing_A_Roadmap_for_Research

Karimi-Haghighi, M., & Castillo, C. (2021). Enhancing a recidivism prediction tool with machine learning: Effectiveness and algorithmic fairness. *Proceedings of the Eighteenth International Conference on Artificial Intelligence and Law*, 210–214. https://doi.org/10.1145/3462757.3466150

Lau, T. (2020, April 1). *Predictive policing explained*. Brennan Center for Justice. https://www.brennancenter.org/our-work/research-reports/predictive-policing-explained

Lee, Y., Ben, B., & Posch, K. (2024, July 5). *Full Article: The Effectiveness of Big Data-Driven Predictive Policing: Systematic Review*. https://www.tandfonline.com/doi/full/10.1080/24751979.2024.2371781

Lee, Y., Bradford, B., & Posch, K. (n.d.). The effectiveness of big data-driven predictive policing: Systematic review. *Justice Evaluation Journal*, 1–34. https://doi.org/10.1080/24751979.2024.2371781

Liu, Y. Y., Yang, M., Ramsay, M., Li, X. S., & Coid, J. W. (2011). A comparison of logistic regression, classification and regression tree, and neural networks models in predicting violent re-offending. *Journal of Quantitative Criminology*, 27(4), 547–573. https://doi.org/10.1007/s10940-011-9137-7

Lynn, J. (2021, April 22). How does A.I. technology exacerbate inequalities in policing? *WHYY*. https://whyy.org/articles/how-does-a-i-technology-exacerbate-inequalities-in-policing/

Madia, J. (2022). Review of predictive policing and artificial intelligence. *International Journal of Police Science*, 1. https://doi.org/10.56331/487529/ipsa5

Mantri, S. (2023, July 25). Need for responsible AI in policing and crime detection. *Forbes India*. https://www.forbesindia.com/article/isbinsight/need-for-responsible-ai-in-policing-and-crime-detection/86965/1

McCarthy, O. J. (2019, February 28). *Turning the tide on crime with predictive policing – our world*. https://ourworld.unu.edu/en/turning-the-tide-on-crime-with-predictive-policing

McConvey, J. R. (2023, July 17). *Global spike in predictive policing draws on AI and biometrics | biometric update*. https://www.biometricupdate.com/202307/global-spike-in-predictive-policing-draws-on-ai-and-biometrics

McCray, T. (2024, April 1). *Even artificial intelligence thinks public safety in San Francisco needs artificial intelligence*. San Francisco Police Officers Association. https://sfpoa.org/node/1638

McDaniel, J. (2022, August 29). *Predictive policing and artificial intelligence*. Routledge & CRC Press.https://www.routledge.com/Predictive-Policing-and-Artificial-Intelligence/McDaniel-Pease/p/book/9780367701369

Moktali, A. (2023, May 18). *Generative AI data privacy with skyflow LLM privacy vault – skyflow*. https://www.skyflow.com/post/generative-ai-data-privacy-skyflow-llm-privacy-vault?kw=ai%20safety&cpn=21370629960&kw=ai%20safety&cpn=21370629960&utm_term=ai%20safety&utm_campaign=APAC:LI:UC:LLM/AI&utm_source=adwords&utm_medium=ppc&hsa_acc=6575335991&hsa_cam=21370629960&hsa_grp=164320521598&hsa_ad=702191782783&hsa_src=g&hsa_tgt=kwd-302905484122&hsa_kw=ai%20safety&hsa_mt=b&hsa_net=adwords&hsa_ver=3&gad_source=1&gclid=EAIaIQobChMI4qv48dCmiAMVeqRmAh0p5gCeEAMYASAAEgIDbvD_BwE

Momsen, C. (2020, May 19). *Big data-based predictive policing and the changing nature of criminal justice – consequences of the extended use of big data, algorithms and AI in criminal law enforcement – KriPoZ*. https://kripoz.de/2020/05/19/big-data-based-predictive-policing-and-the-changing-nature-of-criminal-justice-consequences-of-the-extended-use-of-big-data-algorithms-and-ai-in-the-area-of-criminal-law-enforcement/

Newton, A., May, X., Eames, S., & Ahmad, M. (n.d.). *Economic and social costs of reoffending*. 2019. https://www.gov.uk/government/publications/economic-and-social-costs-of-reoffending

O'Brien, C. (2024, April 9). Protecting the future: The impact of AI on federal law enforcement. *HS Today*. https://www.hstoday.us/subject-matter-areas/ai-and-advanced-tech/protecting-the-future-the-impact-of-ai-on-federal-law-enforcement/

Owen, S. (2018, January 29). Japan wants to predict crimes – but not like "minority report." *South China Morning Post*. https://www.scmp.com/news/asia/east-asia/article/2130980/japan-trials-ai-assisted-predictive-policing-2020-tokyo-olympics

Ozkan, T., Clipper, S. J., & Wolff. (2019, June 6). *Predicting sexual recidivism—Turgut Ozkan, Stephen J. Clipper, Alex R. Piquero, Michael Baglivio, Kevin Wolff, 2020*. https://journals.sagepub.com/doi/abs/10.1177/1079063219852944

Pearsall, B. (2010). *Predictive policing: The future of law enforcement?* (596372010-007) [Dataset]. https://doi.org/10.1037/e596372010-007

Perle. (2023, May 10). *Beyond the badge: Exploring the potential of AI in law enforcement*. Perle Systems. https://perle.com/articles/beyond-the-badge-exploring-the-potential-of-ai-in-law-enforcement-40196867.shtml

Pingen, A. (2023, March 8). *FRA report on use of AI in predictive policing and offensive speech detection*. https://eucrim.eu/news/fra-report-on-use-of-ai-in-predictive-policing-and-offensive-speech-detection/

Purves, D. (2023, June 13). What's wrong with predictive policing? *Public Ethics*. https://www.publicethics.org/post/what-s-wrong-with-predictive-policing

Salo, B., Laaksonen, T., & Santtila, P. (2019). Predictive power of dynamic (vs. static) risk factors in the finnish risk and needs assessment form. *Criminal Justice and Behavior*, 46(7), 939–960. https://doi.org/10.1177/0093854819848793

Sarmah, H. (2019, October 23). Is predictive policing AI a scam? *AIM*. https://analyticsindiamag.com/ai-origins-evolution/is-predictive-policing-ai-a-scam/

Sarzaeim, P., Mahmoud, Q. H., Azim, A., Bauer, G., & Bowles, I. (2023). A systematic review of using machine learning and natural language processing in smart policing. *Computers, 12*(12), Article 12. https://doi.org/10.3390/computers 12120255

Schiff, K. J, Schiff, D. S., Adams, I. T., McCrain, J., & Mourtgos, S. M. (2023). Institutional factors driving citizen perceptions of AI in government: Evidence from a survey experiment on policing. *Public Administration Review.* https://doi.org/10.1111/puar.13754

Shapiro, A. (2019). Predictive policing for reform? Indeterminacy and intervention in big data policing. *Surveillance & Society, 17*(3–4), 456–472. https://doi.org/10.24908/ss.v17i3/4.10410

Shokeen, M., & Sharma, V. (2023). Artificial intelligence and criminal justice system in India: A critical study. *International Journal of Law, Policy and Social Review, 5*(4), 156–162.

Singh, D. (2022). Policing by design: Artificial intelligence, predictive policing and human rights in South Africa. *Just Africa, 7*(1), 41–52. https://doi.org/10.10520/ejc-ajcj_v7_n1_a7

Singh, A., & Mohapatra, S. (2021). Development of risk assessment framework for first time offenders using ensemble learning. *IEEE Access, 9,* 135024–135033. https://doi.org/10.1109/ACCESS.2021.3116205

Söderholm, S. (2023). Fundamental rights control when implementing predictive policing – a European perspective. *Peking University Law Journal, 11*(1), 91–104. https://doi.org/10.1080/20517483.2023.2223850

Stephens, D. (2024, June 27). Forecasting justice: The promise of AI-enhanced law enforcement.*Police1.*https://www.police1.com/tech-pulse/forecasting-justice-the-promise-of-ai-enhanced-law-enforcement

Ting, M. H., Chu, C. M., Zeng, G., Li, D., & Chng, G. S. (2018). Predicting recidivism among youth offenders: Augmenting professional judgement with machine learning algorithms. *Journal of Social Work, 18*(6), 631–649. https://doi.org/10.1177/1468017317743137

Tolan, S., Miron, M., Gómez, E., & Castillo, C. (2019). Why machine learning may lead to unfairness: Evidence from risk assessment for juvenile justice in Catalonia. *Proceedings of the Seventeenth International Conference on Artificial Intelligence and Law,* 83–92. https://doi.org/10.1145/3322640.3326705

Tollenaar, N., & van der Heijden, P. G. M. (2013). Which method predicts recidivism best? A comparison of statistical, machine learning and data mining predictive models. *Journal of the Royal Statistical Society Series A: Statistics in Society, 176*(2), 565–584. https://doi.org/10.1111/j.1467-985X.2012.01056.x

Tollenaar, N., & van der Heijden, P. G. M. (2019). Optimizing predictive performance of criminal recidivism models using registration data with binary and survival outcomes. *PLOS One, 14*(3), e0213245. https://doi.org/10.1371/journal.pone.0213245

Trials, F. (2022, March 1). AI act: EU must ban predictive AI systems in policing and criminal justice. *Fair Trials.* https://www.fairtrials.org/articles/news/ai-act-eu-must-ban-predictive-ai-systems-in-policing-and-criminal-justice/

Verma, P. (2022, July 15). The never-ending quest to predict crime using AI. *Washington Post.* https://www.washingtonpost.com/technology/2022/07/15/predictive-policing-algorithms-fail/

Verte, V. (2024, April 20). Person-based predictive policing under the AI act. *RAILS – Blog*. https://blog.ai-laws.org/person-based-predictive-policing-under-the-ai-act/

Wahab, M. I. (2018). *Artificial intelligence in policing: Use and drawbacks* [Online post]. https://legalserviceindia.com/legal/article-14787-artificial-intelligence-in-policing-use-and-drawbacks.html

Waller, M. A., & Fawcett, S. E. (2013, June). *Data science, predictive analytics, and big data: A revolution that will transform supply chain design and management | request PDF*. https://www.researchgate.net/publication/264340780_Data_Science_Predictive_Analytics_and_Big_Data_A_Revolution_That_Will_Transform_Supply_Chain_Design_and_Management

White, M. (2024, April 1). The future of AI in policing. *Police Chief Magazine*. https://www.policechiefmagazine.org/the-future-of-ai-in-policing/

Xue, J., Chen, J., & Gelles, R. (2019). Using data mining techniques to examine domestic violence topics on Twitter. *Violence and Gender*, 6(2), 105–114. https://doi.org/10.1089/vio.2017.0066

Ziosi, M., & Pruss, D. (2024). Evidence of what, for whom? The socially contested role of algorithmic bias in a predictive policing tool. *Proceedings of the 2024 ACM Conference on Fairness, Accountability, and Transparency*, 1596–1608. https://doi.org/10.1145/3630106.3658991

6

Neurobiological Foundations of AI: Tracing the Evolution of Neural Networks

Vishwas Gupta

6.1 Introduction

It has been seen in the past few years that the development of sciences, and in particular of sciences such as cognitive psychology and artificial intelligence (AI), has been influenced to a large extent by the computer metaphor. Work in these areas also has been focused on various computational mechanisms (e.g., learning and problem-solving) rather than on the mechanisms found in living organisms. The reasons for this are obvious: computation is the most well understood of all processes, and building a computer is much simpler than building a complex living organism. Not to mention that success in understanding the processes of the mind and brain could lead to developments in AI, which would enable us to significantly increase the intelligence of our machines. There are, however, those who would argue against the pursuit of research in this area.

6.1.1 Definition of Artificial Intelligence

Artificial intelligence (AI) is a field that attempts to model, understand, and replicate intelligent behavior (Sarker, 2022). It is an old and venerable field that has gone through many cycles of hype and subsequent disappointment. The definition of AI as "the study of intelligent agents" has endured, and generally, AI is defined as such because success in the field is often taken to imply the successful construction of a "useful" agent – where an agent is something that perceives and acts upon an environment. The breadth of AI is immeasurable as it is an interdisciplinary field taking in psychology, neuroscience, computer science, information engineering, mathematics, linguistics, and many other fields (Rodgers, 2020). Pursuing the "useful" agent has led to many tools and paradigms – from logic-based systems to connectionist models to embodied robotics, each of which has met with some success. However, none of these tools provides a complete picture of intelligence. There is a great divide in AI between the strong AI camp, which believes it is possible to construct a useful simulation of the mind or brain, and the applied AI camp, which simply wants to produce something useful, e.g., a better diagnostic tool for a medical doctor (Dreyfus, 1992). This has led to a somewhat fractious but fundamentally healthy field due to the constant need to re-evaluate and compare techniques in pursuit of the common goal.

AI also refers to developing computer systems capable of performing tasks that typically require human intelligence (Shabbir & Anwer, 2018). These tasks include learning from data, reasoning, problem-solving, perception, understanding natural language, and interacting with the environment (Sarker, 2022). AI systems utilize algorithms, computational models, and large datasets to analyze patterns, make predictions, and autonomously execute tasks with varying degrees of complexity. Machine learning, a subset of AI, enables systems to learn from experience and improve performance over time without explicit programming (Raschka et al., 2020). Natural language processing (NLP) allows computers to understand, interpret, and generate human language, facilitating communication between humans and machines (Khurana et al., 2023). Computer vision enables machines to perceive and interpret visual information from the surrounding environment. Robotics integrates AI technologies with mechanical systems to create intelligent machines capable of interacting with the physical world. As AI advances, it holds profound implications for numerous industries, transforming how we live, work, and interact with technology.

6.1.2 Importance of Neurobiological Foundations in AI

The importance of neurobiological foundations in AI cannot be overstated, as it provides crucial insights into the fundamental principles underlying cognitive processes and behavior (Pfeifer & Bongard, 2006). By understanding the intricate workings of the brain's neural networks, AI researchers can develop more biologically inspired and efficient algorithms, leading to significant advancements in AI technologies. Neurobiological research offers valuable insights into how neurons communicate, process information, and form complex networks within the brain (Sporns, 2011). By emulating these processes in artificial neural networks, AI systems can better mimic human-like capabilities such as learning, perception, and decision-making. This approach, known as biomimicry, enables AI models to exhibit behaviors and functionalities that closely resemble those observed in biological organisms.

Moreover, studying neurobiology can help overcome challenges in AI development, such as scalability, adaptability, and robustness. The brain's remarkable ability to process vast amounts of data efficiently and flexibly serves as a blueprint for designing AI systems capable of handling complex tasks and adapting to diverse environments (Górriz et al., 2020). In addition, insights from neurobiology can inform the design of neuromorphic hardware, which aims to mimic the brain's architecture and processing capabilities. Neuromorphic computing holds promise for creating AI systems that are more energy-efficient, faster, and capable of parallel processing, thus overcoming some of the limitations of traditional computing architectures (Mehonic et al., 2020).

Furthermore, understanding the neurobiological basis of cognition and behavior can lead to ethical advancements in AI, ensuring that AI systems are developed and deployed responsibly, with considerations for human values, privacy, and safety. Finally, integrating neurobiological principles into AI research and development is essential for unlocking the full potential of AI. By leveraging insights from the brain's neural networks, AI technologies can achieve greater sophistication, efficiency, and human-like capabilities, paving the way for groundbreaking innovations across various domains.

The text aims to fill research gaps by addressing the limitations of current AI models, which are heavily influenced by computational mechanisms rather than the biological processes found in living organisms. It highlights the need for more neurobiologically inspired AI research to create models that better mimic human-like intelligence, learning, and decision-making. In addition, the text points out challenges such as scalability, adaptability, and robustness in current AI systems, suggesting that insights from neurobiology can help overcome these hurdles.

The practical implications of these proposed neurobiological insights for AI development include the potential to create more biologically inspired and efficient algorithms. These insights could enhance AI systems' ability to mimic human cognition, making them more adaptable, scalable, and capable of handling complex tasks. Neuromorphic hardware mimics the brain's architecture and could lead to faster, more energy-efficient AI systems with parallel processing capabilities. Moreover, these advancements can inform ethical AI development, ensuring human values, privacy, and safety are considered in AI deployment. Integrating neurobiological principles could lead to more sophisticated AI technologies, opening new possibilities for innovation across industries.

In this chapter, we will try to find the answers to some basic questions, such as how insights from neurobiology can improve the design and development of AI systems. What are the limitations of current AI models primarily based on computational mechanisms, and how can a neurobiologically inspired approach address these limitations? How can the study of neurobiology inform the development of neuromorphic hardware for AI, and what advantages might this hardware have over traditional computing architectures? How can integrating neurobiological principles into AI development contribute to ethical advancements in AI, particularly regarding human values, privacy, and safety? These research questions aim to clarify the study's objectives, guiding readers through exploring how neurobiology can influence and enhance AI development, addressing both technical and ethical aspects.

6.2 Evolution of Neural Networks

6.2.1 Historical Overview of Neural Networks

Table 6.1 shows the historical overview of neural networks.

6.2.2 Biological Inspiration for Artificial Neural Networks

Biological neural networks, the complex networks of interconnected neurons in the brain, have been a key source of inspiration for designing and developing artificial neural networks (ANNs). The fundamental building block in biological and ANNs is the neuron. In biological systems, neurons receive signals from other neurons through dendrites, process these signals in the cell body, and transmit output signals through axons to other neurons. Artificial neurons, or perceptrons, mimic this process by receiving input signals, applying weights to these inputs, and producing an output signal based on an activation function.

In biological neural networks, neurons are interconnected through synapses and specialized junctions where signals are transmitted between neurons. This concept, known as connectionism, is also fundamental to ANNs. In ANNs, the connections between artificial neurons are represented by weighted connections that influence signal transmission strength.

Biological neural networks can learn and adapt through processes such as synaptic plasticity, where the strength of synaptic connections changes in response to experience. This principle is mirrored in ANNs, which are designed to learn from data through various learning algorithms, including supervised learning, unsupervised learning, and reinforcement learning. These algorithms adjust the weights of connections between neurons to reduce errors and enhance task performance.

The hierarchical and modular organization of biological brains, where different regions specialize in processing specific types of information, has also influenced the development of ANNs. In these networks, layers of neurons process information at various levels of abstraction. For instance, convolutional neural networks (CNNs) are inspired by the brain's hierarchical organization of visual processing and are extensively used for image recognition tasks.

The biological neural networks exhibit parallelism and distributed processing, with vast numbers of neurons working parallel to process information and perform computations. ANNs leverage this principle by utilizing

TABLE 6.1

Historical Overview of Neural Networks

Era	Key Developments
Early Foundations (1940s–1950s)	McCulloch and Pitts introduced artificial neurons and mathematical models for neural computation. Laid the groundwork for early neural network architectures.
Perceptron's and the Perceptron Convergence Theorem (1950s–1960s)	Frank Rosenblatt introduced the perceptron, an artificial neural network for binary classification tasks. Developed the perceptron convergence theorem, demonstrating learning of linearly separable patterns.
The AI Winter (1970s–1980s)	Neural network research faced significant challenges, leading to the "AI winter." Limited computational power, lack of large datasets, and theoretical limitations hindered progress. Decreased funding and interest in the field.
Rebirth of Neural Networks (1980s–1990s)	Resurgence of interest in the development of backpropagation for training multilayer networks. Advancements in parallel computing and larger datasets revitalized research.
Deep Learning Revolution (2000s–Present)	The emergence of deep learning focused on hierarchical data representations. Breakthroughs in training algorithms like deep belief networks and convolutional neural networks (CNNs). Widespread adoption in applications like computer vision, NLP, and speech recognition.
Current Trends and Future Directions	Neural networks power a wide range of AI applications. Focus on challenges like interpretability, scalability, and robustness. Exploration of novel architectures and learning paradigms inspired by biological neural networks.

Source: Author's creation.

the parallel processing capabilities of modern computing hardware, which accelerates training and inference tasks and allows for efficient execution of complex computations.

By drawing on these biological principles, ANNs aim to replicate the remarkable capabilities of biological brains. This enables machines to learn, adapt, and perform intelligent tasks across various domains.

6.2.3 Development of Neural Network Models

Neural network models have evolved through theoretical insights, empirical experimentation, and technological advancements. Researchers have proposed various architectures and learning algorithms to address specific challenges and tasks over the years. The evolution of these models began with Frank Rosenblatt's introduction of single-layer perceptrons in the late 1950s. These early models consisted of a single layer of artificial neurons, known as perceptrons, and could learn linearly separable patterns, primarily for binary classification tasks.

The development of backpropagation in the 1980s marked a significant step forward, enabling the construction of more complex models known as multilayer perceptrons (MLPs). MLPs include multiple layers of artificial neurons, such as an input layer, one or more hidden layers, and an output layer. These models can learn nonlinear relationships and have been applied to tasks like pattern recognition, regression, and classification.

In the 1990s, CNNs were introduced as specialized architectures designed for processing structured grid-like data, such as images. CNNs use convolutional, pooling, and fully connected layers to learn hierarchical representations of visual data. They have achieved remarkable success in image classification, object detection, and image segmentation tasks.

Recurrent neural networks (RNNs) were developed to handle sequential data, such as time series or natural language text. Their architecture contains loops, allowing them to maintain a memory of past inputs and process sequences of arbitrary length. Variants like long short-term memory (LSTM) networks and gated recurrent units (GRUs) were introduced to address the vanishing gradient problem, improving the ability to capture long-range dependencies in sequential data.

A more recent advancement in neural network models is the Generative Adversarial Network (GAN), introduced in 2014 by Ian Goodfellow and colleagues. GANs consist of two neural networks, a generator and a discriminator, trained simultaneously through a minimax game. They can generate realistic synthetic data samples and have been applied to tasks such as image generation, data augmentation, and unsupervised representation learning.

Transformers, introduced in 2017, brought a new approach to NLP tasks. Unlike traditional sequence models like RNNs, transformers rely entirely on self-attention mechanisms to process input sequences in parallel. This architecture has achieved state-of-the-art performance in various NLP tasks, including language translation, text summarization, and language understanding.

These examples represent just a portion of the diverse range of neural network models developed over the years. Continued advances in hardware, software, and algorithmic research drive ongoing innovation in the field, resulting in increasingly sophisticated neural network architectures and techniques.

6.3 Neurobiology and Artificial Intelligence

6.3.1 Understanding the Human Brain

Understanding the human brain is one of science's most fascinating and challenging endeavors. The brain, with its billions of neurons and trillions of connections, serves as the command center for all human thoughts, emotions, behaviors, and bodily functions (Olatunji, 2012). Researchers from various disciplines, including neuroscience, psychology, cognitive science, and AI, are dedicated to unraveling its mysteries. Neuroscientists study the structure and function of the brain at multiple levels, from individual neurons and synapses to complex neural circuits and networks (Bassett & Sporns, 2017). Advanced imaging techniques like functional magnetic resonance imaging (fMRI) and electroencephalography (EEG) allow scientists to observe brain activity in real-time and map out the regions responsible for different cognitive functions.

Psychologists and cognitive scientists investigate how the brain processes information, forms memories, makes decisions, and perceives the world around us. Through behavioral experiments and computational models, they seek to understand the underlying principles of human cognition and behavior (Niv, 2021). AI researchers draw inspiration from the brain's architecture and computational principles to develop intelligent machines that can learn, reason, and adapt like humans (Konar, 2018). By studying the brain, AI scientists aim to replicate its remarkable capabilities in machine learning algorithms and neural network architectures.

Despite significant progress, our understanding of the human brain remains incomplete. Many fundamental questions about consciousness, free will, and the neural basis of complex behaviors remain unanswered. However, with continued interdisciplinary collaboration and technological advancements, we are gradually unlocking the secrets of the brain and gaining deeper insights into what makes us human. Ultimately, a comprehensive understanding of the human brain can revolutionize fields ranging from medicine and education to technology and philosophy, ushering in a new era of innovation and discovery.

6.3.2 Implications of Neurobiology in AI Research

The implications of neurobiology in AI research are profound and multifaceted, as insights from the study of biological neural systems continue to shape the development and advancement of AI. Here are some key implications:

1. Biologically Inspired Algorithms: Neurobiology inspires the design of AI algorithms and architectures (Schuman, 2015). By mimicking

the structure and function of biological neural networks, researchers can develop algorithms that exhibit learning, adaptation, and complex information processing capabilities. For example, deep learning architectures, such as CNNs and RNNs, draw inspiration from the hierarchical organization and recurrent connections observed in the brain.

2. Efficient Learning and Adaptation: Biological neural networks excel at learning from experience and adapting to changing environments. By understanding the mechanisms of synaptic plasticity and neural plasticity, AI researchers can develop algorithms that learn from data efficiently and adaptively. Inspired by reward-based learning in the brain, reinforcement learning enables AI systems to learn optimal decision-making strategies through trial and error.

3. Robustness and Generalization: Biological neural systems exhibit robustness and generalization, allowing them to perform effectively in diverse conditions and contexts (Whitacre, 2012). By studying the principles of regularization and ensemble learning observed in the brain, AI researchers can develop algorithms that generalize well to unseen data and resist noise and adversarial attacks.

4. Neuromorphic Computing: Advances in neurobiology have led to the development of neuromorphic computing systems that emulate the parallelism, low power consumption, and fault tolerance of the brain (James et al., 2017). These systems, which leverage hardware implementations of neural network models, hold promise for accelerating AI computations and achieving greater efficiency in real-world applications.

5. Ethical and Societal Considerations: Neurobiology insights raise ethical and societal considerations in AI research and development. As AI systems become more sophisticated and human-like, questions arise about their impact on privacy, autonomy, and the future of work. Understanding the cognitive and emotional aspects of human intelligence can inform the design of AI systems that are transparent, accountable, and aligned with human values.

The implications of neurobiology in AI research underscore the importance of interdisciplinary collaboration between neuroscience, computer science, and related fields. By leveraging insights from the brain, AI researchers can develop more biologically inspired and human-like intelligent systems that benefit society while addressing ethical and societal concerns.

6.3.3 Neural Network Structures in AI

Neural network structures in AI refer to the architectural configurations of ANNs used to model complex relationships and perform specific tasks. Common neural network structures are shown in Table 6.2.

TABLE 6.2

Neural Network Structures in AI

Neural Network Structure	Description	Structure
Feedforward Neural Networks (FNNs)	The simplest type of neural network is one in which information flows in one direction from input nodes through hidden layers to output nodes, with no loops or feedback connections.	Input Layer → Hidden Layers → Output Layer
Convolutional Neural Networks (CNNs)	Designed for processing structured grid-like data, such as images, using convolutional layers to extract features hierarchically and pooling layers to reduce spatial dimensions.	Input Layer → Convolutional Layers → Pooling Layers → Fully Connected Layers → Output Layer
Recurrent Neural Networks (RNNs)	Suited for sequential data processing with feedback connections, allowing the network to maintain a memory of past inputs.	Input Layer → Hidden Layers with Feedback Connections → Output Layer
Long Short-Term Memory (LSTM) Networks	A type of RNN with specialized memory cells capable of capturing long-range dependencies in sequential data, mitigating the vanishing gradient problem.	Input Layer → LSTM Cells (with Memory) → Hidden Layers → Output Layer
Gated Recurrent Unit (GRU) Networks	Similar to LSTMs, but with simplified gating mechanisms for computational efficiency while still capturing temporal dependencies.	Input Layer → GRU Cells (with Simplified Gates) → Hidden Layers → Output Layer
Autoencoders	Neural networks for unsupervised learning are designed to reconstruct input data. Variants include denoising and variational autoencoders.	Input Layer → Encoder Layers → Bottleneck Layer → Decoder Layers → Output Layer
Generative Adversarial Networks (GANs)	It combines two neural networks, a generator, and a discriminator, and is used for generative modeling by playing a minimax game to generate realistic data samples.	Generator Network → Discriminator Network

Source: Author's creation.

These are just a few examples of neural network structures in AI, each tailored to specific types of data and tasks, with ongoing research leading to the development of increasingly sophisticated architectures.

6.4 Neural Network Learning Algorithms

Neural network learning algorithms include backpropagation, which adjusts weights to minimize errors between predicted and actual outputs; reinforcement learning, where agents learn optimal actions through rewards and penalties; and unsupervised learning, which extracts patterns and features from data without explicit supervision.

6.4.1 Supervised Learning

Supervised learning is a type of machine learning in which the algorithm learns from labeled data consisting of input–output pairs. The algorithm learns to map input data to corresponding output labels by minimizing the difference between predicted and actual outputs, allowing it to make predictions on new, unseen data.

6.4.2 Unsupervised Learning

Unsupervised learning is a type of machine learning where the algorithm learns from unlabeled data without explicit supervision or guidance (Patel, 2019). The algorithm aims to identify patterns, structures, or relationships within the data, allowing it to discover hidden insights or representations autonomously (Janiesch et al., 2021). Unlike supervised learning, where the algorithm learns from labeled input-output pairs, unsupervised learning operates solely on input data, making it useful for clustering, dimensionality reduction, and anomaly detection (Usmani et al., 2022). Examples of unsupervised learning algorithms include k-means clustering, principal component analysis, and autoencoders.

6.4.3 Reinforcement Learning

Reinforcement learning is a type of machine learning where an agent learns to make decisions by interacting with an environment (Kulkarni, 2012). The agent receives feedback in the form of rewards or penalties based on its actions, and its goal is to learn a policy that maximizes cumulative rewards over time. Through trial and error, the agent explores different actions and learns which actions lead to favorable outcomes. Reinforcement learning is commonly used in game playing, robotics, and autonomous systems. Key reinforcement learning components include the agent, environment, actions, rewards, and learning algorithm, such as Q-learning or deep Q-networks.

6.5 Neuroplasticity and Adaptability in AI

Neuroplasticity, the brain's ability to adapt and reorganize in response to experiences, inspires AI algorithms to dynamically adjust and learn from new data (Soltoggio et al., 2018). This adaptability enables AI systems to

Neurobiological Foundations of AI

continuously improve performance, simulate learning processes, and adapt to changing environments, mirroring the brain's flexibility.

6.5.1 Role of Neuroplasticity in the Human Brain

Neuroplasticity, the brain's remarkable ability to reorganize and adapt in response to experiences, is pivotal in shaping human cognition and behavior. This adaptability is fundamental in various aspects of our mental and cognitive functions.

One of neuroplasticity's key roles is in learning and memory formation. It underpins the brain's capacity to acquire new knowledge and skills, enabling us to encode and store memories. Through a process known as synaptic plasticity, the connections between neurons are either strengthened or weakened. This dynamic adjustment facilitates the learning of new information and the formation of lasting memories.

In addition to learning and memory, neuroplasticity is crucial for recovery from injury or damage. Neuroplasticity allows for the reorganization and rewiring of neural circuits when the brain suffers an injury or damage, such as a stroke or traumatic brain injury. This adaptive process helps individuals recover lost functions and compensate for deficits, enabling rehabilitation and functional recovery.

Neuroplasticity also plays a significant role in skill acquisition and the development of expertise. Repeated practice and experience reshapes neural circuits, refining skills and mastery in specific domains. This process, called skill learning, involves optimizing task-related networks and enhancing neural representations related to the skill being developed.

Finally, neuroplasticity is integral to emotional regulation and mental health. It influences the structure and function of brain regions involved in emotional processing, such as the amygdala and prefrontal cortex. While maladaptive neuroplasticity may contribute to psychiatric disorders, targeted interventions that leverage neuroplasticity hold promising potential for therapeutic approaches, offering new avenues for improving mental health and emotional well-being.

Neuroplasticity is a fundamental property of the human brain that underlies learning, adaptation, and recovery processes throughout life. By understanding and harnessing the mechanisms of neuroplasticity, researchers aim to develop interventions to enhance learning and cognition, promote recovery from brain injuries, and improve mental health outcomes.

6.5.2 Implementing Neuroplasticity in Artificial Neural Networks

Implementing neuroplasticity in ANNs involves designing algorithms and architectures that mimic the adaptive capabilities of the brain. Here is how neuroplasticity can be integrated into ANNs:

1. **Synaptic Plasticity:** Incorporate mechanisms for adjusting the strength of connections (synaptic weights) between artificial neurons based on activity patterns (Zheng et al., 2013). Algorithms such as Hebbian learning or spike-timing-dependent plasticity can model synaptic plasticity, strengthening connections, or weakening in response to correlated neural activity.
2. **Dynamic Connectivity:** Design ANNs with dynamic connectivity patterns that can change over time in response to learning and experience (Rafiq et al., 2001). Instead of fixed architectures, allow connections between neurons to form, prune, or reconfigure dynamically based on task requirements or environmental changes.
3. **Learning Rules:** Develop learning rules that promote plasticity and adaptation within ANNs. Instead of relying solely on backpropagation, explore reinforcement learning algorithms or unsupervised learning mechanisms that encourage exploration, novelty, and self-organization, mimicking aspects of neural plasticity.
4. **Structural Plasticity:** Introduce mechanisms for structural plasticity, where the topology or organization of neural networks can evolve (Fauth & Tetzlaff, 2016). This may involve adding or removing neurons or layers, adjusting connectivity patterns, or dynamically allocating resources based on task demands or input statistics.
5. **Experience Replay:** Implement techniques such as experience replay, where past experiences are replayed and incorporated into the learning process. This allows ANNs to consolidate knowledge, generalize across tasks, and adapt to changes in the environment more effectively.
6. **Neuromodulation:** Incorporate neuromodulatory signals or mechanisms into ANNs to regulate plasticity processes (Avery & Krichmar, 2017). Neuromodulators such as dopamine, serotonin, or acetylcholine can modulate synaptic strength, excitability, or network dynamics, influencing learning, memory, and attentional processes.

We can develop more adaptive, robust, and flexible learning systems that can learn from experience, generalize across tasks, and autonomously adapt to changes in the environment, much like the human brain.

6.5.3 Benefits and Challenges of Adaptive AI Systems

Adaptive AI systems present a range of benefits that make them increasingly valuable across various applications, although they also encounter notable challenges.

One of the primary benefits of adaptive AI systems is their flexibility. These systems can modify their behavior in response to changing environments, tasks, or user preferences, enabling them to maintain optimal performance across diverse and evolving conditions. This adaptability ensures that the systems remain effective and relevant as circumstances shift.

Another significant advantage is personalization. Adaptive AI systems can tailor recommendations, content, or services based on individual user behaviors and preferences. This personalized approach enhances user satisfaction and engagement by providing a more relevant and customized experience.

In terms of efficiency, adaptive AI systems optimize resource allocation, task scheduling, and decision-making processes. These systems can improve overall efficiency and resource utilization by leveraging real-time data, making operations more streamlined and effective.

Robustness is another key benefit of adaptive AI systems. They are designed to be resilient to uncertainties, noise, and adversarial attacks. Their ability to adapt and self-correct in the face of unexpected events or perturbations ensures continued functionality and accuracy, even under challenging conditions.

Lastly, adaptive AI systems are characterized by their continuous learning capabilities. They can incrementally learn from new data and experiences, allowing them to evolve over time. This ongoing learning process helps them stay relevant and effective in dynamic environments.

Adaptive AI systems offer numerous benefits, including flexibility, personalization, efficiency, and robustness. However, they also face significant challenges that must be addressed to fully realize their potential and ensure their responsible deployment.

One major challenge is data quality and bias. Adaptive AI systems depend heavily on high-quality data for effective learning and adaptation. Issues such as poor data quality, biased datasets, or insufficient data can lead to inaccurate or unfair decisions, which undermine the system's reliability and trustworthiness.

Interpretability is another critical challenge. As adaptive AI systems become more complex and dynamic, understanding and interpreting their decisions or behaviors becomes increasingly difficult. This lack of interpretability can impede accountability, transparency, and user trust, making it harder to validate and justify the system's outputs.

Overfitting and generalization are also concerns. Adaptive AI systems might overfit to specific training data or contexts, which can result in poor generalization and degraded performance when faced with new or unseen data. Striking a balance between adaptation and generalization is essential to ensure that these systems maintain robust and reliable performance across various scenarios.

Ethical considerations pose significant challenges as well. Adaptive AI systems raise concerns related to privacy, autonomy, and fairness. The way these systems adapt based on user behavior or preferences might infringe on privacy rights or perpetuate biases and discrimination if not managed properly. Ensuring that these systems operate ethically is crucial for maintaining trust and equity.

Finally, the computational complexity involved in implementing adaptive AI systems with real-time adaptation capabilities is substantial. These systems require significant computational resources, including processing power, memory, and energy consumption. Addressing scalability and efficiency is essential, particularly in resource-constrained environments.

In summary, while adaptive AI systems bring valuable benefits, addressing challenges related to data quality, interpretability, overfitting, ethical considerations, and computational complexity is vital. This will help in realizing their full potential and ensuring their responsible and effective deployment in real-world applications.

6.6 Neural Network Architectures

Neural network architectures are configurations of interconnected artificial neurons used for modeling complex relationships and performing specific tasks. Common architectures include feedforward, convolutional, recurrent, and generative adversarial networks, each tailored to different types of data and tasks, with ongoing research driving the development of new architectures.

6.6.1 Feedforward Neural Networks

FNNs are the simplest type of ANN, where information flows in one direction, from input nodes through hidden layers to output nodes, with no loops or feedback connections. They consist of multiple layers of artificial neurons, including an input layer, one or more hidden layers, and an output layer. FNNs are commonly used for tasks such as regression, classification, and pattern recognition.

6.6.2 Recurrent Neural Networks

RNNs are a type of ANN designed for sequential data processing (Medsker & Jain, 1999). Unlike FNNs, RNNs have connections that form directed cycles, allowing them to maintain a memory of past inputs. This recurrent connectivity enables RNNs to capture temporal dependencies and process sequences of arbitrary length. RNNs are commonly used in NLP, speech recognition, time-series prediction, and other tasks where sequential information is crucial.

6.6.3 Convolutional Neural Networks

CNNs are a type of ANN specifically designed for processing structured grid-like data, such as images (Khan et al., 2020). CNNs leverage convolutional layers to extract features hierarchically from the input data. These layers apply convolution operations, followed by nonlinear activation functions, to small regions of the input, allowing the network to learn spatial hierarchies of features. Pooling layers are often used to reduce spatial dimensions and capture the most salient information. CNNs have achieved remarkable success in tasks such as image classification, object detection, and image segmentation.

6.7 Neural Network Applications in AI

Neural networks find wide applications in AI, including image and speech recognition, NLP, autonomous vehicles, medical diagnosis, finance, and robotics (Goel et al., 2023). Their ability to learn complex patterns from data enables sophisticated tasks like real-time decision-making, language translation, and autonomous control, revolutionizing various industries and domains.

6.7.1 Image and Speech Recognition

Image and speech recognition are two key applications of neural networks in AI:

1. **Image Recognition:** CNNs are commonly used for image recognition tasks. They can automatically identify objects, people, places, and scenes within images, enabling applications such as facial recognition, object detection, image classification, and medical image analysis.
2. **Speech Recognition:** RNNs and CNNs are utilized for speech recognition tasks. These networks can transcribe spoken language into text, enabling applications such as virtual assistants, dictation systems, voice-controlled devices, and speech-to-text conversion for accessibility purposes.

Neural networks in both cases learn from large datasets of labeled examples, adjusting their internal parameters (weights and biases) through training to improve their accuracy in recognizing patterns and making predictions. These technologies have become increasingly sophisticated, with deep learning architectures achieving state-of-the-art performance in image and speech recognition tasks, driving advancements in various industries including healthcare, automotive, entertainment, and communication.

6.7.2 Natural Language Processing

NLP involves the use of neural networks and other AI techniques to analyze, understand, and generate human language. Neural networks play a crucial role in various NLP tasks, as shown in Table 6.3.

Neural networks in NLP learn from large text corpora, capturing complex linguistic patterns and semantic relationships to perform various tasks accurately. NLP applications are prevalent in virtual assistants, customer service automation, information retrieval systems, and content generation, among others, driving advancements in human-computer interaction and language understanding.

6.7.3 Robotics and Autonomous Systems

Neural networks play a crucial role in robotics and autonomous systems, enabling them to perceive, reason, and act in dynamic environments. Here's how neural networks are used in robotics and autonomous systems:

TABLE 6.3

Neural Networks and Natural Language Processing

Task	Neural Network Models	Description
Text Classification	Convolutional Neural Networks (CNNs), Recurrent Neural Networks (RNNs)	Used for sentiment analysis, spam detection, topic classification, and document categorization
Named Entity Recognition (NER)	RNNs, CNNs	Employed to identify and classify named entities such as names of people, organizations, and locations.
Machine Translation	Sequence-to-Sequence Models (Recurrent, Transformer)	Utilized for translating text from one language to another, as seen in systems like Google Translate.
Text Generation	RNNs, Long Short-Term Memory (LSTM) Networks, Generative Adversarial Networks (GANs)	Generates human-like text for applications such as chatbots, language modeling, and story generation.
Question Answering	Attention-Based Models, Various Neural Networks	Extracts relevant information from text documents to answer user queries.
Text Summarization	Sequence-to-Sequence Models (Transformer-based architectures like Bidirectional Encoder Representations from Transformers or Generative Pre-trained Transformer)	Generates concise summaries of longer documents.

Source: Author's own creation.

1. **Perception:** CNNs are used for visual perception tasks, allowing robots to recognize objects, people, and obstacles in their environment (Ashiq et al., 2022). RNNs and LSTMs are used for processing sensor data, such as lidar or radar readings, to understand spatial relationships and detect patterns over time.
2. **Localization and Mapping:** Neural networks are used for simultaneous localization and mapping, where robots build maps of their surroundings and estimate their own position within these maps (Saeedi et al., 2011). Neural network–based multiple robot simultaneous localization and mapping. Graph neural networks and recurrent architectures are used to fuse sensor data and perform localization and mapping tasks in real-time.
3. **Motion Planning and Control**: Neural networks are used to plan and control the motion of robotic systems, enabling them to navigate through complex environments, avoid obstacles, and perform manipulation tasks. Reinforcement learning algorithms are used to learn optimal control policies, while imitation learning techniques allow robots to mimic human demonstrations.

The neural networks in robotics and autonomous systems enable robots to perceive their surroundings, make informed decisions, and execute tasks autonomously, paving the way for applications in areas such as manufacturing, logistics, healthcare, agriculture, and space exploration.

6.8 Ethical Considerations in AI Development

Ethical considerations in AI development include fairness, transparency, privacy, accountability, and safety. Developers must address biases in datasets and algorithms, ensure transparency and explainability of AI systems, protect user privacy, establish accountability mechanisms, and prioritize safety to mitigate potential risks and ensure responsible AI deployment.

6.8.1 Bias and Fairness in Neural Networks

Bias and fairness in neural networks concern the tendency of these systems to produce or perpetuate discriminatory outcomes based on characteristics such as race, gender, or socioeconomic status. These biases can arise from skewed training data or inherent algorithmic biases, leading to unfair treatment of individuals or groups. To address bias and promote fairness in neural networks, several key strategies are essential.

First, data collection and labeling must be meticulously managed to ensure that training data is diverse, representative, and free from bias. Careful attention to the selection and labeling of data helps to mitigate the risk of reinforcing stereotypes or discriminatory patterns, thus promoting a more equitable model.

Second, bias detection and mitigation techniques are crucial. This involves analyzing model outputs for disparities across different demographic groups and making necessary adjustments to algorithms or training data to enhance fairness. By actively identifying and addressing biases, models can be refined to reduce unfair outcomes.

Fairness metrics play a significant role in this process. Defining and evaluating metrics such as disparate impact, equal opportunity, and demographic parity allow for a systematic assessment of a model's fairness and equity. These metrics provide quantifiable measures to monitor and improve fairness outcomes over time.

Promoting algorithmic transparency is also critical. Enhancing the transparency and explainability of neural network models helps to understand how decisions are made and uncover potential sources of bias. Techniques such as interpretable model architectures and post-hoc explanation methods contribute to shedding light on model behavior, facilitating better insights into its fairness.

Also, fostering diverse representation within AI development teams is essential. A broad range of perspectives and experiences ensures that biases are more readily identified and addressed. Diverse teams are better equipped to consider various viewpoints and challenges, leading to more equitable and effective AI systems.

Addressing bias and promoting fairness in neural networks is fundamental to ensuring equitable outcomes and mitigating potential harm to individuals or groups affected by algorithmic decision-making. Ongoing research and collaboration are necessary to develop robust techniques and frameworks that achieve fairness in AI systems.

6.8.2 Privacy and Data Security

Privacy and data security are critical considerations in the development and deployment of neural networks and AI systems. Addressing these concerns involves several key strategies. First, data protection is paramount, requiring the implementation of measures like encryption, access controls, and data anonymization techniques to safeguard personal data. This prevents unauthorized access or disclosure, ensuring that privacy is maintained. In addition, privacy-preserving techniques such as federated learning, differential privacy, and homomorphic encryption are employed. These methods allow collaborative training on decentralized data sources while preserving individual user privacy.

Compliance with data protection regulations, such as the General Data Protection Regulation and the California Consumer Privacy Act, is also essential.

FIGURE 6.1
Components of data privacy and security

These regulations impose requirements for data handling, user consent, and transparency, which must be strictly adhered to. Ethical data use is another crucial aspect, involving adherence to responsible data use principles, minimizing data collection, obtaining informed consent from users, and ensuring transparency and accountability in data processing practices.

To further enhance security, implementing secure infrastructure and best practices for system design, software development, and network security is necessary to protect against data breaches, cyberattacks, and unauthorized access to sensitive information. Continuous monitoring and auditing of AI systems and data processing pipelines are also important to detect and mitigate security vulnerabilities, data breaches, and compliance violations. This ensures ongoing protection of user privacy and data security (Figure 6.1).

By addressing privacy and data security concerns effectively, organizations can build trust in neural networks and AI systems. Protecting user rights and mitigating the risks of data misuse or unauthorized access are essential for fostering user confidence in AI technologies. Implementing robust privacy and security measures ensures responsible AI deployment and demonstrates a commitment to safeguarding personal information.

6.8.3 Responsibility and Accountability in AI Systems

Responsibility and accountability in AI systems involve ensuring that developers, operators, and users are aware of and accountable for the ethical and legal implications of AI technology. Key considerations include:

1. **Ethical Frameworks:** Establishing ethical guidelines and principles for the development, deployment, and use of AI systems, addressing concerns such as fairness, transparency, privacy, bias, and safety.
2. **Legal Compliance:** Ensuring compliance with relevant laws, regulations, and standards governing AI technology, including data

protection, anti-discrimination, intellectual property, and product liability laws.
3. **Transparency and Explainability:** Promoting transparency and explainability in AI systems to understand how decisions are made, enable accountability, and facilitate trust among users and stakeholders.
4. **Risk Assessment and Mitigation:** Conducting risk assessments to identify potential ethical, social, and legal risks associated with AI systems, and implementing measures to mitigate these risks and prevent harm to individuals or society.
5. **Human Oversight and Control:** Maintaining human oversight and control over AI systems, particularly in high-stakes applications such as healthcare, finance, and criminal justice, to ensure accountability and intervene in cases of errors or malfunctions.
6. **User Education and Empowerment:** Educating users about the capabilities, limitations, and implications of AI technology, empowering them to make informed decisions and advocate for responsible AI use.
7. **Organizational Responsibility:** Holding organizations accountable for the ethical and responsible use of AI technology, including establishing internal governance structures, policies, and processes to ensure compliance with ethical and legal standards.
8. **Regulatory Oversight:** Promoting regulatory oversight and accountability mechanisms to enforce compliance with ethical and legal standards, investigate complaints or violations, and impose sanctions or penalties for noncompliance.

By promoting responsibility and accountability in AI systems, stakeholders can ensure that AI technology is developed and used in a manner that aligns with ethical principles, respects human rights, and benefits society as a whole (Figure 6.2).

6.9 Future Directions in Neurobiologically Inspired AI

Future directions in neurobiologically inspired AI include developing brain-like architectures, spiking neural networks, and neuromorphic hardware. Emphasis on unsupervised learning, continual learning, and cognitive architectures aims to achieve more efficient, adaptable, and human-like AI systems while addressing ethical and societal implications.

Neurobiological Foundations of AI

FIGURE 6.2
Key considerations for responsibility and accountability

6.9.1 Neuromorphic Computing

Neuromorphic computing involves designing hardware architectures that emulate the parallelism, low power consumption, and fault tolerance of the brain (Roy et al., 2019). Future directions include developing neuromorphic chips with spiking neural networks, enabling efficient and scalable implementations of AI algorithms for tasks such as pattern recognition and real-time processing.

6.9.2 Brain–Computer Interfaces

Brain–computer interfaces (BCIs) enable direct communication between the brain and external devices, facilitating control, communication, and interaction without traditional input methods (He et al., 2020). Future directions involve enhancing BCI technology for medical applications like prosthetics and neurorehabilitation, as well as exploring potential for augmenting human capabilities and enabling new forms of human–computer interaction, such as thought-based control and enhanced cognitive function.

6.9.3 Integration of AI and Neuroscience Research

The integration of AI and neuroscience research involves leveraging insights from neuroscience to inform the design and development of more biologically inspired AI algorithms and systems. Future directions include using AI to analyze complex neural data, simulate brain circuits, and model cognitive processes, facilitating discoveries in neuroscience while advancing the development of AI technologies with improved efficiency, adaptability, and human-like intelligence.

6.9.4 Neurosymbolic AI

Integrating symbolic reasoning and logic with neural network models to combine the strengths of connectionist and symbolic AI approaches, enabling AI systems to reason abstractly and perform complex cognitive tasks.

6.9.5 Cognitive Architectures

Developing cognitive architectures that model higher-level cognitive functions such as perception, attention, memory, and decision-making, to achieve more human-like intelligence in AI systems.

6.10 Case Studies

There are some case studies demonstrating the successful application of neurobiological principles in AI, highlighting unique insights and tangible benefits:

1. **DeepMind's AlphaGo**

   Overview: AlphaGo, developed by DeepMind, is an AI program designed to play the board game Go. It successfully defeated top human players, showcasing its advanced decision-making capabilities.

   Neurobiological Principle Applied: AlphaGo combines deep neural networks with reinforcement learning, mimicking the way the human brain learns from experience. The neural networks used in AlphaGo are inspired by the structure and function of the brain's neural connections, allowing the AI to evaluate complex board positions and make strategic decisions.

   Unique Insights: AlphaGo's success demonstrated the power of combining neurobiologically inspired learning mechanisms with advanced computational algorithms. It provided insights into how neural networks can be trained to handle high-dimensional and complex decision-making tasks.

Tangible Benefits: This application has advanced AI research in fields requiring strategic thinking and decision-making, such as financial modeling and autonomous systems, by proving the effectiveness of neurobiologically inspired reinforcement learning.

2. **Neuromorphic Hardware – IBM's TrueNorth Chip**

   Overview: IBM developed the TrueNorth chip, a neuromorphic computing architecture inspired by the brain's structure. It uses a network of neurons and synapses to process information, mimicking the parallel processing capabilities of the human brain.

   Neurobiological Principle Applied: TrueNorth uses a digital design that emulates the event-driven nature of neural spikes, similar to how neurons in the brain fire in response to stimuli. This allows for high-speed, low-power processing.

   Unique Insights: The chip demonstrated that neurobiological principles could be translated into hardware design, creating systems that are not only efficient but also capable of handling complex tasks such as pattern recognition and sensory data processing.

   Tangible Benefits: Neuromorphic hardware like TrueNorth offers significant energy efficiency and speed advantages over traditional computing systems. This has applications in fields like robotics, where real-time processing and low power consumption are critical.

3. **CNNs and Visual Recognition**

   Overview: CNNs have become a cornerstone of visual recognition in AI, used in applications such as image classification, facial recognition, and autonomous vehicles.

   Neurobiological Principle Applied: CNNs are inspired by the visual processing pathways in the human brain, particularly the hierarchical structure of the visual cortex. They use layers of convolutional filters to mimic the way the brain processes visual information, from simple edges to complex patterns.

   Unique Insights: The success of CNNs has shown how layering and hierarchical processing, concepts derived from neurobiology, can significantly enhance an AI system's ability to interpret visual data accurately.

   Tangible Benefits: CNNs have led to breakthroughs in medical imaging, enabling more accurate diagnosis of diseases through pattern recognition in radiology images. They have also enhanced the capabilities of autonomous vehicles in understanding and navigating their surroundings.

6.11 Conclusion

The integration of AI and neuroscience represents a promising frontier, merging insights from two distinct yet complementary disciplines to drive innovation and understanding. By drawing inspiration from the brain's remarkable capabilities, researchers in AI can develop more biologically inspired algorithms and systems capable of learning, reasoning, and adapting in a manner akin to human cognition. This collaboration not only enriches AI technology but also deepens our understanding of the brain's intricate mechanisms and functions. Through neural network models, BCIs, and neuromorphic computing, AI researchers aim to replicate and harness the brain's efficiency, robustness, and adaptability. Concurrently, neuroscience benefits from AI techniques in analyzing complex neural data, simulating brain circuits, and modeling cognitive processes, offering new insights into brain function and disorders. Ethical considerations, such as privacy, bias, and accountability, remain paramount in this endeavor, ensuring responsible development and deployment of AI systems inspired by neuroscience. As these fields continue to converge, the potential for groundbreaking discoveries and transformative applications across healthcare, technology, and society is vast, promising a future where AI and neuroscience together unlock the mysteries of the mind and advance humanity's collective knowledge and capabilities.

References

Ashiq, F., Asif, M., Ahmad, M. B., Zafar, S., Masood, K., Mahmood, T., . . . Lee, I. H. (2022). CNN-based object recognition and tracking system to assist visually impaired people. *IEEE Access*, 10, 14819–14834.

Avery, M. C., & Krichmar, J. L. (2017). Neuromodulatory systems and their interactions: A review of models, theories, and experiments. *Frontiers in Neural Circuits*, 11, 108.

Bassett, D. S., & Sporns, O. (2017). Network neuroscience. *Nature Neuroscience*, 20(3), 353–364.

Dreyfus, H. L. (1992). *What computers still can't do: A critique of artificial reason.* MIT Press.

Fauth, M., & Tetzlaff, C. (2016). Opposing effects of neuronal activity on structural plasticity. *Frontiers in Neuroanatomy*, 10, 75.

Goel, A., Goel, A. K., & Kumar, A. (2023). The role of artificial neural network and machine learning in utilizing spatial information. *Spatial Information Research*, 31(3), 275–285.

Górriz, J. M., Ramírez, J., Ortíz, A., Martinez-Murcia, F. J., Segovia, F., Suckling, J., . . . Ferrandez, J. M. (2020). Artificial intelligence within the interplay between natural and artificial computation: Advances in data science, trends, and applications. *Neurocomputing*, 410, 237–270.

He, B., Yuan, H., Meng, J., & Gao, S. (2020). Brain-computer interfaces. *Neural Engineering*, 131–183.

James, C. D., Aimone, J. B., Miner, N. E., Vineyard, C. M., Rothganger, F. H., Carlson, K. D., ... Plimpton, S. J. (2017). A historical survey of algorithms and hardware architectures for neural-inspired and neuromorphic computing applications. *Biologically Inspired Cognitive Architectures*, 19, 49–64.

Janiesch, C., Zschech, P., & Heinrich, K. (2021). Machine learning and deep learning. *Electronic Markets*, 31(3), 685–695.

Khan, A., Sohail, A., Zahoora, U., & Qureshi, A. S. (2020). A survey of the recent architectures of deep convolutional neural networks. *Artificial Intelligence Review*, 53, 5455–5516.

Khurana, D., Koli, A., Khatter, K., & Singh, S. (2023). Natural language processing: State of the art, current trends, and challenges. *Multimedia Tools and Applications*, 82(3), 3713–3744.

Konar, A. (2018). *Artificial intelligence and soft computing: Behavioral and cognitive modeling of the human brain*. CRC Press.

Kulkarni, P. (2012). *Reinforcement and systemic machine learning for decision making* (Vol. 1). John Wiley & Sons.

Medsker, L., & Jain, L. C. (Eds.). (1999). *Recurrent neural networks: Design and applications*. CRC Press.

Mehonic, A., Sebastian, A., Rajendran, B., Simeone, O., Vasilaki, E., & Kenyon, A. J. (2020). Memristors – from in-memory computing, deep learning acceleration, and spiking neural networks to the future of neuromorphic and bio-inspired computing. *Advanced Intelligent Systems*, 2(11), 2000085.

Niv, Y. (2021). The primacy of behavioral research for understanding the brain. *Behavioral Neuroscience*, 135(5), 601.

Olatunji, L. A. (2012). *Your brain; your power: A scientific guide to mental empowerment throughout life*. AuthorHouse.

Patel, A. A. (2019). *Hands-on unsupervised learning using Python: How to build applied machine learning solutions from unlabeled data*. O'Reilly Media.

Pfeifer, R., & Bongard, J. (2006). *How the body shapes the way we think: A new view of intelligence*. MIT Press.

Rafiq, M. Y., Bugmann, G., & Easterbrook, D. J. (2001). Neural network design for engineering applications. *Computers & Structures*, 79(17), 1541–1552.

Raschka, S., Patterson, J., & Nolet, C. (2020). Machine learning in Python: Main developments and technology trends in data science, machine learning, and artificial intelligence. *Information*, 11(4), 193.

Rodgers, W. (2020). *Artificial intelligence in a throughput model: Some major algorithms*. CRC Press.

Roy, K., Jaiswal, A., & Panda, P. (2019). Towards spike-based machine intelligence with neuromorphic computing. *Nature*, 575(7784), 607–617.

Saeedi, S., Paull, L., Trentini, M., & Li, H. (2011). Neural network-based multiple robot simultaneous localization and mapping. *IEEE Transactions on Neural Networks*, 22(12), 2376–2387.

Sarker, I. H. (2022). AI-based modeling: Techniques, applications, and research issues towards automation, intelligent and smart systems. *SN Computer Science*, 3(2), 158.

Schuman, C. D. (2015). *Neuroscience-inspired dynamic architectures*. PhD diss., University of Tennessee. https://trace.tennessee.edu/utk_graddiss/3361

Shabbir, J., & Anwer, T. (2018). *Artificial intelligence and its role in near future*. arXiv preprint arXiv:1804.01396.

Soltoggio, A., Stanley, K. O., & Risi, S. (2018). Born to learn: The inspiration, progress, and future of evolved plastic artificial neural networks. *Neural Networks*, 108, 48–67.

Sporns, O. (2011). The human connectome: A complex network. *Annals of the New York Academy of Sciences*, 1224(1), 109–125.

Usmani, U. A., Happonen, A., & Watada, J. (2022, July). A review of unsupervised machine learning frameworks for anomaly detection in industrial applications. In *Science and Information Conference* (pp. 158–189). Cham: Springer International Publishing.

Whitacre, J. M. (2012). Biological robustness: Paradigms, mechanisms, and systems principles. *Frontiers in Genetics*, 3, 67.

Zheng, P., Dimitrakakis, C., & Triesch, J. (2013). Network self-organization explains the statistics and dynamics of synaptic connection strengths in cortex. *PLoS Computational Biology*, 9(1), e1002848.

7
The Urgency of Artificial Intelligence (AI) for the Enhancement of Maritime Cultural Heritage Management in Indonesia

Hutomo Putra

7.1 Introduction

With its archipelagic expanse and storied maritime history, Indonesia boasts a wealth of cultural heritage embedded in the intricate tapestry of its coastal landscapes. These include physical artifacts, such as shipwrecks and historic port cities, and intangible cultural heritage, such as traditional navigation techniques and maritime folklore. The maritime cultural heritage of Indonesia is a testament to centuries of seafaring traditions, trade routes, and historical interactions (Adhuri, 2018). Preserving this rich heritage is a matter of national pride and a crucial endeavor to ensure the continuity of cultural legacies for future generations.

The imperative of incorporating artificial intelligence (AI) in maritime cultural heritage management in Indonesia is underscored by its potential to enhance preservation efforts significantly. Indonesia's maritime cultural heritage is vast and multifaceted, encompassing many artifacts, shipwrecks, underwater archaeological sites, and coastal settlements, all deeply intertwined with the nation's historical identity. This heritage's sheer scale and diversity present enormous documentation, conservation, and ongoing management challenges. With their data processing capabilities and pattern recognition algorithms, AI technologies offer streamlined cataloging processes, ensuring accuracy in managing various artifacts, shipwrecks, and cultural sites. This efficiency is crucial for handling the intricacies and scale of Indonesia's maritime heritage.

The utilization of AI in maritime cultural heritage management holds profound implications for preserving and understanding Indonesia's rich and diverse maritime heritage. As a nation endowed with a wealth of maritime cultural treasures, ranging from ancient shipwrecks to coastal archaeological sites, Indonesia faces the challenge of effectively managing and conserving these invaluable assets (Hardjoko, 2017). These treasures, which include ancient shipwrecks, submerged archaeological sites, historical coastal settlements, and traditional maritime practices, represent not only the historical and cultural identity of the Indonesian people but also the broader narrative of human civilization and its relationship with the sea. This discussion explores the urgency of incorporating AI technologies to enhance the management practices associated with Indonesia's maritime cultural heritage, addressing the complexities and opportunities presented by this intersection of technology and cultural preservation.

7.2 The Current Management of Maritime Cultural Heritage in Indonesia

The historic shipwrecks and their material cargoes in Indonesia face imminent threats of permanent damage and disappearance, primarily due to persistent challenges in undertaking effective Underwater Cultural Heritage (UCH) management. Issues such as looting, salvaging, and treasure hunting persist, posing ongoing risks. In addition, the Government of Indonesia's sea toll development, aimed at enhancing maritime connectivity, introduces potential harm to these submerged cultural assets (Putra, 2019). Expanding shipping lanes, dredging activities, and constructing new ports can inadvertently damage or destroy historic shipwrecks and their material cargoes. The lack of comprehensive UCH impact assessments in such projects' planning and implementation phases exacerbates the risk of irreversible harm to these cultural sites. This underscores the need for more integrated approaches to development planning that consider preserving cultural heritage alongside economic objectives.

The dynamic nature of climate change and natural disasters further complicates the preservation efforts, categorizing historic shipwrecks and their material cargo as endangered cultural heritage. Rising sea levels, increasing ocean temperatures, and the intensification of storms and other natural disasters pose significant threats to UCH. Coastal erosion and shifting seabed sediments, driven by changing climatic conditions, can expose shipwrecks to the elements, accelerating their deterioration. In addition, more frequent and severe weather events, such as typhoons and tsunamis, can physically damage or displace submerged artifacts, further endangering these fragile cultural sites. The compounded effects of climate change make it increasingly difficult to predict and manage the risks to UCH, necessitating adopting more resilient and adaptive conservation strategies.

Indonesia's rich maritime history is mirrored in its extensive UCH, including many historic shipwrecks and their material cargoes scattered across the archipelago. However, commercial salvage operations and illegal looting have long threatened this invaluable heritage, a persistent problem in the country. Commercial salvage, driven by the high value of artifacts recovered from shipwrecks, has been documented in various years, with significant instances reported in 1990, 1999, 2002, 2005, 2006, 2008, 2009, and 2010. These activities often occur in Indonesia's vast and largely unregulated waters, where salvagers recover artifacts not for their historical or cultural significance but for profit. This commercialization of cultural heritage has led to the destruction of archaeological sites and the irreversible loss of historical context, which is crucial for understanding Indonesia's maritime past.

Against this backdrop of ongoing threats to UCH, Indonesia has sought to redefine its maritime identity on the global stage. Since 2014, Indonesia has aimed to position itself as the international maritime fulcrum, emphasizing maritime development, economy, connectivity, diplomacy, and security (Al Syahrin, 2018; Diposaptono, 2017). This ambitious initiative reflects Indonesia's recognition of its geographic and strategic advantages as an archipelagic nation at the crossroads of major global shipping routes. The sea toll development, a crucial component of this vision, involves deepening sea channels, constructing principal and sub-feeder harbors, and connecting regions from west to east. However, this program raises concerns about potential harm to undiscovered underwater archaeological remains along the sea toll development route, contradicting the broader goals of maritime fulcrum development (Putra, 2019). The expansion of marine infrastructure, particularly in areas not thoroughly surveyed for cultural resources, poses a risk to undiscovered underwater archaeological remains. The potential harm to these undiscovered sites starkly contrasts the broader goals of the maritime fulcrum development, which include preserving and promoting Indonesia's maritime heritage as a cornerstone of its national identity.

In the long-term development plan for Indonesia 2045, known as Golden Indonesia, cultural aspects emerge as a key element. The plan envisions contributing cultural values to development by capitalizing on national cultural noble values and enhancing a work ethic. This underscores the pivotal role of culture as a top priority in Indonesia's overall development plan, encompassing UCH assets. The legal framework established in the 1945 Indonesian Constitution further reinforces the importance of culture in Indonesia's development. Article 32, paragraph (1) of the Constitution mandates the State to promote national culture within the context of global civilization actively. This includes ensuring the freedom of society to maintain and develop cultural values, emphasizing the preservation of cultural heritage to strengthen national identity, elevate the nation's dignity, enhance people's welfare, and promote the nation's cultural heritage globally. Consequently, safeguarding the values embedded in underwater material cultural remains is integral to achieving the overarching goal of preserving heritage culture in Indonesia. This commitment to culture strengthens national identity and enhances

Indonesia's standing on the global stage, contributing to the nation's dignity and prosperity.

The UCH management domain, administered by the Cultural Heritage Protection Division, is entrenched in scholarly investigation and entails the protracted preservation and conservation of submerged cultural assets. This division operates within the purview of two legislative frameworks, specifically Law No. 5/1992 of Objects of Cultural Heritage and Law No. 11/2010 on Cultural Heritage Protection. The antecedent legislation, promulgated in 1992, was subsequently succeeded by the latter in 2010, a response precipitated by the imperatives of fortifying protections against commercial salvaging endeavors targeting historical shipwrecks. Law No. 11/2010 on Cultural Heritage Protection heralded a substantive paradigm shift prompted by the concerted efforts of the Cultural Heritage Protection and Preservation Unit to stem the illicit trade of materials extracted from historical shipwrecks. Coeval with the enactment of this legislation, the Cultural Heritage Protection Division initiated a moratorium, suspending all commercial survey and salvage activities in Indonesian waters for an indeterminate duration.

The management of UCH in Indonesia, overseen by the Cultural Heritage Protection Division, is deeply rooted in scholarly research and focuses on the long-term preservation and conservation of submerged cultural assets. This division operates under the guidance of two key legislative frameworks: Law No. 5/1992 on Objects of Cultural Heritage and Law No. 11/2010 on Cultural Heritage Protection. The earlier legislation, enacted in 1992, laid the groundwork for protecting cultural heritage objects in Indonesia. However, as the challenges of preserving UCH evolved, it became clear that stronger protections were needed, particularly to combat the increasing threats posed by commercial salvage operations targeting historical shipwrecks.

This law marked a significant shift in the country's approach to safeguarding its cultural heritage, including the valuable artifacts and historical remains in its waters. It was driven by the need to enhance protections against the exploitation of underwater cultural sites and address the illicit trade of materials recovered from them. The extant legislation, Law No. 11/2010 on Cultural Heritage Protection, intricately delineates the protocols for safeguarding and conserving material cultures derived from historic shipwrecks in Indonesia. Provision No. 26 articulates four specific statements about procedures governing cultural heritage survey and excavation within this legal framework. These provisions underscore:

1. The Government assumes responsibility for discovering and locating artifacts, monuments, structures, and/or locales deemed cultural heritage.
2. Government-led search activities related to cultural heritage sites, or those anticipated to hold such status, proscribe public or community engagement in excavation, diving, and/or salvage endeavors on land and underwater.

3. As mentioned, the search is permissible exclusively for research purposes, contingent upon securing legal permits from local governments and subject to the site's specific geographic location.

From 2006 to 2011, the Cultural Heritage Protection Division of the Ministry of Education and Culture conducted a comprehensive archaeological assessment and survey of 33 historical shipwreck sites in Indonesian waters. This extensive project evaluated the condition and significance of these submerged cultural assets, essential to Indonesia's efforts to safeguard its maritime heritage. The financing for this initiative was derived from their annual national budget, ensuring independence from any sponsorship by commercial salvage enterprises. Notably, the investigative approach adopted adhered rigorously to the principles advocated by the 2001 UNESCO Convention on the Protection of Underwater Archaeology, explicitly emphasizing the best practice of in situ preservation (UNESCO, 2001; ICOMOS, 1996). By following these internationally recognized best practices, the Cultural Heritage Protection Division aimed to ensure that the historical shipwreck sites were protected in their natural environments rather than disturbed or removed. The focus on in situ preservation is intended to preserve the historical and cultural context of the shipwrecks, which is crucial for understanding their significance and ensuring that future research can continue to yield valuable insights. This can be seen as described on Table 7.1.

Despite the advancements in legal frameworks and significant efforts to protect Indonesia's UCH, the current legal standing is still far from ideal. Although laws such as Law No. 11/2010 on Cultural Heritage Protection mark an essential step forward, their implementation and effectiveness face several challenges. Enforcement and monitoring of these laws remain inconsistent, partly due to the vast and often remote nature of Indonesia's maritime territories. This makes overseeing and regulating activities challenging, leaving gaps where illegal looting or unauthorized salvage operations persist.

In this context, integrating AI presents a transformative opportunity for enhancing the protection of UCH. AI technologies can significantly improve the efficiency and effectiveness of heritage management in several ways. For instance, AI can aid in monitoring and enforcement by utilizing advanced data processing capabilities to analyze large volumes of information from satellite imagery, sonar scans, and underwater drones. This can help identify unauthorized activities or potential threats in real time, allowing quicker response and intervention.

Furthermore, AI can enhance stakeholder coordination by providing a centralized data-sharing and analysis platform. Machine learning algorithms can process and interpret complex datasets, such as those from archaeological surveys, to provide insights into the condition and location of underwater cultural sites. This can support better planning and management efforts, ensuring conservation strategies are based on accurate and current information. Embracing AI can provide the tools needed to

TABLE 7.1

The Shipwrecks Survey Databases

No	Evidence	Years	Location	Water Depth (m)
1	War Aircraft	2011	Meti Island, North Halmahera	34
2	Hawiamaru Shipwreck	2011	Kao Bay, North Halmahera	6–10
3	Kawimaru Shipwreck	2011	Kao Bay, North Halmahera	6–12
4	Topas Shipwreck Fragments	2011	Solsol Island, North Halmahera	5
5	Barnabas Shipwreck	2011	Wangeotak Island, North Halmahera	6–12
6	Sebira Shipwreck	2011	Sebira Island, Kepulauan Seribu	37
7	Tidung Shipwreck	2011	Tidung Island, Kepulauan Seribu	43
8	The Dutch Shipwreck	2011	Belanda Island, Kepulauan Seribu	40
9	Poso Shipwreck	2011	Gosong Congkak, Kepulauan Seribu	30
10	Tabularasa Shipwreck	2011	Pramuka Island, Kepulauan Seribu	38
11	Papatheo Shipwreck	2011	Papatheo Island, Kepulauan Seribu	15–30
12	Kumbang Shipwreck	2011	Kumbang Island, Kepulauan KarimunJawa	12.5
13	Mati 1 Shipwreck	2011	Batu Lawang Waters, Kepulauan KarimunJawa	53
14	Mati 2 Shipwreck	2011	Batu Lawang Waters, Kepulauan KarimunJawa	53
15	Iron and Metal Fragments	2011	Nyamuk Island, Kepulauan KarimunJawa	3–4
16	Parang Shipwreck	2011	Parang Island, Kepulauan KarimunJawa	28
17	Nusa Indah Shipwreck	2010	Menjangan Island, Kepulauan KarimunJawa	28–30
18	Geleang Shipwreck	2010	Geleang Island, Kepulauan KarimunJawa	48

(Continued)

TABLE 7.1 (Continued)

The Shipwrecks Survey Databases

No	Evidence	Years	Location	Water Depth (m)
19	Taka Menyawakan Shipwreck	2010	Taka Menyawakan Island, Kepulauan KarimunJawa	3–9
20	Kumbang Shipwreck	2010	Kumbang Island, Kepulauan KarimunJawa	2–13
21	Parang Shipwreck	2010	Parang Island, Kepulauan KarimunJawa	34–38
22	Indonoor Shipwreck	2010	Kemujan Island, Kepulauan KarimunJawa	15
23	Seruni Shipwreck	2010	Seruni Island, Kepulauan KarimunJawa	10
24	Ceramic Sherds	2010	Genting Island, Kepulauan KarimunJawa	2
25	Iron and Metal Fragments	2009	Tidore Waters, North Maluku	50
26	Toshimaru Shipwreck	2009	North Halmahera, North Maluku	7
27	Mawali Shipwreck	2009	Lembe Strait, Bitung, North Sulawesi	20–28
28	Aquila Shipwreck	2009	Wayane Beach, Ambon Bay	17–35
29	Unknown Shipwreck	2009	Nangka Island Waters, Kota Kapur, Bangka – Belitung Island	28
30	VOC Shipwreck	2008	Buton Island, Sagori Waters, South East Sulawesi	7
31	WW II Shipwreck	2007	West Sumatera, Pesisir Selatan Waters	22–28
32	Ashigara Shipwreck	2006	Barang Lompo Waters, Makassar, South Sulawesi	32
33	Chinese Shipwreck	2006	Selayar Waters, Kendari, South East Sulawesi	21

Source: The Cultural Heritage Protection and Preservation Division Survey report.

overcome existing gaps and achieve more effective protection and preservation of Indonesia's invaluable UCH.

7.3 The Potencies and Challenges

The incorporation of AI's predictive analytics stands as a pivotal development in the field of risk assessment within maritime cultural heritage management. This integration offers a nuanced understanding of potential threats, thereby empowering the formulation of proactive conservation strategies. Through the comprehensive analysis of environmental factors and historical data, AI systems emerge as invaluable tools for identifying and mitigating risks associated with natural disasters, climate change, and human activities, contributing significantly to the sustainable preservation of UCH. By harnessing the power of AI, maritime heritage professionals can move from reactive to proactive strategies, allowing for better anticipation and mitigation of risks before they materialize.

Applying AI-powered image recognition and sensing technologies in underwater archaeology elevates the efficacy of surveying and documentation processes associated with submerged cultural heritage. Uncrewed vehicles, equipped with sophisticated AI algorithms, streamline data collection, minimizing the necessity for extensive human intervention. This technological synergy not only enhances the efficiency of archaeological endeavors but also allows for the exploration of previously inaccessible or hazardous underwater sites, expanding the scope of knowledge acquisition in maritime archaeology.

Beyond the realm of conservation, the transformative potential of AI extends to public experiences at maritime heritage sites. Virtual reality (VR) and augmented reality (AR) technologies, underpinned by AI capabilities, offer immersive and interactive content. AI-driven VR and AR applications can recreate historical scenes, simulate underwater environments, and offer guided tours of shipwrecks and other submerged cultural sites without needing physical presence. People could explore a digital reconstruction of an ancient shipwreck, walking through its decks and observing artifacts as they would have appeared centuries ago. Moreover, AI can analyze user interactions and adjust the content in real time, offering personalized narratives that cater to each person's interests. For instance, the public interested in the technological aspects of ancient ships might receive detailed information about the construction methods and materials used, while another focused on the cultural exchanges along historical trade routes might be guided through stories of the people and goods that traveled across the seas. This enriches the public experience and fosters a profound understanding and appreciation of Indonesia's maritime history and culture.

However, deploying AI in maritime cultural heritage management is challenging. Ethical concerns, such as the responsible use of AI in archaeological research, data privacy issues, and the potential for cultural misappropriation, demand careful consideration. There is a risk that over-reliance on AI could lead to the commodification or exploitation of cultural heritage, where the focus shifts from preservation to profit-driven initiatives. Data privacy issues raise questions about who owns the data, how it is stored, and who has access to it. This is particularly concerning in a diverse and culturally rich nation like Indonesia, where maritime heritage encompasses many traditions, languages, and historical narratives. Therefore, AI-driven representations must be developed with cultural sensitivity and accuracy, involving local communities and cultural experts to ensure that the digital portrayal of heritage remains faithful to its origins.

The collaborative efforts of archaeologists, cultural heritage experts, and AI specialists become imperative to navigate these multifaceted challenges successfully. By bringing together diverse perspectives, stakeholders can work together to develop ethical guidelines and best practices that govern the use of AI in this context. Establishing a comprehensive framework is essential to seamlessly integrate technological advancements with ethical practices and cultural sensitivity, ensuring AI's harmonious coexistence and preserving maritime cultural heritage. Such a framework would provide clear guidelines on how AI should be used in archaeological research, how data should be managed and protected, and how cultural representations should be handled to avoid misappropriation. This framework would serve as a foundation for the sustainable management of UCH, ensuring that AI is used to support and enhance conservation efforts rather than undermine them. This collaborative and interdisciplinary approach strengthens the efficacy of AI applications and reinforces the ethical foundation necessary for the sustainable management of UCH in Indonesia and beyond.

7.4 The Urgencies

The urgency of incorporating AI into maritime cultural heritage management becomes apparent when considering several key considerations.

7.4.1 Efficient Documentation and Analysis

The sheer volume and intricacy of maritime artifacts necessitate streamlined documentation processes. AI technologies can automate cataloging, enabling comprehensive coverage and accurate analysis of diverse artifacts, shipwrecks, and underwater sites. This efficiency is crucial for meticulously recording and studying Indonesia's maritime cultural heritage. Photogrammetry is one

FIGURE 7.1
150-Year-Old Shipwreck Margaret Muir Found off Algoma, Wisconsin

Source: Zach Whitrock and the Wisconsin Historical Society Maritime Archeology program.

of the alternative technology solutions and the essential recording and documentation tools in maritime archaeology projects. It is a method to produce a three-dimensional (3D) model using computer software for making an animated video, which reconstructs the artifact by uploading several high-quality overlapping two-dimensional (2D) pictures into 3D models (Van Damme, 2015). This technology could exhibit fragile archaeological remains, which are not easy to display to the public due to the in-situ preservation, conservation, and protection. Moreover, it could be instrumental in bringing underwater archaeological sites to the public and a part of utilization in maritime cultural heritage management (Figure 7.1).

Photogrammetry has emerged as a groundbreaking tool in the recording and documentation of maritime archaeology, offering a new dimension of precision and detail in preserving UCH. As highlighted by Drap (2012), Martorelli (2014), and Marín-Buzón et al. (2021), this method represents a significant advancement in the field, providing archaeologists with the ability to create highly detailed 3D models of archaeological objects and materials (Figure 7.2). These models allow for an in-depth examination and analysis that is impossible with traditional 2D documentation techniques. By capturing the intricate details of submerged artifacts, shipwrecks, and other cultural remains, photogrammetry enhances our understanding of these objects' original forms, conditions, and contexts, contributing valuable insights to the study of maritime history.

However, the successful application of photogrammetry in maritime archaeology is not without its challenges. One of the primary technical requirements of this method is the need for skillful diving and photography. Archaeologists must be adept in underwater navigation and the precise art of underwater photography, which involves capturing many high-quality images from

FIGURE 7.2
3-D photogrammetry model

Source: The Author's Documentation.

multiple angles. This process is crucial for generating accurate 3D models, as the software used in photogrammetry relies on these images to reconstruct the shape, texture, and color of the objects in question. Any gaps in the photographic coverage or inconsistencies in image quality can lead to incomplete or distorted models, thereby compromising the integrity of the documentation.

The complexity of photogrammetry is further compounded by the environmental conditions that divers encounter while conducting these surveys. Visibility is a significant factor that can significantly impact the photographs' quality. In many underwater environments, particularly deep or murky ones, visibility can be severely limited, making it difficult to obtain clear images. Sediment disturbances, water turbidity, and low light levels are common issues that can obscure details and reduce the effectiveness of photogrammetry. Divers must often work under challenging conditions, requiring technical expertise and a deep understanding of the specific site dynamics to optimize image capture.

In recent years, a new wave of software advancements has emerged, revolutionizing the field of photogrammetry by integrating it with advanced computer vision algorithms. This new generation of software dramatically simplifies the process of creating detailed 3D models, significantly reducing the need for the labor-intensive manual point measurement typically required in traditional photogrammetric methods. These modern tools are designed to be fully automated, allowing users to generate highly accurate and comprehensive 3D dense point clouds (3Dpc) with just a few straightforward steps. Integrating computer vision techniques with photogrammetry principles has enabled these innovative systems to produce thick, colorized 3D point clouds from numerous photographic images. By leveraging sophisticated algorithms, these tools analyze and interpret photos to reconstruct detailed and accurate 3D representations of surfaces or objects. The result is a highly detailed and precise spatially 3D model that captures the full complexity of the subject, whether it is an underwater archaeological site, a historical artifact, or any other object of interest.

This approach, as outlined by Demesticha et al. (2014) and Skarlatos et al. (2012), represents a significant advancement over traditional methods. Previously, creating such detailed 3D models required extensive manual work, including meticulous point measurements and adjustments. The new software eliminates much of this labor by automating the process, thus streamlining the workflow and enhancing efficiency and accuracy. The automation provided by these advanced software solutions speeds up the documentation process and reduces the potential for human error, leading to more reliable and consistent results. This is particularly valuable in maritime archaeology, where precise documentation of underwater sites is crucial. The ability to quickly and accurately generate 3D point clouds facilitates better analysis, preservation, and presentation of cultural heritage sites, making these modern tools an essential asset for researchers and conservators.

7.4.2 Proactive Conservation Strategies

AI's predictive analytics capabilities play a transformative role in ushering in a proactive era within the field of conservation, particularly in the intricate domain of maritime heritage sites. This advanced technological application goes beyond conventional approaches by leveraging historical data, scrutinizing environmental variables, and assessing potential threats to provide nuanced insights into the vulnerability of these culturally significant sites.

The proactive nature of AI's predictive analytics becomes particularly crucial in maritime heritage management. By analyzing extensive historical datasets, AI systems discern patterns, trends, and potential risk factors that may impact the integrity of underwater cultural assets. This analytical prowess enables authorities to develop a comprehensive understanding of the evolving challenges faced by maritime heritage sites, ranging from the encroachment of climate change to the persistent threats posed by human activities.

One of the primary advantages of AI's predictive capabilities lies in its ability to anticipate and forecast potential risks. For instance, AI systems can assess the likelihood of natural disasters impacting specific maritime heritage sites, such as storms or rising sea levels (Hashemi et al., 2016; Tan et al., 2021). By identifying patterns and trends in these environmental factors, AI can predict potential damage from rising sea levels, increased storm activity, or ocean acidification, enabling heritage managers to implement protective measures in advance. Similarly, predictive analytics can evaluate the impact of climate change on underwater ecosystems, providing authorities with valuable information to formulate adaptive conservation strategies (Plagányi et al., 2011; Payne et al., 2016).

Moreover, AI's ability to analyze historical data enhances its role in assessing risks associated with human activities, such as commercial fishing, underwater construction, and unauthorized salvage operations. By examining patterns in ship traffic, fishing activities, and other maritime operations, AI can identify areas where cultural heritage sites are at higher risk of being disturbed or damaged. This information is crucial for developing targeted conservation strategies, such as designating protected areas, enforcing stricter regulations, or adjusting shipping routes to minimize the impact on sensitive sites.

Another significant potency of AI in this domain is its capacity to model and simulate various scenarios, providing insights into the potential outcomes of different conservation approaches. For example, AI-driven simulations can help predict the effectiveness of artificial reefs or other physical barriers in protecting underwater sites from erosion or human interference. These models can also be used to assess the long-term sustainability of current conservation practices, allowing for adjustments to be made in real-time based on changing conditions. By understanding and predicting potential threats, authorities can enforce regulations, conduct targeted surveillance, and engage in community outreach initiatives to raise awareness and garner support for the conservation of these culturally rich sites.

Furthermore, AI's predictive analytics align with the broader goals of sustainable development (Truby, 2020; Vinuesa et al., 2020). As nations strive to achieve economic progress, this development mustn't come at the expense of cultural and environmental integrity. AI's predictive capabilities support this balance by offering a framework for sustainable management that considers the interconnectedness of economic, cultural, and environmental factors. For example, in areas with maritime heritage sites near developing coastal communities, AI can help assess the potential impacts of urbanization or industrial activities on these sites, guiding policymakers in making decisions that support economic growth and cultural preservation.

AI's predictive analytics herald a new era in maritime cultural heritage management, where technology and conservation efforts work harmoniously to safeguard past treasures for future generations. This synergy empowers authorities to navigate the complexities of UCH management with a level of foresight and resilience that was previously unattainable. By leveraging AI's capabilities, nations can move beyond short-term solutions and embrace a proactive approach that ensures the sustained preservation of their maritime heritage.

7.4.3 Underwater Survey and Exploration

Deepwater archaeology provides a compelling context for showcasing the capabilities and future potential of autonomous underwater vehicles (AUVs). In underwater archaeological exploration, remote sensing technologies play a critical role, and the investigation process generally unfolds in several distinct yet interconnected stages. Initially, the exploration begins with a broad, wide-area survey to map out the general underwater landscape and identify areas of interest. This preliminary stage helps cover large seabed expanses efficiently, often employing advanced AUVs with various sensors and imaging technologies. These wide-area surveys lay the groundwork for subsequent steps by highlighting potential sites that warrant further examination.

Following the wide-area survey, the next step involves target identification. Here, the data collected during the initial study is analyzed to pinpoint specific locations or objects with historical or archaeological significance. This phase requires detailed analysis of the gathered data, often using sophisticated algorithms and machine learning techniques to enhance the accuracy of target detection and classification. Once potential targets are identified, a more detailed site investigation is conducted. This stage focuses on examining the identified sites more closely, employing high-resolution imaging and specialized AUVs to capture intricate details of the underwater environment. The aim is to gather comprehensive data on the site's features, artifacts, and overall condition, which is essential for understanding the historical context and significance of the findings.

Uncrewed vehicles with AI algorithms emerge as pivotal tools in exploring and mapping underwater sites (Tholen, 2021). In addition, Mindell and Bingham (2001) outline these stages as a nested process, emphasizing the importance of each step in the overall framework of underwater archaeological research. The evolving capabilities of AUVs enhance each phase of this process, from broad surveys to detailed site investigations, by providing tools and technologies that enable more precise, efficient, and compelling underwater exploration. As AUV technology advances, its role in deep water archaeology is expected to expand, addressing the ongoing need for innovation in remote sensing, data collection, and site management. These autonomous vehicles, ranging from remotely operated vehicles (ROVs) to AUVs, can precisely navigate the intricate underwater terrain. AI algorithms guide these vehicles, facilitating real-time decision-making and adaptive navigation based on the evolving conditions of the underwater environment.

The deployment of unmanned vehicles empowered by AI extends beyond mere navigation; it includes capturing high-resolution images and data. With advanced sensing technologies, these vehicles can systematically survey underwater archaeological sites, capturing intricate details and generating 3D reconstructions. The result is a comprehensive and detailed dataset that enriches the understanding of submerged cultural heritage. A notable advantage of AI-driven underwater exploration is the reduction of reliance on extensive human intervention. Traditionally, underwater archaeological endeavors necessitate a significant investment of human resources, often constrained by challenges such as limited dive times, depth constraints, and adverse environmental conditions. AI-powered unmanned vehicles mitigate these challenges, operating autonomously to cover larger areas and depths with increased efficiency.

Furthermore, integrating AI in underwater archaeology enhances the safety and accessibility of exploration. Unmanned vehicles can navigate hazardous environments, including deep-sea regions and challenging underwater terrains, mitigating risks associated with human divers (Chen et al., 2021). This ensures the safety of archaeological teams and extends the reach of exploration to previously inaccessible sites. In essence, AI-powered image recognition and sensing technologies, coupled with unmanned underwater vehicles, redefine the landscape of underwater archaeology. This technological synergy accelerates the pace of surveying and documentation and unlocks new possibilities for exploring submerged cultural heritage. As the field continues to embrace these advancements, the rich tapestry of human history preserved beneath the waves becomes increasingly accessible and understandable, enriching our collective understanding of the past.

7.4.4 Development and Utilization

Beyond the realm of preservation, the integration of AI applications unfolds transformative dimensions in maritime heritage assets. Fueled by AI's capabilities, virtual and augmented reality technologies emerge as dynamic tools that transcend traditional modes of storytelling. Through the creation of immersive experiences, these technologies breathe life into historical narratives, simulate maritime journeys, and deliver interactive educational content, enriching the public experience and fostering a profound appreciation of Indonesia's maritime history and culture.

At the forefront of this technological convergence is the utilization of virtual and augmented reality, harnessed and driven by the intelligence of AI algorithms. These applications transcend conventional approaches, offering a multisensory experience that transcends the boundaries of traditional education and engagement methods. VR technologies, powered by AI, enable the recreation of historical scenes with unprecedented accuracy and detail. By leveraging AI algorithms, these simulations can dynamically adapt based on user interactions, providing a personalized and engaging journey through Indonesia's maritime history. The public can virtually step into the past, exploring maritime landscapes, encountering historical figures, and witnessing pivotal events, all curated by intelligent algorithms that tailor the experience to individual preferences.

VR, while often perceived as a contemporary innovation, is not an entirely novel concept. Historically, VR has been known under various terminologies such as synthetic environment, cyberspace, artificial reality, and simulator technology, reflecting its evolving nature and applications. The development of VR has progressively expanded its possibilities, paving the way for its integration into diverse fields, including education (Ausburn & Ausburn, 2004). The evolution of VR has been marked by significant advancements that have transformed it from a theoretical concept into a practical tool for another purpose.

By creating immersive, computer-generated environments, VR provides a platform where the public can engage with content in previously unattainable ways. This immersive experience allows learners to interact with and navigate through virtual spaces, facilitating a deeper understanding of the subject. Simulating complex scenarios and environments in a controlled and engaging manner enables students to grasp principles and concepts more rapidly and effectively. This hands-on interaction makes learning more enjoyable and enhances the retention and application of knowledge (Onyesolu, 2009a, 2009b).

Moreover, VR has been touted for its capacity to create experiences that can be more vivid and compelling than reality itself. According to Negroponte (1995), VR possesses the potential to produce highly realistic simulations that sometimes surpass the sensory detail and immersion of actual experiences. This characteristic allows VR to craft detailed and nuanced environments that can accurately simulate real-world scenarios. Such advanced simulations are particularly valuable in educational contexts where practical experience and experimentation are crucial. For instance, in archaeology, medicine, or engineering fields, VR can provide students and professionals with opportunities to practice and refine their skills in a risk-free, virtual setting.

Technically, building and experiencing VR require two main components: hardware and software components. The hardware components are divided into five sub-components: computer workstation, sensory displays, process acceleration cards, tracking system, and input devices. Meanwhile, the software components are divided into four subcomponents: 3D modeling software, 2D graphics software, digital sound editing, and VR simulation. Systemically, VR is classified into three major types: (1) non-immersive VR systems, (2) semi-immersive VR systems, and (3) immersive (fully immersive) VR systems. Interestingly, VR also developed a low-cost VR technology that gives benefits and positive implications for several sectors, such as hospitals, educational institutions, museums, and other organizations that invest in their technology development, such as mass media, fiction books, television, motion pictures, music videos, games, fine arts, marketing, healthcare, therapeutic uses, and real estates.

Referring to this chapter's context, VR also impacts heritage and archeology. Historically, the first use of a VR presentation in a Heritage aspect occurred in 1994 on the 3D reconstruction of Dudley Castle in England in 1550, which British-based engineer Colin Johnson designed (Sanders, 2008). It became a turning point of VR implementation in Heritage and Archaeology resulting in the enormous potential in museums and public center applications around the world such as National Czech and Slovak Museum and Library, the Pacific Science Centre, the Tate, the San Diego Museum of Art, the Rijksmuseum, the Cleveland Museum of Art, the Dali Museum, the Natural History Museum of Utah, the Australian National Maritime Museum, the Kennedy Space Center Public Complex, the Museo Nazionale della Scienza e della Tecnologia Leonardo da Vinci, the Australian Centre for the Moving Image, the Children's Museum of Indianapolis, the Smithsonian American Art Museum, and the National Museum of Finland (Shehade & Stylianou-Lambert, 2020).

AR, another facet of this technological synergy, enhances the physical environment at maritime heritage sites. AI-driven AR applications overlay digital content onto real-world surroundings, seamlessly blending historical reconstructions with the present landscape. This interactive layer enriches the public experience by providing additional information, context, and interactive elements, creating an educational journey transcending traditional static exhibits.

The potential of AI-driven VR and AR extends far beyond creating immersive experiences. Intelligent algorithms are crucial in analyzing user interactions, preferences, and learning patterns. This data-driven approach enables adaptive content delivery, allowing experiences to be tailored to individual users' unique backgrounds, interests, and learning styles. By personalizing the content, AI ensures that each visitor can engage with maritime heritage in a manner that resonates with their curiosities and needs. This personalized approach enhances the learning experience and ensures visitors of all ages and backgrounds can derive meaningful insights from their interactions with the exhibits.

Moreover, AI applications in both VR and AR enable dynamic and interactive storytelling. As Holloway-Attaway (2020) points out, historical narratives can be presented nonlinearly, allowing visitors to explore different aspects of Indonesia's maritime history according to their interests. Instead of following a predetermined path, users can navigate through various narrative elements, discovering stories and information that are most relevant to them. The intelligent algorithms behind these applications curate content in real-time, adapting to user choices and interactions to maintain an engaging and informative experience. This real-time curation ensures that the narrative remains vibrant, relevant, and responsive to the diverse interests of the audience.

In summary, integrating AI-driven virtual and augmented reality technologies redefines the landscape of public engagement and education at maritime heritage sites. By providing immersive, adaptive, and personalized experiences, these applications contribute to a deeper understanding and appreciation of Indonesia's rich marine history and culture. As the public embark on virtual journeys through time, guided by the intelligence of AI, they become active participants in the exploration and preservation of the nation's maritime heritage.

7.4.5 Ethical Considerations

Integrating AI into managing maritime cultural heritage in Indonesia brings a range of ethical concerns that warrant careful consideration. Achieving a balance between leveraging technological advancements and upholding ethical standards is crucial to ensuring that AI is used responsibly and effectively while preserving Indonesia's rich cultural heritage (Kasmahidayat, 2022). One significant ethical issue revolves around the risk of reducing cultural artifacts to mere data points within AI systems. As AI technologies analyze and interpret information about these artifacts, there is a danger that their cultural and historical significance might be overshadowed. When artifacts are treated solely as inputs for algorithms, their deeper meanings, traditional values, and historical contexts may be overlooked or undervalued. This reductionist approach can diminish the richness and complexity of the artifacts, failing to capture their entire cultural essence.

Moreover, AI's reliance on data-driven models may lead to an oversimplification of cultural narratives. By focusing predominantly on quantitative data and algorithmic outputs, there is a risk that the nuanced and multifaceted aspects of maritime heritage could be lost. This could result in a narrow interpretation of cultural heritage that fails to reflect Indonesia's maritime traditions' diverse and dynamic nature. Such an approach may inadvertently perpetuate stereotypes or inaccuracies, misrepresent the cultural heritage, and diminish its authenticity.

Data privacy is a critical concern in AI applications, mainly when dealing with the sensitive information associated with maritime cultural heritage (Edwards, 2016). As AI technologies generate and analyze large datasets, there is an increased risk that this data may include confidential details about artistic practices, community identities, and traditional knowledge. Protecting this information from unauthorized access is essential to uphold the privacy and dignity of the communities linked to these cultural assets. Unauthorized exposure or misuse of such sensitive data could lead to significant repercussions, including the erosion of trust and potential harm to the artistic integrity of the involved communities.

To address these concerns, implementing AI in maritime heritage management must incorporate a framework that respects and preserves the cultural significance of artifacts. This involves engaging with cultural experts, historians, and community representatives to ensure that AI systems are designed with a deep understanding of the artifacts' historical and cultural contexts. Collaborative efforts can help bridge the gap between technological advancements and cultural preservation, ensuring that AI applications enhance rather than undermine the integrity of maritime heritage. Furthermore, ethical guidelines should be established to govern the use of AI in this field. These guidelines should emphasize the importance of preserving artifacts' cultural and historical value while leveraging AI's documentation, analysis, and conservation capabilities. It is also essential to develop AI systems capable of interpreting artifacts in a way that respects their cultural significance, incorporating qualitative insights alongside quantitative data.

Transparency and accountability are key to addressing ethical concerns (Larsson & Heintz, 2020). By making the processes and methodologies used in AI applications open to scrutiny, stakeholders can ensure that the technology is used to align with ethical standards and cultural sensitivities. Regular reviews and updates of AI systems, informed by feedback from cultural and historical experts, can help maintain the accuracy and respectfulness of the interpretations and representations generated by AI. Community engagement is key to ethical AI implementation (Wilson, 2022). Involving local communities in developing, deploying, and monitoring AI applications ensures the technology aligns with their values and concerns.

While AI offers significant potential for advancing the management of maritime cultural heritage in Indonesia, it is essential to navigate the ethical challenges associated with its use. Adopting a balanced approach that integrates technological innovation with cultural respect and sensitivity makes it possible to harness the benefits of AI while preserving the richness and significance of Indonesia's maritime heritage. Ongoing dialogues among archaeologists, cultural heritage experts, AI specialists, and local communities are necessary. Establishing ethical frameworks and guidelines specific to AI in maritime heritage management is essential for harmonizing technology and cultural preservation. In summary, addressing ethical concerns ensures that AI becomes a tool for responsibly preserving Indonesia's cultural heritage, respecting the profound connections between technology and heritage.

7.5 Conclusion

In conclusion, integrating AI into maritime cultural heritage management in Indonesia is a critical imperative, transcending technological advancements. This strategic necessity arises from the intricate challenges of preserving and safeguarding the extensive and diverse cultural legacy embedded in the nation's maritime history. By harnessing the transformative power of AI and meticulously navigating ethical considerations, Indonesia stands poised not only to elevate its documentation and conservation efforts but also to pioneer innovative and engaging avenues for present and future generations to connect with and sincerely appreciate its invaluable maritime heritage.

The urgency for AI integration stems from the pressing need to address multifaceted challenges, including the impact of human activities, developmental projects, and environmental factors on UCH. Looting, salvaging, and treasure hunting persist as persistent threats, posing risks to the integrity of historic shipwrecks and their material cargoes. In addition, the sea toll development initiated by the Government of Indonesia, while promoting economic progress, introduces potential harm to undiscovered underwater archaeological remains.

AI's predictive analytics stands out as a transformative tool in risk assessment, offering insights into potential threats such as natural disasters, climate change, and human activities. By analyzing environmental factors and historical data, AI contributes to proactive conservation strategies, ensuring the sustainable preservation of UCH.

In underwater archaeology, AI-powered image recognition and sensing technologies enhance surveying and documentation processes. Unmanned vehicles equipped with AI algorithms facilitate efficient data collection, reducing the need for extensive human intervention. This technological synergy improves the efficiency of archaeological endeavors and enables the exploration of previously inaccessible or hazardous underwater sites.

Beyond conservation, AI's transformative potential extends to public experiences at maritime heritage sites. Driven by AI capabilities, virtual and augmented reality technologies offer interactive educational content, fostering a deeper understanding and appreciation of Indonesia's maritime history and culture among the public.

However, implementing AI in maritime cultural heritage management necessitates careful consideration of ethical concerns, data privacy issues, and collaborative efforts between archaeologists, cultural heritage experts, and AI specialists. Establishing a comprehensive framework becomes imperative to integrate technological advancements with ethical practices and cultural sensitivity.

As Indonesia strives to position itself as a global maritime fulcrum, integrating AI aligns with broader national development goals. In the long-term development plan for Indonesia 2045, cultural aspects emerge as a cornerstone, contributing to development by capitalizing on national cultural values. This underscores the significance of culture, including UCH assets, in Indonesia's overall development trajectory.

The urgency of AI integration in maritime cultural heritage management in Indonesia signifies a holistic approach to address present and future challenges. It enhances the technological arsenal for conservation and facilitates a profound and meaningful engagement with the nation's maritime heritage. As Indonesia navigates this transformative journey, careful consideration of ethical dimensions and collaborative efforts will be crucial to ensure the harmonious coexistence of AI and the enduring preservation of its invaluable maritime cultural legacy.

References

Adhuri, D. S. (2018). The state and empowerment of Indonesian maritime culture: The case of traditional marine resource management. *Journal of Ocean & Culture*, 1, 18–34.

Al Syahrin, M. N. (2018). Kebijakan poros maritim Jokowi dan sinergitas strategi ekonomi dan keamanan laut Indonesia. *Indonesian Perspective*, 3(1), 1–17.

Ausburn, L. J., & Ausburn, F. B. (2004). Desktop virtual reality: A powerful new technology for teaching and research in industrial teacher education. *Journal of Industrial Teacher Education*, 41(4), 1–16.

Chen, X., Bose, N., Brito, M., Khan, F., Thanyamanta, B., & Zou, T. (2021). A review of risk analysis research for the operations of autonomous underwater vehicles. *Reliability Engineering & System Safety*, 216, Article 108011.

Colin, J. (n.d.). *Computer visualization of Dudley Castle*. Retrieved October 22, 2024, from http://www.extrenda.net/dudley/index.htm

Demesticha, S., Skarlatos, D., & Neophytou, A. (2014). The 4th century BC shipwreck at Mazotos, Cyprus: New techniques and methodologies in the 3D mapping of shipwreck excavations. *Journal of Field Archaeology*, 39(2), 134–150.

Diposaptono, S. (2017). *Membangun Poros Maritim Dunia Dalam Perspektif Tata Ruang Laut* (M. Budiman (ed.); 3rd ed., Issue 3). Perpustakaan Nasional: Katalog Dalam Terbitan.

Drap, P. (2012). Underwater photogrammetry for archaeology. In *Special applications of photogrammetry*. IntechOpen.

Edwards, L. (2016). Privacy, security and data protection in smart cities: A critical EU law perspective. *European Data Protection Law Review*, 2, 28.

Hardjoko, H. (2017). *Indonesian maritime cultural resources management: A study of salvaged material cultures from historic shipwreck finds in Indonesia* [Doctoral dissertation, Flinders University].

Hashemi, M. R., Spaulding, M. L., Shaw, A., Farhadi, H., & Lewis, M. (2016). An efficient artificial intelligence model for prediction of tropical storm surge. *Natural Hazards*, 82, 471–491.

Holloway-Attaway, L., & Vipsjö, L. (2020). Using augmented reality, gaming technologies, and transmedial storytelling to develop and co-design local cultural heritage experiences. *Visual Computing for Cultural Heritage*, 177–204.

ICOMOS (1996). *ICOMOS charter on the protection and management of underwater cultural heritage*. Sofia.

Kasmahidayat, Y., & Hasanuddin, H. (2022). Collaboration strategy in the development and inheritance of archipelago's arts. *Journal of Indigenous Culture, Tourism, and Language*, 1(1), 1–20. https://doi.org/10.35912/jictl.v1i1.1065

Larsson, S., & Heintz, F. (2020). Transparency in artificial intelligence. *Internet Policy Review*, 9(2).

Marín-Buzón, C., Pérez-Romero, A., López-Castro, J. L., Ben Jerbania, I., & Manzano-Agugliaro, F. (2021). Photogrammetry as a new scientific tool in archaeology: Worldwide research trends. *Sustainability*, 13(9), Article 5319.

Martorelli, M., Pensa, C., & Speranza, D. (2014). Digital photogrammetry for documentation of maritime heritage. *Journal of Maritime Archaeology*, 9, 81–93.

Mindell, D. A., & Bingham, B. (2001, November). *New archaeological uses of autonomous undersea vehicles*. Proceedings of the MTS/IEEE Oceans Conference, Honolulu.

Negroponte, N. (1995). The digital revolution: Reasons for optimism. *The Futurist*, 29(6), 68.

Onyesolu, M. O. (2009a). Virtual reality laboratories: An ideal solution to the problems facing laboratory setup and management. In *Proceedings of world congress on engineering and computer science 2009* (pp. 291–295). Newswood Limited.

Onyesolu, M. O. (2009b). Virtual reality laboratories: The pedagogical effectiveness and use in obtaining cheap laboratories using the computer laboratory. *Journal of Science Engineering and Technology*, 16(1), 8679–8689.

Payne, M. R., Barange, M., Cheung, W. W., MacKenzie, B. R., Batchelder, H. P., Cormon, X., Paula, J. R. (2016). Uncertainties in projecting climate-change impacts in marine ecosystems. *ICES Journal of Marine Science*, 73(5), 1272–1282.

Plagányi, É. E., Bell, J. D., Bustamante, R. H., Dambacher, J. M., Dennis, D. M., Dichmont, C. M., Zhou, S. (2011). Modeling climate-change effects on Australian and Pacific aquatic ecosystems: A review of analytical tools and management implications. *Marine and Freshwater Research*, 62(9), 1132–1147.

Putra, H. (2019). Kebijakan pembangunan tol laut dan potensi dampaknya pada tinggalan kapal asing bersejarah yang karam di wilayah perairan Indonesia. *Paradigma: Jurnal Kajian Budaya*, 9(1), 4.

Sanders, D. (2008, March 13). Why do virtual heritage? Online Features Article, *Archaeology Archive*. Accessed March 10, 2023, from http://archive.archaeology.org

Shehade, M., & Stylianou-Lambert, T. (2020). Virtual reality in museums: Exploring the experiences of museum professionals. *Applied Sciences*, 10(11), Article 4031.

Skarlatos, D., Demestiha, S., & Kiparissi, S. (2012). An "open" method for 3D modeling and mapping underwater archaeological sites. *International Journal of Heritage in the Digital Era*, 1(1), 1–24.

Tan, L., Guo, J., Mohanarajah, S., & Zhou, K. (2021). Can we detect trends in natural disaster management with artificial intelligence? A review of modeling practices. *Natural Hazards*, 107, 2389–2417.

Tholen, C., El-Mihoub, T. A., Nolle, L., & Zielinski, O. (2021). Artificial intelligence search strategies for autonomous underwater vehicles applied for submarine groundwater discharge site investigation. *Journal of Marine Science and Engineering*, 10(1), Article 7.

Truby, J. (2020). Governing artificial intelligence to benefit the UN sustainable development goals. *Sustainable Development*, 28(4), 946–959.

UNESCO (2001). *Annex of the UNESCO convention on the protection of underwater cultural heritage*. Paris.

Van Damme, T. (2015). Computer vision photogrammetry for underwater archaeological site recording in a low-visibility environment. *The International Archives of Photogrammetry, Remote Sensing and Spatial Information Sciences*, 40(5), 231.

Vinuesa, R., Azizpour, H., Leite, I., Balaam, M., Dignum, V., Domisch, S., & Fuso Nerini, F. (2020). The role of artificial intelligence in achieving the sustainable development goals. *Nature Communications*, 11(1), 1–10.

Wilson, C. (2022). Public engagement and AI: A values analysis of national strategies. *Government Information Quarterly*, 39(1), Article 101652.

8

Artificial Intelligence and the Future of Software Development: Transforming the Software Development Lifecycle in the Digital Era

Siddharth Gaikwad, Suneel K. Prasad, and S. Vijayakumar Bharathi

8.1 Introduction

With growing competition and complex markets, software product companies require new methods that help them increase their efficiency and stay ahead in the competitive market. This lead in the market is possible by well-understanding customer needs, delivering the best quality software with minimum errors and bugs, providing releases with minimum time-to-market, and quickly improving as per changing needs and trends in the market. With the advent of artificial intelligence (AI), software product companies look forward to achieving the goal mentioned above by using different AI techniques in the software development lifecycle. Thus, this chapter deals with assessing the use of AI for the industrial purpose of software product development to identify the gaps in the current processes and different phases of software development by reviewing the existing literature and finding out what AI techniques can be recommended for the identified anomalies. With the current processes, gaps can be found in various activities of requirement engineering and how development is carried out. For example, with current testing methods, bug detection could be better, but it can result in bugs and defects on the user end. Project managers need help prioritizing the requirements and activities even with modern tools like JIRA. (A project management software developed by Atlassian.) In this chapter, we explore and propose extensive use of AI techniques such as machine learning (ML), deep learning (DL), data mining (DM), and natural language processing (NLP) in the processes mentioned above and phases, to predict the defects in the software and help the software team to make software with minimum defects to enhance user experience. AI can assist project managers in prioritizing, refining, and understanding requirements so that the right product can be made as per user needs and reduce the iterations, resulting in software development within schedule and providing a competitive advantage. The high-level analytics capabilities of the current era have led to AI that can go beyond the descriptive analytics in current tools and focus more on predictive and prescriptive solutions to help in decision-making during the development (Liu et al., 2021). AI technique integrations in the software product development lifecycle involves evaluating the strategic integration of AI technologies in the software development process to enhance efficiency, innovation, and overall product quality and improve the way software engineering (SE) is exercised (Ozkaya, 2023, pp. 4–9) (Ebert & Louridas, 2023). Thus, the chapter focuses on the use of AI for project management (to predict timelines and resources), AI techniques used in requirement engineering (RE), development and testing phase, and ultimately, how AI can result in software delivery as per customer's need and satisfaction, so the software businesses can get benefitted by the AI boost and be early adopters of AI technology for making efficient and effective software products.

8.2 Study's Objectives

The primary objective of this chapter is to recognize the various phases of the software development lifecycle (SDLC) where AI methods might be implemented to boost organizational productivity and provide the company with a competitive edge. Therefore, this chapter assesses the scope of use of AI techniques in various phases of software product development that will result in AI techniques and methods that organizations can use for efficient software delivery and managing projects. The chapter identifies areas where organizations or people face issues in different phases of software development. The chapter addresses the business point of view, not dwelling in much depth on the individual technical aspects of the mentioned AI techniques, but highlights and acknowledges the opportunity for success if these techniques are used in the mentioned phases of software development. Ultimately, the authors present a mapping of AI techniques applications in different phases of software product development that can guide businesses to use AI techniques for their required processes. Overall, this chapter examines the opportunities for applying AI techniques throughout the various phases of the SDLC. We investigate the potential benefits of AI in SE. Finally, we explain how AI integration in the SDLC can improve customer experience and provide a competitive advantage for the organization. Certain research questions are thus created by the author, considering the research scope, which can be answered with the help of this study.

8.2.1 Research Questions

RQ1: What challenges are encountered in the current software development process that can result in opportunities for applying AI techniques in the SDLC?

RQ2: What AI techniques can be applied at different SDLC phases?

RQ3: Can AI techniques be applied in SE umbrella activities such as project management?

RQ4: How can AI used in SDLC enhance customer experience and competitive advantage for organizations?

8.3 Research Methodology

Research is carried out by studying the existing literature about using AI in different phases of product development. The author mainly focused on two databases, Scopus and Web of Science, due to their volume and content validity. The Institute of Electrical and Electronics Engineers Xplore was also used when links were diverted from Scopus. Content sourced from the above-mentioned databases included various articles, conference papers, and reviews. The search flow for literature, as shown in Figure 8.1, was used to source the content. To identify the most related papers, queries were developed and

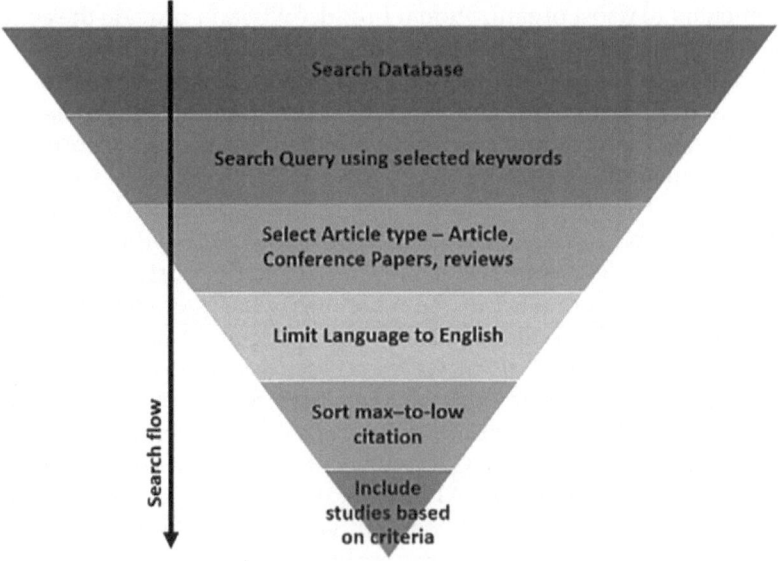

FIGURE 8.1
Search flow for literature (self-compiled)

used to find the most related databases. For example, to identify papers using NLP in the requirement phase, the following Query was used as advanced search in Scopus: *(TITLE-ABS-KEY ("natural language processing" AND "software requirements" AND "product development") OR TITLE-ABS-KEY ("NLP" AND "requirements elicitation"))* and for advance search in Web of Science – TS = *("natural language processing" AND "software requirements") AND TS = ("product development" OR "requirements elicitation")*. A similar method is used for searching content, considering the use of different AI techniques in different phases of software product development. The details of some of the search queries used to search articles for different AI techniques and software development phases are mentioned in Table 8.1. However, it is to be noted that since the scope of the research included various research techniques and phases, it was not possible to search all required articles in just a single search query. Thus, multiple search rounds were executed.

Table 8.1 only mentions a few of those queries, which are provided with many papers as provided in the reference section. Other filters were also applied during the search, such as the focus for the content was derived mainly from articles, conference papers, and reviews; other than these data types, the rest were not considered for the study (Moher et al., 2009). Papers that were open access or available through organization-provided access were only considered for the study. The content search was also limited to the English language only. For better quality of content, filters were applied where papers with a greater number of citations were preferred in the case where a large number of articles were available after searching on the above-mentioned criteria. If only fewer articles were available, they were considered irrespective of their citation and selected based on their adherence to the topic. Finally, the papers were shortlisted and finalized by reading through the paper's content, such as initially focusing on the paper's abstract and, if needed, going through other parts of the paper. The authors also developed a set of inclusion and exclusion criteria, which were considered through the above process of search flow, which assisted in selecting the needed papers and prevented them from going outside the research scope. One hundred forty-six articles were identified using different queries, which were filtered down to 58 and added to this article by applying the whole method and criteria. Table 8.2 lists the inclusion and exclusion criteria. *Point to be noted: To make the content in Table 8.2 more readable, Articles, Conference Papers, and Reviews – all such data source types – are just referred to as "Articles."*

8.4 Software Product Development Lifecycle

Different research works in the area have mentioned different phases of software development. However, considering and going through much of the information regarding the software development lifecycle, the author has

TABLE 8.1

Queries Used for AI Techniques in Software Development Phases

Sr No	AI Technique	Software Phase	Query for Scopus	Query for Web of Science
1	Natural Language Processing (NLP)	Planning and Requirements Gathering	(TITLE-ABS-KEY ("natural language processing" AND "software requirements" AND "product development") OR TITLE-ABS-KEY ("NLP" AND "requirements elicitation"))	TS = ("natural language processing" AND "software requirements") AND TS= ("product development" OR "requirements elicitation")
2	Machine Learning (ML)	Planning and Requirements Gathering	(TITLE-ABS-KEY ("Machine Learning" AND "Requirement Engineering")) AND (LIMIT-TO (DOCTYPE, "cp") OR LIMIT-TO (DOCTYPE, "ar") OR LIMIT-TO (DOCTYPE, "cr"))	TS = ("machine learning" AND "software product development") AND TS = ("feature prioritization")
3	Generative AI and Large Language Models	Software Design and Architecture	(TITLE-ABS-KEY ("generative AI" AND ("software design" OR "software architecture" OR "user experience"))	
4	Machine Learning for Code Completion	Development and Implementation	TITLE-ABS-KEY (machine learning AND code completion) AND (software development OR software engineering)	
5	NLP for Documentation and Testing	Testing and Quality Assurance		TS = (natural language processing AND (software documentation OR software testing)) AND TS = (software development OR software engineering)

Artificial Intelligence and the Future of Software Development 173

TABLE 8.2

Inclusion and Exclusion Criteria

Sr No	Inclusion Criteria	Sr No	Exclusion Criteria
IC1	The article fully available and not just abstract or open access articles	EC1	Articles whose full content is not accessible or locked articles
IC2	Abstract only the above-mentioned journals	EC2	Articles that are book chapters or published for a website.
IC3	Articles are available in English language only	EC3	Articles without references
IC4	Articles should be recent; 2016 to 2024 are preferred	EC4	Articles with searched key terms not mentioned in the Abstract

FIGURE 8.2
Software product development phases (self-compiled)

grouped and prepared a six-phase SDLC (Figure 8.2). While different products may require different phases and activities in customizable order per the organization's need, the six-phase process can be referred to by all businesses (Sofian et al., 2022; Böckle et al., 2005).

8.5 Challenges

For customers' constantly evolving needs in modern world scenarios, an agile method for developing software products is considered an efficient approach that can frequently adapt to the volatility of changing needs and demands and provide a competitive advantage. Out of this, Agile Scrum practice is one of the most dominantly used methods with various benefits such as adapting to changing requirements, reducing development time, and quickly solving problems. However, it possesses some challenges such as identifying requirements, how to do initial planning, lack of attention to RE in analysis and design phases, it lacks adequate version control, configuration management, and traceability in document archives – all of which could be contributing factors to the failure of the project (Lee & Chen, 2023). For a product to succeed, end customers' requirements are to be quickly integrated into the product. However, the existing market lacks faster methods to integrate end customers into this software development process (Humpert et al., 2022). A. Irshad et al. have done detailed and thorough research on the problems and challenges faced in global software development, such as the 4C problem – Communication, Coordination, Collaboration, and Control problems – along with other problems such as project management problems, and requirement change management challenges. All such problems related to our scope are also referred from (Siddique et al., 2023) and mentioned in Table 8.3. R. Simhadri et al. have also done detailed research to identify challenges that are faced in the requirement management phase of SE, out of which all the relatable challenges are included in Table 8.3 after studying

TABLE 8.3

Challenges in Software Development

Sr No	Challenges
1	Challenges in identifying a requirement
2	Difficulty in initial planning
3	Challenges in tracing documents
4	Slow integration of end customers in the development process
5	Requirement change management
6	4C – Communication, Coordination, Collaboration, Control Problems
7	Challenges regarding project management
8	Challenges in project budget and time estimations
9	Challenges in software architecture
10	Challenges in requirement refinements
11	Challenges in decision-making capacity
12	Challenges of security in software development
13	Challenges in conflicting requirements

and filtering (Simhadri & Shameem, 2023). *A. Alghamdi et al.* have taken a different approach by highlighting the security challenges encountered due to complex software development processes (Alghamdi & Niazi, 2022). Thus, we have highlighted a list of significant challenges encountered along with the modern-day software development process and which can be further addressed by using modern AI techniques.

Table.8.3 mainly summarizes the list of challenges discussed in the above section.

8.6 Relevant Artificial Intelligence Techniques

The vast amount of diverse data generated in the last decade, mainly due to the big data environment, has resulted in a growing trend of use of AI (Yang & Wan, 2022) and has demanded the development of new technologies, which also resulted in the development of new AI techniques. AI that can go beyond descriptive analytics in existing tools and concentrate more on predictive and prescriptive solutions to aid in decision-making throughout development has been made possible by the high-level analytics capabilities of the current era (Liu et al., 2021). *Silva et al.* have provided the "CDAC AI Lifecycle, which consists of 19 stages and three phases (design, develop, and deploy)" that cover, address, and account for all challenges from conception to production of AI and measuring return on investment in addition to understanding the various applications of AI (De Silva & Alahakoon, 2022). *Taboada et al.* have provided a detailed review of the use of AI in project management in different domains, mainly focusing on the construction and IT industry, which symbolizes the widespread of AI in today's world and demonstrates its strength to be used in a wide variety of domains; the article provides a literature review based on classification of AI use in sector, function, techniques, and Performance based on different domains (Taboada et al., 2023). *F. Sun. et al.* have developed MdmNet, which can be used for product classification. Thus, motivating and demonstrating the enormous scope of AI/ML techniques in today's era and modern markets and products is imperative. This motivation design model (MDM) for product classification is based on understanding target consumers and their cognitive structure that derives consumer-related information, including incentive, desirability, and willingness, by mining the relationship between consumers' interests and expectations resulting in consumer-centered product classification (Sun et al., 2022). *Kanbach et al.* have also reviewed the boost in generative AI and analyzed its potential in business model innovation and how AI can be adopted for businesses. The paper also provides examples of AI in different industries, such as SE, healthcare, and financial services (Kanbach et al., 2023). *H. Sofian et al.* have developed

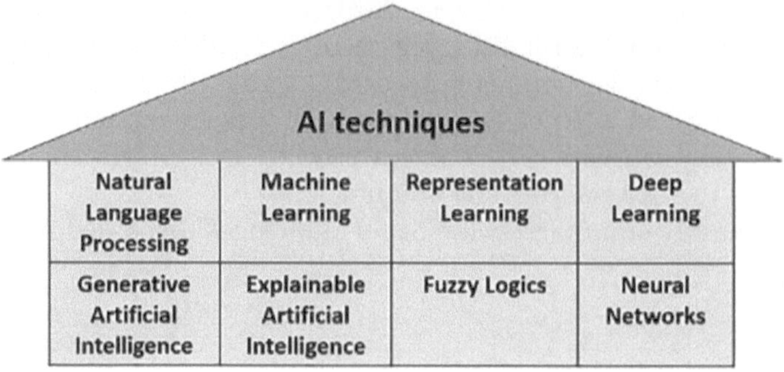

AI techniques			
Natural Language Processing	Machine Learning	Representation Learning	Deep Learning
Generative Artificial Intelligence	Explainable Artificial Intelligence	Fuzzy Logics	Neural Networks

FIGURE 8.3
The housing of different techniques under AI (self-compiled)

a literature review for the systematic mapping of AI techniques in different phases of software development – proposing AI techniques such as ML, (b) heuristic algorithms (HA), DL, DM, (e) data analytics (DA), and NLP that have been widely explored in the SE phases (Sofian et al., 2022). Thus, ensuring the broad scope of AI techniques for different applications throughout the development lifecycle is necessary. *Borges et al.* have thus performed a systematic literature review that explores the interaction between AI and business strategy. It focuses on the strategic use of AI and how it can help organizations. Also, they have explained how different AI techniques like "Machine Learning (ML), Deep Learning (DL), and Representation Learning (RL) are related to one another" (De Fátima Soares Borges et al., 2021). Figure 8.3 represents the housing of different techniques under AI. This article not only focuses on AI as an umbrella term but also discusses the use of AI techniques that come under this AI umbrella and that can be used in different processes of software development.

8.7 AI Integration with Software Products Lifecycle

With the integration of AI in software development, software developers can work more productively and with less cognitive strain by utilizing AI in software development. It entails using AI-based automated technologies to reduce human mistakes and direct human focus toward conceptual activities outside the scope of computer capabilities. AI-augmented software development suggests a multimodal "partnership" between humans and computers in which software engineers and development tools have different responsibilities. AI-based tools can perform more efficiently without altering their flow or finishing tasks differently. AI offers opportunities in both areas (Ozkaya, 2023, pp. 4–9). *Ebert et al.* have mentioned different

GenAI techniques and given an example of how they can be used in software development, such as using large language models for improving data quality, media content, and documentation, using AI tools available in the market for content creation such as audio, video, and demos. Besides this, AI has applications in complex tasks such as code generation in the development phase, generative design in the design phase, test case generation in the testing phase based on the requirements, and debugging and deployment (Ebert & Louridas, 2023). Thus, AI has applications in almost all significant phases of software development, which we will discuss in detail in the upcoming sections.

8.7.1 AI for Requirement Management

AI techniques have wide applications in the requirement and planning phase. As per the literature survey done by the authors for this chapter, it was found that research for AI use in the requirement management phase is one of the most dominant areas in the software development lifecycle. In this section, we will see different applications of AI in RE by studying the current published literature. Once the team gathers the requirements, "classifying requirements" into "functional" and "nonfunctional" requirements is one of the first tasks that need to be completed; automating this is a challenge because of the natural language used in the requirement-gathering process. Therefore, to understand this problem, *Abad et al.* suggested preprocessing techniques that can be used with ML algorithms, which can automatically classify requirements into functional and nonfunctional requirements (Abad et al., 2017). *Y. Zeng et al.* have examined and analyzed research that uses NLP and ML during the requirement elicitation stage. From this, "ML-based requirement elicitation methods were classified into five parts – (a). Data Cleansing and Preprocessing, (b). Textual Feature Extraction, (c). Learning, (d). Evaluation, and (e). Tools" (Cheligeer et al., 2022). Using NLP techniques, ML can also identify requirements in different domains and writing styles in textual requirements specifications. *Abualhaija et al.'s* automated ML approach shows an "average precision of 81.2% and an average recall of 95.7%," much more than simple baselines of demarcated requirements (Abualhaija et al., 2019). Choosing which needs to be addressed foremost and in what sequence is a tactical approach in software development. It is usual to refer to this process as requirements prioritization. To deliver promised advantages, *Perini et al.* describe a needs prioritization method called case-based ranking (CBRank), which blends requirements ordering approximations obtained by ML techniques with preferences from project stakeholders. Thus, it also demonstrates using ML techniques for requirement prioritization (Perini et al., 2013). *Ahmad et al.* have aimed to use a DL bidirectional gated recurrent units (BiGRU) approach to classify requirements into functional and nonfunctional using word and character sequences as tokens (AlDhafer et al., 2022). Risk prediction is one of the most delicate and essential tasks in the SDLC. It could make the difference between the project's success and failure.

Early risk prediction is crucial for maximizing the likelihood of a software project's success. *Vera and Del Carpio* used various ML techniques and tes+ted models for risk prediction (Vera & Del Carpio, 2024).

The core of requirement elicitation is requirement conflict. It is also the main factor in determining whether the planned information system project succeeds or fails. *Elhassan et al.* presented an automated approach for requirements conflict identification based on the Mean shift clustering unsupervised ML model (Elhassan et al., 2022). *Luo et al.* had a different approach to requirement classification that makes use of "BERT-based pre-trained language models (PRCBERT)," which employs "flexible, prompt templates" to accomplish the requirement classification and prompt learning (Luo et al., 2022). To detect privacy requirements in user stories, *Casillo et al.* have suggested an approach that blends DL algorithms with NLP and linguistic resources. Information about the text's semantic and syntactic structure is extracted using NLP technologies. A convolutional neural network that has already been trained on this data subsequently processes the data, opening the door for applying a transfer learning strategy (Casillo et al., 2022). *Siahaan et al.* mentioned a method for extracting user stories from online news in natural language that can help in elicitation (Siahaan et al., 2023). *Varenov et al.* suggested using various models to classify security requirements in natural languages (Varenov & Gabdrahmanov, 2021). Thus, from the content mentioned above, we have focused on the AI techniques that play a key role in the requirement management phase of software development that can help organizations plan and prioritize the correct requirements and avoid errors at a later stage.

8.7.2 AI Integration in Software Design and Development

Going into the further phases of software development, where the actual implementation of the requirements takes place to design, write code, and build a software product, we will explain the use of AI techniques in the development and implementation phases. *Raneri et al.* have developed and tested AI in product design and automated testing. They have focused on predictive technology under AI to provide entrepreneurs in a lean startup with a build-measure-learn loop. When they discovered that the algorithm could forecast the right level of "Product Design Decision" for digital products (Raneri et al., 2022), we can find the use of AI in software product design from this paper. Along with its application in the design phase of product development, AI is also under research for Agile project management for the development of software products, where it can help project managers by providing predictions for assessing risks and analytics for making decisions. *Dam et al.* researched the development of an AI-powered Agile project management assistant to accelerate productivity and increase project success rate (Dam et al., 2019). *Nimmo et al.* discuss the importance of AI skills for project managers and concludes that the field of project management will see a significant impact of AI and ML on both hard and soft skills (Nimmo & Usher, 2020). *P. Hofmann et al.* proposed a five-step method to develop organization-specific AI use cases in the project management domain (Hofmann et al., 2020).

Similarly, like GenAI, Explainable AI has its application in SE, which can be seen in (Tantithamthavorn & Jiarpakdee, 2021), which focuses on the accuracy of the AI/ML predictions that can provide explainable and actionable predictions. AI techniques can be used in various other core activities of software development, as mentioned by *Dehaerne et al.*, where various applications were listed, such as generating code from label, generating GUI code from screenshots, HTML generation from images of hand-drawn mock-ups, automatic program repair (APR), assisting in code translation (CUDA to OpenCL), code refactoring and programming-by-example (Dehaerne et al., 2022). *Benito et al.* have compared various neural network architectures and focused on using DL in code generation (Cruz-Benito et al., 2021). *Shin et al.* have mentioned six DL-based code generation models *(trans, External-Knowledge-Codegen [EK Codegen], CG-RL, Codegen-TAE, TreeCodeGen, PyCodeGPT)* selected based on high BLEU scores that are efficient for normal code generation and evaluated it on various parameters for ML programming tasks; these models can be referred for understanding the code generation applications through DL models (Shin et al., 2023). Other pretrained language models are also under development. They are showing promising results such as "CodeBERT," specifically designed for *understanding and manipulating both "NL-PL,"* i.e., natural language and programming language, which can bridge the gap between NL and PL and can help in the future for many applications such as "code search, code summarization, code completion, and code documentation generation" (Zhou et al., 2021). *Kim et al.* have suggested an "ML system" for "code prediction" by *feeding trees to transformers* that can help in the auto-completion of code or can provide the most potential output needed (i.e., *next token prediction*) (Kim et al., 2021). *Proksch et al.* have developed "pattern-based Bayesian networks (PBN)" based on the practical "best matching neighbor (BMN)" and *Bayesian Networks*, which are comparatively more effective for "code completion" (Proksch et al., 2015). *Aye et al.* checked the effectiveness of models on real-world data sets for code completion and highlighted the use of ML for this purpose (Aye et al., 2021). *Zhou et al.* investigated the robustness problem of the deep neural networks (DNN) when they are used for the SE task of "code comment generation." They suggested the *identifier substitution method known as "ACCENT (Adversarial Code Comment gENeraTor)" for creating adversarial code* (Y. Zhou et al., 2022). Thus, from the above section, we found various areas where different AI techniques, such as ML, NLP, DL, and DNN, can be used for various applications in software development.

8.7.3 AI in Software Testing

AI has been widely used in software testing. *Colakoglu et al.* have proposed a systematic mapping study on software product quality metrics highlighting the importance of quality situations in today's era (Colakoglu et al., 2021). *K. T. Wei et al.* provided a gap analysis for identifying the elements that influence the efficiency of the "software bug detection and prediction" methods now in use and evaluating the contribution of AI techniques to their improvement. The study highlights software development challenges and how AI can be used to improve the efficiency and reliability of software. The study also discusses the importance of communication between AI and SE practitioners (Fadhil et al., 2020). *D. Amalfitano et al.* found and evaluated 20 pertinent secondary papers; the analysis was carried out by mapping the chosen research by established AI and software testing taxonomies (Amalfitano et al., 2023). *Rath et al.* have suggested an approach for bug localization based on analyzing requirements. Here, the approach developed is called "TraceScore," which goes through the project's requirements, prepares bug reports, and traces the defective source code. This technique takes care of the natural language used to make reports and shows efficiency, as mentioned by the author. It makes the concept of "bug localization" easier and time-saving compared to the classical method (Rath et al., 2018).

Other than using AI techniques directly on the software under development, AI techniques such as NLP can be used to assist testers or test engineers in developing various kinds of test cases; *Wang et al.* presented "Use Case Modeling for System-level, Acceptance Tests Generation (UMTG)," where NLP can be used to develop "Acceptance Testcases automatically." This approach can translate the Use Case specifications, which are mainly in natural language, into data for Acceptance test cases (Wang et al., 2022). *Okanović et al.* have presented "PerformoBot," which can assist developers in "load testing" by helping them specify various parameters for the test and then with the help of a load testing tool to execute the test automatically, this can be used right from to configuration to report generation about the test (Okanović et al., 2020). *Riccio et al.* have demonstrated DL capabilities by use of the "DeepMetis" tool, which effectively enhances the provided test set, improving its average capacity to "identify mutants" (Riccio et al., 2021). *Fatima et al.* developed "Flakify, a language model-based predictor," which is tested for predicting "flaky testcases" which mainly works on source code and reduces the risks surrounding using the production code, also making use of CodeBERT for the prediction, which is an efficient way to save resources while testing (Fatima et al., 2023). *Batool et al.* have focused on different models of DL such as long short-term memory (LSTM), bidirectional LSTM (BILSTM), and radial basis function network (RBFN) to compare and study the efficacy of DL models in "Software Fault Predictions" (Batool & Khan, 2023). Moving forward from tests and test cases, *Izadi et al.* have identified the issues related to labelling and managing many issues in software repositories such as GitHub. They have developed a model to predict the objective of opening this issue priority level, which can make the issue-tracking process much easier and more efficient, raising the scope of AI techniques from the test and test case level to the more significant issue-management level (Izadi et al., 2022). All these techniques together recognize the use of AI in the software testing domain.

8.7.4 AI in Software Maintenance and Support

The maintenance and support phase of software development is one of the most essential parts of the software product lifecycle as it ensures the continuous use of the product with various updates and improvements. The current process creates many difficulties, where an organization needs to invest many resources to maintain the existing systems, and it is not easy to consistently provide improvements that meet customers' needs. However, using AI techniques contributes to this phase and provides new methods to provide a competitive advantage to the organization. *Mishra et al.* recommend using "GQM and ISO 9241–11" to quantify "usability expectations for mobile applications" that are M-commerce based on *fuzzy logic*. This AI method analyzes the user's expectations and preferences to determine how the mobile application is utilized. By identifying opportunities for improvement, this technique facilitates ongoing improvement and maintenance of the mobile application or software product (Mishra & Dadhich, 2024). AI technique can go beyond applying requirement elicitation at a business-to-business level. It can also focus on extracting new requirements from the online reviews made by the business-to-customer customers to evolve the product continuously for the user needs and sustain itself in the market. *Buchan et al.* evaluated three ML algorithms, namely naïve Bayes (with multinomial and Bernoulli variants), support vector machines (with linear and multinomial variants) and logistic regression, verifying that semi-automated "extraction of candidate requirements" from a sizable amount of noisy, unstructured web user evaluations is feasible and reliable (Buchan et al., 2018). Going beyond just identifying customer needs from online reviews, *Kilroy et al.* have unveiled a "multi-document keyphrase extraction system" that uses users' *Reddit* social media posts to foresee future consumer demands. This method can gain a competitive advantage by meeting significant consumer requirements that a large multinational firm has identified, with lead periods of up to 25 months before they become popular in the market (Kilroy et al., 2022). *Li et al.* have suggested the use of AI for crowdsourcing RE, which can be used to crowdsource requirements and automatically classify those user requirements; this can be used for improving the product continuously as per the changing needs of customers and makes it easy to analyze the requirements even in the natural language used by the users (Li et al., 2018). *Tizard et al.* mentions feedback's importance, as 71% of software products fail because of the shortness of feedback and its analyses. Thus, the paper suggests using AI in requirement mining in Software Product forums. There is a wide variety of data sources on product platforms, such as users interacting and mentioning their experience and needs about the product and mining, which can be utilized to modify the product as per user needs (Tizard, 2019).

Similarly, *Khan et al.* used the NLP and ML approach for knowledge acquisition from online forums, where the research was carried out on Reddit and requirement information was derived from the forum to help improve the software product (Khan et al., 2020). *Merten et al.* have focused on software feature request detection, an issue tracking system, to improve request management in the same system where bugs are reported, and other tasks are performed. With the traditional process, there is a possibility of delay in getting these requests recognized or even missed due to other prioritized bugs that need to be resolved. However, using ML can improve and avoid such issues, preventing the organization from remaining trapped in the bug resolution cycle and missing essential feature request needs that can lead to satisfied clients and competitive advantage (Merten et al., 2016). Hence, using AI techniques in the maintenance phase of the software product lifecycle can ensure that the organization reaps the fruits of the products and keeps its presence in the market. These techniques are more efficient than the traditional processes and are required to meet the high competition and volatility in the software market.

8.8 Discussion and Recommendation

From the above content, we developed a framework that summarizes and recognizes the significant areas of usage of AI techniques in different phases of software development and the associated applications (Figure 8.4). The proposed framework summarizes the data mentioned in the above sections of this chapter and derives different techniques that organizations can use in different software development phases. This work has analyzed the AI techniques and their application in a particular phase irrespective of the software model followed in the project. The primary intention is to do this due to every software development project's customizable nature, which depends entirely on the company. For example, a company may choose to use a scrum model; in another case, they may use a waterfall, which is entirely project-specific and based on the customer's requirements. Nevertheless, once the model is finalized and the project is planned, the question of using AI-based methods to solve issues arises, which management can choose by referring to our proposed framework. The framework consists of two sections divided by a horizontal line representing the time and progress of the project. The above section represents the waterfall model,

Artificial Intelligence and the Future of Software Development 183

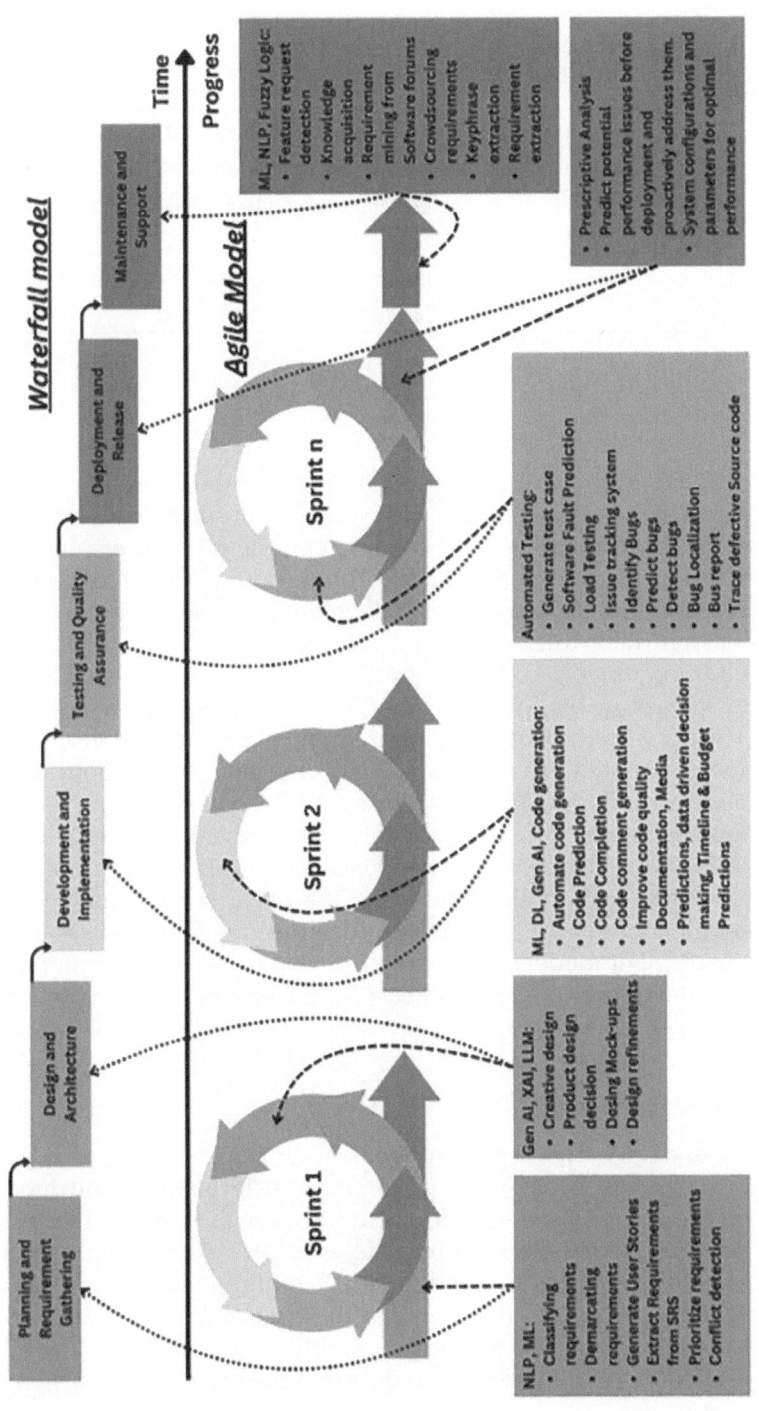

FIGURE 8.4
Mapping of AI technique with software product development

TABLE 8.4

Color Code for Proposed Framework

Color of Phase/Text Box	Name of Corresponding Phase
Blue	Planning and Requirements Gathering
Orange	Design and Architecture
Yellow	Development and Implementation
Green	Testing and Quality Assurance
Red	Deployment and Release
Purple	Maintenance and Support

where all the activities are aligned sequentially, and the following section represents the Agile model, representing different sprints for software development. To better understand the concept, the number of phases is kept the same for activities in the waterfall model and in the circular sprint diagram, representing the same color code followed throughout the framework as shown in Table 8.4.

The dotted body arrow connects the textbox mentioning the AI techniques and Phases in the Waterfall model. The dashed arrow connects phases in sprints with the text box containing relevant applications that AI can solve for the pointed phase. Table 8.5 maps the phases and applications of AI techniques with the technology used for it. The text box represents the techniques and applications that can be used to enhance the phases. Businesses should review the framework while planning and can choose suitable techniques and applications as per their project requirement. The business should identify the problems in their development process using various management models and then select one of the suitable methods mentioned in the framework that can become the best possible solution for the problem.

8.8.1 Proposed Framework

This framework can act as a primary evaluation content before the company approaches any consultancy firm for transformation. The model covers many opportunities a software firm can have to transform its business into a market leader. Hence, our model is helpful as a reference for all organizations facing difficulties and wanting to improve the efficiency of their software development. Incorporating these techniques in areas in the right-most column will make a complete AI-integrated software lifecycle, which will result in better software and faster releases, keeping customer satisfaction at peak.

TABLE 8.5

Mapping Table of AI Techniques with Software Product Development

No.	AI Techniques	Phase of Software Product Development Lifecycle	Description of Mapping (Areas of Scope for AI Implementation in Software Development)
1	Natural Language Processing (NLP)	Planning and Requirements Gathering	Detecting privacy requirements from user stories User story extraction from Natural language Extract requirements from text documents and specifications
2	Machine Learning (ML)	Planning and Requirements Gathering	Predict user behavior and product usage patterns to inform feature prioritization Cluster user feedback to identify common themes and areas for improvement Classifying functional and nonfunctional requirement Demarcating requirements in textual specifications Textual feature extraction Requirement prioritization Risk prediction in software requirements Conflict detection automation Entity extraction from software requirement specification
3	Generative AI	Design and Architecture	Generate creative design ideas for user interfaces and user experiences Design mock-ups and prototypes based on user preferences and desired functionalities Product design decision
4	Explainable AI (XAI)	Design and Architecture	Generated design decisions, ensuring transparency and trust in the process Facilitate collaboration between human designers and AI models for iterative design refinement
5	Code Generation	Development and Implementation	Automatically generate code Translate natural language specifications into executable code Improve code quality and automate code
6	Generative AI	Development and Implementation	Generate test cases Documentations AI/ML predictions Content and media quality Hard skill, soft skill support

(Continued)

TABLE.8.5 (Continued)

Mapping Table of AI Techniques with Software Product Development

No.	AI Techniques	Phase of Software Product Development Lifecycle	Description of Mapping (Areas of Scope for AI Implementation in Software Development)
7	ML, DL, RL	Development and Implementation	Code prediction Code completion Code generation Code comment generation Understanding and manipulating NL-PL Decision-making Data driven insights Predictions and estimations Budget estimations Timeline predictions
8	Automated Testing, ML, DL	Testing and Quality Assurance	Generate test cases and data sets for comprehensive software testing. Bug detection Bug prediction Bug localization Software fault predictions Load testing Acceptance test cases and testing Issue tracking system Predicting flaky test cases Preparing bug report Tracing to defective source code
9	Performance Optimization	Deployment and Release	Predict potential performance issues before deployment and proactively address them System configurations and parameters for optimal performance
10	Prescriptive Analytics	Deployment and Release	Predict potential issues Optimize release timing and rollout strategies based on market and user behavior data
11	ML, NLP	Maintenance and Support	Translate user documentation Support natural languages Analyze feedback from different regions and languages to identify global user needs Feature request detection Knowledge acquisition Requirement mining from software forums Crowdsourcing requirements Key phrase extraction Requirement extraction
12	Fuzzy Logic Techniques	Maintenance and Support	User needs for Mobile application

8.9 Use Cases

Although few examples in the industry are available, here we will demonstrate few use cases which demonstrate the industrial acceptance of AI technology in SDLC

8.9.1 Automated Code Generation

Automated code generation is similarly auto-correct found in today's document type applications but can be considered highly complex, although will similarly assist developers in developing code. Tools like Tabnine can be used for automated code generation and can help code correction.[1]

8.9.2 Project Management Using AI

AI-based Project management tools like Trello's AI assistance tool[2] and ClickUp[3] are good examples for easier management of resources and timelines and can help execute the Project Management Tasks easier. These tools may help in predicting project timeline, resource requirements, and any potential risks.

8.9.3 AI Assistance in Software Testing

Tools with AI assistance in testing can help in detecting and identifying errors or bugs early in the software development lifecycle. This can save later costs and save the reputation of the product when used by the customer. Tools like SonarQube[4] can help in keeping the code clean from bugs and assisting the development team with efficient testing methods. *Kindly Note: Authors do not promote or claim efficiency of any tool, the above are just examples for better understanding of readers. The name of the tools may not be the same in future depending on various industrial scenarios.*

8.10 Conclusion

This chapter mainly focuses on AI and its application in the software product development lifecycle. From this content, authors mapped various AI techniques for different phases of software development that researchers and businesses can refer to for their implementations. The authors developed a framework that can be referred to map different AI techniques in different areas, phases, and development applications. The study referred to a comprehensive set of techniques and application areas. However, it was identified that mainly, as per the current research environment, most of the work is done in ML and NLP techniques. These techniques are not just used for core software product development but also to enhance the product itself, as this will give precise requirements, better code and efficiently tested software. The focus was placed on the requirement management, development, testing, and maintenance phases, mainly related to product development direction, highlighting the importance of user needs or the needs-driven market of today's era. We believe that our proposed framework will enlighten the software development community with a wide range of techniques and areas of improvement at once and act as a primary guide for those who are seeking to make their software development process more efficient by using AI.

8.11 Future Scope

Implementing new technologies for existing processes takes resistance and requires an organization wide acceptance. Although, with the advent of AI technologies we see this trend changing where a lot of organizations are showing interest to get their systems and processes integrated with AI technologies to get a better outcome. In this chapter, we mainly discussed techniques that can be used in industry in the near future and have some existing ongoing research and implementations taking place. With this, setting the direction for future research is important as a guiding path to help us explore the cutting-edge technologies poised to impact the software development projects such as edge AI, autonomous software agents, and quantum computing. These technologies were currently out of scope for our scope because the extent of research is scarce. Moreover, these technologies are in evolving stage and can be separately considered as a focused topic for research. Therefore, we recommend these studies could be included in future studies.

Acknowledgment

The research was conducted at Symbiosis Centre for Information Technology, Pune, India, where the university helped to access various research articles in different databases which led to extraction of valuable knowledge from the available and sourced content.

Notes

1. https://www.tabnine.com/
2. https://support.atlassian.com/trello/docs/automation-overview/
3. https://clickup.com/ai
4. https://www.sonarsource.com/products/sonarqube/

References

Abad, Z. S. H., Karras, O., Ghazi, P., Glinz, M., Ruhe, G., & Schneider, K. (2017). What Works Better? A Study of Classifying Requirements. *2017 IEEE 25th International Requirements Engineering Conference*. https://doi.org/10.1109/re.2017.36

Abualhaija, S., Arora, C., Sabetzadeh, M., Briand, L. C., & Vaz, E. (2019). A Machine Learning-Based Approach for Demarcating Requirements in Textual Specifications. *2019 IEEE 27th International Requirements Engineering Conference (RE)*. https://doi.org/10.1109/re.2019.00017

AlDhafer, O., Ahmad, I., & Mahmood, S. (2022). An End-to-End Deep Learning System for Requirements Classification Using Recurrent Neural Networks. *Information & Software Technology, 147*, 106877. https://doi.org/10.1016/j.infsof.2022.106877

Alghamdi, A. I., & Niazi, M. (2022). Challenges of Secure Software Deployment: An Empirical Study. *The International Conference on Evaluation and Assessment in Software Engineering 2022 (EASE 2022)*, June 13–15. https://doi.org/10.1145/3530019.3531337

Amalfitano, D., Faralli, S., Hauck, J. C. R., Matalonga, S., & Distante, D. (2023). Artificial Intelligence Applied to Software Testing: A Tertiary Study. *ACM Computing Surveys, 56*(3), 1–38. https://doi.org/10.1145/3616372

Aye, G. A., Kim, S., & Li, H. (2021). Learning Autocompletion from Real-World Datasets. *43rd IEEE/ACM International Conference on Software Engineering: Software Engineering in Practice, ICSE-SEIP 2021*. https://doi.org/10.1109/icse-seip52600.2021.00022

Batool, I., & Khan, T. A. (2023). Software Fault Prediction Using Deep Learning Techniques. *Software Quality Journal, 31*(4), 1241–1280. https://doi.org/10.1007/s11219-023-09642-4

Böckle, G., Pohl, K., & Van Der Linden, F. (2005). A Framework for Software Product Line Engineering. In *Springer eBooks* (pp. 19–38). Springer. https://doi.org/10.1007/3-540-28901-1_2

Buchan, J., Bano, M., Zowghi, D., & Volabouth, P. (2018). Semi-Automated Extraction of New Requirements from Online Reviews for Software Product Evolution. *2018 25th Australasian Software Engineering Conference (ASWEC)*. https://doi.org/10.1109/aswec.2018.00013

Casillo, F., Deufemia, V., & Gravino, C. (2022). Detecting Privacy Requirements from User Stories with NLP transfer learning models. *Information & Software Technology, 146*, 106853. https://doi.org/10.1016/j.infsof.2022.106853

Cheligeer, C., Huang, J., Wu, G., Bhuiyan, N., Xu, Y., & Zeng, Y. (2022). Machine Learning in Requirements Elicitation: A Literature Review. *Artificial Intelligence for Engineering Design, Analysis and Manufacturing, 36.* https://doi.org/10.1017/s0890060422000166

Colakoglu, F. N., Yazıcı, A., & Mishra, A. (2021). Software Product Quality Metrics: A Systematic Mapping Study. *IEEE Access, 9,* 44647–44670. https://doi.org/10.1109/access.2021.3054730

Cruz-Benito, J., Vishwakarma, S., Martín-Fernández, F., & Faro, I. (2021). Automated Source Code Generation and Auto-Completion Using Deep Learning: Comparing and Discussing Current Language Model-Related Approaches. *AI, 2*(1), 1–16. https://doi.org/10.3390/ai2010001

Dam, H. K., Tran, T., Grundy, J., Ghose, A., & Kamei, Y. (2019). Towards Effective AI-Powered Agile Project Management. *2019 IEEE/ACM 41st International Conference on Software Engineering: New Ideas and Emerging Results (ICSE-NIER).* https://doi.org/10.1109/icse-nier.2019.00019

De Fátima Soares Borges, A., Laurindo, F. J. B., De Mesquita Spínola, M., Gonçalves, R. F., & De Mattos, C. A. (2021). The Strategic Use of Artificial Intelligence in the Digital Era: Systematic Literature Review and Future Research Directions. *International Journal of Information Management, 57,* 102225. https://doi.org/10.1016/j.ijinfomgt.2020.102225

De Silva, D., & Alahakoon, D. (2022). An Artificial Intelligence Life Cycle: From Conception to Production. *Patterns, 3*(6), 100489. https://doi.org/10.1016/j.patter.2022.100489

Dehaerne, E., Dey, B., Halder, S., De Gendt, S., & Meert, W. (2022). Code Generation Using Machine Learning: A Systematic Review. *IEEE Access, 10,* 82434–82455. https://doi.org/10.1109/access.2022.3196347

Ebert, C., & Louridas, P. (2023). Generative AI for software practitioners. *IEEE Journals & Magazine | IEEE Xplore.* Digital Object Identifier, August 1. https://doi.org/10.1109/MS.2023.3284195

Elhassan, H., Abaker, M., Abdelmaboud, A., & Rehman, M. B. (2022). Requirements Engineering: Conflict Detection Automation Using Machine Learning. *Intelligent Automation and Soft Computing, 33*(1), 259–273. https://doi.org/10.32604/iasc.2022.023750

Fadhil, J. A., Koh, T. W., & Kew, S. N. (2020). Artificial Intelligence for Software Engineering: An Initial Review on Software Bug Detection and Prediction. *Journal of Computer Science, 16*(12), 1709–1717. https://doi.org/10.3844/jcssp.2020.1709.1717

Fatima, S., Ghaleb, T. A., & Briand, L. C. (2023). Flakify: A Black-Box, Language Model-Based Predictor for Flaky Tests. *IEEE Transactions on Software Engineering, 49*(4), 1912–1927. https://doi.org/10.1109/tse.2022.3201209

Hofmann, P., Jöhnk, J., Protschky, D., & Urbach, N. (2020). Developing Purposeful AI Use Cases – A Structured Method and Its Application in Project Management. In *15th International Conference on Wirtschaftsinformatik (WI)* (pp. 33–49). https://doi.org/10.30844/wi_2020_a3-hofmann

Humpert, L., Röhm, B., Anacker, H., Dumitrescu, R., & Anderl, R. (2022). Method for Direct End Customer Integration into the Agile Product Development. *Procedia CIRP, 109,* 215–220. https://doi.org/10.1016/j.procir.2022.05.239

Izadi, M., Akbari, K., & Heydarnoori, A. (2022). Predicting the Objective and Priority of Issue Reports in Software Repositories. *Empirical Software Engineering, 27*(2). https://doi.org/10.1007/s10664-021-10085-3

Kanbach, D. K., Heiduk, L., Blueher, G., Schreiter, M., & Lahmann, A. D. (2023). The GenAI Is Out of the Bottle: Generative Artificial Intelligence from a Business Model Innovation Perspective. *Review of Managerial Science*. https://doi.org/10.1007/s11846-023-00696-z

Khan, J. A., Liu, L., & Wen, L. (2020). Requirements Knowledge Acquisition from online User Forums. *IET Software*, *14*(3), 242–253. https://doi.org/10.1049/iet-sen.2019.0262

Kilroy, D. P., Healy, G., & Caton, S. (2022). Using Machine Learning to Improve Lead Times in the Identification of Emerging Customer Needs. *IEEE Access*, *10*, 37774–37795. https://doi.org/10.1109/access.2022.3165043

Kim, S., Zhao, J., Tian, Y., & Chandra, S. (2021). Code Prediction by Feeding Trees to Transformers. *2021 IEEE/ACM 43rd International Conference on Software Engineering (ICSE)*. https://doi.org/10.1109/icse43902.2021.00026

Lee, W., & Chen, C. (2023). Agile Software Development and Reuse Approach with Scrum and Software Product Line Engineering. *Electronics*, *12*(15), 3291. https://doi.org/10.3390/electronics12153291

Li, C., Huang, L., Ge, J., Luo, B., & Ng, V. (2018). Automatically Classifying User Requests in Crowdsourcing Requirements Engineering. *Journal of Systems and Software*, *138*, 108–123. https://doi.org/10.1016/j.jss.2017.12.028

Liu, G., Wan, H., & Zhang, L. (2021). Application of Artificial Intelligence in Computer Network Technology in the Era of Big Data. *2021 2nd International Seminar on Artificial Intelligence, Networking and Information Technology (AINIT)*. https://doi.org/10.1109/ainit54228.2021.00139

Luo, X., Xue, Y., Xing, Z., & Sun, J. (2022). PRCBERT: Prompt Learning for Requirement Classification Using BERT-Based Pretrained Language Models. *37th IEEE/ACM International Conference on Automated Software Engineering (ASE '22)*. https://doi.org/10.1145/3551349.3560417

Merten, T., Falis, M., Hübner, P., Quirchmayr, T., Bürsner, S., & Paech, B. (2016). Software Feature Request Detection in Issue Tracking Systems. *2016 IEEE 24th International Requirements Engineering Conference*. https://doi.org/10.1109/re.2016.8

Mishra, M., & Dadhich, R. (2024). Fuzzy Logic-Based Quantification of Usability Expectation for M-Commerce Mobile Application by Using GQM and ISO 9241-11. *Journal of Computer Science*, *20*(1), 1–9. https://doi.org/10.3844/jcssp.2024.1.9

Moher, D., Liberati, A., Tetzlaff, J., & Altman, D. G. (2009). Preferred Reporting Items for Systematic Reviews and Meta-Analyses: The PRISMA Statement. *BMJ*, *339*, July 21, b2535. https://doi.org/10.1136/bmj.b2535

Nimmo, L., & Usher, G. (2020). "Job-Ready" Project Managers: Are Australian Universities Preparing Managers for the Impact of AI, ML and Bots? *Project Management Research and Practice*. Fachhochschule Dortmund, *6*, October–December. https://doi.org/10.37938/pmrp.vol6.0014

Okanović, D., Beck, S., Merz, L., Zorn, C., Merino, L., Van Hoorn, A., & Beck, F. (2020). Can a Chatbot Support Software Engineers with Load Testing? Approach and Experiences. *ICPE '20: Proceedings of the ACM/SPEC International Conference on Performance Engineering*. https://doi.org/10.1145/3358960.3375792

Ozkaya, I. (2023). The Next Frontier in Software Development: AI-Augmented Software Development Processes. *IEEE Journals & Magazine | IEEE Xplore*. Digital Object Identifier, August 1. https://doi.org/10.1109/MS.2023.3284169

Perini, A., Susi, A., & Avesani, P. (2013). A Machine Learning Approach to Software Requirements Prioritization. *IEEE Transactions on Software Engineering, 39*(4), 445–461. https://doi.org/10.1109/tse.2012.52

Proksch, S., Lerch, J., & Mezini, M. (2015). Intelligent Code Completion with Bayesian Networks. *ACM Transactions on Software Engineering and Methodology, 25*(1), 1–31. https://doi.org/10.1145/2744200

Raneri, S., Lecron, F., Hermans, J., & Fouss, F. (2022). Predictions Through Lean Startup? Harnessing AI-Based Predictions Under Uncertainty. *International Journal of Entrepreneurial Behaviour & Research, 29*(4), 886–912. https://doi.org/10.1108/ijebr-07-2021-0566

Rath, M., Lo, D., & Mäder, P. (2018). Analyzing Requirements and Traceability Information to Improve Bug Localization. *ACM/IEEE 15th International Conference on Mining Software Repositories, MSR '18*. https://doi.org/10.1145/3196398.3196415

Riccio, V., Humbatova, N., Jahangirova, G., & Tonella, P. (2021). DeepMetis: Augmenting a Deep Learning Test Set to Increase its Mutation Score. *2021 36th IEEE/ACM International Conference on Automated Software Engineering (ASE)*. https://doi.org/10.1109/ase51524.2021.9678764

Shin, J., Wei, M., Wang, J., Shi, L., & Wang, S. (2023). The Good, the Bad, and the Missing: Neural Code Generation for Machine Learning Tasks. *arXiv (Cornell University)*. https://doi.org/10.1145/3630009

Siahaan, D., Raharjana, I. K., & Fatichah, C. (2023). User Story Extraction from Natural Language for Requirements Elicitation: Identify Software-Related Information from Online News. *Information & Software Technology, 158*, 107195. https://doi.org/10.1016/j.infsof.2023.107195

Siddique, S., Naveed, M., Ali, A. M., Keshta, I., Satti, M. I., Irshad, A., Alomari, Z., Edo, O. C., & Diekola, O. A. (2023). An Effective Framework to Improve the Managerial Activities in Global Software Development. *Nonlinear Engineering, 12*(1). https://doi.org/10.1515/nleng-2022-0312

Simhadri, R. S., & Shameem, M. (2023). Challenges in Requirements Gathering for Agile Software Development. *EASE '23: Proceedings of the 27th International Conference on Evaluation and Assessment in Software Engineering*. https://doi.org/10.1145/3593434.3594237

Sofian, H., Yunus, N. A. M., & Ahmad, R. (2022). Systematic Mapping: Artificial intelligence Techniques in Software Engineering. *IEEE Access, 10*, 51021–51040. https://doi.org/10.1109/access.2022.3174115

Sun, F., Luh, D., Zhao, Y., & Sun, Y. (2022). Product Classification with the Motivation of Target Consumers by Deep Learning. *IEEE Access, 10*, 62258–62267. https://doi.org/10.1109/access.2022.3181624

Taboada, I., Daneshpajouh, A., Toledo, N., & De Vass, T. (2023). Artificial Intelligence Enabled Project Management: A Systematic Literature Review. *Applied Sciences, 13*(8), 5014. https://doi.org/10.3390/app13085014

Tantithamthavorn, C., & Jiarpakdee, J. (2021). Explainable AI for Software Engineering. *2021 36th IEEE/ACM International Conference on Automated Software Engineering (ASE)*. https://doi.org/10.1109/ase51524.2021.9678580

Tizard, J. (2019). Requirement Mining in Software Product Forums. *2019 IEEE 27th International Requirements Engineering Conference (RE)*. https://doi.org/10.1109/re.2019.00057

Varenov, V., & Gabdrahmanov, A. (2021). Security Requirements Classification into Groups Using NLP Transformers. *2021 IEEE 29TH International Requirement Engineering Conference Workshops (REW)*. https://doi.org/10.1109/rew53955.2021.9714713

Vera, Y. P., & Del Carpio, Á. F. (2024). Comparing Machine Learning Techniques for Software Requirements Risk Prediction. *Indonesian Journal of Electrical Engineering and Computer Science, 34*(1), 508. https://doi.org/10.11591/ijeecs.v34.i1.pp508-519

Wang, C., Pastore, F., Göknil, A., & Briand, L. C. (2022). Automatic Generation of Acceptance Test Cases from Use Case Specifications: An NLP-Based Approach. *IEEE Transactions on Software Engineering, 48*(2), 585–616. https://doi.org/10.1109/tse.2020.2998503

Yang, J., & Wan, Y. (2022). The Development Trend of Artificial Intelligence in the Big Data Environment. *2022 3rd International Conference on Electronic Communication and Artificial Intelligence (IWECAI)*. https://doi.org/10.1109/iwecai55315.2022.00064

Zhou, X., Han, D., & Lo, D. (2021). Assessing Generalizability of CodeBERT. *2021 IEEE International Conference on Software Maintenance and Evolution (ICSME)*. https://doi.org/10.1109/icsme52107.2021.00044

Zhou, Y., Zhang, X., Shen, J., Han, T., Chen, T., & Gall, H. (2022). Adversarial Robustness of Deep Code Comment Generation. *ACM Transactions on Software Engineering and Methodology, 31*(4), 1–30. https://doi.org/10.1145/3501256

Part 3

Blockchain and Governance
Enhancing Trust and Accountability

9

Immutable Transparency: Leveraging Blockchain Transparency Features to Foster Trust in Decentralized Systems

Manisha Singh and Sonali Srivastava

9.1 Introduction

Blockchain has been gaining significant attention in popular and business press; Information technology research and advisory company Gartner places it in the "peak of inflated expectations" – the beginning of a hype cycle of public attention and expectation (Toufaily et al., 2021). Blockchain refers to a distributed and immutable ledger that permanently records all transactions across a network. It is the technology that underpins digital currencies and has the potential to immensely impact various critical systems, from finance to healthcare to the Internet of Things (IoT) (Komalavalli et al., 2020). One of the key features of blockchain is its use of cryptographic techniques to create a verifiable and permanent data record. Each block in a blockchain contains a cryptographic hash of the previous block, a timestamp, and transaction data. By design, it is "immutable," as the record cannot be changed – any fraudulent changes will be immediately apparent. This permanence and the cryptographic assurance of the integrity of the data provide a high degree of transparency in the system (Rahardja et al., 2021).

In the context of decentralized systems, the problem of fraud is compounded by the lack of any single entity exercising control and by the need to enable a potentially unbounded and unknown set of entities to come to a consensus on the current state of the system (Roszkowska, 2020). Thus, these systems could greatly benefit from a technology that enables not only the decentralization and openness that today's modern systems attempt to achieve but also increased transparency that can address fraud – namely, blockchain technology. Currently, in the centralized systems that dominate today's critical infrastructure, fraud prevention and detection are enabled through various mechanisms, including market regulation, standardization, and auditing and reporting requirements (Alazab et al., 2021). A decentralized network offers some advantages, but it could also lead to some challenges.

First, without centralized control, the network risks fragmentation, resulting in different competing standards, separate markets, and the multiplication of intermediaries, thus damaging user economic consequences. Second, the network's decentralization has made tracing illegal activities more difficult. This could provide advantages for criminals who use technology. Third, it amplifies the effects of operational or group behavioral dynamics of the decision and action of the individual nodes, indicating that where the consequences of a bad decision (such as a cyber-attack or other misuse) are less than the contained detriment, there is an increased potential for more common lousy fruit. Decentralized systems possess inherent models that do not depend on any central trusted third parties, and several application-based decentralized systems built on blockchain technology have emerged. Trust is vital to any multi-agent system, and its absence can lead to catastrophic failures.

As decentralized applications built on blockchain technology become part of day-to-day life, the need for trust in such systems grows. Trust and transparency go hand in hand, where transparency ensures accountability and builds trust amid fear and suspicion. Transparency requires the disclosure of important details, and such mechanisms should be studied to enhance trust in the absence of a central entity. Most existing research concentrates on the technical aspects of blockchain-based decentralized systems, such as consensus protocols and security measures. However, transparency is equally important for building trust in such systems (Alazab et al., 2021). Therefore, blockchain's inherent transparency features and usage in decentralized applications must be studied. Existing analysis of transparency features of blockchain-based systems is limited, and there is no structured study explaining various transparency features and their strength levels.

Blockchain technology gained notable interest due to its transparency feature, enabling all users to view every transaction in the database. The implementation of smart contracts enabled blockchain technology to be applied in various domains, including finance, supply chains, healthcare, IoT, and more. Despite its popularity and widespread implementation, the transparency feature of blockchain technology remains ambiguous to users. Many users do not know how transparency benefits and builds trust in such systems activities (Rejeb et al., 2020). This research considers this gap, examining transparency features concerning blockchain's functionalities to encourage further exploration by researchers and decentralized application builders.

9.2 Overview of Blockchain Technology

Blockchain technology is a decentralized, distributed ledger system that ensures secure and tamper-proof transactions between parties without intermediaries. Blockchain is a peer-to-peer network architecture in which cryptography stores information in blocks. The blocks are organized in a chain based on the consensus protocol followed by the network. Transactions in the blockchain are collected and added in the form of blocks. Every transaction is broadcast to the network and is accepted by the system once a certain number of nodes agree that a transaction is valid. When a block is completed, it also gets its timestamp. Each block includes the prior block's hash and its own timestamp (Komalavalli et al., 2020). As such, a blockchain resists modifying its data: once recorded, the data in any given block cannot be altered retroactively. In that way, blockchains are inherently resistant to modification of the data. The term "distributed ledger technology" is often used interchangeably with blockchain, and the distributed ledger that blockchain technology enables is a more accurate description because it can be utilized in formats that do not involve a chain of blocks, such as hash graphs. HashMap, another type of distributed ledger, does not involve the chain of transactions linked by cryptography and, therefore, is not a blockchain (Akhter et al., 2022).

9.2.1 Trust in Decentralized Systems

The mandate to establish security in decentralized systems is closely followed by the need to develop trust. Trust is a significant factor in every aspect of social, political, and economic exchanges. Institutions do not work effectively without trust, impositions proliferate, and legitimacy is at risk. All these apply also to computers and networks. Over the years, many trust models have been evaluated and adopted for traditional systems. However, it is acknowledged that many of these models do not cater to the complexities, particularly the need to establish and maintain a pervasive level of trust in a decentralized manner (Truong et al., 2021). Whether a peer-to-peer file-sharing service or a community wireless network, decentralized systems rely on multiple participants making localized autonomous decisions.

These systems will become more pervasive and introduce new applications, from pervasive healthcare to environmental management systems. Establishing and maintaining trust in a decentralized environment is not new; the need for secure and effective mechanisms for performing electronic transactions has been widely recognized. The emergence of Bitcoin and its underlying blockchain technology has led to a paradigm change in technical and trust architectures within decentralized systems (Zhang, 2020). Nevertheless, only a few individuals delve into the notion of transparency, which they firmly believe to be the most profound element of this technology. When transparency is mentioned in conjunction with blockchains, it often refers to the fact that the data stored is transparent and visible to all participants. However, transparency in the formation, verification, and execution of the rules, or smart contracts, that govern a blockchain network is key (Centobelli et al., 2022).

9.2.2 Objectives

Demonstrate why transparency is a fundamental property in decentralized systems by leveraging the transparency features of blockchain technology to prevent and detect fraud. Provide a comprehensive explanation of how fraud is currently addressed in decentralized systems and how blockchain transparency features can effectively mitigate fraud.

9.3 Fraud in Decentralized Systems

The challenges and complexity of fraud in decentralized systems are numerous. Such systems lack a centralized authority to prevent and respond to fraudulent activities. Distributed networks are open to anyone, and have no strict requirements for participation or identification, creating an environment in which malicious actors can quickly enter and exit. Furthermore, decentralized systems typically employ some form of consensus mechanism to facilitate decision-making (Tyagi, 2023). These features allow fraud to manifest and evolve beyond mere tampering with transaction records.

9.3.1 Understanding the Challenges of Fraud

All transactions and data in a typical decentralized system are interconnected. However, combining the information production and validation process without a trusted authority often leads to two main inevitable challenges of fraud in those systems. The first is the presence of malicious or dishonest participants. Such fraud neither involves hacking, system misuse, nor abusive behavior; a single entity can defraud the system without others' awareness or approval. Traditional centralized systems also face malicious actions, but the risks are less due to regulations, laws, and accountability mechanisms (Dib & Toumi, 2020). In a decentralized environment, the number of available participants for fraud is large and may not be related to offline analogs.

The second challenge is the lack of a governing body to resolve disputes and issue penalties. In a fraud case, conflicts can arise between different parties. However, there is no clear strategy or mechanism to resolve the issue in a decentralized system. It is because the fraud is distributed, and every single entity is potentially under the threat of being defrauded, including the current dispute resolution provider (Aouidef et al., 2021). As a result of that, the lack of authority to issue penalties in a decentralized environment often leads to the removal of the released content as the only effective punishment. This also deteriorates the trust between the participants.

9.3.2 Impact of Fraud on Decentralized Networks

When fraud incidents occur in a decentralized network, measures that previously worked well in a centralized environment – such as risk prevention, fraud detection, investigation, and reporting – now need to be redefined and even reinvented to suit these new information communication technology networks. Driven by increasing transparency and trust in a decentralized environment, bottom-up monitoring, evidence sharing, and behavior analysis can be amplified. These mechanisms can help build an environment of continuous oversight and collaborative operational risk management (Wu et al., 2023). However, the level of coordination and complexity due to many stakeholders and dynamic network behaviors deepens the impact of fraud in decentralized networks. Since decentralized systems' participants only need to reach an agreement instead of generating their information, the harmful parts have an immensely and historically wide impactful space to exploit.

9.3.3 Need for Transparent Mechanisms to Mitigate Fraud

In traditional systems, such as centralized systems used for financial transactions, transparency is usually achieved by ensuring that any relevant party or authority can view a particular user's transactions and account details. These transparency features are managed by central authorities (Ghode et al., 2020). Fraud detection and prevention can be achieved by keeping evidence of all the transactions as well as account details and user actions and by allowing relevant parties to examine that information in case fraudulent activities have been identified. On the contrary, in a decentralized system where a central authority does not exist, ensuring transparency and executing the right measures to mitigate fraud is much more challenging.

The term "decentralized system" in this section refers to a network in which the processing power is distributed among multiple nodes, and no one can control the whole network. The challenges lie in: first, the lack of a central authority to validate and authorize transactions; second, the difficulty in identifying malicious actors across an extensive network; and last, the issue that in existing decentralized systems, rules and guidelines are either nonexistent or yet to be matured, resulting in limited accountability of every user and hence a higher potential for fraudulent activities (Bodkhe et al., 2020). Given the challenges of implementing fraud prevention measures in such types of networks, fraudsters have been shifting their attention from traditional systems to emerging ones. For instance, reports have emerged that cryptocurrencies, which operate under a decentralized network, have become a common subject for fraudsters. Fraudulent activities such as Ponzi schemes, where returns are paid to existing investors from new capital paid by new investors, have caused substantial financial losses to the market (Alexander & Cumming, 2022). This suggests that crypto-related fraudulent activities tend to be more lucrative and profitable, as the vulnerabilities in the systems have not been successfully or effectively mitigated due to the lack of transparent mechanisms for fraud detection and prevention. All in all, the emergence of decentralized systems and their importance in our society is inevitable.

9.4 Blockchain Transparency Features

In the case of public blockchains, we often refer to their ability to provide an open and transparent environment where all the participants may inspect the given blockchain to ensure its integrity. Such features, which are contrary to the private ones, are said to allow blockchain to foster trust between unknown parties and build trustable decentralized systems. To begin with, let us provide a comprehensive overview of the transparency elements inherent in blockchain technology. Subsequently, we will delve into the correlation between transparency and the inherent trustworthiness of decentralized systems (Centobelli et al., 2022; Zavolokina et al., 2020).

Blockchain technology is famous for its high level of transparency. Information stored on a blockchain can be easily verified by any user of the system. This transparency is considered to be one of the powerful features of blockchain, and it has facilitated many different use cases of blockchain technology. Unlike the real-world physical environment, the physical presence of any physical object cannot be stored in a blockchain platform. In decentralized systems, trust is established by allowing parties to come to a consensus and make decisions. This can be particularly challenging when the parties involved do not have prior knowledge or no reason to trust each other. In such an environment, transparency becomes crucial in building trust among parties. Transparency is the degree to which information is made available in a system. In models of decentralized trust, transparency allows parties to verify, without doubt, the actions and assertions of others. When every action is publicly recorded and made available, parties can independently verify the history of the system.

First and foremost, as mentioned earlier, all records are grouped into blocks that are linked together cryptographically – hence the term "blockchain." These blocks are stored in a sequential, linear database so that it is impossible for anyone to modify a block of records once it has been added to the database. If any alteration is attempted, a hacker would need to change the block itself and every block that comes after it, not just on a single system but most of the systems on the network. Some benefits of immutability are apparent. Once data has been written to the blockchain, it cannot be erased, hidden, or altered. All changes are recorded and so can be audited with ease (Dolev & Liber, 2022). Counterfeiting in the supply chain is a good example of where blockchain technology can be used to ensure immutability.

Every significant stage of a product's lifecycle can be recorded and verified as being correct on the blockchain. Counterfeits simply would not have the correct history, and so could be immediately identified. Also, the use of public key infrastructure (PKI) ensures that all participants are uniquely identifiable and data cannot be decrypted or altered except by the correct individual. This protects the system against fraud. Combining a blockchain with a consensus algorithm makes it possible to achieve an entirely autonomous and democratic system that requires no third-party intervention. An example of such a system would be a blockchain-based election. The security given by the immutability of the vote data and the absence of the need for a person to manually check the validity of the vote makes this a desirable proposition for large-scale and critical administrative processes.

9.5 Mitigating Fraud through Transparent Mechanisms

On decentralized systems, the absence of a centralized authority creates an environment where fraud can easily occur and be sustained. This is due to the lack of a single point of oversight and the need for consensus between multiple independent participants in order to reach or establish a decision. Fraud prevention methods typically fall into one of two categories: data-centric approaches and model-centric approaches. Data-centric approaches focus primarily on ensuring only quality data is observed and processed in the decentralized network, preventing false observations from being made on the network in the first place. Measurement-based detection techniques seek to enforce truthful reporting by observing the reported state and inferring the quality of the observed state from the reports themselves.

When the protocol used in the decentralized network is known a priori, data-centric approaches can be optimal. However, the inability to detect fraud, even with the use of transparency mechanisms, is often a drawback. Model-centric approaches assume that the underlying system model is partially or completely known. In the case where the model is partially known, independent agents are used to cross-reference and verify each other's observations. In the case where the model is completely known, manipulations often require agents to generate additional parallel observations of a variable to fake or omit the observation of the variable altogether. While these approaches extensively explore the use of transparency for fraud detection in centralized systems, the framework is quite different in decentralized network settings and existing mechanisms are often difficult to implement (Xu et al., 2021). Also, as the history of transactions is present and accessible to all participants, the actions committed by any particular user are more accountable. This is particularly important for systems that engage in financial transactions or other mission-critical businesses. With the nature of public verification provided by blockchain, every transaction that involves the movement of assets can be scrutinized and verified for its legitimacy.

9.5.1 Challenges of Fraud in Decentralized Systems

9.5.1.1 Lack of Centralized Authority

Blockchain will no doubt decrease the costs of most transactions by eliminating third parties, shortening process time, and increasing the previous untapped asset liquidity for every industry. Imagine the benefits to finance and accounting if it were possible to use blockchain to replace layers of accountants now required to audit accounts and transactions in a tiered multi-entity business flow. In a decentralized model – where the data and control are distributed – there is no single point of control, and data may be held locally, remotely, or in multiple locations. Ultimately, it is the inability to rely on a centralized authority to verify the authenticity of data and identities in a decentralized system that provides fraudsters with the opportunities they need (Helmrich et al., 2021). The key challenge in trusting decentralized systems is the lack of a central authority that can verify the legitimacy of transactions and identities. Without a central authority, there is no way to independently confirm the accuracy of digital records or the authenticity of virtual identities.

9.5.1.2 Difficulty in Identifying Malicious Actors

A major challenge associated with digital currencies and decentralized systems is the difficulty in identifying malicious actors. This challenge is particularly apparent in various online forms of communication, such as discussion forums and messaging apps, where an inherent level of anonymity can be both beneficial and detrimental. With the proliferation of new technology, payment systems, and assets attempting to usher in a decentralized monetary arrangement, the risks associated with anonymity have been magnified. Without the ability to pore through an entity's online history or identity, problems arise from a lack of familiarity with the actors involved. Unfortunately, bad actors can use this anonymity to their advantage.

For an instance, a group of enthusiasts may come together to create an open-source digital currency, freely available to anyone with the necessary technical expertise. A dedicated development team is formed, an online discussion group is set up, and excitement starts to build. A payment system is independently created to allow novel currency units to be easily traded for either traditional currency systems or goods and services. Clients are designed to enable end users to make and receive transactions with digital currency easily. As the currency gains popularity, the value and volume of transactions grow, drawing attention from others. Some of these new arrivals might have wanted to lend their support or build on the nascent currency. Others may enter with less altruistic intentions.

9.5.1.3 Limited Accountability

On decentralized systems, transactions are easy to hide by obfuscating the connection between user identity and transaction history. Pseudonymity offers limited accountability in decentralized systems since it is difficult for a user to be held accountable for his actions when his identity is hidden behind a pseudonym, which does not link to his real-world identity. If an account is blocked or a user is blacklisted, a malicious actor with a pseudonymous identity can always create a new identity and continue its previous behavior. On the other hand, a non-pseudonymous approach lacks the privacy that users on a decentralized system are granted, exposing them to targeted attacks being connected to their real-world identity (Chatzigiannis et al., 2021).

9.5.2 How Blockchain Transparency Features Mitigate Fraud?

9.5.2.1 Immutable and Auditable Transaction History

One of the foremost transparency features embedded into blockchain technology is the ability for all participants in the network to instantly access an immutable and auditable transaction history. Network participants have access to the exact, unchangeable copy of the blockchain, which documents each and every transaction carried on the blockchain in chronological order so that the entire history of the transaction can be easily retrieved and verified at any point. In utilizing this transparency feature, participants can actively and continuously monitor the assets or information they have transferred to a blockchain in terms of accuracy, ownership, authenticity, and fraud detection Komalavalli et al., 2020. As a result, blockchain systems that maintain an auditable transaction history represent a more secure and transparent method for managing digital assets and financial transactions than traditional systems based on centralized trust authorities and private ledgers. These themes – security, transparency, and centralized trust – will be explored throughout the rest of this section.

9.5.2.2 Public Verification of Transactions

Blockchain users can quickly validate transactions through access to the entire ledger. The need for public verification arises from the fact that anyone can read and write records in the blockchain. Since every transaction can be audited through public verification, it is impossible for a user to spend coins that do not invoice from him/her. Any fraud during validation is easy to spot because the hacker will still need to change all subsequent blocks. Public verification therefore provides the simplest way to detect any fraud during the transaction verification process. If any user attempts to remove a block from the chain, this will be easily spotted by other users. Public verification discourages hacking and fraud because a successful validation requires consensus among all users. This ensures that no fraudulent transaction can be included into the blockchain.

9.5.2.3 Consensus Mechanisms for Fraud Detection

There are several types of consensus mechanisms used in blockchain networks. Nevertheless, blockchains do not utterly eliminate the need for mutual trust among participants. Monitored participants are still able to collude in an attempt to manipulate the transaction history and change the actual ownership of an asset or information. The level of collusion capable of being undertaken by participants differs between different consensus algorithms. In permissionless blockchains utilizing the proof-of-work consensus algorithm, it has been determined that up to 49% of the network participants can collude with one another to conduct a double-spend attack. However, in the event of participants being monitored and audited, the party being audited would not be able to conduct a successful double-spend attack, regardless of the attempt of other participants to collude. That is, the more cryptocurrencies a stakeholder has, the more likely they will be chosen to validate the next block. PoS is considered to be faster and more energy efficient than proof of work. Other consensus mechanisms include delegated proof of stake (DPoS) and practical Byzantine Fault Tolerance (pBFT). DPoS introduces the concept of a validator, who is selected by the stakeholders. Only the validators are trusted to produce blocks, and they receive rewards for doing so. In pBFT, a replica that would like to propose a block on the blockchain is designated as the leader for that view. The leader assigns the order and sequence numbers to each block and sends a proposal to the other nodes to get their votes. There are different voting phases, and the block will be committed to the chain only when more than two-thirds of the nodes agree on the validity of the block.

9.6 Threats to Transparency and Trust in Decentralized Systems

9.6.1 Manipulation of Data and Records

The first common threat to trust and transparency in decentralized systems is the manipulation of data. Because most decentralized networks rely on some form of majority consensus to validate and record information, attackers need to control only the majority, not the entire network, to tamper with the public record. This is especially the case with proof of work systems due to the 51% attack vulnerability. In a 51% attack, an attacker with the computational resources to produce the majority of the hashing power of a blockchain network can maliciously manipulate the public record. This type of attack undermines trust in the information stored in the blockchain, since it is no longer impossible to fraudulently modify the record.

9.6.2 Sybil Attacks and Identity Fraud

In response to the lack of a central authority that can verify the identity of individuals in a network, Sybil attacks and identity fraud are common challenges in decentralized systems. In a Sybil attack, a malicious user creates multiple false identities to gain influence in a network. Since decentralized systems often rely on the principle of "one-identity-one-vote," the attacker can manipulate the system by allocating more than one identity to themselves. Such attacks were first brought to the attention of the computer science community by the developer of a peer-to-peer online community who went by the pseudonym "Sybil." This is the exact outcome that becomes possible through the successful execution of a Sybil attack. Sybil's attacks can also be remarkably damaging. For example, if a service uses a reputation system to build trust between users, a Sybil attacker could submit numerous ratings on their own services, in the hopes of artificially inflating their reputation. The essence of this attack is the ability to fabricate the digital identity of the attacker, rendering the use of identity as a measure of trust valueless. The defining feature of blockchain technology, its immutable public ledger allowing for transparency and traceability, makes it resistant to fraudulent behaviors, such as Sybil attacks. Through the implementation of mechanisms like proof of work or proof of stake – which exploit the transparency of blockchain to verify transactions and mitigate the potential for manipulation – and the requirement for users to disclose their digital signatures in order to submit transactions on a blockchain, the possibility of identity fraud can be significantly reduced.

9.6.3 Collusion among Network Participants

Collusion is defined as an agreement between two or more parties to disrupt the regular operation of a network. In the context of blockchain, it refers to the scenario where coalitions of miners, e.g., control a disproportionately large share of the network's computing power. This might enable the colluding members to prevent new transactions from being approved or even reverse transactions that had been completed, which will be detrimental to the proof-of-work that can be relied on (Xiao et al., 2020). Monitoring and preventing collusion among network participants is a topical and ongoing area of research and will become increasingly crucial as blockchain is being adopted by a wide range of different application areas, which span from the maintaining of land registry, financial transaction processing, and to even the provision of e-voting services and counting. The real problem in solving network participant collusion is that the identity of the attackers is often unknown. However, the transparent nature of the blockchain will often make it possible to trace any malicious activities back to the offending parties, as the audit trail left by the blockchain will help to identify those who attempt to commit the attack. As a result, it does not have any sole controlling party, and therefore, the ability to manipulate a single blockchain instance is extremely limited. This type of architecture makes the manipulation of any blockchain, including all of the tasks and the blocks within, incredibly difficult, even with hardware advances.

9.7 Strategies for Addressing Challenges and Vulnerabilities

The use of a regulated framework incorporating a balance between security and accessibility aspects can optimize e-voting. Governed by a regulatory regime, it would suffice for a framework that sets out best practices, rights, and obligations that apply to the setup and operation of an e-voting solution, along with enforcement and supervision from the demonstration of adherence to the relevant security standards (Essex & Goodman, 2020). This would provide a baseline for proving compliance with legal and international standards in cyber security, as well as offering transparency to the voters in the sense that adequate safeguards are in place which would prevent any tampering.

Now, ways of addressing these challenges facing blockchain and other e-voting platforms could be as follows: encryption and privacy enhancing technologies; governance frameworks and regulation; and continuous monitoring and auditing. By having end-to-end encryption, it ensures that any intermediary nodes, systems, servers, and the election governing body cannot view or tamper with the votes cast by the voter. Security and cryptographic measures such as firewalls, digital signatures, and PKIs can also be deployed to enhance the integrity and authentication of a vote when transmitted across a network (Mullegowda et al., 2024). Such methods provide the means to sign ballots and cast votes in a secure fashion, with the aim of preventing attempts at vote tampering during electronic transmission.

Also, it is necessary to expedite the development of privacy technologies that can be incorporated into the blockchain to better protect user's private data on the ledger. Such technologies include weak blocks that can hide transaction timestamp, confidential transactions that can protect transaction amount and stealth address that can prevent the revealing of a user's public key in a transaction. The integration of privacy-enhancing technologies can be made through soft forks, which can preserve backward compatibility and ensure that all previous and non-upgraded nodes still function well.

Governance refers to the rules, processes or laws by which a blockchain, crypto currency or decentralized system is regulated. One of the main advantages of decentralized technologies, such as blockchain, is that they are not subject to a single jurisdiction or regulatory body. However, this also means that it is necessary to give thought to how such technologies will be governed. This is especially important for public trust in blockchain applications. There are already a number of organizations and decentralized entities petitioning for legal recognition of their governance models. In any organization, good governance includes proper regulatory compliance and a clear framework for decision-making. However, it is early days in the prescriptive governance regulation of blockchain technology. The European Union has recently recognized a "European Blockchain Partnership," and the European Commission is running a "European Blockchain Observatory and Forum."

Blockchain networks require continuous monitoring and auditing mechanisms to ensure the security and integrity of the system. Real-time monitoring of data and network activities can detect and prevent cyber security incidents and promptly initiate responses. Data integrity and consistency checks must be conducted frequently, and any discrepancy should be reported and acted upon. These tasks can be automated at the system level through predefined and well-structured data management procedures. In summary, continuous monitoring refers to the regular and routine checking of the blockchain data, network, and system activities and data integrity, while auditing refers to the examination of blockchain materials, the data, and the network activities with the purposes of identifying and managing risks, and ensuring that the audited system adheres to the relevant policies and regulations. Most importantly, continuous monitoring and auditing are necessary for blockchain and its application-specific network; such comprehensive strategies are also essential features in modern cyber resiliency programs. However, the most important benefit of continuous monitoring and auditing on a blockchain network is the traceability and accountability that can be derived from the transparent nature of the technology.

9.8 The Interplay between Transparency and Trust in Decentralized Systems

An exploration of the interplay between transparency and trust in blockchain systems is undertaken, focusing on the relationship between these critical components of decentralized systems. Transparency and trust are observed as positive moderators in the functioning of blockchain systems. Blockchain systems are considered untrusted environments with certain attacks and vulnerabilities. When it comes to systems of accountability, this principle relies on providing public or institutional access to information about actions taken in the system, along with the ability to verify that those actions align with legitimate standards. There is a need to explore the interaction between transparency and trust in blockchain systems' network and protocol design.

Transparency is a primary construct in blockchain systems, achieved through transaction ledger exposure to all nodes in the network and on-chain governance that involves active participation from network participants in protocol rule decisions. Trust is a widely discussed but poorly understood subjective construct that is difficult to objectively quantify. Trust in blockchain systems can be classified as trust in the underlying technology, trust in self-executing protocols, and trust in participants' characteristics.

Diving deeper into the threefold classification of blockchain trust, trust in the underlying technology refers to how much one understands blockchain technology in terms of its advantages and limitations. This can either be scientific and mathematical trust, which is generally limited to academics and computer scientists, or blind trust, which is dangerous as it can easily mislead nonexperts into believing that blockchain technology is an absolutely trustworthy solution to many problem domains. Trust in self-executing protocols relates to how network participants perceive the preset protocol rules (conditions on which validity of information is decided) and their subsequent execution by machines in a trustless and impartial manner. Trust in participants' characteristics pertains to how participants view the behavior of one another outside the preset self-executing protocol rules, and in having good intentions and taking due diligence to prevent undesirable actions and acts. While blockchain systems are fundamentally built on the assumption of mistrust of participants and prejudice against participants' honest behavior, this subjective construct of mistrust may paradoxically turn into trust in some situations.

9.9 Case Studies and Examples

One cryptocurrency is the first and most well known, designed to enable "peer-to-peer" transactions without intermediaries. It is based on a decentralized, time-stamped, distributed ledger. The network consists of "nodes" (computers) that can confirm the validity of a transaction (Omar et al., 2020). Every node in the entire network has the same copy of the ledger. Transparency was achieved with the use of the blockchain structure. A blockchain is a publicly accessible ledger, immutable, and built sequentially. It contains a mathematical proof of the validity of every transaction ever made. Transparency is the most important feature because it guarantees the security of value in it. As the ledger is visible to everyone (Kshetri, 2021) and cannot be altered retrospectively, this rules out dishonest transaction publishing. Transparency ensures that market prices for goods and services can be determined honestly. Everyone can see what transactions and addresses were processed in the network, and because no one can know the owner of an address, pseudonymity is created.

Another platform is a peer-to-peer blockchain-based decentralized platform constructed to support "smart contracts," consisting of a virtual machine that executes script code using an international network of public nodes. Its blockchain keeps the state of all accounts and contracts worldwide, containing all transactions from the Genesis block. However, there are notable privacy drawbacks. While all states are stored in the blockchain, the execution results (logs and storage modification) are not publicly accessible. Deployed contracts have to maintain account addresses, which are publicly accessible. Hence, with additional off-chain data, reconstruction of transaction semantics for different protocols is feasible. Events that contain acknowledgment with unexpected block times indicate problems in the protocol. This platform combines transparency of the transaction data with the principle of deterministic execution. All nodes have the same transaction history and contract state, maintaining consistency in a "world computer" paradigm (Han et al., 2020). The public exposure of all executions may create privacy issues. Efforts are made to limit the exposure as much as possible. Code in contracts is compiled to Bytecode, making it hard to understand the control flow and resource consumption. Internal storage of contracts (state) is secret as it cannot be accessed directly from other contracts. Still, all modifications within transactions are publicly recorded (Khan et al., 2021).

Another framework is an open-source, permissioned blockchain platform supported by various corporations. Unlike other platforms, this framework aims at business utilization, and privacy among stakeholders is paramount. One of the greatest advantages in this architecture is the "channel" implementation. It enables exchanging transactions between groups of members, hiding them from the others. Each channel has its own ledger and smart contracts. Programs used across different channels can also be instantiated under different names and therefore controlled and executed uniquely. In addition, all endorsers in the network can be assigned to a specific channel, hiding them from the others. Endorsement policies can limit the number of organizations asked to sign a transaction per transaction type (Omar et al., 2020).

9.9.1 Real-World Applications of Transparent Features

Several innovative projects that utilize the transparency features offered by blockchain technology have emerged recently. These projects are at the forefront of addressing trust issues stemming from information asymmetry in a wide array of sectors. At the core of initiatives like Everledger and Chronicled is the concept of using blockchain technology to assign products digital identities and indelible storage of product state. This allows for the inspection of the product and its state updates by multiple stakeholders, as well as a view of the product history and its testing state (Khan et al., 2021). Most importantly, this builds a secondary market where stakeholders can prove product authenticity and traceability unimpeachably.

Food and luxury product fraud addresses the same issues but goes a step further. They also prevent data manipulation problems faced by single blockchain systems. In such a situation, a party with malicious intent can inject untrue or manipulated data into the blockchain, rendering the truth opaque and making the blockchain data meaningless. The circular chicken and beef food fraud addresses this problem with multichain systems where data across multiple chains need to be reconciled (Ferreira et al., 2020). This way, data that seems true in one chain may seem false or suspicious in another, exposing manipulation or untruth. Most recently, a research group and a Belgian bank have deployed a project that makes products linked to mortgages traded on a public chain with full anonymity preservation. This means that, unlike Bitcoin or Ethereum, no transaction can be traced back to any company or person. Therefore, information asymmetries cannot be exploited in fraud attempts, and no party would have an information advantage over the rest of the market.

9.10 Future Perspective and Conclusion

In the exploration of the critical challenges in blockchain transparency, it is clear that the technology provides an incredibly strong base for large scale and trustworthy support. With so much scope for future development, combined with fanatic and somehow enthusiastic underground developer community, blockchain technology will provide many exciting opportunities for the development of future immutable transparency and decentralized systems. These are enormously exciting times to be involved in the field of distributed trust and the future is most certainly bright. The promise of some paradigm shifting breakthroughs makes blockchain technologies a massively exciting emerging technology field. Remember that, above all, a culture of safety is promoted. Consumers will be more protected and, if something does go wrong, accountability of responsible parties will be clearer. It is critical that security, privacy and the value of trust in digital life is recognized which is why it is inevitable that transparency, combined with privacy as a core ethic, is designed to become the ultimate standard.

The future of distributed trust provides many interesting avenues for further research. For example, the global nature of blockchain technology means that, unlike existing trust systems, a single nation state has no oversight or control of the actual technologies in use, in theory facilitating international trade and globalization. The possibilities for various legislative and disruptive legal challenges emerge in an environment where global technology merges with divisive local politics. The rise of the IoT has thus far been characterized by the lack of transparent security: strategies to enhance the security of IoT devices and the exploitation of providing transparent security by adopting a "security and privacy by design" approach will define the next generation of consumer technology. An effort is underway to make transparent security technologies user-friendly and socially compatible. Initiatives to improve consumers' ability to understand the implications of transparent security, a curious multidisciplinary cooperative study that forms the critical mass, and a legal framework to prevent malicious attacks via transparency are some of the future focus in securing a globally interconnected systems. The promises of blockchain platforms have captured the imagination of technologists, business leaders and governing bodies around the world. However, structural and technological development in these platforms has outpaced the development of a body of scientific research to guide the evolution of blockchain systems. The most successful research in digital trust and transparency will embrace a transdisciplinary approach by recognizing the multifaceted and complex problems such as sustainable evolution of trust in a system and governance and the specific discipline resources needed for satisfactory resolution.

References

Akhter Md Hasib, Kazi Tamzid, Ixion Chowdhury, Saadman Sakib, Mohammad Monirujjaman Khan, Nawal Alsufyani, Abdulmajeed Alsufyani, and Sami Bourouis. "Electronic Health Record Monitoring System and Data Security Using Blockchain Technology." *Security and Communication Networks* 2022 (4 February 2022): 1–15. https://doi.org/10.1155/2022/2366632.

Alazab, Mamoun, Swarna Priya Rm, Parimala, Praveen Kumar Reddy Maddikunta, Thippa Reddy Gadekallu, and Quoc-Viet Pham. "Federated Learning for Cybersecurity: Concepts, Challenges, and Future Directions." *IEEE Transactions on Industrial Informatics* 18, no. 5 (May 2022): 3501–9. https://doi.org/10.1109/tii.2021.3119038.

Alexander, C., and D. Cumming. *Corruption and Fraud in Financial Markets: Malpractice, Misconduct and Manipulation.* John Wiley & Sons, 2022.

Aouidef, Yann, Federico Ast, and Bruno Deffains. "Decentralized Justice: A Comparative Analysis of Blockchain Online Dispute Resolution Projects." *Frontiers in Blockchain* 4 (16 March 2021). https://doi.org/10.3389/fbloc.2021.564551.

Bodkhe, U., D. Mehta, S. Tanwar, P. Bhattacharya, P. K. Singh, and W. C. Hong. "A Survey on Decentralized Consensus Mechanisms for Cyber Physical Systems." *IEEE Access* 8 (2020): 54371–401.

Centobelli, Piera, Roberto Cerchione, Pasquale Del Vecchio, Eugenio Oropallo, and Giustina Secundo. "Blockchain Technology for Bridging Trust, Traceability and Transparency in Circular Supply Chain." *Information & Management* 59, no. 7 (November 2022): 103508. https://doi.org/10.1016/j.im.2021.103508.

Chatzigiannis, Panagiotis, Foteini Baldimtsi, and Konstantinos Chalkias. "SoK: Auditability and Accountability in Distributed Payment Systems." In *Applied Cryptography and Network Security*, 311–37. Lecture Notes in

Computer Science. Cham: Springer International Publishing, 2021. https://doi.org/10.1007/978-3-030-78375-4_13.

Dib, Omar, and Khalifa Toumi. "Decentralized Identity Systems: Architecture, Challenges, Solutions and Future Directions." *Annals of Emerging Technologies in Computing* 4, no. 5 (20 December 2020): 19–40. https://doi.org/10.33166/aetic.2020.05.002.

Dolev, Shlomi, and Matan Liber. "Towards Self-Stabilizing Blockchain, Reconstructing Totally Erased Blockchain." *Information and Computation* 285, no. 104881 (May 2022): 104881. https://doi.org/10.1016/j.ic.2022.104881.

Essex, Aleksander, and Nicole Goodman. "Protecting Electoral Integrity in the Digital Age: Developing E-Voting Regulations in Canada." *Election Law Journal Rules Politics and Policy* 19, no. 2 (1 June 2020): 162–79. https://doi.org/10.1089/elj.2019.0568.

Ferreira, João F., Pedro Cruz, Thomas Durieux, and Rui Abreu. "SmartBugs: A Framework to Analyze Solidity Smart Contracts." *arXiv [Cs.SE]*, 8 July 2020. arXiv. http://arxiv.org/abs/2007.04771.

Ghode, Dnyaneshwar J., Rakesh Jain, Gunjan Soni, Sunil K. Singh, and Vinod Yadav. "Architecture to Enhance Transparency in Supply Chain Management Using Blockchain Technology." *Procedia Manufacturing* 51 (2020): 1614–20. https://doi.org/10.1016/j.promfg.2020.10.225.

Han, S., S. Park, S. Park, S. Kim, and M. Cha, M. "Mitigating Embedding and Class Assignment Mismatch in Unsupervised Image Classification." In *European Conference on Computer Vision*, 768–84. Cham: Springer International Publishing, 2020, August.

Helmrich, Alysha, Samuel Markolf, Rui Li, Thomaz Carvalhaes, Yeowon Kim, Emily Bondank, Mukunth Natarajan, Nasir Ahmad, and Mikhail Chester. "Centralization and Decentralization for Resilient Infrastructure and Complexity." *Environmental Research Infrastructure and Sustainability* 1, no. 2 (1 September 2021): 021001. https://doi.org/10.1088/2634-4505/ac0a4f.

Khan, Shafaq Naheed, Faiza Loukil, Chirine Ghedira-Guegan, Elhadj Benkhelifa, and Anoud Bani-Hani. "Blockchain Smart Contracts: Applications, Challenges, and Future Trends." *Peer-to-Peer Networking and Applications* 14, no. 5 (18 April 2021): 2901–25. https://doi.org/10.1007/s12083-021-01127-0.

Komalavalli, C., Deepika Saxena, and Chetna Laroiya. "Overview of Blockchain Technology Concepts." In *Handbook of Research on Blockchain Technology*, 349–71. Elsevier, 2020. https://doi.org/10.1016/b978-0-12-819816-2.00014-9.

Kshetri, Naresh. "Blockchain Technology for Improving Transparency and Citizen's Trust." In *Advances in Intelligent Systems and Computing*, 716–35. Advances in Intelligent Systems and Computing. Cham: Springer International Publishing, 2021. https://doi.org/10.1007/978-3-030-73100-7_52.

Mullegowda, Rakshitha Channarayapatna, Nirmala Hiremani, Mahantesh Birje, and Nataraj Kanathur Ramaswamy. "A Novel Smart Contract Based Blockchain with Sidechain for Electronic Voting." *International Journal of Electrical and Computer Engineering (IJECE)* 14, no. 1 (1 February 2024): 617. https://doi.org/10.11591/ijece.v14i1.pp617-630.

Omar, Ilhaam A., Raja Jayaraman, Khaled Salah, Mecit Can Emre Simsekler, Ibrar Yaqoob, and Samer Ellahham. "Ensuring Protocol Compliance and Data Transparency in Clinical Trials Using Blockchain Smart Contracts." *BMC Medical Research Methodology* 20, no. 1 (7 September 2020): 224. https://doi.org/10.1186/s12874-020-01109-5.

Rahardja, Untung, Achmad Nizar Hidayanto, Ninda Lutfiani, Dyah Ayu Febiani, and Qurotul Aini. "Immutability of Distributed Hash Model on Blockchain Node Storage." *Scientific Journal of Informatics* 8, no. 1 (10 May 2021): 137–43. https://doi.org/10.15294/sji.v8i1.29444.

Rejeb, Abderahman, John G. Keogh, and Horst Treiblmaier. "How Blockchain Technology Can Benefit Marketing: Six Pending Research Areas." *Frontiers in Blockchain* 3 (19 February 2020). https://doi.org/10.3389/fbloc.2020.00003.

Roszkowska, Paulina. "Fintech in Financial Reporting and Audit for Fraud Prevention and Safeguarding Equity Investments." *Journal of Accounting & Organizational Change* 17, no. 2 (2 September 2020): 164–96. https://doi.org/10.1108/jaoc-09-2019-0098.

Toufaily, Elissar, Tatiana Zalan, and Soumaya Ben Dhaou. "A Framework of Blockchain Technology Adoption: An Investigation of Challenges and Expected Value." *Information & Management* 58, no. 3 (April 2021): 103444. https://doi.org/10.1016/j.im.2021.103444.

Truong, Nguyen, Gyu Myoung Lee, Kai Sun, Florian Guitton, and Yike Guo. "A Blockchain-Based Trust System for Decentralised Applications: When Trustless Needs Trust." *Future Generations Computer Systems: FGCS* 124 (November 2021): 68–79. https://doi.org/10.1016/j.future.2021.05.025.

Tyagi, A. K. "Decentralized Everything: Practical Use of Blockchain Technology in Future Applications." In *Distributed Computing to Blockchain*, 19–38. Academic Press, 2023.

Wu, Q., J. Zhu, and Y. Cheng. "The Effect of Cross-Organizational Governance on Supply Chain Resilience: A Mediating and Moderating Model." *Journal of Purchasing and Supply Management* 29, no. 1 (2023): 100817.

Xiao, Yang, Ning Zhang, Wenjing Lou, and Y. Thomas Hou. "Modeling the Impact of Network Connectivity on Consensus Security of Proof-of-Work Blockchain." In *IEEE INFOCOM 2020 – IEEE Conference on Computer Communications*. IEEE, 2020. https://doi.org/10.1109/infocom41043.2020.9155451.

Xu, C., C. Zhang, J. Xu, and J. Pei. "Slimchain: Scaling Blockchain Transactions through off-Chain Storage and Parallel Processing." *Proceedings of the VLDB Endowment* 14, no. 11 (2021): 2314–326.

Zavolokina, Liudmila, Noah Zani, and Gerhard Schwabe. "Designing for Trust in Blockchain Platforms." *IEEE Transactions on Engineering Management* 70, no. 3 (March 2023): 849–63. https://doi.org/10.1109/tem.2020.3015359.

Zhang, P., and M. Zhou "Security and Trust in Blockchains: Architecture, Key Technologies, and Open Issues." *IEEE Transactions on Computational Social Systems* 7, no. 3 (2020): 790–801.

10

The Ethical Ledger: A Review of Literature on the Alignment of Accounting Ethics and Blockchain Technology

Priyanka Koundal, Minie Bhalla, and Manpreet Kailay

10.1 Introduction

Modern digitization trends, known as blockchain, have significantly altered business procedures, industries, and businesses, posing disruptive challenges in our lives (Pugna & Duțescu, 2020; Zutshi et al., 2021). Everyone uses the term "blockchain," and academia and business know how disruptive this technology might be for every aspect of our lives (Angelis & Ribeiro Da Silva, 2019). Blockchain is a decentralized and immutable technology that securely records transactions across a network of computers known as nodes. It operates on a peer-to-peer network, reducing the risk of data manipulation and enhancing Security. The key features of blockchain include decentralization, immutability, transparency, and smart contracts. Originally developed for cryptocurrencies, blockchain technology has become a transformative innovation that could disrupt various industries (Mwandosya & Luhanga, 2020). It is a decentralized, distributed ledger that records transactions immutable and transparently. This technology operates on cryptography, consensus mechanisms, and smart contracts, ensuring data cannot be altered without network consensus (Secinaro et al., 2022). Blockchain removes intermediaries, reduces costs, and enhances efficiency and security. It challenges centralized systems and redefines trust, ownership, and governance (Krichen et al., 2022).

Blockchain has emerged as a significant advancement in the financial sector, mainly where trust is imperative. It enables the development of innovative digital services and platforms through a decentralized ledger and robust security mechanisms (Ali et al., 2020). Blockchain technology, used in cryptocurrencies, corporate governance, and equity finance, provides transparency, security, immutability, and permanence through a network of nodes

(Mohanta et al., 2019; Yu et al., 2018). Blockchain's distributed storage system improves accessibility and transparency of information, ensuring data security by preventing simultaneous attacks on all nodes. This assurance provided by hash chaining makes data fraud virtually impossible, significantly reducing the risk of fraud in new blocks (Benedetti et al., 2021; Iansiti & Lakhani, 2017). Blockchain enhances data accuracy, reduces costs, and promotes trust in financial reporting. Its immutability prevents fraud, and smart contracts enhance data security. Incorporating blockchain into the accounting curriculum can prepare future professionals for ethical practices. The features of blockchain improve accounting operations and considerably strengthen accounting ethics by ensuring transparency, data accuracy, and transaction security. Blockchain technology has the potential to significantly enhance accounting ethics through its core features of transparency, immutability, and fraud reduction (Centobelli et al., 2022).

Accounting ethics guide accountants' behavior, focusing on integrity, objectivity, confidentiality, and professional competence (Yarahmadi & Bohloli, 2015). These principles are crucial for building trust, preventing fraud, maintaining professionalism, complying with regulations, and establishing a strong ethical foundation for new accountants (Septiari et al., 2023). The Institute of Chartered Accountants of India regulates accounting standards in India (Karanth & KT, 2020). It establishes the Ethical Standards Board to maintain efficiency, objectivity, and integrity while safeguarding members' interests and dignity (www.icai.org) (Srivastava & Bhutani, 2012). The International Ethics Standards Board for Accountants is a global organization responsible for developing and maintaining accounting ethics, promoting the International Code of Ethics for Professional Accountants, which serves as a global ethical standard, overseen by Public Interest Oversight Board (PIOB) and supported by International Federation of Accountants (IFAC) (Allen & Bunting, 2008; Sonnerfeldt & Loft, 2018). Accounting ethics are crucial for trust, integrity, regulatory compliance, decision-making, long-term sustainability, professional reputation, fraud prevention, and corporate governance. They foster trust, ensure accurate financial statements, reduce legal penalties, and support sound decision-making. Ethical practices also contribute to long-term relationships and professional reputation, prevent fraud, and ensure financial integrity and accountability.

As blockchain matures, its applications extend beyond digital currencies, with accounting being a particularly compelling area (Pugna & Duțescu, 2020). Blockchain can enhance accounting ethics by promoting transparency and immutability and reducing fraud. It allows all network participants to view and verify transactions, ensuring accuracy and traceability. Immutability preserves the integrity of financial data (Angelis & Ribeiro Da Silva, 2019). Blockchain also reduces opportunities for fraud by securely recording and verifying transactions. Security and transparency can foster trust and reinforce the role of accountants as guardians of financial integrity. Accountants must provide transparent financial reports, enabling stakeholders to evaluate a company's performance, prevent fraudulent activities, and mitigate penalties and fines (Lager, 2009). Ethical accounting practices also enhance corporate reputation, fostering trust and loyalty, increasing customer retention, and providing a competitive advantage in the marketplace. Thus, upholding ethical standards is essential for the long-term success and sustainability of businesses and the economy.

Blockchain technology can potentially address ethical challenges in the accounting profession, including transparency, accountability, professional competence, data security, confidentiality, and regulatory compliance (Ajayi-Nifise et al., 2024). Blockchain technology has the potential to revolutionize financial reporting by increasing transparency, reducing fraud, and enhancing trust among stakeholders. It can address data privacy and misuse concerns while ensuring compliance with financial reporting standards and data protection laws. The immutability and integrity of recorded transactions provided by blockchain can effectively safeguard against data corruption or manipulation (Pilkington, 2016). Utilizing advanced encryption in blockchain technology significantly strengthens the security of financial records, reducing their vulnerability to fraudulent activities and human errors (Yerram et al., 2021). It facilitates streamlined and cost-efficient audits by enabling concurrent verification of transactions by multiple auditors. It reduces the probability of audit failures and misconduct. It ensures that ethical breaches are promptly addressed and shared within the profession.

This chapter explores the similarities between blockchain and accounting ethics, highlighting the historical development of blockchain technology and the principles it shares with accounting, such as transparency, immutability, and fraud reduction. It also discusses the potential benefits of blockchain in accounting, including enhanced accuracy and efficiency. However, this study also acknowledges the challenges and opportunities associated with blockchain adoption in accounting, such as potential risks and the need for updated regulatory frameworks. It emphasizes integrating blockchain technology into accounting and how it can foster ethical practices. Lastly, this chapter speculates on the future of accounting with blockchain, predicting a reshaping of the profession and accountants' role in ethical blockchain design and implementation.

10.2 Key Similarities between Blockchain and Accounting Ethics

This analysis aims to clarify how blockchain can function as a reliable mechanism for enforcing ethical standards in accounting by investigating its technical capabilities and tracing its historical development.

10.2.1 The Historical Development of Blockchain Technology

Haber and Stornetta's (Bayer et al., 1993) article, *How to Stamp a Digital Document*, pioneered computationally efficient techniques for digitally time-stamping easily editable records. They built a cryptographically secured ledger, preventing back- or forward-dating, and kept the documents private. This idea is the basis of blockchain, eliminating the need for third-party records and ensuring document privacy (Pugna & Duțescu, 2020). Satoshi Nakamoto coined the term "blockchain" in 2008 to describe the first digital cryptocurrency, Bitcoin, as a peer-to-peer system that allowed instantaneous transactions without third parties. It led to the development of distributed ledger technology, widely identified as blockchain, which has since been implemented across different platforms (Monti & Rasmussen, 2017).

Blockchain 1.0, a programmable currency like Bitcoin, enables seamless online value transfer. Blockchain revolutionizes how we conduct digital transactions, allowing seamless cross-border payments and removing unnecessary barriers. Its decentralized nature, immutability, and trustworthiness guarantee high security and reliability. This new digital currency has a profound impact on the financial system. Nevertheless, constructing a globally interconnected blockchain network continues to be a significant hurdle (Q. Wang & Su, 2020). Blockchain 2.0, an essential advancement in blockchain technology, has expanded its application to various financial industries, enabling decentralized currency exchange and programmable finance. The core aim is to act as a programmable distributed credit platform for smart contracts with applications beyond virtual currencies. This technology is used in debt certificates, real estate contracts, and intellectual property rights transactions, demonstrating its potential for decentralized financial markets (Wang & Su, 2020). Blockchain 3.0, a technology known for its decentralization and trust properties, has extended its reach beyond the financial sector to encompass various fields, including identity identification, auditing, arbitration, and bidding (Tanwar, 2022). It enhances operational effectiveness by eliminating the need for intermediaries. Scientists are investigating its potential in the Internet of Things (IoT), challenging the fundamental Internet protocol.

Blockchain technology progresses in three stages, influenced by the inclusion or exclusion of specific elements. These changes expand its reach into previously untapped markets and elevate its overall potential. Blockchain 4.0, the newest iteration, merges blockchain technology with artificial intelligence (AI). This cutting-edge combination utilizes deterministic hashing algorithms for consistency, in contrast to AI's probabilistic theory for uncertainty (Angelis & Ribeiro Da Silva, 2019; Mukherjee & Pradhan, 2021). The future of blockchain technology remains uncertain due to its disruptive nature. In the modern era of technology, blockchain has garnered significant attention from various industries. It has multiple uses, from social services to finance, and has dramatically impacted the growing business world.

10.2.2 Accounting Ethics and Blockchain Technology as an Aid to Cultivating Accounting Ethics

There are various interpretations of the terms "ethics" and "morals." Webster's Collegiate Dictionary provides four main definitions for "ethics." "The subject that explores morality, ethics, and responsibilities." A system of values provides a foundation for ethical norms that guide the actions of people or organizations (Duska et al., 2011). Ethics focus on good or bad, right or wrong, and are either values upheld by individuals, communities, or disciplines or the discipline that studies these values, aiming to analyze and assess people's behaviors and practices (Septiari et al., 2023). Adherence to accounting standards dictates the guidelines and formats for producing financial statements and reports in accounting practice. Accounting practices are structured by standards, which outline the guidelines and formats for developing financial statements and reports. The guidelines outline the correct procedures for accurately documenting financial transactions in the financial statements (Reddy, 2024). The appropriate application of accounting principles is shaped by standards, which include established guidelines, processes, and criteria for measurement. The "Financial Accounting Standards Board" (FASB) is responsible for developing accounting standards in the United States. The International Accounting Standards Board is crucial in setting global standards (Kaya & Koch, 2015).

While companies must follow the accounting rules for recording, presenting, and disclosing information in traditional accounting, they still retain control over other aspects of those standards, such as the accounting policies, estimates, and judgments utilized. Listed firms only release routine financial statements to the market; they keep the development of the reports' accounting processes a secret. Although this institutional framework might safeguard businesses' confidential information, there are also several unfavorable adverse effects (Tiron-Tudor et al., 2021). Accounting ethics aid in developing a person's conviction to make moral choices. Despite the perceived importance of accounting ethics, maintaining ethical behavior is difficult. These difficulties include the internal pressure that comes with adhering to a code of ethics and the capacity of a code of ethics to buy morality and absolve people of the most important component of ethical behavior – personal responsibility. Future listed firms may be required to disclose their blockchain accounting data to regulators and stakeholders as it offers the most pertinent information and will further improve the efficiency of the financial markets. It is logical to expect corporations under greater shareholder pressure to choose to increase disclosure, even if it is only a recommendation and not a requirement, or risk negative market equity value implications (Potekhina & Riumkin, 2017).

Accounting professionals frequently encounter situations where their judgment can be ethically or legally problematic, even though accountants are considered the corporate world's regulators, checking the accuracy of financial reports and ensuring they adhere to accepted standards. Due to the increasing number of global ethical crises involving small and large businesses, unethical accounting is becoming a significant concern (Sherif & Mohsin, 2021). Blockchain technologies enable trust, privacy, security, and data integrity without requiring any third-party governing organization because they are a sort of decentralized transaction and data management system (Ayoade et al., 2018). Although it is a fundamental component of a financial statement audit, confirming the existence of a transaction is only one of the crucial elements. An audit evaluates whether recorded transactions are supported by relevant, reliable, objective, accurate, and verifiable information. The admission of a transaction into a reliable blockchain may be sufficient appropriate audit proof for some financial statement statements, such as the transaction's occurrence (Demirkan et al., 2020).

10.2.3 In-Depth Analysis of Specific Shared Principles of Blockchain and Accounting Ethics

This section delves into the core principles shared by blockchain and accounting ethics, such as transparency, accountability, and integrity, highlighting how these values reinforce trust in financial ecosystems (Figure 10.1 and Table 10.1).

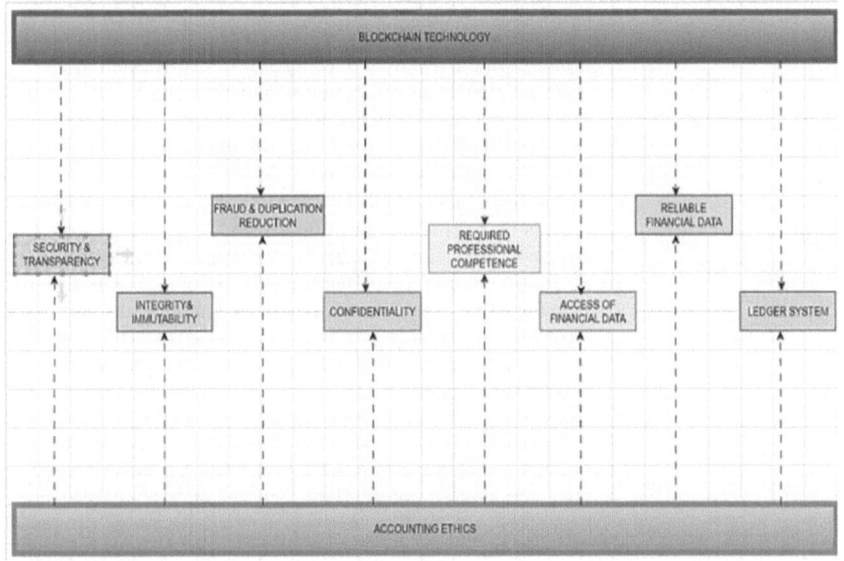

FIGURE 10.1
Author's construction

TABLE 10.1

Key Similarities between Blockchain Technology and Accounting Ethics

Security and transparency	Both accounting ethics and blockchain technology recognize the importance of security and transparency in maintaining trust and integrity. Accounting ethics require accountants to secure financial information and present it transparently, while blockchain technology inherently provides secure and transparent record-keeping through its decentralized and immutable nature. Accounting ethics, as per 410.3 A2 of (IFAC, 2021), "Transparency can better inform the views and decisions of those charged with governance and a wide range of stakeholders." Blockchain technology enhances accuracy, trust, and efficiency in the accounting ecosystem by providing a decentralized, immutable architecture, preventing hacking, freeing up accountants' time, and improving transparency (Javaid et al., 2022). Integrating blockchain technology in accounting practices enhances security and transparency, reduces errors, fraud, and financial misconduct, and fosters trust and confidence in financial markets.
Integrity and immutability	Both accounting ethics and blockchain technology uphold Integrity and Immutability in accounting records. Blockchain technology ensures integrity (honesty) and immutability (cannot change data), and accounting ethics ensures honesty and immutability because it is relevant for end users. On a blockchain, immutable transactions are recorded that cannot be altered or deleted (Politou et al., 2019). The Code of Ethics for Professional Accountants emphasizes the importance of integrity in professional and business relationships. It emphasizes honesty, straightforwardness, and fairness and prohibits involvement in questionable documents, filings, correspondences, or inaccurate statements (Payne et al., 2018). The intersection of integrity and immutability in both domains enhances the transparency and credibility of financial information, reducing the risk of fraud and errors.
Fraud and duplication reduction	Accounting ethics and blockchain technology protect accounting records from fraud and duplication. Blockchain technology assures that it can prevent data tampering and fraud, and accounting standards set by professional organizations also guarantee the same. Documents will be tamper-proof and instantly recognizable even if altered, thus minimizing the risk of fraud (Maffei et al., 2021). Blockchain technology provides a decentralized, open system for transaction verification, eliminating the need for a central authority and enhancing trust in financial records. As per R360.15 of IFAC (2021), the professional accountant must adhere to all applicable requirements under auditing standards, such as those about recognizing and addressing noncompliance, including fraud. It ensures that any potentially fraudulent activities can be effectively identified and dealt with, protecting the integrity of financial reporting and maintaining public trust.

(Continued)

TABLE 10.1 (Continued)

Key Similarities between Blockchain Technology and Accounting Ethics

Confidentiality	Confidentiality is a crucial principle in accounting ethics, as it ensures the trust and integrity of financial information. Accounting ethics and blockchain technology assure confidentiality in accounting records. As per the American Institute of Certified Public Accountants Code of Professional Conduct, Section 301.01, "A member in public practice shall not disclose any confidential client information without the specific consent of the client." This ethical guideline ensures client information confidentiality, fostering trust between accountants and clients, and can lead to legal action and damage to professional reputation. Blockchain technology can offer a business ecosystem security protection and confidentiality preservation by encrypting the transaction data (including the sender, recipient, and amount) using advanced cryptographic techniques. Blockchain technology ensures that only authorized parties can access and verify the information, reducing the risk of unauthorized disclosure (Y. Wang & Kogan, 2018).
Required professional competence	Both accounting ethics and blockchain technology require professionals to possess a high level of competence and educational qualification to ensure the accurate and ethical execution of their responsibilities. In accounting, professional competence is necessary to navigate financial regulations and provide sound financial advice. In contrast, in blockchain technology, professional competence is crucial for designing and managing secure and compliant blockchain systems. The role of a management accountant requires maintaining knowledge and skills, adhering to laws and standards, preparing accurate reports, staying updated with accounting developments, and possessing strong analytical and problem-solving abilities (Kgapola, 2015). The study indicates a significant rise in the demand for blockchain engineers, who are expected to possess strong programming skills, a deep cryptography understanding, and hands-on experience in blockchain solutions (Kassab et al., 2021).
Provide access to financial data to relevant parties	Controlled access is essential in accounting ethics and blockchain technology, ensuring authorized financial data sharing for transparency, accountability, and trust. It is achieved through internal controls and data governance policies. Accounting ethics and blockchain technology jointly guarantee access to financial data to relevant users. Real-time blockchain accounting enables users or regulators to access enterprise information, ensuring transparency and trust while enhancing security measures against unauthorized tampering or manipulation (Dai & Vasarhelyi, 2017). Section 320.1 of the Code of Ethics for Professional Accountants states that "professional accountants in business are often involved in the preparation and reporting of information that may either be made public or used by others inside or outside the employing organization." It highlights the significant responsibility that professional accountants have in ensuring the accuracy and integrity of financial information.

(Continued)

TABLE 10.1 (Continued)

Key Similarities between Blockchain Technology and Accounting Ethics

Provide reliable, authentic data for the users	Accounting ethics and blockchain technology aim to provide reliable, authentic data, focusing on accuracy, transparency, and integrity. Accounting uses strict standards, internal controls, and auditing, while blockchain ensures these qualities through cryptographic security and consensus mechanisms. The central standard of the code is objectivity, which requires the management accountant to "communicate information fairly and objectively" and to "disclose fully all relevant information that could reasonably be expected to influence an intended user's understanding of the reports, comments, and recommendations presented" (Duska et al., 2011). The management accounting code emphasizes objectivity, presenting unbiased, factual information for informed decision-making. Transparency prevents conflicts of interest, while data replication across multiple nodes reduces the risk of single-point failures, thereby enhancing network stability (Singh & Kim, 2018).
Decentralized ledger system	The general ledger in accounting and the distributed ledger in blockchain technology serve the same purpose of accurately recording and tracking financial transactions. They are critical tools for ensuring the integrity of financial records and supporting transparent and accountable financial practices. While the general ledger is centralized and used in traditional accounting (Fullana & Ruiz, 2021), the distributed ledger in blockchain technology is decentralized and provides a highly secure and trustworthy system for recording transactions. Both systems are subject to regular audits and are maintained per ethical standards to ensure accuracy and regulation compliance. Blockchain technology offers a decentralized and secure ledger system that enhances transparency, efficiency, and productivity in networks with multiple participating enterprises (Tanwar, 2022). It eliminates the need for a central authority and allows for real-time financial data updates, making it resistant to tampering or fraud. This technology can potentially revolutionize traditional business transactions and improve accounting ethics.

Thus, the similarities between accounting ethics and blockchain technology highlight their shared emphasis on accuracy, transparency, and trust. Both accounting and blockchain utilize ledger systems to record and verify financial data, ensuring reliability and accessibility. These systems are crucial in supporting ethical decision-making and instilling confidence in stakeholders. As blockchain technology becomes more integrated with accounting practices, it has the potential to enhance the integrity and efficiency of financial reporting, bridging the gap between traditional methods and innovative digital solutions.

10.2.4 Potential Benefits of Blockchain in Accounting: Real-World Examples

Table 10.2 highlights the key similarities between accounting ethics and blockchain technology, emphasizing how these similarities manifest in real-world applications.

TABLE 10.2

Key similarities between Accounting Ethics and Blockchain Technology

Key Similarities	Blockchain Technology	Accounting Ethics	Real-World Applications
Security and Transparency	Blockchain technology offers a secure and transparent system for recording and storing transactions in an immutable ledger.	Ethical accounting practices prioritize the importance of being transparent in financial reporting.	Companies like Walmart use blockchain to track product origins, ensuring transparency in their supply chain (Centobelli et al., 2022; Kamath, 2018).
Integrity and Immutability	The traceability and immutability of blockchain transactions help enhance data integrity.	Accountants are responsible for ensuring that financial statements are accurate and have integrity.	Auditors can use blockchain to verify real-time transactions, improving accountability in financial audits (Patel et al., 2019).
Fraud and Duplication Reduction	The immutability of blockchain records makes it challenging to change or forge data, which helps prevent fraud and duplication.	Ethical accounting is a practice that seeks to prevent fraud and misrepresentation in financial statements.	Using blockchain in cryptocurrency accounting reduces the risk of fraud by providing accurate transaction records (Mahtani, 2022).
Confidentiality	Blockchain technology enables the secure storage and transmission of confidential financial data.	Maintaining client confidentiality is a crucial aspect of ethical accounting.	Companies can use blockchain to share financial information with authorized parties while maintaining confidentiality securely (Y. Wang & Kogan, 2018).

(Continued)

TABLE 10.2 (Continued)

Key similarities between Accounting Ethics and Blockchain Technology

Key Similarities	Blockchain Technology	Accounting Ethics	Real-World Applications
Required Professional Competence	Implementing blockchain in accounting requires continuous learning and the development of new skills.	Ethical accounting practices necessitate that professionals maintain their competence through education qualification.	Accounting firms invest in training their staff on blockchain technology to provide competent and trustworthy services (Tiron-Tudor et al., 2021).
Provide Access to Relevant Parties	Blockchain technology allows all stakeholders with the necessary permissions to have real-time access to data.	Ethical accounting requires providing relevant financial information to authorized parties.	Companies using blockchain can provide stakeholders with real-time financial data, enhancing decision-making (Ko et al., 2018).
Provide Reliable Authentic Data	Blockchain ensures the authenticity and reliability of financial data recorded on the ledger.	Ethical accounting practices aim to provide reliable and authentic financial information.	Everledger's blockchain for diamonds ensures authenticity, building trust in the diamond supply chain (Walker & Kemp, 2019).
Distributed Ledger System	Blockchain operates on a decentralized network, reducing reliance on a single entity.	Ethical accounting promotes maintaining independence and objectivity when reporting financial information.	Decentralized finance (DeFi) platforms allow for peer-to-peer transactions without intermediaries, promoting ethical financial practices (Chen & Bellavitis, 2019).

10.3 Challenges and Opportunities of Blockchain in Accounting

When integrated into accounting practices, blockchain technology faces challenges, including aligning with existing systems, regulatory and compliance issues, scalability and performance issues, and data privacy and confidentiality concerns.

The scalability challenges in blockchain networks, such as transaction processing speed, latency, block size, and network decentralization, hinder their ability to handle more significant economic transactions (Khan et al., 2021). Compared to traditional payment systems, existing blockchain networks have limited transaction processing speeds, leading to slower transaction processing times as the number of transactions increases. The size of each block in a blockchain also limits the number of transactions that can be processed, resulting in higher transaction fees and longer confirmation times. The integration of blockchain technology in accounting presents significant challenges in terms of security and privacy (Alzoubi, 2011). The transparency of blockchain poses a risk to the confidentiality of sensitive financial data, while the immutability of blockchain conflicts with regulations regarding data erasure. The reliance on private keys for transaction authorization introduces security risks, and pseudonymity in blockchain transactions does not guarantee privacy. Metadata leakage and compliance with regulatory frameworks further complicate the adoption of blockchain in accounting. To overcome these challenges, robust privacy-preserving mechanisms, careful regulatory compliance, and advanced security protocols are necessary.

While the implementation of blockchain technology in accounting offers numerous benefits, there are significant challenges that need to be addressed. These challenges include governance and regulation issues, compliance with financial reporting standards and data protection regulations, lack of standardization, reevaluating internal control systems, and the need for auditors to develop new skills and tools (Alzoubi, 2011; Habib et al., 2022). Organizations must remain vigilant in monitoring regulatory changes and overcoming these challenges to successfully integrate blockchain technology in accounting without compromising regulatory compliance and data integrity. The adoption of blockchain technology in accounting faces challenges related to interoperability (Kayıkcı & Subramanian, 2022; Prewett et al., 2020).

Integrating blockchain with existing legacy systems can be difficult due to compatibility issues, leading to data silos and hindering accounting processes. Ensuring data consistency and synchronization between blockchain systems and traditional databases is crucial to avoid inaccuracies in financial reporting. In addition, the absence of standardized protocols for blockchain technology further complicates interoperability, making it challenging for organizations to adopt blockchain solutions effectively.

The lack of knowledge and understanding of blockchain technology among accounting and auditing professionals poses a significant skill gap that can hinder the effective implementation and utilization of blockchain solutions (Abdennadher et al., 2022; Tiron-Tudor et al., 2021). To address this issue, organizations must invest in training programs that provide technical knowledge and educate professionals on how blockchain can transform accounting practices. In addition, organizations must be prepared to continually update their training programs to keep up with the evolving skill requirements as blockchain technology advances. By doing so, organizations can ensure that their workforce remains competent in using blockchain effectively and maximize the potential benefits of blockchain adoption. Implementing blockchain solutions can be costly and require significant investments in technology and infrastructure (Li, 2018). Organizations must consider software development, system integration, and training expenses.

In addition, establishing the necessary technological infrastructure can be challenging, as it may involve upgrading existing systems or investing in new technologies. Furthermore, organizations may struggle to quantify the return on investment for blockchain implementations, making decision-makers hesitant to invest in this technology. Overall, the cost and infrastructure considerations pose barriers for many companies, especially smaller ones, when adopting blockchain solutions.

Blockchain technology offers significant opportunities for enhancing accounting practices, including enhanced transparency and trust, improved accuracy and reduced errors, streamlined auditing processes, cost reduction in transaction processing, enhanced security and fraud prevention, and integration with other emerging technologies such as AI and IoT. These benefits can lead to more reliable financial reporting, efficient audits, lower operational costs, and advanced data analytics, ultimately driving innovation within the accounting industry.

Blockchain technology enhances data integrity by providing a decentralized and immutable framework for recording and managing data. This characteristic is crucial for accurate financial reporting and has the potential to revolutionize data integrity in accounting, as supported by the study (Dai & Vasarhelyi, 2017). Real-world examples, such as Everledger's use of blockchain to track the provenance of diamonds, further demonstrate blockchain's practical application and effectiveness in ensuring accurate and tamper-proof data (Oriekhoe et al., 2024). Blockchain technology has the potential to significantly improve transparency in various industries. By allowing all parties involved in a transaction to access the same information in real-time, blockchain fosters trust among stakeholders and reduces the likelihood of disputes. This transparency also enables efficient audits and compliance with regulatory requirements, as demonstrated by the findings of (Kokina et al., 2017). Furthermore, real-world examples include Walmart utilizing blockchain to track the supply chain of food products and providing transparency about the origins and handling of products, which helps ensure food safety (Astill et al., 2019).

The use of blockchain technology in auditing processes has the potential to streamline the process and increase efficiency (Turker & Bicer, 2020). By providing auditors with direct access to transaction data, blockchain can reduce the time and effort required for audits. In addition, blockchain's immutability and consensus mechanisms make it difficult to alter or falsify information, reducing the risk of fraud in accounting (Yu et al., 2018). Adopting blockchain technology in auditing processes can enhance accountability and improve the accuracy of transaction records.

Blockchain technology offers cost efficiency and enhanced security benefits (Garg et al., 2021). By automating processes through smart contracts, blockchain can reduce administrative costs associated with data reconciliation and auditing (Patel et al., 2019). It can lead to significant cost savings by streamlining operations and reducing the need for intermediaries. In addition, blockchain uses advanced cryptographic techniques to secure data transactions, protecting against unauthorized modifications and cyberattacks. It provides a secure platform for data transactions, protecting sensitive financial information from breaches. As a result, financial institutions are increasingly adopting blockchain to secure transactions and protect sensitive client information, thereby enhancing overall data security.

10.3.1 Potential Risks and Limitations of Blockchain Adoption

Blockchain technology, which has the potential to revolutionize various industries, including accounting, faces several challenges. Scalability issues, high energy consumption, complexity, security vulnerabilities, regulatory challenges, key management risks, and data immutability concerns are some key challenges organizations must address before adopting blockchain solutions. Scalability issues arise from the slow and resource-intensive consensus mechanisms used in traditional blockchains, which can limit transaction throughput and lead to high transaction fees (Liu et al., 2020). High energy consumption is also a concern, requiring substantial computational power for validating transactions (Maitra et al., 2021).

Complexity and technical expertise are also significant barriers to widespread adoption, as many organizations may lack the knowledge or resources to deploy blockchain solutions effectively (Biswas & Gupta, 2019). Security vulnerabilities, such as hacking and security breaches, can damage monetary losses and network integrity. Companies must invest in robust security measures to mitigate these risks. Regulatory and legal challenges arise from the decentralized nature of blockchain, as different jurisdictions have varying laws regarding the technology (Yeoh, 2017). Uncertainty in regulations can hinder adoption, as companies may be reluctant to invest in technology with unclear legal implications. Key management risks arise from the irreversible nature of blockchain transactions, which can result in significant financial losses (Ma et al., 2018). Data immutability concerns arise from the immutability of blockchain data, which cannot be altered or deleted and can conflict with data protection laws, such as GDPR. Therefore, current research and development efforts are necessary to realize the full benefits of blockchain technology.

10.3.2 Adapting Regulatory Frameworks and Accounting Standards for Blockchain Integration

Integrating blockchain technology into accounting practices requires significant regulatory frameworks and adjustments to accounting standards

(Han et al., 2023). It involves developing legal resilience and adaptive governance within blockchain networks to comply with changing regulations while maintaining decentralization. Global standardization is necessary to establish consistent regulations across jurisdictions and facilitate smoother blockchain adoption (Albshaier et al., 2024). Compliance challenges arise due to the unique properties of blockchain, requiring regulators to create frameworks that consider its decentralized and immutable nature. Accounting standards must be adapted to incorporate blockchain's features, recognizing it as a legitimate method for recording and reporting financial transactions (Giang & Tam, 2023). Real-time reporting and auditing can be facilitated by blockchain, necessitating a shift in traditional auditing practices. Training programs are needed to equip accounting professionals with the skills to work with blockchain systems. Overall, adapting regulatory frameworks and accounting standards is crucial for realizing the full potential of blockchain technology in enhancing the integrity, transparency, and efficiency of accounting practices. Continuous collaboration, education, and innovation are essential in navigating the complexities of blockchain integration.

10.3.3 The Integration of Blockchain Technology in the Field of Accounting: Leveraging Blockchain Technology to Foster Accounting Ethics

The term "blockchain" accurately describes the technology's process, where new transactions are added to a chain of previous ones using a challenging cryptographic technique, ensuring the accuracy of the transaction history. Blockchain is a technology that stores the history of transactions in a ledger that is not controlled by a central authority. It allows for the transfer of ownership without the need for verification by a central authority. Instead, it relies on cryptographic validation by many peer-to-peer agents (Fullana & Ruiz, 2021).

The financial sector is experiencing notable transformations, especially in the fields of accounting and auditing, which have not previously encountered disruption driven by technology (Pugna & Duțescu, 2020). Blockchain, a decentralized ledger, has the potential to revolutionize accounting, auditing, and control processes by ensuring traceability and transparency through data validation and relay tasks (Yu et al., 2018) blockchain safeguards information by combining distributed ledger technology and hash chaining, making it immutable, secure, and transparent.

Auditing and accounting experienced a noteworthy change due to the incorporation of blockchain technology. It operates as a decentralized ledger, recording transactions in a public and verifiable manner. This level of transparency helps prevent potential tampering and ensures that transactions remain free from any control by individuals or organizations. The potential of blockchain to enhance the ethicality of accounting is substantial, as it effectively safeguards against any unauthorized tampering or alteration of data. Blockchain technology can transform the accounting industry, but its impact on the current system remains unclear, with challenges and risks still to be identified and the potential for significant changes.

Blockchain technology and accounting ethics share transparency, trust, and integrity. They provide a decentralized ledger for trustworthy record-keeping and prevent transaction fraud. Blockchain technologies provide a decentralized transaction and data management system that offers trust, privacy, security, and data integrity. They eliminate the need for third-party governing organizations (Jasim & Raewf, 2020). Both blockchain technology and accounting ethics also prioritize the concept of accountability. They hold individuals and organizations responsible for their actions and ensure all transactions are correctly recorded and audited.

Furthermore, blockchain technology and accounting ethics strive to enhance financial systems' efficiency and effectiveness by promoting standardized practices and reducing errors or discrepancies. Thus, integrating blockchain technology into accounting practices can help strengthen the ethical framework by providing a transparent and immutable record of financial transactions. It can enhance trust and confidence in financial reporting, streamline processes, and reduce the risk of fraudulent activities. Moreover, using blockchain technology in accounting can improve data accuracy and timeliness, leading to more informed decision-making and better financial management.

10.4 The Future of Accounting with Blockchain

Blockchain technology is expected to impact the accounting profession significantly, revolutionizing how financial transactions are recorded, audited, and reported. Studies suggest that blockchain enables continuous auditing, automates accounting processes through smart contracts, and integrates data analytics for deeper insights into financial performance (Han et al., 2023). Accountants will also be crucial in designing and implementing ethical blockchain systems, collaborating with technologists, and receiving ongoing training and education. New auditing practices built around blockchain will involve real-time audit evidence, enhanced risk assessment, and integration with other technologies like artificial intelligence and cloud computing (Qasim & Kharbat, 2020). Overall, the future of accounting with blockchain technology promises increased transparency, efficiency, and security, with accountants playing a vital role in shaping and adapting to these changes.

Blockchain technology is set to revolutionize accounting by enhancing transparency, automating processes, enabling real-time reporting, and streamlining auditing practices. This decentralized and immutable nature of blockchain reduces fraud and manipulation, fostering trust among stakeholders. Smart contracts – self-executing contracts – can automate accounting processes, reducing human error and increasing efficiency (Akpan, 2024). This shift could lead to cost savings and improved operational efficiency. Real-time financial reporting can enhance responsiveness to market changes and regulatory requirements, improving financial management and strategic planning. Integrating blockchain into accounting practices could revolutionize auditing by providing a complete record of transactions, reducing the time and resources required for compliance activities. However, regulatory adaptation and skill development are still challenges. Organizations must work closely with regulators to ensure compliance and develop standardized practices that enhance the credibility and acceptance of blockchain in accounting. Educational institutions and organizations must invest in training programs to equip accounting professionals with the necessary knowledge and skills.

10.5 Conclusion

This review explores the potential of blockchain technology in the accounting profession, highlighting its potential to enhance ethical practices. It highlights the technology's disruptive nature and ability to promote transparency, immutability, and fraud reduction, aligning with accounting ethics. Integrating blockchain in accounting can create a more trustworthy financial reporting environment. However, it also presents challenges and opportunities that require updated regulatory frameworks and evolving accounting standards. Accounting professionals must adapt to new auditing practices and actively participate in the development of ethical guidelines and standards for blockchain use in accounting.

Further research is needed, and collaboration between accountants, technologists, and regulators is crucial in addressing the complexities of blockchain integration. By fostering interdisciplinary partnerships and promoting continuous education, the accounting profession can position itself at the forefront of this technological revolution and ensure that blockchain catalyzes enhanced ethical practices in accounting (George & Patatoukas, 2020). The study emphasizes the importance of current research and collaboration between accountants and technologists to utilize the benefits of blockchain while fully managing its risks. Future research should focus on developing practical frameworks for integrating blockchain into accounting practices and updating regulatory standards to support this integration. By fostering collaboration and innovation, the accounting profession can effectively navigate the digital age and uphold its ethical responsibilities in a complex financial landscape.

The research suggests that blockchain technology can potentially impact the accounting field significantly. It effectively reduces fraudulent activities in data transmission and provides a secure and transparent system for tracking asset ownership. Adopting blockchain technology in accounting requires a comprehensive perspective, considering technical issues and organizational adoption. Accountants can benefit from blockchain technology by increasing productivity, better understanding of resources and obligations, and lowering the cost of maintaining ledgers. However, accountants must enhance their knowledge of blockchain to incorporate and utilize it effectively. Overall, blockchain technology has the potential to revolutionize the accounting profession, and accountants have the opportunity to influence its future integration and use.

Future studies should be conducted via primary data collecting, as advised by those employing blockchain technology. This study identified a few factors that affect blockchain adoption, but additional research is still required to address these problems. Based on the literature, the suggested framework shows how many elements interact and gives companies a starting point for comparison when creating blockchain applications. Future research should look into, confirm, and test these connections and expand the framework based on empirical findings.

References

Abdennadher, S., Grassa, R., Abdulla, H., & Alfalasi, A. (2022). The effects of blockchain technology on the accounting and assurance profession in the UAE: An exploratory study. *Journal of Financial Reporting and Accounting*, 20(1), 53–71.

Ajayi-Nifise, A. O., Falaiye, T., Olubusola, O., Daraojimba, A. I., & Mhlongo, N. Z. (2024). Blockchain in US accounting: A review: Assessing its transformative potential for enhancing transparency and integrity. *Finance & Accounting Research Journal*, 6(2), 159–182.

Akpan, Dr. M. (2024). Blockchain: Smart contract applications. In Dr. M. Akpan, *Future-Proof Accounting* (pp. 9–18). Emerald Publishing Limited. https://doi.org/10.1108/978-1-83797-819-920241002

Albshaier, L., Almarri, S., & Hafizur Rahman, M. (2024). A review of blockchain's role in E-commerce transactions: Open challenges, and future research directions. *Computers*, 13(1), 27. https://doi.org/10.3390/computers13010027

Ali, O., Ally, M., Clutterbuck, & Dwivedi, Y. (2020). The state of play of blockchain technology in the financial services: A systematic literature review. *International Journal of Information Management*, 54, 102199. https://doi.org/10.1016/j.ijinfomgt.2020.102199

Allen, C., & Bunting, R. (2008). A Global standard for professional ethics. *Journal of Accountancy*, 205(5), 46.

Alzoubi, A. (2011). The effectiveness of the accounting information system under the enterprise resources planning (ERP). *Research Journal of Finance and Accounting, 2*(11).

Angelis, J., & Ribeiro Da Silva, E. (2019). Blockchain adoption: A value driver perspective. *Business Horizons, 62*(3), 307–314. https://doi.org/10.1016/j.bushor.2018.12.001

Astill, J., Dara, R. A., Campbell, M., Farber, J. M., Fraser, E. D., Sharif, S., & Yada, R. Y. (2019). Transparency in food supply chains: A review of enabling technology solutions. *Trends in Food Science & Technology, 91*, 240–247.

Ayoade, G., Karande, V., Khan, L., & Hamlen, K. (2018). Decentralized IoT data management using blockchain and trusted execution environment. *2018 IEEE International Conference on Information Reuse and Integration (IRI)*, 15–22. https://ieeexplore.ieee.org/abstract/document/8424682/

Bayer, D., Haber, S., & Stornetta, W. S. (1993). Improving the efficiency and reliability of digital time-stamping. In R. Capocelli, A. De Santis, & U. Vaccaro (Eds.), *Sequences II* (pp. 329–334). Springer, New York. https://doi.org/10.1007/978-1-4613-9323-8_24

Benedetti, H., Nikbakht, E., Sarkar, S., & Spieler, A. C. (2021). Blockchain and corporate fraud. *Journal of Financial Crime, 28*(3), 702–721.

Biswas, B., & Gupta, R. (2019). Analysis of barriers to implementing blockchain in industry and service sectors. *Computers & Industrial Engineering, 136*, 225–241.

Centobelli, P., Cerchione, R., Del Vecchio, P., Oropallo, E., & Secundo, G. (2022). Blockchain technology design in accounting: Game changer to tackle fraud or technological fairy tale? *Accounting, Auditing & Accountability Journal, 35*(7), 1566–1597. https://doi.org/10.1108/AAAJ-10-2020-4994

Chen, Y., & Bellavitis, C. (2019). Decentralized finance: Blockchain technology and the quest for an open financial system. *Stevens Institute of Technology School of Business Research Paper*. https://papers.ssrn.com/sol3/papers.cfm

Dai, J., & Vasarhelyi, M. A. (2017). Toward blockchain-based accounting and assurance. *Journal of Information Systems, 31*(3), 5–21.

Demirkan, S., Demirkan, I., & McKee, A. (2020). Blockchain technology in the future of business cyber security and accounting. *Journal of Management Analytics, 7*(2), 189–208. https://doi.org/10.1080/23270012.2020.1731721

Duska, R., Duska, B. S., & Ragatz, J. (2011). *Accounting Ethics* (1st ed.). Wiley. https://doi.org/10.1002/9781444395907

Fullana, O., & Ruiz, J. (2021). Accounting information systems in the blockchain era. *International Journal of Intellectual Property Management, 11*(1), 63. https://doi.org/10.1504/IJIPM.2021.113357

Garg, P., Gupta, B., Chauhan, A. K., Sivarajah, U., Gupta, S., & Modgil, S. (2021). Measuring the perceived benefits of implementing blockchain technology in the banking sector. *Technological Forecasting and Social Change, 163*, 120407.

George, K., & Patatoukas, P. N. (2020). The blockchain evolution and revolution of accounting. *SSRN Electronic Journal*. https://doi.org/10.2139/ssrn.3681654

Giang, N. P., & Tam, H. T. (2023). Impacts of blockchain on accounting in the business. *SAGE Open, 13*(4), 21582440231222419. https://doi.org/10.1177/21582440231222419

Habib, G., Sharma, S., Ibrahim, S., Ahmad, I., Qureshi, S., & Ishfaq, M. (2022). Blockchain technology: Benefits, challenges, applications, and integration of blockchain technology with cloud computing. *Future Internet, 14*(11), 341.

Han, H., Shiwakoti, R. K., Jarvis, R., Mordi, C., & Botchie, D. (2023). Accounting and auditing with blockchain technology and artificial Intelligence: A literature review. *International Journal of Accounting Information Systems, 48*, 100598.

IAASB (2021). Irba.Co.Za. https://www.irba.co.za/upload/IAASB-2021-Handbook-Volume-2.pdf

Iansiti, M., & Lakhani, K. R. (2017). The truth about blockchain. *Harvard Business Review 95*(1), 118–127.

Jasim, Y. A., & Raewf, M. B. (2020). Information technology's impact on the accounting system. *Cihan University-Erbil Journal of Humanities and Social Sciences, 4*(1), 50–57. https://doi.org/10.24086/cuejhss.v4n1y2020.pp50–57

Javaid, M., Haleem, A., Singh, R. P., Suman, R., & Khan, S. (2022). A review of Blockchain Technology applications for financial services. *BenchCouncil Transactions on Benchmarks, Standards and Evaluations, 2*(3), 100073.

Kamath, R. (2018). Food traceability on blockchain: Walmart's pork and mango pilots with IBM. *The Journal of the British Blockchain Association, 1*(1). https://jbba.scholasticahq.com/article/3742.pdf#page=47

Karanth, S., & Srinivas. K.T. (2020). The Institute of Chartered Accountants of India V/S national financial reporting authority. *International Journal of Engineering and Management Research, 10*(6), 141–143. https://doi.org/10.31033/ijemr.10.6.19

Kassab, M., Destefanis, G., DeFranco, J., & Pranav, P. (2021). Blockchain-engineers wanted: An empirical analysis on required skills, education and experience. *2021 IEEE/ACM 4th International Workshop on Emerging Trends in Software Engineering for Blockchain (WETSEB)*, 49–55. https://doi.org/10.1109/WETSEB52558.2021.00014

Kaya, D., & Koch, M. (2015). Countries' adoption of the International Financial Reporting Standard for Small and Medium-sized Entities (IFRS for SMEs) – early empirical evidence. *Accounting and Business Research, 45*(1), 93–120. https://doi.org/10.1080/00014788.2014.969188

Kayıkcı, Y., & Subramanian, N. (2022). Blockchain interoperability issues in supply chain: Exploration of mass adoption procedures. In A. Emrouznejad & V. Charles (Eds.), *Big Data and Blockchain for Service Operations Management* (Vol. 98, pp. 309–328). Springer International Publishing. https://doi.org/10.1007/978-3-030-87304-2_13

Kgapola, M. P. (2015). *Professional Accountant's Perspective of Skills Required to Move into a Management Position* [PhD Thesis]. https://repository.nwu.ac.za/handle/10394/171099

Khan, D., Jung, L. T., & Hashmani, M. A. (2021). Systematic literature review of challenges in blockchain scalability. *Applied Sciences, 11*(20), 9372.

Ko, T., Lee, J., & Ryu, D. (2018). Blockchain technology and manufacturing industry: Real-time transparency and cost savings. *Sustainability, 10*(11), 4274.

Kokina, J., Mancha, R., & Pachamanova, D. (2017). Blockchain: Emergent industry adoption and accounting implications. *Journal of Emerging Technologies in Accounting, 14*(2), 91–100.

Krichen, M., Ammi, M., Mihoub, A., & Almutiq, M. (2022). Blockchain for modern applications: A survey. *Sensors, 22*(14), 5274.

Lager, J. M. (2009). Overcoming cultures of compliance to reduce corruption and achieve ethics in government. *McGeorge Law Review, 41*, 63.

Li, S. (2018). Application of blockchain technology in smart city infrastructure. *2018 IEEE International Conference on Smart Internet of Things (SmartIoT)*, 276–2766. https://ieeexplore.ieee.org/abstract/document/8465562/

Liu, Y., Qian, K., Chen, J., Wang, K., & He, L. (2020). Effective scaling of blockchain beyond consensus innovations and Moore's law. *arXiv* arXiv:2001.01865. http://arxiv.org/abs/2001.01865

Ma, S., Hao, W., Dai, H.-N., Cheng, S., Yi, R., & Wang, T. (2018). A blockchain-based risk and information system control framework. *2018 IEEE 16th Intl Conf on Dependable, Autonomic and Secure Computing, 16th Intl Conf on Pervasive Intelligence and Computing, 4th Intl Conf on Big Data Intelligence and Computing and Cyber Science and Technology Congress (DASC/PiCom/DataCom/CyberSciTech)*, 106–113. https://ieeexplore.ieee.org/abstract/document/8511874/

Maffei, M., Casciello, R., & Meucci, F. (2021). Blockchain technology: uninvestigated issues emerging from an integrated view within accounting and auditing practices. *Journal of Organizational Change Management*, 34(2), 462–476.

Mahtani, U. (2022). Fraudulent practices and blockchain accounting systems. *Journal of Accounting, Ethics and Public Policy*, 23(1), 97–148.

Maitra, S., Yanambaka, V. P., Puthal, D., Abdelgawad, A., & Yelamarthi, K. (2021). Integration of Internet of Things and blockchain toward portability and low-energy consumption. *Transactions on Emerging Telecommunications Technologies*, 32(6), e4103. https://doi.org/10.1002/ett.4103

Mohanta, B. K., Jena, D., Panda, S. S., & Sobhanayak, S. (2019). Blockchain technology: A survey on applications and security privacy Challenges. *Internet of Things*, 8, 100107. https://doi.org/10.1016/j.iot.2019.100107

Monti, M., & Rasmussen, S. (2017). RAIN: A bio-inspired communication and data storage infrastructure. *Artificial Life*, 23(4), 552–557. https://doi.org/10.1162/ARTL_a_00247

Mukherjee, P., & Pradhan, C. (2021). Blockchain 1.0 to Blockchain 4.0 – The evolutionary transformation of blockchain technology. In S. K. Panda, A. K. Jena, S. K. Swain, & S. C. Satapathy (Eds.), *Blockchain Technology: Applications and Challenges* (Vol. 203, pp. 29–49). Springer International Publishing. https://doi.org/10.1007/978-3-030-69395-4_3

Mwandosya, M. J., & Luhanga, M. L. (2020). Blockchain: A disruptive and transformative technology of the fourth industrial revolution. *Business Management Review*, 23(2), 16–31.

Oriekhoe, O. I., Ashiwaju, B. I., Ihemereze, K. C., Ikwue, U., & Udeh, C. A. (2024). Blockchain technology in supply chain management: A comprehensive review. *International Journal of Management & Entrepreneurship Research*, 6(1), 150–166.

Patel, B., Mullangi, K., Roberts, C., Dhameliya, N., & Maddula, S. S. (2019). Blockchain-based auditing platform for transparent financial transactions. *Asian Accounting and Auditing Advancement*, 10(1), 65–80.

Payne, D. M., Corey, C. M., & Raiborn, C. (2018). A model code of ethics for decision making in accounting professions. *2017–2018 OFFICERS President President-Elect*, 195. https://swaom.org/wp-content/uploads/2022/02/proceedings-2018-4.pdf#page=216

Pilkington, M. (2016). Blockchain technology: Principles and applications. In *Research Handbook on Digital Transformations* (pp. 225–253). Edward Elgar Publishing. https://www.elgaronline.com/abstract/edcoll/9781784717759/9781784717759.00019.xml

Politou, E., Casino, F., Alepis, E., & Patsakis, C. (2019). Blockchain mutability: Challenges and proposed solutions. *IEEE Transactions on Emerging Topics in Computing*, 9(4), 1972–1986.

Potekhina, A., & Riumkin, I. (2017). *Blockchain–A New Accounting Paradigm: Implications for Credit Risk Management*. https://www.diva-portal.org/smash/record.jsf?pid=diva2:1114333

Prewett, K. W., Prescott, G. L., & Phillips, K. (2020). Blockchain adoption is inevitable – Barriers and risks remain. *Journal of Corporate Accounting & Finance*, 31(2), 21–28. https://doi.org/10.1002/jcaf.22415

Pugna, I. B., & Duțescu, A. (2020). Blockchain – the accounting perspective. *Proceedings of the International Conference on Business Excellence*, 14(1), 214–224. https://doi.org/10.2478/picbe-2020-0020

Qasim, A., & Kharbat, F. F. (2020). Blockchain technology, business data analytics, and artificial intelligence: Use in the accounting profession and ideas for inclusion into the accounting curriculum. *Journal of Emerging Technologies in Accounting*, 17(1), 107–117.

Reddy, S. S. (2024). Impact of Indian Accounting Standards (IND AS) on financial statements. *International Scientific Journal of Engineering and Management*, 03(05), 1–9. https://doi.org/10.55041/ISJEM01744

Secinaro, S., Dal Mas, F., Brescia, V., & Calandra, D. (2022). Blockchain in the accounting, auditing and accountability fields: A bibliometric and coding analysis. *Accounting, Auditing & Accountability Journal*, 35(9), 168–203. https://doi.org/10.1108/AAAJ-10-2020-4987

Septiari, D., Helmayunita, N., & Serly, V. (2023). Accounting ethics: From professionals views. *Jati: Jurnal Akuntansi Terapan Indonesia*, 6(2), 146–156. https://doi.org/10.18196/jati.v6i2.18084

Sherif, K., & Mohsin, H. (2021). *The Effect of Emergent Technologies on Accountants' Ethical Blindness*. http://qspace.qu.edu.qa/handle/10576/38582

Singh, M., & Kim, S. (2018). Branch-based blockchain technology in intelligent vehicles. *Computer Networks*, 145, 219–231. https://doi.org/10.1016/j.comnet.2018.08.016

Sonnerfeldt, A., & Loft, A. (2018). The changing face of ethics – Developing a Code of Ethics for Professional Accountants from 1977 to 2006. *Accounting History*, 23(4), 521–540. https://doi.org/10.1177/1032373217751219

Srivastava, A., & Bhutani, P. (2012). IFRS in India: Challenges and opportunities. *IUP Journal of Accounting Research & Audit Practices*, 11(2). https://search.ebscohost.com/login.aspx?direct=true&profile=ehost&scope=site&authtype=crawler&jrnl=0972690X&AN=78153553&h=eupkbyGmsWZTDFYEEAsDZz%2FpGy1W1fBk3u3r%2Fggtz2S2yTKe51WiUqdNZhKdOcsypgnJvIqiY9S4H4Lx1Tf8xA%3D%3D&crl=c

Tanwar, S. (2022). Blockchain revolution from 1.0 to 5.0: Technological perspective. In S. Tanwar, *Blockchain Technology* (pp. 43–61). Springer Nature Singapore. https://doi.org/10.1007/978-981-19-1488-1_2

Tiron-Tudor, A., Deliu, D., Farcane, N., & Dontu, A. (2021). Managing change with and through blockchain in accountancy organizations: A systematic literature review. *Journal of Organizational Change Management*, 34(2), 477–506.

Turker, I., & Bicer, A. A. (2020). How to use blockchain effectively in auditing and assurance services. In U. Hacioglu (Ed.), *Digital Business Strategies in Blockchain Ecosystems* (pp. 457–471). Springer International Publishing. https://doi.org/10.1007/978-3-030-29739-8_22

Walker, B. J., & Kemp, A. L. (2019). Blockchains are diamonds' best friend: The case for supply chain transparency. In J. Barberis, D. W. Arner, & R. P. Buckley (Eds.), *The RegTech Book* (1st ed.). Wiley. https://doi.org/10.1002/9781119362197.ch47

Wang, Q., & Su, M. (2020). Integrating blockchain technology into the energy sector – From theory of blockchain to energy blockchain research and application. *Computer Science Review, 37*, 100275. https://doi.org/10.1016/j.cosrev.2020.100275

Wang, Y., & Kogan, A. (2018). Designing confidentiality-preserving Blockchain-based transaction processing systems. *International Journal of Accounting Information Systems, 30*, 1–18.

Yarahmadi, H., & Bohloli, A. (2015). Ethics in accounting. *Spectrum: A Journal of Multidisciplinary Research, 4*(8), 1–8.

Yeoh, P. (2017). Regulatory issues in blockchain technology. *Journal of Financial Regulation and Compliance, 25*(2), 196–208.

Yerram, S. R., Goda, D. R., Mahadasa, R., Mallipeddi, S. R., Varghese, A., Ande, J., Surarapu, P., & Dekkati, S. (2021). The role of blockchain technology in enhancing financial security amidst digital transformation. *Asian Business Review, 11*(3), 125–134.

Yu, T., Lin, Z., & Tang, Q. (2018). Blockchain: The introduction and its application in financial accounting. *Journal of Corporate Accounting & Finance, 29*(4), 37–47. https://doi.org/10.1002/jcaf.22365

Zutshi, A., Grilo, A., & Nodehi, T. (2021). The value proposition of blockchain technologies and its impact on Digital Platforms. *Computers & Industrial Engineering, 155*, 107187.

11
Using Blockchain Technology for Audit Trail[1]

Bilal Alagha and İlker Özçelik

11.1 Introduction

An audit trail is a record of all events and activities within a system, often used in accounting and financial systems to track changes to data. Recent audit failures, such as the collapse of Wirecard (Baranidharan, Ajekwe & Nakitende, 2023; Aßländer & Burkatzki, 2023) and the issues faced by Luckin Coffee (Li, 2023), highlight the need for more reliable audit trails. Traditional audit methods expose significant weaknesses, often relying on outdated auditing systems vulnerable to security breaches. Unauthorized access to records can compromise the integrity of the audit process. Moreover, traditional methods are typically time-consuming and costly (Newray, 2023), and they involve manual procedures prone to delays and errors. The lack of real-time verification means that fraudulent activities might remain undetected.

Numerous instances of fraud and financial mismanagement in recent years have emphasized the importance of maintaining a reliable audit trail. For example, a study by the Association of Certified Fraud Examiners found that businesses lose an estimated 5% of their revenue each year due to fraud, and more than $4.7 trillion is lost annually to occupational fraud worldwide.[2] This highlights the need for a robust audit trail to help detect and prevent such incidents.

Government agencies and organizations use audit trails to ensure transparency, compliance, and fraud prevention (Wee, 1999; Olivier & von Solms, 1999). This practice is not only required by federal laws and regulations but also by industry standards. For instance, the General Data Protection Regulation (GDPR) of the European Union and The Personal Information Protection and Electronic Documents Act of Canada mandate maintaining audit trails for auditing, error correction, and internal controls (European Union, 2016; Ringelstein & Staab, 2009). These methods can be useful in monitoring online services and evaluating the quality of service provided by Internet service providers.

A survey by Deloitte found that 53% of respondents believed that blockchain technology would improve audit quality and reduce fraud risks.[3] This indicates that blockchain technology is becoming increasingly significant in the audit trail and can enhance the auditing process by improving efficiency, transparency, and security. Blockchain technology is a decentralized and distributed ledger designed to store and verify transactions between parties. While it is commonly associated with cryptocurrencies such as Bitcoin, its potential applications extend beyond financial transactions. Blockchain has features that make it an attractive technology for audit trails, such as immutability and transparency. Blockchain-based security auditing can provide greater transparency and accountability, as all parties can track and verify audit results.

Blockchain provides a cutting-edge solution to audit trail issues. It functions as a decentralized and immutable ledger; once a transaction is recorded, it cannot be altered or deleted. This creates a secure audit trail, with every transaction being recorded in real time and visible to all parties on the network. This feature enhances transparency and significantly reduces the risk of fraud, providing a more reliable and efficient auditing process. Adopting blockchain in audit trails could enhance the field by improving the integrity and reliability of audit trails. It could also reduce the time and costs associated with traditional and manual record-keeping and enhance operations through automated transaction recording. By addressing many limitations in traditional audit methods, blockchain could contribute to more efficient and reliable auditing practices.

By using blockchain for audit trails, organizations can create a tamper-proof and transparent record of all activities within a system, reducing the risk of fraud and improving trust among stakeholders. This could be achieved by implementing blockchain-based audit logs to record all activities within a system, including access attempts, changes made to data, and other relevant events. Organizations can employ smart contracts to establish the terms and circumstances that must be met for an event to be registered on the blockchain. As a result, it guarantees that noteworthy events are documented, which helps decrease the likelihood of fraudulent activities.

Traditional systems, like centralized databases, often fall short in various criteria, such as ensuring availability and providing comprehensive and tamper-proof records necessary for effective auditing, governance, and record keeping. However, blockchain-based audit trail approaches address these issues by introducing concepts of decentralization and immutability to audit trails. This has the potential to revolutionize the approach to monitoring online and utility services, thereby improving the efficiency of such monitoring processes. This chapter investigates the state of utilizing blockchain technology for audit trails and examines pertinent literature to present a detailed overview of the field. It also offers perspectives on the possibilities and difficulties involved in this developing area.

The rest of the chapter is structured as follows: section 11.2 explores audit trails' historical context and evolution. Section 11.3 examines the advent of blockchain technology, highlighting the key distinctions between public and private blockchains, and their implications for audit trails are covered in section 11.4. Section 11.5 presents a comparative analysis of audit trail systems before and after integrating blockchain technology and reviews existing research on audit trails and blockchain. Theoretical studies focus on the concepts and principles underlying audit trails and blockchain, while practical applications explore how they have been implemented in various industries and use cases. Section 11.6 addresses future directions and innovations in the field, while section 11.7 concludes the chapter by emphasizing the growing significance of audit trails and blockchain in recent years.

11.2 Historical Context and Evolution of Audit Trails

An audit trail is a record of all the events and activities that occur within a particular system. It provides a chronological order of events that allows someone to trace the history of a transaction or activity from its inception to its current state. These transactions or activities may be scientific, financial, or communication by individual people, systems, or other entities. Audit trails are commonly used in finance, accounting, and other industries to ensure compliance with regulations, detect fraud, and maintain accountability.

In information technology (IT), an audit trail may consist of logs that record user activity, system events, or changes to data. The information in the audit trail can be used to troubleshoot issues, investigate security breaches, or analyze system performance. An audit trail is also used to demonstrate compliance with regulations or to provide evidence in legal proceedings. As per the National Institute of Standards and Technology definition, an audit trail is a time-ordered record of system activities that can be used to recreate and review the series of events and actions related to a security-related transaction. It covers the entire process from the start to the end and can provide insight into the steps leading up to the operation, procedure, or event (Hu, Ferraiolo, & Kuhn, 2006).

There are two types of audit trails:

1. **External Audit:** An independent examination of an organization's or department's operational practices by a third-party auditor. It provides an unbiased assessment of an organization's/department's internal controls and compliance with relevant standards and regulations.

2. **Internal Audit:** It is conducted by an organization's internal audit team. It enables an organization/department to examine its progress and implement measures to foster future expansion. It also identifies and mitigates risks and ensures compliance with internal policies and procedures.

All types of audits can be important for an organization's compliance with legal and regulatory requirements. External audits objectively assess an organization's practices, while internal audits can help identify and address internal control weaknesses and risks. Organizations should be prepared to cooperate and provide requested documentation and information for any type of audit they may be subject to for ensuring a thorough and efficient audit process.

11.2.1 Traditional Methods of Creating and Maintaining Audit Trails

Centralized systems have traditionally been the foundation for managing audit trails (Talha, 2024). They provide unified control, allowing for consistent policy implementation and straightforward audit data management. Consolidating information in a single location simplifies access, and organizations have well-established practices for managing these systems. However, these systems have downsides. They are prone to failures due to their single point of failure (Garip et al., 2023), making them vulnerable to data breaches. In addition, they can be tampered with by individuals who can access and compromise the integrity of the audit trail. Limited transparency due to restrictive access and the potential for errors in data further reduces their reliability (Theodorakopoulos, Theodoropoulou, & Halkiopoulos, 2024).

Manual auditing, which is less common nowadays, offers simplicity and flexibility. It does not rely on complex technology and allows for maintaining records in various formats, including paper, which can be useful in specific scenarios. However, manual auditing is prone to human error, which can lead to inaccuracies. The process is also time-consuming and labor-intensive (Verevka & Shen, 2024), and paper documents are vulnerable to loss, theft, or unauthorized access, raising concerns about integrity and security.

11.2.2 Impact of Regulations and Technological Advancements

Regulatory changes have impacted audit trail practices. Increased regulations and compliance requirements now demand more secure and reliable auditing. These regulations aim to enhance audit trails and ensure they meet higher standards (Saleh et al., 2023). Privacy and data protection laws such as GDPR and California Consumer Privacy Act have introduced stricter rules for managing audit trails (Tikkinen-Piri, Rohunen, & Markkula, 2018). These regulations define the scope and process for exercising audit authority, establish criteria for selecting individuals to audit, and protect consumers' personal information from disclosure unless a court order, warrant, or subpoena is issued.[4]

Technology advancements have significantly transformed audit trail management. Blockchain's decentralization feature and the shift from paper to digital records have improved reliability and accuracy by reducing errors. Such advancements have also enhanced the ability to manage and analyze audit trails more effectively. In addition, blockchain technology has revolutionized audit trails by providing immutable and transparent records. Its decentralized nature and inherent properties address many limitations of traditional systems, reducing the risk of tampering and fraud and improving data integrity. An audit trail can provide valuable insights into an organization's activities and help ensure accountability and compliance. By implementing a blockchain-based audit trail, organizations can access many advantages, including transparency, exceptional availability, immutability, and non-repudiation. Hence, they can leverage the numerous benefits that blockchain technology provides. Blockchain is a decentralized digital ledger that stores data and allows secure and transparent peer-to-peer transactions (Rodeck & Curry, 2022). Blockchain can be classified into the following categories:

1. **Public Blockchain:** Anyone can participate in the network, read, and write data (Rodeck & Curry, 2022). Examples of public blockchains include Bitcoin and Ethereum (Guegan, 2017).
2. **Private Blockchain:** Access to the network is restricted to an organization or a group. A permissioned blockchain necessitates that the governing authority grants access privileges to individuals or entities to participate in the network (Rodeck & Curry, 2022). Businesses often use private blockchains for internal operations and supply chain management.

Blockchain serves as a robust tool for creating an audit trail. In a blockchain system, as illustrated in Figure 11.1, users submit transactions, which are then grouped to make a block. Each log and entry, such as auditing or periodic service records, can be represented as a transaction in an audit trail scenario. They form a block when they are combined. To ensure the block's validity, all nodes must approve and accept its proper generation before adding it to the chain. Once a block is created and verified, it is connected to the existing chain with the collaboration of independent parties called miners. The leader is chosen randomly among the miners to provide a secure environment since tampering with the system would require fooling all nodes simultaneously. Selecting the leader can be achieved with the help of consensus algorithms.

A block includes information from the previous block, creating a connection between blocks in the chain. This feature strengthens security, as modifying a single transaction would necessitate updating all subsequent information in the chain, which is challenging. In addition, transactions are

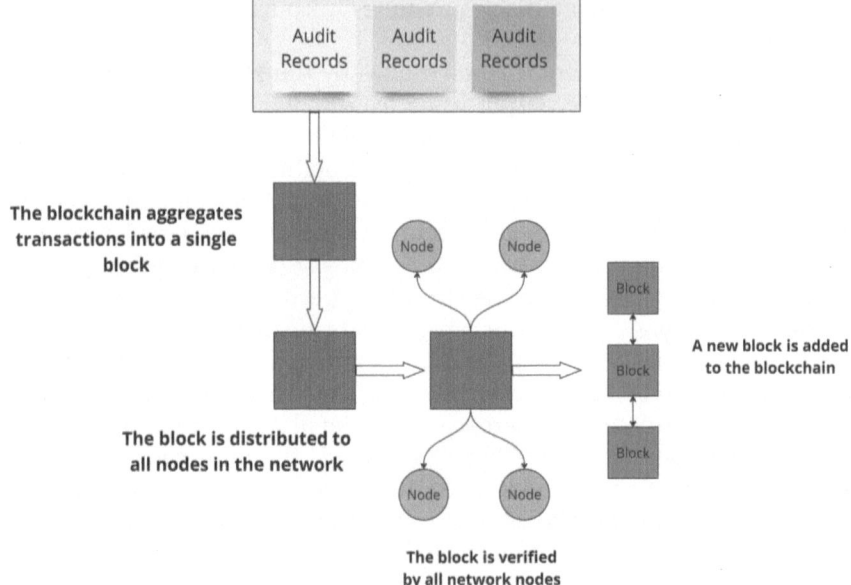

FIGURE 11.1
Blockchain construction

executed within the blockchain without a third-party intervention using automated scripts called smart contracts. Smart contracts operate autonomously on the blockchain, allowing for seamless integration of these procedures during the design of the blockchain system.

11.3 The Advent of Blockchain Technology

Some fundamental aspects characterize blockchain technology. Blockchain is decentralized, a distributing authority with control across a network of nodes rather than relying on a single central entity. This approach enhances resilience and reduces the risk of single points of failure. Blockchain is also an immutable system, so once data is recorded, it cannot be altered or erased (Liu et al., 2023). This feature ensures the data's integrity and prevents tampering. Moreover, all participants in the blockchain network can see and verify transactions, shaping a transparent system that enhances trust and facilitates the detection of fraudulent activities. These features inherent in blockchain enable the creation of a secure and reliable system that can facilitate auditing practices.

Blockchain technology can be broadly categorized into public and private blockchains with distinct characteristics and applications. A public blockchain is open to anyone who wants to read, write, or participate, and they can remain anonymous. It provides high transparency since all transactions are visible to every participant in the network. This openness is essential for creating immutable audit trails, as each transaction can be verified and traced. Public blockchains employ consensus mechanisms such as proof of work or proof of stake to validate transactions (Rosa-Bilbao & Boubeta-Puig, 2023), ensuring data security and preventing tampering. A public blockchain suits decentralized applications, cryptocurrencies, and public record-keeping. In some sectors, such as financial institutions, where regulatory compliance is crucial, public blockchain offers a transparent and verifiable audit trail that can be reviewed by regulatory bodies to verify its integrity.

However, private blockchains have restricted access; only verified participants can join the network (Zahir et al., 2024), and their identities are revealed. A private blockchain is suitable for internal use and restricted data management, such as legal services. It can also be used for specific internal compliance and by internal auditors to provide verifiable and auditable records. Public blockchains are suitable for applications requiring open and decentralized verification (Zahir et al., 2024), such as public financial transactions, where audit trails must be transparent. On the other hand, private blockchains are ideal where controlled access and data privacy are essential, such as internal audits or compliance tracking within organizations, where audit trails can be only accessed by authorized participants. Choosing between public and private blockchain depends on the specific use case and the organization or application's requirements.

11.4 Blockchain's Impact on Audit Trails

Blockchain offers a promising solution to many traditional audit trail issues. Traditional audit trails are often vulnerable to tampering and unauthorized access. Blockchain addresses the idea that using its decentralized nature, the data is distributed across multiple nodes rather than stored in a single central repository. This makes it much more difficult for malicious actors to alter or access the data without detection. Furthermore, each block on the chain is linked to the previous one, creating a chain of blocks that is nearly impossible to alter. In the financial and real estate industries, JPMorgan Chase uses blockchain to enhance transaction processes to be completed in hours compared to their original process, which takes days (Shevchenko & Lunsford,

2023). Companies like Propy use it to facilitate real estate transactions, making the process more efficient and cost-effective (Coinmagazine, 2023).

11.5 Comparative Analysis

Audit trails are essential for maintaining a reliable record of specific events within organizations. Traditional audit trails that rely on centralized systems often encounter challenges related to transparency, immutability, data integrity, and accessibility. The introduction of blockchain has significantly transformed these aspects, offering enhanced capabilities and benefits. Table 11.1 compares audit trails before and after utilizing blockchain technology, illustrating the improvements brought by this adoption.

Blockchain technology has emerged as a promising solution for enhancing audit trails in various domains, including auditing and remote audits, financial audits, enterprise applications, data management, sharing, and record keeping. By utilizing blockchain technology for audit trails, the immutability and integrity of financial records are guaranteed, resilience auditing processes in enterprise applications are ensured, and proper management and sharing of data and protection of records are also verified. This innovative approach to audit trails holds the potential to improve transparency, efficiency, reliability, and integrity in audit trail practices across multiple sectors, offering a sturdy basis for maintaining accurate and dependable audit trails.

TABLE 11.1

Comparing Audit Trails: Before and After Blockchain

Aspect	Before Blockchain	After Blockchain
Transparency	Limited transparency due to restricted access and centralized systems	Inherent transparency with decentralized ledger
Immutability	Prone to tampering; changes or deletions can occur	Immutable records that cannot be tampered with
Data Integrity	Using a centralized system can be prone to errors and susceptible to malicious activities	The decentralized nature helps verify data integrity
Cost	Manual processes are time-consuming and costly	Automated processes; save time and reduce operational costs
Accessibility and Availability	Centralized access, limited remote or external audit capabilities, and limited availability	Decentralized access, cross-organizational audits, remote accessibility, and high availability

The literature review can be divided into four main categories:

1. **Auditing and Remote Audits (Governance):** Auditing and Remote Audits play a critical role in maintaining transparency, accountability, and compliance across diverse domains.
2. **Financial Audits:** Financial Audits concentrate on meticulously examining and evaluating financial records, statements, and transactions to guarantee their accuracy and reliability.
3. **Enterprise Applications:** Enterprise Applications are the applications or solutions employed by corporate bodies to effectively manage a diverse range of business-related processes.
4. **Data and Records:** Data and Records focus on verifying the proper management and sharing of data and protection of records within and across organizations.

11.6 Auditing and Remote Audits (Governance)

Wang, Zhang, and Chang (2020) presented how blockchain technology could affect the auditing profession. Some people raised a debate about whether it could replace auditors, while others thought it would add value to the industry. The authors suggested a conceptual model for an auditing information system that utilizes blockchain's features. The proposed system combines blockchain technology, smart contracts, automated auditing tools, and traditional auditing practices, which should enhance auditing efficiency and be cost-effective by offering some features, such as real-time transaction recording, inventory monitoring, suspicious warnings, and analysis and reporting of auditing data.

Jayashree et al. (2021) proposed utilizing blockchain technology for digital voting (I-Voting) to enhance public elections' speed, cost-effectiveness, and convenience. The proposed I-Voting system depends on blockchain technology and enables registered voters to vote using any internet-connected device. The authors highlighted the drawbacks of traditional voting methods and the advantages of online voting and noted the security issues that prevented many countries from adopting such systems. The proposed I-Voting system uses encryption, smart biometrics, and real-time ID verification to ensure anonymity and security of the voting process. The authors also emphasized blockchain adoption to create tamper-proof audit trails for voting and discussed using hash functions to secure user voting details.

Mccorry et al. (2021) discussed how blockchain technology can be utilized in electronic voting to ensure secure and verifiable results. Traditional paper-based voting systems do not allow voters to confirm that their votes are accurately recorded, and digital voting systems that use direct recording electronic machines could record a different candidate without the voter realizing it. A voter verifiable paper audit trial can help solve this problem of voters not being able to verify their votes are accurately recorded despite the system still not allowing voters to check their votes. The authors thoroughly analyzed secure e-voting over blockchain technology and provided solutions for several voting scenarios.

11.7 Financial Audits

Wang, Huang et al. (2020) presented a solution to the difficulties of verifying energy bills in systems based on Internet of Things (IoT). The challenges arise due to privacy issues and the need for bulk auditing requests. The proposed solution, pAuditChain, utilizes homomorphic encryption and blockchain technology to ensure data auditing and privacy protection. In addition, it uses a certificateless signature approach to enhance the efficiency of bulk auditing requests. Both individual users and authorities can use the system. The theoretical analysis confirms the privacy-preserving and auditing procedures. This is the first solution to secure bills generated by IoT smart meters while maintaining the auditing function. The approach can also be applied to other IoT devices.

Constantinides and Cartlidge (2021) proposed utilizing blockchain technology to safeguard periodic double auctions for financial "dark pool" trading while maintaining the privacy of pre-trade order details and verifying the actions of the auction operator. Dark pools are nondisplayed financial trading venues designed for large-volume traders to avoid market impact, but lack of transparency concerns regulators. Constantinides and Cartlidge (2021) introduced an innovative smart contract protocol for implementing periodic double auctions on a blockchain in a verifiable and privacy-preserving way. Traders first submit encrypted order commitments that the operator cannot read. During the auction matching phase, the orders are revealed to the operator, and the results of the off-chain auction are made public. The protocol offers traders guarantees about the execution of their orders. The smart contract protocol is adaptable and can conveniently convert into a commercial system. The authors evaluated the protocol, which showed clear merits over the closest alternative protocol in the literature. They concluded that a double auction that preserves privacy and has a publicly verifiable audit trail has advantages in dark pool financial trading and various application areas.

Handoko, Arfianti, and Marlinda (2022) discussed how blockchain technology can support auditors in remote audits, ensure data integrity, and detect suspicious financial reporting. Their study involved interviewing experienced auditors and examining relevant literature. It also showed that the characteristics of blockchain enable auditors to maintain audit trails and detect financial fraud. The success of blockchain adoption depends on factors such as human resources, IT control environment, and Certified Public Accountant firm size. However, employing blockchain poses challenges such as cyber-attacks, IT risk, human error, and misuse. Thus, they suggested future research to determine how auditors can address these challenges.

11.8 Enterprise Applications

Ahmad et al. (2019) introduced BlockTrail, a blockchain architecture that reduces the complexity of conventional blockchain systems used in audit trails for enterprise business applications. Blockchain technology provides secure data processing without intermediaries but increases storage costs and lowers transaction throughput. BlockTrail divides the blockchain system into several layers, enabling parallel processing of transactions, which reduces storage required and enhances validation. Their study also discussed the security measures to increase defense capabilities and identify faulty replicas. They aimed to expand the range of BlockTrail from auditing to the hierarchical model of central bank digital currency, which has high scalability and throughput requirements.

Ahmad et al. (2019) proposed a new blockchain design, called BlockTrail, for auditing applications that addresses the challenges of transaction bulk and throughput limitations of existing blockchains. BlockTrail is a blockchain solution that is both scalable and efficient. It breaks down legacy blockchain systems into layers of co-dependent hierarchies, resulting in a reduction in space and time complexity and an increase in throughput. Ahmad et al. (2019) emphasized the significance of audit trails in enterprise solutions, such as government agencies responsible for property appraisal and tax collection, and how current blockchain systems face significant challenges in terms of space and time complexity due to the volume and size of transactions. To address this issue, BlockTrail employs a multichain blockchain model that divides the network into many layers, each capable of processing transactions independently while utilizing the hierarchical structure of eGovernment applications to facilitate parallel transaction processing and reduce storage overhead.

Regueiro et al. (2021) discussed the vulnerabilities of current audit trail implementations and proposed a blockchain-based mechanism to address these vulnerabilities. Audit trails are critical to ensure good internal business control and detect discrepancies and malicious activities. Despite the present implementations, which are vulnerable to attacks compromising their integrity, most organizations maintain audit trails in relational databases that can be manipulated or deleted. Regueiro et al. (2021) presented a comprehensive design and implementation of a blockchain-based system for creating protected audit trails by taking advantage of the security capabilities of blockchain technology. The proposed mechanism is general-purpose and can be used in any ecosystem, such as banking and healthcare.

11.9 Data and Records

11.9.1 Data Management and Sharing

Shafagh et al. (2017) discussed that the current IoT applications' cloud-centric architecture has led to isolated data silos, which restricts the potential of comprehensive data-driven analytics. To solve this problem, the authors proposed a blockchain-based design for IoT as an auditable layer that provides distributed access control and data management. The proposed design aims to give users data ownership and enable secure data sharing while ensuring secure and resilient access control management.

Sanchez et al. (2022) discussed the challenges of ensuring secure and trustworthy data sharing in decentralized environments where participants do not trust each other. Ensuring the accuracy and immutability of access logs is one of their significant challenges, as they hold a comprehensive record of data access for auditing purposes. Sanchez et al. (2022) proposed AuditTrust, a secure audit trail for data sharing in a distributed environment that utilizes blockchain technology, including Hyperledger Besu, InterPlanetary File System, Intel SGX Trusted Execution Environment, and Vault. Their system permits data sharing and requesting by data owners and consumers while maintaining the confidentiality and integrity of access logs. The evaluation of AuditTrust shows its effectiveness and low latency costs. Their system is designed as a framework for various application domains, where data must be exchanged between entities that do not trust each other.

Oakley et al. (2023) discussed the challenges of guaranteeing data reliability in clinical trials. They proposed Scrybe, a permissioned blockchain, as a solution for recording evidence of the source of clinical trial data. The authors contend that the increasing use of context-aware smart devices and wearable IoT devices in clinical trials creates challenges that current electronic data capture and clinical data management systems are inadequate to address. Scrybe aimed to meet the audit criteria that guarantee the confidentiality, integrity, and credibility of clinical trial data collected. Scrybe employs a lightweight mining algorithm and provides improved efficiency and cost-effectiveness. The authors also illustrated how Scrybe satisfies all relevant controls and offered a proof-of-concept integration with Research Electronic Data Capture (REDCap) to demonstrate its resistance to tampering. They concluded that Scrybe has potential applications beyond clinical trial data provenance and that a forthcoming vision of Scrybe will feature smart-contract functionality to enhance its capabilities.

11.10 Record Keeping

Wang and Yang (2021) discussed the utilization of blockchain technology in recordkeeping at the National Archives of Korea (NAK). The NAK built a blockchain recordkeeping platform to conduct research and development in two areas of recordkeeping approaches. The first employs blockchain transaction audit trail technology to ensure the authenticity of audiovisual archives. In contrast, the second leverages blockchain technology to confirm that the datasets of various information systems developed by government agencies were handled without any form of forgery or tampering. They concluded that blockchain-based recordkeeping solutions can provide the record and archive management system with elevated security and stability.

Ermolaev et al. (2020) addressed the difficulties of maintaining data accuracy and dependability nowadays, where information is increasing rapidly. To tackle this issue, authors proposed the integration of a blockchain and a graph database, which can enhance auditing practices and offer a secure and immutable history record (BitFury Group, 2016). They employed two methods for combining these technologies: "apply-and-rollback" and "two-step." In the first approach, the Neo4j database is created to execute modification and change tracking queries before reporting them to the blockchain. In contrast, the latter approach was implemented on the Exonum framework and Neo4j database, creating an auditable trail of data integrity. The blockchain records the changes to nodes in the graph database, including failed transactions. Direct read requests to Neo4j ensure that the system performs optimally, and Java programming language can be used to add business constraints. They noted that the solution has the potential for complete data recovery, which can be used as a reliable solution to ensure data integrity.

Adlam and Haskins (2020) discussed data breaches in electronic health records (EHRs). The current approach cannot ensure patient privacy and medical records security (Kshetri, 2018), and audit logs can identify who is responsible for those breaches or manipulations. The authors proposed Hyperledger Fabric, a blockchain system that creates a tamper-proof audit trail for EHRs. Their experiment demonstrated that blockchain-based audit trails could replace the traditional audit logs used by EHRs. They proposed the system as a diagram that shows how data flows and uses smart contracts to investigate how private blockchain technology could enhance the EHR audit log process. Blockchain-based audit trials improve the security and privacy of EHRs by offering transparency, immutability, audibility, and decentralization (Emmadi et al., 2019).

Sarode, Watanabe, and Bhalla (2022) highlighted the significance of maintaining accurate health records, specifically EHR, and stressed the importance of maintaining the reliability of audit trails in these records. To address this issue, the article proposes a blockchain-based audit management system that allows patients or authorized medical professionals to access a chronological record of all the tests, reports, and medical procedures performed during the patient's treatment. This system can resolve problems such as fragmented medical data across various hospitals and potential data loss due to system failures. The article recommends using smart contracts to store essential information and maintain the data's integrity.

The possibility of an online service quality audit trail and its connection to blockchain technology is an intriguing area that has received limited attention in the literature. In the context of online services, an audit trail could capture various metrics related to service quality, such as response times, downtime occurrences, and billing accuracy. By integrating blockchain technology into this process, tamper-resistant audit trail could be stored, enhancing transparency and immutability. This enables users and service providers to access the audit trail data, maintaining its integrity. Using smart contracts on blockchain could automate processes such as billing, further enhancing the system's efficiency.

While there is limited research on this area, it indicates an unexplored direction for researchers to delve into, offering the potential to improve online service quality monitoring. Exploring the connection between online service quality and blockchain-based audit trails could contribute to developing innovative approaches and frameworks in digital services by improving service reliability, customer satisfaction, and operational efficiency.

11.11 Future Directions and Innovations

Blockchain technology is set to revolutionize various industries, including audit trails. As blockchain networks evolve, they will become more capable of handling many transactions and data without affecting performance. Potential advances in scalability and privacy will enhance blockchain's capabilities, leading to more comprehensive and interconnected audit trail systems. This will enable organizations to maintain detailed audit trails while protecting sensitive information. This will be valuable in industries where data privacy is critical, such as finance and healthcare.

Integrating artificial intelligence (AI) (Vani, 2024), machine learning, and smart contracts is expected to enhance the functionality of audit trails. AI-powered analytics can identify anomalies and predict potential fraud, while smart contracts can allow for more complex and automated audit processes. In addition, integrating blockchain with IoT devices will create new opportunities for real-time audit trails (Ratnayake, Liyanage, & Murphy, 2024). IoT devices generate vast amounts of data that can be securely recorded and verified on a blockchain. This integration will provide immutable audit trails for IoT device processes and transactions, enhancing transparency and accountability in manufacturing and supply chain management industries.

Blockchain's impact on governance structures is significant. Among the potential benefits are decentralized governance models, increased transparency, and compliance processes. Blockchain technology can potentially enhance compliance processes by automating and recording compliance activities. With smart contracts, organizations can automate the enforcement of regulatory requirements. This will reduce the administrative tasks associated with compliance and minimize human error, leading to more accurate reporting. Audit trails on a blockchain will be updated in real time, providing auditors and regulators with immediate access to accurate and verified data, enabling more proactive audits.

Blockchain's global nature will facilitate cross-border compliance by providing a unified and transparent system for verifying international transactions. This will simplify compliance with global regulations and standards, making it easier for multinational organizations to manage and report their activities across different countries. Blockchain technology has the potential to significantly lower compliance costs by automating compliance processes and reducing the need for intermediaries. Organizations will benefit from reduced administrative overhead and fewer resources dedicated to managing compliance, allowing them to allocate resources more efficiently. The future of blockchain holds tremendous potential for transforming audit trails and governance practices. These innovations will enhance the effectiveness of audit trails and transform governance structures and compliance protocols by increasing transparency, accountability, and privacy while mitigating risks.

11.12 Conclusion and Discussion

An audit trail serves as a comprehensive record of activities within a system, essential for tracking changes, particularly in accounting and financial systems. Audit failures have underscored the pressing need for more reliable audit mechanisms. Traditional auditing methods reveal significant vulnerabilities, relying on outdated systems prone to security breaches and unauthorized access, compromising audit integrity. In addition, these methods are often time-consuming, expensive, and susceptible to delays and errors due to manual processes, with the lack of real-time verification increasing the risk of undetected fraud. The significance of maintaining a trustworthy audit trail has been emphasized by numerous instances of fraud and data mismanagement in recent years. The scams and revenue loss businesses have encountered in recent years have turned the world's eyes toward the importance of having a robust audit trail to detect and prevent such incidents.

Blockchain addresses many of the shortcomings of traditional audit methods by providing a tamper-proof, real-time ledger of transactions accessible to all parties involved. This technological advancement offers enhanced transparency, reduced fraud risk, and increased efficiency in auditing processes. By automating transaction recording and eliminating many manual procedures, blockchain can significantly lower the time and costs associated with traditional auditing practices.

The growing significance of blockchain technology in audit trails is evident in many surveys. Blockchain technology offers important features such as immutability, transparency, and availability, making it exceptionally well suited for audit trails. Through the implementation of a blockchain-based audit trail, organizations, and governmental entities can enhance their audits by taking advantage of the features offered by blockchain technology, which enables all stakeholders to track and verify audit results without third-party dependency.

One of the major advantages of blockchain-based audit trails is transparency. Every transaction or activity within the blockchain is recorded on a distributed database accessible only to authorized participants. Ensuring that data cannot be altered without consensus from the network participants enhances transparency and trust among consumers and service providers.

Implementing blockchain for audit trails enables organizations to create immutable and transparent records of all system activities, including data changes and access attempts. Smart contracts can be employed to set specific conditions for recording events on the blockchain, ensuring accurate documentation and reducing the likelihood of fraudulent activities. Unlike traditional centralized databases, which often fall short of providing comprehensive and tamper-proof records, blockchain-based systems introduce essential features of decentralization and immutability, potentially revolutionizing the monitoring of online and utility services. Furthermore, this integration can offer real-time traceability of all transactions and activities within online and utility services, which enhances security by detecting unauthorized access and mitigating fraudulent behaviors that pose risks to these services.

Automating governance and audit processes and eliminating the need for intermediaries minimize administrative and operational costs for service providers. The audit trail enables more efficient resource allocation and decision-making, leading to cost savings and improving service delivery by addressing availability issues. In addition, organizations can establish tamper-proof and transparent records of system activities, thereby mitigating the risk of fraud and enhancing trust among stakeholders. This can be achieved by utilizing blockchain-based audit logs to record all relevant events, including access attempts and data changes. Smart contracts can be utilized to define the terms and conditions necessary for an event to be recorded on the blockchain, ensuring that noteworthy events are documented and reducing the likelihood of fraudulent activities. Researchers explore various application areas to utilize blockchain in audit trails to take advantage of transparency through decentralized and immutable transaction recording. Blockchain technology ensures data integrity and fosters trust in the auditing process. Furthermore, by eliminating intermediaries and minimizing manual tasks, blockchain reduces costs associated with auditing.

However, public blockchains may encounter scalability limitations when handling a high volume of transactions, potentially impacting the performance of audit trail systems. Privacy concerns arise, particularly when sensitive or confidential data is included in audit trails, necessitating a delicate balance between transparency and privacy. Furthermore, integrating blockchain technology with existing systems can present adaptation challenges due to its inherent resistance to change. Ensuring compliance with data protection and privacy regulations also poses a challenge. Addressing these challenges is essential for successfully adopting blockchain technology in audit trails.

The application of blockchain-based auditing systems for utility and online service providers still requires further exploration and research. How does implementing blockchain technology in auditing processes impact overall service quality? Does it enhance accuracy, timeliness, and transparency in auditing activities? What are the potential benefits and challenges of using blockchain for auditing, and how do they impact service quality outcomes? While blockchain is known for its security features, is there a possibility of auditing data being leaked or compromised? What vulnerabilities or attack vectors could potentially expose sensitive auditing information stored on the blockchain? How scalable is the blockchain infrastructure for handling large volumes of auditing data, and are there any performance limitations that need to be addressed for seamless adoption of blockchain-based auditing services? These questions encompass various aspects to explore the risks and benefits of utilizing blockchain in auditing, shedding light on potential research directions and areas for further investigation.

This chapter thoroughly explores the utilization of blockchain technology for audit trails, providing an in-depth overview of the field by examining relevant literature. This examination aims to present a thorough understanding of how blockchain can enhance audit practices and contribute to more secure and efficient auditing processes. It also offers insights into this emerging area's potential opportunities and challenges. In addition, possible areas for future research have also been identified.

Notes

1. No financial or nonfinancial interests are directly or indirectly related to this work submitted for publication.
2. https://www.acfe.com/about-the-acfe/newsroom-for-media/press-releases/press-release-detail?s=2022-RTTN-launch
3. https://www2.deloitte.com/us/en/insights/topics/understanding-blockchain-potential/global-blockchain-survey-2019.html
4. https://cppa.ca.gov/regulations/pdf/cppa_act.pdf

References

Adlam, R., & Haskins, B. (2020, September). A permissioned blockchain approach to electronic health record audit logs. In *Proceedings of the 2nd International Conference on Intelligent and Innovative Computing Applications* (pp. 1–7). ACM.

Ahmad, A., Saad, M., Njilla, L., Kamhoua, C., Bassiouni, M., & Mohaisen, A. (2019, May). Blocktrail: A scalable multichain solution for blockchain-based audit trails. In *ICC 2019–2019 IEEE International Conference on Communications (ICC)* (pp. 1–6). IEEE.

Aßländer, M. S., & Burkatzki, E. (2023). The financial fraud of the German fintech company Wirecard: Structural causes and failures of the supervisory authorities. In *Sustainable Finance and Financial Crime* (pp. 291–306). Cham: Springer International Publishing.

Baranidharan, S., Ajekwe, C. C. M., & Nakitende, M. G. (2023). Accounting fraud and bankruptcy: The case of Wirecard AG. In *Theory and Practice of Illegitimate Finance* (pp. 222–244). IGI Global.

BitFury Group. (2016). On blockchain auditability. *Whitepaper*. https://bitfury.com/content/downloads/bitfury_white_paper_on_blockchain_auditability.pdf

Coinmagazine. (2023, July 6). Propy: The blockchain-powered real estate revolution. *Medium*. https://coinmagazine.medium.com/propy-the-blockchain-powered-real-estate-revolution-7698c47d687c

Constantinides, T., & Cartlidge, J. (2021, December). Block auction: A general blockchain protocol for privacy-preserving and verifiable periodic double auctions. In *2021 IEEE International Conference on Blockchain (Blockchain)* (pp. 513–520). IEEE.

Emmadi, N., Vigneswaran, R., Kanchanapalli, S., Maddali, L., & Narumanchi, H. (2019). Practical deployability of permissioned blockchains. In *Business Information Systems Workshops: BIS 2018 International Workshops, Berlin, Germany, July 18–20, 2018, Revised Papers 21* (pp. 229–243). Springer International Publishing.

Ermolaev, V., Klangberg, I., Madhwal, Y., Vapper, S., Wels, S., & Yanovich, Y. (2020, May). Incorruptible auditing: Blockchain-powered graph database management. In *2020 IEEE International Conference on Blockchain and Cryptocurrency (ICBC)* (pp. 1–3). IEEE.

European Union. (2016). Regulation (EU) 2016/679 of the European Parliament and of the Council of 27 April 2016 on protecting natural persons about the processing of personal data and the free movement of such data (General Data Protection Regulation). *Official Journal of the European Union*, L119, 1–88. Retrieved from https://eur-lex.europa.eu/

Garip, S., Bilgen, M., Altin, N., Ozdemir, S., & Sefa, I. (2023). Reliability analysis of microgrids: Evaluation of centralized and decentralized control approaches. *Electric Power Components and Systems*, 51(19), 2319–2338.

Guegan, D. (2017, December). *Public blockchain versus private blockchain*. HAL Open Science, halshs-01524440, version 1 (pp. 1–6). https://shs.hal.science/halshs-01524440/

Handoko, B. L., Arfianti, F., & Marlinda, S. (2022, December). The utilization of blockchain technology on remote audits ensures audit data integrity and detects potential fraudulent financial reporting. In *Proceedings of the 2022 6th International Conference on Software and e-Business* (pp. 104–112). ACM.

Hu, V. C., Ferraiolo, D., & Kuhn, D. R. (2006). *Assessment of Access Control Systems* (pp. 09–29). Gaithersburg, MD: US Department of Commerce, National Institute of Standards and Technology.

Jayashree, D., Pandithurai, O., Yogeswari, S., Swetha, K. B., & Shalini, A. (2021). I-voting system based on blockchain. *Smart Intelligent Computing and Communication Technology*, 38, 81.

Kshetri, N. (2018). Blockchain and electronic healthcare records [cybertrust]. *Computer*, 51(12), 59–63.

Li, Y. (2023, August). Study the reasons for the failure of the audit of Luckin Coffee and suggestions for countermeasures. In *International Conference on Economic Management and Green Development* (pp. 729–737). Singapore: Springer Nature Singapore.

Liu, Z., Ren, L., Feng, Y., Wang, S., & Wei, J. (2023). Data integrity audit scheme based on quad Merkle tree and blockchain. *IEEE Access*, 11, 59263–59273.

McCorry, P., Mehrnezhad, M., Toreini, E., Shahandashti, S. F., & Hao, F. (2021). On secure e-voting over the blockchain. *Digital Threats: Research and Practice (DTRAP)*, 2(4), 1–13.

Newray, K. L. (2023). Improving public record management system at government ministries and agencies: Factors to consider and action steps. *International Journal for Multidisciplinary Research*, 5(6), 1–17.

Oakley, J., Worley, C., Yu, L., Brooks, R. R., Özçelik, İ. L. K. E. R., Skjellum, A., & Obeid, J. S. (2023). Scrybe: A secure audit trail for clinical trial data fusion. *Digital Threats: Research and Practice*, 4(2), 1–20.

Olivier, W., & von Solms, R. (1999). The effective utilization of audit logs in information security management. In *Information Security Management & Small Systems Security: IFIP TC11 WG11. 1/WG11. 2 Seventh Annual Working Conference on Information Security Management & Small Systems Security September 30–October 1, 1999, Amsterdam, The Netherlands* (pp. 51–61). Springer US.

Ratnayake, R., Liyanage, M., & Murphy, L. (2024, May). Machine learning for data trust evaluations in blockchain-enabled IoT systems. In *2024 IEEE International Conference on Blockchain and Cryptocurrency (ICBC)* (pp. 1–2). IEEE.

Regueiro, C., Seco, I., Gutiérrez-Agüero, I., Urquizu, B., & Mansell, J. (2021). A blockchain-based audit trail mechanism: Design and implementation. *Algorithms*, 14(12), 341.

Ringelstein, C., & Staab, S. (2009, July). DIALOG: Distributed auditing logs. In *2009 IEEE International Conference on Web Services* (pp. 429–436). IEEE.

Rodeck, D., & Curry, B. (2022, April 28). What is blockchain? *Forbes Media*.

Rosa-Bilbao, J., & Boubeta-Puig, J. (2023). Ethereum blockchain platform. In *Distributed Computing to Blockchain* (pp. 267–282). Academic Press.

Saleh, M. A., Amanzholova, S. T., Sagymbekova, A. O., Zaurbek, A., & Almisreb, A. A. (2023). How can blockchain strengthen cybersecurity? Unraveling the promises and challenges. In *DTESI* (workshops, short papers).

Sanchez, H. L., Tysebaert, S., Rath, A., & Riviere, E. (2022, September). AuditTrust: Blockchain-based audit trail for sharing data in a distributed environment. In *European Dependable Computing Conference* (pp. 5–17). Cham: Springer International Publishing.

Sarode, R. P., Watanabe, Y., & Bhalla, S. (2022, December). A blockchain-based approach for audit management of electronic health records. In *International Conference on Big Data Analytics* (pp. 86–94). Cham: Springer Nature Switzerland.

Shafagh, H., Burkhalter, L., Hithnawi, A., & Duquennoy, S. (2017, November). Towards blockchain-based auditable storage and sharing of IoT data. In *Proceedings of the 2017 on Cloud Computing Security Workshop* (pp. 45–50). ACM.

Shevchenko, E., & Lunsford, R. (2023). Blockchain disruption in finance: JPMorgan Chase's success story and the transfer of quorum to ConsenSys. *Journal of Finance and Accountancy*, 32, 1–12.

Talha, M. (2024). Blockchain in accounting: Transforming transparency and security in financial records. *Dandao Xuebao/Journal of Ballistics*, 36(1), 63–73.

Theodorakopoulos, L., Theodoropoulou, A., & Halkiopoulos, C. (2024). Enhancing decentralized decision-making with big data and blockchain technology: A comprehensive review. *Applied Sciences*, 14(16), 1–46. https://doi.org/10.3390/app14167007

Tikkinen-Piri, C., Rohunen, A., & Markkula, J. (2018). EU General Data Protection Regulation: Changes and implications for personal data collecting companies. *Computer Law & Security Review*, 34(1), 134–153.

Vani, V. (2024). Blockchain and AI for secure and sustainable healthcare development. In *Cybersecurity and Data Management Innovations for Revolutionizing Healthcare* (pp. 308–329). IGI Global.

Verevka, T., & Shen, Z. (2024). Key factors in efficient auditing of investment projects in time of digitalization. In *Understanding the Digital Transformation of Socio-Economic-Technological Systems: Dedicated to the 120th Anniversary of Economic Education at Peter the Great St. Petersburg Polytechnic University* (pp. 207–215). Cham: Springer Nature Switzerland.

Wang, H., & Yang, D. (2021). Research and development of blockchain recordkeeping at the National Archives of Korea. *Computers*, 10(8), 90.

Wang, K., Zhang, Y., & Chang, E. (2020, July). A conceptual model for blockchain-based auditing information system. In *Proceedings of the 2nd International Electronics Communication Conference* (pp. 101–107). ACM.

Wang, Q., Huang, L., Chen, S., & Xiang, Y. (2020). Blockchain enables your bill to be safer. *IEEE Internet of Things Journal*, 9(16), 14162–14171.

Wee, C. (1999). Audit logs: To keep or not to keep? In *Recent Advances in Intrusion Detection*. Springer.

Zahir, A., Groshev, M., Antevski, K., J. Bernardos, C., Ayimba, C., & De La Oliva, A. (2024, January). Performance evaluation of private and public blockchains for multi-cloud service federation. In *Proceedings of the 25th International Conference on Distributed Computing and Networking* (pp. 217–221). ACM.

12
A Blockchain-Enabled Digital Strategy for Agriculture Trade

Sneha Kumari, V. G. Venkatesh, and S. Vijayakumar Bharathi

12.1 Introduction

Agriculture trade demands supply chain design, coordination, organization, and monitoring. It considers the economic aspect by optimizing costs and has positive or regenerative impacts on social and environmental aspects. The World Trade Organization developed an agreement on agriculture in 1995 to promote agricultural trade.

12.1.1 Overview of Agriculture Trade Challenges

Exposure to agriculture emissions to carbon price suggests climate policy for agriculture trade (Leahy et al., 2020). Price policies are adopted to address energy, transport, and industry-related CO_2 emissions. Regional agreements and policies have tripled since 2000 to promote agriculture trade. Agriculture trade is influenced by the demand for food, trade agreements, and climate change (Ortiz et al., 2021). In countries, agricultural production has placed a record worldwide for different commodities. Agriculture interventions, schemes, subsidies, and policies have supported the production (Fan et al., 2024). However, with the rise in agriculture production, there is a need to enhance the brand value and market potential. Geographical indicators (GI) and quality parameters are questioned during the agriculture trade. The trade lacks transparency; thus, the producers ignore GI and quality parameters (Li et al., 2023). Another issue is that the farmers never achieve real-time prices. For example, a farmer usually sells agricultural produce at a price much lower than what a regular consumer typically pays in the international retail market. Thus, farmer-level participation in the trade is low mainly due to a lack of direct accessibility to consumers, awareness, and trust. Blockchain can address these issues for trading agricultural produce by allowing farmers access to the consumers, and blockchain, coupled with the Internet of Things (IoT), artificial intelligence (AI), and machine learning (ML), will digitize trust and better traceability (Torky & Hassanein, 2020). An ancillary benefit of blockchain is supporting hi-tech jobs in agriculture, big data analytics, information technology (IT) security, specialized training, and agribusiness. The usage of blockchain is low in emerging economies due to several reasons like lack of awareness, selection of vendors, and development of environmental and security issues (Ganguly, 2024). Blockchain technology can be a game changer as it can provide tamper-proof, accurate data about the farms, inventory, credit scores, and food tracking.

12.1.2 Introduction to Blockchain Technology

As the agriculture trade is always a concern for increasing farmers' income, generating employment opportunities, and attaining sustainability, applying blockchain technology in the supply chain will solve such complex problems (Gupta & Shankar, 2024). Blockchain in agriculture trade will provide an end-to-end solution protecting the GI certification (Bonetti et al., 2024). This will result in a multi-seller e-commerce platform that links farmers directly to sell their agricultural produce. The verifications and certifications can be easily done through AI and ML. The traceability of agricultural produce will lead to a better supply chain.

12.1.3 Rationale for the Application of Blockchain in Agriculture Trade

Blockchain is the digital technology applied to agriculture trade to facilitate better financial transactions with stakeholders (Kamilaris et al., 2019). Blockchain is maintained by a network of machines for managing individual transactions in the agriculture trade. A blockchain is an agreement among the parties for a transparent system. Bitcoin is commonly used as proof of work to solve different tasks. The proof of work helps to digitally verify the records for the task completion. Some companies have applied digital technology in the agriculture trade. AgriDigital Company executed the world's first settlement of the sale of 23.46 tons of grains in the blockchain. AgriDigital served transactions of more than 1.6 million tons of grains (Kamilaris et al., 2019). Louis Dreyfus Co. is also one of the world's biggest foodstuffs traders using blockchain. The digital flow consists of technologies like QR code, RFID, NFC, internet, and web services. The code provides detailed information about the product. Blockchain is an opportunity for transparent delivery with verified documents. It assures quality and food safety by verifying the labels and traceability. Blockchain can mitigate food fraud by identifying the sources. Cargill Inc. aims to trace from store to form, including blockchain. The European Grocer Carrefour uses blockchain to verify the standards and trace food origins. Downstream Beer is the first company to apply blockchain in the beer supply chain. Paddock to Plate is a project on the meat supply chain that helps to track the meat along the chain in Australia.

12.2 Understanding the Agricultural Trade Landscape

12.2.1 Current Challenges in Agriculture Trade

The application of blockchain technology varies among developed and developing countries. The farmers of a developing nation lack experience in digital technology. Developed countries like the United States, Australia, and Europe are digitally competent and have better access to blockchain technology (Kamilaris et al., 2019).

12.2.2 Key Players and Stakeholders Involved

The stakeholders play an important role in blockchain technology implementation (Balci & Surucu-Balci, 2021). Stakeholder mapping is the primary stage where the stakeholders perform based on their potential. The investors assist in providing financial support for the system. Data miners validate the data and add new transactions to the blockchain. The data miners, in return, are awarded cryptocurrency tokens called bitcoins. The node operator ensures the integrity of all transactions by validating and preparing a blockchain ledger. Software developers are responsible for implementing new features for the improvement and monitoring bugs. Buyers in the form of processing companies, wholesalers, distributors, and farmers can interact through the blockchain network by sending and receiving transactions. The strategic manpower is responsible for maintaining the blockchain network rules.

12.2.3 Stakeholder Engagement and Strategies to Involve Farmers, Traders, Regulators, and Technology Providers

Blockchain-enabled digital technology leads to stakeholders' involvement in achieving common goals. The stakeholders' engagement is essential for the implementation of a blockchain. Agriculture trade involves the active participation of the stakeholders as the functional web in trade from producers to sellers is linked in terms of maintaining quality standards, good agricultural practices, grading, sorting, packaging, and selling. Stakeholders have a different understanding of digital technology. Therefore, it is essential to develop strategies for the stakeholders to adapt to the blockchain environment. Table 12.1 presents the strategies.

12.2.4 Market State and Dynamics

Countries have several, though noncritical, technologies required to apply hi-tech to build a mobile-based multi-seller e-commerce platform, QR codes, and IoT. High-tech innovations like blockchain and AI offer revolutionary solutions to agriculture. However, the assimilation of advanced technologies

TABLE 12.1

Strategies for Stakeholder Engagement for Blockchain-Enabled Digital Technology

Stakeholders	Strategies
Farmers	Workshops, training, and webinars can create awareness among farmers about a technology-enabled environment. Pilot projects can be implemented to familiarize the farmers with blockchain technology. The application should be easy to access, as farmers are not digitally literate.
Traders	To improve the supply chain, blockchain demonstration is required. Collaborative efforts are also required with the traders to ensure transparency and trust among the stakeholders.
Regulators	The legal requirements can be regulated through pilot projects through consistent engagements.
Technology Providers	The requirements and objectives of blockchain solutions need to be clearly defined. Technology providers must understand the need from the farmers' and traders' perspective. The stakeholders need to be mapped to understand the implementation of blockchain.

Source: Created by the Authors.

takes time. The emerging economy needs to work on the usage of blockchain among small and medium farmers (Asante Boakye et al., 2023). The basic purpose is to reduce costs and maximize the benefits derived from these technologies. Hence, the farmer clusters in the form of cooperatives or collectives can play an important role in applying blockchain technology. This will also reduce dependence on files and paperwork, digitizing the supply chain.

12.3 Blockchain Technology Fundamentals

12.3.1 Basics of Blockchain Technology

Blockchain technology has brought greater transparency and accountability to the international agriculture supply chain. It promises a reliable source for dealing with the agriculture supply chain stakeholders. It facilitates data-driven technologies for timely payments to producers. This helps address the challenge of complex supply chains (Tsolakis et al., 2023). Technology thus provides solutions to food quality and safety issues, which are highly concerning to consumers and the government.

12.3.2 Features and Benefits of Blockchain in Trade

Blockchain technology can support small farmers by providing traceability in the value chains. It leads to increased transparent transactions, leading to better product quality (Kamilaris et al., 2019). Blockchain helps to bring traceability among the stakeholders of the value chain. The contaminated products can easily be traced using blockchain, resulting in quality management. The price management can be done efficiently using blockchain.

12.3.3 Smart Contracts and Their Role in Agriculture Trade

Smart Contracts regulate the trust between the two parties and the business terms and conditions (Szabo, 1997) using blockchain (Pranto et al., 2021). The parties need to undergo smart contracts to make the process transparent and prevent any breach in the agreements clause. The concept started emerging in 2016 through the Ethereum blockchain. The contract is stored in the blockchain, making the process autogenerative. Autogeneration helps trace the agriculture supply chain. Smart Contracts comprise codes in attributes, events, functions, and modifiers. Attributes lead to the storage of the data in the memory. Function results in the execution of a task, modifiers are the access power, and events represent storage of the data that can be retrieved. Smart contracts equipped with IoT sensors and blockchain lead to the monitoring of agriculture operations. Maintenance of data security is a key concern in smart contracts. Smart contracts can help bring e-agribusiness solutions (Leduc et al., 2021).

12.4 Implementation Framework for Blockchain in Agriculture Trade

Integrating blockchain in agriculture trade demands technology infrastructure for sufficient resources to set up blockchain and technical skilled manpower for proper data storage and validation (Thinakaran et al., 2023). The data sources from the agroecosystem must be brought to one platform. The innovations and integrity capability can result in blockchain-enabled digital strategy resulting in digital agriculture trade. Literature also supports that blockchain-enabled digital strategy can be possible once the linkage is moderated by behavioral control. The intentions to perceive blockchain technology influence the behavior toward the blockchain-enabled strategy in agriculture trade (see Table 12.2).

TABLE 12.2

Building Blocks for Blockchain-Enabled Digital Strategy

Constructs	Definition	Source
Technology Infrastructure	Infrastructure capability refers to the ability of the technology infrastructure (e.g., applications, hardware, data, and networks)	Wamba et al., 2016; Lewis & Byrd, 2003; Byrd & Turner, 2000; Duncan, 1995
Data Sources	Data is defined as the medium through which big data can be generated	Davenport & Dyché, 2013; Jeble et al., 2016; Madhavan & Halevy, 2003; Dickinson et al., 2003
Technical Skills	Human resources refer to individual managers and workers' training, experience, judgment, relationship, intelligence, and insights.	Hatala et al., 2015; Winckel et al., 1994; Barney, 1991
Innovative Capability	Innovative capability is based on reinforcing the firm's practices and processes.	Mendoza-Silva, 2021; Wilson & Daniel, 2007; Persaud, 2005; Lawson & Samson 2001
Integrative Capability	Integrative capability applies to integrating technology, organization structure, culture, and climate to achieve multi-channel customer satisfaction.	Jiang et al., 2015; Wilson & Daniel, 2007; Lawson & Samson, 2001

12.4.1 Traceability and Provenance of Agricultural Products Using Blockchain

Blockchain can help address the traceability and provenance of agricultural produce in the following manner:

- Quality Improvement: The trace of quality parameters can help in better quality management of agricultural produce.
- Adopting Scientific Methods: Scientific methods in handling sorting, and grading of agricultural produce should be involved.
- Technology Infusion: Technology infusion will lead to the application of IoT, AI, and ML.
- Expansion of Quality Testing: Blockchain can lead to monitoring the quality testing of agricultural produce.

12.4.2 Improving Trust and Transparency among Stakeholders in Agriculture Trade

Blockchain-enabled e-commerce platform that is live 24 × 7 as it is automated. On Amazon, an end consumer enjoys carefree shopping without concern about the seller's identity, as Amazon assumes responsibility for establishing trust, enabling tracking, and providing verification. A blockchain, therefore, helps to overcome issues like lack of direct access to the end consumer, democratizing trust, and scan-based verification of credentials (Werbach, 2018). Blockchain helps in modules for verification, fraud detection, and farm-to-fork traceability (Ellahi et al., 2023). It can support multi-seller, payment gateway-integrated e-commerce platforms robustly.

12.4.3 Enhancing Food Safety and Quality Assurance through Blockchain-Based Solutions

Food safety and quality assurance are challenging today (Creydt en Fischer, 2019). Blockchain can provide efficient solutions at different supply chain stages to ensure quality management (Kamilaris et al., 2019). Contaminants can be easily identified, thereby preventing health risks. The blockchain integration has led to real-time data monitoring and tracing based on hazard analysis and critical control points.

12.4.4 Synergy between Blockchain and Other Technology

Blockchain technology integrates with the IoT for agriculture applications. IoT sensors track the soil, moisture, and temperature conditions required for agriculture. Blockchain data records help trace agricultural produce. The IoT helps in preventing malpractice by ensuring transparency and efficiency. IoT sensors establish standards to ensure compatibility. Blockchain integration with AI helps in predictive analytics for yield, demand, and supply chain. AI helps forecast, plan, and reduce waste. Integration of blockchain with AI leads to meeting agriculture trade needs. Blockchain integration with big data helps to provide insights into supply chain strategies. The blockchain helps in data security and data-driven decision-making. The blockchain sets protocols for data entry, accuracy, and management.

12.5 Case Studies and Examples

Walmart is the world's leading retailer, integrating blockchain technology into the agriculture supply chain. The food safety collaboration center can track and trace the supply chain of sliced mangoes from South and Central

America to North America (Kamath, 2018). The blocks provide information related to the farm, batch number, soil quality, fertilizer, storage temperature, and shipping details. This information is then uploaded, and an e-certificate is provided to the packed product. The product carries a quick response (QR) code that can be easily scanned, and detailed information can be accessed. Axio Zen has integrated blockchain for marine conservation through awareness creation using a blockchain-based collectible digital asset. The digital asset resembles a sea turtle and helps identify critically endangered species (Howson, 2020). Barclays' Blockchain is a UK-based financial service provider that helps bring transparency to the agricultural trade finance for the export of goods. TradeLens platform results in traceability of the cut flowers and avocados from Africa to Europe (McDaniel & Norberg, 2019). The platform also traces the global supply chain for meat and processed food (Maersk, 2021). Provenance Platform is another example where consumers can trace the seafood products to monitor the quality and eco-label certifications of seafood. Global Food Safety Initiative helps make the food supply chain secure and traceable using blockchain technology. The Agri Chain platform helps monitor agricultural trade using blockchain. Ripe.io helps control the quality of agricultural products in the supply chain. The Agri Wallet platform is an example of prioritizing the correct payment to the farmers for the right produce. FarmShare is a platform that creates digital identifications for farmers for supply chain services.

The CarbonChain platform helps track carbon credits in agroforestry. Nori platform tracks the carbon sequestration in soil through blockchain. The AgriTech Hub platform uses blockchain to track the land records for farmers' credit facilities. Food Security Blockchain Lab helps monitor resources. Bean Chain in Antioquia Colombia uses blockchain to enable an efficient supply chain. IBM Food Trust uses blockchain solutions to ensure transparency in the food supply chain. The solution provides access to the data stored for the food supply chain. IBM Food Trust enables access to blockchain data based on the Global trade item number or universal product code for agricultural produce. The organization has control over who can access the data on the network.

Golden State Food ensures the supply chain of processed products, such as meat and dairy products.

12.5.1 Real-World Applications of Blockchain in Agriculture Trade

The application of mobile devices for data gathering barcodes, QR codes, and radio-frequency identification (RFID) has helped in the real-world application of blockchain in agriculture trade (Khan et al., 2022). Businesses consistently differentiate in terms of improvement in data management for real-world applications of blockchain in agriculture trade. For blockchain implementation in the agriculture supply chain, it is essential to convince the farmers of its usability. The priority of farmers in different parts of the world is different; therefore, the uniform application of blockchain is challenging. Blockchain, being a computing equipment, requires sufficient resources. Resource availability has been a challenge in developing countries (Zhao et al., 2021). The challenge is due to the gap in digital competencies and access to blockchain technology (Maru et al., 2018).

12.5.2 Success Stories and Lessons Learned

Implementing blockchain in agriculture has led to traceability, security, trust, and prevention of agro-product frauds in agriculture (Bhusal, 2021). There are agriculture start-ups, farmer-producer companies, cooperatives, and private firms that have integrated blockchain with the agriculture supply chain. Blockchain results in data records followed by verifications by the participating nodes. The first step is the receival of any transaction request wherein a block is created. As a next step, the new block is broadcasted to all the nodes in the network. The transaction verification is done once it reaches the consumer. The block is added to the existing blocks with a new data block. This helps make the agricultural supply chain efficient and sustainable. There are agriculture startups that have been using blockchain. Agridigital is one of the startups that use the Ethereum blockchain, enabling real-time payment to the farmers. Agrileder uses mobile applications based on R3's Corda. TeFood has implemented identification tags and QR codes.

Blockchain was implemented for food businesses in 2016. China has also tried to improve its quality by undergoing different experiments with blockchain. India's Walmart has embraced the technology. Blockchain technology also provides enjoyment if one is familiar with the topic. The products we grow must adapt to meet consumer demand, and technology plays a key role in facilitating this development. In addition, microbiology, multi-trade, biological commerce, precision agriculture, and nutrients for management are made possible by big data and advanced analytics. Technology is already well established, and it is critical to recognize that blockchain has primary branches: public, private, consortium, and hybrid. The network is open to anyone to join. The only participants in a private blockchain are those connected to the value chain.

Emerging economies like India have also used blockchain in seed distribution. Jharkhand, a state in India, through a global blockchain company, SettleMint, has led to transparent seed distribution among farmers. The seed distribution from the producing agencies to different stakeholders like retailers, cooperatives, primary agriculture credit societies, and farmer producer organizations can be traced and finally can reach farmers (News, 2022). Blockchain technology can track the seed distribution under all schemes, helping in real-time monitoring. This will result in timely availability of the seeds. Each farmer must register in the blockchain along with the Aadhar card and mobile numbers. Seed distribution is logged in through a one-time password generated on a registered mobile number. The platform thus helps monitor the quantity of seeds purchased, variety, and number of times the farmers purchase seeds in different districts. This will create a robust farmers' database, enhancing the delivery. This will lead to strategic planning and controlling the seed distribution.

12.5.3 Challenges Encountered and Solutions Implemented

The blockchain owner and permissions require a process to be followed. The parameters for monitoring the food quality require research. There are high risks related to loss of funds and privacy issues. Every transaction is recorded, which leads to the identification of the users. Accessibility of the blockchain is a challenge in agriculture trade. Looking at the complexity of digital technology, blockchain integration in the form of IoT, RFID, sensors, big data, and robots is difficult in developing countries. This is because the drivers for implementing blockchain must be explored in developing countries. Integrating blockchain in agriculture is necessary to build trust among the stakeholders and simplify the process. Substantial research is required on blockchain and agriculture. The information infrastructure required for blockchain is a barrier to its integration, as new users are incompatible with its adoption. Though blockchain can measure food quality parameters, not all quality parameters can be measured. This brings another challenge for the implementation. Data visibility and too much information sharing are also problems, as there are a lot of competitors in the food industry.

The privacy issues must be handled properly, or the competitors can easily benefit from transparent data sharing. Governance in the blockchain process is a core element of the agriculture supply chain. Capacity building for understanding the technical skills needs to be taken care of regarding permissions, blockchain ownership, accessibility, flexible approach, scalability, and audit. Blockchain data, once entered, cannot be tampered with, even if it is false. The data credibility depends on the user entering the information (Tyagi, 2023). Therefore, data verification will be required to understand the credibility of the data. There is an issue of hacking the entire system that may compromise all the data and information stored. The problem of hacking the entire system is endemic in the public blockchain (Ganne, 2018).

12.5.4 Proposed Theoretical Model

Blockchain implementation in agriculture trade varies across countries due to differences in the IT infrastructure, technical skills, and the competency to accept blockchain technology. Therefore, designing a framework for blockchain depends on macroenvironmental conditions. The framework for blockchain-enabled digital strategy can be grounded in resource-based view theory (Barney, 1991) and dynamic capability theory (Wilson & Daniel, 2007; Teece et al., 1997). The resource-based view posits that to bring traceability and trustworthiness to the agricultural supply chain, it is essential to implement blockchain technology while considering the resources. Resources include financial, physical, human, technological, and organizational resources (Barney, 1991). Blockchain integration into agriculture supply chains requires financial capital for building technology infrastructure and technical skills for running the blockchain and bringing farmers and other stakeholders into a platform. Grant (1991) considers resources and capabilities crucial for the firm's remaining profitable and execution of its business strategy. Dynamic capability theory can also help in building the framework. Dynamic capability is the ability to grow and restructure competencies to adapt to changing business scenarios (Prieto-Sandoval et al., 2019). It can also be referred to as an innovative way to attain competitive advantage (Leonard-Barton, 1992). Durability, transparency, transferability, and replicability determine how long advantages can be sustained. In the oil industry, a recent invention of an alternate technique to drill oil led to the collapse of oil prices across the globe. Wal-Mart gained considerable market share with its low cost and global sourcing strategy, a feature not easy to replicate. The evolution of internet-based supply chains from Amazon has challenged their business model. Agri Startups leadership in developing innovative technology products is challenged by competitors who catch up with them by replicating technology and processes. Figure 12.1 and Table 12.1 derive the building blocks for blockchain-enabled digital strategy in agriculture trade.

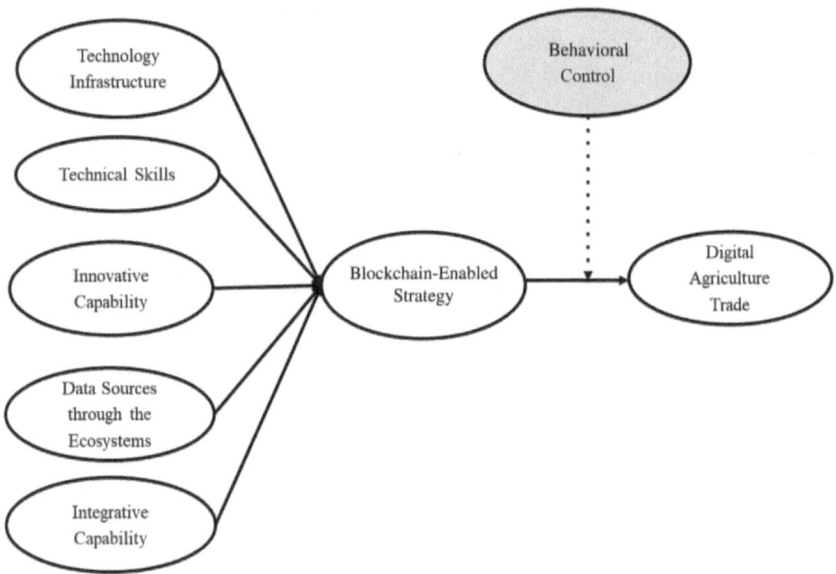

FIGURE 12.1
Proposed model for blockchain-enabled digital strategy

The proposed model can be empirically validated. The study proposes the following questions for future research on blockchain-enabled digital strategies for agriculture trade.

1. How is the proliferation of blockchain technology associated with the development of the Internet and digital devices, specifically in the agriculture supply-chain context?
2. What are the fundamental motivations for applying blockchain technology in agriculture trade, as evidenced by various case studies with success and failure stories?
3. What challenges do stakeholders face in implementing and adopting blockchain solutions in the agriculture trade sector, and how can these challenges be addressed to maximize the potential of blockchain technology?
4. How can a framework be developed to enable blockchain digital strategy to facilitate agricultural trade?
5. How does the application of blockchain technology in the agriculture supply chain contribute to developing and enhancing dynamic capabilities within organizations?
6. What are the key factors influencing the successful implementation of blockchain digital strategies in agriculture trade, and how do they relate to the concept of dynamic capabilities?
7. How do different stakeholders in the agriculture supply chain perceive the potential value of blockchain technology, and how does this perception influence their willingness to invest in and adopt blockchain solutions?
8. To what extent does the integration of blockchain technology in agriculture trade enhance transparency, traceability, and trust among stakeholders, as suggested by the dynamic capability theory?

12.6 Regulatory and Ethical Issues Around Blockchain Adoption in Agriculture Trade

Blockchain adoption has regulatory issues like data protection and privacy. The implementation of blockchain helps in information security to keep the confidentiality of the data. Blockchain has different regulations that help maintain quality management standards in the agriculture trade. The blockchain also helps dispute resolution mechanisms and legal frameworks for agriculture trade. The blockchain also ensures good data management practices. Small and marginal farmers are not digitally literate; therefore, there is a need to build a technology infrastructure for participation in the blockchain system. The farmers need to be provided education and affordable technology for better participation. The consumption of high energy by blockchain technology concerns environmental sustainability. Blockchain can adhere to the ethical standards for monitoring a fair-trade practice. The primary concerns surrounding blockchain technology are security and cyber threats. There is a need for assurance for blockchain technology for protection against cyber threats. There is a need to implement a strategy to collaborate with the regulators, create industry standards, and maintain transparency, stakeholder involvement, and frameworks for the ethical adoption of blockchain.

The blockchain has altered the structure of international trade. There is a deficiency in sustainability, integrity, and trust. The adoption of a blockchain is a positive step. Approximately one-third of the items are thrown away. Climate change presents another difficulty. Simply put, a blockchain refers to the procurement of computer-assisted public personnel. Data with a hash value is contained in every trade block that distinguishes blockchain from conventional data. There are particular guidelines for entering data. One person cannot unilaterally alter. Once entered, data cannot be changed. Extra care must be taken with traceability.

12.6.1 Recommendation for Navigating the Challenges

The challenges associated with blockchain in agriculture trade must be understood to manage strategies to overcome them. Table 12.3 depicts the upcoming challenges and the strategies to overcome them. Small marginal farmers only receive 30% to 40% of the value and are exploited in the agriculture trade. Aurohill is engaged in project identification. Pomegranates are available everywhere because people have built trust in the system. There is a need for widespread knowledge and a large labor force who knows this technology. It is necessary to have a database of farmers.

TABLE 12.3

Navigating the Challenges for Strategies

No.	Challenges	Strategies
1	It is difficult to maintain privacy for sensitive information.	Security audits can help blockchain function better.
2	Blockchain technology does not work the same way with agriculture.	Blockchain solutions should be developed to integrate with the functions of the agriculture supply chain.

(Continued)

TABLE 12.3 (Continued)
Navigating the Challenges for Strategies

No.	Challenges	Strategies
3	There are technical challenges like handling the big data and maintaining security.	The blockchain platforms must be evaluated, and necessary investments should be made to increase efficiency.
4	There are frauds in blockchain.	Consistent monitoring is required to address unethical practices.
5	Blockchain technology requires a lot of energy consumption.	There is a need to understand the environmental impact for minimizing energy consumption and carbon footprints.
6	Blockchain solutions are not accessible to farmers.	Farmers require proper training and capacity building to handle blockchain solutions.
7	Blockchain solutions for agriculture trade are stolen.	Protocols should be built to protect intellectual property rights for blockchain solutions.
8	The agriculture sector has a lot of regulatory frameworks in the supply chain.	The development of a comprehensive framework is required for the solutions.
9	There are reports highlighting legal issues with the data.	The involvement of legal experts can help address the requirements.
10	There are cases of compliance with the data privacy legal system.	The blockchain solutions should comply with the data privacy regulations.
11	Industry requirements are not met at times.	There is a need for regular improvements and updates on blockchain solutions. Consistent monitoring will help advance the industry's emerging trends.

12.6.2 Compliance Strategies and Ethical Considerations

Implementing blockchain in agriculture trade requires the development of compliance strategies and ethical regulations to maintain regulatory alignments in the trading system. Data privacy must also be maintained in the agriculture trading system. Industrial standards must be followed for proper reliability and validity of the data source. Firms must also follow regular audits to address any data flaws and errors.

Blockchain, IoT, AI, and ML technologies coupled with broad access to smartphones and the internet under "Digital" have made it possible to advance the significant socioeconomic interests of farmers. The digital-enabled strategy aims to design, develop, and implement a blockchain-based, IoT-enabled, and AI- and ML-powered e-commerce technology demonstrator platform for agriculture commodities. The farmer is at the core of blockchain. It is designed to solve farmers' key problems (Figure 12.2).

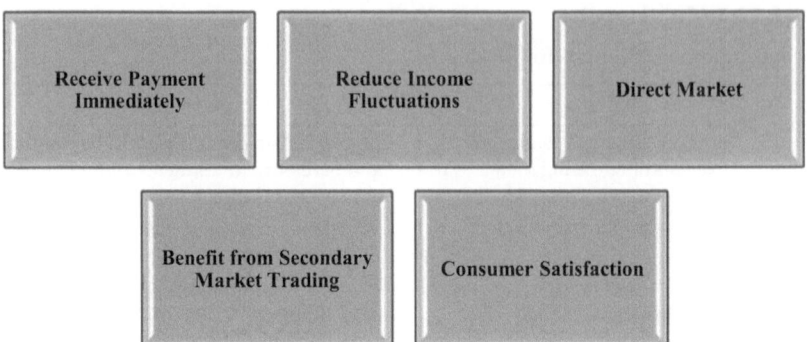

FIGURE 12.2
What do farmers want?

1. Receive Payment Immediately: In the traditional supply chain, the farmer gets paid many months later for the harvest and sale of the produce. The informal settlement channels and weak tracing of quantity sold to the originating farmer create issues for the farmers. An active e-commerce platform will resolve these issues and shorten payment time to a few days.
2. Reduce Income Fluctuations: Cycles of excessive spending and scarcity are a prime cause of debt traps. This happens because farmers are not connected to the year-round consumer market but only to a few post-harvest buyers. Blockchain helps to sell a part of the future harvest when desired, further stabilizing the income stream. The system brings farmers in direct contact with buyers and enables forward selling.
3. Direct Market: Traceability and grade can be provided quickly. The e-commerce platform mitigates monopoly and democratizes trust by assuming responsibility and extending it to all members, thus raising farmer income.
4. Benefit from Secondary Market Trading: Secondary trading is trading commodities without involving physical delivery, i.e., the trades are cash-settled. Secondary markets are an essential component of liquid markets. For example, Farmer "F" sells forward to Trader "T" at a given price. Instead of taking a delivery, Trader A sells it to a retailer, "R" at a price that makes a capital gain. The farmer cannot benefit from the sale from T to R. However, with a proof of ownership chain established by blockchain and fraud detection and control enabled by AI and ML, will give farmers a new way to earn money and discourage too much speculation.
5. Consumer Satisfaction: The applications hence lead to consumer satisfaction.

12.7 Future Perspectives and Conclusion

12.7.1 Concluding Remarks and Recommendations for Stakeholders

The study of organization, planning, coordination, and monitoring of agriculture commodities from farm to fork can be managed through technology. The supply chain is a web of functions, from production to distribution. Technology applications in agriculture supply chains ensure food security and sustainable agricultural development (Kumari et al., 2023). In addition to focusing on cost reduction, technology applications for sustainable supply chains have significant positive effects on the social and environmental spheres. Global suppliers and sustainability are influenced by Institutional dimensions (Pereira et al., 2023). These institutional dimensions help sustain the supply chains by minimizing waste and its detrimental impacts. However, these supply chains are often challenged by various factors such as climate change, market volatility, and supply chain disruptions. Agriculture production activities are driven by risks that have a social and environmental impact (Yazdani et al., 2021). Technology can help reduce the risks. The information revolution has changed business firms deriving different insights from the data. D is also important in predicting food fraud levels in the agriculture supply chain. The most commonly used data mining methods are neural networks, decision trees, case-based reasoning, statistical methods, and fuzzy methods. Data mining leads to data verification and the development of blocks.

12.7.2 Potential Impact of Blockchain on Agriculture Trade

Wide and cheap access to smartphones and the internet has made it possible to advance farmers' major socioeconomic interests by integrating blockchain, IoT, AI, and ML technologies. The goal is to design, develop, and implement a blockchain-based, IoT-enabled, and AI- and ML-powered e-commerce technology demonstrator platform for agricultural commodities.

1. Increase Farmers' Income: E-commerce platform resolves the issues of traditional supply chain wherein the farmers get a delayed payment. The delay in the payment is due to informal channels and weak traceability. The blockchain intervention helps in reducing the payment duration. Transparency in the payment system results in increase in the farmers' income.
2. Transparent Payment Systems: Blockchain interventions result in faster and transparent payment systems. Unlike most professions, a farmer is paid only once a year for an agricultural commodity. This creates excessive spending and scarcity cycles – a prime cause of *debt traps*. This happens as he is not connected to the *year-round consumer*

market but only to a few post-harvest buyers. If he could *sell a part of the future harvest when desired*, the income stream would further stabilize. The blockchain can address both problems by bringing farmers in direct contact with buyers and enabling forward selling.

3. Reduction in the Intermediaries: A farmer gets a low payment because authenticity, traceability, and grade are monopolies of trusted retailers, which a farmer cannot provide. The e-commerce platform *democratizes trust* by assuming responsibility for establishing it and extending it equally to all members, thus raising farmer income without triggering a rise in consumer price inflation.
4. Efficient Trade: Blockchain is an essential component for an efficient trade. Blockchain will result in a reduction in the intermediaries involved in the trading system. The proof of ownership chain established by blockchain, rules such as "farmer gets the capital gains of trading" are easy to establish. This helps to create an efficient trading system for the farmer.
5. Combatting Adulterated Products: Blockchain helps to verify the product and protect the farmers as well as consumers from fake products and the contents.
6. Efficient Supply Chain Management: Blockchain interventions lead to a reduction in paper work. This will minimize duplication and low risks.

12.7.3 Emerging Trends in Blockchain Technology

Blockchain has been integrated with IoT devices and sensors. These devices and sensors help record climate parameters like temperature and humidity and sensitize the requirements for agricultural commodities in the storage system. The sensors also help in tracking records for crop production. Some sensors race human or animal footprints in the agricultural field.

Blockchain, when integrated with AI, helps promote precision agriculture. Sensors help analyze soil moisture conditions, agri input requirements, and other factors to improve crop yield. Research trends can be observed by collecting research databases on agriculture trade and blockchain and analyzing them using the R programming language to depict the themes and keywords treemap.

The emerging trend in blockchain in agriculture trade, as shown in Figure 12.3, is prone to application of blockchain in agriculture, supply chain, food supply chain, agriculture resilience, food traceability, and the IoT. The blockchain-enabled technology is moving toward the agriculture supply chain as traceability and quality standards are major concerns in agriculture.

A Blockchain-Enabled Digital Strategy for Agriculture Trade 277

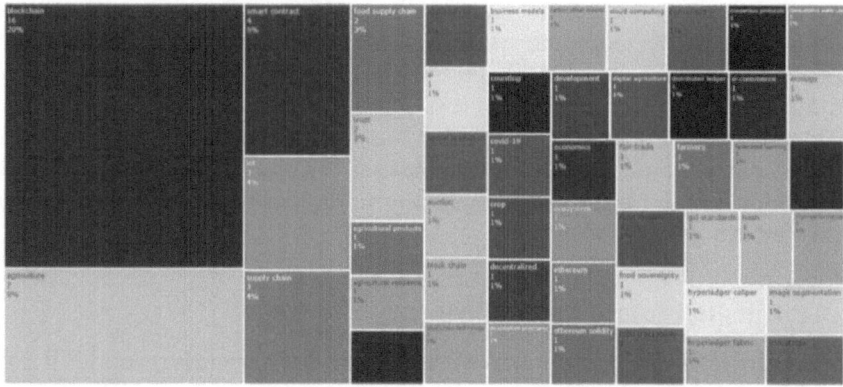

FIGURE 12.3
Emerging trends in blockchain in agriculture trade

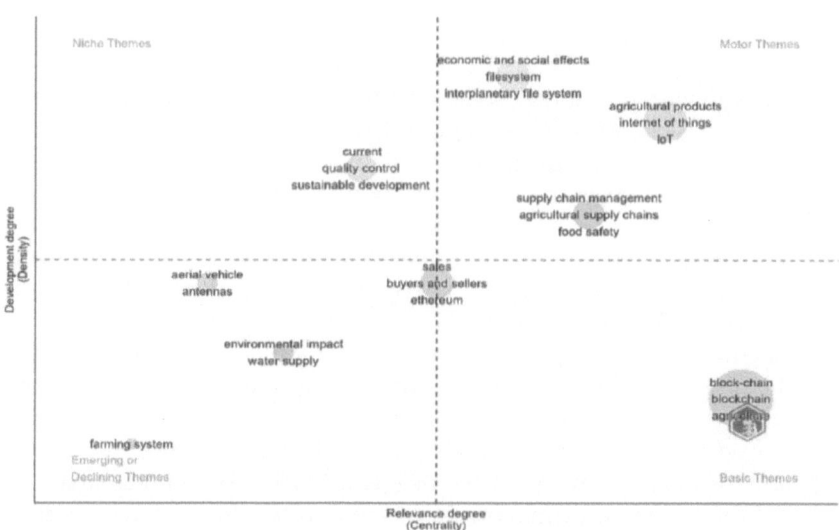

FIGURE 12.4
Themes for blockchain research in agriculture trade

Figure 12.4 shows the distribution of key research in the different themes based on the relevance and development degree. Blockchain and agriculture have been taking the space for research in recent years. It can be observed that aerial vehicles have emerged as emerging themes while sales, buyers, and sellers have declined over the years. Research has been more prone toward hi-technology than focusing on basic sales analysis. Quality control and sustainable development in the agriculture trade have been the major concerns; therefore, they have been identified as niche themes. Agriculture commodities are often rejected across borders if they are not able to meet quality standards. The quality standards can now be easily traced with the help of a blockchain. The relevant themes for the blockchain digital strategy can be found in agriculture supply chain management, the IoT, food safety, and economic and social effects.

12.7.4 Potential Future Applications

Blockchain technology promises solutions in the agriculture trade. It can help map the agricultural commodities with the requirements. Blockchain solutions can help trace the agricultural commodity, its production details, and geographical coverage. From agriculture production to processing, the flow of the commodity can be easily traced with the number of stakeholders involved and the quality parameters. This will help get the right product quality at the right time.

There is also potential to map the blockchain technology to monitor the climatic conditions in the storage structures or during transportation. IoT sensors have been used for onion storage, where the emission of gases from the onions indicates that they are getting spoiled. Blockchain can help reduce the number of intermediaries in the supply chain by linking farmers and buyers through direct marketing. Based on the records, the farmers can receive automated payments. Predictive analytics used in agriculture can help forecast crop yield and estimate demand and supply for agricultural commodities. The predictions can also help build better marketing strategies.

Blockchain can also help manage transactions in the agriculture supply chain, helping keep records for an efficient agriculture trade. High-tech innovations like blockchain and AI offer revolutionary solutions to agriculture. However, the assimilation of advanced technologies takes time. Emerging Economies need to work on the usage of blockchain among small and medium farmers. The essential purpose is to reduce costs and maximize the benefits derived from these technologies. Hence, the farmer clusters in the form of cooperatives can play an important role in applying blockchain technology. Blockchain can digitalize the supply chain, reducing the paperwork.

12.7.5 Future Research Directions

Blockchain is one of the fastest-growing technologies implemented to transform the agriculture industry. The usage of blockchain is low in emerging economies due to a number of reasons like lack of awareness, selection of vendors, and development of environment and security issues. Blockchain technology will clearly be a gamer changer as it can provide tamper-proof, accurate data about the farms, inventory, credit scores, and food tracking.

Blockchain can be one of the pillars of the 2030 Agenda for Sustainable Development Goals (SDGs). SDG 2 ensures food security, and SDG 3 ensures health and well-being can be well managed through the interaction of blockchain in the agriculture trade (Tyagi, 2023). The blockchain stakeholders and players need to work on the proposed integrated framework for blockchain-enabled digital strategy in agriculture trade. Blockchain integration is dependent upon the behavioral control patterns of the stakeholders. Therefore, there is still a need for research to determine the factors for understanding the perception and intention to use blockchain technology among the stakeholders. The integrated framework proposed in this chapter can also be validated to understand the country's acceptability.

References

Asante Boakye, E., Zhao, H., & Ahia, B. N. K. (2023). Blockchain technology prospects in transforming Ghana's economy: A phenomenon-based approach. *Information Technology for Development, 29*(2–3), 348–377.

Balci, G., & Surucu-Balci, E. (2021). Blockchain adoption in the maritime supply chain: Examining barriers and salient stakeholders in containerized international trade. *Transportation Research Part E: Logistics and Transportation Review, 156*, 102539.

Barney, J. (1991). Firm resources and sustained competitive advantage. *Journal of Management, 17*(1), 99–120.

Bhusal, C. S. (2021). Blockchain technology in agriculture: A case study of blockchain start-up companies. *International Journal of Computer Science & Information Technology (IJCSIT), 13*.

Bonetti, E., Bartoli, C., & Mattiacci, A. (2024). Applying blockchain to quality food products: A marketing perspective. *British Food Journal, 126*(5), 2004–2026.

Byrd, T. A., & Turner, D. E. (2000). Measuring the flexibility of information technology infrastructure: Exploratory analysis of a construct. *Journal of Management Information Systems, 17*(1), 167–208.

Creydt, M., & Fischer, M. (2019). Blockchain and more-algorithm driven food traceability. *Food Control, 105*, 45–51.

Davenport, T. H., & Dyché, J. (2013). Big data in big companies. *International Institute for Analytics, 3*, 1–31.

Dickinson, D. M., Ellison, M. D., & Webb, R. L. (2003). Data sources and structure. *American Journal of Transplantation, 3*, 13–28.

Duncan, N. B. (1995). Capturing flexibility of information technology infrastructure: A study of resource characteristics and their measure. *Journal of Management Information Systems, 12*(2), 37–57.

Ellahi, R. M., Wood, L. C., & Bekhit, A. E. D. A. (2023). Blockchain-based frameworks for food traceability: A systematic review. *Foods, 12*(16), 3026.

Fan, T., Feng, Q., Li, Y., Shanthikumar, J. G., & Wu, Y. (2024). Output-oriented agricultural subsidy design. *Management Science, 70*(3), 1448–1464.

Ganguly, K. K. (2024). Understanding the challenges of the adoption of blockchain technology in the logistics sector: The TOE framework. *Technology Analysis & Strategic Management, 36*(3), 457–471.

Ganne, E. (2018). *Can Blockchain Revolutionize International Trade?* Geneva: World Trade Organization.

Grant, R. M. (1991). The resource-based theory of competitive advantage: Implications for strategy formulation. *California Management Review, 33*(3), 114–135.

Gupta, R., & Shankar, R. (2024). Managing food security using blockchain-enabled traceability system. *Benchmarking: An International Journal, 31*(1), 53–74.

Hatala, R., Cook, D. A., Brydges, R., & Hawkins, R. (2015). Constructing a validity argument for the Objective Structured Assessment of Technical Skills (OSATS): A systematic review of validity evidence. *Advances in Health Sciences Education, 20*, 1149–1175.

Howson, P. (2020). Building trust and equity in marine conservation and fisheries supply chain management with blockchain. *Marine Policy, 115*, 1–6.

Jeble, S., Kumari, S., & Patil, Y. (2016). Role of big data and predictive analytics. *International Journal of Automation and Logistics, 2*(4), 307–331.

Jiang, W., Mavondo, F. T., & Matanda, M. J. (2015). Integrative capability for successful partnering: A critical dynamic capability. *Management Decision, 53*(6), 1184–1202.

Kamath, R. (2018). Food traceability on blockchain: Walmart's Pork and Mango Pilots with IBM. *JBAA Case Study, 1*(1), 47–54.

Kamilaris, A., Fonts, A., & Prenafeta-Boldú, F. X. (2019). The rise of blockchain technology in agriculture and food supply chains. *Trends in Food Science & Technology, 91*, 640–652.

Khan, H. H., Malik, M. N., Konečná, Z., Chofreh, A. G., Goni, F. A., & Klemeš, J. J. (2022). Blockchain technology for agricultural supply chains during the COVID-19 pandemic: Benefits and cleaner solutions. *Journal of Cleaner Production, 347*, 131268.

Kumari, S., Venkatesh, V. G., & Shi, Y. (2023). Virtual technologies adoption to sustain quality in agricultural sector: An emerging economy perspective. *Journal of Cleaner Production, 388*, 135988.

Lawson, B., & Samson, D. (2001). Developing innovation capability in organisations: A dynamic capabilities approach. *International Journal of Innovation Management, 5*(03), 377–400.

Leahy, S., Clark, H., & Reisinger, A. (2020). Challenges and prospects for agricultural greenhouse gas mitigation pathways consistent with the Paris Agreement. *Frontiers in Sustainable Food Systems, 4*, 69.

Leduc, G., Kubler, S., & Georges, J. P. (2021). Innovative blockchain-based farming marketplace and smart contract performance evaluation. *Journal of Cleaner Production, 306*, 127055.

Leonard-Barton, D. (1992). Core capabilities and core rigidities: A paradox in managing new product development. *Strategic Management Journal, 13*(S1), 111–125.

Lewis, B. R., & Byrd, T. A. (2003). Development of a measure for the information technology infrastructure construct. *European Journal of Information Systems, 12*(2), 93–109.

Li, L., Chen, Y., Gao, H., & Li, C. (2023). How to regulate the infringements of geographical indications of agricultural products – an empirical study on judicial documents in China. *International Journal of Environmental Research and Public Health, 20*(6), 4946.

Madhavan, J., & Halevy, A. Y. (2003, January). Composing mappings among data sources. In *Proceedings 2003 VLDB Conference* (pp. 572–583). Morgan Kaufmann.

Maersk. (2021). Case Study: How blockchain technology is beefing up supply chain visibility. *Maersk.* https://www.maersk.com/news/articles/2021/07/27/how-blockchain-technology-is-beefing-upas retrieved on 23rd April 2024.

Maru, A., Berne, D., De Beer, J., Ballantyne, P., Pesce, V., Kalyesubula, S., . . . & Chaves, J. (2018). Digital and data-driven agriculture: Harnessing the power of data for smallholders. *F1000Research, 7*(525), 525.

McDaniel, C., & Norberg, H. C. (2019). *Can Blockchain Technology Facilitate International Trade?* Mercatus Research: Mercatus Center at George Mason University, p. 16, https://www.mercatus.org/publications/trade-and-immigration/can-blockchaintechnology-facilitate-international-trade as retrieved on 23rd April 2024.

Mendoza-Silva, A. (2021). Innovation capability: A systematic literature review. *European Journal of Innovation Management, 24*(3), 707–734.

News. (2022). *This State Is India's 1st to Use Blockchain to Distribute Seed to Farmers.* https://www.ndtv.com/india-news/jharkhand-is-indias-1st-to-use-blockchain-technology-to-distribute-seed-to-farmers-3266915 as retrieved on 23rd April 2024.

Ortiz, A. M. D., Outhwaite, C. L., Dalin, C., & Newbold, T. (2021). A review of the interactions between biodiversity, agriculture, climate change, and international trade: Research and policy priorities. *One Earth, 4*(1), 88–101.

Pereira, M. M., Silva, M. E., &a Hendry, L. C. (2023). Developing global supplier competences for supply chain sustainability: The effects of institutional pressures on certification adoption. *Business Strategy and the Environment.* https://onlinelibrary.wiley.com/doi/abs/10.1002/bse.3363.

Persaud, A. (2005). Enhancing synergistic innovative capability in multinational corporations: An empirical investigation. *Journal of Product Innovation Management, 22*(5), 412–429.

Pranto, T. H., Noman, A. A., Mahmud, A., & Haque, A. B. (2021). Blockchain and smart contract for IoT enabled smart agriculture. *PeerJ Computer Science, 7*, e407.

Prieto-Sandoval, V., Jaca, C., Santos, J., Baumgartner, R. J., & Ormazabal, M. (2019). Key strategies, resources, and capabilities for implementing circular economy in industrial small and medium enterprises. *Corporate Social Responsibility and Environmental Management, 26*(6), 1473–1484.

Szabo, N. (1997). Formalizing and securing relationships on public networks. *First Monday, 2*(9).

Teece, D. J., Pisano, G., & Shuen, A. (1997). Dynamic capabilities and strategic management. *Strategic Management Journal,* 509–533.

Thinakaran, J., Paul, S., Beulah Christalin Latha, C., & Jacob, G. (2023). Blockchain in big data for agriculture supply chain. In *Blockchain and Its Applications in Industry 4.0* (pp. 257–291). Singapore: Springer Nature Singapore.

Torky, M., & Hassanein, A. E. (2020). Integrating blockchain and the internet of things in precision agriculture: Analysis, opportunities, and challenges. *Computers and Electronics in Agriculture, 178*, 1–23.

Tsolakis, N., Schumacher, R., Dora, M., & Kumar, M. (2023). Artificial intelligence and blockchain implementation in supply chains: A pathway to sustainability and data monetisation? *Annals of Operations Research, 327*(1), 157–210.

Tyagi, K. (2023). A global blockchain-based agro-food value chain to facilitate trade and sustainable blocks of healthy lives and food for all. *Humanities and Social Sciences Communications, 10*(1), 1–12.

Wamba, S. F., Gunasekaran, A., Akter, S., Ren, S. J. F., Dubey, R., & Childe, S. J. (2016). Big data analytics and firm performance: Effects of dynamic capabilities. *Journal of Business Research, 70*, 356–365.

Werbach, K. (2018). Trust, but verify: Why the blockchain needs the law. *Berkeley Technology Law Journal, 33*(2), 487–550.

Wilson, H., & Daniel, E. (2007). The multi-channel challenge: A dynamic capability approach. *Industrial Marketing Management, 36*(1), 10–20.

Winckel, C. P., Reznick, R. K., Cohen, R., & Taylor, B. (1994). Reliability and construct validity of a structured technical skills assessment form. *The American Journal of Surgery, 167*(4), 423–427.

Yazdani, M., Gonzalez, E. D., & Chatterjee, P. (2021). A multi-criteria decision-making framework for agriculture supply chain risk management under a circular economy context. *Management Decision, 59*(8), 1801–1826.

Zhao, H., Chang, J., Havlík, P., Van Dijk, M., Valin, H., Janssens, C., . . . & Obersteiner, M. (2021). China's future food demand and its implications for trade and environment. *Nature Sustainability, 4*(12), 1042–1051.

13
Blockchain Accountability Strategy of ESG-Focused Cryptocurrency Projects

K. Pallavi and Sonali Srivastava

13.1 Introduction

Investors worldwide are focusing more on adding digital currencies to their portfolios. Such digital currencies, also known as cryptocurrency, are not regulated by government-imposed legal laws or private sources (Xie, 2019). Cryptocurrencies are easier to handle as they do not need to be maintained and take control of their monetary transactions, unlike other stocks (Lipton & Treccani, 2021). Blockchain techniques in securitizing help prevent forgery or alteration (Khan et al., 2019; Conesa, 2019). Cryptocurrency cannot be regulated with its monetary transaction; thus, the government does not issue it, making it impossible for the government to interfere and manipulate. Still, the danger with cryptocurrencies is that they are very volatile and are not dependent on any underlying asset like derivatives stocks or traditional currency (Teichmann & Falker, 2020).

Environmental, social, and corporate governance (ESG) is a concept that analyzes how the organization sets goals for the benefit of society apart from just keeping the profit motive. ESG not only considers social benefits but also environmental benefits (Levillain & Segrestin, 2019).

Concerning ESG concerns in cryptocurrency, investors and governments of various companies are showing interest in investing in cryptocurrencies. The principles for responsible investment of the United Nations have pledged to undertake ESG considerations in investment and their management policies and procedures. In the year 2016, many rating agencies like Definitive and Morgan Stanley Capital International published ESG data publish data for their investors (Hoepner et al., 2021).

ESG goals concerning environmental considerations include stabilizing the effects of climatic change and attaining sustainability of the achieved objectives (Nawaz et al., 2021). Some common examples of ESG are diversity, equality, rights of consumers, and investment (Corbet et al., 2019). Cryptocurrencies like Bitcoin, Ripple, Stellar, Cardano, and others do not have a strong transaction verification mechanism. The only biggest first-mover advantage that a cryptocurrency like bitcoin has is that anyone at the ease of his place can access and manage his digital currency just by having an adequate internet connection to connect with, which also tends to promote financial inclusion. Whereas considering the viewpoint of corporate governance, cryptocurrencies tend to be controversial assets. It is contended that cryptocurrencies like Bitcoin follow decentralized systems as no central authority regulates them, but a few crypto assets are centralized, with a single organization managing them (Teichmann & Falker, 2021).

This chapter analyzes the need and importance of loopholes in managing socially responsible investments. The literature also shows blockchain technology's breakthrough role in this field. This chapter develops a model for understanding how blockchain technology has impacted ESG investments and analyzes the importance of blockchain technology in ESG reporting measures.

13.2 Understanding ESG in Cryptocurrency Projects

Unlike nonfinancial criteria, investing in ESG is typically an investment criterion considering the investment's ESG dimensions (Koenigsmarck & Geissdoerfer, 2021). These investments are based on ESG investment scores, which investors tend to be cautious and sensitive about (Ceccarelli et al., 2021). ESG acts as an umbrella term for the investors' concerns from all three viewpoints, including the social, environmental, and governance dimensions, which are unrelated. ESG investing leans more toward corporate social responsibility (CSR), which ultimately leads to sustained growth and development of society as a whole (Chamorro-Mera & Palacios-González, 2019). Though this investing in ESG is dominantly carried by institutional investors (Meunier & Ohadi, 2022), the contribution of individual investors can lead to its thorough implementation. There are a few determinants of ESG investments which are discussed as follows.

13.2.1 Financial Concerns of Investors

The first and foremost concern of investors related to ESG investments is the profitability of the investment, which can cause a negative attitude toward investing in it. It is identified that approximately 40% of the investors in the UK and the US consider ESG investments to be low-performing when compared to traditional investment instruments (Meunier & Ohadi, 2022; Palacios-González & Chamorro-Mera, 2020). Some researchers have highlighted that ESG investments deliver similar profitability to conventional investments. A few studies have shown that besides the market downfall due to the outbreak of COVID-19, ESG investments were relatively stable in their stock prices (Albuquerque et al., 2019; Pástor & Vorsatz, 2020). On the other hand, a few studies have shown that the risk exposure of firms to ESG-related issues has significantly impacted the investment patterns of institutional investors (Hoepner et al., 2021). However, it is agreed that out of the three pillars of ESG investment, investing in social and environmental criteria is more important to ensure long-term impacts (Huang et al., 2023).

13.2.2 Investors' Nonmonetary Utility

Studies have identified the nonpecuniary utility, also known as "moral satisfaction," of ESG investors as an important aspect where investors tend to ordinate their investment patterns with social preferences and balance nonpecuniary utility and their returns. As per the model suggested by Fama and French (2007), the investors who pick socially responsible investments included in assets of their choice tend to make a lower degree of alpha (profits). Conversely, the Capital Asset Pricing Model developed by Baker et al. (2022) suggests that investors with green bond holdings have moral satisfaction because these green bonds are kept at a premium price. It is also observed that within the context of ESG bonds, there lies a weak relation between fund flows and past performance of the fund, unlike conventional bonds that exhibit strong correlations; this implies that ESG bonds' fund performance cannot be predicted through historical trends which give its investors benefit of the doubt to pick these investments over conventional bonds.

Studies also investigate the link between the likelihood of holding socially responsible funds and the trust associated with holding them. While investing in such bonds, investors prefer to opt for ethical banking practices; they either emphasize the risk they take against higher financial returns or focus more on the facility to withdraw money earlier (Chamorro-Mera & Palacios-González, 2019). Evidence from studies shows that investors who invest in socially responsible funds willingly toward a social cause can adjust to the negative externalities that come with such funds (Humphrey et al., 2021). In places like the Dutch, participants of pension plan funds prefer their investments to be focused on socially responsible investments attaining sustainable development (Bauer et al., 2021; Brodback et al., 2019).

13.2.3 The Salience of ESG Scores

Investors are pretty sensitive to fluctuations in ESG scores. It was found that in 2016, a financial services firm, Morningstar, categorized firms as low and high sustainability. The firms categorized as low sustainable earned less returns than those categorized as high sustainable. Similar patterns have been observed when the same Morningstar established climate-focused mutual funds (Ceccarelli et al., 2021). Sometimes, these investors interested in socially responsible investments may or may not figure out which investment is sustainable or which is not. They need assistance in this case to identify whether these investments are sustainable or not, plus whether these investments precisely match their social preferences.

13.2.4 ESG and Industry

The industry is brimming with the latest technological advancements that amalgamate cyber and physical systems (CPS), which frame a virtual model enabling real-time monitoring and decision-making. This amalgamation of cyber and physical systems produces digital twins (Aheleroff et al., 2021), which is a virtual representation of physical systems empowered by machine learning techniques and simulation for decision-making updated from real-time data (Verdouw et al., 2021). This kind of smart system is capable of immense storage, data collection, analysis, and communication techniques, which can be helpful in ESG disclosure.

Firms, while in their disclosure policies, release a considerable database of ESG reporting, which third-party companies use to generate ESG scores or ratings. The companies that release such ESG are bound to follow some standardized stringent policy "frameworks" to check what information to disclose and how to disclose it so that the investors accessing it can verify the information. A few such disclosure frameworks are the Global Reporting Initiative, the Sustainability Accounting Standards Board, and the Task Force on Climate-related Financial Disclosures. Besides this, there are a few ESG reporting issues. Below are the ESG reporting issues taken into consideration by the firms:

13.2.4.1 Authenticity

ESG data is extracted from both internal and external sources. Third-party companies, when conducting verification of such data, can only do so based on the supplied data. This questions the authenticity of the ESG disclosure data. The motives of ESG are rooted in stakeholder theory and legitimacy theory, which promotes stakeholders' role in enhancing a firm's social utility, alignment, and congruence (Reber et al., 2022). However, firms aligning with the ESG disclosure structures, practices, and compliances may have to bear associated costs. If they are ready to bear it, it can be a competitive advantage for such firms over other rivals. As institutional theory suggests, firms, due to the normative, mimetic, and coercive forces, adopt ESG initiatives (DiMaggio & Powell, 1983). Under such pressures from legitimate authorities and stakeholders, firms implement ESG only symbolically (window-dressing). This decoupling process signifies the gap between a firm's shallow ESG reporting and actual processes. This process of decoupling is also known as "CSR-washing," "pinkwashing," "green-washing," and "corporate hypocrisy." This creates a gap in the authenticity issues in ESG disclosure, which can impact the credibility of ESG processes.

13.2.4.2 Retrospective Reporting

ESG builds real-time and prospective data. The reports that ESG generates are only valid for the duration of data collection. Concerning the ever-changing and dynamic environment of firms, it is practically impossible to consider retrospective data (Castka et al., 2020), considering the time-to-time demands of consumers and regulators (Reid & Castka, 2023). Also, with the onset of digital and advanced technologies and the data evaluation within the perspective velocity, volume, variety, and veracity of data, it is important to keep in check the updated data requirements (Asif et al., 2022). Retrospective reporting stands obsolete as real-time data keeps users informed and updated, and prospective reports can be used to predict future trends in processes and alert them in case of any upcoming danger.

Organizational information processing theory (OIPT), which aligns with such a system of prospective reporting, implies that a firm should invest in and build robust structures for information processing capability to adopt real-time and prospective data reporting needs. Structural contingency theory advocates the same concept (Lawrence & Lorsch, 1967). This is possible with Industry 5.0, the latest digital advancements like AI, cloud computing, and machine learning, and digital twins (Asif et al., 2022; Castka & Searcy, 2023).

13.2.4.3 Customizability of Reports

ESG is helpful for decision-making tactics and risk analysis for investment managers (Reber et al., 2022). When such investment managers and stakeholders are given the liberty to choose the customizability of these reports, it becomes easier for them to choose their preferences based on parameters of interest, information depth, etc. This process of servicing users with customized services is mass personalization. Mass Personalization as a Service, abbreviated as MPaaS is a process of delivering tailor-made services to the users with their preferences, which can be made possible with the help of I5.0 (Aheleroff et al., 2021). However, in contrast to this, the capability of human information processing is limited and is bound to affect rational choices in decision-making. This emerged from a concept known as Bounded Rationality, which forms from three factors, viz. cognitive limitations, time constraints, and imperfect information, which collectively may lead to imperfect decision-making. Customizing ESG can require a huge amount of data and cost.

13.2.4.4 ESG Reporting Scope

Disclosure in ESG has limitations only up to reporting companies. This ESG disclosure from company to company depends on the supply chain pattern of interdependent companies that work in unison by mutually exchanging information. One of the biggest threats to ESG compliance is the risk of off-tracking information supply chains (Thomson Reuters, 2021). An ideal ESG disclosure must contain the multi-suppliers' social and environmental concerns, including the supply chain and the concerned stakeholders. Otherwise, there is a chance that these risks can be carried forward to other interconnected firms. This error of carrying forward risk on proper ESG reporting can lead to Type II error (false negative). Thus, the need for firms to take responsibility for their actions and related entities is evident in discussions on parent companies' duty of care to protect people and the environment from the harm incurred by a firm's operations and activities. European Commission (2022) also endorses a framework for making companies accountable and responsible for human rights violations committed by their contractors or subsidiaries. These issues can be addressed with the use of I5.0. Contingency theory and OIPT advocate the need to build up robust supply chains and data-sharing networks to keep the ESG disclosure reporting objectives of the firms in check.

13.2.4.5 Cost Incurred with ESG

ESG reporting requires numerous informational, human, financial, and technological resources and is thus costly (Drempetic et al., 2020). Technologies that generate and analyze vast amounts of ESG data and build a structure for reporting such data costs are incurred, and this cost increases as the size of the firm expands. This is addressed by the transaction cost economics theory, which states that when firms are involved in business-related transactions and information sharing with other firms, it leads to incurring huge costs (Williamson, 2007). Data collection, verification of information, managing knowledge repositories, benchmarking, establishing information and communication channels, and providing infrastructural support incur costs that can account for one of the most significant budgets in corporate departments. This cost incurring of ESG within the context of data handling can be done using I5.0 as I5.0 can efficiently manage the data generation, data processing, generating real-time reports, predicting prospective insights, and conducting retrospective audits. In parlance, network economics theory says that if firms opt to develop their ESG disclosure processes on shared platforms with that of the interconnected firms along with offering services to individuals and corporate users, it can cause them to cut operational costs, improve transparency, and benefit from greater economies of scale in shared infrastructure, standardized data formats, and collaborative compliance mechanisms. This implies that the more users are shared and the bigger the network, the more distributed costs are.

13.2.4.6 Efficacy of ESG Disclosures

Efficacy is fetching insightful, information-oriented, and contextual ESG reports. A few studies have identified companies with higher ESG scores besides indulging in malpractices. From the operational viewpoint of the firms, the inability to manage ESG data complexities and quantifying risk leads to lower ESG efficacy (Wolters Kluwer, 2022). OIPT here gives a clearer picture to the firms that while dealing with ESG efficacy, they need to either reduce the generation of voluminous information by using mechanized structures or improve their information processing capacities. Mechanistic structures are known to take care of the information needs of such firms by implementing stringent rules, standardizing processes with defined frameworks, systems, and hierarchies, and multiplying interconnection and coordination among related bodies (Courtright et al., 1989). This data, once generated, also needs to be transformed into valuable insights and information (Selim, 2020). This OIPT advocates firms' robust information processing capacity.

13.2.4.7 Role of Blockchain in ESG Accountability

Blockchain is an important part of I5.0 that keeps decentralized transactions intact. It also keeps a network of peer-to-peer interconnected computer systems. It helps keep transactions secure and prevents unauthorized tampering, protecting their authenticity. One such prominent use of blockchain was undertaken by a renowned firm, Global Fishing Watch, which employed blockchain technology to monitor and combat illegal fishing attempts (The Guardian, 2021). Blockchain can also be used to improve governance (Coindesk, 2020) and the management of digital contracts (Respol, 2023).

13.2.5 Blockchain as General Purpose Technology

It is a prime concern that investors or consumers are protected against risks arising from cryptocurrency investing and security risks and that cryptocurrency should not further harm the economy, considering the retrospective collapses during 2022 (Jalan & Matkovskyy, 2023). Many investors are unaware of the risks accompanying modern technologies in the crypto industry. This gap is offset using the blockchain technology. Blockchain is not merely a modern fintech but also serves the purpose of a general-purpose technology (GPT). Blockchain serves in carbon credits, financial services, and supply chains, enabling 5G service slicing (Sun et al., 2022) and many more. GPT can serve the economy by acting as a generalized productivity enhancer and being used as input to many downstream sectors, technical improvements, and innovational complementarities (Bresnahan & Trajtenberg, 1995).

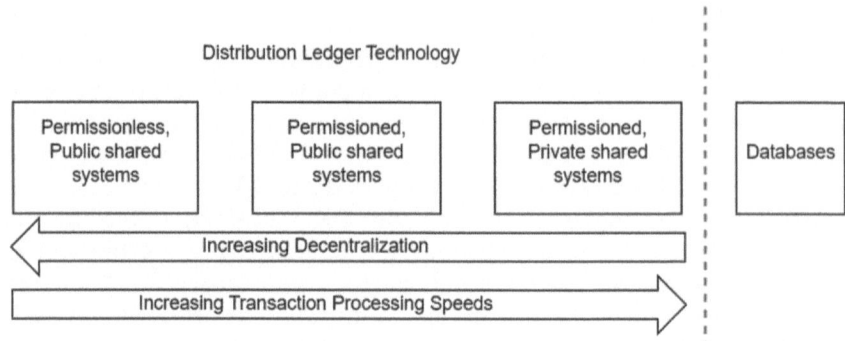

FIGURE 13.1
The distributed ledger technologies typologies

Source: Authors Compilation.

Blockchain has been used in distributed systems, known as "distributed ledger technologies" (DLTs). There are a few types of DLTs concerning blockchain (Figure 13.1). They are:

- Public: These are accessible to all. Anyone can read and manipulate the transactions on the network.
- Private: These are closed systems. One needs permission to access the transactions in the network.
- Permissioned: In this, the user gaining the permission can read and write the transactions in the network.
- Permissionless: Anyone can join the network without requiring any permission.
- Shared: In this, the ledger is shared on several nodes across the network.

13.2.6 Blockchain in Sustainability

Blockchain is widely used to attain sustainability using different types of DLT. Blockchain is segmented into three layers: Layer 1, Layer 2, and the intermediary service layer.

- Layer 1: This is the basic layer of the blockchain network, which includes a peer-to-peer network of nodes that store the ledger itself. This layer depicts how transactions are understood and segmented into new blocks. It also has cryptographic algorithms that keep the transactions secure.

- Layer 2: This layer comprises the solutions and applications built by the blockchain within the previous layer.
- Intermediary layer: These are the intermediary providers between Layers 1 and 2. They provide custody and wallet management services.

Blockchain gives its users the liberty to communicate transactions with each other without any centralized authority (Nofer et al., 2017). A public ledger records the details of the transactions and duplicates them to each node so that they are accessible to all network members (Sunny et al., 2020). Each transaction is end-to-end encrypted by the participants; thus, information security and traceability are ensured (Casino et al., 2019). Blockchain is strengthened by synergizing the physical and digital spaces using breakthrough technologies like digital twin, Internet of Things (IoT), CPS, cloud/fog/edge computing, and big data (Da et al., 2020; Aoun et al., 2021). These systems, which are used by blockchain, are empowered by data, making them robust and giving better productivity, efficiency, flexibility, resilience, and cost-effectiveness (Hajjaji et al., 2021).

The integration of blockchain with ESG can only be done by using IoT with blockchain technology, which makes it one of the most effective platforms, namely, BI-ESG (blockchain–Internet of Things–environmental, social, and governance). This BI-ESG attempts to bring authenticity, security, and transparency from ESG data collection until the ESG reporting. This is done using intelligent systems to keep stakeholders' confidence and benefit them.

The first and foremost layer is the perception layer, which is the bottommost layer of the architecture that automatically assembles the voluminous ESG data generated. This layer has, by default, the function of data analyzing capability that is efficient enough to make quick and effective decisions at the operational level within the layer (Figure 13.2). The second layer, interoperation, bridges the connecting gap between smart objects and blockchain networks. The data collected is sent to IoT gateways individually from each node; the IoT then converges all the data it receives and interconnects the network protocols. The gateway operating systems consolidate and process this data. The third layer is a synchronized consortium blockchain network that keeps transactions secure, authentic, and accessible. Each layer node comprises communication channels for easier and faster data processing and output, low transaction costs, and efficiency. Practically, each node consists of a data ledger as a decentralized base to record, replicate, and synchronize all information transactions within the network. The data processed as information is then formatted in standardized form using JavaScript. The top and the last layer is the application layer, which enables the users to be authorized to access ESG-based services powered by web applications. The ESG knowledge base has been established to provide industry analysis and firm performance appraisal. Report manager and tracker ensure timely submission and progress tracking system. Besides this, the platform keeps up with a review

Layer 4	APPLICATION LAYER
Layer 3	SYNCHRONIZATION LAYER
Layer 2	INTERCEPTION LAYER
Layer 1	PERCEPTION LAYER

FIGURE 13.2
The P-I-S-A architecture

Source: Authors compilation.

system to ensure double checking of the processes and evaluate and analyze the information to assist investors in making quality investment decisions.

Stakeholders can also suggest necessary changes and offer their viewpoints on the company's ESG performance. Concerning service accessibility, listed companies are the top authorities who command ESG data generation and processing. In contrast, ESG professional consultants seek these listed companies to access the ESG raw data. This BI-ESG platform with its P-I-S-A architecture enhances transparency, security, and efficiency of the ESG reporting and evaluation process.

13.3 Develop a Sustainable Blockchain Model for ESG-Focused Projects

It is observed that ESG factors and practices that contribute to ESG are important when considering investments and business management because they can develop productivity and give sustained growth. In order to justify the firm's performance concerning the ESG aspects, a standard model needs to be developed. The model in Figure 13.3 shows the ESG framework of how Blockchain can enhance the working of ESG-based crypto funds.

Strategy of ESG-Focused Cryptocurrency Projects

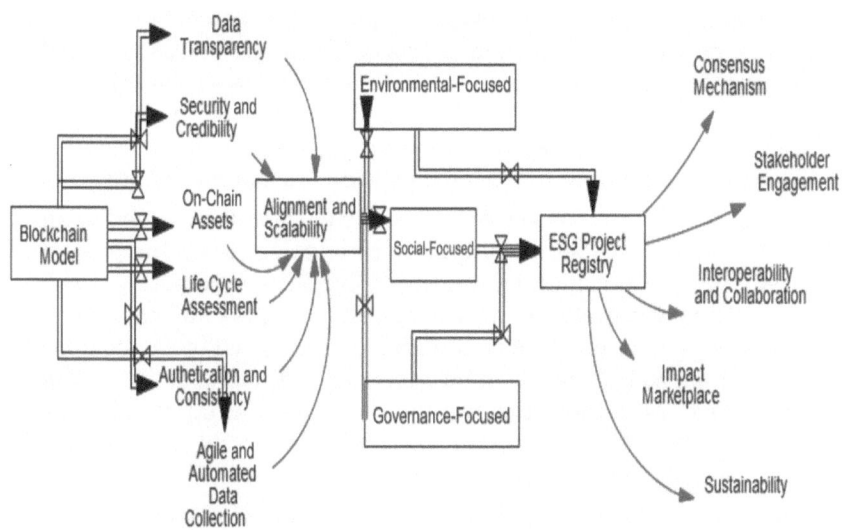

FIGURE 13.3
The framework of blockchain implications in ESG projects

Blockchain is a technology that provides complete transparency and authentication across the entire supply chain of transactions. Apart from dealing with data transparency, blockchain also provides uncontrolled data access. The various elements of the blockchain model are:

1. Data Transparency: Data transparency is the facility to access and work on data efficiently (Bertino et al., 2019) by anyone and from anywhere, irrespective of who created it and where they are located. Data transparency is essential for quality data requirements so that it can be used for operational, decision-making, and planning purposes. All in all, data transparency is a mechanism that can be used to provide fine-grained metadata that could be used for effective data quality metrics.

2. Security and Credibility: Blockchain helps attain transparency and gives much-needed security and credibility to the transactions. The voluminous data generated during transactions is protected by the use of distributed ledger systems of blockchain, and it also helps in data evaluation for decision-making purposes. The transactions that occur in blockchain networks are verified on each node. Only then is the information transmitted, which ensures the data's security and credibility and that the transactions are safe and secure from unauthorized access.

3. On-Chain Assets: Since blockchain purely works on the principle of virtual networks, the on-chain assets or digital assets are traded only on transaction networks of blockchain. As these assets are traded on virtual platforms without the intervention of a physical counterpart, they are safe and secure from unauthorized access. Since these transactions occur on a public ledger, they keep track of every transaction.
4. Life Cycle Assessment: While ESG reporting, companies tend to greenwash ESG reports by manipulating them due to undue pressure from higher authorities. However, life cycle assessment (LCA) techniques help integrate the data obtained from ESG and then evaluate them for understanding the ESG performance of the complete value chain as LCA needs to be effectively utilized as it is not easier to manage, as without the high-quality data and input, LCA may abruptly give insignificant, incorrect and biased results. Using blockchain and IoT here can lead to cross-validation of ESG disclosures.
5. Authentication and Consistency: With the help of IoT, blockchain can help authenticate transactions and data. The ESG reports are proposed to use token-based or coin-based mechanisms, which can help verify the data and clean it for further assessment. Since blockchain is adept at managing voluminous data, it can consistently process transactions to a large extent, keeping the security and authenticity of the transactions intact.
6. Agile and Automated Data Collection: As blockchain produces transparent, agile, efficient, and automated data collection processes, it can effectively manage the processing and packaging of ESG reports. Since the data generated is voluminous and the most significant benefit of blockchain is that it deals with digital transactions, data generation, recording, and analysis are automatic by systems.
7. Alignment and Scalability: It is important to align the transactions with real-time data requirements and control and manage the voluminous data generated by increasing the load of transactions as the number of nodes increases. This comes as the number of users of crypto assets increases, as the number of users of the information in the distributed ledger system of blockchain increases. Thus, this blockchain and IoT can help manage the alignment and scalability. We need to gauge the sustainability of these systems concerning the different perspectives that have been obtained.
8. Environment-Focused: When discussing sustainability, the environment and activities must be considered. The world faces drastic climatic changes, such as the depletion of forests and natural resources, change of seasons, global warming, pollution, and increasing sea levels leading to natural calamities, among many more. This may be why technologies have advanced at the cost of loss of environment

and nature. Thus, investors and stakeholders expressing their concerns have shown interest in investing in financial decisions leading to sustainable development and environmental protection.

9. Social-Focused: Besides environmental concerns, investors are increasingly making investment decisions based on factors such as employee health and safety, product quality, and corporate responsibility toward consumers. The focus is also on positively impacting the community to frame and maintain appropriate labor standards and human rights. When these decisions are taken, society benefits, causing inclusion and diversity of beings.

10. Governance-Focused: The governance perspective of sustainable investing discusses the standard rules and regulations laid out and implemented to control and manage legitimate systems. It involves hedging against the market and other associated risks, stringently implementing anti-corruption and bribery, implementing and practicing business ethical standards, keeping up with a transparent tax system in the economy, and keeping the leadership and corporate governance affirmed.

11. ESG Project Registry: The investments, when made keeping concern ESG parameters with the help of blockchain technologies, lead to some desired outcomes such as:

    a. Consensus Mechanism: Blockchain is a proven technique for collecting and processing substantial transaction datasets and managing the network supply chain. The DLT and the consensus mechanisms of blockchain technology allow users to visualize the data and standards that should be followed during the data collection process for ESG evaluation.

    b. Stakeholder engagement: Blockchain tracks numerous transactions in supply chain networks and keeps an immutable and transparent ledger system that enables stakeholders to track transaction data, analyze the information collected, and make quality decisions. Parallelly, it provides access to only the users who are authorized to use it.

    c. Interoperability and Collaboration: Since blockchain deals with vast amounts of transaction data, cross-chain interoperability protocols can help reduce the burden of these transactions by distributing the transactions to multiple chains, thus improving networks' overall scalability and efficiency. Also, after decentralizing these transactions on different chains, developers can collaborate on the functionalities from various blockchains, increasing the ambit of innovation and decentralized systems in blockchains.

d. Impact Marketplace: Impact marketplaces are where impact tokens are traded. Impact tokens are digital assets that contribute to the Sustainable Development Goals endorsed by United Nations and represent a specific metric, like the number of vaccination doses, tonnes of carbon dioxide, and the number of children attending school. These tokens can be registered on the blockchain and monitored on the supply chain. They generally invest in health, education, energy, or agriculture to improve these sectors.

e. Sustainability: When blockchain is considered in relation to ESG-investing strategies, the ESG collectively discusses sustainability. These ESG-investing strategies aim to contribute to ESG development, thus attaining sustainability. Digital assets reduce the burden of handling physical assets and increase connectivity among users from different parts of the world. It keeps records of the transactions and maintains smooth transactions in the supply chain through a distributed ledger system. Any amount of historical information can be obtained from any user at any point, thus enhancing the sustainability and efficiency of transactions.

This model was developed with the idea of how blockchain contributes to ESG-based investment opportunities. This model considered the factors of blockchain technology that can be used to make ESG investments more authentic and reliable. When these ESG investments in real life become authentic, investors become more confident investing in ESG investment. This also contributes to monitoring ESG legal compliances and can help stakeholders in ethical considerations.

13.4 Impact on Stakeholder Engagement Strategies in Cryptocurrency Projects

Stakeholders play a vital role in decision-making processes and, thus, in the value creation of an asset. The studies have tried to identify the relationship between ESG ratings and stakeholder values and have found a positive relationship between both. Investors use ESG ratings to evaluate how companies treat their stakeholders, and thus, ESG scores can be considered a good measure of social (Brogi & Lagasio, 2019) and stakeholder responsibility. However, ESG ratings are based on many factors other than stakeholder value. It is argued that considering the stakeholders' view of the corporation, a performance analysis of the corporation merely based on shareholders' value can be a drawback (Chakravarthy, 1986). On the other hand, stakeholder management can be considered a way of maximizing shareholders' sustainable wealth. ESG ratings have been used in stakeholders' context to identify whether higher stakeholders' performance can lead to higher financial performance of the company (Choi & Wang, 2009; Mattingly, 2017).

The model of essential stakeholder synergies for sustainable competitive advantage also considers social purpose as an important aspect in the value creation of stakeholders (Tantalo & Priem, 2016). Further, it has been identified that implementing corporate governance appropriately and managing ESG-related risks effectively can also influence value creation for stakeholders (Adams, 2017). Addressing the ecological aspects creates value for the stakeholders and aligns business practices with sustainable development goals (Schaltegger et al., 2012). Freeman and Dmytriyev (2017) state that a firm's total value includes values created by suppliers, financiers, customers, employees, and related communities. Companies usually create value by choosing the manufacturing company's customers and the quality of the goods and services they are willing to pay (Bowman & Ambrosini, 2000). It is essential to note the distribution of value on the level of wealth creation to those who have contributed to the firm's value creation.

13.5 Future Trends and Challenges

13.5.1 Challenges

ESG-focused digital currencies strive to prioritize social responsibility. However, ensuring that these currencies uphold their ESG objectives poses the following challenges:

1. Using wallet addresses of names in blockchain transactions leads to a lack of transparency. This hinders efforts to trace the entities or businesses involved in transactions, making it challenging to hold them accountable for their ESG commitments.
2. Due to the data storage capacity of blockchains, there are constraints on storing ESG-related data on the chain. This limitation makes it difficult to monitor and validate a project's social impact
3. The regulatory environment surrounding ESG-oriented currencies continuously evolves, creating uncertainty. This dynamic landscape makes it hard for projects to establish accountability measures that align with future regulations.
4. There is a risk of "greenwashing" within ESG-focused projects, where unfounded or deceptive claims about benefits are made. Due to the absence of standardized transparency requirements, projects may exaggerate their impacts or downplay negative aspects.

5. Despite having verifiable ESG data, enforcing accountability on projects remains complex. Decentralized blockchains operate without the authority to enforce penalties for failing to meet ESG objectives. These difficulties underscore the importance of finding ways to guarantee that cryptocurrency initiatives focused on ESG adhere to their social obligations. In order to ensure accountability in ESG-focused cryptocurrencies, the difficulties mentioned above indicate that innovative solutions are needed. They include key recommendations and possible future trends.
6. The entire industry should develop standardized ESG reporting and verification frameworks. These frameworks should provide clear indicators for measuring environmental and social impact, thus enabling developers to follow a roadmap.
7. ESG-native blockchains are beginning to emerge, and they offer exciting possibilities. Blockchains can have built-in features such as transparent structures, data repositories for extensive information on ESG issues, and governance systems enabling responsibility enforcement.
8. Encouraging active involvement from investors, NGOs, or regulatory authorities is vital. By opening lines of communication and fostering collaborations, transparency will be nurtured, and projects will be held accountable based on their ESG objectives.

While ESG investments encounter these challenges, it is of utmost importance to understand the future trends they can have. This section addresses these future trends.

13.5.2 Future Trends

Future trends should focus on the following:

1. One of the most exciting developments in blockchain has been the rise of DAOs, where communities are governed by collective decision-making. In these organizations, token holders can vote on ESG initiatives and ensure that those responsible for them are held to account.
2. The tokenization of environmental or social impact could be a game-changer. This would mean that carbon offsets or achievements in social development could be turned into tokens, allowing investors to invest directly in beneficial ESG outcomes.
3. AI and machine learning can improve data analysis and verification regarding companies' ESG claims. They will also detect any attempts at "greenwashing" and ensure that reports containing ESG data are accurate.

By implementing these guidelines and being alert to new trends, accountability issues faced by ESG-focused cryptocurrency projects can be overcome, unlocking their maximum potential for positive environmental and social impacts.

13.6 Conclusion

The accountability of ESG-focused cryptocurrencies is a complex issue with no easy solutions. However, by acknowledging the challenges and working toward solutions, the industry can build trust and ensure these projects deliver on their sustainability and social responsibility promises. Collaboration between project developers, regulators, and the broader crypto community is key to ushering in a future where ESG-focused cryptocurrencies are not just a financial innovation but a powerful force for positive change. This chapter has a few limitations, such as the availability of information and data. Based on the limitations, future researchers can work on data-based methods to validate the information conveyed through this article.

References

Adams, C. (2017). *Understanding integrated reporting: The concise guide to integrated thinking and the future of corporate reporting.* Routledge.

Aheleroff, S., Xu, X., Zhong, R. Y. and Lu, Y. (2021). Digital twin as a service (DTaaS) in industry 4.0: An architecture reference model. *Advanced Engineering Informatics,* 47, p. 101225.

Albuquerque, R., Koskinen, Y. and Zhang, C. (2019). Corporate social responsibility and firm risk: Theory and empirical evidence. *Management Science,* 65(10), pp. 4451–4469.

Aoun, A., Ilinca, A., Ghandour, M. and Ibrahim, H. (2021). A review of Industry 4.0 characteristics and challenges, with potential improvements using blockchain technology. *Computers & Industrial Engineering,* 162, p. 107746.

Asif, M., Searcy, C. and Castka, P. (2022). Exploring the role of Industry 4.0 in enhancing supplier audit authenticity, efficacy, and cost-effectiveness. *Journal of Cleaner Production,* 331, p. 129939.

Baker, M., Bergstresser, D., Serafeim, G. and Wurgler, J. (2022). The pricing and ownership of US green bonds. *Annual Review of Financial Economics,* 14(1), pp. 415–437.

Bauer, R., Ruof, T. and Smeets, P. (2021). Get real! Individuals prefer more sustainable investments. *The Review of Financial Studies,* 34(8), pp. 3976–4043.

Bertino, E., Kundu, A. and Sura, Z. (2019). Data transparency with blockchain and AI ethics. *Journal of Data and Information Quality (JDIQ),* 11(4), pp. 1–8.

Bowman, C. and Ambrosini, V. (2000). Value creation versus value capture: Towards a coherent definition of value in strategy. *British Journal of Management*, 11(1), pp. 1–15.

Bresnahan, T. F. and Trajtenberg, M. (1995). General purpose technologies "Engines of growth"? *Journal of Econometrics*, 65(1), pp. 83–108.

Brodback, D., Guenster, N. and Mezger, D. (2019). Altruism and egoism in investment decisions. *Review of Financial Economics*, 37(1), pp. 118–148.

Brogi, M. and Lagasio, V. (2019). Environmental, social, governance, and company profitability: Are financial intermediaries different? *Corporate Social Responsibility and Environmental Management*, 26(3), pp. 576–587.

Casino, F., Dasaklis, T. K. and Patsakis, C. (2019). A systematic literature review of blockchain-based applications: Current status, classification, and open issues. *Telematics and Informatics*, 36, pp. 55–81.

Castka, P. and Searcy, C. (2023). Audits and COVID-19: A paradigm shift in the making. *Business Horizons*, 66(1), pp. 5–11.

Castka, P., Searcy, C. and Mohr, J. (2020). Technology-enhanced auditing: Improving veracity and timeliness in social and environmental audits of supply chains. *Journal of Cleaner Production*, 258, p. 120773.

Ceccarelli, V., Fremout, T., Zavaleta, D., Lastra, S., Imán Correa, S., Arévalo-Gardini, E., Rodriguez, C. A., Cruz Hilacondo, W. and Thomas, E. (2021). Climate change impacts cultivated and wild cacao in Peru and the search for climate change-tolerant genotypes. *Diversity and Distributions*, 27(8), pp. 1462–1476.

Chakravarthy, B. S. (1986). Measuring strategic performance. *Strategic Management Journal*, 7(5), pp. 437–458.

Chamorro-Mera, A. and Palacios-González, M. M. (2019). Socially responsible investment: An analysis of the structure of preferences of savers. *Corporate Social Responsibility and Environmental Management*, 26(6), pp. 1423–1434.

Choi, J. and Wang, H. (2009). Stakeholder relations and the persistence of corporate financial performance. *Strategic Management Journal*, 30(8), pp. 895–907.

Coindesk (2020). Digital voting is coming. Let's do it right [online]. *Coindesk*. Available: https://www.coindesk.com/markets/2020/11/10/digital-voting-is-coming-lets-do-it-right/ (Accessed March 17, 2024).

Conesa, C. (2019). Bitcoin: A solution for payment systems or a solution in search of a problem? *Banco de Espana Occasional Paper*, (1901).

Corbet, S., Cumming, D. J., Lucey, B. M., Peat, M. and Vigne, S. (2019, May 3). *Investigating the dynamics between price volatility, price discovery, and criminality in cryptocurrency markets*. Price Discovery and Criminality in Cryptocurrency Markets.

Courtright, J. A., Fairhurst, G. T. and Rogers, L. E. (1989). Interaction patterns in organic and mechanistic systems. *Academy of Management Journal*, 32(4), pp. 773–802.

Da R. R., R., Alberti, A. M. and Singh, M. (2020). *Blockchain technology for Industry 4.0*. Springer Singapore.

DiMaggio, P. J. and Powell, W. W. (1983). The iron cage revisited: Institutional isomorphism and collective rationality in organizational fields. *American Sociological Review*, 48(2), pp. 147–160.

Drempetic, S., Klein, C. and Zwergel, B. (2020). The influence of firm size on the ESG score: Corporate sustainability ratings under review. *Journal of Business Ethics*, 167(2), pp. 333–360.

European Commission (2022). Just and sustainable economy: Commission lays down rules for companies to respect human rights and environment in global value chains [Online]. *European Commission*. Available: https://ec.europa.eu/commission/presscorner/detail/en/IP_22_1145 (Accessed March 17, 2024).

Fama, E. F. and French, K. R. (2007). Disagreement, tastes, and asset prices. *Journal of Financial Economics*, 83(3), pp. 667–689.

Freeman, R. E. and Dmytriyev, S. (2017). Corporate social responsibility and stakeholder theory: Learning from each other. *Symphonya. Emerging Issues in Management*, (1), pp. 7–15.

Hajjaji, Y., Boulila, W., Farah, I. R., Romdhani, I. and Hussain, A. (2021). Big data and IoT-based applications in smart environments: A systematic review. *Computer Science Review*, 39, p. 100318.

Hoepner, A. G., Majoch, A. A. and Zhou, X. Y. (2021). Does an asset owner's institutional setting influence its decision to sign the principles for responsible investment? *Journal of Business Ethics*, 168, pp. 389–414.

Huang, A. H., Wang, H. and Yang, Y. (2023). FinBERT: A large language model for extracting information from financial text. *Contemporary Accounting Research*, 40(2), pp. 806–841.

Humphrey, V., Berg, A., Ciais, P., Gentine, P., Jung, M., Reichstein, M., Seneviratne, S. I. and Frankenberg, C. (2021). Soil moisture–atmosphere feedback dominates land carbon uptake variability. *Nature*, 592(7852), pp. 65–69.

Jalan, A. and Matkovskyy, R. (2023). Systemic risks in the cryptocurrency market: Evidence from the FTX collapse. *Finance Research Letters*, 53, p. 103670.

Khan, A. G., Zahid, A. H., Hussain, M. and Riaz, U. (2019, November). Security of cryptocurrency using hardware wallet and QR code. In *2019 international conference on innovative computing (ICIC)* (pp. 1–10). IEEE.

Koenigsmarck, M. and Geissdoerfer, M. (2021). Mapping socially responsible investing: A bibliometric and citation network analysis. *Journal of Cleaner Production*, 296, p. 126376.

Lawrence, P. R. and Lorsch, J. W. (1967) *Organization and environment: Managing differentiation and integration*. Division of Research, Graduate School of Business Administration, Harvard University, Boston.

Levillain, K. and Segrestin, B. (2019). From primacy to purpose commitment: How emerging profit-with-purpose corporations open new corporate governance avenues. *European Management Journal*, 37(5), pp. 637–647.

Lipton, A. and Treccani, A. (2021). *Blockchain and distributed ledgers: Mathematics, technology, and economics*. World Scientific.

Mattingly, J. E. (2017). Corporate social performance: A review of empirical research examining the corporation–society relationship using Kinder, Lydenberg, Domini social rating data. *Business & Society*, 56(6), pp. 796–839.

Meunier, L. and Ohadi, S. (2022). Misconceptions about socially responsible investments. *Journal of Cleaner Production*, 373, p. 133868.

Nawaz, M. A., Seshadri, U., Kumar, P., Aqdas, R., Patwary, A. K. and Riaz, M. (2021). Nexus between green finance and climate change mitigation in N-11 and BRICS countries: Empirical estimation through difference in differences (DID) approach. *Environmental Science and Pollution Research*, 28, pp. 6504–6519.

Nofer, M., Gomber, P., Hinz, O. and Schiereck, D. (2017). Blockchain. *Business & Information Systems Engineering*, 59, pp. 183–187.

Palacios-González, M. M. and Chamorro-Mera, A. (2020). Analysis of socially responsible consumption: A segmentation of Spanish consumers. *Sustainability*, 12(20), p. 8418.

Pástor, Ľ. and Vorsatz, M. B. (2020). Mutual fund performance and flows during the COVID-19 crisis. *The Review of Asset Pricing Studies*, 10(4), pp. 791–833.

Reber, B., Gold, A. and Gold, S. (2022). ESG disclosure and idiosyncratic risk in initial public offerings. *Journal of Business Ethics*, 179(3), pp. 867–886.

Reid, J. and Castka, P. (2023). The impact of remote sensing on monitoring and reporting: The case of conformance systems. *Journal of Cleaner Production*, 393, p. 136331.

Respol (2023). Blockchain technology for the energy sector [Online]. *Respol*. Available: https://www.repsol.com/en/press-room/repsol-news/32/index.cshtml (Accessed March 17, 2024).

Schaltegger, S., Lüdeke-Freund, F. and Hansen, E. G. (2012). Business cases for sustainability: The role of business model innovation for corporate sustainability. *International Journal of Innovation and Sustainable Development*, 6(2), pp. 95–119.

Selim, O. (2020). ESG and AI: The beauty and the beast of sustainable investing. In *Sustainable investing* (pp. 227–243). Routledge.

Sun, Y., Jiang, S., Jia, W. and Wang, Y. (2022). Blockchain as a cutting-edge technology impacting business: A systematic literature review perspective. *Telecommunications Policy*, 46(10), p. 102443.

Sunny, J., Undralla, N. and Pillai, V. M. (2020). Supply chain transparency through blockchain-based traceability: An overview with demonstration. *Computers & Industrial Engineering*, 150, p. 106895.

Tantalo, C. and Priem, R. L. (2016). Value creation through stakeholder synergy. *Strategic Management Journal*, 37(2), pp. 314–329.

Teichmann, F. M. J. and Falker, M. C. (2021). Cryptocurrencies and financial crime: Solutions from Liechtenstein. *Journal of Money Laundering Control*, 24(4), pp. 775–788.

The Guardian (2021). Plate hook: How blockchain tech could turn the tide for sustainable fishing [Online]. *The Guardian*. Available: https://www.theguardian.com/environment/2021/jun/09/hook-to-plate-how-blockchain-tech-can-turn-the-tide-for-sustainable-fishing-aoe (Accessed March 17, 2024).

Thomson Reuters (2021). ESG and the global supply chain [Online]. *Thomson Reuters*. Available: https://insight.thomsonreuters.in/business/posts/thomson-reuters-2021-social-impact-esg-report-progress-on-key-esg-activities (Accessed March 17, 2024).

Verdouw, C., Tekinerdogan, B., Beulens, A. and Wolfert, S. (2021). Digital twins in smart farming. *Agricultural Systems*, 189, p. 103046.

Williamson, O. E. (2007). The economic institutions of capitalism. Firms, markets, relational contracting (pp. 61–75). Gabler.

Wolters Kluwer (2022). *The five biggest hurdles to effective ESG reporting* [Online]. Available: https://www.wolterskluwer.com/en/expert-insights/the-5-biggest-hurdles-to-effective-esg-reporting (Accessed March 17, 2024).

Xie, R. (2019). Why China had to ban cryptocurrency, but the US did not: A comparative analysis of crypto-market regulations between the US and China. *Washington University Global Studies Law Review*, 18, p. 457.

Part 4

Cryptocurrencies

Strategizing in a Decentralized Financial Landscape

Part 4

14

Cryptocurrency Integration in the Web 3.0 Ecosystem: Opportunities, Challenges, and Future Directions

Adarsh Chandra Nigam and Ruby S. Chanda

14.1 Introduction

The digital landscape is undergoing a transformative shift propelled by the emergence of Web 3.0, a paradigm characterized by applications leveraging blockchain and decentralized systems. This evolution marks a departure from the centralized structures of Web 2.0, ushering in a new era of trustless interactions and peer-to-peer transactions (Bergquist Mcneil, 2022). At the heart of Web 3.0 lies blockchain technology, a decentralized ledger system that ensures data transparency, security, and immutability (Alkhuary et al., 2020). Unlike its predecessors, Web 3.0 prioritizes user autonomy and data sovereignty, empowering individuals to take control of their digital identities and assets.

While Web 2.0 brought about unprecedented connectivity and the rise of user-generated content, it also exposed significant vulnerabilities. The centralized nature of Web 2.0 platforms has led to high-profile data breaches, privacy violations, and issues of monopolistic control. One of the most notorious examples is the 2017 Equifax data breach, where the personal information of 147 million Americans was compromised due to centralized data storage vulnerabilities (Bernard et al., 2017). Similarly, the Marriott International data breach in 2018 exposed the sensitive information of approximately 500 million guests, highlighting the risks associated with centralization (Godage, 2023). The Facebook-Cambridge Analytica scandal in 2018 further exemplifies the dangers of centralized control over data, where the personal data of up to 87 million users was harvested without consent and used for political advertising, sparking global outrage (ur Rehman, 2019). These incidents underscore the inherent risks associated with centralization, where a single point of failure can result in massive security breaches. The monopolistic control exercised by a few tech giants over user data has raised privacy concerns and limited competition and innovation within the digital economy. Antitrust investigations into companies like Google and Amazon reveal how centralized control can stifle market competition and maintain monopolistic power (Palmer & Novet, 2020).

Consumer Behavior and Expectations: These challenges have significantly influenced consumer behavior, driving a demand for more decentralized and secure digital ecosystems. Modern consumers, particularly digital-native millennials and Gen Z, prioritize transparency, data sovereignty, and privacy in online interactions. They seek platforms that offer greater control over their digital identities and assets, moving away from the centralized models that dominate the current web.

Web 3.0 builds upon the shortcomings of Web 2.0 by integrating decentralized technologies. It allows for both reading and writing data in a distributed and secure manner through blockchain-based interactions and transactions (Ragnedda & Destefanis, 2019) (see Figure 14.1). By leveraging blockchain technology, Web 3.0 ensures that data is distributed across a network, reducing the likelihood of large-scale data breaches and empowering users with control over their digital information.

Web 3.0 and cryptocurrency integration can help achieve sustainability goals, leveraging blockchain for transparency and decentralization, aligning with Sustainable Development Goal (SDG) targets such as responsible consumption and production (SDG 12), climate action (SDG 13), and industry innovation (SDG 9). The shift toward Web 3.0 is driven by the demands of digital-native consumers who prioritize hyper-personalization, convenience, and sustainability in online interactions (Barassi & Treré, 2012). These consumers seek seamless experiences that transcend geographical

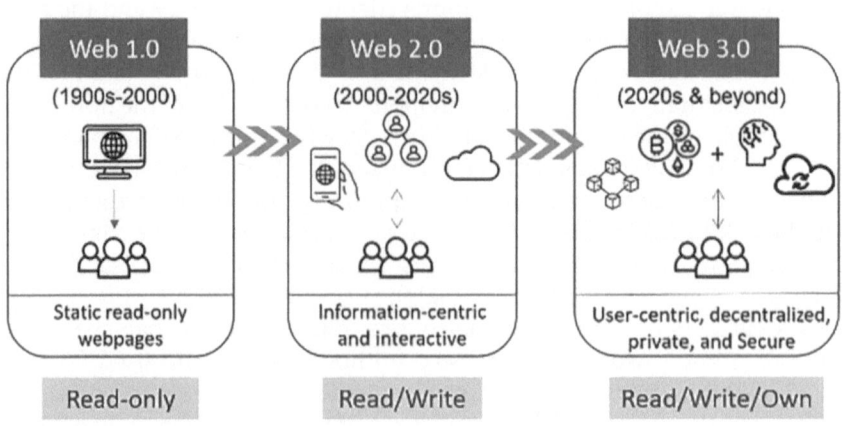

FIGURE 14.1
The evolution of web interactivity (Illustration by the Authors)

boundaries and traditional intermediaries, demanding greater transparency and accountability from digital platforms (Ragnedda & Destefanis, 2019). In response, businesses must adopt innovative approaches to customer engagement within the Web 3.0 landscape, leveraging decentralized applications (dApps) and token economies to meet evolving consumer expectations (Mougayar, 2016).

Web 3.0's core principles of decentralization and tokenization address specific challenges that current centralized systems fail to solve efficiently. Decentralization enhances security and reduces the risk of single points of failure by distributing control across a network. Tokenization democratizes access to assets, enabling fractional ownership and creating new opportunities for liquidity in traditionally illiquid markets.

Cryptocurrency integration emerges as a cornerstone of the Web 3.0 ecosystem, offering a viable solution to the challenges posed by traditional payment systems. Cryptocurrencies, such as Bitcoin and Ethereum, facilitate borderless transactions, expedite settlements, and enhance security through cryptographic encryption (Nica et al., 2017). Moreover, the decentralized nature of cryptocurrencies ensures resilience against censorship and government control, fostering a more inclusive and accessible financial ecosystem (Srokosz & Kopciaski, 2015).

The building blocks of Web 3.0 encompass a suite of transformative technologies that underpin its decentralized architecture and functionality:

- Blockchain technology forms the cornerstone, providing a secure and immutable ledger for transactions and data storage (Lai et al., 2023). This addresses the challenge of ensuring data integrity and trust in transactions, offering opportunities for more transparent and secure digital interactions. Digital assets, represented as tokens on the blockchain, enable the creation and exchange of value in a decentralized manner (Lee, 2019). These tokens address challenges related to traditional asset management, such as liquidity and accessibility, by allowing fractional ownership and more effortless transfer of assets. Blockchain creates opportunities for democratizing investment and expanding access to financial resources.
- Smart contracts are self-executing contracts with the terms of the agreement directly written into code. They automatically enforce and execute agreements once predetermined conditions are met, without the need for intermediaries. Smart contracts address challenges in trust and inefficiency within traditional contract execution by automating processes and eliminating the need for intermediaries. Smart contracts reduce transaction costs, increase efficiency, and minimize the potential for human error or fraud, creating opportunities for streamlined and more reliable business operations (Yerram, 2022).

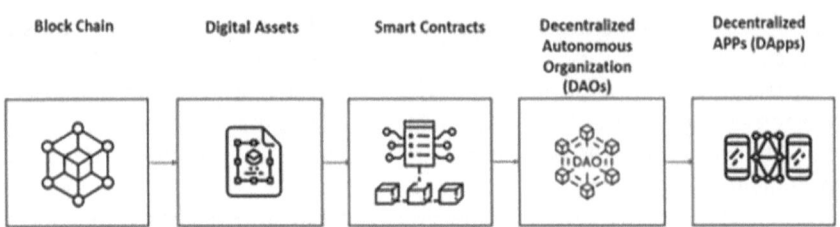

FIGURE 14.2
Building blocks of Web 3.0 (Illustration by the Authors)

- Decentralized autonomous organizations (DAOs) are entities governed by smart contracts, self-executing codes operating on a blockchain. DAOs address centralized governance and transparency challenges by functioning without centralized control and enabling democratic decision-making processes. This model makes organizations more secure and resistant to corruption or manipulation, creating opportunities for more equitable and efficient operations (Santana & Albareda, 2022).
- dApps run on a blockchain or peer-to-peer network instead of being hosted on centralized servers. Unlike traditional applications, dApps are open-source, operate autonomously, and are not controlled by any single entity. dApps address challenges such as censorship, downtime, and data breaches by removing central control points. They contribute to the robustness and resilience of the Web 3.0 ecosystem, creating opportunities for innovation in application development and greater user autonomy (Lundberg & Petrén, 2022).

Together, these building blocks form the foundation of Web 3.0, driving innovation and empowering users with greater control over their digital interactions and assets (see Figure 14.2).

14.1.1 Motivation

This chapter is motivated by the pressing need to address several fundamental challenges within the current financial systems, which are increasingly becoming inadequate in the face of growing digitalization and consumer demands. One of the primary concerns is privacy. Traditional economic systems rely heavily on centralized databases, which are vulnerable to data breaches and unauthorized access, as seen in numerous high-profile incidents. Web 3.0, with its decentralized architecture, offers a promising solution by enhancing data privacy and security, thereby restoring trust in digital financial transactions.

Another significant challenge is the high transaction costs associated with traditional financial services, particularly cross-border transactions. These costs are often a result of multiple intermediaries, slow processing times, and currency conversion fees. Web 3.0, through the use of blockchain and smart contracts, has the potential to drastically reduce these costs by eliminating intermediaries and enabling near-instantaneous transactions across borders.

Moreover, access barriers in the current financial systems continue to exclude large portions of the global population, particularly in developing regions. These barriers include stringent regulatory requirements, lack of economic infrastructure, and limited access to banking services. Web 3.0 technologies, exceptionally decentralized finance (DeFi), offer a pathway to financial inclusion by providing decentralized platforms accessible to anyone with an internet connection, thus democratizing access to financial services.

The potential impact of Web 3.0 on various sectors is profound. For instance, Web 3.0 could lead to more efficient, transparent, and inclusive financial markets in the financial sector. In the supply chain industry, blockchain could enhance transparency and traceability. In healthcare, decentralized networks could ensure the security and privacy of patient data. By addressing these specific challenges, Web 3.0 aims to improve existing systems, foster innovation, and create new opportunities across industries, making the study of its integration into the digital economy both timely and crucial.

This chapter critically examines the integration of cryptocurrency within the Web 3.0 ecosystem, exploring opportunities, challenges, and future directions. Through real-world case studies and scholarly insights, we aim to elucidate the transformative potential of cryptocurrency integration in reshaping the digital economy. By fostering a deeper understanding of Web 3.0 and cryptocurrency integration, we endeavor to contribute to the scholarly discourse and pave the way for future research in this burgeoning field.

14.2 Web 3.0 Wallets: Enhancing Digital Asset Management

Decentralized wallets (Web 3.0 wallets) are the cornerstone of DeFi and token economies, providing users with a secure and efficient way of managing their digital assets. These wallets leverage blockchain technology to offer many functionalities, from storing and transferring digital assets to participating in dApps and earning yields through DeFi protocols. Decentralized wallets encompass a range of functionalities that empower users to manage their digital assets securely and efficiently within the decentralized landscape. These functionalities are presented in Table 14.1.

Web 3.0 wallets are pivotal in digital asset management, providing users with enhanced control and security over their cryptocurrencies (Marbouh

TABLE 14.1

Functionalities of Web 3.0 Wallets

Functionality	Description
Storing and Transferring Cryptocurrencies	Secure storage and seamless transfer of various cryptocurrencies ensure user control and transaction transparency
Participating in Decentralized Applications (dApps)	Seamless interaction with diverse, dApps, including DeFi, NFTs, DEXs, and gaming, empowers users with autonomy and accessibility in digital interactions
Earning Yields through DeFi Protocols	Participation in DeFi protocols for yield generation through lending, borrowing, staking, and liquidity provision, maximizing returns while contributing to ecosystem growth
Multichain Support	Management of cryptocurrencies across multiple blockchain networks from a unified interface, enabling easy navigation and access to diverse, decentralized services
Token Management	Advanced management of various digital assets, encompassing tokens for collectibles, utility, and security, enhancing asset visibility and control
Privacy Features	Integration of privacy-enhancing measures for safeguarding sensitive information and transactions, ensuring confidentiality and security
Integration with Hardware Wallets	Seamless integration with hardware wallets for enhanced security of private keys, enabling secure management and transactions of digital assets

et al., 2020). Enterprises, ranging from small-scale internet shops to multinational corporations, are increasingly embracing cryptocurrency payments to capitalize on the unique advantages offered by Web 3.0 technologies (Turi, 2020). However, the transition to Web 3.0 is challenging as businesses grapple with regulatory uncertainties, scalability issues, and the seamless integration of DeFi with traditional financial systems (Lee, 2019).

14.3 Web 3.0: Transformative Opportunities for Businesses

Businesses are increasingly recognizing the transformative potential of decentralized technologies. By leveraging dApps and token economies built upon blockchain, Web 3.0 offers businesses enhanced security, efficiency, and accessibility. From streamlined trade processing to cost reduction and scalability, Web 3.0 presents many technical advantages that empower enterprises to innovate and thrive in the digital economy. Table 14.2 illustrates some potential benefits businesses could leverage from Web 3.0.

TABLE 14.2

Business Benefits of Web 3.0

Benefit	Description	Source
Enhanced Security	Web3 technology fosters self-sufficiency in decentralized markets, reducing the likelihood of security vulnerabilities.	Hooks, 2019
Automated Trade Processing	Integrating self-executing intelligent contracts in Web3 optimizes trade processes, accelerating transactions.	Petcu et al., 2023
Asset Tokenization	Web 3.0 enables asset tokenization, simplifying access to digital tokens for various objects and eliminating the need for fractional ownership.	Bashir, 2020
Scalable Platforms	Entrepreneurs and Web 3.0 development companies are encouraged to create scalable platforms to accommodate growing user bases.	Nasar, 2023
Efficiency and Accessibility	Web 3.0 introduces new business models with enhanced efficiency, openness, user-friendliness, speed, and security.	Lundberg & Petrén, 2022
Cost Reduction	Development costs are expected to decrease with the popularity of Web 3.0 and related trade platforms, benefiting from streamlined and personalized experiences.	Lacity & Lupien, 2022

14.4 The Role of Cryptocurrencies in Web 3.0

Cryptocurrencies play a pivotal role in shaping the decentralized landscape of Web 3.0, facilitating trustless transactions and fostering greater autonomy for users (Chen et al., 2022). By eliminating intermediaries and establishing decentralized networks, cryptocurrencies enable seamless collaboration and data sharing across various platforms and applications, thus mitigating data silos and enhancing interoperability. The decentralized nature of cryptocurrencies enhances security and trust in the Web 3.0 ecosystem, reducing the risk of cyberattacks and providing individuals with complete ownership over their digital assets (Debe et al., 2019). Moreover, cryptocurrencies prioritize user privacy and data protection, addressing significant concerns in the digital age (Bai et al., 2022). Emerging solutions such as zero-knowledge proofs (ZKPs) and decentralized identity systems further reinforce privacy and empower users with increased control over their data (Nita & Mihailescu, 2024).

The cryptocurrency ecosystem is diverse and inclusive, encompassing a wide range of participants vital to the growth and evolution of blockchain networks. Miners validate transactions and maintain network security, while developers drive innovation through the creation of dApps and improvements to blockchain protocols. Traders contribute to market liquidity and dynamics by engaging in cryptocurrency transactions on digital asset exchanges. Users interact with cryptocurrencies through wallets and applications, participating in DeFi protocols, non-fungible token (NFT) marketplaces, and other dApps. In addition, customers utilize cryptocurrencies for purchases, suppliers accept digital assets as payment, banks integrate cryptocurrency services, retailers adopt digital payment options, and processing units ensure the decentralized nature of blockchain networks. Together, these participants form a dynamic ecosystem that fosters innovation, adoption, and utilization of cryptocurrencies and blockchain technology.

The integration of tokenization and smart contracts within the cryptocurrency and Web 3.0 frameworks heralds a significant paradigm shift in various domains. Tokenization enables the creation of digital replicas of real-world assets, facilitating seamless financial transactions across sectors such as art, intellectual property, and real estate (Series, 2020). This innovation leverages blockchain technology to ensure transparency and security in asset management. In addition, smart contracts automate procedures by executing transactions based on predefined conditions, effectively eliminating the need for intermediaries (Bashir, 2020). Their deployment in dApps fosters innovation and generates new possibilities, further enhancing the efficiency and reliability of blockchain-based systems. Together, tokenization and smart contracts offer transformative potential, revolutionizing traditional processes and unlocking novel opportunities in the digital landscape.

14.5 Case Studies: Implementations of Web 3.0 and Cryptocurrency in Business

This section examines real-world case studies highlighting the implementation of Web 3.0 technologies and DeFi across various industries. By analyzing both the successes and challenges of these projects, we aim to identify effective strategies and best practices for harnessing the transformative potential of decentralized platforms. These case studies provide empirical evidence of how blockchain, smart contracts, NFTs, DAOs, and other crypto concepts solve concrete business problems and drive innovation in diverse applications.

The collection of case studies presented provides a comprehensive overview of the diverse applications of blockchain technology, smart contracts, DAOs, and NFTs across various industries, as given in Table 14.3. These examples highlight both the transformative potential and the inherent challenges associated with integrating decentralized technologies into traditional and emerging systems. In **supply chain finance**, blockchain has significantly improved credit reporting accuracy and credit scoring of small and medium enterprises (SME), although challenges such as high resource consumption

TABLE 14.3

Case Studies on Blockchain and Decentralized Technology Applications

Source	Case Study	Technology	Outcomes	Challenges
Zheng et al. (2022)	Supply Chain Finance	Blockchain and smart contracts	Enhanced credit reporting accuracy, improved SME credit scoring, and reduced information asymmetry	High resource consumption, integration with existing systems, and ensuring privacy and security
Agrawal et al. (2021)	Supply Chain Management	Blockchain and smart contracts	Improved traceability and transparency of organic cotton, data sharing across the textile supply chain, and increased trust among supply chain partners	Integration complexities, maintaining data privacy, ensuring compliance with regulations
Gourisetti et al., (2021)	Energy Sector: Distributed Energy Resources Integration	Distributed ledger technologies, industrial NFT, and DLT cybersecurity sack for secure, peer-to-peer, and peer-to-market energy transactions	Improved grid management, enhanced security, streamlined settlement processes	Ensuring robust data integrity through real-time monitoring and smart contracts
Angrish et al. (2018)	Manufacturing: Cybermanufacturing System (FabRec)	Ethereum smart contracts	Ensures secure, transparent manufacturing relationships by providing an immutable log of critical events within a permissioned network	Challenges in standardizing protocols across diverse systems, integrating with existing manufacturing IT infrastructure
Sigalov et al. (2021)	Construction: Automated Payment and Contract Management	Integration of building information modeling (BIM) with blockchain-based smart contracts	Improved transparency and traceability in payment processes and reduced delays in construction payments	Complexity in integrating BIM with blockchain, high initial setup costs, and ensuring legal compliance

(Continued)

TABLE 14.3 (Continued)

Case Studies on Blockchain and Decentralized Technology Applications

Source	Case Study	Technology	Outcomes	Challenges
Uchani Gutierrez and Xu (2022)	Smart Cities – Secure Property Transactions	Blockchain and smart contracts	Enhanced transaction security, improved autonomy, and reduced gas fees in smart cities	Economic viability concerns, integration challenges with existing infrastructure, the need for inclusive criteria, and the importance of stakeholder participation.
Mendoza Arvizo et al. (2023)	Healthcare	Blockchain and smart contracts	Enhanced security and privacy of medical records, reduced execution time of smart contracts by 14%, improved data integrity and traceability, ensured compliance with legal regulations, and reduced computational power usage with a 22% faster hash function	Integration challenges, economic viability concerns, the need for proper smart contract lifecycle management, and the importance of adhering to healthcare regulations
Wang et al. (2024)	Agriculture: Cotton Lint Traceability	Blockchain, NFTs, smart contracts, InterPlanetary File System (IPFS)	Enhanced traceability, specific gas costs (e.g., 523,440 gas for deployment), secure data storage via IPFS, and automated validation of processes using NFTs and smart contracts	Economic efficiency concerns with Ethereum gas fees, challenges in integrating NFTs with existing supply chains, and the need to adapt to local policies and regulations
Omar et al. (2021)	Healthcare Supply Chain	Blockchain, Ethereum network, smart contracts	Streamlined procurement, reduced pricing discrepancies, and enhanced transparency, with gas costs under $1.20 for fast execution	Managing gas costs, ensuring security, handling exceptions, and adapting smart contracts for different industries

(Continued)

TABLE 14.3 (Continued)

Case Studies on Blockchain and Decentralized Technology Applications

Source	Case Study	Technology	Outcomes	Challenges
Huh and Kim (2020)	Real Estate	Blockchain smart contracts, AI-based blockchain, ElGamal encryption, quantum cryptography, hyperledger, Practical Byzantine Fault Tolerance	Secure handling of down payments, reduced need for real estate agents, enhanced verification processes with 4,000 transactions per second performance in tests	Managing complex encryption algorithms, ensuring cross-platform cryptographic consistency, high computational requirements for nodes
Quy et al. (2023)	Healthcare	NFTs, blockchain (Ethereum Virtual Machine-compatible platforms), smart contracts	Medical document sets with privacy; transaction costs varied across platforms: Build and Build (BNB) (originally Binance Coin), BNB smart chain ($8.43 for creation), Fantom ($0.001849), Polygon ($0.01), Celo ($0.004)	Addressing dynamic transaction costs, managing platform-specific constraints, and ensuring secure data privacy
Brennecke et al. (2022)	MakerDAO in Decentralized Finance (DeFi)	Blockchain, DAO, Stablecoin (Dai), Governance Token (MKR) Smart contracts, DAO, Dai, multi-asset collateralization, partial decentralization	Implemented a stable cryptocurrency with multi-asset collateralization, maintaining 1:1 USD stability, achieving lower volatility, and significant DeFi adoption. Implemented a stable cryptocurrency with multi-asset collateralization and lower volatility, positioned as a potential future alternative to the gold exchange standard	Challenges in stability, governance, collateral diversification, adoption, regulation, and market adaptation

(Continued)

TABLE 14.3 (Continued)

Case Studies on Blockchain and Decentralized Technology Applications

Source	Case Study	Technology	Outcomes	Challenges
Chen et al. (2024)	Information Technology (IT)	Blockchain, DAO, and NFT	Enhanced DAO governance security, reducing manipulation risks by 51%, while motivating high-quality, unique e-document creation through an optimized incentive mechanism	Addressed centralized vulnerabilities, improved plagiarism detection, balanced whale voting*, ensured scalability across platforms Securing the system, improving plagiarism detection, and optimizing DAO governance to prevent manipulation
Ferreira et al. (2024)	Information Technology (IT)	Hyperledger Fabric with smart contracts	20% faster transactions, 100% traceability, 30% time, and 15% cost reduction via smart contracts	Blockchain complexity, immaturity, IT infrastructure needs, staff training, payment integration limitations
Muthe et al. (2020)	Gaming	Ethereum, IPFS, ERC-1155, smart contracts	Enhanced gaming network reliability and reduced latency through decentralized proxy computation	Scalability and security issues with Ethereum 1.0 and solidity, requiring large proxy node networks
Andronache and Aciobănitei (2024)	Fitness: Mobile health application with cryptocurrency	Blockchain technology and cryptocurrency (DAnkeCoin)	Increased physical activity levels and positive user feedback on usability and rewards	Technical complexities in integrating blockchain with health data tracking and ensuring sustained user engagement

* Whale voting refers to a situation in blockchain governance systems – especially in decentralized autonomous organizations (DAOs) – where large token holders (a.k.a. "whales") can disproportionately influence or control voting outcomes.

and integration with existing systems persist. In **supply chain management**, blockchain enhances the traceability and transparency of products like organic cotton, fostering greater trust among stakeholders, but faces complexities in maintaining data privacy and regulatory compliance. The **energy sector** benefits from blockchain-enabled transactive energy systems that improve grid management and security, though issues like cybersecurity threats, including DoS attacks, require attention. In **manufacturing**, blockchain and smart contracts facilitate transparency and automated verification processes, though integrating these technologies with existing infrastructure remains challenging. **Construction** sees improved payment transparency and reduced delays through the integration of BIM with blockchain-based smart contracts, yet faces high initial costs and legal compliance issues. In **healthcare**, blockchain secures medical records and enhances data integrity, with smart contracts reducing execution time by 14%, though economic viability and regulatory compliance pose significant challenges. **Agriculture** uses blockchain and NFTs for enhanced traceability, but high Ethereum gas fees and integration with supply chains are major concerns. **Real estate** transactions benefit from blockchain security enhanced with artificial intelligence (AI), achieving high transaction speeds, though managing complex encryption algorithms remains a challenge.

Crypto-enabled fitness apps like DAnke incentivize user engagement and healthier lifestyles by integrating blockchain rewards systems, driving both health improvements and user retention in the business. These case studies illustrate that while Web 3.0 technologies offer substantial improvements in efficiency, transparency, and security across sectors, overcoming integration, regulatory, and technical challenges is essential for their widespread adoption. By analyzing the lessons learned and best practices from these case studies, we can derive valuable insights into the mechanics of how crypto technologies enable these solutions, as well as the measurable outcomes they produce.

Performance Improvements and Financial Outcomes: One of the most compelling outcomes observed across multiple case studies is the significant improvement in transaction efficiency and cost reduction. For instance, the healthcare sector's adoption of blockchain and smart contracts led to a 22% faster hash function and a 14% reduction in smart contract execution time, as shown in the study by Mendoza Arvizo et al. (2023). Similarly, the integration of Hyperledger Fabric in a real-life additive symbiotic network (Ferreira et al., 2024) resulted in 20% faster transactions, alongside a 30% reduction in time and a 15% reduction in costs. These metrics underscore the efficiency gains that blockchain-based solutions can deliver, particularly in environments where transaction speed and cost-effectiveness are critical. In the financial sector, Brennecke et al. (2022) demonstrated how MakerDAO, a DeFi platform, successfully maintained the stability of its Dai stablecoin at a 1:1 ratio with the US dollar through over-collateralization strategies. This achievement highlights the role of DAOs and smart contracts in creating resilient financial instruments that can operate with reduced volatility. The emphasis on collateralization rates above 150% in MakerDAO's governance model illustrates the importance of robust risk management frameworks in maintaining stability within decentralized financial ecosystems.

User Engagement and Trust: The case studies also reveal how blockchain and smart contracts enhance user engagement and trust, particularly in industries where transparency and data integrity are paramount. Agrawal et al. (2021) showed that blockchain and smart contracts significantly improved traceability and transparency in the supply chain management of organic cotton, fostering greater trust among supply chain partners. This increase in transparency is a direct result of blockchain's immutable ledger, which ensures that all participants have access to accurate and unalterable records of transactions. In the real estate sector, Huh and Kim (2020) demonstrated how blockchain smart contracts, combined with advanced encryption techniques, achieved transaction speeds of up to 4,000 transactions per second across 250 nodes, while simultaneously enhancing security and transparency. This case underscores the potential for blockchain to not only streamline complex transaction processes but also to build trust among stakeholders by ensuring data security and consistency across platforms.

Mechanics of Crypto-Enabled Solutions: The integration of blockchain, smart contracts, and NFTs into various systems has been shown to address specific pain points and enhance operational efficiency. For example, Wang et al. (2024) utilized blockchain, NFTs, and the InterPlanetary File System (IPFS) in agriculture to enhance the traceability of cotton lint. The use of NFTs for process validation, combined with IPFS for secure data storage, showcases how these technologies can work together to create a transparent and verifiable supply chain.

Another notable example is the decentralized framework for e-document sharing proposed by Chen et al. (2024). By leveraging DAOs and NFTs within a blockchain-based system, the framework achieved a 51% reduction in manipulation risks and ensured robust copyright protection.

This case highlights how decentralized governance and tokenization can be used to safeguard digital assets and promote fair practices in digital content management. While the benefits of blockchain and related technologies are evident, the case studies also highlight several challenges that must be addressed to achieve widespread adoption. For instance, the complexity of integrating blockchain with existing systems, as noted in the energy sector (Gourisetti et al., 2021) and supply chain management (Agrawal et al., 2021), presents significant barriers. The best practices to overcome these challenges include adopting standardized protocols and ensuring interoperability between blockchain networks and legacy systems. Moreover, the high resource consumption and privacy concerns associated with blockchain, as seen in the supply chain finance sector (Zheng et al., 2022), necessitate ongoing research into more energy-efficient consensus mechanisms and privacy-preserving technologies like ZKPs. By focusing on these areas, future implementations can mitigate the environmental impact of blockchain and protect user data from unauthorized access. The case studies analyzed demonstrate that blockchain, smart contracts, DAOs, and NFTs offer powerful tools for improving efficiency, transparency, and trust across a wide range of industries. The lessons learned from these implementations highlight the need for careful planning and the adoption of best practices, such as ensuring interoperability, standardizing protocols, and addressing privacy and security concerns.

14.6 Adoption Trends in Enterprises

Enterprises are navigating a transformative landscape as they embrace decentralized technologies and integrate cryptocurrencies into their operations. This strategic shift reflects a convergence of market forces, technological advancements, and evolving consumer preferences across various industries. A nuanced analysis of adoption trends reveals both convergent and divergent viewpoints, highlighting the multifaceted nature of enterprise responses to decentralized platform integration. Across sectors such as healthcare, education, and supply chain management, there is a convergence of adoption trends driven by common imperatives, including the pursuit of decentralization, transparency, and efficiency. For instance, in healthcare, the decentralization of patient records through blockchain technology offers secure and interoperable data management, aligning with the industry's imperative for data privacy and accessibility (Kuo et al., 2017). Similarly, in education, blockchain-based solutions for credential verification converge with the need for trustworthy and streamlined credentialing systems (Li et al., 2022). These convergent adoption trends underscore the universal appeal of decentralized technologies in addressing industry-specific challenges and opportunities.

However, divergent viewpoints emerge when examining adoption trends in industries such as finance, real estate, and e-commerce. While some enterprises embrace DeFi for banking services and tokenization of real estate assets, others remain cautious due to regulatory uncertainties and security concerns (Barde, 2023; Joshi & Choudhury, 2022). Similarly, e-commerce enterprises exhibit varying degrees of readiness to adopt cryptocurrency payments, with concerns over price volatility and integration complexities (Lai et al., 2023). These divergent perspectives underscore the heterogeneous nature of enterprise responses to decentralized platform integration, shaped by industry-specific dynamics, regulatory environments, and risk appetites.

To navigate these divergent adoption trends effectively, enterprises must adopt a nuanced approach that balances risk and innovation. Future research should explore the factors influencing divergent adoption trajectories, including regulatory landscapes, technological maturity, and organizational readiness. By identifying common challenges and best practices across industries, researchers can offer valuable insights to enterprises seeking to navigate the complexities of Web 3.0 adoption.

14.7 Challenges and Limitations

Despite the transformative potential of Web 3.0 and cryptocurrency integration, enterprises face a myriad of challenges and limitations in their adoption journey. Regulatory hurdles emerge as a common challenge across industries, with evolving regulatory frameworks posing uncertainty and compliance burdens (Chuen & Deng, 2017). Moreover, scalability issues inherent in blockchain technology hinder the seamless integration of decentralized solutions into enterprise workflows, particularly in high-volume industries such as finance and supply chain management (Chang et al., 2022). Interoperability concerns further compound adoption challenges, as enterprises grapple with integrating decentralized systems with existing infrastructure and legacy systems. Achieving interoperability requires standardized protocols, cross-industry collaboration, and technological innovation (Treiblmaier et al., 2021). In addition, security remains a paramount concern, with enterprises facing threats from cyberattacks, data breaches, and vulnerabilities inherent in decentralized architectures (Ghosh et al., 2023).

To address these challenges effectively, future research should explore holistic solutions that encompass regulatory frameworks, technological innovations, and organizational strategies. By examining successful case studies and identifying common pitfalls, researchers can offer actionable insights to enterprises seeking to navigate the complexities of Web 3.0 adoption.

14.8 Implications

14.8.1 Ethical Implications

14.8.1.1 Data Privacy and Individual Tracking

Web 3.0 technologies, particularly blockchain, offer unprecedented transparency and immutability, which raise ethical concerns regarding data privacy and the potential misuse of individuals' data. The transparent nature of blockchain could lead to scenarios where sensitive information is permanently recorded and accessible, posing risks to privacy. To address these concerns, it is essential to explore the implementation of privacy-preserving technologies like ZKPs and confidential transactions. These methods can help ensure that individuals' data is protected while still maintaining the transparency and security that blockchain offers. Ethical guidelines must also be developed to govern how data is collected, stored, and shared, ensuring that users' rights to privacy are respected.

14.8.1.2 Decentralized Finance and Global Financial Stability

The rise of DeFi offers significant opportunities for financial inclusion and innovation but also presents risks to global financial stability. The lack of centralized oversight in DeFi systems can lead to market manipulation, fraud, and systemic risks that could affect global economies. An ethical approach to DeFi must include the development of governance frameworks that incorporate checks and balances to prevent abuse and ensure financial stability. In addition, it is crucial to consider the ethical implications of financial inclusion efforts, ensuring that these technologies do not exploit vulnerable populations or exacerbate existing inequalities.

14.8.2 Legal Implications

14.8.2.1 Smart Contracts and Legal Frameworks

Smart contracts, which are self-executing contracts with the terms directly written into code, present challenges for existing legal frameworks. The legal enforceability of smart contracts is still a grey area, particularly when it comes to issues such as jurisdiction, contract law, and dispute resolution. Moreover, the possibility of a backlash against decentralization could emerge as platforms grow larger and more influential, potentially leading to new forms of centralized control. To navigate these challenges, it is essential to explore how existing legal concepts can be adapted to smart contracts and to propose new legal frameworks that address the unique characteristics of these technologies.

14.8.2.2 Regulatory Challenges

The regulatory landscape for Web 3.0 technologies is still evolving, with many jurisdictions struggling to keep pace with the rapid development of these technologies. There is a need for new regulations that address the specific challenges posed by Web 3.0, including data protection, financial transactions, and intellectual property rights. Proposing legal frameworks that draw from existing regulations in similar technologies can help provide a foundation for regulating Web 3.0. In addition, research should focus on the potential unintended consequences of these regulations, such as the possibility of stifling innovation or creating new forms of inequality.

14.9 Future Research Directions

The future of DeFi and token economies is both promising and complex, characterized by opportunities for innovation and significant challenges. As DeFi platforms grow, they are expected to democratize financial services globally, enabling wealth creation and participation in previously inaccessible markets. However, regulatory uncertainties and technical challenges, such as scalability and security, pose threats to their sustainable adoption. Similarly, the advancement of token economies – driven by blockchain technology – offers transformative potential in value exchange and asset ownership but faces hurdles in regulatory compliance and user comprehension. To fully realize the potential of DeFi and tokenized ecosystems, ongoing research and collaboration are critical.

Building on the current understanding of decentralized platforms and their integration across industries, the following are specific areas where future research can advance the field.

14.9.1 Enhancing Interoperability and Standardization

Research Question: How can interoperability be enhanced across diverse blockchain networks in industries such as healthcare, supply chain management, and real estate without compromising on data integrity and security?

Direction: The industry currently faces challenges with fragmented blockchain systems that struggle to communicate with each other. Future research should focus on developing cross-chain communication protocols, such as Polkadot's interoperability framework, and standardized smart contract interfaces, as seen in the Ethereum Request for Comment-20[1] token standard. Empirical research should involve creating simulation environments where different blockchain networks interact, followed by stress-testing these environments to identify weaknesses in data exchange and standardization efforts. This can lead to more robust frameworks that facilitate seamless data interoperability across platforms, thus promoting wider adoption across industries.

14.9.2 Addressing Regulatory Challenges

Research Question: What regulatory frameworks can be developed to support innovation in decentralized ecosystems while ensuring compliance, particularly in data protection and financial transactions?

Direction: As decentralized technologies become more pervasive, their regulatory oversight becomes crucial. Research should investigate the development of adaptive regulatory sandboxes, like those employed by the UK Financial Conduct Authority, to test new blockchain applications under controlled conditions. Comparative studies of regulatory approaches across jurisdictions, such as the European Union's General Data Protection Regulation (GDPR) versus the U.S. regulatory landscape, can provide insights into how different models impact innovation. In addition, research should explore the creation of automated compliance mechanisms using smart contracts that can dynamically adjust to regulatory changes, ensuring that decentralized platforms remain compliant as regulations evolve.

14.9.3 Exploring Scalability Solutions

Research Question: How to enhance the throughput and latency of blockchain networks, particularly in high-transaction environments like finance and supply chain management?

Direction: Scalability remains a significant bottleneck for blockchain adoption. Research should focus on the practical implementation and testing of layer-2 solutions, such as Optimistic Rollups and zk-Rollups, which have shown promise in increasing transaction throughput on networks like Ethereum. In addition, evaluating the effectiveness of sharding techniques, as proposed in Ethereum 2.0, through empirical studies in real-world deployments will be crucial. Future studies could involve deploying these solutions in pilot projects with financial institutions or supply chain networks, assessing their performance under varying transaction loads to determine their viability at scale.

14.9.4 Advancing Privacy and Security

Research Question: How can privacy-preserving technologies such as ZKPs and multiparty computation (MPC) be optimized for specific use cases in DeFi and blockchain applications?

Direction: As the use of blockchain technology expands, so does the need for robust privacy solutions. Research should explore the practical applications of ZKPs in financial transactions, such as implementing "Zero-knowledge succinct non-interactive argument of knowledge" (zk-SNARKs) in decentralized exchanges (DEXs) to ensure transaction confidentiality. In addition, the integration of MPC in identity verification processes within dApps can enhance user privacy without sacrificing usability. Future research should focus on optimizing these cryptographic protocols for performance, reducing their computational overhead, and making them more accessible for widespread deployment in real-world scenarios. Case studies on platforms like Zcash and their use of ZKPs can provide valuable insights into the practical challenges and solutions in this area.

14.9.5 Integration of AI with Web 3.0

Research Question: How can AI be effectively integrated with Web 3.0 technologies to enhance dApps' decision-making capabilities?

Direction: The convergence of AI and Web 3.0 offers new opportunities but also introduces complex challenges. Research should focus on developing AI algorithms tailored for decentralized environments, such as Federated Learning models that allow AI to function without centralized data collection, thereby preserving user privacy. In addition, exploring the use of AI in smart contract execution – where AI models predict and prevent contract breaches or fraud – can significantly enhance the security and efficiency of decentralized platforms. Future studies could involve collaborative projects that integrate AI models with blockchain-based applications in sectors like finance or healthcare, evaluating their effectiveness in real-world conditions.

14.9.6 Examining Social and Economic Impacts

Research Question: What are the long-term socioeconomic impacts of widespread adoption of DeFi and Web 3.0 technologies, particularly in terms of financial inclusion, wealth distribution, and digital rights?

Direction: The adoption of Web 3.0 technologies has far-reaching social and economic implications. Research should conduct longitudinal studies to examine how decentralized platforms impact income inequality, access to financial services, and community empowerment. For example, studies could analyze the effects of decentralized lending platforms on financial inclusion in underserved communities, using real-world data from platforms like Aave or Compound. In addition, research could explore the implications of decentralized governance models on digital rights and privacy, providing a framework for balancing innovation with social equity. By examining these factors, researchers can inform policy interventions that maximize the positive societal outcomes of decentralized platform adoption.

14.10 Framework for Handling Ethical Concerns in Web 3.0

In the context of Web 3.0, addressing ethical concerns requires a comprehensive and technically robust framework that integrates various decentralized technologies such as smart contracts and distributed ledger technologies. The proposed ethical framework for Web 3.0 technologies is designed to ensure that ethical considerations are embedded throughout the lifecycle of technological development and deployment (Figure 14.3). The process begins with Ethical Planning and Identification, where advanced threat modeling and stakeholder analysis are employed to systematically identify potential ethical

Cryptocurrency Integration in the Web 3.0 Ecosystem 325

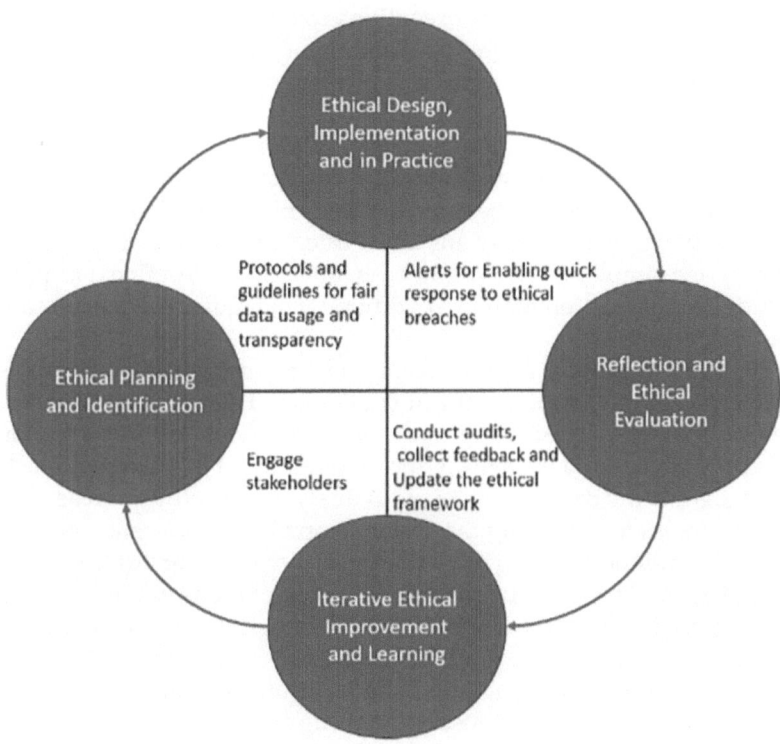

FIGURE 14.3
Ethical management framework for Web 3.0 (Illustration by the Authors)

challenges unique to Web 3.0. This might involve assessing risks related to data privacy in dApps and ensuring compliance with relevant regulations like GDPR, which are crucial for protecting user rights in a decentralized environment. Following this, Ethical Design and Implementation focuses on embedding these identified ethical principles directly into the system architecture. For example, smart contracts can be designed to enforce fairness in transactions within DeFi platforms, preventing exploitative fees or practices. In addition, decentralized governance mechanisms, such as DAOs, are implemented to give community members a voice in decision-making processes, ensuring that governance remains transparent and inclusive. Privacy-enhancing technologies like zk-SNARKs also incorporated to protect user data, ensuring that privacy is upheld as a fundamental aspect of the system. Once these systems are operational, ethics in practice and real-time monitoring becomes essential. This stage involves the continuous oversight of the system's ethical performance through real-time monitoring tools and blockchain audit capabilities. For instance, using blockchain explorers and security audit tools like Certik or Quantstamp, stakeholders can track transactions and smart contract executions to ensure they adhere to established ethical standards. This helps in the timely detection and rectification of any ethical breaches, such as unfair resource distribution or biased algorithmic decisions.

The next phase, Reflection and Ethical Evaluation, critically assesses the effectiveness of the implemented ethical measures. This involves reviewing whether the privacy and fairness measures in place are adequately protecting users and whether there are any new ethical dilemmas or gaps that have emerged. For example, a dApp might be evaluated to determine if its privacy protections are robust enough or if additional safeguards are necessary to prevent data leaks.

Finally, Iterative Ethical Improvement and Learning ensures that the system remains adaptive to new ethical challenges. This stage involves using upgradeable smart contracts and machine learning models to continuously refine and enhance the system's ethical standards. For example, machine learning algorithms can be employed to analyze past ethical breaches and predict future issues, allowing the system to evolve proactively. Continuous integration/continuous deployment pipelines that incorporate ethical checks at every stage of development ensure that new iterations of the system consistently uphold these ethical standards. By integrating these stages into a cyclical process, the proposed framework ensures that Web 3.0 technologies are not only ethically sound at launch but continue to adapt and respond to emerging ethical challenges, thus maintaining trust and integrity in decentralized systems.

14.11 Conclusion

The integration of cryptocurrency within the Web 3.0 ecosystem represents a profound shift in how financial transactions and digital interactions are conducted. This exploration has highlighted the transformative potential of blockchain technology and dApps in creating a more secure, efficient, and inclusive financial landscape. Throughout this chapter, we have examined the critical elements that define Web 3.0, including decentralization, tokenization, and the role of cryptocurrencies in fostering innovation across various sectors. Real-world case studies have been analyzed to critically evaluate the tangible benefits of Web 3.0 technologies in enhancing transparency, security, and efficiency across industries such as supply chain management, healthcare, real estate, and more. These examples underscore the practical advantages of adopting blockchain and DeFi solutions, offering significant improvements over traditional systems in terms of cost reduction, process automation, and enhanced user trust.

However, the journey toward fully realizing the potential of Web 3.0 is fraught with challenges. Regulatory uncertainties, scalability issues, and the complexities of integrating decentralized systems with existing infrastructures remain significant barriers. As these technologies continue to evolve, it is essential that stakeholders across industries collaborate to address these challenges. The development of robust regulatory frameworks, advancements in privacy-preserving technologies, and the enhancement of interoperability across blockchain networks are critical areas requiring ongoing research and innovation.

Looking ahead, the future of Web 3.0 will be shaped by how effectively these challenges are addressed. The potential for decentralized platforms to democratize access to financial services, enhance data security, and create new economic opportunities is immense. However, achieving these outcomes will require a concerted effort from policymakers, industry leaders, and researchers to ensure that the benefits of Web 3.0 are realized while mitigating the risks.

As we conclude this exploration, it is clear that Web 3.0 and cryptocurrency integration hold the promise of a more transparent, equitable, and innovative digital economy. The insights gained from this chapter provide a foundation for future research and implementation strategies that can guide the continued development of decentralized technologies, ensuring their success in reshaping the global financial landscape.

Note

1. ERC-20 is a technical standard used for creating and issuing fungible tokens on the Ethereum blockchain.

References

Agrawal, T. K., Kumar, V., Pal, R., Wang, L., & Chen, Y. (2021). Blockchain-based framework for supply chain traceability: A case example of textile and clothing industry. *Computers & Industrial Engineering, 154*, 107130.

Alkhuary, R., Brusset, X., & Fenies, P. (2020). Blockchain in general management and economics: A systematic literature review. *European Business Review. 32*(4), 765–783.

Andronache, G., & Aciobănitei, L. (2024, May). DAnke-An application for promoting a healthy lifestyle using gamification and blockchain. In *2024 IEEE 18th International Symposium on Applied Computational Intelligence and Informatics (SACI)* (pp. 000365–000370). IEEE.

Angrish, A., Craver, B., Hasan, M., & Starly, B. (2018). A case study for Blockchain in manufacturing:"FabRec": A prototype for peer-to-peer network of manufacturing nodes. *Procedia Manufacturing*, 26, 1180–1192.

Bai, Y., Lei, H., Li, S., Gao, H., Li, J., & Li, L. (2022, August). Decentralized and self-sovereign identity in the era of blockchain: A survey. In *2022 IEEE International Conference on Blockchain (Blockchain)* (pp. 500–507). IEEE.

Barassi, V., & Treré, E. (2012). Does Web 3.0 come after Web 2.0? Deconstructing theoretical assumptions through practice. *New Media & Society*, 14(8), 1269–1285.

Barde, K. (2023). Transforming the FinTech Landscape: The Web 3.0 Revolution and its Implications. *SSRG International Journal of Computer Science and Engineering*, 10(11), 36–42.

Bashir, I. (2020). *Mastering Blockchain: A Deep Dive into Distributed Ledgers, Consensus Protocols, Smart Contracts, DApps, Cryptocurrencies, Ethereum, and More*. Packt Publishing Ltd.

Bergquist Mcneil, L. (2022). Blockchains, smart contracts, and stablecoins as a global payment system: The rise of web 3.0. https://www.diva-portal.org/smash/get/diva2:1671071/FULLTEXT01.pdf

Bernard, T. S., Hsu, T., Perlroth, N., & Lieber, R. (2017, September 7). Equifax says cyberattack may have affected 143 million in the U.S. *The New York Times*. https://www.nytimes.com/2017/09/07/business/equifax-cyberattack.html

Brennecke, M., Guggenberger, T., Schellinger, B., & Urbach, N. (2022). The de-central bank in decentralized finance: A case study of MakerDAO. *Proceedings of the 55th Hawaii International Conference on System Sciences*.

Chang, A., El-Rayes, N., & Shi, J. (2022). Blockchain technology for supply chain management: A comprehensive review. *FinTech*, 1(2), 191–205.

Chen, C., Zhang, L., Li, Y., Liao, T., Zhao, S., Zheng, Z., ... & Wu, J. (2022). When digital economy meets web3. 0: Applications and challenges. *IEEE Open Journal of the Computer Society*, 3, 233–245.

Chen, L., Zhu, J., Xu, Y., Zheng, H., & Su, S. (2024). A framework based on the DAO and NFT in blockchain for electronic document sharing. *CMES-Computer Modeling in Engineering & Sciences*, 140(3).

Chuen, D. L. K., & Deng, R. H. (2017). *Handbook of Blockchain, Digital Finance, and Inclusion: Cryptocurrency, Fintech, Insurtech, Regulation, Chinatech, Mobile Security, and Distributed Ledger*. Academic Press.

Debe, M., Salah, K., Rehman, M. H. U., & Svetinovic, D. (2019). IoT public fog nodes reputation system: A decentralized solution using Ethereum blockchain. *IEEE Access*, 7, 178082–178093.

Ferreira, I. A., Palazzo, G., Pinto, A., Pinto, P., Sousa, P., Godina, R., & Carvalho, H. (2024). A blockchain architecture with smart contracts for an additive symbiotic network-a case study. *Operations Management Research*, 1–17.

Ghosh, P. K., Chakraborty, A., Hasan, M., Rashid, K., & Siddique, A. H. (2023). Blockchain application in healthcare systems: A review. *Systems*, 11(1), 38.

Godage, R. D. (2023). Marriott international data breach 2018. https://www.researchgate.net/publication/372524901_Marriott_International_Data_Breach

Gourisetti, S. N. G., Cali, Ü., Choo, K. K. R., Escobar, E., Gorog, C., Lee, A., ... & Sani, A. S. (2021). Standardization of the distributed ledger technology cybersecurity stack for power and energy applications. *Sustainable Energy, Grids and Networks*, 28, 100553.

Hooks IV, J. B. (2019). The mesh economy: How blockchain and alternative networks can bridge the digital divide and facilitate economic inclusion. *Blockchain Economics: Implications of Distributed Ledgers-Markets, Communications Networks, and Algorithmic Reality, 1*, 251.

Huh, J. H., & Kim, S. K. (2020). Verification plan using neural algorithm blockchain smart contract for secure P2P real estate transactions. *Electronics, 9*(6), 1052.

Joshi, S., & Choudhury, A. (2022). Tokenization of real estate assets using blockchain. *International Journal of Intelligent Information Technologies (IJIIT), 18*(3), 1–12.

Kuo, T. T., Kim, H. E., & Ohno-Machado, L. (2017). Blockchain distributed ledger technologies for biomedical and health care applications. *Journal of the American Medical Informatics Association, 24*(6), 1211–1220.

Lacity, M. C., & Lupien, S. C. (2022). *Blockchain Fundamentals for Web 3.0*. University of Arkansas Press.

Lai, Y., Yang, J., Liu, M., Li, Y., & Li, S. (2023). Web3: Exploring decentralized technologies and applications for the future of empowerment and ownership. *Blockchains, 1*(2), 111–131.

Lee, J. Y. (2019). A decentralized token economy: How blockchain and cryptocurrency can revolutionize business. *Business Horizons, 62*(6), 773–784.

Li, Z. Z., Joseph, K. L., Yu, J., & Gasevic, D. (2022, August). Blockchain-based solutions for education credentialing system: Comparison and implications for future development. In *2022 IEEE International Conference on Blockchain (Blockchain)* (pp. 79–86). IEEE.

Lundberg, L., & Petrén, M. (2022). *DApp revolution: An investigation into the nature and business models of web 3.0 decentralized applications* (Master's thesis). Chalmers University of Technology. https://odr.chalmers.se/server/api/core/bitstreams/7674c621-d0f4-42da-8322-9b202229bb94/content

Marbouh, D., Abbasi, T., Maasmi, F., Omar, I. A., Debe, M. S., Salah, K., ... & Ellahham, S. (2020). Blockchain for COVID-19: Review, opportunities, and a trusted tracking system. *Arabian Journal for Science and Engineering, 45*, 9895–9911.

Mendoza Arvizo, A. I., Avelar Sosa, L., García Alcaraz, J. L., & Cruz-Mejía, O. (2023). Beneficiary contracts on a lightweight blockchain architecture using smart contracts: A smart healthcare system for medical records. *Applied Sciences, 13*(11), 6694.

Mougayar, W. (2016). *The Business Blockchain: Promise, Practice, and Application of the Next Internet Technology*. John Wiley & Sons.

Muthe, K. B., Sharma, K., & Sri, K. E. N. (2020, November). A blockchain based decentralized computing and NFT infrastructure for game networks. In *2020 Second International Conference on Blockchain Computing and Applications (BCCA)* (pp. 73–77). IEEE.

Nasar, M. (2023). Web 3.0: A review and its future. *International Journal of Computer Applications, 185*(10), 41–46.

Nica, O., Piotrowska, K., & Schenk-Hoppé, K. R. (2017). Cryptocurrencies: Economic benefits and risks. *University of Manchester, FinTech Working Paper*, (2).

Nita, S. L., & Mihailescu, M. I. (2024). A novel authentication scheme based on verifiable credentials using digital identity in the context of web 3.0. *Electronics, 13*(6), 1137.

Omar, I. A., Jayaraman, R., Debe, M. S., Salah, K., Yaqoob, I., & Omar, M. (2021). Automating procurement contracts in the healthcare supply chain using blockchain smart contracts. *IEEE Access, 9*, 37397–37409.

Palmer, A., & Novet, J. (2020, October 6). Amazon bullies partners and vendors, says antitrust subcommittee. *CNBC*. https://www.cnbc.com/2020/10/06/amazon-bullies-partners-and-vendors-says-antitrust-subcommittee.html

Petcu, A., Pahontu, B., Frunzete, M., & Stoichescu, D. A. (2023). A secure and decentralized authentication mechanism based on Web 3.0 and Ethereum blockchain technology. *Applied Sciences, 13*(4), 2231.

Quy, T. L., Khanh, H. V., Huong, H. L., Khiem, H. G., Phuc, T. N., Ngan, N. T., . . . & Khoa, D. T. (2023). Decentralized management of medical test results utilizing blockchain, smart contracts, and NFTs. *International Journal of Advanced Computer Science and Applications, 14*(8).

Ragnedda, M., & Destefanis, G. (2019). *Blockchain and Web 3.0* (Vol. 11). London: Routledge, Taylor and Francis Group.

Santana, C., & Albareda, L. (2022). Blockchain and the emergence of Decentralized Autonomous Organizations (DAOs): An integrative model and research agenda. *Technological Forecasting and Social Change, 182*, 121806.

Series, O. B. P. (2020). The tokenisation of assets and potential implications for financial markets. *The Secretary General of the OECD, 107*.

Sigalov, K., Ye, X., König, M., Hagedorn, P., Blum, F., Severin, B., . . . & Groß, D. (2021). Automated payment and contract management in the construction industry by integrating building information modeling and blockchain-based smart contracts. *Applied Sciences, 11*(16), 7653.

Srokosz, W., & Kopciaski, T. (2015). Legal and economic analysis of the cryptocurrencies impact on the financial system stability. *Journal of Teaching and Education, 4*(2), 619–627.

Treiblmaier, H., Leung, D., Kwok, A. O., & Tham, A. (2021). Cryptocurrency adoption in travel and tourism–an exploratory study of Asia Pacific travellers. *Current Issues in Tourism, 24*(22), 3165–3181.

Turi, A. N. (2020). *Technologies for Modern Digital Entrepreneurship*. Berkley: Apress.

Uchani Gutierrez, O. C., & Xu, G. (2022). Blockchain and smart contracts to secure property transactions in smart cities. *Applied Sciences, 13*(1), 66.

ur Rehman, I. (2019). Facebook-Cambridge Analytica data harvesting: What you need to know. *Library Philosophy and Practice*, 1–11.

Wang, L., Sun, W., Zhao, J., Zhang, X., Lu, C., & Luo, H. (2024). A non-fungible token and blockchain-based cotton lint traceability solution. *Applied Sciences, 14*(4), 1610.

Yerram, S. R. (2022). Smart contracts for efficient supplier relationship management in the blockchain. *American Journal of Trade and Policy, 9*(3), 119–130.

Zheng, K., Zheng, L. J., Gauthier, J., Zhou, L., Xu, Y., Behl, A., & Zhang, J. Z. (2022). Blockchain technology for enterprise credit information sharing in supply chain finance. *Journal of Innovation & Knowledge, 7*(4), 100256.

15

Cryptocurrency Regulations in India: Opportunities and Challenges

Maneesh Yadav and Gurudev Sahil

15.1 Introduction

In the era of the global financial meltdown in 2008, Bitcoin came into the picture of the economic network describing the payment system and peer-to-peer transfer based on blockchain technology and verification of cryptography. The published white paper on Bitcoin has given birth to the concept of digital currency. The notion of the no boundaries and delimitation of the national regulatory environment in virtual currencies has acquired futuristic momentum in adopting the currency. The currencies' database and transactions have been stored concurrently in different jurisdictions. Internationally, regulators have adopted various mechanisms to regulate the virtual currencies in their jurisdiction with approvals and rejections. Indian regulators denied the virtual currency in the initial phase; however, later, it was allowed with no legal recognition as a currency. The most significant apprehension is the siphoning of funds from one boundary to another without any regulation or disclosure. This is reflected in the approach that few countries have accepted as a currency, and certain have denied it. The evolution of digital currency can be traced back to the article by David Chaum (Chaum, 1982, 1983).

The term used for digital currency is "cryptocurrency," and it is globally recognized for transactions. The virtual currencies are also labeled as "forex," "digital coins," "virtual forex," "digital forex," or "cryptocurrency." The primary genesis of the creation of crypto is the facilitation of trade by the third party to the buyer and the seller on the digital platform. The first testing of virtual currency failed in 1999, which was started in 1990, and it was called "DigiCash" (Trautman & Harrell, 2017). In 1996, multiplayer online games initiated a conceptual virtual world of assets, trade, and production similar to a real-life economy (Trautman, 2018). The creator(s) of "Bitcoin," namely Satoshi Nakamoto (pseudonym), released the Bitcoin white paper on October

31, 2008, "A P2P Electronic Cash System," and harbingered the concept of cryptocurrency, thus forwarding an entente with digital cash and with no central controlling authority based on a peer-to-peer network system in the year 2008. Interestingly, the first Bitcoin was used to purchase pizza from a well-known brand, Papa John's. The Bitcoin software was also released in 2009 (Tandel & Mestry, 2018).

The industry expansion of digital currency has been increasing tremendously recently due to lucrative investment opportunities for investors with high-risk aversion. It increased the number of cryptocurrencies available in the market, i.e., more than 20,000 currencies. The idea is based on creating different hashes by using encryption algorithms. With the help of the verified internet network and connected users, it can be exchanged like physical currency. It facilitates hassle-free trade in the country and on the international level. Interestingly, the UN Conference on Trade and Development Report 2021 tabled the data on the percentage of Indians owning/holding cryptocurrency, which was more than seven. The data shows that market capitalization reached 1 trillion dollars in January 2023.

15.2 Terminology of "Cryptocurrency" Elucidated

The monetary system and its regulations strengthen the country's economic structure and social stability. The country's key functional area is defining the rules and maintaining the economic ecosystem's viability. Every country has a designated central bank to monitor and control the currency transactions in the country (Dahlberg et al., 2019). The world governments are regulating virtual currency with a cautious mindset based on local laws and socio-legal perceptions. There are debates about the future of digital currency and its regulation within the changing environment (Shubber, 2015). In digital currency, the ledger is the blockchain on which cryptocurrencies are recorded, and these blockchains are on the public platform. The blockchain is the complete record of the assets in the virtual space, such as ownership and transfer of the records, along with a private key. The transfer of the virtual asset from one individual to another is only possible with the private key when it matches with the blockchain in the public domain. After the match with the public blockchain, it will be recorded on the blockchain with no reversal mechanism. The mechanism is to avoid multiple transactions and duplicates of the trade (Chu, 2018). It can also be treated as a virtual accounting system where the blockchain safely keeps buying and selling records. The cryptocurrency has no intrinsic value to determine the value of the underlying asset (Jeffrey, 2017).

Cryptocurrencies, as a digital medium of value exchange that relies on decentralized blockchain technology, offer increasing business opportunities in creating network-based trust-enabling environments and have experienced an increase in market value from zero to more than $1 trillion. Cryptocurrency uses cryptography to validate transactions on the public blockchain. Various esteemed institutions have, in their own way, tried to define virtual currencies. The European Commission presently offers an operating definition of digital forex as follows:

> [It is] a virtual illustration of price this is neither issued via way of means of a vital financial institution or a public authority nor always connected to fiat forex, however, is widespread via way of implies of herbal or criminal humans as a method of charge and may be transferred, saved or traded electronically.
>
> *European Commission*

Likewise, the IRS (internal revenue service, hereinafter referred to as IRS) department of the United States is also defined as:

> A digital asset is a digital representation of value recorded on a cryptographically secured distributed ledger or similar technology. If a particular asset has characteristics of a digital asset, it's treated as one for federal income tax purposes.

In a few regulatory setups of sovereignties, digital assets are used as currency just like regular regulated currency. However, they have no legal tender status in countries like the United States. They are based on the medium of exchange with a unit of account having a store of value like other recognized legal tender.

From the legislative perspective, the global regulators have different standpoints in legalizing and regulating cryptocurrency as a legal tender. For example, Canada is a crypto-friendly country, whereas Chinese regulators have a stern stance on the use of cryptocurrency for trading. Malaysia, on the other hand, has a relatively favorable environment toward cryptocurrency. There seems to be a growing interest among Malaysian consumers in adopting cryptocurrency. Because of this development, Malaysian regulators are establishing a framework to monitor the activities of cryptocurrency exchangers. Existing studies in Malaysia on cryptocurrency focus on policies, regulations, and technologies from the perspectives of the government, financial institutions, and businesses using various theories. Despite the growth and increased attention toward cryptocurrencies in Malaysia, there is still a lack of research on cryptocurrency adoption focusing on Malaysian consumers.

Cryptocurrency versus Fiat/Traditional Currency: Cryptocurrencies lack legal tender and lawful standing, and even after that, market popularity demonstrates their value, accessibility, and simplicity of acceptance in the industry. Based on a distributed record ledger, blockchain technology is used by cryptocurrencies to process transactions and get around the flaws in the present monetary system. Let us examine some of the benefits of using blockchain technology in cryptocurrencies: (1) Blockchain uses the SHA 256 hash algorithm, which makes it one of the most secure forms. (2) The ledger is transparent since all transactions are broadcast to all peers. (3) No one peer may change the history of transactions, making a blockchain immutable. (4) The ledger is resilient since it is distributed. You can still view the material even if many of your peers log off. Cryptocurrency has been calibrated to be the best-case scenario for any financial transaction because of its ingrained properties of immutability, security, verifiability, resilience, and transparency with privacy. The Atlantic Council's Geo-economics Centre has released a significant update to its central bank digital currency (CBDC) tracker. According to the tracker, 105 nations are exploring CBDCs) and 50 are in an advanced research stage (development, pilot, or launch). A digital currency has been fully introduced in 10 nations. A CBDC is being considered by 19 of the G20 nations, with 16 being in the planning or trial stages. South Korea, Japan, India, and Russia are among those mentioned. China's richest man, Jack Ma, has said that blockchain technology has the potential to revolutionize the world more than anyone can fathom. He has, though, issued a Bitcoin bubble warning. Bill Gates considered Bitcoin to be a technological tour de force.

Digital assets are not issued or backed by government authority but are based on the agreement by the community of the users of the assets. Virtual digital assets are not similar to fiat or e-money issued and circulated by the governing state. Digital currency is a digital portrayal of worth not offered nor guaranteed by any central financial establishment; however, it is widespread as it is traded electronically. The data on transactions is saved at the software program platform blockchain, or allotted ledger generation; it underpins many digital currencies; it can also be used inside nonpublic, allowed ledger structures – monetary establishments, governments, and cross-enterprise can utilize variations of public and personal structures.

15.3 Indian Regulatory Environment

The Indian regulatory environment is unregulated in terms of cryptocurrency trading and settlements. The Reserve Bank of India (RBI) has also not approved it as a "legal tender" and involves complete risk to the crypto-holder in the case of buying and selling. The Indian government has shown a direct willingness to govern the virtual currency. It is reflected in various regulations, bills, and RBI decisions showing commitment to strengthening the cryptocurrency norms. In the same context, RBI is supposed to introduce a "Digital Rupee" in the form of a "CBDC" supported by RBI. In support of the digital rupee, RBI has also released a concept note in the year 2022 to give more clarity and effecting factors that would be considered to formulate the policy in India. It has also conducted various pilot surveys at retail and wholesale levels. The recent step toward regulating the currency is the bill presented in the parliamentary house, i.e., Cryptocurrency and Regulation of Official Digital Currency Bill, 2021 ("2021 Bill"). The bill is unavailable in the public domain, but effective regulations are expected.

As per the Government's slated version, the Bill aims "To create a facilitative framework for creating the official digital currency to be issued by the Reserve Bank of India ('RBI'). The Bill also seeks to prohibit all private cryptocurrencies in India. However, it allows certain exceptions to promote cryptocurrency's underlying technology and uses." The contemplated options include a complete ban on private cryptocurrencies and recognizing all or some categories of crypto products under a prescribed regulatory framework. The proposed crypto law is likely to align with the guidance of the Financial Action Task Force (FATF). In October 2018, FATF added two new definitions to the glossary: virtual asset (VA) and virtual asset service provider ('VASP'). The said guidance was updated in October 2021 to assist both National Authorities as well as Private Sector entities in understanding and developing regulatory and supervisory responses to VA and VASPs and in understanding relatable anti–money laundering and countering the financing of terrorism (AML/CFT) obligations.

In the recent development of the Indian Companies Act, 2013, Schedule III has been amended and prescribed for companies to disclose the gain or loss in cryptocurrencies in their annual financial statements from April 2021. In the same line of action, the Indian budget 2022–2023 has proposed the tax percentage for the earnings out of digital currencies in the financial year. It is mandated that the tax on profit will be charged at the rate of 30%, and in the case of loss, it will not be adjusted with the other income source. It was also proposed that the transfer of digital currency as a gift to the receiver be taxed. Under Indian income tax, tax deduction at source will be levied of 1% of the total value of the asset transfer subject to transactions exceeding INR 50,000 or INR 10,000 in a single financial year. The provision of penalty has been introduced under Sections 271C and 276B of the act in case of default in the filing of the TDS. The income tax department has clarified Section 115BBH, which provides no offset in case of loss in the trade of digital assets against the gains from other income or income from other digital assets. Only exemptions to the deduction of the cost of acquisition are allowed. Section 2(47A) has been introduced to define digital assets legally.

Proposals of Budget 2022 tax on transfer of VDAs (virtual digital assets, hereinafter referred to as VDAs) with effect from April 1, 2022: Tax should be levied at 30% on the transfer of VDA. Only the cost of acquisition will be allowed as a deduction. No set off of loss shall be allowed while computing income from VDA. Also, loss arising from the transfer of any VDA shall not be allowed to be set off against any other income. The definition of VDA is broad enough to cover any information or code or number or token generated through cryptographic means or otherwise and which provides a digital representation of value exchanged with or without consideration, with the promise or representation of having inherent value, or functions as a store of value or a unit of account including its use in any financial transaction or investment, but not limited to an investment scheme. It can be transferred, stored, or traded electronically. Any currency (whether Indian or foreign) is not covered within the ambit of VDA. VDAs also include NFTs or any other token of a similar nature. The government may further notify or exclude any other digital asset from the definition of VDA. Withholding tax provisions will be effective from July 1, 2022, and the tax will be deducted at 1% on the payment made for transferring VDA to a resident. These provisions would apply even if the consideration is paid partly or wholly. TDS (Tax Deducted at Source, hereinafter referred to as TDS) is not required in cases where aggregate consideration in a financial year is below INR 50,000 if payment is made by a specified individual/Hindu undivided family and INR 10,000 in all other cases.

TDS Provisions Section 194S was also inserted by the Finance Act 2022. The section says:

> Payment on transfer of virtual digital asset. 194S. (1) Any person responsible for paying any resident any sum by way of consideration for the transfer of a virtual digital asset shall, at the time of credit of such sum to the account of the resident or at the time of payment of such sum by any mode, whichever is earlier, deduct an amount equal to one percent of such sum as income-tax thereon: Provided that in a case where the consideration for transfer of the virtual digital asset is –
>
> (a) wholly in kind or in exchange of another virtual digital asset, where there is no part in cash; or
>
> (b) partly in cash and partly in kind but the cash part is not sufficient to meet the liability of deduction of tax in respect of the whole of such transfer,
>
> the person responsible for paying such consideration shall, before releasing the consideration, ensure that tax required to be deducted been paid in respect of such consideration for the transfer of virtual digital asset.
>
> (2) The provisions of sections 203A and 206AB shall not apply to a specified person.

(3) Notwithstanding anything contained in sub-section (1), no tax shall be deducted in a case where –

(a) the consideration is payable by a specified person and the value or aggregate value of such consideration does not exceed fifty thousand rupees during the financial year; or

(b) the consideration is payable by any person other than a specified person and the value or aggregate value of such consideration does not exceed ten thousand rupees during the financial year.

(4) Notwithstanding anything contained in section 194-O, in case of a transaction to which the provisions of the said section are also applicable along with the provisions of this section, then tax shall be deducted under subsection (1).

(5) Where any sum referred to in subsection (1) is credited to any account, whether called "Suspense Account" or by any other name, in the books of account of the person liable to pay such sum, such credit of the sum shall be deemed to be the credit of such sum to the account of the payee and the provisions of this section shall apply accordingly.

(6) If any difficulty arises in giving effect to the provisions of this section, the Board may, with the prior approval of the Central Government, issue guidelines to remove the difficulty.

(7) Every guideline issued by the Board under sub-section (6) shall be laid before each House of Parliament and binding on the income-tax authorities and the person responsible for paying the consideration on transfer of such virtual digital asset.

Explanation. – For this section, "specified person" means a person, – (a) being an individual or a Hindu undivided family whose total sales, gross receipts, or turnover from the business carried on by him or profession exercised by him does not exceed one crore rupees in case of business or fifty lakh rupees in case of the profession, during the financial year immediately preceding the financial year in which such virtual digital asset is transferred; (b) being an individual or a Hindu undivided family, not having any income under the head "Profits and gains of business or profession."

From the above provisions, it can be understood that the liability of deducting tax lies with the exchange. Numerous exchanges in India are working online. Some centralized exchanges, such as WazirX, also deal with fiat money. Still, DEXs, such as Defi Swap, Uniswap, Pancakeswap, and Curve, deal with crypto-to-crypto transaction. It is difficult for a regulating agency to collect information from DEXs through banking channels as these do not maintain bank accounts. The above provisions of TDS have taken care of the profit at the time of consideration paid to the resident in cash/cheque or even crypto. This means that when a person shifts from one crypto to another, the provisions are applicable, but this transaction cannot be mapped as the amount is not credited to the bank account.

Guidelines for the advertisement of digital assets were issued in 2022 by the Advertising Standards Council of India, i.e., *Guidelines for the Advertising of Virtual Digital Assets and Linked Services*. The standards prescribed that the full disclosure and disclaimer related to the assets should be released. The Prevention of Money Laundering Act, 2002, and the Foreign Exchange Management Act, 1999 have been mandatory in the disclosure of the Indian platforms. In the CASE *Internet and Mobile Association of India v. Reserve Bank of India*, it was observed that the RBI has failed to prove the damage caused to the regulated currency by the authority due to the trade of virtual assets. Also, the apex court has quashed the impugned circular by the RBI in 2020. In light of the judgment, RBI issued a fresh circular in 2021 to clarify the validity of the previous circular.

The position as of date is that VCs (virtial currencies, hereinafter referred to as VCs) are not banned. Still, the trading in VCs and the functioning of VC exchanges are sent to comatose by the impugned circular by disconnecting their lifeline, namely, the interface with the regular banking sector. What is worse is that this has been done (1) despite RBI not finding anything wrong about how these exchanges function and (2) even though VCs are not banned.

In forming regulations related to digital currency, the RBI will play a pivotal role in the management and governance of the currency along with the Ministry of Corporate Affairs. Companies and other legal bodies dealing with digital currency will be regulated by the registrar of the companies under the ministry. Other regulators, such as the Income Tax Department, the Securities Exchange Board of India, and the Advertising Standards Council of India, will also play a critical role in the proposed digital currency regulations.

The approach of the RBI concerning digital currency refers to various benefits of using it, which are not limited to but include financial inclusion, lowering of transaction costs, and efficient payment structure, among others. It is most apposite to mention that felicitating a trial and testing of the currency before widespread launch would be appropriate. It is observed that countries are finding it challenging to integrate digital currency into the financial mainstream and regulate it simultaneously. However, it would be best to have an effective regulatory environment to weed out or combat cyber-related or illicit threats.

15.4 Money Laundering via Crypto Trading

In their research, Brenig and Müller (2015) focused on the economic aspects of crypto money laundering based on the decentralized ecosystem and cryptography. The research was focused on the transactional and contextual factors affecting digital assets used for money laundering. Different categories of money laundering activities, such as Nested services, gambling platforms, mixers, and privacy coins, are used. Even in the United States, there are regulations related to AML, which were drafted a decade ago, and only some amendments after a crisis, like the terrorist attacks of September 11, 2001, related to the due diligence of the banks (Arnold, 2022). The modus operandi of money laundering via crypto starts from buying tokens or chips or currency for gaming from gaming websites. After the gaming process, they encash the amount from the websites. By the process of encashing, they convert the token into white money.

In the other mode, the crypto exchanges hide the money via blockchain. They use Data anonymization services like artificial intelligence (AI) governance design and engineering services or expert data opinion services and privacy consulting for tracking pixels. The use of services is to break the money trail between the two transactions on the crypto exchange. The regulated mechanism of the initial public offering of the regulated capital market is reflected in the initial coin offering in the crypto exchanges, which is used to convert one cryptocurrency to another. It creates multilayer transactions to hide the illegal money. The other money transfer mechanism, like mixing or tumblers, is used to erase the trace of the money from one source. It will create difficulty in tracing the money from the source. After mixing, the currency will transfer from one address to different addresses. The criminal can encash the money across the globe in any jurisdiction to hide the money or invest in legal businesses. Online social platforms like Facebook and Telegram channels are used to generate cryptocurrencies by unlawful organizations to fund drug business or terrorism. The transfer of funds is usually through wallets on different exchanges, which makes the fund origin untraceable.

The existence of a large number of unregulated cryptocurrency exchanges across the world subsequently results in criminal activities. The reluctance to conduct "know your customers" (KYC) or identity checks of transactions or the customers is one of the primary reasons for the lack of deterrence. The mandates are few and far between, encouraging perpetrators to launder cryptocurrencies. Specifically, launderers use illegal money in fiat currency to open an online account with currency exchanges. The money launderers deploy a layered approach by continually transferring illicit currency to multiple accounts or positing it from one currency to another, consequently making it appear as cleansed money. The perpetrators send the cleansed currency to an external cryptocurrency wallet as a last step. The other method used is converting cryptocurrency as cash using crypto automated teller machines, making it easy to fund other illicit activities, leaving state agencies perplexed and thus creating threats against security without leaving any traceable path.

With the help of the brokers, over-the-counter facilities are provided to the crypto trades to siphon the funds without the trail of money. With the charge of some brokerages, brokers are making money, and illegal money transfers are completed without the regulator's knowledge. Money launders form online companies to legalize cryptocurrencies by taking them as a permitted payment source. Input money via crypto will be adjusted against the business ledger or shown in the purchase of assets.

15.5 Areas That Need to Be Answered

Wonglimpiyarat (2016), in his research, observed the answer to a cashless and virtual currency-based society and witnessed that the need for regulation is important to recognize the effectiveness of Bitcoin or similar currencies. The study reveals that digital currency is the start of revolutionary advancement in the banking sector in developing countries, but cash will remain a need in society. The unregulated digital currency has potential security risks, counterparty, legal, shallow market issues, privacy, governance, etc. The other risk category is from the cybercriminals who use it for terror funding and other illegal activities like Ponzi schemes and drug deals in the black market. The regulatory and compliance disparities are the primary concern of virtual currency globally. Due to no support from the enforcement agencies, it is difficult to trace the illicit trail of money hiding in the blockchain and governance issues in the trade like no customer trade records and trade risk management (Nigh & Pelker, 2015).

Collating the issues to zero in the regulatory gaps could be the most appropriate exercise. As discussed previously, the grant of legal standing of virtual currencies in a competent jurisdiction is the most indispensable component. First, establishing a crystal clear legal stance aids the imposition of regulations and safeguards the interests of the investors. Therefore, adhering to a standard that whether it signifies a legal tender, commodity, or a piece of property is most pertinent. Second, the burgeoning cross-border transactions prove it difficult for the regulatory authorities to exercise the jurisdiction. The sanctions of international laws limited to the regional applicability of state consortiums do not bring answers to global jurisdictional issues. The jurisdictional problems, cross-border payments, and reluctance in international cooperation have a big say in the inadequacy of legal regulations. The harmonization of legislation, standardization, and uniformity have gross apertures, providing tech-smart perpetrators with a haven. A consensus on a model law based on the coming together of central banks of major states could be a starting point to counter the above-stated menace (Cheun, 2015).

Third, data protection, mining, and privacy are riddled with complexities. The counterbalancing of security with privacy and the ever-need of a suitable data protection regime concoct to formulate behaviors, regulations, and implementation in a complex web of questions. The extent of privacy concerns and the grant of liberty to utilize data in the crypto universe is an area of unknown territories (Arslanian & Fischer, 2022). Fourth, the snowballing of AI tech has brought the world to a stage where tech smarts can hold the world as their marionettes. The author does not want to paint a bleak picture; however, it is no longer a far-fetched future where AI and blockchain will pervade every aspect, and virtual currencies will be at the frontline and germination points. The concerns with the use of AI relate to the concerns of virtual currency, which declares a lot. The fifth area/concern flows as a corollary to the previous moot point and relates to public awareness (Prasad, 2021). Education-related initiatives are lagging, and the strengthening of the general public's comprehension of virtual currency is a role that states must take seriously.

15.6 Conclusion and Suggestions

Chainalysis (2021) observed that India adopted digital currency the fastest way and ranked second in the adoption of the overall world comparison. There is no central authority over virtual currencies, either within or across jurisdictions, and each regulator's response is apt according to that regulator's narrow perspectives of the markets and traditional regulations. Optimally regulatory structures might emerge and converge with time, but it is only chaos and confusion around virtual currencies. Indian regulators have made it mandatory for Indians to disclose their complete identity before buying assets via KYC and AML laws.

To deal with the associated potential risk of illegal activities via the sale and purchase of cryptocurrencies, it is suggested that strict regulations be imposed on the digital assets market intermediaries, i.e., wallets, exchanges, and brokerage. Indian regulators have imposed precautionary measures in case of taxation and income disclosure norms, but focused parliamentary legislation is needed in the current situation. The current crypto scams and insolvency by the major operators worldwide result from the lack of disclosure and regulatory audit processes.

However, to put things in perspective, there needs to be a nuanced regulatory approach that fosters a balanced approach to investor protection with financial stability necessitated by the changing contours of cryptocurrency regulations, presenting a dynamic interplay of challenges and opportunities in India. The avenues abound with the prospect of financial inclusion, a significant advantage of financial growth, and a transparent regulatory advancement that can create a conducive environment, fostering investor confidence and creating space for entrepreneurial ventures in entities related to virtual currencies. Particularly in the Indian context, the legislative machinery and the central bank should unite to navigate the challenges with the collaborative efforts of stakeholders and legal experts and create a roadmap for the virtual currency ecosystem. This ecosystem should not be bereft of innovation and its transformative benefits to harness its true potential of a sustainable digital economy. In light of the current discussion, it is recommended that future research study the impact of tax regulations on the future of digital currency in India. Regulation of virtual currency will lead to digital innovations in the country.

References

Arnold, A. (2022). Stolen billions from errant mouse clicks: Crypto requires new approaches to attack money laundering. *Bulletin of the Atomic Scientists, 78*(4), 191–197. https://doi.org/10.1080/00963402.2022.2087374

Arslanian, H., & Fischer, F. (2022). *The future of finance: The impact of FinTech, AI, and crypto on financial services*. Palgrave Macmillan.

Brenig, C., & Müller, G. (2015). *Economic analysis of cryptocurrency-backed money laundering*. Twenty-Third European Conference on Information Systems (ECIS).

Chainalysis. (2021, October 14). The 2021 global crypto adoption index: Worldwide adoption jumps over 880% with P2P platforms driving cryptocurrency usage in emerging markets. *Chainalysis*. https://www.chainalysis.com/blog/2021-global-crypto-adoption-index/#

Chaum, D. (1982). *Computer systems established, maintained, and trusted by mutually suspicious groups*. Dissertation, Computer Science, UC Berkeley.

Chaum, D. (1983). Blind signatures for untraceable payments. *Advances in Cryptology, 82*, 199–203. Boston, MA: Springer. https://doi.org/10.1007/978-1-4757-0602-4_18. ISBN 978-1-4757-0604-8

Cheun, D. L. (2015). *Handbook of digital currency: Bitcoin, innovation, financial instruments, and big data*. Academic Press.

Chu, D. (2018). Broker-dealers for virtual currency: Regulating cryptocurrency wallets and exchanges. *Columbia Law Review, 118*(8), 2323–2359.

Dahlberg, T., Bolívar, R., & Scholl, H. J. (2019). What blockchain developers and users expect from virtual currency regulations: A survey study. *Information Polity: The International Journal of Government & Democracy in the Information Age, 24*(4), 453–467. https://doi.org/10.3233/IP-190145

Jeffrey, M. (2017). Demystifying cryptocurrencies, blockchain, and ICOs. *Toptal*. https://www.toptal.com/finance/financial-consultants/cryptocurrency-market

Nigh, B., & Pelker, C. A. (2015). FBI – virtual currency: Investigative challenges and opportunities. *FBI Law Enforcement Bulletin*, 21–30.

Prasad, E. S. (2021). *The future of money: How the digital revolution transforms currencies and finance*. Harvard University Press.

Shubber, K. (2015). The regulators. *New Scientist, 225*(3006).

Tandel, P., & Mestry, S. (2018). Cryptocurrency-the world of cryptocurrencies. *AADYA-National Journal of Management and Technology, 8*, 83–92.

Trautman, L. J. (2018). Bitcoin, virtual currencies, and the struggle of law and regulation to keep pace. *Marquette Law Review, 102*(2), 447–538.

Trautman, L. J., & Harrell, A. J. (2017). Bitcoin versus regulated payment systems: What gives? *Cardozo Law Review, 38*, 1041.

Wonglimpiyarat, J. (2016). The new Darwinism of the payment system: Will bitcoin replace our cash-based society? *Journal of Internet Banking and Commerce*, 1–15.

16

A Case Study on Cryptocurrency Strategy and Regulation in the Asia Pacific

Sandy Arief and Wikan Karis Basutama

16.1 Introduction

The term "Cryptocurrency" refers to a digital currency that utilizes a tool known as cryptography to regulate the generation of currency units and verify the execution of payment transactions on a decentralized network (Geva & Geva, 2019) known as a distributed ledger, such as the blockchain. This decentralized network allows online payments to take place directly from one cryptocurrency wallet holder to another without going through a bank or any other centralized third party (Nian & Chuen, 2015). Cryptography also utilizes encrypted algorithms to maintain both security and fidelity of a cryptocurrency, which enables it to function as both a form of currency and a virtual accounting system (FATF, *Virtual Currencies: Key Definitions and Potential AML/CFT Risks*, 2014). One of the most notable examples of cryptocurrencies is Bitcoin (Hanl, 2018). The creation of Bitcoin is attributed to an entity or group that adopted the pseudonym "Satoshi Nakamoto," who released a white paper under the title *Bitcoin: A Peer-to-Peer Electronic Cash System*, which delineated a blueprint for a decentralized cryptographic currency, leveraging blockchain technology to resist centralized control (Nakamoto, 2008). This differentiates cryptocurrency from "Fiat Currency," a government-issued centralized currency (You, 2022). Unlike cryptocurrency, the value of a fiat currency hinges on the intricate dynamics of supply, demand, and the stability of the issuing government, which provides central banks with enhanced control over the economy by influencing the money supply through printing (Gross & Siebenbrunner, 2019).

This chapter compares three jurisdictions: Indonesia, China, and Japan. Determining the classification of cryptocurrencies and the appropriate forum for their regulation enables this study to provide an analysis of the regulation of cryptocurrencies and showcase ways to improve consumer protection and financial crime prevention. This chapter focuses on how cryptocurrency could be regulated, whether as a security, commodity, or property and who should regulate cryptocurrency, whether domestically or internationally. This chapter argues that the regulatory methods that are being used on a domestic scale need to be addressed and evaluated for international effectiveness to efficiently regulate the global threat that cryptocurrency has the potential to be. The remainder of the chapter is structured as follows: the analysis of Indonesia, China, and Japan. Finally, a comparative analysis and conclusion are also discussed.

16.2 Indonesia

Whereas some countries have adopted a consistent policy for regulating cryptocurrency regardless of classification, Indonesia has taken a mixed approach. In countries where cryptocurrency is accepted, it is legal for citizens to use it, whether as a means of payment or a store of value. Meanwhile, in countries where it is banned, it becomes illegal to utilize it, whatever the form. In Indonesia, it is important to distinguish between having cryptocurrency as money (means of payment) or as an investment asset. The latter has allowed the term "crypto asset" to spread widely among regulators and the community. Through its central bank, Bank Indonesia, the Indonesian government has firmly and repeatedly reaffirmed its stance that cryptocurrency, which falls under the broader scope of virtual currency, cannot be used for payment within the territories of the Republic of Indonesia. At the same time, the government has allowed the use of virtual currencies as crypto assets to be traded as commodities in the futures market. The government has been very consistent in developing this mixed-policy approach in the past decade. The prohibition of virtual currencies has been followed with a subsequent reiteration of existing regulations that exclude them from payment processing. At the same time, the futures market has been augmented with exchanges, clearing houses, storage institutions, and registered traders to form a robust ecosystem suitable for investors to buy and sell crypto assets quickly and securely. The crypto industry in Indonesia has developed into a multi-billion dollar industry and continues to show potential for growth in the future. Further challenges have arisen regarding the taxation of crypto transactions and the development of alternative digital currencies. The Indonesian government has adequately responded to these promptly and proportionately.

Indonesia has maintained a strong statement regarding the need to maintain the sovereignty of its currency, the Rupiah (currency code "IDR"), against potential alternatives including virtual currencies. Amid the rising popularity of Bitcoin and the likes in the early 2010s, their adoption as currency for payment began to gain traction. This also sparked a hot debate in Indonesia.

Early adopters of this technology wanted to see its widespread use for payment, due to its ease and anonymity. However, new types of risks associated with the use of these products also surfaced. To clarify any confusion and speculation, Bank Indonesia, in February 2014, came forward with a concise but very firm statement through a press release (Bank Indonesia, 2014). It stated that Bitcoin and other virtual currencies are not considered currencies or legal payment instruments in Indonesia. The statement calls upon existing regulation, namely Law No. 7 of 2011 on Currency, which states that the Rupiah is the sole currency that can be used for transactions in Indonesia. Using another currency for payment would be a violation of this law. The statement ends by urging the community to take extra precautions when dealing with virtual currencies and bear any negative consequences.

In January 2018, the central bank released another public statement reaffirming the 2014 statement (Bank Indonesia, 2018). This time, with a more detailed explanation of virtual currency's use or misuse risks and implications. The press release states, "Every transaction that has the purpose of payment, or other obligations which need to be fulfilled with money, or other financial transactions conducted within the territory of the Republic of Indonesia, has to be fulfilled with Rupiah." The statement then outlines the three main reasons why using virtual currencies brings about a series of new risks. First, given that virtual currencies are not governed and administered by a specific authority and have no underlying assets to base their price owning them is a highly risky activity that entails speculation. Second, the value of virtual currency is highly volatile and prone to bubbles, which can seriously strain the financial system's stability. Any negative impact from the bursting of such a bubble can be devastating for the economy. Third, due to its anonymous nature, virtual currencies can be abused by criminals to perpetrate acts of money laundering and terrorist financing (ML/TF). In addition to restating its ban as currency, the statement warns payment system providers against processing virtual currency. This is because Article 34 of Bank Indonesia Regulation No. 18/40/PBI/2016 on Payment Transaction Processing specifically prohibits payment system providers from processing virtual currency. Thus, through the 2018 statement, the Indonesian government has made it unequivocally clear that there is no place for virtual currency in the Indonesian payment system.

Other government institutions have supported Bank Indonesia's prohibition. The Ministry of Finance released a statement outlining similar justifications for Bank Indonesia's decision not to acknowledge virtual currency as legal tender (Ministry of Finance, 2018). Furthermore, the National Financial Intelligence Unit (FIU) also released a similar statement, underlining the ML/TF risks that virtual currency brings (PPATK, 2018). Since the 2018 statement, there have been several reforms to the payment system regulation. However, the prohibition of virtual currencies remains consistent and was even further specified in Bank Indonesia Regulation No. 22/23/PBI/2020 on

Payment System and Bank Indonesia Regulation No. 23/6/PBI/2021 on Payment System Providers.

The government's decision to prohibit the use of virtual currencies as a means of payment was not unjustified. The rise in the use of Bitcoin worldwide created a new breed of criminal activities, even in Indonesia (BBC, 2017). In October 2014, a university student in Jakarta was arrested for buying drugs online from Mexico. It was indicated that the perpetrator paid for the goods with Bitcoin. A year later, a terrorist by the initials LWK threatened to bomb Alam Sutera Mall, asking for a ransom to be paid also in Bitcoin (Jakarta Post, 2015). In 2017, the national police arrested several individuals involved in a cryptocurrency Ponzi scheme called "Bitconnect." This scheme promised high returns to investors who lent Bitcoin and was fraudulent, causing significant financial losses (Suud, 2021). It is quite clear that Bitcoin and other virtual currencies possess characteristics that are desirable to criminals (Foley et al., 2019). They are easy to transfer, thus reducing transport and storage costs. Above all, they maintain anonymity, allowing the perpetrators to be relatively untraceable. In the grand scheme of things, the deliberate legalization of virtual currencies as legal tender would blur the lines between legal and illegal use of these currencies.

The Indonesian government's move to establish a secure ecosystem for buying and selling crypto in the form of assets began in the latter half of 2018. A group of ministries and government agencies met under the lead of the Coordinating Ministry for Economic Affairs in September 2018 to discuss the way forward with regard to regulating cryptocurrency. These discussions led to an agreement outlined in a letter by the coordinating ministry no. S-302/M.EKON/09/2018 signed on September24, 2018 (BAPPEBTI, 2020). The agreement reaffirms the prohibition of the use of crypto as currency but allows its use as an investment asset classified as a commodity that can be traded in the futures market. This was a landmark decision that opened the gateway for legal active trading of crypto assets in the Indonesian market. The decision was made in view that crypto assets provided substantial investment opportunities, and its complete prohibition may result in huge capital outflows. This is because investors always seek markets that benefit them the most, and an unwelcoming market will drive away potential investors.

Some of the reasons that motivated the central bank to prohibit the use of virtual currencies for payment would then evolve into the rationale for regulating them. In general, the decision to regulate the trading of crypto assets is based on four considerations (BAPPEBTI, 2020). First, to minimize the risk of abuse of crypto assets for illegal purposes such as money laundering, terrorist financing and financing of the proliferation of weapons of mass destruction. Completely banning crypto in both realms of payment and investment would keep its use within the underground economy. A large part of these transactions would go undetected, thus allowing criminal activities to thrive. Second, to provide protection to genuine consumers from excessive losses incurred from trading crypto assets. Buying and selling crypto in an unregulated environment exposes its investors to risks from the volatility of the instrument itself and the legitimacy of the trading platforms. Third, to provide a legal basis for crypto traders to conduct their business in Indonesia. On the business side, many tech companies were ready to jump on the bandwagon. This would not be possible if setting up crypto trading company or platform were prohibited. Fourth, to facilitate innovation and growth of the crypto asset trading industry. The creation of Bitcoins and other virtual currencies is only the beginning of a wave of innovation in more complex products using blockchain and distributed ledger technologies. Innovation creates jobs and growth, and the profits generated could contribute to the economy through taxes. In short, the decision to regulate crypto assets can be attributed to an attempt at minimizing risks while promoting growth.

Establishing a well-regulated crypto asset industry within the commodity futures market would prove to be momentous task that would take years to realize. Some may argue that it is still transforming to this date. The government agency tasked to oversee this process was the Indonesian Commodity Futures Trading Regulatory Agency (CoFTRA) under the Ministry of Trade. The first step was to grant CoFTRA the authority to regulate the crypto market. This was done through Ministry of Trade Regulation No. 99 of 2018 on General Policy on Organizing the Crypto Asset Term Trade. This new law established the crypto asset as a new class of commodity subject to a futures contract, tradable on the futures exchange. The law then gives CoFTRA the authority to produce subsequent regulations related to crypto asset trading. After gaining authority, CoFTRA placed several restrictions on crypto asset trading. The agency holds full authority to designate crypto assets that can be traded by crypto asset traders in the crypto market. The head of CoFTRA publishes a decree periodically that updates the list of coins or other types of virtual assets legally tradable in the market. These must fulfill several criteria, namely: (1) uses distributed ledger technology, (2) is a utility crypto or asset-backed crypto, and (3) has been assessed using an analytical hierarchy process set by the CoFTRA. As of 2024, there are 545 registered crypto asset products in Indonesia (Heaptalk, 2024). Moreover, the subjects that are allowed to trade crypto assets are limited to natural persons; legal persons are prohibited from trading crypto assets (unless they are registered crypto traders supervised by CoFTRA). The framework for developing the crypto market involves defining several new categories of industry players, such as Futures Exchanges "Bourses," Futures Clearing Institutions, Crypto Asset Traders, Depository Institutions, Crypto Asset Customers, and Crypto Asset Committees. These parties collectively form the new ecosystem for trading crypto assets.

The early years of regulating the crypto asset industry faced several challenges, notably the complexity of establishing the ecosystem. In some ways, the activation of the market took place parallel with the establishment of the institutions. After ratifying the regulations for the requirements of the crypto institutions, CoFTRA began onboarding crypto traders. The number of registered traders grew gradually, reaching a total of 35 traders as of early 2024 (Ministry of Trade, 2024). Meanwhile, it was not until July 2023 that the first crypto exchange was granted a license by the agency. CoFTRA granted the first crypto bourse license to PT Bursa Komoditi Nusantara (Reuters, 2023). Around the same time, the first clearing institution and depository institution were also granted license, namely PT Kliring Berjangka Indonesia and PT Tennet Depository Indonesia respectively. Upon the establishment of these institutions, CoFTRA urged registered crypto traders to apply to become full-fledged traders and to register on the exchange (Tempo, 2023). Toward the end of 2023, another pair of clearing institutions and depository institutions was granted a license. However, as of this writing, there is still only one crypto exchange licensed by CoFTRA.

As has been extensively discussed in other countries, the next step in regulating the crypto industry is finding a way to impose taxes on crypto transactions. The year 2021 was particularly a boom for Indonesia's crypto industry, as it recorded its highest annual trading value to date at IDR 859.5 trillion. With the global economy filled with uncertainty amid the COVID-19 pandemic, many individuals attempted to seek refuge and potential gains in the crypto market. A total of 11.2 million investors were registered in that year. This was a huge fiscal potential that the government could tap into. Thus, in 2022, the Ministry of Finance ratified Decree No. 68/PMK.03/2022 effective May 1, 2022, which governed the imposition of value added tax (VAT) and income tax on crypto transactions. This regulation set the rate on crypto purchases at 0.11% on registered platforms and 0.22% on unregistered platforms. Meanwhile, the rate set on sale transactions were slightly less at 0.1% and 0.2% respectively on registered and unregistered platforms. Through this, the government also incentivizes investors to use registered crypto traders. The regulation also stipulates VAT and income tax rates on miners and mining pools.

Further developments in Indonesia's crypto market have been made in the last few years. Being a Muslim-majority country, Indonesia's financial sector places great significance on the value of products that fulfill Sharia principles. Meanwhile, due to the nature of crypto assets, many of their products cannot be categorized as sharia-compliant (Meera, 2018). This has led to the development of gold-backed crypto assets that have gained popularity in Indonesia. Moreover, the central bank has taken steps to facilitate virtual payments through the development of its own digital currency. This is known globally as central bank digital currencies (CBDC). Bank Indonesia has issued a white paper in 2022 and subsequent consultative papers on this topic (Bank Indonesia, 2024). The CBDC currently in development will hopefully provide people with a new form of currency that can benefit from the advantages of virtual currencies without incurring the drawbacks. Lastly, in early 2023, the government ratified Law No. 4 of 2023 regarding the Development and Strengthening of the Financial Sector (the "Financial Sector Omnibus Law"). This law defines Inovasi Teknologi Sektor Keuangan (ITSK) which includes every product, service, and activity in the digital financial ecosystem. The law will gradually transfer the regulatory and supervisory authority of crypto assets, which falls under the ITSK, to the Otoritas Jasa Keuangan (OJK) (Arum & Nataniel, 2023). In response to this, OJK has coordinated with BAPPEBTI to ensure a smooth transition.

16.3 China

Cryptocurrencies and digital assets have developed exponentially and become significantly complex in recent years. Despite their potential growth, volatility, and evolving technologies, cryptocurrency regulations have been slow to catch up with the pace of the market. Some countries have ratified laws and regulations regarding cryptocurrency. The People's Republic of China can be seen as having the most unique approach toward crypto asset regulation. In 2013, the Central Bank of the People's Republic of China (PBOC) issued the "Notice on Preventing Bitcoin Risk," which was the first official document in China to address the legal status of cryptocurrencies (Ju et al., 2016). The notice was created to protect the legal tender status of China's currency, the Renminbi (RMB), prevent money laundering risks and maintain financial stability. The notice stipulated that Bitcoin does not hold the same legal status as the RMB and that Bitcoin is a specific virtual commodity and cannot and should not be used as a currency in the market. The notice then went on to state that the trading platform of Bitcoin is required to be filed with the telecommunications regulatory authority following the provisions of the Telecommunications Regulations of the People's Republic of China and the Measures for the Administration of Internet Information Services (Burgess, 2024). However, cryptocurrency regulation in China still encounters challenges. China's central bank defined cryptocurrency as a specified virtual commodity (Huang & Mayer, 2022). The legal attribute is unclear, which brings consumer protection and criminal identification difficulties. Cryptocurrencies are built on a blockchain, an open, distributed ledger technology that can record transactions between two parties efficiently and in a verifiable and permanent way (Halaburda & Gandal, 2016).

The earliest sign of crypto-related restrictions came in December 2013, when the Central Bank of the People's Republic of China (PBOC) and four agencies jointly issued the *Notice on Precautions Against the Risks of Bitcoins*.[3] .[1] It defined a token as "a specially designated virtual commodity" that does not possess "the same legal status of a currency." Hence, Chinese financial and payment institutions were prohibited from engaging in any Bitcoin-related activities or services to "protect the status of the RMB as the statutory currency, prevent risks of money laundering and protect financial stability" (PBOC et al., 2013).

In September 2021, the Central Bank of the People's Republic of China (PBOC) announced that all activities related to cryptocurrencies and stablecoins are illegal (Hu, 2024). Globally, no overarching and centralized regulatory frameworks regarding cryptocurrencies and stablecoins exist (Borri & Shakhnov, 2020). This lack of regulatory clarity at the national and international levels has created risks and uncertainties (Griffith & Clancey-Shang, 2023). Chinese authorities passed new, more restrictive regulations: First, initial coin offerings (ICOs) were banned in China (Borri & Shakhnov, 2020). ICOs signify an innovative financial mechanism that has garnered significant attention recently. They predominantly serve as a fundraising tool for projects within the blockchain and cryptocurrency realms. ICOs originated as a decentralized method of fundraising wherein new cryptocurrency projects would sell a portion of their newly minted tokens to early supporters and investors in exchange for more established cryptocurrencies, predominantly Bitcoin and Ethereum. Second, cryptocurrency exchanges were prohibited from converting RMB into cryptocurrencies, or vice versa, purchasing or selling cryptocurrencies, and setting prices. Third, financial and nonbank payment institutions were prohibited from directly or indirectly providing services for ICOs and cryptocurrencies (Borri & Shakhnov, 2020).

The PBOC describes its cryptocurrency ban as a way to navigate financial crime and prevent economic instability and uncertainty (Allen et al., 2022). However, China's cryptocurrency ban comes amid fears that cryptocurrencies facilitated capital flight from its markets, bypassing conventional restrictions (Shin, 2022). Chinese policy on the issue of cryptocurrency is motivated by a rational calculation of the costs and benefits of each element that influences the development of cryptocurrency in China (Cheng, 2019).

In addition to banning all private-issued cryptocurrencies and stablecoins in China, the PBOC has issued its own CBDC, a digital version of a country's central bank money or fiat currency) and is experimenting with a partial implementation in several major cities (Allen et al., 2022). This mechanism could alleviate the challenges in China's financial system, as more credit would be made accessible to those previously "underserved" small and medium enterprises and start-ups, allowing the Chinese financial systems to grow more rapidly (with more efficient and more inclusive lending and payment systems outside the banking sector) to keep pace with the size of its real economy (Jagtiani et al., 2021). This transformation could not be achieved without the risk of highly volatile currency valuation and significant uncertainties if relying on private-issued cryptocurrencies (Allen et al., 2022).

Finally, there are critical considerations in designing cryptocurrency regulations:

1. China should actively formulate international standards related to blockchain and digital finance and connect with open-source organizations and organizations of global standards. In addition, China strengthens exchanges between national and international standards and continuously improves China's international voice regarding blockchain and digital currency standards (Huang & Mayer, 2022; Cheng, 2019).
2. For corporate managers involved in cryptocurrencies, using the financial industry qualification certificate system issued by financial regulatory agencies as a reference can prevent illegal fund-raising and other activities, establishing a blockchain and digital financial access standard system (Shin, 2022).
3. For investors in blockchain finance, it can be learned from the Securities and Futures Investor Suitability Management Measures issued by the China Securities Regulatory Commission and the division of investors in the U.S. Equity Crowdfunding Act. It can make blockchain financial companies honestly "know your customers (KYC)" and sell appropriate products to investors with equivalent investment ability and investment level to prevent financial risks (Hu, 2024).

16.4 Japan

Japan has established itself as one of the leaders in the digital asset domain through its comprehensive and proactive approach to cryptocurrency regulation and supervision. The premise of its strategy is simple: promoting innovation while maintaining the protection of investors and market stability. However, due to the inherent complexity of virtual-based assets and currencies, multiple layers of intricacies arise from this strategy. Japan's approach requires it to adopt a framework adaptable to technological advancements and ever-changing market factors, ensuring a balance between fostering the industry's growth and mitigating emerging risks (FSA, 2022). Indeed, dealing with anything that lacks physical presence poses certain challenges. In this case, the regulators must deal with specific cryptocurrency risks. As Hu et al. (2019) Explain that these risks include market volatility, fraud, and cyber threats. The mitigating measures need to be designed to address these risks adequately.

As a country that regulates cryptocurrency, the presence of a powerful regulatory and oversight agency is paramount. The body tasked with such responsibility in Japan is the Financial Services Agency (FSA). The FSA fulfils its duty by formulating regulations and enforcing compliance with financial institutions and crypto exchanges. This agency plays a pivotal role in policing the industry through policy development, guidelines issuance, and industry alignment (Amaya, 2022). The FSA is also tasked with regulating the industry. On-site inspections and audits are conducted regularly to ensure market integrity and investor protection. As with the practice in other countries, regulatory agencies do not operate independently. The same is true with the FSA, as they collaborate with other institutions to promote inter-sectoral coordination and the effectiveness of policies targeting digital currency markets.

Japan's legal basis for regulating cryptocurrency transactions revolves around several notable laws and provisions. Many of these provisions are essential to enhance transparency and improve investor protection. The landmark decision the country made that allowed cryptocurrency transactions to occur within its borders was the amendment of the Payment Services Act (PSA) and Fund Settlement Law in 2016, which took effect in 2017. This amendment recognizes virtual currencies as "property of value" and thus a valid form of payment and requires crypto exchanges to register with the FSA. The registration process involves the FSA scrutinizing the exchanges for their measures related to operations and security and ensuring they have complied with standards of transparency and fund protection (Goto et al., 2019). Further complexities of having crypto-based products are addressed by the Financial Instruments and Exchange Act, which imposes disclosure requirements and sets minimum standards for trading platforms (Omagari & Sako, 2019). This regulation applies to products such as crypto derivatives and ICOs. This was an attempt on the Japanese government's behalf to prevent malicious practices against investors. In addition, as with any financial product that blurs the relationship between fund source and beneficiary, money laundering risks become somewhat of a tangible concern. Thus, Japan addressed this issue by updating its anti–money laundering (AML) laws to require crypto exchanges to implement KYC measures, including customer verification and monitoring of suspicious transactions or activities. These provisions have allowed Japan to comply with global AML best practices and maintain the financial system's integrity (Iwashita, 2019).

Regulating cryptocurrency requires that it be defined in a very clear and unambiguous way. Japan defines cryptocurrency as an asset that is neither money nor equated with fiat currency (Nagase et al., 2024). It is also not listed as a type of "security." Rather, the PSA defines two definitions of "crypto assets," categorized as Type I and Type II. First, Type I is defined as "proprietary value that may be used to pay an unspecified person the price of any goods, etc. purchased or borrowed or any services provided and that may be sold to or purchased from an unspecified person (limited to that recorded on electronic devices or other objects by electronic means and excluding Japanese and other foreign currencies and Currency Denominated Assets; the same applies in the following item) and that may be transferred using an electronic data processing system." Meanwhile, Type II is defined as "proprietary value that may be exchanged reciprocally for proprietary value specified in the preceding item with an unspecified person and that may be transferred using an electronic data processing system." In short, these two definitions establish the foundation of what cryptocurrency can be used for in Japan: to be used as a means of payment and to be exchanged with or transferred to another person. On a related note, "crypto asset exchange services" are also defined by the PSA as activities such as (1) sale or purchase of crypto assets or the exchange of a crypto asset for another; (2) intermediating, brokering, or acting as an agent in respect of those activities; (3) management of customers' money is connected with the aforementioned activities; (4) management of customers' crypto assets for the benefit of another person. These are the activities that allow the crypto market to operate.

By allowing cryptocurrency exchanges to operate in Japan, the country has, by default, allowed the trading of cryptocurrencies. This is because the users of these exchanges not only use them to acquire currencies but also actively trade them to gain profit. The PSA has given the government the tools necessary to select highly qualified financial institutions to operate exchanges (Kaur, 2023). In addition, some freedom is also given for foreign-based exchanges. The government allows international cryptocurrency exchanges to operate only if they can prove that they have passed through an equally rigorous registration process. Japan's FSA is committed to increase checks and balances through various efforts. Obtaining the license to trade requires an entity to register with the FSA and fulfil strict AML and cybersecurity requirements. In Japan, AML standards are set by two main authorities namely the Japan FIU and the Japan Financial Intelligence Center. As part of these standards, countering financing of terrorism (CFT) measures must also be implemented. In general, the domestic AML/CFT regulation requires a minimum of (1) record-keeping and verification of the customer's identity, (2) record keeping and verification of transactions, (3) reporting of suspicious activities to the FSA, and (4) monitoring for politically exposed persons. These measures are essential to ensure that perpetrators of illicit transactions do not abuse these platforms. Any harm that may be caused to retail investors ought to be prevented. Thus, it is in the best interest of the financial system that these efforts be put in place despite the additional costs it creates.

The fact that Japan has legalized cryptocurrencies as a means of payment can cause some confusion. This is because cryptocurrencies are still not recognized as legal tender under the country's regulatory framework (PILnet, 2023). The only official legal tender recognized by Japan remains the Japanese yen. Nevertheless, cryptocurrencies can be used in lieu of money, in the sense that one may complete payment by transferring cryptocurrencies to a vendor. The lack of recognition as legal tender creates an interesting caveat: businesses have the final decision of whether to accept or reject cryptocurrencies to complete a transaction. This is a reflection of Japan's conservative approach to regulating virtual currencies. Allowing their use to promote economic growth can be done without jeopardizing the yen's sovereignty and financial stability in general. This way, the business sector can get the best of both worlds: those who want to embrace cryptocurrencies can delve within their own spheres, while those more traditional business owners can stay true to their tried-and-tested fiat money.

Another policy question that arises from regulating cryptocurrencies relates to how they are taxed. Generally, taxation on financial assets can be done through various ways. Japan has taken the approach of taxing cryptocurrency gains using income tax (Pravdiuk, 2021). Any profit yielded from a cryptocurrency transaction is considered miscellaneous income and must be reported on annual tax returns. This allows the government to extract tax income from various ways investors or customers can generate income from virtual assets, which is consistent with the country's broader tax policy. Despite this general approach to taxation, the government has also taken initiatives through tax incentives. In Japan, cryptocurrency transactions are exempt from consumption tax (Singh & Shukla, 2022). This is an attempt to promote the adoption of digital currencies by reducing transaction costs.

Japan's stance to actively promote cryptocurrency transactions has shown desirable results reflected by promising growth in the industry. The country has achieved a sizable market and rapid adoption rate. A survey in 2021 showed that around 11% of the population owns cryptocurrency, comparable to Germany and Spain (Finder, 2021). The industry is supported by many registered exchanges through which voluminous trading activities are carried out daily. Some of the main determining factors of this impressive feat are advanced technological infrastructure and a supportive regulatory environment (Lim et al., 2019). In addition, the growing acceptance of virtual currencies in general has also contributed from the demand side.

Despite all the positive effects cryptocurrencies have brought to the country, Japan ought to still be wary of the risks arising from criminal activities. Looking back at its first breach in 2014, the hacking of the Mt. Gox exchange remains one of the biggest security breaches the Japanese cryptocurrency industry has ever seen. It caused a financial loss of around 850,000 Bitcoins (Arora, 2020). The scale of this event became one of the driving factors for the government to regulate the industry. Another notable event occurred in 2018 when a cryptocurrency exchange, Coincheck, was hacked and lost more than $500 million worth of coins (Cheng, 2018). One of the root causes identified was that the exchange stored the New Economy Movement coins in "hot" wallets, a cryptocurrency storage method linked to the internet. Besides those mentioned previously, there have been other notable cases, including fraud, theft, money laundering, and illegal trading activities (Panda & Jani, 2019). These issues undermine the importance of robust security measures and strict oversight from regulatory authorities. Any vulnerabilities identified must immediately be addressed to protect investors from financial losses. This remains one of the country's challenges.

Japan has displayed many success stories as one of the leading countries adopting and regulating cryptocurrencies. Their robust regulatory framework emphasizing transparency and investor protection has allowed the industry to flourish with manageable downsides. However, the virtual currency landscape is continuously evolving. The advent of new technologies, such as decentralized finance platforms and advanced blockchain technologies, may pose difficult policy questions. Furthermore, cross-border issues may arise in an increasingly reliant era on online activities. These must be answered adequately with the correct tools and timing to maintain Japan's lead in the digital domain.

16.5 Comparative Analysis

Regulating cryptocurrency adequately has become a challenge for most countries due to the novel nature of the technology and the rapidly evolving types of products available. Added to the fact that multiple geographical, political, and cultural factors are at play, we can be certain that there is no one-size-fits-all for any country. According to De Araujo Consolino et al. (2018), there are four main policy questions that countries need to answer when they want to regulate cryptocurrency. First, whether they consider cryptocurrencies legal tender. Legalizing cryptocurrencies can ease payment transactions but undermine the local currency's sovereignty. Second, whether they allow cryptocurrency exchanges to operate. Cryptocurrency exchanges need to be regulated and supervised by a dedicated agency. Third, should ICOs be allowed? ICOs are particularly challenging because they can take on many forms and be used by unscrupulous individuals to defraud investors. Fourth, whether they allow mining. Like traditional mining, mining virtual coins poses questions about electricity consumption and its environmental impact. Considering them, it is quite possible that there will be a substantial combination of regulatory approaches. One country can be loose in certain aspects but very strict in others. One country can take a very strong stance against cryptocurrencies, while another can be very accommodative and lax. This has not even considered the possibility that some countries may change their stance occasionally, depending on the political landscape. The possibilities are endless.

Even within the context of the Asian Pacific Region, there is great diversity regarding the regulatory approach to cryptocurrency. Two extremes have been identified in this region: China on one end, which has become progressively more restrictive against cryptocurrencies and their institutions, and Japan on the other extreme, which has taken great lengths to regulate transactions and exchanges (De Araujo Consolino et al., 2018). Other countries can be placed on a spectrum somewhere in between these two. To discuss the different approaches, we can conveniently categorize these countries into three categories: those that ban cryptocurrencies outright, those that regulate them, and those that somewhat accept them. The first two will be discussed first, while the latter will be discussed separately due to their many intricacies.

China remains one of its strongest contenders among the countries that have banned cryptocurrencies. The country has ruled that cryptocurrencies lack legal basis and have taken steps in the past few years to shut down exchanges. In addition, little room has been given to miners by cutting off the power available to them. Bangladesh takes a similar approach to China, publicly announcing that using cryptocurrencies within the country has financial and legal consequences (Mahbub & Rahman, 2018). Other countries that prohibit cryptocurrencies include Iran, Thailand, and Kazakhstan. On the other side of the spectrum is Japan, leading worldwide in cryptocurrency regulation. Cryptocurrency is legal in Japan as a means of payment, and exchanges and ICOs are well regulated. Another example is the Philippines, which has allowed the use of virtual assets as a medium of exchange (Bangko Sentral ng Pilipinas, 2021). They also have regulations for cryptocurrency exchanges and ICOs. Furthermore, South Korea and Russia have placed some limitations in the past (Kim, 2017), but have now generally embraced cryptocurrencies for payment and trading.

The countries that have taken a mixed approach are just as diverse, and their policies illustrate different priorities from those of the government. For example, Kyrgyzstan has taken a strong stance to prohibit using cryptocurrencies within its borders. However, it is said that the country will consider using virtual currencies for government transactions (Tassev, 2018). This, among many other reasons, is to improve transparency. India previously took a strong stance, unlike that of its neighbor, Bangladesh. However, this view has shifted since early 2018, when efforts to regulate began, particularly about ICOs (Ohri, 2024). Hong Kong and Malaysia have taken approaches that discourage the use of cryptocurrencies for transactions and trading. Meanwhile, they regulate ICO activities quite strictly, focusing on investor protection. Singapore, usually known for its liberal business policies, has greatly emphasized AML/CFT measures regarding cryptocurrencies. Having banned cryptocurrencies as a means of payment, Indonesia has opened its gates to trading activities through registered exchanges.

A mixed approach can benefit a country somewhat because the policy can be tailor-made to best fit the domestic situation. Any country should be discouraged from replicating another country's approach merely because it has been proven successful in that country. Many factors need to be considered. Formulating policies requires time, research, and – at times – trial and error. The best policies are not made overnight but through rigorous deliberations, discussions, and testing. Indeed, even today, we still find many countries in the middle of this process. The landscape keeps evolving; the process continues. Some may think it is somewhat futile to attempt to control something ever changing. However, it is unwise to think it is a project that is not worth undertaking.

16.6 Conclusion

The overall aim of this chapter was to address the regulation of cryptocurrencies by establishing how different countries classify and regulate cryptocurrencies and then analyze how the regulation of cryptocurrencies in different countries has an impact on improving consumer protection and financial crime prevention. This grounded a discussion on the current state of international regulation and underscored the need for cohesion and harmonization between regulatory frameworks. By exploring the different crypto crazes and crashes, this work demonstrated the dangers of cryptocurrency regarding a lack of consumer protection and financial crime prevention. It then analyzed the regulation and classification of cryptocurrency in Indonesia, China, and Japan. The analysis of each jurisdiction showed an integration-based approach shared by Indonesia, China, and Japan, which slowly integrated crypto asset regulation into existing regulatory frameworks. This integration approach seemed to prioritize addressing the lack of consumer protection and financial crime prevention by affording the same protection to crypto actors afforded to the traditional banking systems.

This work is subject to several limitations. First, this literature review is limited by its utilization of articles that examine research on cryptocurrencies. This poses the risk of excluding articles that could provide meaningful contributions to the study. Furthermore, the deficiency of research in accounting and auditing about cryptocurrencies can partly be attributed to the limited data available for analysis. Cryptocurrencies are a relatively new phenomenon; hence, the available information on their impact on accounting and auditing procedures is limited. Future research could involve a comparative analysis of alternative accounting treatments for entities that acquire cryptocurrencies either as a medium of exchange or as an investment, focusing on examining the impact of these treatments on financial results.

Note

1. PBOC, MIIT, CBRC, CSRC, & CIRC. (2013, December 5). *Guanyu Fangfan Bitebi Fengxian de Tongzhi* (关于防范比特币风险的通知) [*Notice on Precautions Against the Risks of Bitcoins*]. The Central People's Government of the People's Republic of China. http://www.gov.cn/gzdt/2013–12/05/content_2542751.htm.

References

Allen, F., Gu, X., & Jagtiani, J. (2022). Fintech, cryptocurrencies, and CBDC: Financial structural transformation in China. *Journal of International Money and Finance, 124*, 102625. https://doi.org/10.1016/j.jimonfin.2022.102625

Amaya, T. (2022). *Regulating the Crypto Assets Landscape in Japan.* Financial Services Agency. https://www.fsa.go.jp/en/news/2022/20221207/01.pdf

Arora, G. (2020). *Cryptoasset Regulatory Framework in Japan.* Available at SSRN 3720230. http://dx.doi.org/10.2139/ssrn.3720230

Arum, D., & Nataniel, R. (2023). *Key Points on the Financial Sector Omnibus Law: General Overview.* Arma Law. https://www.arma-law.com/news-event/newsflash/undang-undang-omnibus-law-sektor-keuangan

Bangko Sentral ng Pilipinas. (2021, January 21). *Guidelines for Virtual Asset Service Providers (VASP).* https://www.bsp.gov.ph/Regulations/Issuances/2021/1108.pdf

Bank Indonesia. (2014, February 6). *Statement of Bank Indonesia Related to Bitcoin and Other Virtual Currency.* Bank Indonesia. https://www.bi.go.id/en/publikasi/ruang-media/news-release/Pages/SP_160614.aspx

Bank Indonesia. (2018, January 12). *Bank Indonesia Warns All Parties Not to Sell, Buy, or Trade Virtual Currency.* Bank Indonesia. https://www.bi.go.id/en/publikasi/ruang-media/news-release/Pages/sp_200418.aspx

Bank Indonesia. (2024). *Project Garuda: Navigating The Architecture Of Digital Rupiah.* Bank Indonesia. https://www.bi.go.id/en/rupiah/digital-rupiah/default.aspx

BAPPEBTI. (2020). *Crypto Asset.* Jakarta: BAPPEBTI. https://bappebti.go.id/resources/docs/brosur_leaflet_2001_01_09_o26ulbsq.pdf

BBC. (2017, December 7). Bitcoin is prohibited by the Indonesian financial authorities; these are the facts. *BBC News Indonesia.* https://www.bbc.com/indonesia/indonesia-42265038

Borri, N., & Shakhnov, K. (2020). Regulation spillovers across cryptocurrency markets. *Finance Research Letters, 36*, 101333. https://doi.org/10.1016/j.frl.2019.101333

Burgess, T. (2024). A multi-jurisdictional perspective: To what extent can cryptocurrency be regulated? And if so, who should regulate cryptocurrency? *Journal of Economic Criminology, 5*, 100086.

Cheng, E. (2018, January 26). *Japanese Cryptocurrency Exchange Loses more than $500 Million to Hackers.* Retrieved from CNBC: https://www.cnbc.com/2018/01/26/japanese-cryptocurrency-exchange-loses-more-than-500-million-to-hackers.html

Cheng, Y. (2019). Review of Chinese policy against cryptocurrency growth. *International Journal of Science and Society, 1*(1), 38–44. https://doi.org/10.54783/ijsoc.v1i1.8

De Araujo Consolino, A., Pedrosa-Garcia, J. A., & Winther, Y. (2018). *Regulation of Cryptocurrencies: Evidence from Asia and the Pacific.* WP/18/03. MPFD Working Papers. United Nations ESCAP. https://hdl.handle.net/20.500.12870/1212

FATF. (2014). *FATF Report, Virtual Currencies, Key Definitions, and Potential AML/CFT Risks.* Financial Action Task Force. http://bit. ly/2M0pj1d

Finder. (2021). *Cryptocurrency Adoption Rates.* https://dvh1deh6tagwk.cloudfront.net/finder-us/wp-uploads/sites/5/2021/06/Crypto_Adoption_final-compressed-1.pdf

Foley, S., Karlsen, J. R., & Putniņš, T. J. (2019). Sex, drugs, and bitcoin: How much illegal activity is financed through cryptocurrencies? *The Review of Financial Studies, 32*(5), 1798–1853.

FSA. (2022). *Regulatory Framework for Crypto-assets and Stablecoins*. Financial Services Agency. https://www.fsa.go.jp/inter/etc/20220914-2/02.pdf

Geva, B., & Geva, D. (2019). Non-state community virtual currencies. In: Fox, D., & Green, S. (Eds.), *Cryptocurrencies in Public and Private Law*. Oxford University Press, pp. 281–306. Osgoode Legal Studies Research Paper.

Goto, I., Kuribayashi, Y., & Saito, T. (2019). Virtual currencies: Regulators make their move. *International Financial Law Review*, 75.

Griffith, T., & Clancey-Shang, D. (2023). Cryptocurrency regulation and market quality. *Journal of International Financial Markets, Institutions, and Money*, 84, 101744. https://doi.org/10.1016/j.intfin.2023.101744

Gross, M. M., & Siebenbrunner, C. (2019). *Money Creation in Fiat and Digital Currency Systems*. International Monetary Fund.

Halaburda, H., & Gandal, N. (2016). *Competition in the cryptocurrency market*. Updated version published as "Can we predict the winner in a market with network effects", 14–17.

Hanl, A. (2018). *Some Insights into the Development of Cryptocurrencies (No. 04-2018)*. MAGKS Joint Discussion Paper Series in Economics.

Heaptalk. (2024, February 23). *CoFTRA Releases the 545 Legal Crypto Assets in Indonesia*. Heaptalk. https://heaptalk.com/industry/coftra-releases-the-545-legal-crypto-assets-in-indonesia/

Hu, A. S., Parlour, C. A., & Rajan, U. (2019). Cryptocurrencies: Stylized facts on a new investible instrument. *Financial Management*, 1049–1068.

Hu, J. (2024). The regulation of cryptocurrency in China. *International Journal of Digital Law and Governance*, 1(1), 53–79. https://doi.org/10.1515/ijdlg-2024-0007

Huang, Y., & Mayer, M. (2022). Digital currencies, monetary sovereignty, and U.S.–China power competition. *Policy & Internet*, 14(2), 324–347. https://doi.org/10.1002/poi3.302

Iwashita, N. (2019). *Regulation of Crypto-Asset Exchanges and the Necessity of International Cooperation*. T20/TF2 Policy Brief, March, 15, 2019. https://t20japan.org/wp-content/uploads/2019/03/t20-japan-tf2-3-regulation-crypto-asset-exchanges.pdf

Jagtiani, J., Papaioannou, M., Tsetsekos, G., Dolson, E., & Milo, D. (2021). Cryptocurrencies: Regulatory perspectives and implications for investors. In: Rau, R., Wardrop, R., Zingales, L. (Eds.), *The Palgrave Handbook of Technological Finance*. Cham: Springer International Publishing, pp. 161–186. https://doi.org/10.1007/978-3-030-65117-6_7

Jakarta Post. (2015, October 30). Alam Sutera bomber says he was trying to repay debts. *The Jakarta Post*. https://www.thejakartapost.com/news/2015/10/30/alam-sutera-bomber-says-he-was-trying-repay-debts.html

Ju, L., Lu, T., & Tu, Z. (2016). Capital flight and bitcoin regulation. *International Review of Finance*, 16(3), 445–455.

Kaur, G. (2023, September 24). An overview of the cryptocurrency regulations in Japan. *Cointelegraph*. https://cointelegraph.com/learn/crypto-regulations-in-japan

Kim, C. (2017, September 29). South Korea bans raising money through initial coin offerings. *Reuters*. https://www.reuters.com/article/business/south-korea-bans-raising-money-through-initial-coin-offerings-idUSKCN1C40FE/

Lim, C., Wang, Y., Ren, J., & Lo, S.-W. (2019). A review of fast-growing blockchain hubs in Asia. *The Journal of the British Blockchain Association*. https://jbba.scholasticahq.com/article/9959.pdf

Mahbub, S., & Rahman, R. (2018, July 10). Legality of bitcoin in Bangladesh. *The Daily Star*. https://www.thedailystar.net/law-our-rights/law-analysis/bitcoin-legality-in-bangladesh-bank-1602583

Meera, A. K. (2018). Cryptocurrencies from Islamic perspectives: The case of bitcoin. *Bulletin of Monetary Economics and Banking, 20*(4), 475–492.

Ministry of Finance. (2018, January 22). *Warning Against the Use of Virtual Currency*. Ministry of Finance Republic of Indonesia. https://www.kemenkeu.go.id/informasi-publik/publikasi/siaran-pers/siaran-pers-peringatan-penggunaan-mata-uang-virtual

Ministry of Trade. (2024, March 22). *CoFTRA Encourages Transparent Trading of Crypto Assets*. Ministry of Trade Republic of Indonesia. https://www.kemendag.go.id/berita/pojok-media/bappebti-mendorong-perdagangan-aset-kripto-secara-transparan

Nagase, T., Fukui, T., & Hatano, K. (2024). *Blockchain & Cryptocurrency Laws and Regulations 2024*. Global Legal Insights. https://www.globallegalinsights.com/practice-areas/blockchain-laws-and-regulations/japan/

Nakamoto, S. (2008). *Bitcoin: A Peer-to-Peer Electronic Cash System*. Satoshi Nakamoto.

Nian, L. P., & Chuen, D. L. K. (2015). Introduction to bitcoin. In: *Handbook of Digital Currency*. Academic Press, pp. 5–30.

Ohri, N. (2024, May 16). Exclusive: India's SEBI is open to oversight of crypto trade, in contrast to the Reserve Bank. *Reuters*. https://www.reuters.com/world/india/indias-sebi-open-oversight-crypto-trade-contrast-reserve-bank-2024-05-16/

Omagari, T., & Sako, Y. (2019, November 26). *Japan's New Crypto Regulation: 2019 Amendments to Payment Services Act and Financial Instruments and Exchange Act of Japan*. K&L Gates. https://files.klgates.com/files/publication/c04281aa-b40c-4fcb-931d-ff301e085571/presentation/publicationattachment/7443e764-03c4-4621-9022-4c6258979449/japans_new_crypto_regulation.pdf

Panda, P. C., & Jani, N. (2019). Growth of cryptocurrency and illegal activities. In: *5th International Conference on Economic Growth and Sustainable Development: Emerging Trends*, pp. 15–16. https://www.researchgate.net/profile/Nisarg-Jani-2/publication/343229318_Growth_of_Cryptocurrency_and_Illegal_Activities/links/5f1e53d8299bf1720d6801cf/Growth-of-Cryptocurrency-and-Illegal-Activities.pdf

PBOC, MIIT, CBRC, CSRC, & CIRC. (2013, December 5). *Guanyu Fangfan Bitebi Fengxian de Tongzhi*（关于防范比特币风险的通知）*[Notice on Precautions Against the Risks of Bitcoins]*. The Central People's Government of the People's Republic of China. http://www.gov.cn/gzdt/2013-12/05/content_2542751.html

PILnet. (2023). *Legal Regulation of Cryptocurrency and NFTs*. https://www.pilnet.org/wp-content/uploads/2023/12/Japan-Cryptocurrency-and-NFTs-Guide_formatted.pdf

PPATK. (2018, February 14). *Beware of The Use of Virtual Currency*. Pusat Pelaporan dan Analisis Transaksi Keuangan. https://www.ppatk.go.id/siaran_pers/read/764/siaran-pers-hati-hati-penggunaan-virtual-currency-.html

Pravdiuk, M. (2021). International experience in cryptocurrency regulation. *Norwegian Journal of Development of the International Science, 31*, 37.

Reuters. (2023, July 21). Indonesia launches new crypto bourse, clearing house. *Reuters*. https://www.reuters.com/technology/indonesia-launches-new-crypto-bourse-clearing-house-2023-07-21/

Shin, F. (2022, January 31). *What's Behind China's Cryptocurrency Ban?* https://www.weforum.org/agenda/2022/01/what-s-behind-china-s-cryptocurrency-ban/ Accessed 15th April 2024.

Singh, A. P., & Shukla, D. (2022). A comparative review of taxation policies concerning cryptocurrencies. *Prayagraj Law Review*, 45.

Suud, Y. A. (2021, November 18). *Compensating BitConnect Coin Fraud Victims, US Department of Justice Immediately Disburses $57 Million in Confiscated Assets.* Cyberthreat.id. https://cyberthreat.id/read/12868/Ganti-Rugi-Korban-Penipuan-Bit-Connect-Coin-Depkeh-AS-Segera-Cairkan-Aset-Sitaan-57-Juta

Tassev, L. (2018, February 5). Kazakhstan, Kyrgyzstan, and Uzbekistan on the crypto radar. *Bitcoin.com News*. https://news.bitcoin.com/kazakhstan-kyrgyzstan-and-uzbekistan-on-the-crypto-radar/

Tempo. (2023, July 29). *Indonesia Launches Crypto Exchange; 23 Prospective Traders Have Been Registered.* Tempo.co. https://en.tempo.co/read/1753609/indonesia-launches-crypto-exchange-23-prospective-traders-have-been-registered

You, R. (2022). A new dimension in the world economy – fiat digital currencies: A review. *BCP Business & Management, 30,* 705–711.

Part 5

Navigating the Legal and Ethical Landscapes of the Metaverse

17
Navigating the Legal Landscape of the Metaverse

Aji Baskoro and Annisa Hafizhah

17.1 Introduction

In an era of continuous development, technology has become the backbone of modern society. Innovation flows ceaselessly, changing how we communicate, work, and interact with the surrounding environment. Today, society has become a digital society, where every aspect of life seems intertwined within a framework of sophisticated technology (Brownsword, 2022). Daily interactions are no longer confined to physical meetings but have expanded into the nonphysical world. The latest innovation at present is the virtual world known as the Metaverse.

The Metaverse, as the latest technological innovation, has garnered global attention and sparked discussions worldwide. By leveraging augmented reality (AR) and virtual reality (VR) technology, the Metaverse is formed as a three-dimensional (3D) virtual world that provides profound digital experiences (Dwivedi et al., 2022). Within the Metaverse, users can interact and collaborate in the virtual world, resulting in experiences resembling real life (Mogaji et al., 2023). Avatars representing users can be created in the Metaverse, used to attend digital meetings, and even engage in collaborative activities online (Gao & Lyu, 2023). The uniqueness of the Metaverse lies in its ability to create experiences that closely resemble real life, opening up new opportunities in communication, entertainment, and business (Ariza-Montes et al., 2023).

However, behind this extraordinary potential, several challenges arise, including data security, user privacy, and ethical considerations related to Metaverse usage (Cheng-Han & Kiat-Boon, 2023). These challenges are quite serious and require answers with adaptive regulations. Effective and adaptive regulations must be able to keep up with technological advancements, provide a solid foundation to maintain a balance between technological progress and legal certainty and protect society (Riha & Maj, 2009).

So far, studies on law and the Metaverse remain scarce. However, the author found several studies on the relationship between law and Metaverse technological innovations. First, research on the three waves of technology disruption on legal authority and the demand to respect the law (Clark et al., 2023). Second, research on the essence and framework of new technology and challenges in the Metaverse (Shi et al., 2023). Third, studies on law enforcement in the Metaverse cover private law, such as personal data protection and intellectual property, and public law, such as sexual harassment (Miraj & Zen, 2023). These three studies play a crucial role, and their findings can enrich research on law and technology. However, existing studies need to be enriched through further research on the challenges and legal strategies to respond to the advancement of Metaverse technological innovations. Therefore, this study is a development of several existing studies.

The term "Metaverse," as identified through existing research, originated from the science fiction novel titled "Snow Crash," published in 1992 (Kayakoku, 2023). In this novel, Stephenson depicted the Metaverse as a virtual environment closely linked to the real world, where users interact through digital avatars (Sektiyaningsih, 2022). Since then, this term has garnered the attention of researchers from various sectors. In terms of etymology, the term "Metaverse" consists of two words, namely "meta" and "verse." "Meta" means "beyond," while "verse" means "universe" (Ayanti, 2022). Meanwhile, according to the Great Dictionary of the Indonesian Language (Kamus Besar Bahasa Indonesia, KBBI), the word "metaverse" is defined as "metamesta" (Kamus Besar Bahasa Indonesia, Edisi Kelima).

Topics surrounding the Metaverse have received more attention since Mark Zuckerberg, the founder of Facebook, announced the company's transformation by changing its name from Facebook to Meta (Endarto & Martadi, 2022). This step created a project that provides an overview of the future direction of the internet and social media, where there is closer integration between reality and the virtual world (Shi et al., 2023). Moreover, this action created a new paradigm where the boundaries between the real world and the virtual world are becoming increasingly blurred and narrowed by the concept of Metaverse, which is based on the application of VR and AR technologies (Endarto & Martadi, 2022).

Various studies, discussions, and other aspects emerge in the public domain to show the implications of the Metaverse's development. Whether in economic, political, legal, sociocultural sectors, or education, the Metaverse becomes a profound context with broad impacts (H. Gao et al., 2023). Metaverse holds significant potential for innovation in education.

Utilizing the Metaverse in education is extensive. As emphasized by the World Bank, there are at least four ways in which the Metaverse can positively impact learning and skill development, including learning and connecting in an immersive virtual campus, enhancing real-world skills in virtual and hybrid environments, exploring different worlds through visualization and storytelling, and building human capabilities in interpersonal or difficult situations (Jagannathan, 2022).

Simulation of learning environments can be conducted within the Metaverse. Teachers and students can interact directly in the virtual world to demonstrate lesson materials more realistically. Interaction between teachers and students in the Metaverse can be done as avatars. An avatar represents a person, or in this case, the user, in the digital world. Teachers and students can interact with their respective avatars in an immersive environment. This immersive environment surrounds the user and is presented in 3D, unlike 2D technologies such as video calls, making users feel as if they are physically present in a digital space (Ayanti, 2022).

The Metaverse concept has already been implemented in several educational institutions worldwide. Some universities, such as BrainSTEM University, CEU University, Amman Arab University, Khon Kaen University (KKU), University of Nicosia (UNIC), and the University of Nigeria, have integrated Metaverse into their systems (Endarto & Martadi, 2022). However, educational institutions in Indonesia are still relatively slow to adopt the Metaverse.

Particularly from a legal perspective, privacy, data security, and copyright issues become the focus in the Metaverse. Protection of personal data, freedom of speech, and other individual rights in the virtual world require special attention in terms of legal regulations. The enforcement of security standards and ethics in data usage becomes crucial to maintaining trust and integrity in the Metaverse environment. Furthermore, concerning creative content such as copyright and ownership of assets in the virtual world.

Therefore, the reason for writing this becomes very clear when looking at the disruptive impact of Metaverse in the legal realm. This chapter is expected to uncover emerging legal challenges and formulate effective strategies for responding to the Metaverse. Hopefully, this work can significantly contribute to designing regulations that protect individual rights, including privacy and freedom of speech, in an increasingly complex Metaverse world and benefit stakeholders in formulating good policies. Furthermore, this study is urgent for the development of adaptive regulations. Because the sustainability of Metaverse development requires responsive regulations, this chapter is expected to guide answering regulations that are adaptive to technological changes and Metaverse dynamics.

17.2 Exploring the Impact of Metaverse Beyond Virtual Reality

The Metaverse, as the latest technological innovation, is receiving significant global attention. The Metaverse introduces a new paradigm in digital interaction, using AR and VR technologies to create a 3D VR (Deniz, 2023). The uniqueness of the Metaverse lies in its ability to make a virtual world that users can access and explore. From a technological perspective, the Metaverse integrates AR and VR to provide profound digital experiences (Kraus et al., 2023). AR adds virtual elements to the real world, while VR creates entirely virtual environments.

Combining these two technologies creates a 3D virtual world that allows users to interact, communicate, and collaborate (Ng, 2022). Metaverse users can utilize this platform to interact digitally, create representations of themselves in the form of avatars, and collaborate in virtual environments (Ng, 2022). The 3D environment allows users to engage in digital meetings, collaborative activities, and experiences that emulate real-life scenarios.

Simulations in the Metaverse can be classified into four main types: AR, Lifelogging, Mirror World, and VR. These four types of simulations provide unique dimensions in the Metaverse user experience, each with different characteristics and functions. The simulations as shown in Figure 17.1 (Kye et al., 2021) are described as follows:

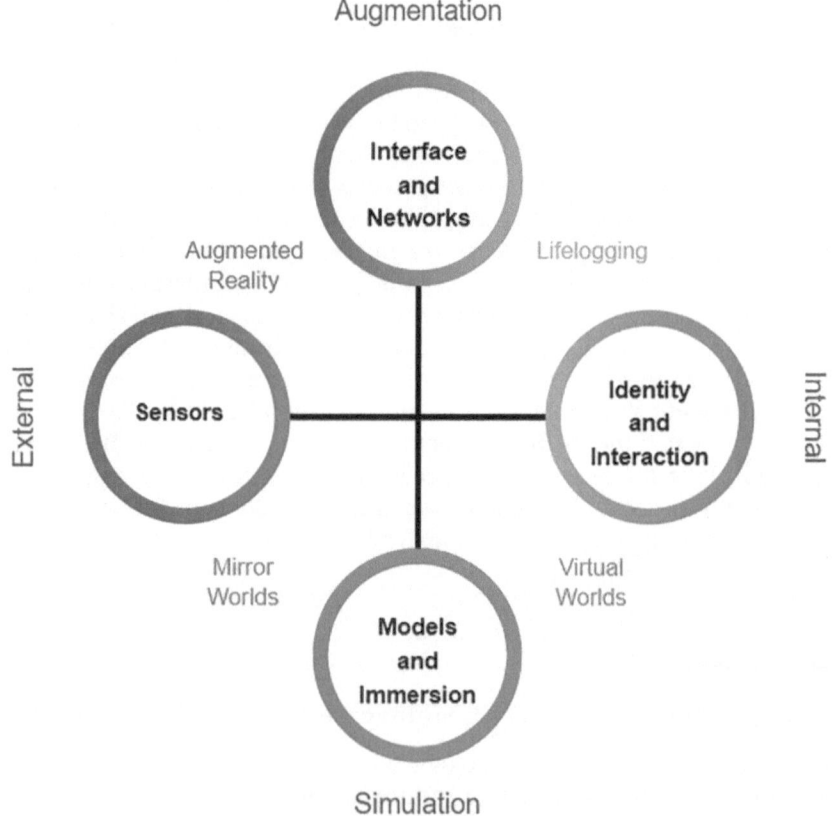

FIGURE 17.1
Simulations of technology and the Metaverse (Kye et al., 2021)

1. **AR:** AR is the simulation of artificial objects in the real environment. This technology combines real-world conditions with human-made objects (Mulati, 2023). AR brings additional virtual elements into the real world. In the context of the Metaverse, AR allows users to see and interact with virtual objects integrated into their physical environment. For example, users can view additional information about objects around them through AR-enabled devices.
2. **Lifelogging:** Lifelogging is similar to other social media platforms. Lifelogging in the Metaverse can capture, collect, store, and share daily experiences and acquired data objects (Mulati, 2023). This involves recording and storing users' daily data, creating digital records encompassing various aspects of their lives. In the Metaverse, lifelogging can provide experiences of sharing memories through digital representations of users' daily lives.
3. **Mirror World:** The simulation of the Mirror World is more futuristic. The virtual model presented involves the refinement of real-world information or "reflection" involving virtual mapping, modeling, annotation tools, and other geospatial sensor technology, as well as location-based lifelogging technology (Mulati, 2023). Mirror World creates a digital copy of the real world. In the Metaverse, Mirror World allows users to explore and interact with digital representations that reflect their physical environment. This creates opportunities for collaboration in a digital world, replicating the real world.
4. **VR:** VR differs from AR. VR technology visually represents virtual worlds using advanced graphics and rendering techniques. AR and VR can combine to create engaging 3D virtual experiences (Mulati, 2023). VR immerses users in an entirely virtual environment. In the Metaverse, VR technology lets users experience deep and immersive experiences in a virtual world. Interaction in this environment occurs entirely within the virtual world.

Furthermore, the Metaverse can be classified into realistic, unrealistic, and fused environments. A fused environment is defined as a combination of elements that are not entirely realistic but are based on conditions that exist in the real world (Schroeder et al., 2001). However, avatars in the Metaverse also face real-world physical limits, such as being unable to exist in multiple places simultaneously. While sensory aspects like atmosphere and touch are hard to replicate, visual and auditory elements can closely mimic reality (Dwivedi et al., 2022).

To ensure sustainability, the Metaverse must operate with many users, and services must be accessible without limits. Even through mobile devices with relatively low specifications (Dwivedi et al., 2022). In designing the Metaverse environment for the long term, scalability needs to be considered, which is the ability to grow and operate on a larger scale than the existing capacity (Dwivedi et al., 2022).

Meanwhile, in the privacy and security of Metaverse data, the Metaverse system can collect much more sensitive information than traditional systems. Thus, it can pose a significant risk of privacy violations for users (Dwivedi et al., 2022). Users known as avatars generate various data, including intimate information such as messages, voice, and video, as well as proprietary business information used in the workplace (Dwivedi et al., 2022). However, as a consequence, threats to data security will continue to exist. Personal information and content stored in the virtual Metaverse environment may face risks of forgery and leakage. For example, Metaverse headset devices can record all conversations and videos in users' private spaces. In addition, eye-tracking technology can record what users see (Dwivedi et al., 2022). Some of the applications of Metaverse are as follows:

1. **Metaverse Integration in Education and Immersive Learning Sector**

   The Metaverse offers immersive learning through AR and VR, extending beyond traditional classrooms. For instance, the European Institute of Administration in France utilizes VR to enhance lesson engagement, like in virtual labs for risky experiments (Contreras et al., 2022). Students worldwide can collaborate on projects in virtual spaces, making education more inclusive. In Indonesia, there is currently a junior high school with the concept of Metaverse, namely MTs Negeri 1 Kebumen with the tagline MATANSA LAND, which helps in the learning program of religion and science (Kebumen24.com, 2022).

   Despite its potential, challenges also arise regarding the adaptation of educational institutions to this technology. Adequate technology infrastructure, teacher training, and providing access for all students are key factors for implementing Metaverse in education. In addition, data security and student privacy in the virtual environment must also be considered to maintain the integrity and security of the learning experience in cyberspace.

2. **Metaverse in Transforming Digital Economy and E-Commerce**

   The Metaverse transforms the digital economy and e-commerce by moving beyond physical limitations. Consumers can now interact with virtual stores, explore 3D products, and use avatars for personalized shopping experiences. Many businesses are adopting virtual showrooms and VR-based product exhibitions, creating immersive environments where social interaction, entertainment, and shopping blend seamlessly. This enhances customer engagement and personalization, allowing businesses to tailor recommendations through artificial intelligence (AI) and behavioral data analysis (Ltifi, 2025).

New business models, including token-based economies and cryptocurrencies, are emerging alongside these developments. Tokenization, via non-fungible tokens (NFTs), enables users to buy, sell, and own digital assets, bringing new value to virtual goods and collectibles. This evolution is reshaping retail and creative industries like entertainment and advertising. Moreover, the Metaverse generates new job opportunities in virtual design, software development, and platform management, further driving its economic impact.

3. **Metaverse and Challenges in the Legal World**

   Implementing Metaverse technology presents several legal challenges, particularly around digital property rights, data protection, and jurisdiction. Users can own digital assets like NFTs, but questions remain about ownership enforcement in a virtual world. Intellectual property rights are also a concern, especially when reproducing digital content, such as art and music, requiring updated copyright laws (Mengual, 2024). Privacy issues are heightened by collecting biometric data in VR devices, leading to concerns about misuse and security.

   Jurisdiction is a significant issue due to the Metaverse's lack of geographical boundaries. Crimes like fraud or harassment in virtual environments raise complex questions about which country's laws should apply. Addressing these challenges requires international regulatory cooperation, as no single country can claim jurisdiction in the Metaverse. Furthermore, Metaverse platforms are typically owned by corporations focused on profit, not adhering to the moral and legal standards expected of governments, raising ethical concerns (Johan, 2022).

4. **Metaverse Opportunities and Challenges in Healthcare**

   The Metaverse offers significant opportunities in healthcare, mainly through AR and VR technologies that enhance medical training and patient care. These technologies allow medical professionals to simulate emergencies, practice complex surgeries, and conduct VR-based therapy for mental health issues like anxiety and trauma. Immersive environments help patients confront fears in a controlled space, improving therapy outcomes. Sensory-rich VR environments also enhance experiential learning for medical professionals (Jane Patel, 2024).

   However, concerns exist regarding the potential negative impacts on users' mental and physical health. Prolonged engagement with virtual worlds may lead to issues like disorientation, technology addiction, or social isolation, especially when users become more comfortable with their virtual identities. Physical health risks, such as eye strain or injury, also arise from extended use of VR devices. Researching the long-term health effects and establishing guidelines for safe usage to mitigate these risks is crucial.

Metaverse, the latest technological innovation, has attracted global attention by offering a new paradigm in digital interaction through AR and VR technologies. With the ability to create 3D virtual worlds that can be accessed and explored, Metaverse integrates AR and VR to provide immersive digital experiences. AR adds virtual elements to the real world, while VR creates an entirely virtual environment, allowing users to interact, communicate, and collaborate in a dynamic virtual space.

However, the use of the Metaverse also poses significant challenges in the legal and health fields. Issues related to digital property rights, personal data protection, and jurisdiction in virtual worlds require special attention and the development of adaptive regulations. On the health side, Metaverse technology can be used for medical training and mental health therapy. Still, it also poses potential risks, such as reality disorientation and physical health issues due to prolonged use of VR devices. Overall, the Metaverse offers vast potential for transformation in various sectors but also requires a cautious approach to its challenges. The application of this technology must be balanced with attention to legal and health aspects to ensure optimal benefits for its users.

17.3 Putting Digital Strategy into Action: Metaverse's Role in Digital Sphere

Technological innovation continues to progress rapidly, shifting the paradigm of human life from traditional to digital and from the real to the virtual world. This transformation significantly impacts various sectors, including the legal world. Therefore, it is not surprising that the legal profession has changed. According to Richard Susskind, there are three driving factors: challenges, liberalization, and information technology (Susskind, 2023). The complex challenges faced in the context of the economy and global changes, along with liberalization that changes legal regulations and policies and the development of information technology, are the primary dynamics that drive transformation in legal practice. In addition to the factors mentioned by Susskind, other factors such as politics, globalization, economic conditions, and history also play an essential role in shaping legal developments (Kusumawardani, 2019).

Therefore, collaboration between law and technology is increasingly becoming a necessity. The collaboration model between law and technology is designed to provide adequate legal certainty and protection (Riswandi, 2016). Through the integration of law and technology, stronger and more efficient mechanisms can be created to respond to rights violations. By supporting each other, law and technology can work together to identify, prevent, and prosecute harmful online actions against individuals and the public (Webley et al., 2019). This creates a more substantial legal environment and gives authorities the power to protect citizens' rights in the virtual world (Johnson & Post, 1996).

In addition, this collaboration can potentially restore violated rights as they should be. For example, the right to receive payment for the information created can be carried out more effectively by combining legal and technological aspects. This can provide fair compensation for those whose rights have been neglected or abused in the digital environment. Therefore, the law must be able to respond to the challenges of the times that arise from technological transformation. Along with the potential of technology to disrupt all sectors, it is essential for the law to have specific and in-depth studies regarding the legal impact and implications of technological advances (Camacho, 2023).

The collaboration between law and technology needs to cover various aspects, ranging from privacy protection and data security to regulations related to developing and implementing new technologies (Guihot, 2019). This will help create a strong and adaptive legal foundation in line with the continuing development of technology (Dwivedi et al., 2023). Thus, the law can effectively maintain justice, human rights, and a balance between technological innovation and societal interests.

In facing rapid and complex changes in various layers of society, especially in the context of technological development and social dynamics, responsive legal involvement is needed. The theory of responsive law, developed by Nonet et al. (2017), introduces essential concepts about integrating social sciences into the legal structure (Asa et al., 2021). They argue that for the law to respond to ongoing challenges and changes, legal strategies must involve elements and influences from the social sciences (Nonet et al., 2017). By integrating social science perspectives into legal science, Nonet and Selznick emphasize the importance of treating the legal experience as dynamic and fluid, not static and rigid, but constantly changing depending on its context. Understanding the law cannot be separated from the evolving social reality (Teubner, 2017). Thus, responsive law proposes a paradigm in which law is not only an entity that enforces rules but also functions as a tool for understanding, responding to, and creating solutions to ever-changing societal issues (Nonet et al., 2017). Some of the ways in which Metaverse affects digital space are as follows:

1. **Technological Innovation and Strategic Digital Transformation**

   The emergence of the Metaverse marks a fundamental transformation in how we understand and utilize technology. Built on the foundation of AR and VR, the Metaverse paves the way for digital experiences beyond mere interaction on a flat screen. The Metaverse blurs the boundaries between the physical and virtual worlds, creating a space where personal, social, and professional activities can be conducted immersively. This represents a significant leap from the traditional digital paradigm, dominated by two-dimensional spaces, toward a 3D world that enables far more prosperous and deeper interactions.

This technological innovation requires companies and organizations to develop new digital strategies that adapt to the changing environment. Digital strategies that were successful in the past may no longer be relevant in the context of the Metaverse as user demands and expectations have shifted. Users in the Metaverse seek more personal, intuitive, and immersive interactions. Therefore, organizations must redefine their digital presence and branding approach and consider radical changes in their business models to remain competitive.

One of the biggest challenges in the Metaverse is establishing a strong and authentic presence in the virtual world. Physical stores, traditional websites, and mobile apps may no longer be enough to capture users' attention. Companies must create virtual spaces in the Metaverse that offer memorable user experiences, from interactive virtual stores and product showcases to live events in 3D spaces. Presence in the Metaverse is not just passive but involves interactions that allow users to experience the value of products or services through simulations and direct experiences. Digital branding in the Metaverse will also heavily depend on how a brand conveys its narrative through avatars, NFTs, and other virtual objects that reflect its identity.

The Metaverse also shifts business models from what we have traditionally known to virtual commerce (v-commerce). In this world, goods and services can be digital assets, such as NFTs, allowing users to buy or trade unique virtual items, such as clothing, virtual property, or digital artwork. Companies need to rethink how they sell products and provide services in a digital format. Business transactions will also shift from traditional models to blockchain transactions, offering greater transparency and security in the virtual environment. Virtual commerce can encompass everything from simple daily transactions to immersive customer experiences like product trials in the virtual world, enabling users to interact directly with products before making a purchase decision.

2. **Integration of Law and Technology: Legal Implications in the Metaverse**

Along with digital transformation, the rise of the Metaverse introduces new legal challenges that must be anticipated. The shift of activities from the real world to the virtual world introduces legal complexities not fully covered by existing laws. Collaboration between law and technology becomes essential, especially in addressing data privacy, intellectual property rights, and digital ownership issues. If not adequately addressed, legal gaps in the Metaverse can expose users and companies to various risks, ranging from virtual fraud and copyright infringement to cybercrime.

Digital assets such as NFTs are becoming increasingly popular in the Metaverse. However, while users can own these virtual assets, the ownership rights and legal protections surrounding them are often questioned. These virtual assets are often tied to unique blockchain systems, where ownership and transactions are recorded transparently. However, without clear legal protection, creators and users remain vulnerable to plagiarism, fraud, or digital theft. Therefore, developing a legal framework to protect digital ownership and copyright is crucial. Such regulations must be global, considering the Metaverse's borderless environment and the cross-country interactions that occur within it.

The immersive nature of the Metaverse amplifies concerns about user privacy and data security. With VR and AR technologies collecting personal data, such as body movements, facial expressions, and social interactions in the virtual world, the data collected can be far more personal than typically gathered through ordinary digital platforms. In this context, personal data protection must be a top priority, especially in securing sensitive information that could be exploited for unethical purposes. Companies and Metaverse developers must comply with international standards such as General Data Protection Regulation (GDPR) and develop privacy policies that protect users. Furthermore, cybersecurity must be a primary concern, with the development of systems capable of detecting and preventing cybercrimes, such as identity theft, eavesdropping, and fraud in virtual transactions.

In addition to security and privacy challenges, there is also the issue of law enforcement in the Metaverse. As a borderless platform, legal jurisdiction becomes a significant issue. If a crime or violation occurs in the virtual world, the key question is, which country's law applies? In this case, international cooperation is crucial to establish rules and procedures that can be applied globally in enforcing laws in the Metaverse. Dispute resolution, such as claims of virtual asset ownership or intellectual property violations, will also require new legal procedures tailored to the nature of the virtual world.

Regarding data privacy, the Metaverse places significant pressure on the current legal landscape and strengthens the argument for recognizing data privacy rights under the U.S. Constitution. As the Metaverse is established and evolves, it is evident that the legal landscape will change to respond to emerging contemporary demands. However, how these adaptations will affect and revise the U.S. legal framework remains unclear. U.S. law seeks to regulate privacy and intellectual property on technology platforms such as the Metaverse (Flannery, 2022). Yet, challenges remain in clarifying the ownership of digital assets like NFTs and providing more detailed protections for data related to avatars and virtual identities. On the other hand, the European Union, through implementing the GDPR, takes a more decisive approach to data privacy. The GDPR, which serves as a reference for data privacy matters, ensures stronger protection of personal data collected in the Metaverse. However, challenges persist in ensuring that data collected through technologies such as AR and VR comply with privacy rules across various member states (Menéndez González & Bozkir, 2024).

3. Responsive Law and the Metaverse

The development of the Metaverse has significant implications for the legal field, necessitating a more adaptive and responsive approach. In this context, the theory of responsive law, introduced by Nonet et al. (2017), becomes highly relevant. Responsive law teaches that the legal system must evolve by societal needs and social changes. In the era of the Metaverse, where technology is rapidly advancing and influencing nearly every aspect of human life, a dynamic and flexible legal approach is crucial to addressing the new challenges that arise. The Metaverse introduces unique challenges, including new forms of social interaction, virtual identities, digital economies, and legal violations in the virtual world. Traditional approaches to law, which tend to be static, will struggle to keep pace with these changes.

Therefore, responsive law is the ideal approach, where the law not only enforces existing rules but also adapts to the new dynamics created by technology. The Metaverse presents cross-border legal challenges, where users from various countries can interact within the same virtual space. This raises issues related to jurisdiction, cross-border intellectual property rights, and cybercrime. To address these challenges, the legal framework in the Metaverse must be dynamic and globally cooperative. Strong international collaboration is needed to establish regulations governing data transfers, digital transactions, and protecting rights in the virtual world. This also requires cross-jurisdictional legal mechanisms to handle disputes arising within the Metaverse.

4. The Metaverse as a Platform for Legal Practice

In addition to its challenges, the Metaverse also opens up new opportunities for legal practice. The Metaverse can become a platform where law firms, lawyers, and other legal professionals can operate more efficiently and without geographical boundaries. This virtual space enables various forms of global collaboration and offers new legal training and simulation approaches. The Metaverse enables the emergence of virtual law firms that operate exclusively in the virtual world. In these virtual law firms, lawyers and clients can meet, discuss, and collaborate in immersive spaces without having to meet face-to-face in the physical world. This will facilitate more efficient cross-border interactions, especially in handling cases involving clients from various jurisdictions. Legal transactions can be conducted in a secure virtual environment, including digital contract signing, online arbitration, or legal consultations. One of the significant benefits of the Metaverse is its potential to be used for legal training and simulation. Universities and law firms can utilize this virtual environment to simulate complex legal cases or trials in realistic settings. These simulations can provide a more profound and interactive learning experience for law students or young lawyers, allowing them to practice facing various real-world legal scenarios.

5. **Regulatory Strategy and Governance in the Metaverse**

The growth of the Metaverse cannot be separated from the issues of governance and regulation within its virtual ecosystem and real-world law. Regulatory strategies in the Metaverse must account for the speed of technological innovation and the need for user protection while ensuring healthy and ethical growth within the virtual world. The Metaverse may be internally regulated by platform providers (such as Meta or Decentraland) or its user community. A user-based governance model implemented through blockchain technology could create a more democratic ecosystem where users have control over the rules and regulations applied in the virtual world. However, this self-governance also requires strong oversight to ensure compliance with international legal standards and the protection of user rights.

Regulation in the Metaverse also requires the adaptation of traditional governance models. Governments and regulatory bodies must explore new legal frameworks or establish unique regulatory bodies responsible for overseeing activities within the Metaverse. These bodies must have global authority and collaborate with national governments to monitor and ensure legal compliance in the virtual world, including addressing copyright violations, data privacy issues, and cybercrime. Furthermore, governance in the Metaverse must consider ethical implications, including freedom of speech, data privacy, and individual liberty. Unbalanced regulations could stifle innovation or, on the other hand, sacrifice user rights. Therefore, a well-considered and balanced regulatory strategy is needed to ensure the law protects users while allowing virtual innovation to flourish.

The Metaverse is a space for technological innovation and significantly impacts strategic digital transformation and legal governance. In this context, the law must follow the changes and actively shape this virtual environment by protecting rights, promoting ethical behavior, and facilitating innovation. Responsive law, flexible regulations, and integration of social sciences are key to creating a sustainable and equitable virtual ecosystem.

17.4 Understanding the Legal Challenges of Metaverse

Metaverse, as a rapid technological innovation, presents several significant legal challenges that must be addressed to ensure sustainability and balance in its use. Here is an analysis of some legal challenges that arise with Metaverse innovation:

1. **Privacy and Data Security:** The main challenge in Metaverse is protecting user privacy and data security. The risk of privacy violations and personal data theft increases with increasingly intensive interactions in the virtual world. The law must meet the demands to ensure Metaverse platforms have high-security standards and effective data protection mechanisms.
2. **Copyright and Ownership of Virtual Assets:** the concepts of copyright and ownership of virtual assets become complex in the Metaverse. Questions about copyright of virtual works, ownership of assets in the digital environment, and regulations on transfer of ownership need to be addressed. The law must evolve to accommodate the rights and obligations related to creative content and virtual assets created and traded in the Metaverse.
3. **Legal Responsibility in the Virtual World:** The Metaverse presents challenges in determining legal responsibility in the virtual world. Questions about punishment for illegal or harmful actions in the Metaverse, such as hacking or damaging behavior, require clear legal regulations. Law enforcement in the virtual world also requires an effective approach.
4. **Ethical and Moral Norms:** The existence of the Metaverse raises new ethical and moral questions. The law must answer questions about ethical boundaries in creating and using Metaverse technology. Debates about users' rights and obligations and norms of behavior

in the digital environment require ethical guidelines and adaptive legal regulations.
5. **User Engagement and Public Participation:** The law needs to address user engagement and public participation in Metaverse development. The regulatory process and policymaking must involve relevant stakeholders to ensure fair representation and protect public interests.
6. **Security and Accidents in the Virtual Environment:** Legal challenges related to security and accidents in the virtual environment must be addressed. Regulations must cover responsibility and compensation in accident or incident situations in the Metaverse.

In responding to these challenges, the law must remain responsive and adaptive and incorporate existing legal principles with Metaverse dynamics. Continuity of dialogue between stakeholders, legal experts, and policymakers is key to effectively and sustainably addressing these challenges. The Metaverse, as a rapidly evolving technological innovation, presents numerous legal challenges that must be addressed to ensure its sustainable and balanced use. One of the foremost issues is privacy and data security, as the immersive nature of the Metaverse allows for intensive data collection, raising concerns about user privacy and personal data protection (Flannery, 2022). With interactions becoming more complex, the risk of data breaches and privacy violations increases, necessitating the development of legal frameworks that enforce high-security standards and robust data protection mechanisms. Another critical challenge is copyright and ownership of virtual assets. Creating, owning, and transferring digital assets – such as virtual real estate or NFTs – introduce new legal questions regarding intellectual property rights. Current copyright laws must evolve to address the unique context of virtual goods and ensure that creators and consumers are adequately protected.

In addition, the issue of legal responsibility in the virtual world is complex, as determining accountability for illegal or harmful activities such as hacking or harassment requires clear legal guidance. Questions around jurisdiction further complicate this, as the Metaverse transcends geographical boundaries, making it challenging to decide which legal system governs disputes. Ethical considerations also arise, with the Metaverse posing new dilemmas regarding acceptable behavior, content regulation, and the ethical use of emerging technologies like AI-driven avatars. Legal frameworks must be established to define boundaries for virtual conduct and safeguard against harmful behavior. Moreover, ensuring user engagement and public participation in shaping the regulatory landscape of the Metaverse is crucial for fostering transparency and protecting the public interest. Developing inclusive policies will be essential to building trust between users and platforms.

Finally, security and accidents in the virtual environment present further legal challenges. As the Metaverse grows, so do the risks of cyberattacks and technical malfunctions that could result in real-world harm or damage. Legal systems must determine liability for accidents occurring in virtual spaces and establish security standards to mitigate these risks. In conclusion, the Metaverse demands innovative and responsive legal solutions. Continuous collaboration between legal professionals, technologists, and policymakers is vital to addressing these challenges effectively, ensuring that legal principles evolve alongside the digital transformations shaping the future.

17.5 Aligning Existing Legal Principles with the Promised Feature of Metaverse

The Metaverse is a concept of the future virtual world, also known as Web 3.0, intended to complement or potentially replace the Web 2.0-based internet we use daily. The Metaverse provides a virtual space where users can engage in various activities, including purchasing digital assets such as virtual land, buildings, and artwork (Ruhtiani et al., 2022).

The Metaverse enables individuals to interact in virtual worlds using digital technology. However, recent developments have turned the Metaverse into an investment vehicle for entrepreneurs. Major technology companies have spent tens of billions of dollars acquiring global gaming brands. In contrast, others have invested billions of dollars in research and development of Metaverse technology and infrastructure. In addition, investors and entrepreneurs are spending millions of dollars to purchase digital land in the Metaverse to create virtual business spaces where consumers can buy and sell goods and host shows and art exhibitions (Ruhtiani et al., 2022).

The development of the Metaverse itself has been a phenomenal breakthrough in the development of NFTs, which serve as digital assets within the Metaverse. One of the notable Metaverse projects is Decentraland, which began development in late 2015 by Ari Meillich and Esteban Ordano, two individuals from Argentina. Therefore, the relationship between NFTs and the Metaverse is closely intertwined. The Metaverse also influences the sustainability of NFTs. Someone who owns an NFT will possess valuable assets in the digital environment, equivalent to owning valuable assets or goods in the physical world. NFTs have various applications, including gaming and branded products. The use of NFTs is diverse, including integration with the Metaverse world and physical products in the real world, such as collecting and trading digital assets, including artworks like paintings, music, and images, issuing online event tickets, selling items in Metaverse games, or even as proof of ownership of an asset like a land ownership certificate (Alexander Sugiharto et al., 2022).

With the growing popularity of NFTs and digital art, copyright disputes have become increasingly prominent in the Metaverse. Many creators find their digital assets being copied, sold, or misused without their consent. A notable case for copyright disputes in the Metaverse is *Hermès vs. Mason Rothschild*, where the luxury brand sued the digital artist for creating and selling "MetaBirkins," NFT versions of the Birkin bag. Hermès argued that the NFTs infringed on their trademark, leading to a lawsuit in U.S. federal court. Rothschild defended his work as artistic expression protected by free speech. However, the court ruled in favor of Hermès, establishing a precedent that traditional intellectual property laws apply even in the virtual realm (Johnson, 2024).

Furthermore, another real-world issue in the Metaverse involves privacy concerns and data breaches, as seen with Meta's (formerly Facebook) Horizon Worlds. Since Metaverse platforms collect vast amounts of personal data – such as biometric data, user behavior, and financial information – breaches can expose sensitive details to hackers. In 2022, Meta faced issues over its handling of biometric data, including facial recognition and user movements, raising alarms among privacy advocates such as the European Union's GDPR watchdogs. As a response, Meta introduced stricter data protection measures and allowed users to opt out of certain data collection practices, complying with regulations like GDPR. These cases show how real-world legal frameworks and data privacy regulations are being adapted to address challenges in the evolving digital landscape. Meta complied with international data protection regulations, like GDPR and the U.S. privacy laws, to avoid legal penalties. Meta enhanced encryption standards, adopted data anonymization techniques, and gave users better control over their privacy settings (McDonald, 2022).

Both examples (copyright dispute and data breaches in the Metaverse) demonstrate how real-world legal frameworks are applied to emerging problems in the Metaverse. However, technological solutions and regulatory compliance continue to evolve as these platforms grow. In responding to Metaverse innovation, legal strategies need to be developed considering the theory of responsive law proposed by Philippe Nonet, Philip Selznick, and Robert A. Kagan. This theory offers a foundation for responding to ongoing social dynamics and creating adaptive law. Here is an analysis of legal strategies in the context of Metaverse based on responsive law theory:

1. **Interdisciplinary Engagement:** Responsive law theory emphasizes integrating social sciences into legal science. In the context of Metaverse, legal strategies can involve collaboration between legal experts, information technology specialists, psychologists, and social scientists to holistically understand Metaverse's social and technological impacts. This interdisciplinary engagement supports the development of more contextual and relevant regulations.

2. **Flexibility and Adaptability of Law:** The flexibility and adaptability of law in responsive theory become important in responding to rapid changes in the Metaverse. Regulations must adapt to technological developments and changes in user behavior. Strategies that allow for quick and timely regulation revisions will provide sustainability and effectiveness in addressing Metaverse challenges.
3. **Public Participation and Stakeholder Engagement:** Responsive law theory emphasizes public participation in policy-making. Legal strategies in Metaverse must involve users, technology companies, academics, and advocacy groups to create fair regulations that accommodate various interests. Public participation ensures more representative regulations that understand the community's needs.
4. **Legal Education and Public Awareness:** Legal strategies in the Metaverse can include proactive legal education approaches and increasing public awareness of rights and obligations in the digital environment. This aligns with the concept of social responsibility inherent in responsive law theory.
5. **Balance between Regulation and Innovation:** Responsive law theory emphasizes the balance between regulation and innovation. Legal strategies in Metaverse must recognize the need to promote innovation while maintaining security and individual rights. Formulating rules that do not hinder technological progress yet protect societal values is challenging.

By guiding legal strategies with the principles of responsive law theory, it is hoped that regulations in the Metaverse can create a dynamic, fair, and adaptive legal environment capable of accommodating rapid developments in the digital world. Continuity of dialogue between policymakers, legal experts, and the community is essential in successfully implementing these strategies.

17.6 Conclusion

In conclusion, integrating law and technology, particularly in response to the innovation of the Metaverse, presents both opportunities and challenges. The legal strategies proposed based on the theory of responsive law emphasize interdisciplinary collaboration, flexibility, public participation, legal education, and maintaining a balance between regulation and innovation. These strategies aim to create a dynamic and adaptive legal framework capable of addressing the evolving social and technological landscape of the Metaverse while safeguarding individual rights and societal values.

By adopting these strategies, policymakers, legal experts, and stakeholders can work together to navigate the complexities of the Metaverse and ensure that legal systems remain relevant and effective in the digital age. Continuous dialogue and engagement with the community are crucial for successfully implementing these strategies and fostering a harmonious relationship between law and technology in the ever-evolving digital world.

After all, this chapter provides a general overview of legal issues in the Metaverse, highlighting key challenges but recognizing the need for more in-depth research. Future studies should explore specific legal frameworks to address issues like intellectual property, privacy, and jurisdiction in virtual spaces. An interdisciplinary approach, incorporating legal, technological, and societal perspectives, will be essential to develop comprehensive solutions. Further research could focus on creating robust legal structures that account for the complexities of the Metaverse, ensuring both innovation and user protection.

References

Alexander Sugiharto, S. H., Muhammad Yusuf Musa, M. B. A., & Mochamad James Falahuddin, S. T. (2022). *NFT & Metaverse: Blockchain, Dunia Virtual & Regulasi*. Indonesian Legal Study for Crypto Asset and Blockchain.

Ariza-Montes, A., Quan, W., Radic, A., Yu, J., & Han, H. (2023). Human values and traveler behaviors: Metaverse for conferences and meetings. *Journal of Travel & Tourism Marketing*, 40(6), 490–511. https://doi.org/10.1080/10548408.2023.2263766

Asa, A. I., Munir, M., & Ningsih, R. S. M. (2021). Nonet and Selznick's responsive law concept in a historical philosophy perspective. *Crepido*, 3(2), 96–109. https://doi.org/10.14710/crepido.3.2.96–109

Ayanti, N. (2022). Metaverse dalam Pembelajaran *cross cultural understanding* di Jurusan Bahasa Inggris Politeknik Negeri Sriwijaya. In *Sistem Informasi dan Teknologi Digital Era Metaverse*. Akademia Pustaka.

Brownsword, R. (2022). Law, authority, and respect: Three waves of technological disruption. *Law, Innovation and Technology*, 14(1), 5–40. https://doi.org/10.1080/17579961.2022.2047517

Camacho, A. E. (2023). In the anthropocene: Adaptive law, ecological health, and biotechnologies. *Law, Innovation and Technology*, 15(1), 280–312. https://doi.org/10.1080/17579961.2023.2184133

Cheng-Han, T., & Kiat-Boon, D. S. (2023). The metaverse beyond the internet. *Law, Innovation and Technology*, 15(2), 313–356. https://doi.org/10.1080/17579961.2023.2245677

Clark, T., Hamilton, O., Morris, M., & Vereen, E. (2023). Mission, morals and the metaverse: How Morehouse College is transforming undergraduate education in the sciences and humanities with virtual reality. In *Ethical Considerations of Virtual Reality in the College Classroom*. Routledge.

Contreras, G., González, A., Fernández, M., Cepa, C., & Escobar, J. (2022). The importance of the application of the metaverse in education. *Modern Applied Science*, 16(3), Article 3. https://doi.org/10.5539/mas.v16n3p34

Deniz, K. (2023). Metaverse and new narrative: Storyliving in the age of metaverse. In *The Future of Digital Communication*. CRC Press.

Dwivedi, Y. K., Hughes, L., Baabdullah, A. M., Ribeiro-Navarrete, S., Giannakis, M., Al-Debei, M. M., Dennehy, D., Metri, B., Buhalis, D., Cheung, C. M. K., Conboy, K., Doyle, R., Dubey, R., Dutot, V., Felix, R., Goyal, D. P., Gustafsson, A., Hinsch, C., Jebabli, I., . . . Wamba, S. F. (2022). Metaverse beyond the hype: Multidisciplinary perspectives on emerging challenges, opportunities, and agenda for research, practice, and policy. *International Journal of Information Management*, 66, 102542. https://doi.org/10.1016/j.ijinfomgt.2022.102542

Dwivedi, Y. K., Kshetri, N., Hughes, L., Slade, E. L., Jeyaraj, A., Kar, A. K., Baabdullah, A. M., Koohang, A., Raghavan, V., Ahuja, M., Albanna, H., Albashrawi, M. A., Al-Busaidi, A. S., Balakrishnan, J., Barlette, Y., Basu, S., Bose, I., Brooks, L., Buhalis, D., . . . Wright, R. (2023). Opinion paper: "So what if ChatGPT wrote it?" Multidisciplinary perspectives on opportunities, challenges, and implications of generative conversational AI for research, practice, and policy. *International Journal of Information Management*, 71, 102642. https://doi.org/10.1016/j.ijinfomgt.2023.102642

Endarto, I. A., & Martadi, M. (2022). Analisis potensi implementasi metaverse Pada media Edukasi Interaktif. *BARIK – Jurnal S1 Desain Komunikasi Visual*, 4(1), 37–51.

Flannery, C. B. (2022). Philosophical and practical privacy in the metaverse: A case for data privacy protection under the United States Constitution. *Cornell JL & Pub. Pol'y*, 32, 133.

Gao, H., Chong, A. Y. L., & Bao, H. (2023). Metaverse: Literature review, synthesis, and future research agenda. *Journal of Computer Information Systems*, 0(0), 1–21. https://doi.org/10.1080/08874417.2023.2233455

Gao, Z., & Lyu, X. (2023). Planet Anima: A virtual graduation experience in the metaverse. *Digital Creativity*, 34(3), 248–263. https://doi.org/10.1080/14626268.2023.2254750

Guihot, M. (2019). Coherence in technology law. *Law, Innovation and Technology*, 11(2), 311–342. https://doi.org/10.1080/17579961.2019.1665792

Jagannathan, S. (2022). *How Could the Metaverse Impact Education?* https://www.weforum.org/agenda/2022/12/metaverse-impact-education-learning/ accessed at 15-09-2024.

Jane Patel, N. (2024). Exploring the implications of the metaverse: Opportunities and challenges for dance movement therapy. *Body, Movement, and Dance in Psychotherapy*, 0(0), 1–12. https://doi.org/10.1080/17432979.2024.2306581

Johan, S. (2022). Metaverse and its implication in law and business. *Jurnal Hukum Progresif*, 10, 153–166. https://doi.org/10.14710/jhp.10.2.153-166

Johnson, D. R., & Post, D. (1996). Law and borders: The rise of law in cyberspace. *Stanford Law Review*, 48(5), 1367–1402. https://doi.org/10.2307/1229390

Johnson, H. (2024). *Case review: Hermès International v. Rothschild*. https://itsartlaw.org/2024/05/07/case-review-hermes-v-rothschild/ accessed at 15-09-2024.

Kayakoku, H. (2023). History and development of virtual worlds and metaverse. In F. S. Esen, H. Tinmaz, & M. Singh (Eds.), *Metaverse* (Vol. 133, pp. 19–30). Springer Nature Singapore. https://doi.org/10.1007/978-981-99-4641-9_2

Kebumen24.com. (2022, Desember). *Resmi Dilaunching, Madrasah Metaverse Diharapkan Jadi Percontohan MTS Lain – Kebumen24.com*. https://kebumen24.com/2022/12/09/resmi-dilaunching-madrasah-metaverse-diharapkan-jadi-percontohan-mts-lain/

Kraus, S., Kumar, S., Lim, W. M., Kaur, J., Sharma, A., & Schiavone, F. (2023). From moon landing to metaverse: Tracing the evolution of technological forecasting and social change. *Technological Forecasting and Social Change, 189*, 122381. https://doi.org/10.1016/j.techfore.2023.122381

Kusumawardani, Q. D. (2019). Hukum Progresif dan Perkembangan Teknologi Kecerdasan Buatan. *Veritas et Justitia, 5*(1), 166–190. https://doi.org/10.25123/vej.3270

Kye, B., Han, N., Kim, E., Park, Y., & Jo, S. (2021). Educational applications of metaverse: Possibilities and limitations. *Journal of Educational Evaluation for Health Professions, 18*, 32. https://doi.org/10.3352/jeehp.2021.18.32

Ltifi, M. (Ed.). (2025). *Advances in Digital Marketing in the Era of Artificial Intelligence: Case Studies and Data Analysis for Business Problem Solving* (1st ed). CRC Press.

McDonald, T. (2022). *Will Meta's VR "Horizon Worlds" Threaten Your Information Privacy & Online Safety?* https://www.ask.com/news/meta-horizon-worlds-vr-information-privacy-and-online-safety accessed at 15-09-2024.

Menéndez González, N., & Bozkir, E. (2024). Eye-tracking devices for virtual and augmented reality metaverse environments and their compatibility with the European Union general data protection regulation. *Digital Society, 3*(2), 39.

Mengual, L. A. (2024). Legal status for avatars in the metaverse from a private law perspective. *InDret, 2*, 102–135. Scopus.

Miraj, I. M., & Zen, A. P. (2023). The legal status of metaverse law and its implementation in the modern era. In *Sustainable Development in Creative Industries: Embracing Digital Culture for Humanities*. Routledge.

Mogaji, E., Dwivedi, Y. K., & Raman, R. (2023). Fashion marketing in the metaverse. *Journal of Global Fashion Marketing, 0*(0), 1–16. https://doi.org/10.1080/20932685.2023.2249483

Mulati, Y. (2023). Analisis Penggunaan Teknologi metaverse terhadap Pembentukan Memori pada Proses Belajar. *Ideguru: Jurnal Karya Ilmiah Guru, 8*(2).

Ng, D. T. K. (2022). What is the metaverse? Definitions, technologies, and the community of inquiry. *Australasian Journal of Educational Technology, 38*(4), Article 4. https://doi.org/10.14742/ajet.7945

Nonet, P., Selznick, P., & Kagan, R. A. (2017). *Law and Society in Transition: Toward Responsive Law*. Routledge.

Riha, D., & Maj, A. (2009). *The Real and the Virtual: Critical Issues in Cybercultures*. BRILL. https://doi.org/10.1163/9781848880122

Riswandi, B. A. (2016). Hukum dan Teknologi: Model Kolaborasi Hukum dan Teknologi dalam Kerangka Perlindungan Hak Cipta di Internet. *Jurnal Hukum IUS QUIA IUSTUM, 23*(3), Article 3. https://doi.org/10.20885/iustum.vol23.iss3.art1

Ruhtiani, M., Naili, Y. T., Wahyuni, H. A., & dan Purwono, P. (2022). Perlindungan aset digital Pada era metaverse dalam Perspektif Hukum Positif di Indonesia. *Literasi Hukum, 6*(2) https://jurnal.untidar.ac.id/index.php/literasihukum/article/view/6804

Schroeder, R., Huxor, A., & Smith, A. (2001). Activeworlds: Geography and social interaction in virtual reality. *Futures, 33*(7), 569–587. Scopus. https://doi.org/10.1016/S0016-3287(01)00002-7

Sektiyaningsih, I. S. (2022). Tren Nft Dan Defi Dalam Bisnis Di Era Metaverse. *JMBA Jurnal Manajemen dan Bisnis*, *8*(2). http://journal.ibmasmi.ac.id/index.php/JMBA/article/view/493/332

Shi, F., Ning, H., Zhang, X., Li, R., Tian, Q., Zhang, S., Zheng, Y., Guo, Y., & Daneshmand, M. (2023). A new technology perspective of the metaverse: Its essence, framework, and challenges. *Digital Communications and Networks*. https://doi.org/10.1016/j.dcan.2023.02.017

Susskind, R. (2023). *Tomorrow's Lawyers: An Introduction to Your Future* (3rd ed). Oxford University Press.

Teubner, G. (2017). Substantive and reflexive elements in modern law. In *Luhmann and Law*. Routledge.

Webley, L., Flood, J., Webb, J., Bartlett, F., Galloway, K., & Tranter, K. (2019). The profession(s)' engagements with LawTech: Narratives and archetypes of future law. *Law, Technology and Humans*, 6–26. https://doi.org/10.5204/lthj.v1i0.1314

18

Virtual Rape: Parallels between Physical and Virtual Violation in the Metaverse

Stephin Sinu Oommen and Anushka Datta

18.1 Introduction

Humanity steps into an entirely new arena with a hyper-realistic environment, and the users facilitate the medium of experiencing it through physical sensations. This virtual experience is termed a Metaverse, essentially a parallel dimension where individuals can partake in various activities via a virtual medium, from gaming to attending meetings. A survey conducted by PwC (PwC, 2022) stated that subjects, including about 5,000 U.S. business leaders, half of the consumers expressed their eagerness about the metaverse, while two-thirds of the executives stated that their companies are currently involved in it. Moreover, according to the World Economic Forum (WEF) (World Economic Forum, 2010), a quarter of individuals are projected to dedicate a minimum of one hour per day to activities in the metaverse by 2026 (Masterson, 2022).

There is apparent anticipation around the metaverse, bringing in the aspects of many possible legal complexities, with the questions of safety and security rising as a result. In a recent instance of January 2024, a 16-year-old girl from the United Kingdom suffered from extreme emotional trauma when her virtual avatar got gang raped by other users (Belagere, 2024). This has become the first-ever case in the country and has brought to light the issue of criminal conduct in the virtual world and its effect on real-life people, as it can have real psychological and physical consequences (George, 2024). It is noted that virtual reality (VR) is a comprehensive digital realm where various actions can be rendered to feel authentic and sensory perceptions can be greatly enhanced (Wang et al., 2021).

This chapter discusses and holds that the gravity of such an offense cannot be put aside, as the same act in the real-life context is recognized as a punishable offense. Thus, it becomes imperative to take measures regarding the legal framework of these criminal actions committed in the metaverse and the legal remedies available for the victim.[1]. The empirical survey is intended to examine whether legal measures can safeguard the rights or interests of avatars or whether accountability for misconduct lies solely with the avatars or the users perpetrating the misconduct in the real world.

This chapter observes, by looking at the present structure of legislation, a lack of adequate attention to the new development in the metaverse recognized that is consequential to the pertaining issue and the need for an introduction to new standards and regulations about the crimes in the metaverse arises. The virtual nature of the metaverse has become a double-edged sword (Chawki, 2024). While technological advancement has introduced more reach toward the audience and an enriching experience, it has also posed a new challenge of dealing with the mental and emotional impact via these highly realistic simulations and the legality of the acts committed in such virtual space (Yu et al., 2024). It is noted that the discussion on the crime being committed in the metaverse brings forth the issue of the support systems being dispensed within virtual spaces regarding seeking justice for the victims (Athena, 2024). Furthermore, to tackle the legal procedure of a metaverse crime, it becomes essential to determine if users can be held responsible for the actions of their digital counterparts, and if so, then what shall be the extent of the same (Gómez-Quintero et al., 2024).

This chapter focuses on whether India's legal framework is sufficient to address these challenges individuals face in the virtual space (Fortune Business Insights, 2024). It is studied that due to technological development, there was a report conducted in India by Fortune Business, which concluded the report with a result of an overall growth of 35.3% over the forecasted period of 2023–2030. There is a sudden boom in India because these devices' prices have been relatively low, so more and more people are getting access to the metaverse.

18.2 Related Works and Literature Review

The body of research on **"Virtual Rape"** has expanded significantly; several studies have explored various facets, each contributing unique insights. Research work ranging from international authors and authors from India have contributions offering diverse perspectives and insights.

Bellini (2024) addressed the punishments and penalties for sexual assault in the metaverse and, along with that, discusses the challenges that are present regarding regulating the crimes in the metaverse and their jurisdiction. This chapter also addresses the physical and physiological harm and the role of emotional dilemma in the current legal system and how it affects humans. This study briefly introduces the metaverse and tells us about an individual's immersive experience in these virtual spaces. The use of haptic suits gives us a sensory feeling of the activities that we face in the metaverse; thus, due to this technological development, the possibility of mental and physical harm raises concerns over the real-world harm that an individual can cause upon himself. This chapter raises concerns over the inadequacy of the legal frameworks and also about the evolving nature of virtual interactions and offers suggestions for understanding the implications of these technologies.

Sarkar and Rajan (2021) explored the concept of cybercrimes against women in India from a female's viewpoint in their work, *Materiality and Discursivity of Cyber Violence Against Women in India*. The cyberactivities women encounter tend to be an act that automatically leads women to stop using this software and online participation for their safety. This study takes account of this crime as a gender-based and abuse of their digital bodies by an individual from the rest of the world or an intimate partner they trust. This work touches upon the various causes of cyber abuse and online victimization. It has research consisting of interviews with 30 survivors of these offenses committed in cyberspace. It also provides a broad scope of understanding of the magnitude of these offenses in the metaverse and presents a balanced view of the metaverse, recognizing its transformative potential and significant risks to women in the global south.

Chawki (2024), in his work, *Redefining Boundaries in the Metaverse: Navigating the Challenges of Virtual Harm and User Safety*, raises concerns over user safety in the metaverse. This work mainly focuses on the legal framework to combat the challenge regarding sexual exploitation in the metaverse. The authors have provided constructive feedback on the challenges and solutions to tackle them. Introducing the metaverse concept has attracted a new set of challenges. It has invoked interest in various academic fields and a multifaceted approach to the implication of user security. The authors have suggested various methods and safety methods to enhance the safety protocol. The author, taking reference from work scholars like Qin et al. (2022), suggested a comprehensive global framework ensuring a safer environment for individuals in the metaverse. The author also suggests regulating bodies to create laws by taking sufficient time rather than making laws hastily. This research also tells us to update existing laws rather than create new laws for existing crimes in cyberspace.

Singh (2015) provides us a glimpse of what one can encounter in the metaverse, including acts like cyber victimization – actions of stalking, slander, and hacking expressly targeting women. The proof is absent, and the concern of defamation creates barriers to identifying possible offenders. This research addresses numerous facets of cyber violence targeting women, utilizing evidence from diverse regions to offer a thorough knowledge of the problem. Cybercrimes that aim at women include online abuse, impersonation, and emotional dishonesty. These actions are often the result of tight connections and former partners using shared knowledge for vengeance or extortion. Women are more likely to be victims of cybercrimes compared to men. Statistical data suggests that roughly 75% of those who fall victim to cybercrime are categorized as female, yet the true figures may be more prominent due to underreporting. Several instances go unheard because there is no direct harm involved in those acts, making it difficult to scale the level of harm. Singh's work raises concerns regarding the extent of legislation to tackle cyber-crimes that affect women in cyberspace. The lack of precise regulation creates a sense of impunity among offenders, as demonstrated by occasions when culprits dodge considerable penalties due to legal loopholes.

Karthika and Vijayalakshmi (2021) focus on one of the instances that occurred to a celebrity; this work investigates the cyberbullying of actress Parvathy for voicing anti-misogyny ideas. Cybermob targeted Parvathy with rape threats after her controversial speech. The "Virtual Rape Through Facebook" addresses different issues of cyberbullying, trolling, and their ramifications in the digital era. The author focused on the development of the internet and social media, and the role of trolls and cyberbullying in the literature on these phenomena has been surprisingly minimal. This anonymity eliminates the fear of real-world consequences. The study explores how platforms like Facebook and Twitter might facilitate recognizable threats, particularly among youngsters who may misunderstand the hazards involved with their online actions. The research also highlights that there are gender differences in the perceptions of cyberbullying, with male respondents being more likely than their female counterparts to view such episodes as entertaining. In contrast, the latter tends to pay more attention to the negative consequences. The study finds that a good number of the respondents understand the negative impacts of cyberbullying, with some going further to claim that the victims are constantly attacked for no apparent reason. This literature review covers the previously conducted studies on cyberbullying and trolling, which broadens the framework in which the case of Parvathy and its reception will be investigated.

Rigotti and Malgieri (2023), in their work, analyze the impact of the metaverse on the mental and physical aspects of the users and recipients. It elucidates the risks and challenges of applying metaverse technology in the real world. It focuses on the need for specifically vulnerability-sensitive design and protection of human rights. These aspects are crucial to assessing the metaverse's effects on individuals based on their situations. There is a need to consider the unpredictable impacts of the metaverse, especially the risks associated with "meta-vulnerability," presented by the author. The insights gained from this body of work highlight the topic's complexity and establish a solid foundation for further exploration.

18.3 Introduction to the World of Metaverse

Metaverse is a parallel universe where individuals can play video games or participate in events through their digital avatars. It is a three-dimensional, computer-generated environment that has been the common link between the physical and digital worlds. According to the WEF, 25% of people spends at least an hour daily in the metaverse by 2026 (Wright, 2022).

The metaverse concept encompasses a virtual realm that merges through the convergence of physical and digital reality. Within this space, individuals can engage in immersive interactions with both other people and digital content. Key technologies facilitating the development of the metaverse include VR, augmented reality, and artificial intelligence (Zhu, 2022). Metaverse first gained attention in 1992, when it was portrayed as a virtual universe accessible through VR headsets. Since then, this idea has been explored in various works of fiction, including Ernest Cline's novel Ready Player One (2011), in which individuals seek refuge from a dystopian reality by immersing themselves in a virtual world.

The metaverse is not a single virtual world but a network of interconnected 3D worlds that can be accessed through different sources, devices, and platforms (Stephenson, 2021). Some examples of existing or emerging metaverse platforms are Roblox, Fortnite, Minecraft, and Meta Horizon. Users can create and explore virtual worlds, connect with different people in the metaverse, engage in gaming experiences, buy and sell digital and physical products, and many other activities beyond human thinking can be done with the assistance of the metaverse. The metaverse is still in its early stages of development, and many challenges and opportunities are ahead. Some issues that need to be addressed are its feasibility, privacy, safety, regulation, and social impact.

18.4 Legal Implications

Virtual Rape in the metaverse raises issues concerning governance cases across multiple platforms, countries, and cultures as a result of the wide reach of the virtual space. Law enforcement becomes a challenge because of the lack of clarity of jurisdiction in virtual spaces. In terms of identifying and tracking the perpetrators, anonymity is a hindrance in the process of investigations. Thus, an effective mechanism becomes important to hold violators accountable. Introducing the compensation system for victims becomes another key aspect that requires attention. Even though it takes place in a digital space, the psychological and emotional impact has caused trauma in some instances that adversely affected their participation in the metaverse. Consent and privacy issues are among the most significant factors that raise concern. Although VR platforms are actively taking respective initiatives in establishing clear methods for regulating virtual interactions, safeguarding users' privacy on a policy level, with the user's personal information being so accessible, also becomes particularly vital.

18.5 Definition of Virtual Rape: The Horrific Crime in the Realm of Virtual Reality

There is no uniform definition of rape committed in the metaverse, as different virtual worlds may have different rules and regulations. The laws that are existing in the physical world relating to rape are one of the possible ways that can also apply to the virtual world, with some changes and modifications. Although the Information Technology Act of 2000 (IT Act) recognizes certain cybercrimes and could be extended to cyberstalking cases, these laws cannot be explicitly imposed in cases of VR crimes. The possibility of extending the Indian Penal Code (IPC) to VR is not possible as the penal code only applies to living persons and digital avatars are not covered under the term "living persons." The Bharatiya Nyaya Sanhita (BNS), 2023, which replaced IPC, shall also not be applicable as the principle continues to remain the same as of the IPC regarding defining offenses in the old manner (Bakshi & Narang, 2024).

According to the BNS, 2024, rape has been defined under Section 63 which provides that a man is said to commit rape when he penetrates to any extent into the vagina of the woman; even the slightest penetration by a man into a woman's vagina amounts to rape.[2]

In the metaverse, however, physical penetration may not be possible or relevant, depending on the nature of the virtual world and the technology used. In such a world, rape may be committed by using a tool that makes a user appear to perform sexual and violent acts toward another user without their consent. This could be seen as a form of psychological rape, as it causes emotional distress and violation to the victim (Chalmers, 2022).

VR headsets and haptic suits give users a stronger sense of presence and actualization in virtual avatars. In such a universe, rape may be committed by physically touching or grabbing another user's avatar sexually without their consent, as happened in a recent case in 2022 (Das, 2022). This could be seen as a form of Virtual Rape, as it causes physical discomfort and violation to the victim. Therefore, users who commit such acts should be held accountable and face appropriate consequences.

There was a case of Mr. Bungle in LambdaMOO (Beresford, n.d.). In this case, Mr. Bungle used a tool that made him appear to perform sexual and violent acts toward other users without their consent. The impact of these sexual acts on the victims was severe, as they felt violated, humiliated, and traumatized by the experience. They also felt powerless and helpless to stop or escape from the attack. Some even questioned their identity and reality in the virtual world.

Mr. Bungle had no remorse or apology for his actions, while the victims had varying responses ranging from attempting to forget to seeking justice or revenge. The platform's response was lacking since it did not have clear rules for preventing or punishing such behavior. The law was nonexistent since it didn't recognize the rights or interests of virtual citizens and failed to protect them. This is just one of the nuances surrounding digital avatars in the metaverse involving heinous crimes like rape.

18.5.1 Forms of Virtual Rape

Some of the forms of Virtual Rape are discussed as follows:

1. **Unwanted Sexual Advances:** Unwanted sexual advances in the metaverse are any actions or words that express sexual interest or desire toward another user without their consent or in violation of their boundaries. In extended reality spaces, one can force another user to partake in sexual imagery or interactions. This can involve making them view explicit videos or engage in virtual sex. In addition, one can manipulate a user's avatar, using tools or scripts, to perform sexual or violent acts without their consent, thus deceiving others into thinking they are consenting (Hinduja, 2022).

    Sharing explicit content in the metaverse without someone's consent violates their privacy. This could involve distributing or exposing intimate images, videos, or messages of another user in various ways – from hacking into their account or device to accessing their personal data or digital assets such as photos, videos, or messages and sharing them with others or posting them online (Todd et al., 2022). In addition, this may occur by recording an avatar or virtual activity without the user's knowledge, sharing it with others, or posting it online. In the metaverse, one can seize instances of intimate and brutal encounters, facial expressions, or feelings. Sharing undesirable content in the metaverse without consent may negatively impact the individuals involved, causing trauma, humiliation, and violation. Regrettably, the victims might even lose faith in the virtual communities and platforms (Todd et al., 2022).

2. **Forced Participation in Sexual Activities:** In VR, forcing someone into sexual activities is entirely nonconsensual. It can happen in a few ways. One way to do it is by taking someone's belongings on purpose, like touching and grabbing another user's avatar sexually without their consent or using haptic suits to create an endless feeling of touch, which may cause discomfort. This is known as nonconsensual forced participation in the metaverse. The victim can feel the sensation of assault and violation caused by the person who did this act. An example of this form of forced participation is the case of a 21-year-old woman in Horizon Worlds, a metaverse platform by Meta (formerly Facebook), in 2022 (Diaz, 2022).

The metaverse is not all fun and games in the case of Amanda Todd, a Canadian teenager who was blackmailed and bullied online for showing her breasts on a webcam. She eventually took her life in 2012 (Proctor, 2022). This forced participation is a serious offense that should never be tolerated or ignored. The impact it has on the mental health and well-being of victims is irrefutable.

3. **Virtual Groping and Touching:** In the metaverse, virtual groping and touching refer to the act of physically touching or seizing another user's avatar sexually without their consent. The presence and embodiment provided by VR headsets and haptic suits make this very real for victims. They could also experience the effects of the assault on their body as if that weren't enough. Unfortunately, it is not uncommon to see virtual groping and touching in the metaverse. A woman claimed she was virtually groped by someone on Horizon Worlds, a metaverse platform created by Meta (formerly Facebook) in 2022. She reported it on a Facebook group and said that "sexual harassment is no joke already, but when you're in VR, it adds a whole other layer to it." Meta responded by introducing a Personal Boundary feature that creates 4-foot safety bubbles around avatars.

Another incident happened back in 2016 when a gamer wrote an open letter on Medium about being groped in Quivr, which is a VR game where players shoot zombies with bows and arrows. She felt violated because another player made pinching motions near her chest and crotch that made her feel "violated, humiliated, and traumatized" by the experience. The game developers apologized and added an in-game fix that allowed players to push away offenders with a gesture (Sparks, 2021).

18.6 Analysis of Survey

A survey curated and circulated by the authors aimed to determine the subjects' opinions regarding the virtual platform and simulations. The survey dealt with 142 subjects to analyze the familiarity and suggestions that the sample of subjects could provide about the current status of Metaverse. The subjects taken for the survey were of a free age bracket, inclining toward the younger age range. The gender ratio obtained in the survey constituted 46 percent female and 54 percent male subjects. The survey results suggest that most respondents engage with digital environments or VR platforms, with 22.5% indicating they do not. Furthermore, 26.8% of respondents responded

Virtual Rape

that they had heard about the term "Virtual Rape" in the context of the metaverse or digital environments. It can be deduced that the subjects are well versed in the presence and impact of the metaverse in their day-to-day lives. In terms of understanding the concept of "Virtual Rape," 23.2% of respondents feel very familiar with it, while 28.9% feel somewhat familiar, and 47.9% are not familiar with it (Figure 18.1).

Interestingly so, when the subjects were asked about the seriousness of "Virtual Rape" compared to physical rape, the responses varied, with 48.6% considering it more serious. In comparison, 15.5% deemed it much less severe. This discrepancy highlights the complex nature of assessing harm within digital contexts, where traditional concepts of violence intersect with virtual realities. Regarding experiences of distressing or traumatic events in digital environments, 30.3% of respondents indicated they or someone they know had experienced such incidents. Examples provided include instances of cyberbullying, online harassment, or blackmail. These findings underscore the importance of addressing digital safety concerns and implementing effective measures to mitigate harm in virtual realms (Figure 18.2).

Furthermore, upon enquiring about safety measures and guidelines to protect oneself from digital harassment, 51.4% of respondents stated they were aware, while 48.6% were not. Concerning reporting distressing events, 42.3% of respondents said they or someone they know have reported it to platform administrators or authorities, while 30.3% have not, and 27.5% indicated it was not applicable. The questionnaire ended by asking about awareness of support services or resources available for victims of digital harassment; 54.9% of respondents were aware, while 45.1% were not (Figure 18.3).

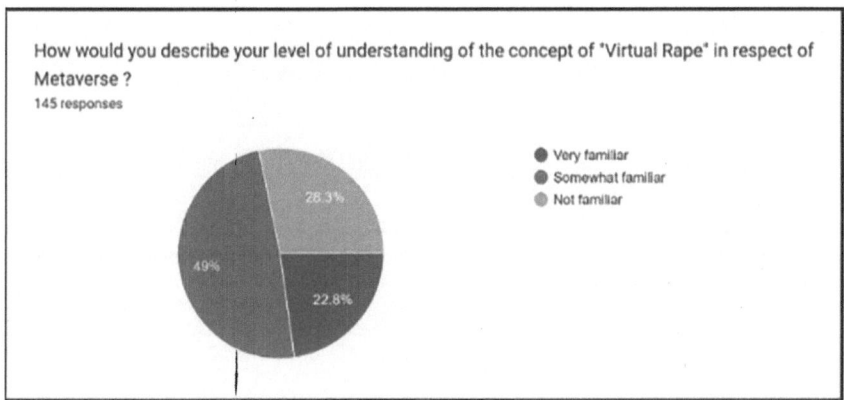

FIGURE 18.1
A screenshot from the survey that we conducted where the respondents told us about their level of understanding regarding Virtual Rape in the metaverse.

On asking about any possible suggestions that the subjects would like to propose for the betterment of the handling of the instances of Virtual Rape, they persistently stated that awareness of such issues is required to be made. Acknowledging the problem becomes the first step in determining the cure or the social issue. Despite suggestions that insisted on focusing on the regulation and security in such virtual space, some subjects had not placed as much importance on addressing the issue. This raises the pertinent issue of spreading knowledge on the topic (Figure 18.4).

Another key factor observed is the dearth of a structured legal framework on which users who have faced violations of their rights can rely. A specialized initiative at the policy level will further solidify a particular legal protection that exclusively provides redressal and protection in this space.

18.6.1 Impact of Virtual Rape on Victims

The impacts of Virtual Rape in victims include the following:

1. **Emotional Trauma:** One of the key issues that crop up time and again in the study is the concern regarding the emotional trauma endured by the users of the gadgets facilitating the virtual real-life-like

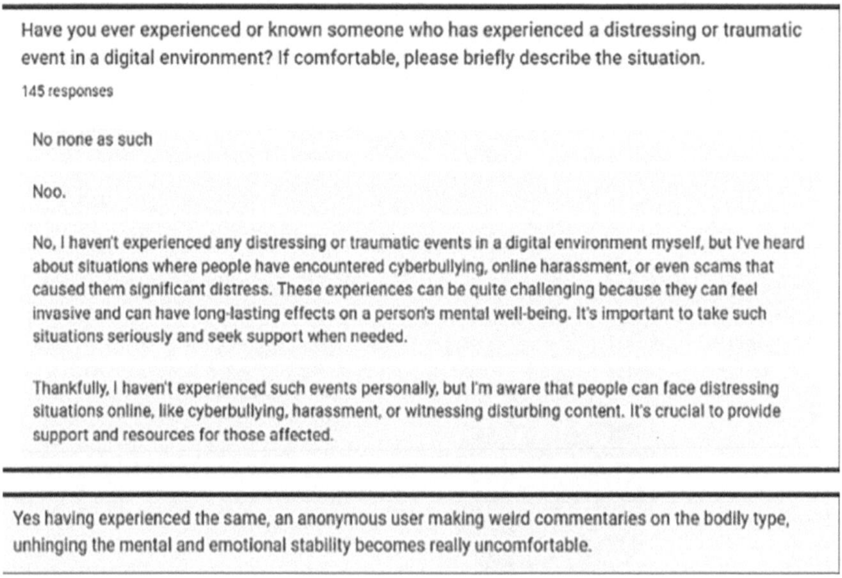

Have you ever experienced or known someone who has experienced a distressing or traumatic event in a digital environment? If comfortable, please briefly describe the situation.

145 responses

No none as such

Noo.

No, I haven't experienced any distressing or traumatic events in a digital environment myself, but I've heard about situations where people have encountered cyberbullying, online harassment, or even scams that caused them significant distress. These experiences can be quite challenging because they can feel invasive and can have long-lasting effects on a person's mental well-being. It's important to take such situations seriously and seek support when needed.

Thankfully, I haven't experienced such events personally, but I'm aware that people can face distressing situations online, like cyberbullying, harassment, or witnessing disturbing content. It's crucial to provide support and resources for those affected.

Yes having experienced the same, an anonymous user making weird commentaries on the bodily type, unhinging the mental and emotional stability becomes really uncomfortable.

FIGURE 18.2
A screenshot from the survey that we conducted where people provided their experiences regarding the distress they faced in the digital environments

Virtual Rape

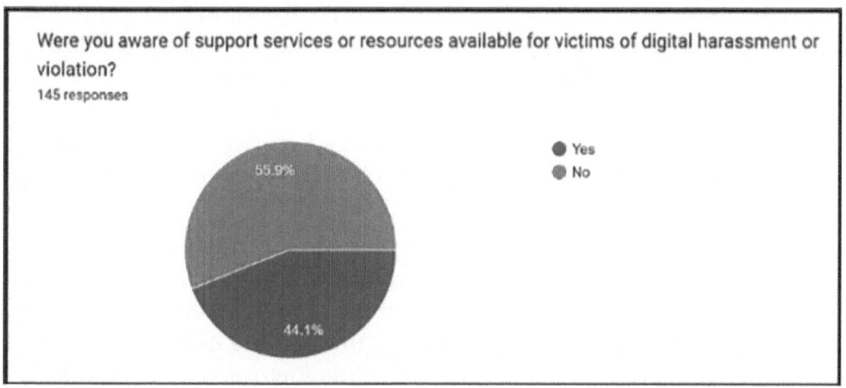

FIGURE 18.3
A screenshot from the survey that we conducted where the respondents were asked if they were aware of redressal mechanisms. The survey's findings further suggest a need for more comprehensive education and dissemination of information regarding digital safety practices. Emphasizing the importance of enhancing awareness, reporting mechanisms, and support infrastructure to effectively address digital harassment and ensure the well-being of individuals in online environments is required.

> Do you think there should be more awareness and legal measures in place to address the issue of "Virtual Rape" in the metaverse and other digital environments?
>
> 145 responses
>
> Yes, people should be made aware about this .
>
> Lawmakers, law enforcement, mental health professionals, and technology companies must collaborate to establish robust legal frameworks, safety protocols, and support systems to protect users, especially vulnerable populations like children, from the psychological harms of virtual sexual assault. Raising public awareness is also crucial to ensure victims feel empowered to report such incidents. Overall, the potential risks posed by virtual rape require a comprehensive, multifaceted response.
>
> Yes, absolutely. Increasing awareness and implementing legal measures to address virtual rape and other forms of digital harassment and assault are essential steps in safeguarding individuals in digital environments like the metaverse. This could involve educating users about consent, establishing clear guidelines and policies within virtual platforms, and ensuring that laws extend to protect individuals from harm in online spaces. Collaborative efforts between technology companies, policymakers, and advocacy groups are necessary to create safer digital spaces for everyone.
>
> Yes, increased awareness and legal measures are essential to address the issue of "Virtual Rape" in the metaverse and other digital environments. As virtual interactions become more prevalent, the potential for digital harm, including virtual sexual assault, grows. Heightened awareness can help individuals recognize

FIGURE 18.4
A screenshot from our survey where the respondents were asked about their inputs and suggestions.

experience. In a simulation that presents even certain physical sensations, the possibility of Virtual Rape emerges as an important issue, being a serious crime in the real world and the world of VR. Virtual Rape is the act of sexually assaulting or in a VR environment, such as the metaverse. The metaverse is a shared space for virtual interaction, where people can interact through realistic people representing alter egos (Patrick, 2023).

Virtual Rape can cause emotional trauma to the victims, as they may experience some of the same mental and emotional responses as in real life. This is because VR transports our brains into an electronic device to trick us into experiencing an alternate existence in real-time. When another touches a user in the metaverse, the hand controllers vibrate, creating a disturbing physical experience that causes a virtual assault (Patrick, 2023). Some of the psychological effects of Virtual Rape may include:

- It causes fear and anxiety in the person toward whom Virtual Rape is caused. Posttraumatic stress disorder, flashbacks, and nightmares are other effects. This also causes relationships to come to an end.
- It also creates a sense of anger and hostility, which causes unstable mental situations. Victims self-blame themselves, and they make themselves believe that they are the ones who caused the situation to occur.
- Victims isolate themselves. Confusion and disbelief occur among victims, along with dissociation, detachment, and numbness. Depression, sadness, and hopelessness are also some of the side effects.

These effects can differ based on a person's personality, and victims may recover quickly and move on, but some may struggle for many years and need therapists as well. Virtual Rape is not only a personal issue but also harms the safety of the metaverse community. It can discourage people from using VR platforms or limit their freedom of expression and exploration. It also causes toxicity and misogyny and harms the reputation and potential of the metaverse (Patrick, 2023).

Therefore, it is important to combat Virtual Rape in the metaverse by raising forming and implementing proper rules and policies and developing reporting mechanisms and giving support and resources to help victims, and holding perpetrators accountable. Hence, it is a more respectful, inclusive, and positive metaverse for everyone.

2. **Distress Similar to Physical Assault:** The impact of Virtual Rape on victims can be very distressing and similar to physical assault in the metaverse. The metaverse is a highly immersive and realistic VR environment where users can feel a sense of presence. When a user is

digitally raped in the metaverse, their sense of presence, agency, and embodiment can be violated and disrupted. Victims may feel powerless and violated and witness and experience something against consent. It causes a feeling of betrayal, humiliation, and violation as their digital body is harmed and assaulted by a person. They face physical pain and unwanted arousal along with a disturbed mental state. They may also experience psychological distress such as fear, anger, shame, guilt, or trauma that remain even after the VR ends.

Research has shown that Virtual Rape can have a similar effect as actual rape. A study found that females who were victims of Virtual Rape in VR had increased activity of negative emotions in the brain along with pain and perception. Another study noted that that men who faced VR rape showed increased activity in brain areas that were related to empathy and moral reasoning. We can hereby conclude that this form of rape, irrespective of gender of the victim, has similar brain responses to it.

Therefore, Virtual Rape is not harmless and is a serious type of hurt that can cause significant distress to the victims. It is required to be dealt with in the same way as we deal with physical rape and should not ignore as it is against human rights and therefore be prevented and punished in the metaverse.

3. **Compromised Safety and Privacy:** The impact of Virtual Rape on victims can also compromise their safety and privacy in the metaverse. The metaverse is a VR world where users can interact through their realistic selves. However, this also means that users may expose their data, such as their appearance, voice, identity, location, preferences, and behaviors, to other users or third parties who misuse or abuse them (World Economic Forum, 2023).

Virtual Rape can also convert into a form of cyberbullying, harassment, or blackmail, where perpetrators may threaten to expose or share the victim's virtual assault or gain monetary favors through them (Albawaba, 2022). We can also say that it is a form of identity theft where the person's virtual self can be copied, and their data can be used for malicious purposes to use them for their malicious intent such as committing crimes and other unlawful activities. Moreover, Virtual Rape can help criminals to keep surveillance, where perpetrators may track or monitor the victim's every move in the metaverse and use them to stalk or harm them in the real world; Virtual Rape can be used to manipulate, where perpetrators may influence victim's opinions in the metaverse, and thereby use this information to cause harm in the actual world. Therefore, Virtual Rape is a grave threat to human security and privacy in the world of metaverse. It is essential to safeguard users from virtual rape by proper measures, consent, and reporting. Hence, we can ensure that people using these applications can benefit from the metaverse without compromising their safety and privacy.

4. **Impaired Trust:** The impact of Virtual Rape on victims can also impair their trust in the metaverse. The metaverse, a VR world, allows users to interact with one another through life avatars. However, this also risks encountering individuals who may not be genuine or have harmful intentions (BBC, 2022). Among the deceptive and aggressive behaviors, Virtual Rape stands out as an extreme form where assailants exploit the vulnerabilities of the VR system. They use fake or stolen identities to sexually assault or harass other users' avatars (Shen, 2022). Virtual Rape can damage the trust that users have in the metaverse, as it might cause them to feel violated in a space that is supposed to be fun. They may lose their personality or feel unvalued by others due to it. This may cause them to lose trust and, ultimately, friendships. They may become suspicious, paranoid, or isolated and avoid social gatherings (BBC, 2022).

   Trust is the secret to enjoying the benefits of the digital world without hesitation or fear. As a result, trust produces pleasant emotions. When users share their thoughts, works, and criticism with others, trust can improve the caliber and diversity of the metaverse content. In addition, it may confidently encourage the expansion of e-commerce and advertising prospects (BBC, 2022).

   Therefore, it is essential to prevent and address Virtual Rape in the metaverse through the establishment and enforcement of ethical standards and norms for user behavior, the provision of efficient safety and security features and tools for user protection and empowerment, the creation of supportive environments for well-being and recovery, and the dissemination of information about the repercussions of virtual rape.

5. **Stigmatization and Victim Blaming:** The impact of Virtual Rape on victims can also involve stigmatization and victim blaming in the metaverse. The metaverse is a VR world where users can interact through realistic avatars representing alter egos (Diaz, 2022). Users, who experience Virtual Rape, may be subjected to social stigma and blame due to a lack of understanding or empathy from others. Nonetheless, this also implies that Virtual Rape is becoming more prevalent in our society. Stigma is a wrong belief and a characteristic, behavior, or reputation that socially discredits someone in a certain way by their actions, choices, or motives (Diaz, 2022). Some people may not be aware of the existence and prevalence of Virtual Rape in the metaverse or may not consider it a serious or harmful issue. Stigmatization and victim blaming are just two reactions to virtual rape, which some may view as mere horseplay or a figment of one's imagination. Even if they have never undergone such an ordeal

themselves, others may still not be empathetic to the assault's psychological and emotional aftermath for its victims.

They will probably judge the victims without taking into account their viewpoints and emotions in favor of applying their prejudices or stereotypes. Tragically, giving in to these responses prevents victims from seeking support or comfort from a wide range of sources, including family members, friends, internet forums, or qualified counselors. They may increase their reluctance to share their experiences, report abuse, or use services. In addition, they may make it harder for them to find healthy and effective coping mechanisms for their trauma. Stigmatization and victim-blaming can damage the trust and confidence that the victims of Virtual Rape have in themselves, others, and the metaverse. They can make them feel more insecure, vulnerable, and violated in a space that is supposed to be fun, creative, and social. They can also reduce their willingness and motivation to engage in social interactions or activities in the metaverse. Therefore, it is important to prevent and challenge stigmatization and victim blaming of Virtual Rape victims in the metaverse by raising awareness.

18.6.2 The Way Ahead for Preventing Crimes Like Virtual Rape in the Metaverse

Some of the ways to prevent Virtual Rape is discussed as follows:

1. **Reporting Mechanism:** Reporting mechanism in the metaverse in the case of Virtual Rape is a topic that has gained attention and urgency because more people are using VR platforms to interact and socialize (Gromek, 2023). Virtual Rape can cause emotional distress in real life as VR is designed to transport our brains into a virtual body to trick us into experiencing an alternate existence in real-time. When another touches a user in the metaverse, the hand controllers vibrate, creating a very disorienting and even disturbing physical experience during a virtual assault (Gromek, 2023).

   Users should be able to adjust their boundary settings, determining how close other users can get to their avatars. If another user crosses the boundary, they will be automatically blocked and reported. Meta, the company formerly known as Facebook, has added this feature to its metaverse platform after a woman reported being virtually gang-raped by other users (Gromek, 2023). Users should be able to easily block and report any user who harasses or assaults them in the metaverse. The block button should prevent the user from seeing or interacting with the offender again. The report button should send a detailed complaint to the platform moderators or authorities, who should investigate and take appropriate actions. Users should also be able to access their data and privacy settings and control who can access or share their information. Users should be able to access support and resources after experiencing Virtual Rape in the metaverse. This may include counseling, therapy, legal advice, or online communities. Users should also be able to receive feedback and updates on their reports and cases and know their rights and options.

These are some of the possible features and steps for reporting mechanisms in the metaverse in case of virtual rape. However, many challenges and limitations exist to implementing and enforcing legal complexities.

2. **Evolving Legal Framework – Cross-Jurisdictional Challenges:** Cross-jurisdictional challenges are one of the most complex and unresolved issues in the metaverse, especially in cases of virtual rape (Wilson, n.d., 2023). Cross-jurisdictional challenges arise when either the victim or the perpetrator (or both) of Virtual Rape are in different states or regions that have their laws. For example, few states may consider it as a form of cyberbullying, and others may not consider it as a crime at all. Some states may have very harsh data protection and privacy laws that protect the user's personal information and identity in the metaverse. In contrast, others may have weak laws or no laws regarding this. These jurisdictional challenges pose several problems and questions for solving Virtual Rape cases:

- How to determine which country's laws and authorities apply to a Virtual Rape case in the metaverse? How do we ensure that they are consistent and compatible with each other?
- How to identify, track, and locate the perpetrators of Virtual Rape in the metaverse? How do we collect and preserve evidence of their actions and intentions?
- How to protect, support, and compensate the victims of Virtual Rape in the metaverse? How can we provide them with legal advice, counseling, therapy, or other resources?
- How to enforce the laws and sanctions against the perpetrators of Virtual Rape in the metaverse? How do we ensure they are effective and proportional to the harm caused?
- How to prevent and deter future incidents of Virtual Rape in the metaverse? How to educate and raise awareness among users about the risks and consequences of Virtual Rape?

These important questions can be addressed by developing and adopting a standard definition and classification of Virtual Rape in the metaverse that can be recognized and accepted by all countries (Arnaldi et al., 2018). Establishing and implementing a universal reporting mechanism for Virtual Rape cases in the metaverse and having established and proper jurisdictional laws can facilitate communication and collaboration among different countries' authorities. Creating and enforcing a global code of conduct for users and providers of VR platforms and services can set ethical standards and norms for behavior in the metaverse. Promoting and supporting research and innovation on VR technologies that can enhance safety and security features and tools for users in the metaverse. Providing and facilitating access to support and resources for victims of Virtual Rape in the metaverse can help them cope with their trauma and recover from their experiences (Mado and Bailenson, 2022).

3. **Preventive Measures:** VR platforms and services should have clear and explicit community guidelines defining acceptable and unacceptable behavior in the metaverse. These guidelines should also specify the consequences and sanctions for violating the rules, such as warnings, suspensions, bans, or legal actions. Users should be required to read and agree to these guidelines before accessing the metaverse and be reminded of them periodically. VR platforms and services should have an effective and responsive moderation system that can monitor, detect, and respond to incidents of Virtual Rape in the metaverse (Arnaldi et al., 2018). This system should include human and artificial intelligence moderators who can review reports, verify evidence, intervene in situations, and take appropriate actions. Users should be able to easily report any user who harasses or assaults them in the metaverse and receive feedback and updates on their cases.

Customizable content filters that can allow users to control what they see and hear in the metaverse. These filters should enable users to block or mute any user, content, or feature they find offensive, disturbing, or triggering. Users should also be able to adjust their boundary settings, determining how close other users can get to their avatars. If another user crosses the boundary, they will be automatically blocked and reported. This program should include tutorials, videos, articles, quizzes, or games that can teach users about the concept and impact of virtual rape, the importance of consent and privacy, the rights and responsibilities of users, and the reporting mechanisms and resources available for victims (Ghosal & Ghosa, 2009).

Collaboration of VR platforms and services with law enforcement agencies to prevent and combat Virtual Rape in the metaverse. This collaboration should involve sharing information, data, and evidence of Virtual Rape cases with the relevant authorities, complying with legal requests and orders, and supporting investigations and prosecutions. This collaboration should also respect the privacy and security of users and follow the applicable laws and regulations of different countries. VR platforms and services should provide a support network for victims of Virtual Rape in the metaverse. This network should include counselors, therapists, lawyers, or online communities that can offer victims emotional, psychological, legal, or social support. Users should be able to access this network through various channels, such as phone calls, chats, emails, or websites. Users should also be able to receive feedback and updates on their reports and cases and know their rights and options (EKO, 2022).

4. **Policy Level Protection:** Although the introduction of VR gaming has been recent in India, it is observed that the protection of users in this virtual space needs to be structured at the policy level. Despite being an area that is ever evolving in its environment, a specialized provision catering to the needs is needed to address the infringement and violation of the users and further ensure the protection of the individual's rights in the virtual arena.

18.7 Conclusion

Upon deeper inspection, a somewhat distorted reality is observed. Due to the continuous presence of crime against women, it has somewhat become normalized in society. The crimes persisting around us have resulted in women being oblivious to the very act of crime that is being committed against them. In many cases, the victim, in fact, seems completely unaware of the crime. This mentality, in turn, has become an impediment to recognizing the disturbing nature of the crimes, which have become the extension of the ones stated in the conventional books of law. Hence, the oppressed mindset of the females has subsisted even in the modern timeline and thus has brought in the dilemma concerning acknowledging the infringement of a person's right, even if it is in the virtual space.

The fact that the integration of VR into the discussion of crimes against women amplifies the potential for exploitation and victimization cannot be disregarded. Due to the very nature of VR technology allows users to engage with highly immersive and interactive digital environments, blurring the lines between the virtual and real worlds. When we look at the same in the context of crimes against women, VR has been used to create simulated scenarios of harassment, assault, or abuse, further desensitizing individuals to such behaviors or even normalizing them. It is also noted that the anonymity afforded by VR platforms tends to embolden perpetrators to commit harmful acts with reduced fear of consequences or accountability. As VR continues to evolve and become more accessible, addressing the ethical implications and ensuring safeguards are in place to protect vulnerable populations, including women, from exploitation and harm within virtual spaces is essential.

Consequentially, the need for the implementation of effective laws to protect victims from various forms of violence, including mental harassment and sexual violence, within virtual environments comes into the picture.

Thus, by granting legal rights to avatars, users may be afforded more excellent protection and recourse against harassment or abuse within virtual spaces. This legal framework would establish responsibilities for users and platform operators, ultimately contributing to developing mechanisms to prevent such crimes. In essence, the conclusion highlights the urgency of addressing the intersection of technology and gender-based violence, advocating for proactive measures to safeguard women's rights and ensure their safety in both physical and virtual realms.

Notes

1. Hadžihasanović and Kubura, The case before the ICTY (IT-01–47-A), April 22, 2008.
2. A man is said to commit "rape" if he penetrates his penis, to any extent, into the vagina, mouth, urethra, or anus of a woman or makes her to do so with him or any other person; or inserts, to any extent, any object or a part of the body, not being the penis, into the vagina, the urethra, or anus of a woman or makes her to do so with him or any other person; or manipulates any part of the body of a woman so as to cause penetration into the vagina, urethra, anus, or any part of body of such woman or makes her to do so with him or any other person; or applies his mouth to the vagina, anus, urethra of a woman, or makes her to do so with him or any other person.

References

Albawaba. (2022, February 10). First rape case in the metaverse inspires new digital rules. *The Node*. https://www.albawaba.com/node/first-rape-metaverse-inspires-new-digital-rules-1465829

Arnaldi, B., Guitton, P., & Moreau, G. (Eds.). (2018). *Virtual reality and augmented reality: Myths and realities*. Wiley.

Athena. (2024). *Metacrimes: The need for laws to govern the metaverse*. Legal Service India. https://www.legalserviceindia.com/legal/article-15110-metacrimes-the-need-for-laws-to-govern-the-metaverse.html

Bakshi, G. K., & Narang, P. (2024, January 5). Is India's legal framework ready to deal with sexual violence in virtual reality? *The Leaflet*. https://theleaflet.in/is-indias-legal-framework-ready-to-deal-with-sexual-violence-in-virtual-reality/

BBC. (2022, May 25). *Female avatar sexually assaulted in Meta VR platform, campaigners say*. https://www.bbc.com/news/technology-61573661

Belagere, C. (2024, January 7). Teen UK girl virtually "gang raped" in metaverse: Are Indian laws equipped to handle similar cases? *The South First*. https://thesouthfirst.com/news/teen-uk-girl-virtually-gang-raped-in-metaverse-are-indian-laws-equipped-to-handle-similar-cases/

Bellini, O. (2024). Virtual justice: Criminalizing avatar sexual assault in metaverse spaces. *Mitchell Hamline Law Review*, 50(1). https://open.mitchellhamline.edu/mhlr/vol50/iss1/3

Beresford, T. (n.d.). Facts about the Mr. Bungle LambdaMOO cybercrime. *Ranker*. https://www.ranker.com/list/lambdamoo-mud-facts/trilby-beresford

Chalmers, D. (2022, January 28). What should be considered a crime in the metaverse? *Wired*. https://www.wired.com/story/crime-metaverse-virtual-reality/

Chawki, M. (2024). Redefining boundaries in the metaverse: Navigating the challenges of virtual harm and user safety. *MDPI Laws*, 13(3), Article 33. https://www.mdpi.com/2075–471X/13/3/33

Das, A. (2022, February 8). Woman recalls "gang rape" in metaverse; concerns grow over making VR platforms safe from sexual predators. *CNBC TV18*. https://www.cnbctv18.com/technology/woman-recalls-gang-rape-in-metaverse-concerns-grow-over-making-vr-platforms-safe-from-sexual-predators-12396992.htm

Diaz, A. (2022, May 27). Women are being sexually assaulted in the metaverse. *New York Post*. https://nypost.com/2022/05/27/women-are-being-sexually-assaulted-in-the-metaverse/

EKO. (2022). *Metaverse: Another cesspool of toxic content*. https://www.eko.org/images/Metaverse_report_May_2022.pdf

Fortune Business Insights. (2024). *India virtual reality market share & research report*. https://www.fortunebusinessinsights.com/india-virtual-reality-market-107618

George, A. S. (2024). *Virtual violence: Legal and psychological ramifications of sexual assault in virtual reality environments*. ResearchGate. https://www.researchgate.net/publication/378150588_Virtual_Violence_Legal_and_Psychological_Ramifications_of_Sexual_Assault_in_Virtual_Reality_Environments

Ghosal, S. G., & Ghosa, S. G. (2009). Socio-political dimensions of rape. *The Indian Journal of Political Science*, 70(1), 107–120. https://www.jstor.org/stable/41856499

Gómez-Quintero, J., Johnson, S. D., Borrion, H., & Lundrigan, S. (2024). A scoping study of crime facilitated by the metaverse. *Futures*, 157, Article 103338. https://doi.org/10.1016/j.futures.2024.103338

Gromek, M. (2023, May 8). Are we ready for avatars reporting sexual harassment in the metaverse police stations? *Forbes*. https://www.forbes.com/sites/digital-assets/2023/05/08/are-we-ready-for-avatars-reporting-sexual-harassment-in-the-metaverse-police-stations/

Hinduja, S. (2022, June 2). *Child grooming and the metaverse – issues and solutions*. Cyberbullying Research Center. https://cyberbullying.org/child-grooming-metaverse

Karthika, C., & Vijayalakshmi, P. P. (2021). Trolls to cyber mob: The virtual rape through Facebook. *Indian Journal of Mass Communication and Journalism*, 1(1), Article A1002091121.

Mado, M., & Bailenson, J. (2022). The psychology of virtual reality. In *The psychology of technology: Social science research in the age of big data* (pp. 155–193). American Psychological Association. https://doi.org/10.1037/0000290–006

Masterson, V. (2022, March 31). *Metaverse: We'll soon spend an hour a day in virtual worlds*. World Economic Forum. https://www.weforum.org/agenda/2022/03/hour-a-day-in-metaverse-by-2026-says-gartner/

Patrick, W. L. (2023, January 3). Sexual assault in the metaverse: Virtual reality, real trauma. *Psychology Today*. https://www.psychologytoday.com/us/blog/why-bad-looks-good/202301/sexual-assault-in-the-metaverse-virtual-reality-real-trauma

Proctor, J. (2022, June 6). Accused in Amanda Todd cyberbullying case alleged to have used 22 accounts to sextort teen. *CBC News*. https://www.cbc.ca/news/canada/british-columbia/amanda-todd-sextortion-trial-1.6479407

PwC. (2022). *Metaverse survey: Capitalizing on metaverse business opportunities*. https://www.pwc.com/us/en/tech-effect/emerging-tech/metaverse-survey.html

Qin, Y., Wang, P. H., & Hua, X. (2022). Identity, crimes, and law enforcement in the metaverse. arXiv. https://arxiv.org/abs/2210.06134

Rigotti, C., & Malgieri, G. (2023). *Human vulnerability in the metaverse*. Leiden University. https://scholarlypublications.universiteitleiden.nl/access/item%3A3677017/view

Sarkar, S., & Rajan, B. (2021). Materiality and discursivity of cyber violence against women in India. *Journal of Creative Communications*, 18(1), 109–123. https://doi.org/10.1177/0973258621992273

Shen, M. (2022, January 31). Sexual harassment in the metaverse? Woman says she was virtually raped. *USA Today*. https://www.usatoday.com/story/tech/2022/01/31/woman-allegedly-groped-metaverse/9278578002/

Singh, J. (2015). Violence against women in cyber world: A special reference to India. *International Journal of Advanced Research in Management and Social Sciences*, 4(1), 8.

Sparks, H. (2021, December 17). Woman claims she was virtually "groped" in Meta's VR metaverse. *New York Post*. https://nypost.com/2021/12/17/woman-claims-she-was-virtually-groped-in-meta-vr-metaverse/

Stephenson, N. (2021, November 10). Metaverse explained: What is it, and when will it get here? *USA Today*. https://www.usatoday.com/story/tech/2021/11/10/metaverse-what-is-it-explained-facebook-microsoft-meta-vr/6337635001/

Todd, E., Gates, T., Bruce, K. S., Splittgerber, A., Bruno, S. L., Becker, J., & Bartnick, W. J. (2022). *Data protection and privacy*. Reed Smith Guide to the Metaverse. https://www.reedsmith.com/en/perspectives/metaverse/2022/08/data-protection-and-privacy

Wang, Q. J., Escobar, F. B., Da Mota, P. A., & Velasco, C. (2021). Getting started with virtual reality for sensory and consumer science: Current practices and future perspectives. *Food Research International*, 145, Article 110410. https://doi.org/10.1016/j.foodres.2021.110410

Wilson, W. (n.d.). Challenges in the metaverse jurisdiction and international treaty law. *IRPJ: EUCLID's Intergovernmental Research and Policy Journal*. https://irpj.euclid.int/articles/challenges-in-the-metaverse-jurisdiction-and-international-treaty-law/

World Economic Forum. (2010). *Global competitiveness report 2010–2011*. https://www.weforum.org/publications/global-competitiveness-report-2010-2011/

World Economic Forum. (2023). *Privacy and safety in the metaverse*. https://www.weforum.org/publications/privacy-and-safety-in-the-metaverse/

Wright, K. (2022, February 08). A quarter of people will have spent time in the metaverse by 2026: Research. *COINTELEGRAPH*. https://cointelegraph.com/news/a-quarter-of-people-will-spend-time-in-the-metaverse-by-2026-research

Yu, J., Dickinger, A., Kam, K. F. S., & Egger, R. (2024). Artificial intelligence-generated virtual influencer: Examining the effects of emotional display on user engagement. *Journal of Retailing and Consumer Services*, 76, Article 103560. https://doi.org/10.1016/j.jretconser.2023.103560

Zhu, L. (2022). *The metaverse: Concepts and issues (report no. R47224)*. Congressional Research Service. https://crsreports.congress.gov/product/pdf/R/R47224

Part 6

Policy and Governance in the Digital Era

19
An Analysis of Meta's Political Ad Policy Enforcement: Perspectives from Bangladesh

Mohammad Pizuar Hossain, Miraj Ahmed Chowdhury, and Partho Protim Das

19.1 Introduction

Facebook is an interactive online platform that has evolved into a crucial space for public discourse and advertising. The increasing significance of online advertising in political elections has sparked the interest of organizations and individuals seeking to persuade voters before elections in various countries worldwide. Advertisements on Facebook have a resemblance to sponsored posts in that, with their textual content, images, or videos, they consistently include the name and profile picture of a Facebook page as their "author" (Edelson et al., 2020). Facebook's "political advertisement" (also referred to as "political ad") denotes a sponsored message published on a Facebook page, with the intention of conveying information related to matters such as the state, politics, government, and justice (Silva et al., 2020). These messages may pertain to various subjects, including political campaigns, human rights, political activism, political news, federal programs, initiatives and regulations, politicians' public agendas, judicial rulings, public expenditures, and crimes against public administration (Silva et al., 2020).

The Meta Ad Library, which was launched in May 2018, initially included only advertisements related to politics or policy issues (Constine, 2019). However, as of March 2019, the archive now displays all active advertisements on any topic as well as inactive political and social issues (Constine, 2019). Meta started archiving political advertisements related to Bangladesh in its Ad Library on September 7, 2022, which marked the beginning of data collection in our research (Meta, 2023c). As detailed in the next section, political advertisements refer to advertisements on social issues, elections, or politics under Meta's political policy. These advertisements are considered such when they have been appropriately declared with a disclaimer or identified as political by Meta, even in the absence of a disclaimer.

This chapter examines the enforcement of Meta's political ad policy to deal with Facebook advertisements related to political, electoral, and social issues in Bangladesh. To carry out our research, we first gathered a one-year database of advertisements labelled as "political" from the Meta Ad Library in Bangladesh. The database includes data from September 7, 2022, to September 7, 2023. We also made use of a list of 30 keywords associated with political parties, organizations, personalities, and other relevant political topics in Bangladesh to search the Meta Ad Library and find active advertisements that met the criteria for political relevance. Moreover, we gathered insights from pertinent scholarship and five key informants from civil society, academia, law, and the news media.

This study makes three significant contributions to the literature: First, it reveals distinct patterns pertaining to the over-enforcement of political advertisements on Facebook in Bangladesh, indicating that approximately 25% of the advertisements identified as political by Facebook were not of a political nature. Second, it highlights the under-enforcement of Meta's political ad policy by pointing out 50 active advertisements that clearly featured political content, which Meta failed to categorize appropriately. Finally, it offers specific recommendations to improve the accountability of Meta concerning political advertising on Facebook in the context of Bangladesh.

19.2 Meta's Relevant Policies and Enforcement Approaches

This section provides an overview of Meta's political advertising policy and the methods employed to enforce it. It also discusses Meta's tools to ensure transparency in the implementation of its policies regarding political advertisements as part of its enforcement strategy.

19.2.1 Meta Political Ad Policy

Meta has established comprehensive guidelines to ensure transparency in advertising, including advertisements pertaining to political candidates across all levels of public office, as well as those addressing electoral and societal concerns. Meta categorizes an ad as about social issues, elections, or politics when that ad: (1) is made by, on behalf of, or about a candidate for public office, a political figure, a political party, and a political action committee that advocates for the outcome of an election to public office; (2) is about any election, referendum, or ballot initiative, including "get out the vote" or election information campaigns; (3) is about any social issue in any place where the ad is being run; and (4) is regulated as political advertising (Meta, 2023a, 2023g).

Advertisers are now obligated to verify their names and locations and disclose the source of funding for the advertisements. In other words, to engage in advertising pertaining to social issues, elections, or politics in a country, advertisers are required to undergo an authorization procedure that includes verifying their identification and confirming their location (Meta, 2023a, 2023h, 2023i). After obtaining authorization, users can generate "disclaimers" that specify the funding source (person, page, or organization) responsible for financing a particular advertisement (Bolden et al., 2020; Meta, 2023b, 2023j). In the process of running a political advertisement, the advertiser is required to designate it as a "Special Ad Category" and include a "disclaimer" (Meta, 2023h).

19.2.2 Enforcement of Meta Political Ad Policy

Meta (2023b) mandates advertisers to take responsibility for assessing whether their advertisements align with the platform's policies on social issues, elections, or politics. Prior to advertisers being able to assert that an advertisement is of a political nature, they are required to undertake a thorough vetting procedure that includes authentication of their identification. As an integral component of this procedure, the individuals involved also generate "disclaimers," referred to as disclosure strings. After the completion of the screening procedure, ad sponsors have the option and obligation to indicate the political nature of each new advertisement they create by choosing a checkbox. When an advertisement is classified as political, it is stored in Meta's publicly accessible Ad Library for seven years. In addition, the disclosure string is shown alongside the advertisement when presented to viewers on Facebook.

Meta undertakes the task of reviewing all submitted advertisements to ensure compliance with its policies (Meta, 2023b). The evaluation process mostly depends on an automated assessment, namely artificial intelligence. In addition, in some instances, human reviewer teams worldwide have been trained to assess certain advertisements. If an advertisement without a stated purpose is identified during a preliminary evaluation, it will not be published or stored in the Ad Library (Pochat et al., 2022). Consequently, the attempted violation remains undisclosed to the public.

However, if an undeclared advertisement, successfully through review, becomes active, it is susceptible to being identified as political either by artificial intelligence detection or through reports submitted by the Meta community (Meta, 2023b). Subsequently, Meta proceeds to reject the advertisement retrospectively, deactivate it, and render it inaccessible to all users. Furthermore, Meta stores the noncompliant advertisement in the Ad Library and accompanies it with a notification stating that "this advertisement was displayed without a disclaimer," irrespective of whether the advertiser has fulfilled the ad permission procedure (Meta, 2023a, 2023k). Although advertisements will continue to be publicly stored even during periods of inactivity, the advertiser's identity will remain undisclosed. Pages that engage in violations may face restrictions on placing new political advertisements or may be disabled (Meta, 2023a).

19.2.3 Meta's Tools for Transparency

Meta tries to enhance transparency by mandating that ad sponsors categorize each advertisement as political and divulge the identity of the advertiser responsible for its funding (Edelson et al., 2020). It emphasizes transparency to establish accountability for itself and for advertisers (Meta, 2023b). Facebook offers three fundamental transparency tools: an Ad Library, Ad Library Application Programming Interface (API), and an Ad Library Report.

19.2.3.1 Ad Library

The Meta Ad Library, an online platform, enables users to search for presently live advertisements associated with Facebook globally (Meta, 2023c). Currently, websites are available without charge and feature many forms of advertising media, including textual content, images, and videos. However, automatic access through mechanisms such as web crawlers is prohibited. It provides access to both active and inactive advertisements on social issues, elections, or politics. In the case of the latter, it is necessary for the metadata to contain the appropriate disclaimer, identification of an authorized advertiser along with the verification process, and categorized approximations of advertising expenditure, audience reach, and impressions. A nonpolitical advertisement is removed from the Ad Library once it becomes inactive; however, a political advertisement is stored for seven years, starting in May 2018 (Meta, 2023k).

19.2.3.2 Ad Library API

The Ad Library API offers a means for automated inquiries pertaining to current and inactive advertisements concerning social issues, elections, or politics on any particular website in a particular nation (Meta, 2023d). The API includes distinct identifiers, impression counts, expenditure figures, and campaign durations for each advertisement. Meta provides advertisement impression and expenditure statistics in broad ranges, which lack precision; for example, displaying spend amounts between $0 and $100, or impressions ranging from 1,000 to 5,000 (Meta, 2023d). In particular, the accessibility of ad pictures and videos was not automatically enabled.

19.2.3.3 Ad Library Report

In addition to Meta's Ad Library, it also releases a daily "Ad Library Report," which encompasses all pages that have sponsored political advertisements (Meta, 2023e). The report gathers advertiser data on social issues, elections, and politics in countries where Meta requires disclosure. It provides a comprehensive list of pages that feature at least one political advertisement during the selected timeframe. It also includes the disclosure strings used by these sites and the precise monetary expenditure incurred (beyond $100).

19.3 Research Methodology and Limitation

This section describes the research design and methods employed in this study. It also brings attention to the ethical considerations and limitations of this study.

19.3.1 Data Collection and Sampling Methods

The qualitative data collection process in this study was conducted in three parts, as described below.

First, the database that we collected from the Meta Ad Library covers the period from September 7, 2022, to September 7, 2023. The research sample consisted of 355 pages from the Meta Ad Library database, which has spent over US$100 on each of their political advertisements. These pages collectively serve 48,760 advertisements. Of the 355 pages, 72 pages identified themselves as political, while the remaining 283 pages did not make any such declaration. We employed a "content analysis" technique to analyze 1,420 ad samples randomly selected from 283 pages. These advertisements were categorized as "commercial," "news and media," "others," and "unavailable" to understand the platform's enforcement of political ad policy (*refer to Annexure 1 for page category specifics*; see Figure 19.1). A research team consisting of three independent volunteers evaluated each piece of content by addressing the indicators that were in line with Meta's political ad policy to label the advertisements as political or nonpolitical.

Second, the advertisements on Facebook, which are flagged as nonpolitical, are visible in the Meta Ad Library only when they are active. Consequently, Facebook advertisements containing politically relevant content, which, however, Meta does not identify as political, are available in the Ad Library for a limited period of time. Therefore, to identify advertisements that were politically relevant, but Meta could not detect them, between June 20 and September 10, 2023, we used a list of 30 keywords concerning political

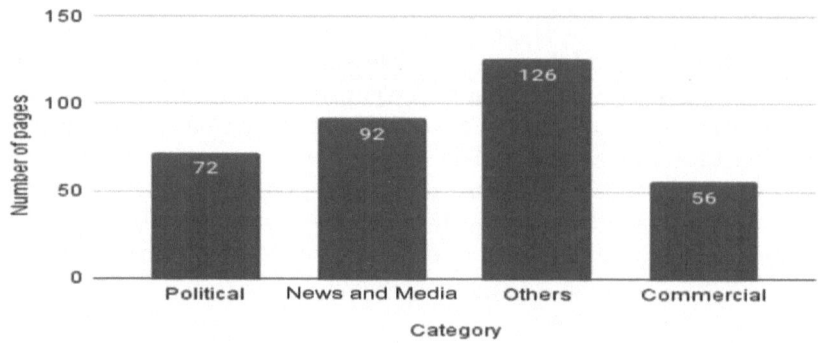

FIGURE 19.1
Number of sample pages by category

parties, organizations, personalities, and other relevant political topics (*refer to Annexure 2 for keyword details*).

Finally, we gathered insights from existing scholarship and five key informants from civil society, academia, law, and news media. Academics have investigated similar issues as this study, but in a different context. Legal experts specialize in researching matters related to constitutional law in Bangladesh. Civil society representatives are advocating for strengthening the implementation of Meta's political ad policy in their specific countries. The journalist focuses on, among others, reporting news about Meta's content moderation, specifically regarding political advertisements, discrepancies, and their effects on Bangladeshi and international affairs. The key informants were interviewed using a semi-structured questionnaire through "Zoom video conferencing." Each interview lasted between 35 and 40 minutes.

19.3.2 Ethical Considerations

We concentrated our data collection efforts on gathering information about advertisements. We did not collect any data related to friends' lists, likes, images, videos, or regular timeline postings of Facebook page owners. Furthermore, the advertisements used in our study were obtained from open-access platforms, specifically the Meta Ad Library, which means they are easily accessible to the public. Regarding interviews with key informants, participants were asked to submit individual "consent forms" with their signatures prior to the interviews. To protect the privacy of key informants, their identities were kept anonymous in this study.

19.3.3 Research Limitations

First, the sample size of this research was limited compared to the total amount of available data in the Meta Ad Library. Second, we employed a restricted set of keywords to identify advertisements that satisfied the requirements for inclusion in the Ad Library, as these advertisements did not disclose their content voluntarily and were not detected by Meta. Third, it is difficult to accurately measure the number of political advertisements that go undetected, as some advertisers may intentionally keep their spending below $100 to avoid inclusion in advertisement library reports. Fourth, the Meta political ad policy fails to deal sufficiently with social issues that are widespread in Bangladesh. Consequently, this research does not adequately address data pertaining to social issues within the specific context of Bangladesh. Finally, this study lacks a comparative analysis between Meta and other social media policies that influence political advertising policies.

19.4 Assessing Enforcement of Meta's Political Ad Policy

This section presents an analysis of the research data pertaining to Meta political ad policy, focusing on two distinct themes: over-enforcement and under-enforcement. It also integrates specific subthemes that have surfaced while discussing the findings.

19.4.1 Over-Enforcement

Over-enforcement, as discussed in this research, refers to advertisements detected or declared on Meta platforms as political when their content does not meet the platform's definition of political ad. This situation may arise when advertisers voluntarily declare an ad as political, and when the machine learning algorithms employed by Meta may inaccurately detect an ad as political, prompting advertisers to provide a disclaimer.

This research analyzed 1,420 advertisement samples from the Ad Library that were posted by pages in the nonpolitical category, as according to Meta, all advertisements from political parties and politicians were considered political. The analysis revealed that approximately 25% of the advertisements from nonpolitical pages (i.e., commercial, news, media, and other categories) were incorrectly detected as political, suggesting over-enforcement.

Among the advertisements categorized as "news and media," 19% were incorrectly detected as political, while 22% of the advertisements in the "others" category faced the same misclassification. However, the highest rate of false positives (i.e., advertisements erroneously identified), at 43%, occurred on "commercial" pages, making it the most adversely impacted by over-enforcement (see Figures 19.2 and 19.3).

Meta's political advertising policy states that if advertisements lack a disclaimer and the content pertains to social issues, elections, or politics, they will be disapproved during the review process (Clegg, 2023). In the case

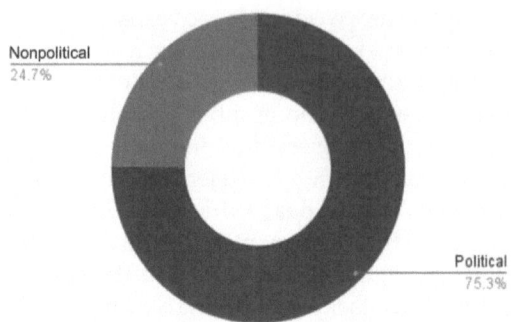

FIGURE 19.2
Around 25% of the political advertisements from nonpolitical pages are over enforced

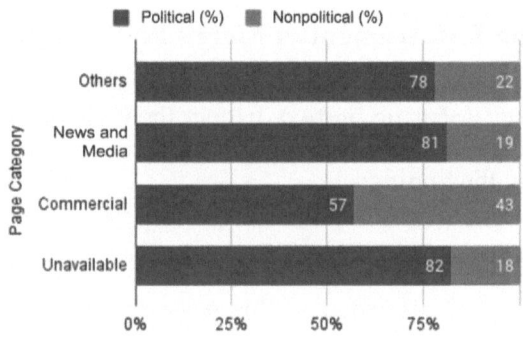

FIGURE 19.3
False detection by category of pages

of advertisements already running, if automated systems or community reports flag them and they are found to violate Meta's policy due to a missing disclaimer, the advertisements will be disapproved and added to the Ad Library.

Considering the Meta political advertising policy and analysis of selected advertisements' content, we highlighted three key findings. First, it identified misdetections where advertisements from commercial pages associated with political figures as even simple product promotions from companies owned by those political figures faced incorrect categorization. Second, advertisements promoting the sale of guidebooks, textbooks, novels, stories, magazines, and services related to employment opportunities, studying abroad, and visa applications were mistakenly categorized as political. Finally, commercial pages faced challenges due to keyword-related issues, where seemingly innocuous terms such as "Minister" triggered the classification of electronic appliance advertisements and marriage matchmaking services as political advertisements. Keywords, for example, "winner" and references to specific events led to the misclassification of advertisements.

What is responsible for such over-enforcement is often difficult to comprehend, as outsiders have little knowledge of how detection algorithms work, but the following sections with specific case studies provide a glimpse of the problem.

19.4.1.1 Inconsistency

Nagad, a digital financial services company based in Bangladesh, spent US$ 35,846 on advertisements during the research period, the highest amount among all pages, and Facebook classified 137 of its advertisements as political. Some of these contents featured photos or names of prominent political figures and contained keywords such as *shorkar* (government), pension scheme (a government scheme), and "Smart Bangladesh" (a political vision turned slogan). While these factors might justify the classification of these advertisements as political, there are instances of simple product promotions being enforced. In September, an analysis was carried out of 24 *Nagad* advertisements that Facebook had ceased running due to the absence of disclaimers. It was revealed that the majority of these advertisements pertained to activities such as Internet and electricity bill payments, as well as mobile recharges, which were not connected to political matters.

The potential correlations between the enforcement of advertisements and the ownership or management of a company remain uncertain, especially when the company is owned or managed by political figures. *Nagad* has been repeatedly reported in the media for its political connections, and its Managing Director, Tanvir A. Mishuk, whose personal page is also listed for running political advertisements, was prominently featured in most *Nagad's* advertisements (The Economist, 2020).

In the case of the *"Beximco* Group," which is owned by Salman F Rahman, a political personality and an adviser to the Bangladeshi prime minister's Private Sector Industry and Investment, a similar pattern was observed. Approximately 130 advertisements from the Beximco Group page were classified as political. Many of these advertisements include posts celebrating festivals, such as Eid (religious festival in Islam), Bengali New Year, and *Buddha Purnima* (birth anniversary of Gautam Buddha, the founder of Buddhism), or promoting its business.

19.4.1.2 Social Issues

In the commercial category, *Panjeree* Publications ranks second with 471 political advertisements and an expenditure of over US$ 7,000. None of the 23 advertisements from this publication, which were stopped from running because of the absence of disclaimers, contained any political pitches or statements. All *Panjeree* Publications' advertisements focused on promoting the sale of guidebooks or textbooks with a simple message regarding how these materials would aid in preparation for secondary school certificate and higher secondary certificate examinations.

Facebook also categorized advertisements from 20 other publications and bookstores as political. While some of these books touch on political topics, the majority are simply novels, stories, magazines, and guidebooks for job-related or public exam preparation. Another example is "migration." Advertisements from six pages specializing in career possibilities, studying abroad, and visa applications were also categorized as political.

Facebook does not publicly provide a comprehensive catalogue of social issues particular to Bangladesh, unlike its operations in 14 other countries, including India and Myanmar (Meta, 2023e). Nevertheless, a review of advertising data clearly indicates the application of political ad classifications to a variety of social issues, including civil and social rights, crime, the economy, education, environmental politics, health, immigration, and governance, categories that exist on India's list (Meta, 2023f).

Social issues play a significant role in shaping political discourse. The data on political advertisements in Bangladesh prompts the question of whether Meta should provide a comprehensive list of social issues for Bangladesh to enhance its accountability and transparency.

19.4.1.3 Keyword Difficulty

According to Meta's political advertising policy, "Advertisments where the primary purpose is the sale of a product or promotion of a service might not be considered social issue advertisements and might not require authorisations and a disclaimer" (Meta, 2023f). However, a review of the number of advertisements discontinued for not having disclaimers suggests that commercial entities frequently become victims of keyword-related issues. "Minister" is an example of such a case. This research's findings suggest that Meta has considered "Minister" as a political keyword and eventually, it marked seven advertisements from "Minister Hi-Tech Park," a company that sells electronic appliances such as TVs, fridges, AND fans and promotes their products exclusively – as political advertisements. One of their political advertisements was simply wishing everyone a happy Eid (greeting the Muslim community at the biggest religious festival).

The "*Biyer Khoj* Marriage Media" page serves as another instance where political ad detection relied solely on specific keywords in the advertisements. The page, identified as "Marriage Therapist," runs advertisements claiming to find life partners. The advertisements claim to have identified suitable matches for professionals such as physicians, engineers, Bangladesh Civil Service cadres, and army officers, as well as for those who are the offspring of Secretaries, members of parliaments (MPs), and Ministers. Evidently, the use of the terms "Secretaries," "MPs," and "Ministers" contributed to the identification of these advertisements as political.

"*Prachurja*: Automated Prize Bond Checker" is another page that spent US$ 1,156 on 27 advertisements during the period examined in this study. They provide SMS services to prize bond winners through the app, and advertisements running from their page are strictly related to the service. Facebook has flagged these as political advertisements. It seemed "bijoyi" (winner) was a keyword that triggered this categorization. This study found about 24 advertisements promoting different competitions, with the keyword "winner" flagged as political.

In addition, a page ran 31 advertisements in honor of the International Collegiate Programming Contest held in Dhaka in 2022. Out of the 31 advertisements, Zunaid Ahmed Palak – Minister of State for Posts, Telecommunications, and Information Technology – could be seen in six, while the rest included the names of the prizewinners and messages about the contestants' experiences and evaluations. Irrespective of this, Meta marked all 31 advertisements as political advertisements.

19.4.2 Under-Enforcement

Under-enforcement is much worse in ramifications because it undermines the entire purpose of political ad transparency. Under-enforcement represents a pure failure of the transparency system, which hinders the ability to study and leads to missing significant portions of political advertising on the platform, including key elements. To understand under-enforcement in political advertisements targeting Bangladesh, this study relied on keyword searches within the Meta Ad Library.

The Meta Ad Library archives political, electoral, and social issue advertisements, whether active or inactive, and retains them for seven years. Political advertisements, however, are only accessible in the Ad Library when they are active. If an ad includes a political message that Meta does not categorize as political, it will no longer be available in the Ad Library once the campaign ends.

19.4.2.1 Undetected Political Advertisements

Several active pages from politicians and political parties managed to evade identification even though the ad content included political messages and images. We identified three key findings based on the study of such content. First, the study found that 50 active advertisements contained clear political messages and content that escaped Meta's detection system. These advertisements ran without a disclaimer and were not added to the Ad Library after their campaigns had concluded. It includes personal political campaigns of politicians and members of parliaments, promotion of political activities such as rallies, and comments on political situations. Second, interestingly, 48% of these pages, which ran these advertisements, self-identified as political organizations, or political figures in the "about" section of pages. Finally,

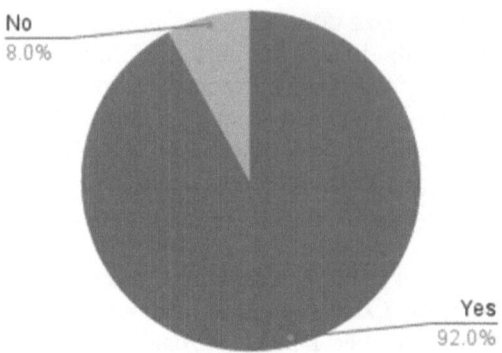

FIGURE 19.4
About 92% of the undetected ads had names of a party or politician

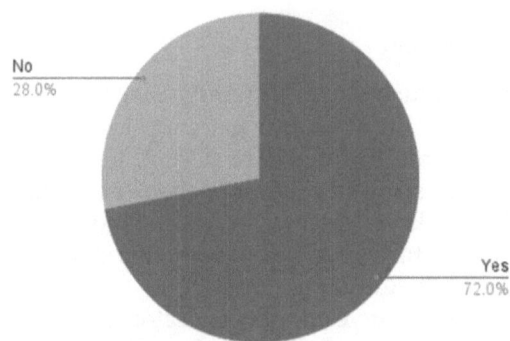

FIGURE 19.5
About 72% of the undetected ads had images of politicians or logo of a party

over 90% (see Figure 19.4) of the undetected advertisements prominently displayed the names of a political party or a political person, while 72% of these advertisements included photos of a political leader or the insignia of a political organization (see Figure 19.5).

19.4.2.2 Inconsistent Detection

The findings reveal that the enforcement of political and electoral advertising rules often lacks consistency when applied to both individuals and commercial pages. First, the same advertisement, containing a political message, was identified as political when it was shared by a page affiliated with a political group, but was undetected when disseminated by one of its followers. Second, in at least two cases, one page shared two identical political advertisements on the same day. One was categorized as political, while the other was not. Third, three posts by self-identified political activists were advertised with calls to participate in a political rally by the student wing and affiliate of the ruling party. Despite the strong political connotations of the content, it was neither identified as political nor added to the library. Finally, on at least five occasions, pages purporting to be news and fashion platforms managed to evade detection while displaying political advertisements, including political demands and featuring prominent political individuals.

19.4.2.3 Slow Response

If an ad is not declared political and Meta later identifies it as such, the ad is deactivated with the note: "These advertisements run without a disclaimer," and added to the Ad Library. Meta often requires many months, and sometimes even a year, to identify an advertisement as political and to prevent it from appearing without disclaimers. For example, a state minister has ran 30 advertisements from his official and verified pages, and only without any disclaimers since 2018. Facebook added disclaimers advertisements on this page only from April 2023. Meta detected three similar advertisements on this page in 6, 8, and 18 days, respectively. In another specific instance, an advertisement conveying a political message remained undetected for 372 days, despite a modest expenditure of around US$ 300 and the accumulation of over a million impressions. Meta took between one week and 79 days to add a disclaimer to the advertisements in at least 30 cases.

19.5 Existing Work and Discussion of Findings

In the present research, out of the 355 pages in the Meta Ad Library database, those that have spent more than US$ 100 on political advertising account for over 90% of the total spending. According to the self-declared identifications of these pages, four categories of pages were classified: political, commercial, news, and media. We also found a minimum of nine pages that were classified as "unavailable" owing to the removal of their advertisements from the platform. Notably, the average expenditure per ad on political and commercial pages was nearly three times higher than that for news, media, and other categories.

According to Edelson et al. (2020), transparency provided by Facebook ad libraries can help deter the spread of political misinformation; however, as mentioned earlier, it comes with flaws. For instance, many advertisements can run repeatedly without a disclaimer of nature. The authors suggest implementing a more effective threat model, conducting an exhaustive background check of the pages that issue political content frequently, and, more importantly, using the content clustering method to assess all advertisements with similar content. Pochat et al. (2022) found in their study that the method of detection adopted by Meta to identify political advertisements is deeply flawed. They also pointed out that while in some countries there was over-enforcement, in others political advertisements were able to run without the presence of a disclaimer. This research finds that Facebook not only fails to consider the underlying political purpose of advertisements, but its policy itself is vague and thus hard to follow, resulting in erroneous assessments. A key informant (academic) of the current research stated:

> After conducting a study of Meta's Ad Library, we discovered that a large number of advertisements were most likely not political. We find a great deal of both over- and under-enforcement of political advertising. At the very least, it is somewhat more difficult to ascertain precisely what causes overenforcement.

Similarly, this research shows specific trends related to the over-enforcement of political advertisements on Facebook and, in particular, suggests that around 25% of the advertisements flagged by Meta as political advertisements were not actually political in nature.

By examining commercial pages such as *Beximco* Group and *Nagad*, it tries to determine if there are any links between a company's ownership or management, especially when political figures are involved, and the enforcement of advertisements. However, it remains unclear whether such connections exist, causing inconsistent implementation of Facebook's political ad policies. For instance, Meta identified 24 *Nagad* advertisements as "political" and requested the inclusion of a disclaimer in the advertisements, even though these advertisements were unrelated to any political indicators.

Commercial pages that promote the sale of books, such as those belonging to publishers and bookstores as well as consulting services for studying or working abroad, have been mistakenly classified as political. For example, of the 23 advertisements sampled from *Panjeree* Publications, none contained political promotions or messages. Therefore, the classification of these advertisements as political advertising is incorrect, as there are no connections between these pages and political campaigns. In fact, these matters pertaining to civil and social rights, economy, education, environmental politics, health, immigration, and governance are considered social issues that are not included in the list of issues determined by Meta concerning political discourse in the context of Bangladesh.

This research highlights the frequent vulnerability of commercial entities to issues related to keywords, such as Ministers, MPs, and Secretaries. It does so by reviewing the number of advertisements discontinued because of the absence of disclaimers. The company "Minister Hi-Tech Park" is an important company in the market for electronic appliances such as TVs, fridges, and fans. However, one of their advertisements, which extended Eid greetings, was deemed political. Regarding susceptibility to keywords, a key informant (civil society representative) expressed the following:

It is difficult to say for sure, but it makes sense that it would be the result of machine learning algorithms focusing on a certain keyword. There are instances where machine learning systems misinterpret a word's context: Politics in Canada differs from politics in the United States (US). As a result, guns are a highly politicized topic in the US, but they are not particularly politicized in Canada. Facebook's machine learning was catching these guns' advertising and forcing them to be political in both countries.

Sosnovik et al. (2023) suggested automated systems to detect false portrayals of policies on social media platforms because of the large amount of data available. Unfortunately, although automated methods can identify political speech when it belongs to any single policy category, the detection is no longer accurate when several policies are involved in a single speech.

Silva et al. (2020) advocate the presence of independent auditors to detect political advertisements. This study identifies the main reason for numerous political advertisements being absent from the ad library is due to the fact that the advertisements itself did not come with a disclaimer that they were political. On the other hand, another study conducted by Jost et al. (2022) found that, despite the existence of a disclaimer on a political ad, regardless of how much information is provided on that disclaimer, users tend to not comprehend the information provided on the disclaimer and rather focus on the ad itself.

Another study showed that although social media platforms show transparency by providing information, there are still discrepancies (Ofcom, 2021). For instance, data are accessible via multiple routes on a platform, and there seems to be a clear difference in observations and the number of active advertisements across the platform. These discrepancies led to a flawed interpretation of the data.

This study posits that Meta's inaccurate data interpretations lead to both under- and over-enforcement of political advertisements. Using 30 keywords, we discovered 50 active advertisements that clearly displayed political content that Meta had not classified as such. It is noteworthy that in their "about" sections, 48% of these pages identified themselves as political organizations or political figures, and the content they disseminated was also of a political nature. On the other hand, over 90% of the nonpolitical advertisements, as classified by Meta, featured a political party or figure and 72% contained images of a political leader or party logo.

Pochat et al. (2022) claimed that Meta not only fails to consider the underlying political purpose of the advertisements, but its policy itself is vague and thus difficult to follow, resulting in erroneous assessments. A key informant (civil society representative) asserted that:

> I believe that allowing a system that permits virtually unlimited spending on political advertisements without transparency regarding the individuals or groups funding those advertisements poses a significant threat to democracies worldwide.

In line with this, Jain and Wood (2020) point out that the tone and sentiment behind an advertisement are adversely different when political advertisers are at risk of being held accountable for their speech. Furthermore, they argue that the tone of an ad depends on the transparency of the sponsorship and the target audience of the ad.

19.6 Conclusion and Recommendations

Both over- and under-enforcement of Meta's political advertising policy are revealed to be a result of the policy's relatively weak enforcement by Meta. Thus, this final part of the article indicates a few additional areas for research as well as recommendations for Meta.

19.6.1 Conclusion

This research primarily evaluates issues involving the enforcement of political advertising policy on Facebook in the context of Bangladesh. It found the presence of over- and under-enforcement of Meta's political advertising policy. The analysis of the data shows that along with pages classified as political, there are also numerous pages impertinent to politics that run political advertisements. It shows that at times, certain advertisements bore the brunt of over-enforcement simply for containing certain keywords or due to the company being affiliated with a politician despite the ad itself not containing any political message. At the same time, under-enforcement was identified as political advertisements from self-declared political pages that were able to escape detection, and the same advertisements ran from different pages receiving contradictory categorization from Meta.

For further research, it is worth noting that Facebook has been the subject of more research than other platforms, such as YouTube and TikTok. This is primarily due to the availability of additional tools and the inclusion of more comprehensive information in Facebook's advertising library. Consequently, research on Facebook is easier than that on other platforms. On the other hand, TikTok lacks political ad transparency, as it claims to have no political advertisements on its platform. Without transparency of advertising on a platform, political advertising is nonexistent. Therefore, the ability to compare and contrast various platforms is a valuable tool. Expanding the current research to include other platforms with high risks will be useful.

19.6.2 Recommendations

This study identified certain constraints in the implementation of Meta's political advertising policy. Based on these results, the following recommendations are proposed:

First, platforms such as Meta should conduct regular audits on keywords tailored to the context of Bangladesh to ensure accurate labelling in classifying political advertisements on Facebook. These audits may focus on refining training datasets that inform algorithms and minimize over-enforcement.

Second, Meta should collaborate with local stakeholders to establish and publicly disclose a comprehensive list of relevant social issues specific to each country, including Bangladesh. In all countries where political advertising policy is implemented, it is important for them to clearly define what constitutes political and social issues. This allows third-party auditors to assess whether pages have overlooked the issue.

Third, Meta can invest in more human reviewers with specific knowledge of the local political landscape and language. Having more human reviewers enables a deeper understanding of local nuances, languages, and political dynamics, leading to effective early detection of political advertisements and verification of disclaimers that may otherwise go undetected by automated systems.

Finally, the government of Bangladesh has the opportunity to foster a collaborative model involving multiple stakeholders such as academics, researchers, and civil society. Engaging in processes like "red teaming," where these stakeholders evaluate the effectiveness of platforms' policies, can provide valuable insights, and contribute to a more robust monitoring system for Facebook political advertisements.

19.7 Acknowledgment

We appreciate the support of the team members at Digitally Right for their assistance during this research. We are grateful to all key informants for their valuable participation in this research. We acknowledge that this chapter includes primary data analysis used for this research project report, which can be accessed at Digitally Right (Chowdhury, M.A., Hossain, M.P., & Das, P.P. (2023). Hits and misses: An examination of meta's political ad policy enforcement in Bangladesh. *Digitally Right*. https://digitallyright.org/wp-content/uploads/2023/12/Hits-And-Misses.pdf).

References

Bolden, S.E., McKernan, B., & Stromer-Galley, J. (2020). Facebook political advertising transparency report. 5 October, *Illuminating*. Retrieved from https://news.illuminating.ischool.syr.edu/2020/10/06/facebook-political-advertising-transparency-report/

Clegg, N. (2023). New features and additional transparency measures as the digital services act comes into effect. 22 August, *Meta*. Retrieved from https://about.fb.com/news/2023/08/new-features-and-additional-transparency-measures-as-the-digital-services-act-comes-into-effect/

Constine, J. (2019). Facebook launches searchable transparency library of all active ads. 29 March, *TechCrunch*. Retrieved from https://techcrunch.com/2019/03/28/facebook-ads-library/

The Economist. (2020). *A new mobile-money firm in Bangladesh is benefiting from special treatment*. 5 March. Retrieved from https://www.economist.com/asia/2020/03/05/a-new-mobile-money-firm-in-bangladesh-is-benefiting-from-special-treatment

Edelson, L., Lauinger, T., & McCoy, D. (2020). A security analysis of the Facebook Ad Library. *IEEE Symposium on Security and Privacy (SP)*. Retrieved from https://ieeexplore.ieee.org/document/9152626

Jain, S., & Wood, A.K. (2024). Facebook political ads and accountability: Outside groups are most negative, especially when hiding donors. *Proceedings of the International AAAI Conference on Web and Social Media, 18*(1), 717–735. https://doi.org/10.1609/icwsm.v18i1.31346

Jost, P., Kruschinski, S., Sülflow, M., Haßler, J., & Maurer, M. (2022). Invisible transparency: How different types of ad disclaimers on Facebook affect whether and how digital political advertising is perceived. *Policy and Internet, 15*(2), 204–212. Retrieved from https://doi.org/10.1002/poi3.333

Kaur, M., Salim, F.D., Ren, Y., Chan, J., Tomko, M., & Sanderson, M. (2020). Joint modelling of cyber activities and physical context to improve prediction of visitor behaviors. *ACM Transactions on Sensor Networks, 1*(1), 1–25. https://doi.org/10.1145/3393692

Meta. (2023a). *Ads about social issues, elections or politics*. Retrieved from https://transparency.fb.com/en-gb/policies/ad-standards/SIEP-advertising/SIEP/

Meta. (2023b). *Election integrity*. Retrieved from https://www.facebook.com/business/m/election-integrity

Meta. (2023c). *Ad library*. Retrieved from https://www.facebook.com/ads/library/

Meta. (2023d). *Ad library API*. Retrieved from https://www.facebook.com/ads/library/api/

Meta. (2023e). *Ad library report*. Retrieved from https://www.facebook.com/ads/library/report/

Meta. (2023f). *Availability for ads about social issues, elections or politics*. Retrieved from https://www.facebook.com/business/help/2150157295276323?id=288762101909005

Meta. (2023g). *About social issues*. Retrieved from https://www.facebook.com/business/help/214754279118974?id=288762101909005

Meta. (2023h). *Choosing a special ad category*. Retrieved from https://www.facebook.com/business/help/298000447747885

Meta. (2023i). *Get authorized to run ads about social issues, elections, or politics*. Retrieved from https://www.facebook.com/business/help/208949576550051?id=288762101909005

Meta. (2023j). *Create disclaimers and link Ad accounts*. https://www.facebook.com/business/help/488070228549681?id=288762101909005

Meta. (2023k). *About the Meta ad library*. https://www.facebook.com/business/help/2405092116183307?id=288762101909005

Ofcom. (2021). *Insights for online regulation: A case study monitoring political advertising*. Retrieved from https://www.ofcom.org.uk/__data/assets/pdf_file/0019/212860/tools-for-online-regulation-welsh.pdf

Pochat, V.L., Edelson, L., Goethem, T.V., Joosen, W., McCoy, D., & Lauinger, T. (2022). An audit of Facebook's political ad policy enforcement. 10–12 August, *USENIX*. Retrieved from https://www.usenix.org/system/files/sec22-lepochat.pd

Silva, M., de Oliveira, L.S., Andreou, A., de Melo, P.O.V., Goga, O., & Benevenuto, F. (2020). *Facebook ads monitor: An independent auditing system for political ads on Facebook*. Retrieved from arXiv:2001.10581 [cs.SI].

Sosnovik, V., Kessi, R., Coavoux, M., & Goga, O. (2023). *On detecting policy-related political ads: An exploratory analysis of Meta ads in 2022 French election*. ACM Digital Library. Retrieved from https://dl.acm.org/doi/10.1145/3543507.3583875

19.8 Key Terms

Terminology	Explanation
Awami League (AL)	AL is one of the political parties in Bangladesh. It was founded as the Awami Muslim League in 1949 and renamed the Awami League in 1972.
Bangladesh Election Commission	The Bangladesh Election Commission, an independent constitutional body, is entrusted with the enforcement of election laws and rules in Bangladesh.
Bangladesh Nationalist Party (BNP)	BNP is one of the political parties in Bangladesh which was founded in 1978.
Digital platforms	Google search engines, Facebook, Spotify, YouTube, and similar Internet and web-based virtual spaces are digital platforms that use unique business models to exchange information, knowledge, goods, ideas, and services for financial or nonfinancial gains (Kaur et al., 2020).
Facebook	Facebook is a social networking platform that is owned by Meta.
Facebook advertisement (or Facebook ad)	An advertisement on Facebook has a resemblance to sponsored posts in that, with their textual content, images, or videos, they consistently include the name and profile picture of a Facebook page as their author.
Keywords	A keyword is any meaningful term or phrase, particularly one that is used to define the contents of a document.
Meta	Meta Platforms Inc., doing business as Meta, and formerly named Facebook Inc., is the company that owns and operates Facebook, Instagram, Threads, and WhatsApp, among other products and services.
Over-enforcement	Over-enforcement by Facebook in the case of a political ad signifies undue takedown of the ad, which does not fall under the Meta political ad policy.

(Continued)

(Continued)

Terminology	Explanation
Paid for by	Meta has introduced a requirement to add a "Paid for by" disclaimer to political advertisements on Facebook to accurately document the individuals or organizations responsible for running these advertisements.
Political ad policy	Meta flags an ad as political when that: (a) is made by, on behalf of or about a candidate for public office, a political figure, a political party, a political action committee, or advocates for the outcome of an election to public office; (b) is about any election, referendum, or ballot initiative, including "get out the vote" or election information campaigns; (c) is about any social issue in any place where the ad is being run; or (d) is regulated as political advertising.
Political advertisement (or Political ad)	A political advertisement on Facebook refers to a sponsored message that includes content about social issues, elections, or politics and corresponds to the Meta Political Ad Policy.
Under-enforcement	Under-enforcement occurs when political advertisements on Facebook are made available due to incorrect enforcement of the Meta political ad policy.

Annexure 1: Broad and Narrow Categories of Facebook Pages

In the following table, five categories of research pages are outlined. First, pages on Facebook that have indicated their political affiliation or declared as political during the category selection process are classified as "Political" pages. Second, a wide range of news and media-related pages have been categorized as News and Media. Third, pages involved in the online sale of goods, services, or products are classified as "commercial." Fourth, in addition to the three categories mentioned, this study's list of 355 pages includes 126 pages that have been categorized as "Other" considering they do not belong to any specific larger category. This category includes various entities, such as government organizations, nonprofit organizations, communities, digital creators, and personal blogs. Last, there is another category this study named as "unavailable" to include pages that, when opened, notify that the "page has been unpublished or deleted," or that "the content is currently unavailable."'

SL	Broad Category	Total Count	Narrow Category	Total Count
1	Political	72	Politician	53
			Political Candidate	03
			Political Organization	09
			Political Party	07
2	News and Media	92	News and Media Website	42
			Media/News Company	26
			Newspaper	14
			Journalist	04
			News Personality	02
			Media	01
			Media Agency	01
			Broadcasting and Media Production Company	01
3	Commercial	56	Bookstore	12
			Publisher	06
			Apparel and Clothing	06
			Financial Service	03
			Shopping Service	03
			Software	03
			Business Service	03
			Consulting Agency	02
			Graphic Designer	02
			Travel Agency	01
			Advertising Agency	01
			Architectural Designer	01
			Book and Magazine Distributor	01
			Chemical Company	01
			Construction Company	01
			E-commerce Website	01
			Electronics Company	01
			Industrial Company	01
			Internet Marketing Service	01
			Local Business	01
			Marriage Therapist	01
			Organic Grocery Store	01
			Toy Store	01
			Wholesale and Supply Store	01
4	Other	126	Public Figure	19
			Nonprofit Organization	18
			Community	15
			Interest	11

(*Continued*)

(Continued)

SL	Broad Category	Total Count	Narrow Category	Total Count
			Government Official and Organization (7)	08
			Digital Creator	05
			Social Service	05
			Personal Blog	05
			College and University	04
			Cause	04
			Sports	03
			Entertainment Website	02
			Religious Organization	02
			Entrepreneur	02
			Education	02
			Arts and Humanities Website	02
			Actor	01
			Animals and Pets	01
			App Page	01
			Armed Forces	01
			Community Center	01
			Community Organization	01
			Consulate and Embassy	01
			Educational Consultant	01
			E-Sports Team	01
			Event	01
			Fan Page	01
			Media Critic	01
			Medical and Health	01
			Nursing School	01
			Party Entertainment Service	01
			Personal Coach	01
			Public and Government Service	01
			RV Park	01
			Youth Organization	01
5	Unavailable	09	–	

Total: 355

Annexure 2: Keywords

The keywords used included: Sheikh Hasina, Khaleda Zia, Sajeeb Wazed, Tarique Rahman, Awami League/AL, BNP (Bangladesh Nationalist Party), Jatiya Party, Jamaate-e-Islami, Bangladesh Chatra League, Bangladesh Jatiotabadi Chatra Dal, Bangladesh Islami Chhatrashibir, Bangladesh Awami Jubo League, Bangladesh Jatiotabadi Jubo Dal, Islamic Movement Bangladesh, Islamic Student Movement Bangladesh, Bangladesh Gono Odhikar Porishod/Bangladesh People's Rights Council, National Leader, People's Leader, Election – Bangladesh, Public Meeting, Assembly – Bangladesh, Activists, Ballot, Vote, Smart Bangladesh, Digital Bangladesh, Rally – Bangladesh, #TakeBackBangladesh, #StepDownHasina, and #OnceAgainHasina.

Please note that this study used Bengali texts of the above keywords, except for the last three hashtag campaigns.

This research underscored the keywords that are mostly connected to political figures, political parties, and political personalities, and the terms or words that are rarely used outside of political contexts or commentary in Bangladesh. For example, four names, such as "Sheikh Hasina" is the name of the former Prime Minister in the Government of Bangladesh, "Khaleda Zia" is the name of chairperson and leader of the BNP since 1984, Sajeeb Wazed is the name of son of Sheikh Hasina, Tarique Rahman is the name of son of Khaleda Zia and acting chairman of BNP since February 2018, have been used as keywords involving political figures.

There are 12 active and relevant political parties and organizations in Bangladesh: Awami League, BNP, Jatiya Party, Jamaat-e-Islami, Bangladesh Chhatra League, Bangladesh Jatiotabadi Chatra Dal, Bangladesh Islami Chhatrashibir, Bangladesh Awami Jubo League, Bangladesh Jatiotabadi Jubo Dal, Islamic Movement Bangladesh, Islamic Student Movement Bangladesh, and Bangladesh People's Rights Council.

Ten keywords, selected outside of political figures and parties, are frequently used in political campaigns, speeches, and commentaries in Bangladesh: national leaders, people's leaders, elections, public meetings, assemblies, activists, ballots, votes, Smart Bangladesh, and Digital Bangladesh. The last keywords associated with English hashtags were selected because they have been widely used in recent political campaigns: #TakeBackBangladesh, #StepDownHasina, and #OnceAgainHasina.

20
Regulating E-Waste Management in the Digital Era: A Legal and Policy Analysis

Ridoan Karim, Md. Shah Newaz, and Andrea Appolloni

20.1 Introduction

In a world increasingly driven by technology, the tale of electronic waste, or e-waste, unfolds as a poignant narrative of our times. E-waste encompasses the vast array of electrical or electronic devices that have reached the end of their lifecycle, often referred to as waste electrical and electronic equipment (WEEE) or end-of-life electronics (Karpagaraj et al., 2023; Townsend, 2011). While the definition of e-waste has remained relatively stable over time, it only scratches the surface of a complex issue.

This story of e-waste is not just about the physical pile-up of discarded gadgets and components. In today's time, it goes deeper into the realm of digital footprints as these abandoned devices are not just silent relics of our past consumption; they are vaults containing sensitive data. Without proper erasure or handling, this data can seep out, leading to breaches of privacy and security that haunt individuals and organizations alike (Das et al., 2023; Kapoor et al., 2021; Newaz & Appolloni, 2023a). Similarly, improper e-waste management may lead to the violations of growing global privacy and data protection laws (Das et al., 2023; Zingerle & Kronman, 2019). The above-mentioned narrative is particularly interesting as it explores the connection between e-waste and data privacy, and how regulations on one can affect the other. However, when we talk about "e-waste," we still limit the discussion to discarded electronic devices and fail to address its broader implications in contemporary times.

Proper e-waste management opens avenues for innovation in recycling technologies and processes. It also creates economic opportunities through the recovery of valuable materials and the growth of recycling industries (Debnath, 2020; Newaz & Appolloni, 2023b; Van Yken et al., 2021). Electronic devices contain valuable materials like gold, silver, copper, and rare earth metals (Li et al., 2019). Efficient recycling and recovery processes supported by effective e-waste regulation can conserve resources and reduce the need for virgin material extraction, aligning with sustainable development goals (Kaya & Tita, 2023; Sa & Korinek, 2021). However, at the governmental level, very few policies consider the channeling of e-waste toward economic prosperity (Patil & Ramakrishna, 2020).

Discussing e-waste in the context of digital strategies involves exploring these opportunities and the legislative frameworks that can support them. The focus often remains on the environmental and health hazards, overshadowing the possibilities for resource recovery and economic gain. Then again, setting up e-waste recycling and recovery facilities requires significant investment in technology and infrastructure (Van Yken et al., 2021). The process of extracting valuable materials from e-waste is technically complex and often expensive (Van Yken et al., 2021). Nevertheless, the main issue is that in many cases, existing laws fail to create a conducive environment for e-waste recycling initiatives (Gollakota et al., 2020; Pariatamby & Victor, 2013). This is because they are outdated, lack enforcement mechanisms, or are misaligned with the current technological landscape (Patil & Ramakrishna, 2020).

The global nature of e-waste, where waste is often exported from developed to less developed countries, complicates regulatory efforts. Such practices, sometimes illegal, exploit weaker environmental protections and labor standards in certain countries, making it difficult to establish a unified approach to e-waste management that benefits all parties economically (Abalansa et al., 2021; Little & Lucier, 2017; Van Erp & Huisman, 2010). As such, effective governance requires international cooperation and strong local legislation to prevent illegal dumping and to ensure sound management of e-waste. This aspect of e-waste regulation is pivotal in global digital strategy discussions. Then again, strategies for e-waste management can also include refurbishing and redistributing electronic devices to bridge the digital divide (Raghavan, 2013). Regulations can encourage practices that extend the life of devices and make technology more accessible to underprivileged communities.

In essence, regulating e-waste is a multidimensional challenge that intersects with broader discussions on sustainable development, digital equity, cybersecurity, and global governance. However, most laws regarding e-waste only address its hazardous impact on the environment and human health, without going beyond that (Patil & Ramakrishna, 2020). Today's e-waste management requires a holistic approach that balances technological progress with environmental sustainability, social justice, and economic viability. As such, the existing legal and regulatory framework for managing e-waste needs a significant paradigm shift to achieve these goals.

To understand how that paradigm shift is possible, this chapter analyzes the legal gaps in the existing global e-waste scenario and proposes recommendations to formulate effective e-waste policies and laws for the contemporary world. Given the global nature of e-waste generation and disposal, this chapter provides a comparative analysis of different legal and policy frameworks around the world. This would offer readers a nuanced understanding of how different jurisdictions approach the challenge of e-waste, highlighting the importance of international collaboration and policy harmonization in the digital era.

To accomplish the abovementioned goals of this chapter, a thorough narrative review has been performed, guided by Templier and Paré (2015), to ensure the inclusion of pertinent empirical studies. This not only situates this work within the existing literature but also reinforces the rationale behind the approach and underscores its contributions to the field. Rather than introducing new concepts or critiquing existing theories, via narrative review this study serves as a crucial link, consolidating dispersed research on e-waste management in the policy and legal realm for readers who may lack the time or resources to explore it comprehensively. Thus, we employed a "configuration of logic" approach to weave together complementary findings, creating a coherent narrative. Therefore, by synthesizing key studies and empirical data from the perspectives of privacy, economic development, and sustainability, we developed a comprehensive legal and policy analysis that identifies trends and supports broader generalizations in the regulatory landscape. Figure 20.1 illustrates the process we followed.

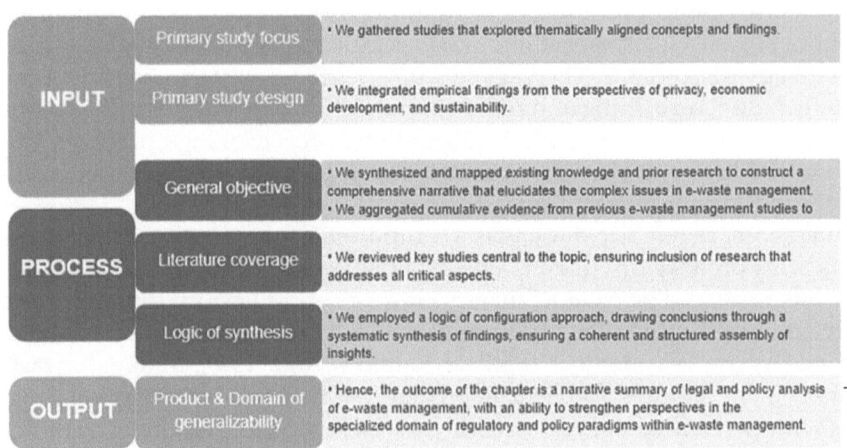

FIGURE 20.1
Structured framework of the chapter

Source: Adapted from Templier and Paré (2015).

20.2 Integrating E-Waste Management into the Circular Economy Framework

By 2026, the electronic recycling industry is projected to reach a value of $65.8 billion, with an annual growth rate of 12.7% (Seif et al., 2024). The international market for consumer electronics recycling is set to surge from $14.5 billion in 2020 to $35.4 billion by 2026, with China experiencing the most rapid growth (Seif et al., 2024). China's recycling market is forecasted to expand to $15.3 billion, with Canada and Japan not far behind, showcasing growth rates of 9% and 8.9%, respectively (Seif et al., 2024). Germany and the rest of Europe are also on track for substantial expansion, with Europe at the forefront of recycling innovation. This leadership is attributed to the rapid adoption of new recycling technologies across various sectors, including security, automotive, marketing, healthcare, retail, IT, and telecommunications (Seif et al., 2024). The Asia Pacific region is also anticipated to see a market size of $5.8 billion by 2026, while Latin America's market is also expected to witness rapid growth (Seif et al., 2024).

Electronic waste encompasses a variety of discarded or obsolete electronic devices. European directives categorize this waste into ten distinct groups, ranging from computers and household appliances to toys and medical devices (Arya et al., 2023). The composition of e-waste varies greatly by device type, with a significant portion consisting of household appliances and communication devices. The significance of electronic waste lies in the valuable metals it contains. For instance, mobile phones include over 40 types of materials, such as precious metals like gold and silver, and common metals like tin and copper (Singh et al., 2018). Rapid technological advancements and consumer demand lead to shorter lifespans for electronic products, contributing to increased waste (Newaz & Appolloni, 2023a). Printed circuit boards from these devices are particularly valuable for recycling due to their metal content, but there is also the presence of hazardous substances like lead (Tembhare et al., 2022). This situation underscores the urgent need for secure, sustainable methods to recycle and reclaim materials from electronic waste.

Hence, the push for better management of e-waste is driven by not only the increasing need for recycling but also the potential economic benefits. However, the current methods of managing e-waste are complex and give rise to a host of social, political, and legal issues. As the influx of broken or outdated electronic devices like phones and computers continues to grow, a significant portion is being shipped off to developing countries. Without formal recycling systems, these electronics enter the informal sector, compounding global human rights issues (Perkins et al., 2014). The informal e-waste recycling sector often operates within communities that are already marginalized and face economic vulnerabilities. The influx of hazardous waste exacerbates existing social inequalities, as the poorest and most vulnerable populations are forced to engage in dangerous recycling activities to earn a livelihood (Heacock et al., 2016).

This situation reflects a broader global pattern of environmental racism and injustice, where the burdens of pollution and hazardous industries are disproportionately borne by marginalized communities. Unfortunately, the global trade in e-waste is driven by economic disparities, where it is cheaper to export broken electronics to developing countries than to recycle them responsibly in developed nations (Abalansa et al., 2021; Sthiannopkao & Wong, 2013). This trade reflects broader patterns of global inequality, the exploitation of cheap labor, and lax environmental regulations in poorer countries. And as a result, we can witness improper handling of toxic substances, which eventually leads to environmental contamination, with severe health consequences for local populations in developing countries dealing with e-waste, including cancer, neurological damage, and reduced intelligent quotients (Awere et al., 2020; Lin et al., 2022). In many cases, the introduction of e-waste recycling in developing countries also goes beyond human rights and environmental issues, and can have profound cultural impacts, altering traditional ways of life, family structures, and social norms. For instance, child labor in e-waste recycling can disrupt traditional paths of education and childhood, affecting community structures and future generations' prospects (Masud et al., 2019; Perkins et al., 2014).

Addressing the challenges of electronic waste management reveals multiple layers of complexity. Many regions lack the necessary infrastructure for proper e-waste recycling, burdened by outdated waste management practices, dense urban populations, and insufficient resources. For instance, India discards over 2 million tons of e-waste annually, with less than 3% undergoing recycling (Arya & Kumar, 2020). The difficulty and expense of extracting valuable materials from electronic devices exacerbate the issue, as does the rapid evolution of technology that recycling facilities struggle to keep pace with. Furthermore, global recycling rates for e-waste hover around a mere 17.4%, hindered by inadequate disposal habits and the illegal trade of e-waste (Gassner, 2021). The absence of stringent regulations for the collection, dismantling, and eco-friendly processing of e-waste poses another significant hurdle.

Within these discarded electronics lies a wealth of valuable resources such as iron, copper, and gold, estimated at $57 billion (Sakhuja et al., 2022). Yet, only a fraction, worth $10 billion, is reclaimed in an environmentally responsible manner, leaving the vast majority to contribute to landfills and environmental degradation (Mukherjee et al., 2023). This scenario underscores the potential benefits of shifting toward a circular economy in electronics, a model focused on minimizing waste and extending the lifecycle of resources. This approach not only offers a more sustainable alternative to the traditional "take-make-use-dispose" model but also opens up new financial and business opportunities.

The transition toward a circular economy is gaining momentum as businesses and consumers alike recognize the urgent need to address the environmental challenges posed by traditional linear economic models. This linear approach, characterized by a "take-make-use-dispose" model, has led to significant waste and resource depletion. In contrast, the circular economy aims to redefine growth, focusing on positive society-wide benefits. It entails gradually decoupling economic activity from the consumption of finite resources and designing waste out of the system. Underpinned by a transition to renewable energy sources, the circular model builds economic, natural, and social capital by embracing three principles: design out waste and pollution, keep products and materials in use, and regenerate natural systems.

The concept of leasing electronics embodies the essence of the circular economy by prioritizing the reuse and recycling of devices at the end of their lifecycle (van Loon et al., 2018). This model allows businesses to retain ownership of the electronics, thereby ensuring that once the lease term ends, devices can be returned, refurbished, and re-leased or recycled, extracting valuable materials for future use. Such an approach not only extends the lifecycle of electronic devices but also significantly reduces e-waste, a critical concern in the digital age.

The benefits of leasing electronics are multifold. For consumers, it offers the flexibility to upgrade to the latest technology without the burden of disposing of old devices. For businesses, it opens up new revenue streams while promoting sustainable practices. Importantly, it contributes to the conservation of valuable resources like rare earth metals, which are finite and increasingly difficult to extract. However, challenges such as establishing efficient return and recycling logistics, encouraging consumer participation, and designing devices suitable for refurbishment and recycling need to be addressed to fully realize the potential of this model (Islam et al., 2022).

Another approach, which is the product-as-a-service (PaaS) model, represents a paradigm shift in the way we perceive product ownership. Instead of purchasing products, consumers pay for the use of a product or a service, with the manufacturer retaining ownership (Szwarc et al., 2024). This model incentivizes manufacturers to design products that are durable, easier to maintain and repair, and more straightforward to recycle at the end of their life, as the responsibility for the product remains with them throughout its lifecycle. PaaS has the potential to significantly reduce waste and promote the reuse of products. It encourages a shift from a disposable culture to one where products are valued for their functionality and longevity. This model can be particularly effective in industries where technology evolves rapidly, such as consumer electronics, where products can become obsolete quickly. By retaining ownership, manufacturers can refurbish and upgrade devices, thereby extending their lifecycle and reducing the need for new materials.

It is not that we cannot keep the conventional model, or we just have to deviate from it; rather, even within the conventional product ownership model, there is considerable scope for companies to drive sustainability. By designing products that are easier to recycle and encouraging consumers to participate in recycling programs, businesses can significantly reduce the environmental impact of their products. This approach requires integrating sustainability into product design, such as using recyclable materials, modular design for easy disassembly, and clear labeling to facilitate recycling.

Consumer incentivization plays a crucial role in this model (Simpson et al., 2019). Programs that offer discounts, trade-ins, or other benefits for returning used products can motivate consumers to recycle. Education and awareness campaigns can further enhance participation rates by highlighting the environmental benefits of recycling and explaining how consumers can contribute (Shevchenko et al., 2019). However, adopting circular economy principles presents challenges as well. On the one hand, it requires significant upfront investment in redesigning products, establishing new business models, and building the infrastructure for product return and recycling. On the other hand, there are also logistical and regulatory hurdles to overcome, especially when dealing with the cross-border movement of used and recycled goods. Still, the circular economy opens up new avenues for innovation and competitiveness. It can lead to cost savings in the long term through efficient resource use and waste reduction. Moreover, businesses that adopt circular practices can enhance their brand reputation and customer loyalty by positioning themselves as environmentally responsible (Patil & Ramakrishna, 2020).

Nevertheless, despite the efforts to create a circular economy and address the contemporary challenge of e-waste, there is a real problem that needs to be resolved. The problem lies in the application and implementation of proper laws and policies to support the circular economy and effectively manage e-waste. In the next section of this chapter, we analyze the existing laws and policies related to e-waste management and identify the gaps that make it difficult to achieve circular economy strategies with e-waste management.

20.3 E-Waste Laws and Policies: Prospects and Challenges

E-waste laws are now in place in many countries, including those with large populations, meaning that around two-thirds of the world's people are currently protected by some form of e-waste regulation (Patil & Ramakrishna, 2020), resulting in significant progress in sustainable e-waste management. Laws relating to e-waste have been developed in the European Union (EU), the United States, the United Kingdom, Oceania (including Australia and

New Zealand), and several Asian nations such as China, India, Japan, South Korea, Taiwan, and Singapore (Nnorom & Osibanjo, 2008). However, these laws are a result of years of development and were shaped by significant world events.

The urgency to confront the transboundary movement of hazardous waste was spurred by notorious episodes like the Khian Sea waste disposal in Haiti in 1986,[1] and the Koko incident in Nigeria in 1988,[2] where toxic waste from richer countries was illicitly dumped in less prosperous nations in Asia and Africa. In response, the United Nations assembled 186 countries to endorse the Basel Convention on the Control of Transboundary Movements of Hazardous Wastes and their Disposal (hereinafter "Basel Convention") in Basel, Switzerland, in 1989. The Basel Convention is dedicated to environmental preservation by prohibiting the exchange of hazardous waste among member states. While this convention has significantly reduced the hazardous waste trade, it has not entirely ceased the illegal trafficking of e-waste from developed to developing countries (Ahmed, 2019).

Following the Basel Convention, the EU swiftly enacted the Waste Shipment Regulation in 1993, barring the export of dangerous e-waste to non-Organisation for Economic Co-operation and Development (OECD) countries. Subsequently, the Commission introduced the Restriction of Hazardous Substances Directive 2012/95/EC, advocating for alterations in product and packaging designs to reduce the use of toxic substances and encourage the adoption of greener alternatives. This directive sought to boost the recycling of WEEE produced within domestic boundaries.

By 2012, the EU Commission had put forth the WEEE Directive (2012/19/EU), aiming to synchronize e-waste management practices across its member states by overseeing the processes of collection, recycling, and resource recovery. This directive advocates for a methodical and distinct collection system to enhance the efficiency of recycling and the recovery of recyclable e-waste components, requiring that processed e-waste be accurately reported to the National Enforcement Authority. It further promotes the design and manufacturing of electrical and electronic equipment (EEE) that is more straightforward to dismantle and recycle, establishing precise treatment criteria for e-waste materials, components, and storage facilities. The directive embraces the extended producer responsibility (EPR) principle, obligating producers to oversee the recycling of their products at the end of their life cycle.

EPR places the onus on manufacturers to manage the environmental impact of their products throughout their lifecycle, addressing costs that are often ignored (Sachs, 2006). This typically involves mandating that producers retrieve their products at the end of their life, usually linking this with recycling objectives. Within the framework of international e-waste legislation, EPR plays a pivotal role, serving as a prelude to addressing broader e-waste management challenges. As defined by the OECD, EPR is a strategic approach that broadens the accountability of producers to include the disposal and recycling phase of a product, beyond its usage (OECD, 2021).

The essence of EPR lies in obligating manufacturers to oversee the collection and recycling of their products at the end of their functional life. This obligation includes both the financial costs and the logistical operations involved in recycling and collection efforts. Producers might undertake these duties individually or through collective initiatives, often by enlisting a dedicated body known as a producer responsibility organization to manage the recycling and disposal processes collaboratively.

These EPR tools have seen varied implementation across the EU, where despite the shared EU WEEE Directive, individual member states tailor their legislation and execution according to national requirements (Favot et al., 2022). The EU directives offer a foundational framework, but it is the national laws that detail the operational facets of EPR systems. EPR systems for e-waste management have been adopted by all EU members and several non-EU countries (Patil & Ramakrishna, 2020).

Across Asia, the management of e-waste displays a broad spectrum of approaches, reflecting the diverse economic landscapes of the continent. The continent has historically battled with unauthorized e-waste imports and ad hoc recycling practices. However, recent developments have led countries such as China, India, Japan, Korea, Taiwan, and Singapore to establish laws aimed at improving e-waste management, inspired by the EU's systematic approach to e-waste regulations. Notably, China is recognized as Asia's leading e-waste producer and a significant recipient of global e-waste. As of January 1, 2018, China has banned the importation of 24 types of solid waste, including waste plastics and slag, due to the influx of discarded EEE from wealthier nations (Liu et al., 2023). This measure has substantially decreased the variety and quantity of waste imports into the country (N. Song et al., 2023). This decision aligns with a wider international initiative aimed at curbing the global movement of such hazardous waste. In an effort to address e-waste more efficiently, China has also revised its legislation to reduce waste generation and to promote improved recycling practices, transitioning from informal to formally regulated recycling processes. In 2012, following Europe's lead, China implemented the EPR law, which requires manufacturers to recycle their products and incorporate recycled materials into new ones (Patil & Ramakrishna, 2020). Neighboring China, Taiwan's e-waste management is governed by the regularly updated "Waste Disposal Act" (Rasnan et al., 2016). The "4-in-1 recycling program" demonstrates Taiwan's commitment to effective and secure e-waste recycling, engaging the community, the recycling sector, local authorities, and a specialized recycling fund (Tsai et al., 2007).

India, another giant e-waste producer in Asia, did not have specific regulations for managing electronic waste until 2011. Instead, it was typically governed by broader environmental and hazardous waste laws. That year, however, marked a significant change with the introduction of e-waste management and handling rule (Thakur & Kumar, 2022). This new policy/rule required manufacturers of EEE to adopt recycling responsibilities, aligning

India with European standards. Another big e-waste producer – Japan – manages its e-waste with two major laws: the Law for the Promotion of Effective Utilization of Resources (LPUR) and the Law for the Recycling of Specified Kinds of Home Appliances (LRHA) (Herat & Agamuthu, 2012). The LPUR encourages manufacturers to voluntarily reduce waste and recycle more, while the LRHA imposes stringent recycling requirements on both consumers and manufacturers, including fees for the recycling of older computers (Herat & Agamuthu, 2012). Korea, being a similar developed economy to Japan, has introduced several innovative approaches to improve e-waste recycling, including the Waste Deposit-Refund System, the Eco-Assurance System, and EPR (Manomaivibool & Hong, 2014). These programs are designed to foster recycling, limit hazardous substances in EEE, and compel manufacturers to report their recycling efforts. Singapore, being another developed economy in Asia, has strictly controlled the transit of hazardous waste through its ports since the 1990s, adhering to the Basel Convention (Shad et al., 2020). The country is now advancing toward specific e-waste management legislation that incorporates EPR principles and encourages voluntary recycling partnerships, leveraging its strategic geographic location (Patil & Ramakrishna, 2020).

In the Americas, the absence of federal e-waste legislation in the United States, coupled with its nonratification of the Basel Ban,[3] has led to disparate state regulations and ongoing e-waste exports. Similarly, Canada and several Latin American countries lack cohesive e-waste policies, though some are making progress toward adopting EPR principles (Patil & Ramakrishna, 2020). Different from the Americas, Oceania – which includes Australia, New Zealand, and the Pacific Islands – recognizes the importance of proper e-waste legislation (Patil & Ramakrishna, 2020). Australia sets a precedent with the Product Stewardship Act for recycling televisions and computers, inspiring the region (Jayasiri et al., 2023).

In Africa, the influx of EEE from developed countries exacerbates the e-waste challenge, resulting in prevalent informal recycling practices (Maphosa & Maphosa, 2020). Nevertheless, nations like Kenya, Ghana, Madagascar, and Nigeria are advancing with new e-waste regulations, featuring import bans and the EPR principle (Patil & Ramakrishna, 2020). South Africa is also in the process of developing a comprehensive e-waste management policy (Patil & Ramakrishna, 2020).

While many countries are at different phases of developing electronic waste (e-waste) legislation, drawing inspiration from the EU's model for crafting their e-waste management strategies, there exists a notable disconnect between these laws and the central theme of the circular economy. Current laws often fail to incentivize the design of recyclable, durable, and repairable electronic products (Patil & Ramakrishna, 2020). For example, many existing e-waste laws are based on the EPR principle, which holds producers accountable for the environmental impacts of their products throughout the product lifecycle. However, these regulations frequently focus more on the end-of-life phase of products, such as recycling and disposal, rather than on the initial design and production stages. This approach does not strongly encourage manufacturers to consider the lifecycle impacts of their products, leading to a missed opportunity to promote the design of more sustainable electronics. Then again, the concept of EPR exhibits considerable variation across the EU. Each EU member state adheres to the EU WEEE Directive but adapts its laws and implementation strategies to suit local needs. While EU directives establish a foundational framework, the intricate details of EPR systems – including take-back schemes for e-waste management – are largely delineated by national legislation (Patil & Ramakrishna, 2020).

Then again, in Europe, despite comprehensive legislation, the enforcement of e-waste laws is lackluster, fostering a clandestine market of illegal waste trading (Patil & Ramakrishna, 2020). The ambiguity in defining recyclable e-waste exacerbates this issue, as different nations hold divergent views on what constitutes recyclable materials, leading to inconsistencies and loopholes in enforcement. These loopholes are not only limited to Europe, as it can be seen in Australia as well. Australia's approach to e-waste legislation exemplifies a narrowed focus that predominantly targets specific categories such as TVs and computers, neglecting other crucial types of e-waste (Patil & Ramakrishna, 2020). This limitation leads to significant volumes of electronic products ending up in landfills or being illegally exported due to the absence of clear directives for local authorities and the public on proper e-waste management.

On the other hand, in North America, the formation and application of EPR policies in the United States and Canada occur primarily at the state or provincial level. Only a handful of states, such as California, New York, and Vermont, have enacted mandatory EPR laws targeting specific items like batteries, mercury thermostats, and switches. Elsewhere, EPR is often voluntary or entirely lacking (OECD, 2016). This inconsistency impedes the effective management of e-waste. Consequently, there is a growing demand for the federal government to implement a uniform and obligatory EPR policy that would support and enhance the regulatory framework at the state or provincial level. In addition, in developing nations like India, although EPR take-back regulations are included in the legislation, their implementation is subpar (Patil & Ramakrishna, 2020). The formal e-waste recycling sector in India struggles significantly, primarily due to inadequate financial support for developing essential infrastructure. Moreover, most of the EPR laws in other countries do not adequately address the participation of all stakeholders, including manufacturers, consumers, and recyclers, in the lifecycle management of electronics. For example, South Korea's EPR regulations, which also utilize a take-back approach, are not exhaustive and do not effectively delineate responsibilities among all stakeholders (Chung & Murakami-Suzuki, 2008).

There are also several different challenges that particularly relates to less affluent countries, where there is often a dire lack of funding and strategic planning for e-waste management (Patil & Ramakrishna, 2020). These countries frequently resort to primitive disposal methods, which are not only environmentally detrimental but also squander valuable resources that could otherwise be recovered. For instance, the rudimentary burning of e-waste in open pits, common in some regions, releases toxic substances into the environment, posing severe health risks to nearby communities and degrading natural ecosystems. Asia, in particular, faces significant challenges due to the illegal importation of e-waste, predominantly in countries like China and India. While some Asian regions, like Japan, South Korea, and Taiwan, possess more sophisticated recycling infrastructures, they are not devoid of issues. These include legal loopholes that facilitate unlawful dumping and inadequate handling of hazardous materials. Furthermore, child labor and unsafe recycling practices in some regions highlight the critical need for comprehensive regulatory oversight and enforcement (Priyashantha et al., 2022).

There are also limited specific legal standards mandating that electronic products be designed for durability, repairability, and recyclability (Maitre-Ekern & Dalhammar, 2016). Without stringent requirements, manufacturers may prioritize cost savings or aesthetic considerations over environmental sustainability. This results in products that are difficult to repair or recycle and that have shorter lifespans due to planned obsolescence. Then again, economic incentives such as tax breaks, subsidies, or grants for companies that design environmentally friendly products are often lacking in current legislation (M. Song et al., 2020). Without financial motivations, manufacturers might not invest in the research and development needed to create products that are easier to repair, reuse, or recycle.

Another growing concern that e-waste legislation often overlooks is the protection of sensitive data when disposing of electronics (Alghazo et al., 2018). E-waste legislation has historically focused on the environmental impact of discarded electronic devices, such as preventing hazardous substances from polluting the environment and promoting the recycling of materials. In contrast, data protection laws aim to secure personal information against unauthorized access, use, or disclosure. Hence, there remains a regulatory and policy gap about the risks to data privacy posed by improperly discarded electronic devices.

In addition, properly addressing data protection in the context of e-waste requires understanding both the technical aspects of data storage and deletion and the environmental considerations of e-waste management. This complexity can be a barrier to integrating these considerations into a single legislative framework. Then again, government agencies responsible for environmental protection often handle e-waste management, while different regulatory bodies oversee data protection. This separation leads to a lack of coordination and integration between these two important areas.

Lastly, the international trade and movement of e-waste complicate the enforcement of data protection measures. Devices discarded in one country can end up being processed in another, where laws and enforcement mechanisms regarding data protection may be weaker or nonexistent.

20.4 The Way Forward

The narrative of e-waste is a poignant reflection of our technological era, highlighting the urgent need for a comprehensive approach to managing the lifecycle of electronics. The current landscape of e-waste legislation, characterized by inconsistencies and gaps in enforcement, underscores the necessity for a paradigm shift toward integrated and stringent regulatory frameworks. By adopting a holistic approach that encompasses not only environmental concerns but also data privacy, economic viability, and social equity, policymakers can craft regulations that not only mitigate the impact of e-waste but also harness its potential as a resource.

It is imperative for countries both within and outside the EU to enhance EPR frameworks. Regulations should not only enforce recycling but also encourage manufacturers to design for durability, repairability, and recyclability from the outset. These initiatives should be bolstered by international standards to ensure consistency and effectiveness across borders. There is also a need for strengthening enforcement of existing e-waste legislation through more robust monitoring and compliance mechanisms. This includes greater transparency and accountability in e-waste tracking and stricter penalties for noncompliance to deter illegal waste trading and dumping.

Fostering international cooperation to combat the global challenges of e-waste management is also important. There is a significant need for an international entity to supervise and coordinate e-waste management efforts worldwide. A major challenge faced by countries attempting to establish their e-waste policies is the absence of global standards for manufacturing and recycling electronic devices. An international organization could assist by establishing universal standards for electronics manufacturers and recycling operations.

In addition, the intersection of data protection and e-waste management presents a critical area of concern in the digital age, particularly as the Internet of Things (IoT) devices become ubiquitous in our daily lives. Without proper data erasure processes, sensitive information can be recovered from disposed devices, leading to potential data breaches. Legal frameworks for e-waste currently lack robust regulations that specifically address the intersection of e-waste management and data protection. While the General Data Protection Regulation (GDPR) covers data protection comprehensively in the EU, it does not directly address the specific risks associated with the disposal of data-bearing devices.

Hence, legislation concerning e-waste should be expanded to include mandatory data destruction requirements before the disposal of electronic devices. This could be modeled after data protection regulations, which specify how data should be securely processed and erased. In addition, there should be a collaborative framework between agencies responsible for data protection and environmental regulation. This integration would ensure that e-waste management policies consider both the environmental impact and the data security implications of disposed electronic devices. Lastly, developing and implementing international standards for data destruction could help harmonize the approaches to e-waste management, making it more effective globally. Such standards should be enforceable and include specific guidelines on how to handle data securely at the end of a device's lifecycle.

In addition, concerns relating to child labor and unsafe recycling practices that have an environmental impact in developing countries also require to be addressed. This requires harmonizing the national laws relating to child labor and environmental protection with international standards. Drawing parallels with the Paris Agreement, the world requires a "Paris Agreement"-style international framework focused on recycling to preserve the Earth's resources, which will also address the concern relating to data protection and child labor relating to e-waste management.

Lastly, smart technologies integrated with IoT should be utilized to enhance optimizing e-waste management processes. For instance, smart bins equipped with IoT sensors can automatically detect when they are full and signal for collection, reducing the risk of improper disposal. In addition, IoT-enabled devices can monitor the condition of electronic products, alerting users when maintenance is needed, or when the device is nearing the end of its lifecycle. This proactive approach not only extends the lifespan of electronic products but also reduces the volume of e-waste generated.

Implementing blockchain technology into the process also offers a transformative approach to managing e-waste by providing transparent and traceable systems for tracking electronic products throughout their lifecycle. Blockchain's decentralized and immutable ledger can record every transaction and movement of electronic products, from manufacturing to disposal, ensuring accountability at every stage. This transparency is particularly valuable in addressing the problem of illegal e-waste dumping and the illicit trade of electronic components. By recording the origin, ownership, and condition of electronic products on a blockchain, stakeholders can verify the legitimacy of e-waste transactions and ensure that e-waste is being disposed of or recycled responsibly. This level of traceability also supports compliance with international regulations, such as the Basel Convention, which governs the transboundary movements of hazardous wastes. Moreover, blockchain can facilitate the creation of digital passports for electronic products, containing detailed information about the materials used, the energy consumed during production, and the product's environmental impact. These digital passports can inform consumers about the sustainability of their electronics, encouraging more responsible purchasing decisions and promoting a circular economy.

Big data analytics can also be utilized to revolutionize e-waste management by providing insights into waste generation patterns, consumer behavior, and the effectiveness of recycling programs. By analyzing large datasets from various sources, including IoT devices, consumer surveys, and recycling facility records, big data analytics can identify trends and predict future e-waste generation. Predictive analytics can also be particularly valuable for policymakers and waste management companies. For example, by analyzing data on electronic product sales, usage patterns, and disposal rates, predictive models can forecast the volume of e-waste that will be generated in a particular region or timeframe. This information can help waste management companies plan their operations more effectively, ensuring that they have the resources and infrastructure needed to handle future e-waste flows.

20.5 Conclusion

Moving forward, it is essential for stakeholders across the spectrum – from government bodies and industries to consumers and nongovernmental organizations – to collaborate in fostering an environment that values and actualizes principles of the circular economy. Such collective efforts are crucial in ensuring that the tale of e-waste transitions from a story of challenges to one of opportunities, where technological advancements and responsible consumption and production pave the way for a sustainable and prosperous digital future.

In navigating the complexities of e-waste management, we are reminded of the interconnectedness of our actions and their repercussions on the planet. It is through informed policies, innovative solutions, and cooperative endeavors that we can achieve the dual goals of environmental sustainability and technological advancement. This chapter ahead in our e-waste narrative is ours to write, with the hope that it will be marked by greater accountability, sustainability, and inclusivity in the face of rapid technological change.

Notes

1. The Khian Sea waste disposal incident involved a Liberian-flagged cargo ship, the Khian Sea, which in 1986 was loaded with over 14,000 tons of incinerator ash from Philadelphia, Pennsylvania. Struggling to find a disposal site after New Jersey

rejected further waste, the vessel spent 16 months seeking a dumping location across the Atlantic, facing rejections from multiple countries. Eventually, 4,000 tons of ash were illegally dumped in Haiti in 1988, misleadingly labeled as "topsoil fertilizer." When the Haitian government discovered the deception, the ship had already fled. Despite changing its name in attempts to offload the remaining ash, the Khian Sea secretly disposed of the rest in the Atlantic and Indian Oceans later that year. The incident led to legal actions, with two owners of the involved shipping company convicted of perjury in 1993. Although the ship was scrapped in 1992, the ash in Haiti remained a problem until 2000, when efforts facilitated by Eastern Environmental Services and pressure from Greenpeace and Haitian groups led to the removal of 2,500 tons of the waste, eventually deemed nonhazardous and disposed of in Pennsylvania in 2002. This event underscored the challenges of international waste disposal and contributed to the establishment of the Basel Convention, aimed at regulating the transboundary movement and disposal of hazardous waste.

2. The Koko incident in Nigeria vividly illustrates the severe environmental and health hazards posed by the illegal dumping of toxic waste in developing countries. In this case, a local farmer was manipulated by an Italian businessman into storing hazardous industrial by-products on his land for a paltry sum. This clandestine operation, which involved over 9,000 chemical drums, came to light in 1988 thanks to investigative journalism and the vigilance of the Nigerian diaspora in Italy. The dump contained carcinogens and other toxic substances, posing an immediate threat to the local community, who was unaware of the danger and had been using the contaminated land for agriculture and repurposing the chemical containers for household use. In response, the Nigerian government declared the area a disaster zone, evacuating residents and initiating a cleanup operation with international assistance, including teams from the United States, the United Kingdom, Japan, and the International Atomic Energy Agency. The operation, which involved repackaging and shipping the waste back to Italy for safe disposal, highlighted the critical need for global cooperation in managing hazardous waste and protecting vulnerable communities from environmental exploitation.

3. The United States signed the Basel Convention in 1990. The U.S. Senate provided its advice and consent to ratification in 1992. The United States, however, has not ratified the Convention because it does not have sufficient domestic statutory authority to implement all of its provisions.

References

Abalansa, S., El Mahrad, B., Icely, J., & Newton, A. (2021). Electronic waste, an environmental problem exported to developing countries: The GOOD, the BAD and the UGLY. *Sustainability, 13*(9). https://doi.org/10.3390/su13095302

Ahmed, I. (2019). The Basel convention on the control of transboundary movements of hazardous wastes and their disposal: A legal misfit in global ship recycling jurisprudence. *Wash. Int'l LJ, 29,* 411.

Alghazo, J., Ouda, O. K. M., & Hassan, A. E. (2018). E-waste environmental and information security threat: GCC countries vulnerabilities. *Euro-Mediterranean Journal for Environmental Integration*, 3(1), 13. https://doi.org/10.1007/s41207-018-0050-4

Arya, S., & Kumar, S. (2020). E-waste in India at a glance: Current trends, regulations, challenges and management strategies. *Journal of Cleaner Production*, 271, 122707. https://doi.org/10.1016/j.jclepro.2020.122707

Arya, S., Kumari, D., Narzari, R., & Kumar, S. (2023). Chapter 1 – A global glance on waste electrical and electronic equipments (WEEEs). In S. Arya & S. Kumar (Eds.), *Global E-Waste Management Strategies and Future Implications* (pp. 1–11): Elsevier.

Awere, E., Obeng, P. A., Bonoli, A., & Obeng, P. A. (2020). E-waste recycling and public exposure to organic compounds in developing countries: a review of recycling practices and toxicity levels in Ghana. *Environmental Technology Reviews*, 9(1), 1–19. https://doi.org/10.1080/21622515.2020.1714749

Chung, S.-W., & Murakami-Suzuki, R. (2008). A comparative study of e-waste recycling systems in Japan, South Korea and Taiwan from the EPR perspective: implications for developing countries. In M. Kojima (Ed.), *Promoting 3Rs in Developing Countries: Lessons from the Japanese Experience* (Vol. 21, pp. 11–23).

Das, S., Hosain, A. S., & Debnath, B. (2023). A review of security threats from E-waste: Issues, challenges, and sustainability. In *Development in E-waste Management* (1st ed., pp. 165–188). CRC Press.

Debnath, B. (2020). Towards sustainable E-waste management through industrial symbiosis: A supply chain perspective. In R. Salomone, A. Cecchin, P. Deutz, A. Raggi, & L. Cutaia (Eds.), *Industrial Symbiosis for the Circular Economy: Operational Experiences, Best Practices and Obstacles to a Collaborative Business Approach* (pp. 87–102). Cham: Springer International Publishing.

Favot, M., Grassetti, L., Massarutto, A., & Veit, R. (2022). Regulation and competition in the extended producer responsibility models: Results in the WEEE sector in Europe. *Waste Management*, 145, 60–71. https://doi.org/10.1016/j.wasman.2022.04.027

Gassner, F. (2021). "To listen to the language of nature and to act accordingly": Natural law as beacon guiding to human flourishing and ecological civilization. *Orientis Aura: Macau Perspectives in Religious Studies*, 6, 3–21.

Gollakota, A. R. K., Gautam, S., & Shu, C.-M. (2020). Inconsistencies of e-waste management in developing nations – facts and plausible solutions. *Journal of Environmental Management*, 261, 110234. https://doi.org/10.1016/j.jenvman.2020.110234

Heacock, M., Kelly Carol, B., Asante Kwadwo, A., Birnbaum Linda, S., Bergman Åke, L., Bruné, M.-N., . . . Suk William, A. (2016). E-waste and harm to vulnerable populations: A growing global problem. *Environmental Health Perspectives*, 124(5), 550–555. https://doi.org/10.1289/ehp.1509699

Herat, S., & Agamuthu, P. (2012). E-waste: A problem or an opportunity? Review of issues, challenges and solutions in Asian countries. *Waste Management & Research*, 30(11), 1113–1129. https://doi.org/10.1177/0734242X12453378

Islam, M. T., Iyer-Raniga, U., & Trewick, S. (2022). Recycling perspectives of circular business models: A review. *Recycling*, 7(5). https://doi.org/10.3390/recycling7050079

Jayasiri, G., Herat, S., & Kaparaju, P. (2023). Management of small WEEE: Future directions for Australia. *Sustainability*, 15(18). https://doi.org/10.3390/su151813543

Kapoor, N., Sulke, P., & Badiye, A. (2021). E-waste forensics: An overview. *Forensic Science International: Animals and Environments, 1*, 100034. https://doi.org/10.1016/j.fsiae.2021.100034

Karpagaraj, A., Gopikrishnan, T., & Singh, S. K. (2023). Reuse and recycling of electronic waste from a global solution perspective. In S. Kumar & V. Kumar (Eds.), *Electronic Waste Management: Policies, Processes, Technologies, and Impact* (pp. 104–123). John Wiley & Sons, Inc.

Kaya, M., & Tita, A. M. (2023). Electronic waste recycling in maintaining a circular economy. In S. Kumar & V. Kumar (Eds.), *Electronic Waste Management: Policies, Processes, Technologies, and Impact* (pp. 301–316). John Wiley & Sons, Inc.

Li, Z., Diaz, L. A., Yang, Z., Jin, H., Lister, T. E., Vahidi, E., & Zhao, F. (2019). Comparative life cycle analysis for value recovery of precious metals and rare earth elements from electronic waste. *Resources, Conservation and Recycling, 149*, 20–30. https://doi.org/10.1016/j.resconrec.2019.05.025

Lin, S., Ali, M. U., Zheng, C., Cai, Z., & Wong, M. H. (2022). Toxic chemicals from uncontrolled e-waste recycling: Exposure, body burden, health impact. *Journal of Hazardous Materials, 426*, 127792. https://doi.org/10.1016/j.jhazmat.2021.127792

Little, P. C., & Lucier, C. (2017). Global electronic waste, third party certification standards, and resisting the undoing of environmental justice politics. *Human Organization, 76*(3), 204–214. https://doi.org/10.17730/0018-7259.76.3.204

Liu, K., Tan, Q., Yu, J., & Wang, M. (2023). A global perspective on e-waste recycling. *Circular Economy, 2*(1), 100028.

Maitre-Ekern, E., & Dalhammar, C. (2016). Regulating planned obsolescence: A review of legal approaches to increase product durability and reparability in Europe. *Review of European, Comparative & International Environmental Law, 25*(3), 378–394. https://doi.org/10.1111/reel.12182

Manomaivibool, P., & Hong, J. H. (2014). Two decades, three WEEE systems: How far did EPR evolve in Korea's resource circulation policy? *Resources, Conservation and Recycling, 83*, 202–212. https://doi.org/10.1016/j.resconrec.2013.10.011

Maphosa, V., & Maphosa, M. (2020). E-waste management in Sub-Saharan Africa: A systematic literature review. *Cogent Business & Management, 7*(1), 1814503. https://doi.org/10.1080/23311975.2020.1814503

Masud, M. H., Akram, W., Ahmed, A., Ananno, A. A., Mourshed, M., Hasan, M., & Joardder, M. U. H. (2019). Towards the effective E-waste management in Bangladesh: A review. *Environmental Science and Pollution Research, 26*(2), 1250–1276. https://doi.org/10.1007/s11356-018-3626-2

Mukherjee, S., Mukhopadhyay, A., & Bhattacharjee, P. (2023). A global perspective on E-waste: From cradle to grave. In S. Kumar & V. Kumar (Eds.), *Electronic Waste Management: Policies, Processes, Technologies, and Impact* (pp. 66–80). John Wiley & Sons, Inc.

Newaz, M. S., & Appolloni, A. (2023a). Evolution of behavioral research on E-waste management: Conceptual frameworks and future research directions. *Business Strategy and the Environment, 33*(2), 477–503. https://doi.org/10.1002/bse.3503

Newaz, M. S., & Appolloni, A. (2023b). Worldwide E-waste management models: Delving into pros and cons and the way forward. In S. Kumar & V. Kumar (Eds.), *Electronic Waste Management: Policies, Processes, Technologies, and Impact* (pp. 33–51). John Wiley & Sons, Inc.

Nnorom, I. C., & Osibanjo, O. (2008). Overview of electronic waste (e-waste) management practices and legislations, and their poor applications in the developing countries. *Resources, Conservation and Recycling, 52*(6), 843–858. https://doi.org/10.1016/j.resconrec.2008.01.004

OECD. (2016). *Extended Producer Responsibility: Updated Guidance for Efficient Waste Management*. Paris, France: OECD Publishing.
OECD. (2021). *Extended Producer Responsibility*. https://www.oecd.org/environment/extended-producer-responsibility.htm
Pariatamby, A., & Victor, D. (2013). Policy trends of e-waste management in Asia. *Journal of Material Cycles and Waste Management*, 15(4), 411–419. https://doi.org/10.1007/s10163-013-0136-7
Patil, R. A., & Ramakrishna, S. (2020). A comprehensive analysis of e-waste legislation worldwide. *Environmental Science and Pollution Research*, 27(13), 14412–14431. https://doi.org/10.1007/s11356-020-07992-1
Perkins, D., Drisse, M., Nxele, T., & Sly, P. (2014). E-waste: A global hazard. *Annals Global Health*, 80(4), 286–295.
Priyashantha, A. K. H., Pratheesh, N., & Pretheeba, P. (2022). E-waste scenario in South-Asia: an emerging risk to environment and public health. *Environ Anal Health Toxicol*, 37(3), e2022022–2022020. https://doi.org/10.5620/eaht.2022022
Raghavan, S. (2013). Reboot systems: Bridging digital divide – the green way. *Emerald Emerging Markets Case Studies*, 3(6), 1–33. https://doi.org/10.1108/EEMCS-06-2013-0077
Rasnan, M. I., Mohamed, A. F., Goh, C. T., & Watanabe, K. (2016). Sustainable E-waste management in Asia: Analysis of practices in Japan, Taiwan and Malaysia. *Journal of Environmental Assessment Policy and Management*, 18(04), 1650023. https://doi.org/10.1142/S146433321650023X
Sa, P. D., & Korinek, J. (2021). *Resource Efficiency, the Circular Economy, Sustainable Materials Management and Trade in Metals and Minerals* (Vol. 139). OECD Library. https://doi.org/10.1787/18166873
Sachs, N. (2006). Planning the funeral at the birth: Extended producer responsibility in the European Union and the United States. *Harv. Envtl. L. Rev.*, 30, 51.
Sakhuja, D., Ghai, H., Bhatia, R. K., & Bhatt, A. K. (2022). Management of E-waste: technological challenges and opportunities. In C. Baskar (Ed.), *Handbook of Solid Waste Management: Sustainability through Circular Economy* (pp. 1523–1557). Springer Nature.
Seif, R., Salem, F. Z., & Allam, N. K. (2024). E-waste recycled materials as efficient catalysts for renewable energy technologies and better environmental sustainability. *Environment, Development and Sustainability*, 26(3), 5473–5508. https://doi.org/10.1007/s10668-023-02925-7
Shad, K. M., Ling, S. T. Y., & Karim, M. E. (2020). Comparative study on E-waste management and the role of the Basel convention in Malaysia, Singapore, and Indonesia: A way forward. *Indonesia Law Review*, 10, 63. https://doi.org/10.15742/ilrev.v10n1.596
Shevchenko, T., Laitala, K., & Danko, Y. (2019). Understanding consumer E-waste recycling behavior: Introducing a new economic incentive to increase the collection rates. *Sustainability*, 11(9). https://doi.org/10.3390/su11092656
Simpson, D., Power, D., Riach, K., & Tsarenko, Y. (2019). Consumer motivation for product disposal and its role in acquiring products for reuse. *Journal of Operations Management*, 65(7), 612–635. https://doi.org/10.1002/joom.1049
Singh, N., Duan, H., Yin, F., Song, Q., & Li, J. (2018). Characterizing the materials composition and recovery potential from waste mobile phones: A comparative evaluation of cellular and smart phones. *ACS Sustainable Chemistry & Engineering*, 6(10), 13016–13024. https://doi.org/10.1021/acssuschemeng.8b02516

Song, M., Wang, S., & Zhang, H. (2020). Could environmental regulation and R&D tax incentives affect green product innovation? *Journal of Cleaner Production, 258*, 120849. https://doi.org/10.1016/j.jclepro.2020.120849

Song, N., McLellan, I., Liu, W., Wang, Z., & Hursthouse, A. (2023). The waste ban in China: What happened next? Assessing the impact of new policies on the waste management sector in China. *Environmental Geochemistry and Health, 45*(4), 1117–1131. https://doi.org/10.1007/s10653-021-01101-y

Sthiannopkao, S., & Wong, M. H. (2013). Handling e-waste in developed and developing countries: Initiatives, practices, and consequences. *Science of The Total Environment, 463–464*, 1147–1153. https://doi.org/10.1016/j.scitotenv.2012.06.088

Szwarc, E., Golińska-Dawson, P., Bocewicz, G., & Banaszak, Z. (2024). *Proactive Resource Maintenance in Product-as-a-Service Business Models: A Constraints Programming Based Approach for MFP Offerings Prototyping.* Paper presented at the Advances in Manufacturing IV, Cham.

Tembhare, S. P., Bhanvase, B. A., Barai, D. P., & Dhoble, S. J. (2022). E-waste recycling practices: A review on environmental concerns, remediation and technological developments with a focus on printed circuit boards. *Environment, Development and Sustainability, 24*(7), 8965–9047. https://doi.org/10.1007/s10668-021-01819-w

Templier, M., & Paré, G. (2015). A framework for guiding and evaluating literature reviews. *Communications of the Association for Information Systems, 37*(1), 6. https://doi.org/10.17705/1CAIS.03706

Thakur, P., & Kumar, S. (2022). Evaluation of e-waste status, management strategies, and legislations. *International Journal of Environmental Science and Technology, 19*(7), 6957–6966. https://doi.org/10.1007/s13762-021-03383-2

Townsend, T. G. (2011). Environmental issues and management strategies for waste electronic and electrical equipment. *Journal of the Air & Waste Management Association, 61*(6), 587–610. https://doi.org/10.3155/1047–3289.61.6.587

Tsai, W.-T., Chou, Y.-H., Lin, C.-M., Hsu, H.-C., Lin, K.-Y., & Chiu, C.-S. (2007). Perspectives on resource recycling from municipal solid waste in Taiwan. *Resources Policy, 32*(1), 69–79. https://doi.org/10.1016/j.resourpol.2007.06.004

Van Erp, J., & Huisman, W. (2010). Smart regulation and enforcement of illegal disposal of electronic waste. *Criminology Pubic Policy, 9*(3), 579.

van Loon, P., Delagarde, C., & Van Wassenhove, L. N. (2018). The role of second-hand markets in circular business: A simple model for leasing versus selling consumer products. *International Journal of Production Research, 56*(1–2), 960–973. https://doi.org/10.1080/00207543.2017.1398429

Van Yken, J., Boxall, N. J., Cheng, K. Y., Nikoloski, A. N., Moheimani, N. R., & Kaksonen, A. H. (2021). E-waste recycling and resource recovery: A review on technologies, barriers and enablers with a focus on Oceania. *Metals, 11*(8). https://doi.org/10.3390/met11081313

Zingerle, A., & Kronman, L. (2019). *Information Diving on an E-Waste Dump in West Africa–Artistic Remixing of a Global Data Breach.* Paper presented at the Conference on Computation, Communication, Aesthetics & X, Milan, Italy.

Index

A

accountability, 50–51, 64–65, 77, 79–80, 85–86, 109–111, 118, 131, 135, 137–139, 142, 163, 195, 198, 200–201, 205, 209, 212–213, 217–218, 223, 225, 228, 231, 234, 237, 240–241, 243, 247, 253, 263, 283, 289, 297–299, 307, 379, 388, 404, 412, 414, 420, 428, 441, 446–448
adaptive AI systems, 130–132
adversarial attacks, 126, 131
agile methodologies, 15–16
artificial intelligence (AI), 4, 26, 45, 73, 89–90, 94, 119, 145, 168, 219, 252, 260, 317, 339, 370
asset tokenization, 311
audit trails, 239–256
automated code generation, 187
automated testing, 178, 186

B

bias detection, 136
big data, 5–6, 14, 22–24, 26–28, 31, 40, 46, 67–68, 114–118, 175, 191, 193, 235–236, 258, 261, 265–266, 268–269, 273, 279–282, 291, 301, 342, 406, 448
blockchain, 4–6, 20, 25–27, 45–46, 51–59, 61–69, 86, 195, 197–200, 202–284, 289–302, 305–334, 339–342, 344, 348, 350–352, 356, 360–361, 374–375, 377, 383, 447
bug detection, 168, 180, 186, 190

C

circular economy, 281–282, 437–440, 443, 448–452
cloud computing, 6, 8, 45–46, 52, 54–56, 61–68, 231, 234, 258, 287
code completion, 172, 179, 186, 192
code generation, 12, 177, 179, 185–187, 190, 192
cognitive architectures, 138, 140, 143
compliance, 15, 19, 38, 55–56, 58, 60, 76, 109, 136–138, 208–209, 214, 217–218, 224, 226–228, 230, 232, 235, 238–239, 241–243, 245, 247, 253, 255, 273, 288, 313, 317, 320, 322–323, 325, 340, 352, 377, 381, 413, 446–447
consensus mechanisms, 206, 213, 216, 224, 228–229, 245, 295, 319
continuous improvement, 9, 16, 32
cross-jurisdictional challenges, 402
cryptocurrency, 52, 54, 59–61, 63, 67–68, 210, 219, 225, 256–257, 262, 283–285, 287, 289, 291, 293, 295–302, 305–307, 309–313, 315, 317, 319–321, 323, 325–335, 337, 339, 341–345, 347, 349–362
cryptography, 56, 65, 199, 213, 216, 223, 315, 331, 333, 339, 344
cybersecurity, 37, 213, 258, 313, 317, 328, 354, 375, 435

D

data integrity, 3, 55, 62, 209, 221, 227–228, 231, 243, 246, 248, 251, 255, 257, 307, 313, 317–318, 322
data management, 6, 14, 57, 209, 221, 231, 234, 242, 245, 246, 250, 258, 267, 271, 319
data privacy, 5, 18, 31, 68, 80, 84–86, 89, 116, 137, 153, 163, 165, 218, 226, 245, 252, 273, 308, 313, 317, 319–320, 325, 375–377, 381, 384, 434, 445–446
data security, 15, 45, 49, 51, 54, 63, 65, 85, 87, 136–137, 213, 217–218, 229, 245, 264, 266, 318, 327, 365, 367, 370, 373, 375, 378–379, 447

455

decentralized autonomous organizations, 308, 316, 330
decentralized finance, 46, 234, 309, 321, 328, 356
decentralized systems, 197–207, 209, 212, 284, 295, 305, 320, 326–327
deep learning, 45–46, 55, 62, 68, 73, 88, 95, 123, 126, 133, 143, 168, 176, 189–190, 192
digital assets, 63, 205, 294, 296, 307, 309–312, 318, 333–336, 338–339, 341, 350, 371, 374–376, 379–381, 393
digital identity, 53, 207, 329
digital strategy, 3–25, 28–32, 34–38, 40–42, 44–69, 74, 76, 78, 80, 82, 84, 86, 88, 90, 92, 96, 98, 100, 102, 104, 106, 108, 110, 112, 114, 116, 118, 120, 122, 124, 126, 128, 130, 132, 134, 136, 138, 140, 142, 144, 146, 148, 150, 152, 154, 156, 158, 160, 162, 164, 166, 170, 172, 174, 176, 178, 180, 182, 184, 186, 188, 190, 192, 198, 200, 202, 204, 206, 208, 210, 212, 214, 218, 220, 222, 224, 226, 228, 230, 232, 234, 236, 238, 240, 242, 244, 246, 248, 250, 252, 254, 256, 258, 260–282, 284, 286, 288, 290, 292, 294, 296, 298, 300, 302, 306, 308, 310, 312, 314, 316, 318, 320, 322, 324, 326, 328, 330, 332, 334, 336, 338, 340, 342, 346, 348, 350, 352, 354, 356, 358, 360, 362, 366, 368, 370, 372, 374, 376, 378, 380, 382, 384, 386, 388, 390, 392, 394, 396, 398, 400, 402, 404, 406, 412, 414, 416, 418, 420, 422, 424, 426, 428, 430, 432, 434, 436, 438, 440, 442, 444, 446, 448, 450, 452
distributed ledger, 5, 23, 198–199, 210, 216, 219, 224, 226, 230, 240, 290, 293–294, 296, 313, 324, 328–329, 333, 344, 348, 350

E

edge computing, 28, 56–57, 65, 68, 69, 291
encryption, 55, 136, 208, 218, 247–248, 307, 315, 317–318, 332, 381

environmental sustainability, 73–74, 80, 86, 272, 435, 445, 448, 452
Ethereum, 53, 56, 63, 212, 243, 258, 264, 268, 307, 313–317, 322–323, 328, 330, 351
ethical AI, 74, 79, 86, 121, 163
ethical considerations, 38–39, 49–50, 54, 65–66, 76–77, 92, 131–132, 135, 142, 162–164, 273, 296, 324, 365, 379, 383, 415–416
e-waste management, 31, 434–452
explainable AI, 86, 108, 179, 185, 192
extended producer responsibility (EPR), 441–442

F

financial audits, 225, 247–248
fintech, 90, 215, 256, 289, 328–329, 342, 359
fraud detection, 49, 60, 64, 201–203, 205–206, 266, 274
fraud prevention, 197, 201, 203, 215, 217, 228, 239

G

general data protection regulation (GDPR), 50, 80, 239, 323, 375, 446
generative adversarial network, 124
generative AI, 6, 116, 172, 175, 185, 191
governance, 4, 6, 8, 10–12, 14–16, 18, 20, 22, 24–25, 28, 30, 32, 34, 36, 38, 40, 42, 44–46, 48, 50–54, 56, 58, 60, 62, 64–68, 74, 76, 78, 80, 82, 84, 86, 88, 90, 92, 96, 98, 100, 102, 104, 106, 108, 110, 112, 114, 116, 118, 120, 122, 124, 126, 128, 130, 132, 134, 136, 138, 140, 142, 144, 146, 148, 150, 152, 154, 156, 158, 160, 162, 164, 166, 170, 172, 174, 176, 178, 180, 182, 184, 186, 188, 190, 192, 195, 198, 200, 202, 204, 206, 208–210, 212–218, 220, 222–224, 226–228, 230, 232, 234, 236, 238, 240–242, 244, 246–248, 250, 252–256, 258, 262, 264, 266, 268–270, 272, 274, 276, 278, 280, 282–284, 286, 288–292, 294–298,

Index

300–302, 306, 308, 310, 312,
314–316, 318, 320–322, 324–326,
328, 330, 332, 334, 336, 338–340,
342, 346, 348, 350, 352, 354, 356,
358, 360, 362, 366, 368, 370, 372,
374, 376–378, 380, 382, 384, 386,
388, 390–392, 394, 396, 398, 400,
402, 404, 406, 409, 412, 414, 416,
418, 420, 422, 424, 426, 428, 430,
432, 434, 436, 438, 440, 442, 444,
446, 448, 450, 452
graph database, 251, 256
green computing, 84, 92

H

hacking, 108, 200, 205, 222, 229, 269, 355, 378–379, 389, 393
haptic, 388, 392–394
hash functions, 247
Hyperledger, 250, 251, 316–317

I

immutable records, 45, 246
integration, 3–5, 12–13, 17, 23, 25, 46–51, 54–59, 63–66, 73–74, 76, 80–82, 84, 140, 142, 152, 159–160, 164–165, 169, 174, 176, 178, 190, 208, 227–234, 236, 244, 250–251, 253, 254, 266, 269–271, 279, 291, 301, 305–307, 309–327, 329, 358, 366, 370, 372, 374, 378, 380, 404, 445, 447, 449
internet of things (IoT), 4, 26, 56, 197, 219, 248, 260, 291, 446
interoperability, 3, 12–13, 23–24, 27, 39–40, 53, 227, 235, 295, 311, 318–320, 322, 327

L

legal frameworks, 51, 66, 73, 75, 149, 271, 321, 377, 379, 381, 383, 389, 446

M

machine learning, 8, 22, 40, 43, 45–46, 48, 55, 62, 65, 68, 74–75, 84, 89, 91, 94–95, 113–115, 117, 120, 125, 128, 142–144, 149, 158, 168, 172, 176, 185, 189–193, 252, 257, 260, 286–287, 298, 326, 417, 425
metaverse, 363, 365–395, 398–407
model training, 56

N

natural language processing, 43, 75, 88, 117, 120, 134, 143, 168, 171
neural networks, 46, 75, 101, 115, 119–124, 126–127, 129–130, 132–141, 143–144, 179, 189, 275
neurobiological foundations, 119–121, 123, 125, 127, 129, 131, 133, 135, 137, 139, 141, 143
neuromorphic computing, 121, 126, 139, 141–143
neuroplasticity, 128–129
non-fungible tokens (NFTs), 371

P

political advertising, 305, 412–413, 417–418, 420–421, 423–424, 426–430
privacy, 3, 5, 14–15, 18, 31, 38, 49–51, 53, 55, 58, 63, 66, 68, 74, 76–82, 84–87, 89, 116, 121, 126, 131, 135–137, 142, 153, 163, 165, 178, 185, 189, 205, 208, 211–213, 218–219, 221, 226–227, 231, 236, 242, 245, 248, 251–253, 255–256, 269, 271–273, 305–306, 308–311, 313–315, 317–321, 323–327, 334, 339–340, 365, 367, 370–371, 373, 375–379, 381, 383–385, 391–393, 399–400, 402, 403, 407, 416, 428, 434, 436, 445–446
project management, 22, 168–170, 174–175, 178–179, 187, 190–192

Q

quantum computing, 4, 6, 9–10, 20, 26–27, 40, 56–58, 65–66, 188

R

real-time processing, 141
regulatory compliance, 15, 55, 58, 209, 217–218, 227, 245, 317, 322, 381
remote audits, 246–248, 257
resource recovery, 435, 441, 453
risk assessment, 64, 82, 85, 94, 98–99, 102–103, 105, 107, 110, 113, 117, 138, 152, 164, 231

S

scalability, 6, 8, 13, 55, 57, 59, 61–62, 64–65, 120–121, 123, 132, 226–227, 229, 235, 249, 252, 255, 269, 294–295, 310, 316, 320, 322–323, 327, 369
security protocols, 227
smart contracts, 52–55, 62, 198–199, 211, 214, 216–217, 219, 229, 231–232, 240, 244, 247, 251–255, 264, 307–309, 312–313, 315, 317–319, 321, 323–326, 328–330
social impact, 297–298, 391
software development, 137, 168–189, 191–193, 228, 371
software testing, 172, 180–181, 186–187, 189
supervised learning, 114, 122, 128
sustainable development, 25, 44, 158, 167, 278–279, 285, 295–297, 302, 306, 361, 385, 435

T

technology integration, 4
transparency, 14, 50–54, 56–57, 62, 64–66, 74, 76–79, 84, 86–87, 109, 112, 118, 131, 135–138, 163, 166, 185, 197–203, 205–218, 222–225, 227–228, 230–235, 238–240, 242–243, 245–248, 252–255, 258, 260, 263, 266–267, 270–272, 275, 288, 291–293, 297–299, 302, 305–310, 312, 317–321, 326, 334, 353, 356–357, 374, 379, 412, 414, 420–421, 423, 425–428, 446–447

U

unsupervised learning, 122, 127–128, 130, 138, 143
user experience, 16, 20, 168, 172, 368

V

virtual assets, 338, 348, 355, 357, 375, 378–379
virtual reality, 6, 152, 165–166, 365, 367, 383, 385, 387, 392, 405–407
virtual worlds, 369, 371–373, 380, 384, 391–392, 406
voting systems, 54, 247–248

W

waste management, 31, 434–438, 440–453
web 3.0, 305–313, 315, 317, 319–321, 323–330, 380

Z

zero-knowledge proofs, 311